1,027

GRE®

Practice Questions

Fifth Edition

The Staff of The Princeton Review

PrincetonReview.com

Penguin
Random
House

The Princeton Review
110 East 42nd Street, 7th Floor
New York, NY 10017
Email: editorialsupport@review.com

Published in the United States by Penguin Random House
LLC, New York, and in Canada by Random House of Canada,
a division of Penguin Random House Ltd., Toronto.

ISBN: 978-0-525-56759-2
ISSN: 1943-4855

Editor: Aaron Riccio
Production Editors: Kathy Carter, Emily Epstein White
Production Coordinator: Deborah Weber

Printed in the United States of America on partially
recycled paper.

10 9 8 7 6 5 4 3 2 1

Fifth Edition

Editorial
Rob Franek, Editor-in-Chief
Mary Beth Garrick, Executive Director of Production
Craig Patches, Production Design Manager
Selena Coppock, Managing Editor
Meave Shelton, Senior Editor
Colleen Day, Editor
Sarah Litt, Editor
Aaron Riccio, Editor
Orion McBean, Associate Editor

Penguin Random House Publishing Team
Tom Russell, VP, Publisher
Alison Stoltzfus, Publishing Director
Amanda Yee, Associate Managing Editor
Ellen Reed, Production Manager
Suzanne Lee, Designer

Acknowledgments

Our sincerest appreciation goes out to John Fulmer, the talented and fearless National Content Director for the GRE at The Princeton Review, and developers Becky Robinson, Bobby Hood, Cathy Evins, Jake Schiff, Karen Hoover, KB Hollingsworth, Kyle Fox, Martin Cinke, Nicole Pirnie, Sarah Woodruff, Scott Thompson, David Bucy, Sionainn Marcoux, David Falls, Jerry Mason, Kevin Kelly, Chris Chimera, and Eric Bertolozzi. We'd also like to extend a word of gratitude to our marvelous production team of Kathy Carter, Emily Epstein White, and Deborah Weber, for their assistance throughout this Fifth edition.

A very special thanks to Adam Robinson, who conceived of and perfected the Joe Bloggs approach to standardized tests and many of the other successful techniques used by The Princeton Review.

Contents

Get More (Free) Content

1 Go to **PrincetonReview.com/cracking**.

2 Enter the following ISBN for your book: 9780525567592.

3 Answer a few simple questions to set up an exclusive Princeton Review account. (If you already have one, you can just log in.)

4 Click the "Student Tools" button, also found under "My Account" from the top toolbar. You're all set to access your bonus content!

Need to report a potential **content** issue?

Contact **EditorialSupport@review.com**.
Include:

- full title of the book
- ISBN
- page number

Need to report a **technical** issue?

Contact **TPRStudentTech@review.com** and provide:

- your full name
- email address used to register the book
- full book title and ISBN
- computer OS (Mac/PC) and browser (Firefox, Safari, etc.)

Once you've registered, you can...

- Take a full-length practice GRE exam

- Read important advice about the GRE and graduate school

- Access a special bonus guide to GRE vocabulary excerpted from *GRE Power Vocab*

- Check to see if there have been any corrections or updates to this edition

Look For These Icons Throughout The Book

 GOING DEEPER

 WATCH OUT

 OTHER REFERENCES

Introduction

Lawful Admission

Though it's still uncommon, some law schools have recently started to accept GRE scores in lieu of LSAT scores. Always check a school's admission page for up-to-date options. Your grad school options may have opened up even further!

SO YOU'VE DECIDED TO GO TO GRAD SCHOOL...

Much like the SAT or ACT that you probably took to get into college, the GRE—or the Graduate Record Exam, as it is officially known—is required for admissions by many graduate programs. GRE test takers include future engineers, historians, philosophers, psychologists, nurses, even veterinarians. In short, the GRE is used by just about any graduate program that is not medical or business school. It may seem odd that a student who is applying for an advanced degree in architecture must take the same exam as a student applying for a degree in comparative literature. In many respects, it is. Because a wide variety of gradate programs rely upon the GRE rather than their own proprietary exam, GRE results are used in a wide variety of ways.

Some programs simply have a minimum combined score that all applicants must achieve. Other programs, such as a creative writing program, care far more about the Verbal score than they do about the Math score. One would think that engineering programs would care more about the Math score, as some do, but most engineering applicants score in the very highest percentiles on the GRE quantitative section and therefore Verbal scores, not Math scores, become a more effective tool for comparing one candidate to another.

If you are frustrated that the skills you have to dust off and polish for the GRE bear little resemblance to the subjects you will be studying in grad school, remember three things. First, the GRE is not a content test. It does not test a body of knowledge, like U.S. history or French. It is designed to test a very specific way of thinking. Second, taking the GRE is a skill, and like any other skill, it can be learned. That is what this book and *Cracking the GRE* are all about. With diligence and practice you can learn everything you need to know for the GRE, and you can do it in a surprisingly short period of time. Far less time, in fact, than it took you to learn physiology, Renaissance poetry, or whichever subject you plan to pursue in your graduate studies. The last thing to remember is that the GRE is only one factor of many that will be considered for admissions, and it is often the easiest to change.

The first task in preparing for the GRE is doing your graduate school research.

Every GRE score has two components: a scaled score and a percentile rank. GRE scores fall on a 130–170 point scale. However, your percentile rank is more important than your scaled score. Your percentile rank indicates how your GRE scores compare to those of other test takers. For example, a scaled score of 150 on the GRE translates to roughly the 43rd percentile, meaning that you scored better than 43 out of every 100 test takers—and worse than the other 57 percent of test takers. A score of 152 is about average, while scores of 163 and above are very competitive. Get the latest reported scores and percentiles at PrincetonReview.com and at www.ets.org/gre, the official ETS (Educational Testing Service) website for the GRE.

How schools weight the scores, assuming they can even answer this question, will differ not only from school to school, but even from student to student. Schools may use GRE scores to validate the verbal abilities of international students with really fantastic essays. GRE scores may be used in lieu of work experience for applicants who are only a year or two out of undergrad, or as a more recent snapshot for adult students returning to school after a decade or so. Mostly they are just there so that schools have an apples-to-apples comparison of applicants with a wildly divergent range of undergrad, work, and life experiences. Also, most applicants are well qualified. Often the scores are there as an easy way to narrow down the pool.

How your program uses your scores will determine quite a bit about how you prepare for the test. The following is a list of questions to ask when you call up your target school.

How Much Do GRE Scores Count?

Schools generally do a pretty good job of telling applicants what is required (application, recommendation, essays, portfolios, test scores, transcripts), but how one factor is weighed against another is a murky science. Typically a GPA or current work experience will weigh far more heavily than a GRE score. On the other hand, if your GPA is on the low side, you will want your GRE scores to be as high as possible to prove that you can do the work.

What Is Your Acceptance Rate?

In other words, how competitive is your program? If the acceptance rate is high, the program may not weigh GRE scores that heavily; however, if they're rejecting 60 percent of their applicants, every number they see will matter and your GRE scores might give you the extra boost needed to make your application stand out.

What Do You Do with Multiple Scores?

When dealing with scores, some schools look at only the most recent and others combine them, but most prefer to use the highest. The computer adaptive test is not like any other test most students have ever taken. The first time people take it is often not their best. The second time, however, students are more comfortable, and scores tend to jump up—even if it is only a week or two later. Plan on taking the test twice.

Do You Use, Look At, or Care About My Analytical Writing Scores?

If schools don't, and most don't, you won't have to spend valuable time practicing this portion of the test.

Do You Care About My Math/Verbal Score?

This is for programs like engineering or English lit, which are clearly weighted toward one side of the test or another. It would be great news if you found out that you could blow off the Math section altogether, no?

Do You Have a Cut-Off Score, and/or What Were the Average Scores or Percentiles for Last Year's Incoming Class?

How do you rank? Are you below the average or above it? Larger programs may have and publish these ranking and cut-off score numbers; smaller ones may not. This will tell you a lot about how much work you have to put in between now and test day.

It is in a school's interest to have a well-informed, serious applicant. Students who drop out of grad school because they've chosen the wrong career path, can't manage the workload, don't like the program, or simply found that the program in particular (or grad school in general) was not what they'd hoped it would be, have wasted both the school's time and money as well as their own. In many ways, the application process is all about identifying those students who will stay in the field and go on to rain glory down upon their alma mater. Students who don't fit that description are far more likely to drop out of the program. Those students and that tuition are hard to replace (advanced standing and executive programs are often a way for schools to take advantage of excess capacity freed up by vacating students).

In short, don't be afraid to pick up the phone and start your research. The more you know, the easier the process becomes, and the more likely it is that you get accepted—and the more likely it is that you make a wise choice with this investment of time (years), money (hundreds of thousands of dollars), and opportunity costs (how far would those same two years get you if you stayed where you are?). This is important.

If you have done your research and you know exactly where you want to go and why, then the GRE simply becomes a small hurdle that you must cross on your way. The GRE is an eminently surmountable hurdle. If you are not committed to the end game, the GRE may become a barrier rather than just a hurdle. If you are not clear on why you are going through this very long, expensive, and onerous process, then going out for drinks with friends on a Thursday night may seem far more worthwhile than sitting down to take another practice test, and therein lies the problem.

Getting serious about the research is the first step toward getting serious GRE scores.

THE TEST—OVERVIEW

You will receive a Math score, a Verbal score, and an Analytical Writing score. These correspond to the three types of sections you will see on the test. Section by section, here's how the test breaks down:

Section	Time	# of Questions
Biographical Information	+/– 10 minutes	–
Issue Essay	30 minutes	1
Argument Essay	30 minutes	1
Section 1	30 or 35 minutes	20
Section 2	30 or 35 minutes	20
Break	10 minutes	–
Section 3	30 or 35 minutes	20
Section 4	30 or 35 minutes	20
Section 5	30 or 35 minutes	20
Possible Research Section	Optional	Depends
Select Schools/Programs	5 minutes	Up to 4
Accept Scores	1 minute	–
Receive Scores	1 minute	–

Your essay sections will always come first. These are two back-to-back essays, each 30 minutes. After the essays you will have two multiple-choice sections, and then you get your one and only proper break.

Most students will see five sections, either two verbal and three math or three verbal and two math. Two Verbal sections and two Math sections will always count. The extra section is experimental. It may be math or verbal; it will look just like the other sections, but it will not count. These five sections, including the experimental, could occur in any order. There is no way to know which section is experimental. You will have a one-minute break between each of these sections.

Occasionally they will give you a research section in place of the experimental section. If so, it will come last; they will identify it as a research section and will tell you that it does not count. If you see one of these, your test is over and your first four sections counted.

Give Yourself a Break
You don't have to take this break, but you absolutely should. This is your one chance to reset your brain before diving back into the test. When you come back after those 10 minutes, you should feel as if you are just sitting down at the computer for the first time, refreshed and ready to go.

The Test Experience

The total testing time is close to four hours. It is a long four hours full of intense concentration. For those who are not prepared, it can also be full of lots of stress, and the atmosphere in the testing centers is not exactly designed to put you at ease.

When you are taking practice tests, make sure to complete all sections, even the essays, because stamina is an issue. Frequently students will focus just on areas of weakness or blow off the essay because they're not concerned about the essay score. This is a mistake. **Knowing how your brain works after two to three hours of close concentration is a big part of being prepared.**

The testing center can be an intimidating place. You will be asked to show ID when you come in. You will be issued a locker where you can store your belongings, since you cannot take anything with you into the test center. Then you will be asked to fill out a questionnaire and a legal disclaimer stating that you are who you say you are and that your reasons for taking the test are on the up and up (no taking it just for fun!). The test center caters to people taking a wide variety of tests, including TOEFL tests, citizenship tests, and others. This means that you will be sitting in a very plain institutional waiting room with a bunch of other fidgety, stressed-out people until you are called to the testing room.

In the testing room you will be issued a cubicle with a computer, six sheets of scratch paper, two pencils, and a set of headphones. The GRE does not have an audible component, but the headphones provided can be used to block out the noises from the cubicles around you. This is usually a good thing, since you will hear people smacking their foreheads, reading out loud, cursing, crying, and occasionally laughing. The fellow testing next to you may be watching his future dissolve before his very eyes. He may find the fact that you are humming to yourself, chuckling, and generally having a swell time—since you are so well prepared—a bit unnerving. That's why they have headphones.

In the beginning of the test, you will be given a tutorial on how to use the computer (scrolling, clicking with the mouse, accepting answers, and other tasks). We certainly hope that you feel prepared enough to skip this section (everyone is so nervous that they might miss something—although, in truth, almost no one does). If you have taken a few practice tests, you know what to do. Save yourself the extra eyeball time and skip the section.

The first section you will see is the 30-minute Analyze an Issue essay. You will be given a choice between two issue topics. The clock starts as soon as the two topics appear on screen. A complete list of the issue topics can be found on the ETS website. The tester has a basic word-processing function that will allow you to cut, paste, erase, and scroll. It does not have a spell-checker, but spelling is not tested on the GRE.

The second section is the 30-minute Analyze an Argument essay. In this section, you cannot choose your argument. A complete list of potential arguments can be found on the ETS website in the same place. The two essays are considered your

You can find more information about the essay tasks on the GRE's website here:

https://www.ets.org/gre/revised_general/prepare/analytical_writing/issue

https://www.ets.org/gre/revised_general/prepare/analytical_writing/argument

first section. You will then get two multiple-choice sections; they could be math or verbal, in any order. After your third section, you will be offered an optional 10-minute break. Use it to flap your arms a bit to get your blood flowing or rest your eyeballs. You could use it to go to the bathroom, but you'd have to be quick. Take as much time as you need to refresh yourself, but the more time you take the longer you'll be stuck in your cubicle. Technically you are not allowed to use your scratch paper during untimed sections, but this is not always enforced.

Most students will have five multiple-choice sections. All five will look like typical Verbal or Math sections, but only four of the five will count. The uncounted section is experimental. The experimental section may be either math or verbal and may occur anywhere between sections two and six. Occasionally ETS will identify the experimental section. They typically do this when they have really strange stuff to test and don't want to entirely freak out the test takers. For the most part, the experimental section is used to gather data on new questions so that they can be added to the general pool of scored questions. In other words, you are paying ETS to do their R&D for them and you are doing it when you are at your most stressed and your time is the most valuable. Sorry.

ETS may also add a "research" section. If they do this, it will come after the multiple-choice sections and they will attempt to bribe you with an infinitesimally small chance at winning a pathetically small scholarship ($500) toward your grad school tuition. Unless you are a particularly generous soul, don't bother.

After you have taken the scored portion of the exam, you will be given the opportunity to cancel your scores. After four hours, everyone tends to believe that they did worse than they actually did. Unless you passed out mid section, left five to ten questions blank, or started hallucinating while on the clock, there is not much to be gained from canceling the scores. If you cancel, you will never know how you did. Your test fee is non-refundable. Your record will reflect that you took the test on this day but that you cancelled your scores. At this point, you should know how your programs will deal with multiple scores. Unless you have a really compelling reason to believe that your scores were a disaster, accept them.

In addition to the dubious honor of contributing to ETS's research and development, your registration fee also buys you score reporting for up to four schools. Normally, if you wish to have scores sent to schools, ETS will charge you approximately $15 per school. On test day, however, the first four schools are included. This will be the last section of your test. You might as well take advantage of it. Some students are reluctant to send scores to first-choice schools because they don't yet know their scores. Send them anyway. If you are planning to apply to a particular school, they will see all of your prior scores, even if you take the test five times. If you don't apply, they'll put the scores in a file and, after a year or two, they'll throw them away. You have nothing to lose from sending out the scores. If you happen to know the school and department code for the schools of your choice, this part will go a bit faster. If not, no problem; you will have to negotiate a series of drop-down menus by state, school, and department.

You will have one minute between sections. You cannot skip questions, and you cannot go back to a question once you have entered and accepted an answer. Once you have completed the test, the computer will give you the option to accept your scores. Once you accept, they will show you your Math and Verbal scores only. Writing scores and percentiles will come about 10 days later in the mail. You must turn in your scratch paper and collect your ID on your way out (and you have to leave the headphones there too).

It is a long and grueling process. The more you have prepared, the less stress you will feel on test day. You can walk out of the test center feeling elated that it's over and good about your scores. Every math or verbal concept that you might see on the test is contained in this book. For the well-prepared student, there should be no surprises on test day. You should know precisely what your target score is and how to achieve it.

Scores

The GRE General Test is scored on a 130–170 point scale in one-point increments. A student might get a 159 on the Math and a 152 on the Verbal. The scale includes only 40 gradations between the highest possible score and the lowest.

Essays are scored on a 1–6 point scale in half-point increments. Students will receive a single averaged essay score for both essays. Quarter point increments are rounded up.

RESOURCES

In addition to this book you have some other worthwhile resources to consider:

Power Prep—There is a new Power Prep sample test on the ETS website. It is not adaptive, but it does mimic the functionality and style of the new GRE Revised General Test.

PrincetonReview.com contains one full-length, free GRE Revised General Test and a free online course demo.

Cracking the GRE—While the book you're reading is primarily about providing additional practice items for each subject, *Cracking the GRE* is like a full course in your hands. It contains all of the strategies, tips, and advice that have the made The Princeton Review the best standardized test-preparation company in the world.

Verbal Workout for the GRE—This book gives you everything you need to tackle the verbal portion of the GRE test. It includes hundreds of practice exercises to sharpen your skills, as well as the Hit Parade for the GRE, a list of the 300 vocabulary words that most frequently appear on the exam.

Math Workout for the GRE—This book goes into greater depth on each of the key math skills you will need on the test and contains multiple drills for each skill you may encounter on test day.

Crash Course for the GRE—This slim volume summarizes all of the major approaches. It is a great and focused review for those who are short on time.

HOW TO USE THIS BOOK

This book is all about building good test-taking habits, not about finding answers.

Over four hours of testing, your brain will get tired. When it gets tired, it will get sloppy. You might find yourself reading a question twice before it registers in your brain. You might start to skip small but key words, or you might find yourself staring at a problem for 30 seconds before you realize what you have to do. When you get tired, you begin to do things by habit without really thinking about them actively. If your habits are good, they will help carry you even when your brain starts to check out. If you have not taken the time to create good test-taking habits, well, you just get sloppy. Sloppiness will kill your score.

The creation of habits requires repetition and that's where this book comes in. You have large groups of similar question types that you can do over and over again until you learn to instantly recognize the situation and respond correctly.

There is a finite quantity of GRE practice material on the market. It is entirely possible to burn through all of it without improving your score by as much as one point. In fact, you may end up further reinforcing bad habits rather than creating new good ones. This happens when you focus on finding answers to each individual question without looking for larger patterns, working to practice and refine your approach, or using the practice material as an opportunity to create good GRE habits. Use *Cracking the GRE* to establish your approach to different question types. Then work your way through this book to cement those approaches into an automatic habit. When you do this, time and large score fluctuations will cease to be an issue. There will be no such thing as having a good or bad day on test day. You will be in control and will have your scores right where you want them.

If you want to change your score, you must change the way you take the test.

WHAT TO EXPECT FROM THIS BOOK

This book is for practicing questions.

In the pages to come, you will receive advice and strategies for how to handle common question types. This book will provide a high-level view of content typically found on the GRE and it is loaded with questions for you to practice.

For all the things this book is intended to be, it is not intended to be a deep-dive into the content. If you are looking for nuance and to learn the intricacies of the different types of content, may we suggest *Cracking the GRE* or the *Math Workout* and *Verbal Workout* books. If you are in a pinch for time and need a slightly more in-depth review than what is provided here, check out *Crash Course for the GRE*.

This book is intended to give you a place to learn some new stuff, develop some stamina, and try out some new skills. But it is mostly intended for you to practice, practice, practice.

Assessment

If you are under a time crunch or just need to shore up some weaknesses, this is your first step. Take the math and verbal assessment tests provided at the beginning of the book. Check your scores and find your areas of weakness. Pick two or three to focus on. The number of questions in a drill represents the frequency with which the question type shows up on most GRE General Tests. Focus on the high-frequency topics first.

Practice

In this book, each of the verbal question types (Text Completion, Reading Comprehension, Sentence Equivalence) and all of the math topics covered on the test gets its own section and set of drills. Each section begins with a brief synopsis of the basic approach. Read these sections carefully. These approaches have been tried, tested, and refined by hundreds of test takers over the years. They are here because they work. They represent good habits. How does the approach described by the book differ from your own? Can yours be improved?

Now is the time to take risks and try out different ways to solve these problems. On test day, it's about the answers, but today, you're not being graded. These items don't count. Take the opportunity to try new approaches. Some of the new techniques may feel awkward at first, but they're here because they've worked for others, so stick with it and really give them a try. Use your scratch paper, stick to your approach, and drill it until it becomes habit. By the time you are done, every time a question of that type pops up, your hand and your mind will know instinctively what to do, no matter how tired you get. This is powerful.

The One-Two Punch

If you are just starting your GRE prep, need more than 50–60 points, or don't yet have an approach, this book is not the place to start. This book is not for teaching. It is a workbook for practice and drilling. *Cracking the GRE* goes into the test and the techniques in far more depth. It breaks down the approach to each question in a step-by-step manner with plenty of examples. *Cracking the GRE* is where you go to learn *how* to take the test; this is where you go to practice it.

THE TEST

The problem you're working on will be in the middle of the screen. If there is additional information, such as a chart or graph or passage, it will be on a split screen either above the question or to the left of it. If the entire chart(s) or passage or additional information does not fit on the split screen, there will be a scroll bar.

Questions with only a single answer will have an oval selection field. To select an answer, just click on the oval. A question with the potential for multiple correct answers will have square answer fields. An X appears in the square when you select the answer choice. At the bottom of the screen, under the question, there may be some basic directions, such as "Click on your choice."

A readout of the time remaining in the section will be displayed in the upper right corner. Next to it is a button that allows you to hide the time. No matter what, the time will return and will begin to blink on and off when you have five minutes remaining on a particular section. At the top center, the display will tell you which question number you are working on, out of the total number of questions. The top of the screen will also contain the following six buttons:

Exit Section: This button indicates that you are done with a particular section. Should you finish a section early, you can use this button to get to the next section. Once you've exited a section, however, you cannot return to it. Note that the two essays are considered a single section. If you use this button after your first essay, you will have skipped the second essay.

Review: This button brings up a review screen. The review screen will indicate which questions you've seen, which ones you've answered, and which ones you've marked. From the review screen, you can return to the question you've just left, or you can highlight a particular question (once you've seen it) and Go To Question.

Mark: The mark button is just what it looks like. You may mark a question for whatever reason you choose. This does not answer the question. You may mark a question whether you've answered it or not. Marked questions will appear as marked on the review screen.

Help: The help button will drop you into the help tab for the particular question type you are working on. From there, there are three additional tabs. One gives you "Section Directions." This is an overview of the section, including the number of questions, the amount of time allotted, and a brief description of the function of ovals vs. boxes. The second is "General Directions" on timing and breaks, test information, and the repeater policy. The last additional tab is "Testing Tools." This is an overview of each of the buttons available to you during a section. Note that the help button will not stop the clock. The clock continues to run even if you are clicking around and reading directions.

Back/Next: These two buttons take you forward to the next question or back to the prior question. You can continue to click these as many times as you like until you get to the beginning or end of the section. If you return to a question you have answered, the question will display your answer.

We will talk more about strategies for pacing on the test and ways to use the mark and review buttons. You should never need the help button. Ideally you will be familiar enough with the functions of the test that you don't have to spend valuable test time reading directions.

How the Computer-Adaptive Test Works

The GRE is now adaptive by section. Your score is determined by the number of questions you get right and their difficulty level. On the first Verbal section, the test will give you a mix of medium questions. Based upon the percentage of questions you get right on that first section, the computer will select questions for the second section. The more you get right on the first section, the harder the questions you will see on the second section, but the more potential points you can get.

Everything is determined by the number of questions you get right, not by the number of questions you answer. Accuracy, therefore, will always trump speed. It makes no sense to worry about the clock and to rush through a section if your accuracy suffers as a result.

Take the Easy Test First!

On the GRE, some questions are a breeze, while others will have you tearing your hair out. You can answer these in any order you like, and the questions you get on the second section will depend upon the number of questions you get right on the first section. You can maximize that number by doing the questions you like first! Remember that every question counts equally toward your score. As you work through a section, if you see a question you don't know how to answer, skip it. If you see one that looks as if it will take a long time, skip it. If you love geometry, but hate algebra, do all of the geometry questions first and leave the algebra questions for last.

Unless you are shooting for a score in the highest percentile, you should NOT attempt to answer every single question.

As long as you are going to run out of time, you might as well run out of time on the questions you are least likely to get right. By leaving time-consuming and difficult questions for the end, you will be able to answer more questions overall and get more of them right. Do not mark questions you skip; we will use the mark function for something else. Just click "Next" and move on to the next question. The review screen will tell you which questions you have not answered.

Note: There is no guessing penalty on the GRE. They don't take points away for a wrong answer. When you get to the two-minute mark, therefore, stop what you're doing and bubble in any unanswered questions.

Answer Questions in Stages

Anytime you practice for a test, you end up getting a few wrong. Later, when reviewing these questions, you end up smacking your forehead and asking yourself, "What was I thinking?" Alternatively, you may find a problem utterly impossible to solve the first time around, only to look at it later and realize that it was actually quite easy; you just misread the question or missed a key piece of information.

On a four-hour test, your brain is going to get tired. When your brain gets tired, you're going make mistakes, like not noticing that the word "to" was missing from the previous clause. Typically these mistakes consist of misreadings or simple calculation errors. A misread question or a calculation error will completely change the way you see the problem. Unfortunately, once you see a question wrong, it is almost impossible to see it correctly. As long as you stay with that question, you will continue to see it wrong every time. Meanwhile, the clock is ticking and you're not getting any closer to the answer.

On the flip side, once you've spotted the error, solving the problem correctly requires only a moment. A question that bedeviled you for minutes on end in the middle of a test may appear to be appallingly obvious when viewed in the comfort of a post-test review. The trick is to change the way you see the question while you still have the opportunity to fix it.

> Step 1—Recognize that you're stuck.
> Step 2—Distract your brain.
> Step 3—See the problem with fresh eyes and fix it.

Step 1—Recognize that you're stuck. This is often the hardest part of the process. The more work you've put into a problem, the more difficult it is to walk away from it. Once you get off track on a problem, however, any additional work you invest in that problem is wasted effort. No problem on the GRE, if you understand what's being asked, should ever take that much time; you have only 30 to 35 minutes, after all! If you find yourself working too hard, or plowing through reams of calculations, you are off track. Get out.

Here are a few warning signs:

- You've found an answer, but it is not one of the choices they've given you.
- You have a half page of calculations, but are no closer to an answer.
- Your hand is not moving.
- You're down to two answer choices, and you would swear on your life that both are correct.
- There is smoke coming out of your ears.

If you find yourself in any of these situations, stop what you're doing and get out. You've got better things to do with your time than sitting around wrestling with this question.

Step 2—Distract your brain. When you find yourself faced with an immovable object, walk away. Think of it this way: you could spend four minutes on a question even when you know you're stuck, or you could walk away and spend those same four minutes on three other easier questions and get them all right. Why throw good minutes after bad? Whether they realize it or not, ETS has actually designed the test to facilitate this process. This is where the mark button comes into play. If you don't like a problem or don't know how to solve it, just skip it. If you start a problem and get stuck, mark it and move to the next question before you waste too much time. Do two other problems (three tops) and then return to the problem that was giving you trouble. We're fishing for that flash of insight here, giving it a chance to occur.

When you walk away from a problem, you're not walking away entirely; you're just parking it on the back burner. Your brain is still chewing on it, but it's processing in the background while you work on something else. Sometimes your best insights occur when your attention is pointed elsewhere. Walk away from a problem early and often. You want to always have questions to use to distract your brain. If you take the test in order, you will not have questions available at the tail end of a section. On some difficult problems you may walk away more than once. It is okay to take two or three runs at a hard problem.

Step 3—See the problem with fresh eyes and fix it. You use other problems to distract your brain so that you can see a troublesome problem with fresh eyes. You can help this process out by trying to read the question differently when you return to it. Use your finger on the screen to force yourself to read the problem word for word. Are there different ways to express the information? Can you use the answer choices to help? Can you paraphrase the answer choices as well? If the path to the right answer is not clear on a second viewing, walk away again. Why stick with a problem you don't know how to solve?

Scratch Paper

After pacing, the next most important global skill is the use of your scratch paper. On a regular test you can solve problems with a pencil right on the test page. On the GRE, you don't have that luxury. Remember that taking the GRE is a skill, and like any other skill it can be practiced and learned. Your physical habits as a test taker are as important as your mental ones. In fact, your physical habits will be used to reinforce your mental ones. Remember that the test is chock-full of tricks and answer choices designed to tempt the tired mind. **If your hand is not moving, it means that you are answering questions in your head.** That is precisely what ETS wants because they have a million students a year testing out their tricks on the experimental section. They are extremely good at it. Your one head cannot beat a-million-students-a-year's worth of trial and error and refinement—but your hand can.

Your use of scratch paper can set you up to approach a question that you might not otherwise know how to approach, it can protect against careless errors, it can have a remarkable effect on efficiency, and, best of all, it can relieve an enormous amount of the mental stress that occurs during testing.

Tip #1—You can separate all GRE questions into two categories. The first category is for questions that you are supposed to get right. These questions are in your scoring range; you know the math or the vocabulary. Not only can you get these questions right, but it is critical to your score that you do so. The second category is for questions that you're not supposed to get correct. They have been tested and proved to be hard; they have difficult vocabulary words and difficult math. Within this categorization, the techniques have two functions. The first is to ensure that the questions you are supposed to get right, you do get right. This is not to be dismissed lightly. Careless errors, especially in the first 10 questions, will kill your score. Rushing through problems that seem easy will kill your score. The second function of the techniques is the use of Process of Elimination to ensure that any and all students will get correct a guaranteed percentage of even those questions that they are not supposed to get correct. Proper use of scratch paper ensures that techniques are happening and happening correctly.

Tip #2—On the Verbal section, the scratch paper has two primary functions. The first is to allow you to park your thinking on the page, to externalize it, to commit to it. If you are doing even an easy question in your head, you are really doing two jobs. The first is the work of solving the question. The second is the work of keeping track of which answer choices are still in and which ones are out. Not only is this mental multitasking extremely inefficient, it can also be quite stressful. Frankly, it's twice the work. By parking your thinking on the page, you efficiently remove wrong answers from consideration, identify your potential answer choices, and move on. You create clarity and organization. Both things lead to less stress, less mental effort, and ultimately less mental fatigue. Students who are doing the work in their heads will spend 20 percent of their time per question just looking at the screen, keeping track of what is in, out, or a maybe.

Tip #3—On the Math section are a number of question types that provoke very specific set-ups on your scratch paper. Once you see the question types, before you have even fully read the question, you make your set-ups and start filling in information. When you have done this, you are halfway into the question, you have organized your thinking and approach, and you have set yourself up to succeed on the problem. All that remains is to fill in the numbers. This is stress-free living on the GRE. It all starts with the scratch paper.

Tip #4—On the Verbal section, use your scratch paper as a place to park your thinking. Quickly evaluate each answer choice with a simple check for one that could work, an X for one that will not, an M or horizontal squiggle for a maybe, and a question mark for one you do not know. Once you have evaluated each answer choice, select from the ones which remain and move on. This will ensure that you don't spend too much time getting stuck trying to assess a difficult answer choice. **You can always spend more time on an answer choice IF you have to, but you never want to spend more time than you HAVE to.**

Tip #5—Learn the set-ups for each type of question. Keep your page organized with space on one side for the question set-up and the other side for calculations. Once you have completed a question, draw a horizontal line across the page and start the next one in a clean space. Do your work on the page. If you get off track you will be able to find out why and where.

VERBAL QUESTION TYPES

Text Completion—These used to be Sentence Completion, but now they've gotten longer, and you must work with each blank independently. Questions may have between one and five sentences and one to three blanks. A one-blank question will have five answer choices. A two- or three-blank question will have three choices per blank. You must select the correct word for each blank to get credit for the question.

Sentence Equivalence—These look like Sentence Completion questions but with one blank and six answer choices. You must select two answer choices from the six provided. Each correct answer will complete the sentence and keep the meaning the same.

Reading Comprehension—Reading Comp supplies you with a passage and then asks you questions about the information in the passage, the author's intent, or the structure. There are three distinct question types that could occur here. They are as follows:

- **Multiple Choice**—You must select one correct answer from five choices.
- **Select All That Apply**—These questions used to number three choices with roman numerals and you had to pick I, I and II only, and so on. Now you simply select the correct answer or answers from a group of three choices.
- **Select in Passage**—You will be asked to click on an actual sentence in the passage. You may click on one word to select the whole sentence. Only one sentence is correct. These will occur primarily on short passages. If they occur in a long passage, the question will specify a particular paragraph.

MATH QUESTION TYPES

Quantitative Comparison—Quant Comps, for short, give you information in two columns. Your job is to decide if the values in the two columns are the same, if one is larger, or if it is impossible to say. (Tip: If there are no variables in either column, eliminate (D).)

Problem Solving—These are the typical five-answer, multiple-choice questions you probably remember from the SAT or ACT. You must correctly select one of the five answer choices to get credit. (Tip: They've given you the answers. One of them is correct. Use the answer choices to help answer the question.)

Select All That Apply—This is a new twist on the old multiple-choice question. In this case, you may have anywhere from three to eight answer choices, and one or more will be correct. You must select ALL of the correct answer choices to get credit. (Tip: The answer choices are generally in ascending or descending order, so start in the middle and look to eliminate as many wrong answer choices as possible.)

Numeric Entry—Alas, these are not multiple choice. It is your job to come up with your own number and type it into the box provided. For fractions, you will be given two boxes and you must fill in the top and the bottom separately. (Tip: You don't have to reduce your fractions. The computer reads 44/88 the same as 1/2, so save yourself a step.)

The Calculator

The GRE provides an on-screen calculator. Like the calculator you might find on your computer, this one will add, subtract, multiply, divide, and find a square root. It also has a transfer number button that allows you to transfer the number on the calculator screen directly to the box on a Numeric Entry question. This button will be grayed out on a multiple-choice question.

Since we all use calculators in our daily life, it's about time they provided one on the GRE. Certainly this should cut down on basic calculation errors and save a bit of time on questions that involve things like averages or percentages. The GRE, however, is not generally a test of your ability to do large calculations, nor is the calculator a replacement for your brain. The test makers will look for ways to test your analytic skills, often making the calculator an unnecessary temptation, or, at times, even a liability. Be particularly careful of questions that ask you to provide answers in a specific format. A question may ask you to provide an answer rounded to the nearest tenth, for example. If your calculator gives you an answer of 3.48, and you transfer that number, you will get the question wrong. Or a question may ask you for a percent and will have the percent symbol next to the answer box. In this case they are looking for a whole number. Depending upon how you solve the problem on your calculator, you may end up with an answer of .25 for 25%. If you enter the decimal, you will get the question wrong.

Here are a few tips for when to use and when not to use your calculator on the GRE:

Good Calculator

- Multiplying two- and three-digit numbers
- Finding percentages or averages
- Solving questions involving Order of Operations (The calculator will understand Order of Operations. If you type in 3 + 5 × 6, it will know to prioritize multiplication over addition.)
- Solving questions that ask you to work with decimals

Bad Calculator

- Converting fractions to decimals in order to avoid working with fractions (better that you know the rules and are comfortable with fractions)
- Attempting to solve large exponents, square roots, or other calculation-heavy operations. There is almost always a faster way to do the problem.
- Solving questions involving adding or subtracting negative numbers if you're not sure of the rules
- Solving charts problems with multiple questions. Write all information down on your scratch paper and label everything. Information you find on one problem might help on another. If you do everything on your calculator, you will have to recalculate.

Calculating

In general, ETS is not interested in testing your ability to do lots of calculations. They like to think that they are testing how well you think rather than how well you can calculate. Therefore, if you find yourself doing lots of calculating on a particular question, you are probably off track. You can often calculate your way to the correct answer if necessary, but usually there is a better way. Your success depends upon how quickly and readily you can spot the opportunities.

Algebra is one math concept that shows up all over the test. There are dozens of different ways to ask an algebra question, some more obvious than others. The sooner you recognize it as an algebra question and make the correct set-up on your scratch paper, the better. This will buy you more time for the occasional question on which you do get hung up. That is where this book comes in. The first 10 algebra questions may look hard. By the time you've seen 60, however, you begin to see them all as variations on a theme. When you can do that, you're ready.

Reading

In many ways, the math portion of the test is as much a test of reading as the verbal. Many of the math problems you will see start out as large blocks of text. When you see a large block of text, break it down into bite-sized pieces and solve the problem meticulously, one step at a time. Skipping or combining steps leads to trouble. Don't be afraid to read the problem out loud to yourself or to use your pencil to follow along with the text on the screen as you're reading. Reading too quickly leads to trouble, skipping words when you read (something all good readers do) leads to trouble, and careless errors will kill your score.

Ballparking

As a general rule, Ballpark first and calculate second. Naturally you should end up Ballparking more at the end of the section and calculating more at the beginning, but it's a good rule of thumb. Ballparking can take many forms. The first benefit to Ballparking is that you can't do it if you don't understand the question. The basic process of trying to come up with a range for an answer involves arriving at a conceptual understanding of what the question is asking. If you are at the tail end of a section, you might stop here and pick an answer. If you are in your first 10, you might use this as a way of figuring out how to go about determining the actual answer.

Ballparking is a valuable way to check your work. GRE questions tend to make sense. The correct answer to a question asking for the number of students in a class will not contain a fraction (ETS won't generally chop a student in half). A question in which a person bicycles uphill one way and downhill on the way home, will not involve a distance greater than the distance a person could or would bike to work in a day. If you are asked for time, and you know that the round trip of 20 miles took two hours, then each leg would average 60 minutes. If you are looking for the downhill leg, any answer greater than 60 is wrong and any answer less than the amount of time an average person could reasonably bike 10 miles is wrong. This is Ballparking. It won't necessarily eliminate four out of five wrong answers (although it could), but it will eliminate a few—and it will tell you the answer you generated actually makes sense.

Diagnostic Test

MATH

Directions: For Questions 1 through 8, compare Quantity A and Quantity B, using additional information centered above the two quantities if such information is given, and select one of the following four answer choices.

(A) *Quantity A is greater.*
(B) *Quantity B is greater.*
(C) *The two quantities are equal.*
(D) *The relationship cannot be determined from the information given.*

A symbol that appears more than once in a question has the same meaning throughout the question.

Question 1

$$y \neq 0$$

Quantity A	Quantity B
$5y^2$	$-\dfrac{y^2}{7}$

○ Quantity A is greater.
○ Quantity B is greater.
○ The two quantities are equal.
○ The relationship cannot be determined from the information given.

Question 2

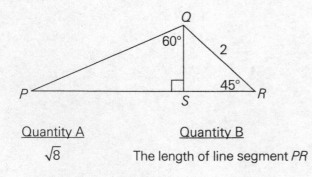

Quantity A	Quantity B
$\sqrt{8}$	The length of line segment *PR*

○ Quantity A is greater.
○ Quantity B is greater.
○ The two quantities are equal.
○ The relationship cannot be determined from the information given.

Question 3

Tony has $3,500 more in his bank account than Brad.

Courtney has $4,700 more in her bank account than Jenny.

Brad has $1,200 more in his bank account than Jenny.

Quantity A	Quantity B
The amount of money in Tony's bank account	The amount of money in Courtney's bank account

○ Quantity A is greater.
○ Quantity B is greater.
○ The two quantities are equal.
○ The relationship cannot be determined from the information given.

Question 4

A computer manufacturer builds 1,000 computers and all of them are sold at a retail store for the same price. The total profit from all of the computer sales is $20,000, or 40% of the total cost of production for all the computers.

Quantity A	Quantity B
The cost of one computer at a retail store	$50

○ Quantity A is greater.
○ Quantity B is greater.
○ The two quantities are equal.
○ The relationship cannot be determined from the information given.

Question 5

Quantity A	Quantity B
The least prime factor of 7^2	The least prime factor of 2^7

- ○ Quantity A is greater.
- ○ Quantity B is greater.
- ○ The two quantities are equal.
- ○ The relationship cannot be determined from the information given.

Question 6

The average (arithmetic mean) of a, b, c, and d is 7.

Quantity A	Quantity B
15	The average (arithmetic mean) of $4a - 5c$, $b - 24$, $8c - a$, and $3d + 2b$

- ○ Quantity A is greater.
- ○ Quantity B is greater.
- ○ The two quantities are equal.
- ○ The relationship cannot be determined from the information given.

Question 7

The length of the width of the larger square is equal to the length of the diagonal (not shown) of the smaller square.

Quantity A	Quantity B
The area of the smaller square	The area of the shaded region

- ○ Quantity A is greater.
- ○ Quantity B is greater.
- ○ The two quantities are equal.
- ○ The relationship cannot be determined from the information given.

Question 8

x and y are both integers
$$xy \neq 0$$
$$x < y$$

Quantity A	Quantity B
x^2	y^2

- ○ Quantity A is greater.
- ○ Quantity B is greater.
- ○ The two quantities are equal.
- ○ The relationship cannot be determined from the information given.

Question 9

The volume of a cube with edge of length 2 is how many times the volume of a cube with edge of length $\sqrt{2}$?

- ○ $\sqrt{2}$
- ○ 2
- ○ $2\sqrt{2}$
- ○ 4
- ○ 8

Question 10

BILLIE'S TIME SHEET FOR JULY 2

Time in:	8:57 in the morning
Time out:	5:16 in the afternoon
Time spent stacking shelves:	80% of total time spent at work

According to the time sheet above, Billie spent approximately how many hours stacking shelves on July 2 ?

○ $5\dfrac{1}{3}$

○ $6\dfrac{2}{3}$

○ $7\dfrac{1}{3}$

○ $8\dfrac{2}{3}$

○ $9\dfrac{1}{3}$

Question 11

What is the probability that the sum of two different single-digit prime numbers will NOT be prime?

○   0

○ $\dfrac{1}{2}$

○ $\dfrac{2}{3}$

○ $\dfrac{5}{6}$

○   1

Question 12

To fill a large concert hall, a madrigal singing group consisting of sopranos, altos, and basses, in a 5 : 7 : 3 ratio, needs at least 40 singers. What is the least number of basses the group needs?

Question 13

If $mx + qy - nx - py = 0$, $p - q = 2$, and $\dfrac{y}{x} = -\dfrac{1}{3}$, then which of the following is true?

○ $n - m = \dfrac{2}{3}$

○ $n - m = -\dfrac{2}{3}$

○ $m + n = \dfrac{2}{3}$

○ $m + n = \dfrac{3}{2}$

○ $m + n = -\dfrac{3}{2}$

Question 14

The "hash" of a three-digit integer with three distinct digits is defined as the result of interchanging its units and hundreds digits. The absolute value of the difference between a three-digit integer and its hash must be divisible by which of the following integers?

○   9
○   7
○   5
○   4
○   2

Questions 15-16 refer to the following graphs.

SENIOR MANAGEMENT OF COMPANY Y

Average Salaries of Senior Managers at Company Y

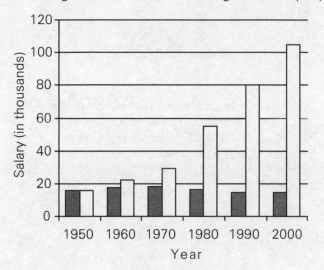

Number of Senior Managers at Company Y

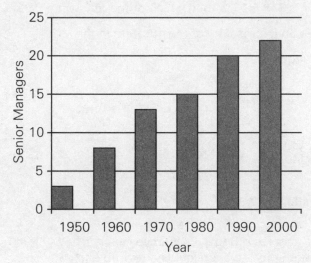

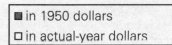

■ in 1950 dollars
□ in actual-year dollars

Question 15

If the number of senior managers increased by 60 percent from 1980 to 2007, what was the increase in the number of senior managers from 2000 through 2007, inclusive?

○ 2
○ 4
○ 6
○ 9
○ 12

Question 16

Which of the following statements can be inferred from the charts above?

Indicate all such statements.

☐ From 1990 to 2000, the average salary, in actual-year dollars, increased by more than 10%.

☐ In 1960, there were fewer than 5 senior managers.

☐ For the decades shown, the number of senior managers increased by the greatest percentage between 1980 and 1990.

Question 17

The sequence of positive numbers $s_1, s_2, s_3 \ldots s_n \ldots$ is defined by $s_n = s_{n-1} + 5$ for $n \geq 2$. If $s_1 = 7$, then which of the following is an expression for the nth term in the sequence?

- ○ $5n - 5$
- ○ $5n - 2$
- ○ $5n$
- ○ $5n + 2$
- ○ $5n + 7$

Question 18

Rachel and Rob live 190 miles apart. They both drive in a straight line toward each other to meet for tea. If Rachel drives at 50 mph and Rob drives at 70 mph, then how many miles apart are they exactly 45 minutes before they meet?

- ○ 50
- ○ 60
- ○ 70
- ○ 90
- ○ 100

Question 19

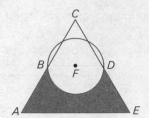

Triangle ACE is equilateral with side lengths of 8. Points B and D are the midpoints of line segments AC and CE respectively. Line segment BD is a diameter of the circle with center F. What is the area of the shaded region?

- ○ $8\sqrt{2} - 4\pi$
- ○ $12\sqrt{3} - 2\pi$
- ○ $12\sqrt{3} - 4\pi$
- ○ $16\sqrt{3} - 2\pi$
- ○ $16\sqrt{2} - 4\pi$

Question 20

If $x = 3^2$, then what is the value of x^x ?

- ○ 3^4
- ○ 3^8
- ○ 3^9
- ○ 3^{12}
- ○ 3^{18}

VERBAL

For each of Questions 1 to 5, select one entry for each blank from the corresponding column of choices. Fill all blanks in the way that best completes the text.

Question 1

British modernists used the literary tropes of fragmentation and failure to explore the impending (i)_____ of British colonialism, illustrating the imminent (ii)_____ of the empire through their literature.

Blank (i)	Blank (ii)
avarice	sunset
castigation	rise
dissolution	wealth

Question 2

The development of hydrogen-powered cars will always be (i)_____ by the physical fact that hydrogen, while containing more energy per gallon than does gasoline, is much less dense than gasoline; hydrogen thus carries less energy per pound, making it (ii)_____ for any vehicle to carry enough hydrogen on board for long trips.

Blank (i)	Blank (ii)
enhanced	convenient
hindered	austere
parodied	ungainly

Question 3

One of the rarest of celestial events, the total solar eclipse, happens only when the Moon, in its orbit around the Earth, fully (i)_____ the view of the sun from a particular location on Earth. Because the Moon is relatively small, in celestial terms, and its umbra, the central part of the Moon's shadow caused by its blocking the sun, traces only a narrow path on the Earth, total eclipses are such (ii)_____ occurrences that they have been known to draw hundreds of thousands of onlookers.

Blank (i)	Blank (ii)
secularizes	atypical
epitomizes	desultory
occludes	momentous

Question 4

To (i)_____ people accurately, census workers must be (ii)_____: because there are often residents of a household with the same name, or people whose names have unusual spellings, workers who are anything less than (iii)_____ in following correct procedures and reviewing cases may result in the same resident getting counted multiple times, or not at all.

Blank (i)	Blank (ii)	Blank (iii)
rectify	derivative	meticulous
tally	fastidious	perfunctory
impute	industrious	inexact

Question 5

The journalist was (i)_____ in his pursuit of the scandal he suspected: despite a lack of support from his editors, he was determined to investigate day and night, follow every lead, and write until dawn to (ii)_____ the big news agencies and release the story first.

Blank (i)	Blank (ii)
decorous	surmount
digressive	forestall
indefatigable	deprecate

For each of Questions 6 to 10, select <u>one</u> answer choice unless otherwise instructed.

Question 6

Over the last several decades, the demand for Country Y's automobiles increased in Country X, but demand for Country X's automobiles in Country Y has remained stagnant. Despite the successful attempts by County X's manufacturers to close the gap in technology so that the automobiles from each country are now equivalent to each other in this respect, Country X's manufacturers fail to acknowledge that drivers in Country Y drive on the left side of the road. Clearly, to help lessen this trade imbalance, Country X manufacturers should produce more cars with right-side steering wheels.

Which of the following is an assumption made by the argument?

○ Reversing the trade imbalance requires making cars with right-side steering wheels.

○ If Country X makes automobiles with right-side steering wheels, most consumers from Country Y will choose to purchase a car from Country X.

○ If consumers from Country Y drive on the left side of the road, these consumers are less inclined to buy steering wheels found on the left-side of the car.

○ The fuel efficiency and maintenance costs of cars from Country X will continue to improve.

○ The government of Country Y requires all its citizens to purchase cars with right-side steering wheels.

Questions 7-10 refer to the following passage.

Comparative historian Marc Ferro claims that the largest discrepancy in knowledge between what academic historians and what the average citizen knows about history is found in the United States. How has this situation come about? Certainly the problem does not lie with the secondary literature. Whereas in the past, American historians were handicapped by secondary literature that was clearly biased towards a European viewpoint, since the civil rights movement of the 1950s and 60s, the secondary literature in American history has become far more comprehensive. And it cannot be simply a matter of space constraints; the average high school history textbook is well over a thousand pages in length.

One theory holds that American history textbooks are simply the socializing instruments of a controlling elite. The stratification of American society is preserved, according to this theory, by the creation of what Marx termed "false consciousness." The theory holds that the way people think about their society and their history is crucial to maintaining the status quo. If the power elites come to believe that their success is the deserved product of their hard work and ingenuity, then there will be no desire to change the system. Similarly, if the lower classes are taught that their plight is solely due to their failings, they will be more likely to accept their fate and less likely to rise up in revolution. Griffin and Marciano contend that history textbooks promote nothing more than hegemony.

Many educational theorists share this viewpoint, which in their discipline is often known as critical theory. Proponents of this view, including Kozol, Freire, and Giroux, argue that the dominant classes would never create or foster an educational system that taught subordinate classes how to critically evaluate society and the injustices it contains. As long as schools serve to transmit culture, the power elite will never allow any real reform in the system.

It is all too easy to blame citizens' poor understanding of American history on some shadowy coterie of cultural aristocracy. But critical theory and other theories that lay the blame for American ignorance of history on the doorstep of the elites cannot explain their own success. Is it not a paradox that critical theory scholarship dominates its field? If the titans of society had as much power as the critical theorists contend, they would surely censor or marginalize the works of social scientists in this field. Furthermore, graduates of "elite" preparatory schools are exposed to alternative interpretations of history, subversive teachers, and unfiltered primary source materials more frequently than are students at public institutions. This would seem to indicate that the power-brokers have little control over what happens at their very own schools, let alone far flung rural schools or schools deep in urban territory. The real culprit may be something not as insidious as a vast upper class conspiracy, but more along the lines of pernicious forces working at a highly local level. Almost half of the states have textbook adoption boards consisting of members of the community. These boards review and recommend what books are taught in neighborhood schools. And because textbook publishers are first and foremost seeking to maximize profit, it is these local boards that they must appease.

Question 7

For the following question, consider each of the choices separately and select all that apply.

According to the passage, proponents of the critical theory believe which of the following?

☐ The creation of a false consciousness is a significant element in maintaining the stratification of American society.

☐ It is not in the interests of the powerful classes of society to engender critical reflection among the majority of citizens.

☐ Alternative interpretations of history may be taught to members of the upper classes, but not to members of the subordinate classes.

Question 8

It can be inferred from the passage that

○ Marx was an early proponent of critical theory

○ textbooks are not solely designed as teaching instruments

○ the secondary literature on American history is no longer biased

○ textbook publishers do not take the views of the power elite into account

○ under the current system, real education reform is impossible

Question 9

For the following question, consider each of the choices separately and select all that apply.

Which of the following statements about critical theory can be supported by the passage?

☐ It is simply another means by which the power elite preserves the stratification of American society.

☐ It does not contain any of the same biases which had appeared in the secondary literature prior to the civil rights movement.

☐ It is not unique in its attempts to attribute Americans' poor knowledge of history to the machinations of a particular class of individuals.

Question 10

Select the sentence in the first paragraph that explains why a problem is less severe for current American historians now than it was a century ago.

Question 11

Not only did the exhibit clearly show the health benefits of a vegetarian diet, it showed how those benefits often translate into a greater sense of _____.

- ☐ vitality
- ☐ mendacity
- ☐ remorse
- ☐ vigor
- ☐ contrition
- ☐ persecution

Question 12

Contemporary authors are more at liberty to be candid than were authors of previous centuries, but modern writers nevertheless often find themselves _____ portions of their works.

- ☐ emancipating
- ☐ censoring
- ☐ refuting
- ☐ lauding
- ☐ ameliorating
- ☐ expurgating

Question 13

While the author clearly identifies the importance of Victorian culture to twentieth-century technological advances, he _____ the importance of British Regency to the development of the social factors that influenced Victorian culture.

- ☐ intimates
- ☐ corroborates
- ☐ neglects
- ☐ placates
- ☐ trumpets
- ☐ omits

Question 14

The writer, though restrained and terse in his prose, had a tendency to be a _____ speaker.

- ☐ eloquent
- ☐ elegant
- ☐ bombastic
- ☐ gregarious
- ☐ verbose
- ☐ affable

Question 15

Given that conditions were quite amenable to fruit trees during the growing season this year, the _____ of apples this fall is surprising.

- ☐ dearth
- ☐ countenance
- ☐ surfeit
- ☐ spate
- ☐ amalgamation
- ☐ paucity

Questions 16-17 refer to the following passage.

Critics of Mark Twain's novel _Huckleberry Finn_ view the protagonist's proclamation "All right, then, I'll go to hell" in chapter 31 as the story's climax. Twain's novel lent itself to such radical interpretations because it was the first major American work to depart from traditional European novelistic structures, thus providing critics with an unfamiliar framework. The remaining twelve chapters act as a counterpoint, commenting on, if not reversing, the first part in which a morality play receives greater confirmation. Huck's journey down the Mississippi represents a rite of passage, in which the character's personal notions of right and wrong come into constant conflict with his socially constructed conscience by the various people and situations the protagonist encounters.

The novel's cyclical structure encourages critics to see the novel's disparate parts as interlinked; the novel begins and ends with the boys playing games. Granted, this need not argue to an authorial awareness of novelistic construction; however, it does facilitate attempts to view the novel as a unified whole. Nevertheless, any interpretation that seeks to unite the last few chapters with the remaining book is bound to be tenuous. This is not because such an interpretation is unnecessarily rigid, but because _Huckleberry Finn_ encompasses individual scenes of the protagonist's self-recognition that are difficult to accommodate in an all-encompassing interpretation. In this respect, the protagonist can best be likened to the Greek tragic figure, Oedipus.

Question 16

The author mentions the "novel's cyclical structure" in order to

- ○ demonstrate that Twain was keenly aware of novelistic construction
- ○ show that the remaining twelve chapters have little connection to the rest of the novel
- ○ support the critic's position that Twain was unaware of novelistic construction
- ○ provide support for a particular critical interpretation of Twain's work
- ○ argue that Twain's protagonist has much in common with Oedipus

Question 17

Which of the following best expresses the main idea of the passage?

- ○ In order to understand Twain's novel, critics must compare its protagonist to Oedipus.
- ○ Twain's novel contains some chapters that resist easy inclusion into a unified interpretation.
- ○ The unconventional structure of _Huckleberry Finn_ indicates a lack of authorial awareness.
- ○ Twain's novel was the first major American novel to discard traditional European structures.
- ○ The protagonist of _Huckleberry Finn_ is considered a modern-day Oedipus by critics.

Questions 18-19 refer to the following passage.

One of the most noxious wind-borne allergens is ragweed *(Ambrosia)*, as evidenced by an estimated 30 million sufferers in the United States alone and a societal cost of over $3 billion. Each plant is able to produce more than a billion grains of pollen over the course of a season, and the plant is the prime cause of most cases of hay fever in North America. Although the plant produces more pollen in wet years, humidity rates above seventy percent tend to depress the spread of pollen by causing the grains to clump.

Ragweed spreads rapidly by colonizing recently disturbed soil, such as that engendered by roads, subdivisions, and cultivation and has adapted to a multitude of climatic conditions, including desert and high mountain areas. Complete elimination is virtually impossible. Physical removal is undone by even one seed or one bit of root left behind. Ragweed regenerates in about two weeks from only a half-inch of stem, usually with additional branching and flowering, so mowing can actually be counterproductive. Ragweed is susceptible to only the most aggressive herbicides, and because ragweed tends to cover large areas, control would mean widespread use of highly toxic chemicals. Control by natural predators? No known mammal browses on ragweed. Some species of *Lepidoptera* (butterflies, skippers, and moths) larvae feed on ragweed, but this arena of control is not well-funded, and consequently not well-researched. Given the health issues and costs occasioned by ragweed, government funding for natural control research is warranted.

Question 18

For the following question, consider each of the choices separately and select all that apply.

Which of the following can be inferred about the spread of ragweed pollen?

☐ Ragweed plants adapted to desert and mountain climates tend to spread fewer grains of pollen than do plants in other locations.

☐ Some attempts to control ragweed pollen may exacerbate the problem.

☐ The clumping of pollen grains caused by high humidity levels affects the ability of the wind to carry the grains.

Question 19

The author mentions some species of *Lepidoptera* in order to

○ detail a species that may be more effective at controlling ragweed than are the most aggressive herbicides

○ suggest a potential research avenue to the problem of controlling ragweed that is at present poorly explored

○ discuss a type of mammal that feeds on ragweed plants and may be successful at controlling the spread of ragweed

○ plead with the government to spend more money and put more research efforts into finding a natural control for ragweed

○ argue that complete elimination of the ragweed plant will only be possible if the government funds research into natural controls of ragweed

Question 20 refers to the following passage.

Friedrich Nietzsche's *Twilight of the Idols* expanded on the problem of the preponderance of reason in ancient Greek society, an issue he first broached in *The Birth of Tragedy.* The radical idea that Socrates was symptomatic of a declining Greek society based on the deification of rationality was almost unique among Enlightenment thinkers. Reaction to the idea in *The Birth of Tragedy,* in fact, was so negative among German academics that Nietzsche himself vacillated in his support, referring to the work as "impossible" and "embarrassing" in a preface to the second edition before returning to the notion in his later works. The antipathy of his peers is not surprising given that he took aim at such pillars of Western thinking as Plato, Socrates, even Christianity. Though originally widely refuted at the time of writing, themes related to the conflict between the rationality on one hand and the power of the senses on the other, were revisited time and time again by his successors.

Question 20

According to the author, proponents of Nietzsche's work would most likely agree that

○ human reason is infallible whereas the senses decay along with the body and are therefore subservient to the mind

○ there is a conflict between Socrates and traditional Christian thought

○ Nietzsche had little influence on later thinkers

○ privileging reason over the senses had a deleterious effect on Greek society at the time of Socrates

○ Nietzsche found Plato to be embarrassing

ANSWERS

Math

1. A
2. B
3. C
4. A
5. A
6. C
7. C
8. D
9. C
10. B
11. C
12. 9
13. A
14. A
15. A
16. A
17. D
18. D
19. B
20. E

Verbal

1. dissolution, sunset
2. hindered, ungainly
3. occludes, atypical
4. tally, fastidious, meticulous
5. indefatigable, surmount
6. C
7. A, B
8. B
9. C
10. Whereas in the past, American historians....
11. vitality, vigor
12. censoring, expurgating
13. neglects, omits
14. bombastic, verbose
15. dearth, paucity
16. D
17. B
18. B, C
19. B
20. D

EXPLANATIONS

Math

1. **A** The question states that $y \neq 0$, so Plug In values for y. If y is 2, then Quantity A is $5(2^2) = 5(4) = 20$

   and Quantity B is $-\dfrac{2^2}{7} = -\dfrac{4}{7}$, so Quantity A is greater than Quantity B and you can elimi-

   nate (B) and (C). Plug In again using a FROZEN number such as $y = -\dfrac{1}{2}$. Quantity A is

   $5\left(-\dfrac{1}{2}^2\right) = 5\left(\dfrac{1}{4}\right) = \dfrac{5}{4}$ and Quantity B is $-\dfrac{\left(-\dfrac{1}{2}\right)^2}{7} = -\dfrac{\frac{1}{4}}{7}$. It is unnecessary to further simplify

   Quantity B, as Quantity A is positive, and Quantity B is negative. Because y^2 is always positive and

   there is a negative sign in front of the fraction for Quantity B, Quantity A is always positive and

   Quantity B is always negative. Quantity A is greater than Quantity B and the correct answer is (A).

2. **B** Straight angle PSR measures 180 degrees, so angle QSR is 90 degrees, and angle SQR is 45

   degrees. This makes triangle QSR a 45-45-90 triangle. Dividing QR by $\sqrt{2}$ yields the lengths

   of QS and SR, that is, $\dfrac{2}{\sqrt{2}}$, which equals $\sqrt{2}$. Angle QPS measures 30°, so triangle PQS is a

   30-60-90 triangle, and PS is found by multiplying QS by $\sqrt{3}$, which is $\sqrt{6}$. Add the lengths of SR

   and PS to find the length of PR, and the value for Quantity B, which is $\sqrt{2} + \sqrt{6}$. Compare this

   to Quantity A by simplifying $\sqrt{8}$ to $2\sqrt{2} = \sqrt{2} + \sqrt{2}$. Each quantity contains at least one $\sqrt{2}$, so

   one can be ignored in each quantity. Because $\sqrt{6}$ is greater than $\sqrt{2}$, Quantity B is greater and the

   correct answer is (B).

3. **C** This problem asks for specific values and gives relationships about those values. It would be more
   easily solved if those values were known, so this is a Hidden Plug In problem. Choose a number
   for the amount of money in Tony's bank account that makes the numbers easy to work with. If
   Tony has $7,000 in his bank account, then Brad has $3,500. Brad has $1,200 more than Jenny, so
   Jenny has $2,300 in her bank account. Courtney has $4,700 more than Jenny, so $4,700 + $2,300
   = $7,000. Courtney and Tony both have $7,000. Eliminate (A) and (B). Because this is a Quant
   Comp Plug In problem, remember to Plug In more than once. If Tony has $10,000 in his bank

account, then Brad has $6,500 and Jenny has $5,300. So, Courtney has $5,300 + $4,700 = $10,000. Courtney and Tony still have the same amount of money in their accounts, so eliminate (D) and select (C).

4.　A　A computer manufacturer builds 1,000 computers and sells all of them which yields a profit of $20,000. The amount of $20,000 is 40% of the cost of production, so the total cost of production is $20,000 = $\frac{40}{100}x$; therefore, x = $50,000. Determine the cost of one computer at the retail store to find the value for Quantity A. All computers are sold for the same amount of money, so determine the total amount of money spent at the retail store. If the total profit is $20,000 and the total cost of production is $50,000, then the total amount of money spent on the computers at the retail store is $70,000. The cost of one computer is $\frac{\$70,000}{1,000}$ = $70. So, Quantity A is $70 and Quantity B is $50, which means that Quantity A is greater and the correct answer is (A).

5.　A　The quantities are already represented as the product of prime factors: 7^2 = (7)(7), so the least prime factor of Quantity A is its only prime factor, 7. Similarly, 2^7 = (2)(2)(2)(2)(2)(2)(2), so Quantity B is 2. The answer is (A).

6.　C　This problem asks for the average of a list of variables, so draw an Average Pie. The problem states that the average of the variables a, b, c, and d is 7, so place 7 in the average section of the pie. There are 4 variables that make up this average, so the number of things is 4. Therefore, the total is 7×4 = 28. So $a + b + c + d$ = 28. There are variables under Quantity B that are consistent with the variables in the question stem, so plug in a number for each of the variables that makes the math easy, such as using the number 7 for all the variables. $\frac{4(7) - 5(7) + 7 - 24 + 8(7) - 7 + 3(7) + 2(7)}{4} = 15$. Both quantities are equal, so eliminate (A) and (B). Now check between (C) and (D) by plugging in a = 1, b = 1, c = 25, and d = 1. The sum of Quantity B with these variables is 4 – 125 – 23 + 199 + 5 = 60 which, when divided by 4, equals 15. The quantities are still equal, so eliminate (D) and select (C).

7.　C　Plug in an easy number for the width of the smaller square, such as 3. So the area of the smaller square is $s^2 = 3^2$ = 9. The diagonal of a square forms two 45-45-90 triangles, so the diagonal (the hypotenuse of either triangle) has length $3\sqrt{2}$. Because the hypotenuse is the width of the larger square, the area of the larger square is $s^2 = \left(3\sqrt{2}\right)^2 = 18$. The area of the shaded region is the result when the area of the smaller square is subtracted from that of the larger: 18 – 9 = 9. Thus, both quantities are equal, and the answer is (C).

8. **D** Plug In values for x and y. Neither x nor y can be equal to 0, as indicated by the statement that $xy \neq 0$. Choose $x = 2$, $y = 3$. Quantity A is 4, Quantity B is 9, so eliminate (A) and (C). Any two positive numbers always results in Quantity B being greater than Quantity A. So try negative numbers. If $x = -5$ and $y = -4$, then Quantity A is 25 and Quantity B is 16. Eliminate (B) and the correct answer is (D).

9. **C** The volume of the larger cube is $s^3 = 2^3 = 8$ and the volume of the smaller cube is $s^3 = \left(\sqrt{2}\right)^3 = 2\sqrt{2}$. To determine how many times greater the volume of the larger cube is than that of the smaller cube, divide the larger number by the smaller, which yields $\dfrac{8}{2\sqrt{2}} = \dfrac{4}{\sqrt{2}} = \dfrac{4\sqrt{2}}{2} = 2\sqrt{2}$. The correct answer is (C).

10. **B** First, figure out how many hours Billie worked. From 9 a.m. to 5 p.m. is 8 hours. She started work 3 minutes before 9 a.m. and finished at 16 minutes after 5 p.m., for a total of 19 more minutes, which is close to 20 minutes, or $\dfrac{1}{3}$ of an hour. So Billie worked approximately $8\dfrac{1}{3}$ hours. To take 80 percent of this, multiply by $\dfrac{80}{100} = \dfrac{4}{5}$. This means she spent $\left(\dfrac{4}{5}\right)\left(8\dfrac{1}{3}\right) = \left(\dfrac{4}{5}\right)\left(\dfrac{25}{3}\right) = \dfrac{100}{15} = 6\dfrac{2}{3}$ hours. The correct answer is (B).

11. **C** The single-digit primes are 2, 3, 5, and 7. Be systematic in listing the results. Start with 2, adding it to the other numbers, then move to 3, and so forth: $2 + 3 = 5$; $2 + 5 = 7$; $2 + 7 = 9$; $3 + 5 = 8$; $3 + 7 = 10$; $5 + 7 = 12$. Out of these six results, 5 and 7 are prime, but the other four results are not, so the probability is $\dfrac{4}{6} = \dfrac{2}{3}$, and the correct answer is (C).

12. **9** This problem provides a ratio, so draw a ratio box. With a ratio of $5 : 7 : 3$, the total number of singers is at least 15. If you double the number, and keep the ratio, there are 30 singers. To have at least 40 singers with the same ratio, the actual total is 45, or 3 times 15, which means there are three times the number of basses (3) in the ratio, or 9.

13. **A** Notice that the question gives information about p and q, and the answer choices refer to m and n. Therefore, isolate those from the variables x and y by factoring. Regrouping the first given equation yields $(m - n)x + (q - p)y = 0$. Because $p - q = -(q - p)$, the second equation shows that $q - p = -2$. Work with the third equation to find that $\dfrac{y}{x} = -\dfrac{1}{3}$, so $x = -3y$. Substituting the last two results into the regrouped first equation yields $(m - n)(-3y) + (-2)y = 0$. Moving the second expression

to the other side of the equation produces $(m - n)(-3y) = 2y$. Inspecting this equation reveals that $(m - n)(-3) = 2$, so $m - n = -\dfrac{2}{3}$. Because $m - n = -(n - m)$, then $n - m = \dfrac{2}{3}$, and the correct answer is (A).

14. A Plug in a three-digit integer, such as 341. Interchanging the 1 and the 3 yields 143. Subtracting 143 from 341 is 198 (which is already positive, so its absolute value is also 198). Since 198 is not divisible by 7, 5, or 4, eliminate (B), (C), and (D). Plug in another number, such as 546. Its hash is 645. Subtracting 546 from 645 is 99, which is not divisible by 2, so eliminate (E). Even if the hundreds digit or the units digit is zero, the absolute value of the difference between a three-digit integer and its hash is divisible by 9. The correct answer is (A).

15. A The number of senior managers in 1980 is 15. To find 60 percent of this, multiply $\dfrac{60}{100}(15) = \dfrac{3}{5}(15) = 9$. This means that in 2007, there are $15 + 9 = 24$ senior managers. In 2000, there are 22, so the increase from 2000 to 2007 is 2. The correct answer is (A).

16. A In the first chart, the average salary, *in actual-year dollars,* in 1990 is 80, and 10% of 80 is 8. The average salary in 2000 is 12 more, which is more than 10%, so (A) is true. According to the second chart, there are 8 managers in 1960, so (B) is false. Finally, from 1980 to 1990, the number of managers increased by 5, which represents a percent change of $\dfrac{5}{15}$ or 33.33%. From 1950 to 1960, the number of managers more than doubled, which is a much greater percent increase. Eliminate (C) and the correct answer is (A).

17. D Plug in 2 for n to find the second term in the sequence: $s_n = s_{n-1} + 5$ so $s_2 = s_{2-1} + 5 = s_1 + 5 = 12$, which is the target number. Now plug 2 into the answer choices for n to see which equals 12. The only answer choice that equals 12 is (D), which is the correct answer.

18. D Together, Rachel and Rob cover 120 of the 190 miles in one hour. Set up a proportion to find out how long the whole trip takes, so $\dfrac{120\,miles}{60\,minutes} = \dfrac{190\,miles}{x\,minutes}$ and $120x = 11{,}400$. Therefore, $x = 95$ minutes for the whole trip. Since the whole trip takes 95 minutes, a separate proportion can be set up to figure out how many miles they cover in 45 minutes. $\dfrac{120\,miles}{60\,minutes} = \dfrac{y\,miles}{45\,minutes}$, so $60y = 5{,}400$ and $y = 90$ miles, and the correct answer is (D).

19. B To find the shaded region, subtract the unshaded region (the triangle and semicircle) from the entire triangle. First, find the area of the big triangle. Drawing a line straight down from the height creates a 30-60-90 triangle, so, because of the side to angle relationship of 30-60-90 triangles, the height is $4\sqrt{3}$. Now, find the area of the triangle. Area $= \dfrac{1}{2}bh = \dfrac{1}{2}(8)\left(4\sqrt{3}\right) = 16\sqrt{3}$. The smaller triangle is also equilateral and creates a 30-60-90 triangle when split down the middle, so the

base of that triangle is 4 and the height is $2\sqrt{3}$. The area of the smaller triangle is therefore $\frac{1}{2}(4)\left(2\sqrt{3}\right) = 4\sqrt{3}$. The radius of the circle is 2, so find the area of the circle. Area = $\pi r^2 = \pi(2^2) = 4\pi$. Don't forget to subtract out only half the circle, so the shaded area is $16\sqrt{3} - 4\sqrt{3} - 2\pi = 12\sqrt{3} - 2\pi$, which is (B).

20.   E   First, determine the value of x, which is 3^2, or 9. The problem asks for the value of x^x, so substitute 9 for x, which makes the expression 9^9. This is not an answer choice. In fact, all the answer choices are written with a base of 3, so convert 9^9 to a base of 3. This yields $9^9 = (3^2)^9$, or 3^{18}. This matches (E), which is the correct answer.

Verbal

1.   **dissolution** and **sunset**

This sentence employs parallel structure, and the comma tells you that both blanks will go in the same direction; either of your two clues, *fragmentation* or *failure*, can be recycled into both blanks. For the first blank, only *dissolution* makes sense; for the second blank, only *sunset* matches the clues, *fragmentation* and *failure*.

2.   **hindered** and **ungainly**

The trigger *while* introduces two conflicting aspects of hydrogen-powered cars. The first clue states that hydrogen contains *more energy per gallon than does gasoline*, which would seemingly aid *the development of hydrogen-powered cars*; since the trigger changes the direction of the sentence, however, a word that means *made more difficult* would make sense in the first blank. Only *hindered* fits. Both the semicolon and the *thus* tell you that the second blank agrees with the first, so you need a word that means something like *difficult* or *awkward*. Only *ungainly* makes sense.

3.   **occludes** and **atypical**

The first blank describes what the Moon does to the Sun; the second sentence tells you that the Moon's shadow is caused by *blocking the sun*, so you are looking for a word that means *blocks*. Only *occludes* means *blocks; secularizes* means *separates from religious connection* and *epitomizes* means *typifies*. The second blank describes the *occurrence*, and the clue is in the first line of the passage: *one of the rarest of celestial events*. Therefore, you need a word that means *rare*. Only *atypical* means *rare; desultory* means *random,* but not necessarily *rare*, and *momentous* means of *far-reaching importance.*

4.   **tally, fastidious,** and **meticulous**

The first blank describes what *census workers* do, so you need a word for the blank that means *count*. Only *tally* means *count*. The second blank describes accurate *census workers*; the part after the colon outlines some of the problems associated with not paying attention to details, so a word that means something like *attentive to details* would make sense. Here, *fastidious* is the best fit. The third blank, like the second, describes the ideal census worker, so once again you need a word that means *attentive to details*. Only *meticulous* means *attentive to detail;* both *perfunctory* and *inexact* are nearly the opposite of what you need.

5. **indefatigable** and **surmount**

The first blank describes the journalist's *pursuit* of the story; since he's investigating *day and night* and writing *until dawn*, a word like *tirelessly* would make sense in the blank. Here, *indefatigable*—literally, not able to be fatigued—is the best fit. The clue for the second blank is *get the story first*; one of the meanings of *surmount* is *to prevail over,* so that is the best answer.

6. **C** Choice (A) strengthens the argument. In fact, it guarantees that the conclusion is true, but it's not the assumption. For (B), the wording is too strong because fixing the trade imbalance does not require that most consumers from Y purchase cars from X. Choice (C) says that if consumers are not inclined to buy automobiles, then the plan is no good. Thus, this is essential to the plan working. Choices (D) and (E) are not necessary to lessening the trade imbalance.

7. **A, B** Be sure to use both the second and third paragraphs to answer this question: Although the term *critical theory* doesn't appear until the latter, it's used to describe the viewpoint discussed in the previous paragraph. Choice (A) is supported by the sentence in the second paragraph that states that *American society is preserved...by the creation of what Marx called "false consciousness."* Choice (B) is also supported by the sentence in the third paragraph that states that *dominant classes...and the injustices it contains.* Choice (C), however, is contradicted by information in the final paragraph.

8. **B** Choice (B) is supported by the final lines of the passage, which indicate that textbook publishers are *first and foremost* seeking to maximize profit. Thus, textbooks are not just teaching instruments, but money makers. Choice (A) is not supported by the passage. The theorists use Marx's term, but that doesn't mean he was a member of the school. Choice (C) is wrong; the passage simply says the literature is *more comprehensive.* That's not the same as saying it is no longer biased. Choice (D) is not supported by the passage. Although the author rejects the idea that the power elites are in control of textbooks, it may still be true that publishers take their views into account. Choice (E) is put forth by the critical theorists, but it is not necessarily true.

9. **C** Choice (C) is supported by the reference in the third paragraph to *critical theory and other theories... on the doorstep of the elites*; if there are other theories that similarly lay blame, then critical theory is *not unique.* Choice (A) is not supported: critical theory is used by *educational theorists*, not the *power elite.* Choice (B) is also not supported: critical theory is discussed as an attempt to explain Americans' alleged ignorance of history, which can no longer be attributed to the less comprehensive secondary sources that were common before the civil rights movement.

10.   Whereas in the past, American historians...

After introducing the main idea, most of the first paragraph is spent dismissing possible causes for the discrepancy that Ferro claims. The third sentence absolves the secondary literature as a suspect; if you selected this sentence, you may have failed to clarify that the problem asked for the sentence that *explains why*. The fourth sentence gives the desired reason: the secondary literature became *more comprehensive* after *the civil rights movement of the 1950s and 60s*. If you chose the fifth sentence, note that the passage doesn't state whether space constraints were ever a problem.

11.   **vitality** and **vigor**

Not only tells you that the second part of the sentence will continue in the same direction as, and expand upon, the first part of the sentence. The first part says an exhibit showed a vegetarian diet is healthy, so the second part will also say the exhibit showed something positive about a vegetarian diet, and it will likely be relevant to health. *Remorse* and *contrition* are synonymous but are too negative. *Mendacity*, which means *deception*, and *persecution*, which means *an attack on an ethnic group*, are also too negative to be extensions of *health benefits*. On the other hand, *vitality* and *vigor* both mean *having lots of energy*, which is a congruous and logical extension of the health benefits of a diet.

12.   **censoring** and **expurgating**

The clue in the sentence is *more at liberty to be candid*. The triggers are *but* and *nevertheless*. Both triggers are opposite-direction triggers, so the correct answer must mean something that relates to the opposite of *to be candid*. A good word for the blank therefore might be *deleting*. *Emancipating* means *setting free*, which is not the same as *deleting*, so you can eliminate (A). *Censoring* means *deleting*, so (B) is a correct answer. *Refuting* means *proving false*, so (C) is incorrect. *Lauding* means *to praise*, so you can eliminate (D). *Ameliorating* means *easing or lessening*, and does not mean *deleting*, so you can eliminate (E). *Expurgating* means *changing by removing words*, so (F) is also correct.

13.   **neglects** and **omits**

While is a trigger word, so you know that the second clause will contrast with the first. The first clause states that the author does identify Victorian culture, so the second clause will be about a failure to identify something. Thus, (A) and (E) can be eliminated, since they suggest successfully communicating something. *Corroborates* means *validates a story;* eliminate (B). *Placates* means *appeases*, so (D) doesn't make sense here. *Neglects* and *omits* both suggest a failure; (C) and (F) are correct.

14.   **bombastic** and **verbose**

The trigger *though* tells you that the latter part of the sentence will contrast with *restrained* and *terse*, so you're looking for words that indicate the difference between the way he writes and the way he speaks. That difference is that his speaking style is the opposite of *restrained* and *terse*, so look for something that means *long-winded. Eloquent* and *elegant* are not the opposite of *restrained* and *terse,* so eliminate (A) and (B). *Gregarious* and *affable* both mean *highly social,* and so are too positive as well as irrelevant to the sentence; eliminate (D) and (F). *Bombastic* and *verbose* both mean *long-winded,* so (C) and (E) give you appropriate, equivalent sentences.

15. **dearth** and **paucity**

The trigger word comes at the very end of this sentence: since the speaker indicates *surprise,* the second half of the sentence will contrast with the first, which says that conditions for apples were good. So you're looking for words that indicate the apples are poor in some way, and both *dearth* and *paucity* indicate a lack or shortage. *Surfeit* and *spate* are also synonyms, but they have the opposite meaning: an abundance or excess. Neither *countenance,* which means *the look on one's face,* nor *amalgamation,* which means *combination,* fits here. Choices (A) and (F) are the best answers.

16. **D** According to the author, *The novel's cyclical structure encourages critics to see the novel's disparate parts as interlinked…however, it does facilitate attempts to view the novel as a unified whole.* Thus, the cyclical structure supports a critical interpretation of the novel. Choice (D) best summarizes this idea.

17. **B** In the first paragraph, the author states, *The remaining twelve chapters act as a counterpoint, commenting on, if not reversing, the first part in which a morality play receives greater confirmation.* According to the second paragraph of the passage, *Huckleberry Finn encompasses individual scenes of the protagonist's self-recognition,* that resist inclusion into an all-encompassing interpretation. Throughout the passage, the author shows that the novel has certain elements that do not fit nicely into a unified vision of the book. Choice (B) is the best restatement of the information given in the passage.

18. **B, C** Choice (A) is not supported, because the passage never compares the rates of pollen production in plants in different climates. Choice (B) is supported by the phrase *mowing can actually be counterproductive.* Choice (C) is supported by the statement that high humidity rates reduce the spread of ragweed, a *wind-borne* allergen, *by causing the grains to clump.* The clumping must have some negative effect on the wind's ability to carry the pollen, making (C) true.

19. **B** The answer to this question lies in the line, *Some species of Lepidoptera (butterflies, skippers, and moths) larvae feed on ragweed, but this arena of control is not well-funded, and consequently not well-researched.* The author mentions the species to indicate that there may be a potential answer to the problem of controlling ragweed, but this answer has not been fully explored. This most closely matches (B). Choice (A) is wrong because the author doesn't make a comparison between the methods of control. Choice (C) is wrong because the species discussed are not mammals. The author does suggest the government explore natural remedies, but (D) doesn't properly answer the question. The mention of *some species of Lepidoptera* is not used to *plead with the government.* Choice (E) is incorrect because earlier in the passage the author indicates that complete elimination of the ragweed is unlikely.

20. **D** The passage tells us that Socrates was an example of the type of thinker who led to a decline in Greek society. His thinking placed great importance on rationality. Later in the passage, we are told that there is a conflict between rationality and the senses. Thus, the author implies that Nietzsche felt that Socrates's excessive rationality was a problem. The answer is (D).

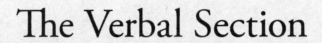

The Verbal Section

Text Completion

TEXT COMPLETION

Text Completion questions occupy a middle ground between Sentence Equivalence and Reading Comprehension. You will be given a small passage—one to five sentences—with one, two, or three blanks. If the passage has one blank, you will have five answers to choose from. If it has two or three blanks, you will be given three answer choices per blank. You have to independently fill in each blank to get credit for the question.

The overall approach is the same. Ignore the answer choices. Find the story being told (there will always be a story), and come up with your own words for the blank. Here's what a three-blank Text Completion will look like:

Question 5

> Proponents of the International Style in architecture called for reducing buildings to purely functional form and found beauty in highlighting (i)_____ features. They rejected references to (ii)_____ and historical styles and offered designs indifferent to location, a quality subsequently (iii)_____ by those who viewed the style as bland or unappealing.

Blank (i)	Blank (ii)	Blank (iii)
structural	oracular	disparaged
aesthetic	vernacular	embraced
hackneyed	secular	reclaimed

Step 1: Find the Story

There will always be a story. There must be a complete enough story that you can identify what's missing. The answer choices are there to mislead you, so don't look at them. Stay with the passage until the story comes into focus. Pay particular attention to trigger words (see Sentence Equivalence). They will indicate the direction of the sentence and will help to fill in blanks. If the sentence does not come into focus, skip it and come back after doing a few other questions.

Step 2: Prep Your Scratch Paper

As opposed to columns of A's, B's, C's, D's, E's, and F's, Text Completion scratch paper will look like this:

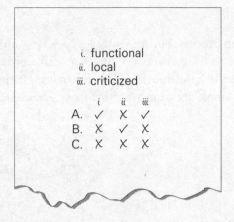

Step 3: Pick a Blank

Some blanks will be easier to fill in than others. In general, blanks have two roles. They test either vocabulary or comprehension. A blank testing vocabulary may be easy to fill in with your own words, but then the answer choices may consist of difficult vocabulary words. A blank testing comprehension may depend upon what you put into another blank, or may contain multiple words, including a few trigger words and prepositions. Start with whichever blank seems the easiest.

Step 4: Speak for Yourself

The answer choices will all fit grammatically into the sentence and quite a few of them will make some sense. Plugging them in to see which one "sounds" right, is just what ETS wants you to do. Sooner or later, with this approach, they will tempt you into a wrong answer. Instead, stay with the sentence until the story becomes clear and then come up with your own word for the blank. If you don't know exactly what word will fit, at least figure out whether the word in the blank will change the direction of the sentence or keep it the same.

Step 5: Use POE

Keep your hand moving. Do not do this process in your head. That leads to mental stress and unnecessary mistakes. Park your thinking on your scratch paper.

Step 6: Rinse and Repeat

Repeat this process for each blank. Remember that some blanks will test vocabulary, but others will test comprehension. Often the information you need for one blank may happen to be another blank. For this you will need to identify the relationship between the blanks.

That may seem like a long process, but it's really just a way of thinking. Find the story. Play close attention to trigger words. Come up with words for the blank or establish direction. Keep the hand moving and eliminate. Putting it all together, the best answers for the sample question are *structural, vernacular,* and *disparaged.*

Text Completion Drills

DRILL 1

Question 1

Just as different people can have very different personalities, so too can pets—even those of the same species and breed possess varied _____.

initiations
implementations
aptitudes
rationalizations
temperaments

Question 2

Frustrated by her husband's lack of (i)_____, Lisa tried to motivate him to (ii)_____ for greater things.

Blank (i)	Blank (ii)
initiative	mitigate
lassitude	invigorate
eloquence	strive

Question 3

At the edges of the universe astronomers have discovered (i)_____ objects called quasars, which have given scientists the first direct (ii)_____ of the existence of stars in distant galaxies.

Blank (i)	Blank (ii)
remote	corroboration
paranormal	distortion
viscous	intuition

Question 4

If one were asked who transmitted the first radio broadcast of the human voice, one might guess the _____ inventor Guglielmo Marconi, but in fact the feat was accomplished by the much less well-known Reginald Fessenden.

infamous
renowned
contingent
cogent
insistent

Question 5

The difference in economic terms between a bond and a note is still observed by the United States Treasury, but in other markets the (i)_____ the two terms has become unimportant and the two words are used (ii)_____.

Blank (i)	Blank (ii)
distinction between	statistically
similarity of	interchangeably
usefulness of	differentially

Question 6

Now known as Administrative Professionals' Day, Secretaries' Day was created in 1952 by Harry F. Klemfuss, a public relations professional who _____ the value and significance of administrative assistants in order to attract more women to the profession.

proscribed
touted
refuted
undermined
admonished

Question 7

When editing manuscripts, literary scholars must remain acutely aware of textual (i)_____; the differences among extant versions of the same work—resulting from printing errors, editing demands, or constant revisions—often make it (ii)_____ for scholars to publish truly (iii)_____ texts.

Blank (i)	Blank (ii)	Blank (iii)
conformities	pejorative	cosmetic
anomalies	daunting	innovative
congruities	banal	authoritative

Question 8

With a similar contrast between a partly cloudy sky and a dark street, the cover of the recent rock CD _____ a famous surrealist painting from the early 1900s.

admires
obfuscates
evokes
disenchants
sanctions

Question 9

Although John F. Kennedy was known for his carefree flag football games, Gerald Ford should be _____ as our football president: He turned down offers to play for two National Football League teams in order to pursue a career in public service.

excepted
abrogated
incorporated
criticized
canonized

Question 10

Though many _____ endlessly praised his work, Dan often wished for some honest criticism.

sycophants
pedants
benefactors
adversaries
mavericks

Question 11

The losing game show contestant experienced a strange mix of (i)_____ and (ii)_____; although she was disappointed that she didn't win the million dollar prize, she was still (iii)_____ about returning to her normal life.

Blank (i)	Blank (ii)	Blank (iii)
despondency	ambivalence	confounded
fruition	elation	complacent
decisiveness	equivocation	euphoric

Question 12

The magazine article from 1956 decrying the
(i)_____ of sequels and remakes flooding
the nation's movie theaters that summer
(ii)_____ the claim that such derivative
films are a uniquely 21st-century
phenomenon.

Blank (i)	Blank (ii)
dearth	underscored
quality	belied
glut	predicted

Question 13

Although considerable (i)_____ resources
had already been expended on the new drug,
development had to be halted due to adverse
effects during human testing; once hailed as
a kind of (ii)_____ that could be used to
treat numerous physical and mental ailments,
the drug will likely be remembered only as
a financial albatross that bankrupted its
developers.

Blank (i)	Blank (ii)
assiduous	sinecure
pecuniary	mendicant
wholesome	panacea

Question 14

Sheila would often _____ her boyfriend's
habits, but everyone could tell that her
seemingly bitter complaints were mostly
facetious.

waffle about
rail against
cater to
grieve over
mince about

Question 15

Although the stress tests given to European
banks are supposed to reassure (i)_____
investors by distinguishing the reliable
financial institutions from the more
(ii)_____ ones, the lack of candor from
those reporting has made the test results
(iii)_____.

Blank (i)	Blank (ii)	Blank (iii)
prolix	precarious	monetary
cantankerous	staunch	suspect
timorous	venerated	sound

DRILL 2

Question 1

Carey and Skylar's constant bickering dismayed their mother, who had grown weary of their _____.

squabbles
laudations
affectations
procrastinations
humor

Question 2

The mayor was so _____ by the long trial that, despite his eventual acquittal, he admitted his failing health and declined to run for re-election.

distraught
exonerated
inspired
debilitated
vindicated

Question 3

Despite her hearing loss and (i)_____ painful arthritis, Maj was a pleasant and surprisingly (ii)_____ dog.

Blank (i)	Blank (ii)
mildly	enervated
chronically	agile
sympathetically	acute

Question 4

While any bird egg will suffice for the tradition of egg decorating, those with _____ shells are preferred, so as to prevent breaking when their contents are hollowed.

tenuous
pristine
permeable
resilient
obtuse

Question 5

Handcuffing the two (i)_____ men stopped the (ii)_____ violence, but did nothing to cease the volley of (iii)_____ they continued to yell at each other.

Blank (i)	Blank (ii)	Blank (iii)
prevaricating	corporeal	epithets
moiling	rhetorical	blows
belligerent	histrionic	projectiles

Question 6

Though she willingly admitted that the (i)_____ town was scenically beautiful, Christine could not help but feel it was (ii)_____ backwater compared to her previous home in the city.

Blank (i)	Blank (ii)
sprawling	a cultural
desolate	an attractive
bucolic	a picaresque

Question 7

The Roman Empire's military and political _____ was often challenged by the smaller but ambitious Persians, who for centuries fought wars intended to usurp Rome's dominion.

heterodoxy
methodology
hegemony
impotence
timorousness

Question 8

The chairman's (i)_____ comments about the environmental disaster caused people to grow even angrier at the company, (ii)_____ a situation that was already (iii)_____.

Blank (i)	Blank (ii)	Blank (iii)
compassionate	edifying	parlous
glib	exacerbating	inured
solicitous	mollifying	compliant

Question 9

Allowing distinguished figures to (i)_____ on their experiences, lives and wisdom learned, the memoir genre has given us such significant works as Ulysses S. Grant's *Personal Memoirs*, an interesting, well-written account of his days as a general and a president. At the opposite end of the spectrum, the genre also provides an outlet for anyone who wants to share any (ii)_____ experience, as evidenced by the (iii)_____ release of a fly-by-night internet celebrity's memoir next month.

Blank (i)	Blank (ii)	Blank (iii)
extemporize	apocryphal	laudable
expatiate	petty	laughable
exagitate	eccentric	impending

Question 10

Although Father's Day, first celebrated in 1908, is now an honored tradition in the United States, it did not always enjoy such (i)_____ ; rather, the unofficial (ii)_____ of prominent figures such as Woodrow Wilson and William Jennings Bryan were required before Americans embraced the holiday.

Blank (i)	Blank (ii)
decorum	opprobrium
ennui	approbation
esteem	hyperbole

Question 11

Some conservative theologians subscribe to the belief of Biblical (i)_____ as far as the Scripture never being wrong when it comes to revealing God, his vision, and his news to humanity. However, other literalist Christians believe the (ii)_____ refers to the Bible being without error in every way, including matters of chronology, history, biology, sociology, politics, et cetera.

Blank (i)	Blank (ii)
inerrancy	centurion
fallacy	erudition
interpretation	doctrine

Question 12

When he was alive, the magnate was described as arrogant, bitterly critical, and (i)_____. Nevertheless, at the memorial, the speaker, who was often the victim of his legendary (ii)_____, was able to find (iii)_____ things to say about him.

Blank (i)	Blank (ii)	Blank (iii)
efficacious	diatribes	magnanimous
bellicose	encomiums	imperious
chastened	eulogies	vindictive

Question 13

When the mother (i)_____ the disruptive child, she did not expect his siblings to encourage malevolent behavior; rather, she anticipated that the children would mock and (ii)_____ their troublesome brother and through this punishment, he would refrain from harassing others.

Blank (i)	Blank (ii)
touted	deride
calumniated	laud
pilloried	renege

Question 14

Many city-dwellers have a _____ of knowledge about their food sources: indeed, a number of people have never even seen a live chicken or cow.

pith
dross
surfeit
culture
dearth

Question 15

Most fans dismissed the press release detailing the comedian's ill health as a hoax, as she had frequently _____ her audience by feigning a physical ailment as part of her stage routine.

reconnoitered
hoodwinked
lambasted
vitiated
derided

DRILL 3

Question 1

An aloe plant may be an excellent choice for those who are interested in gardening but keep busy schedules; aloes easily _____ without frequent watering or careful maintenance.

facilitate
ingest
consume
flourish
advance

Question 2

Howard's friends recognize that his nervous (i)_____ on meeting strangers belies an underlying gregariousness, while new acquaintances often (ii)_____ perceive him as taciturn.

Blank (i)	Blank (ii)
chatter	falsely
silences	accurately
banter	quickly

Question 3

The artist, who specialized in _____ scenes, eagerly sat down to paint his favorite landscape—a peaceful pasture surrounded by hills and valleys.

luminous
perennial
bucolic
eclectic
quiescent

Question 4

Her performance review noted that Jill suffers from a lack of (i)_____, and often makes insulting remarks despite her best efforts to be polite; worse, the review went on to point out that it happens regularly, even though she has no intention of (ii)_____ anyone.

Blank (i)	Blank (ii)
candor	exacerbating
tact	lauding
deference	denigrating

Question 5

The administration had nothing but contempt for the ultimate Frisbee team and frequently spoke _____ of it.

didactically
affably
jocularly
morosely
disdainfully

Question 6

By disclosing and explaining the details of her personal finances before they could be used against her, the council member (i)_____ her opponent's attacks during the campaign. Rather than waiting to react to the inevitable criticism should her opponent find something questionable, her campaign manager thought this strategy would be more (ii)_____.

Blank (i)	Blank (ii)
prefigured	enigmatic
decried	pragmatic
precluded	dogmatic

Question 7

Lindsay, cognizant of the effects of second-hand smoke but hesitant to inconvenience her party guests, _____, as she was unsure whether to ask people to smoke outside during the party.

dissembled
vacillated
equivocated
disparaged
concurred

Question 8

The literary agent took (i)_____ at the statement that slush piles are nothing but (ii)_____; he argued that several major authors, including Stephenie Meyer, Judith Guest, and even Anne Frank, were discovered in such piles of unsolicited, soon-to-be-rejected manuscripts.

Blank (i)	Blank (ii)
gratification	requisitions
accession	dross
umbrage	compendiums

Question 9

While some academics applaud the modernist movement in many universities to treat history and fiction as inherently related fields, there remains a vocal group of traditional historians and literary critics who (i)_____ such a worldview as (ii)_____ and insist that the (iii)_____ nature of the two disciplines must be inviolate.

Blank (i)	Blank (ii)	Blank (iii)
venerate	dogmatic	separate
deride	axiomatic	logical
celebrate	heretical	intertwined

Question 10

Adventures of Huckleberry Finn was one of the first major American novels to be written in _____ voice, using the unaffected language of the common person describing everyday events.

an erudite
a reticent
an urbane
a candid
a quixotic

Question 11

The question of when, if ever, history can be considered (i)_____ is contentious, to say the least. For example, while any evaluation of the 180-year-old presidency of Andrew Jackson should be (ii)_____ the inevitable controversies that arise when evaluating contemporary leaders, his administration remains the subject of polarizing debates. Ultimately, the only historical certainty is that any given judgment must inevitably be a (iii)_____ one.

Blank (i)	Blank (ii)	Blank (iii)
apolitical	characteristic of	disinterested
tendentious	free from	mellifluous
unexpurgated	mired in	subjective

Question 12

The (i)_____ state of the city's public schools certainly demands immediate attention, but it is important that our remedies be thoughtful and comprehensive. While appropriate measures of teacher performance and subsequent accountability will undoubtedly play a vital role in revitalizing our schools, it would be (ii)_____ the many other factors at play, factors as widely divergent as the system's deteriorating physical capital and students' home lives. Even the most talented teachers are challenged, for example, to (iii)_____ of an unstable or abusive home environment on a student's ability to learn.

Blank (i)	Blank (ii)	Blank (iii)
execrable	an error to neglect	terminate the ability
tendentious	a solution to ignore	mitigate the effects
transient	a panacea to solve	exacerbate the influence

Question 13

With his relentless energy but equally diminutive attention span, Garlin (i)_____ his talents on several potentially exciting but uncompleted projects, much to the dismay of his friends who, while venerating his enthusiasm, (ii)_____ his unfocused nature.

Blank (i)	Blank (ii)
squandered	impugned
evinced	parried
burnished	defrauded

Question 14

The origins of La Tomatina, an annual Spanish event in which participants hurl overripe tomatoes at one another for up to two hours, are _____, with possible theories including a friendly food fight and a volley aimed at a bad musician.

esoteric
ephemeral
apposite
nebulous
ubiquitous

Question 15

The _____ group in the adjoining room made it difficult for students taking the mid-term examination to concentrate.

obstreperous
quiescent
rapacious
enervated
antagonistic

DRILL 4

Question 1

Susan _____ the theater; she bought tickets for all the shows put on by the local drama group.

abhorred
cherished
owned
loathed
managed

Question 2

The so-called "thieves' cant" was a (i)_____ language created by thieves, beggars, and swindlers in England in the 1530s to allow them to communicate without the authorities knowing what was going on. Although the cant was widely used by criminal subcultures five hundred years ago, it is now mostly (ii)_____, found only in literature and fantasy role-playing games.

Blank (i)	Blank (ii)
clandestine	obsolete
bourgeois	pervasive
sacrilegious	contemporary

Question 3

Currently _____ in philately, Roger decided to pursue his new hobby because he had already become an expert numismatist.

a dilettante
a philanderer
a mentor
a specialist
an eccentric

Question 4

While the (i)_____ structures of Lego projects are often impressive, it's the internal (ii)_____ such as flower pots, sink fixtures, and working windows that make them truly magical.

Blank (i)	Blank (ii)
august	minutiae
external	stratagems
incidental	proboscises

Question 5

Prior to taking on the new invader, the defending army had engaged in arduous combat; it is likely that the _____ resulting from waging two battles in two days played a part in its subsequent defeat.

bellicosity
pugnacity
pacification
enervation
aggravation

Question 6

Often considered one of the best films in cinematic history, *Breakfast at Tiffany's* faced several (i)_____ during production. The film's star, Audrey Hepburn, almost refused the part, afraid it would (ii)_____ her pristine image; further, the film faced intense scrutiny from censors, and the director had to make several compromises to (iii)_____ them.

Blank (i)	Blank (ii)	Blank (iii)
complications	augment	assuage
harbingers	tarnish	refute
advancements	peruse	discomfit

Question 7

The (i)_____ of medieval papal power was the pontificate of Innocent III, whose immense personal prestige cowed monarchs from the powerful Philip II "Augustus" of France to the (ii)_____ John of England, who earned such derisive epithets as "Lackland" and "Softsword." Even before Innocent's tenure, though, the involvement of Pope Henry IV in the Investiture Conflict had begun to hint at the tension between spiritual and (iii)_____ leadership that would eventually boil over in the Protestant Reformation.

Blank (i)	Blank (ii)	Blank (iii)
zenith	feckless	archaic
perigee	intemperate	temporal
antipathy	resplendent	consecrated

Question 8

Ironically, the myth of Martin Van Buren's _____ was due largely to circumstances that had little to do with Van Buren himself; in reality, of all the U.S. presidents since Andrew Jackson, Van Buren exceeded the average in education, intellect, and experience.

profundity
stoicism
mediocrity
aptitude
malleability

Question 9

Some argue that making money from terrible suffering by publishing photographic books about natural disasters is shameless (i)_____, but perhaps the practice has the (ii)_____ effect of helping us to appreciate the humanity of people living far way.

Blank (i)	Blank (ii)
presumptuous	salutary
idolatrous	specious
profiteering	sedulous

Question 10

While she may have answered him truthfully—in the strictest sense of the word—it became clear to Sergei after the incident that Sheryl had actually been trying to _____.

vituperate
obfuscate
illuminate
covet
desiccate

Question 11

Certainly a roundabout narrative, the book—much like the others in the author's pseudo-autobiographical series—proved to be unpopular among those who preferred _____ to loquaciousness.

succinctness
enlargement
garrulousness
gregariousness
perspicacity

Question 12

During training to handle (i)_____ arguments, the students on the debate team practiced techniques for quickly coming up with remarks that were (ii)_____ even when they might know very little about the topic and would have only a few minutes to prepare.

Blank (i)	Blank (ii)
spurious	sanctimonious
extemporaneous	germane
contentious	seditious

Question 13

Although they stood with the congressman in a tenuous display of solidarity, the incensed commissioners could not conceal their _____.

camaraderie
rancor
adulation
facetiousness
hubris

Question 14

The (i)_____ with which the second-string quarterback managed to turn the tide of the game shocked even those who were familiar with his skills. Previously, he was more infamous for his deceitful (ii)_____ off the field than for anything he had accomplished with a ball in his hand, but his immediate impact on the decisive game is likely to turn some of his erstwhile doubters into (iii)_____ fans.

Blank (i)	Blank (ii)	Blank (iii)
indolence	petulance	recumbent
alacrity	chicanery	ardent
probity	recidivism	fetid

Question 15

The magazine article was (i)_____ about the police commissioner's accomplishments. Although some lawyers' groups argued against the appropriateness of his tactics, the double-digit drop in the crime rate since his appointment suggests that all the journalist's praise was (ii)_____.

Blank (i)	Blank (ii)
effusive	specious
tentative	presumptuous
bombastic	apposite

DRILL 5

Question 1

Rich found the chance shift in the path of the storm (i)_____ , as he was hoping to use the excuse of heavy weather to (ii)_____ more much needed time. With the deadline (iii)_____ and his credibility on the line, he will have to find a way to get the presentation done.

Blank (i)	Blank (ii)	Blank (iii)
hilarious	deplete	deferred
disappointing	garner	nigh
successful	refuse	audacious

Question 2

The defense attorney's _____ closing statement was not enough to sway the jurors in his client's favor; stirring words could not conceal the defendant's evident guilt.

deceptive
eloquent
lengthy
crafty
impromptu

Question 3

A recent Harris Poll indicated that many professions have seen a decline in their (i)_____ over the past several years; teaching, in contrast, has (ii)_____ more respect over the same time period.

Blank (i)	Blank (ii)
ranks	reflected
prestige	squandered
fortunes	reaped

Question 4

In 1770s colonial New England, Puritans _____ the celebration of Christmas, which they considered to be an odious reminder of the Pope's tyranny.

placated
extolled
circumscribed
tempered
repudiated

Question 5

The thin (i)_____ that lines the interior of an eggshell is (ii)_____, and this is the reason using salt water to boil an egg can make the egg taste salty. For the same reason, it is important not to store eggs in the refrigerator with uncovered, strong-smelling food items since the scents can (iii)_____ the egg, causing it to taste bad.

Blank (i)	Blank (ii)	Blank (iii)
yolk	impermeable	permeate
membrane	flexible	addle
albumen	porous	infect

Question 6

Many dog owners treat their pets too _____, forgetting that canines have evolved in competitive environments in which emotional coddling was a sign of weakness.

aggressively
quixotically
fortuitously
indulgently
belligerently

Question 7

As part of Marina Abramović's ground-breaking exhibition at the Museum of Modern Art in New York City, the artist herself logged 700 hours over the course of 3 months in a small chair. Visitors were invited to sit across from the performance artist's stolid countenance, for whatever (i)_____ they desired, the (ii)_____ sitting for only a few moments and the bold sitting for several hours; the visitors thus became (iii)_____ components of the piece, wittingly or unwittingly.

Blank (i)	Blank (ii)	Blank (iii)
motive	timorous	integral
duration	boorish	culpable
approbation	genial	nascent

Question 8

Repulsed by _____ employees, the executive informed his staff that he preferred constructive criticism to calculated flattery.

natty
profligate
rapacious
sententious
obsequious

Question 9

Students may consider modernist works such as James Joyce's *Finnegan's Wake* to be more _____ than Victorian prose: Victorian narratives are linear and predictable, while Joyce's tortuous plots are fragmented and fickle, and they confound the reader.

banal
recondite
elegiac
mundane
panegyric

Question 10

It struck Professor Steele as (i)_____ that the eighteenth-century Bavarians devoted such effort to building houses of worship because at the same time, the rest of Europe's religious fervor was (ii)_____, while movements such as nihilism gained steam.

Blank (i)	Blank (ii)
felicitous	weltering
anomalous	forswearing
querulous	dissipating

Question 11

Ancient generals, lacking modern technologies such as radio and satellite communication, often found that one of the most significant challenges in warfare was accurate _____ of the myriad changes on the battlefield or in the campaign.

fortification
adulteration
appraisal
accretion
adumbration

Question 12

In psychological literature, the "sleeper effect" refers to the phenomenon in which a persuasive message from a trustworthy source loses _____ over time, while the efficacy of a message from a less credible source simultaneously increases.

prescience
erudition
evasiveness
control
cogency

Question 13

Pundits do not believe that the sporadic calls for her ouster—outcries spurred by both her unusual lifestyle and social policies—have compelled the monarch to seriously consider _____.

abnegation
vacillation
castigation
asceticism
misanthropy

Question 14

For some time, scientists refused to believe that Earth's continents are made of moving tectonic plates. Physicists, who could not devise a theory to explain the now-accepted process, rejected the theory outright, as did geologists, who were far too (i)_____ in their thinking, thereby (ii)_____ the advancement of science for a time.

Blank (i)	Blank (ii)
officious	checking
assiduous	limning
dogmatic	asseverating

Question 15

E.L. Doctorow argues that the role of artists in the 21st century is to provide a reminder that even in (i)_____ world, one thing is (ii)_____: America will always be a nation of (iii)_____ free expression.

Blank (i)	Blank (ii)	Blank (iii)
an arcadian	egregious	unfettered
an idiosyncratic	autonomous	circumscribed
a volatile	immutable	jingoistic

DRILL 6

Question 1

Dolly Madison, the wife of President James Madison, was known especially for her _____, remaining calm even as the British invaded Washington D.C. during the War of 1812.

impracticality
cynicism
equanimity
zeal
malevolence

Question 2

Seth was extremely _____, and did not enjoy activities that required effort to meet new people.

extroverted
introverted
gregarious
lackluster
jaded

Question 3

Though Denise's colleagues occasionally took the distant look on her face to mean that she was (i)_____, she was actually thoroughly (ii)_____ of what was happening in the office at all times.

Blank (i)	Blank (ii)
truant	insensible
oblivious	sedulous
fetching	cognizant

Question 4

Some religious leaders have declared inaction on environmental issues to be _____, because it may now be considered a sin to pollute the earth.

fathomable
splenetic
iniquitous
diaphanous
dilatory

Question 5

Julie dismissed DeRay's weight loss scheme as _____ since it relied upon consuming high-calorie snacks while riding on an exercise bike.

fatuous
pithy
indolent
hackneyed
precarious

Question 6

Marty could not help but view the glass as half-empty: for example, when the economy turned around and jobs began to (i)_____, Marty insisted to all who would listen that the good news would be quite transient, that another recession was (ii)_____, and that those who doubted him would later appreciate his unwillingness to celebrate.

Blank (i)	Blank (ii)
proliferate	superfluous
aggrandize	imminent
pique	odious

Question 7

The recent convert, still a _____ with respect to the rites of her church, did not yet feel completely comfortable in her new faith.

pilgrim
iconoclast
ascetic
tyro
poseur

Question 8

Veeder claims that the very notion of the existence of synonyms is (i)_____, as words depend on (ii)_____, connotation, and linguistic and cultural context for their (iii)_____ meanings.

Blank (i)	Blank (ii)	Blank (iii)
veracious	denotation	subjective
fallacious	cogitation	distinct
maladaptive	mastication	interchangeable

Question 9

Politicians' tendency to (i)_____ their own virtues by demeaning their opponents is (ii)_____: what if voters forget the name of the candidate and remember only that of his adversary?

Blank (i)	Blank (ii)
enfeeble	injudicious
tout	ostentatious
democratize	apt

Question 10

Video game enthusiasts know that while advances in computer graphics can make games more fun to play, such a result is by no means _____.

desultory
endemic
salient
ineluctable
seminal

Question 11

Middlemarch author George Eliot reportedly bemoaned the dearth of (i)_____ women, of which her well-educated main character, Dorothea, was a (ii)_____. Therefore, Eliot scholars have long debated the author's purpose in marrying Dorothea to the elderly preacher Casaubon and having him exploit his bride for mundane and (iii)_____ needs.

Blank (i)	Blank (ii)	Blank (iii)
captious	paradigm	menial
erudite	misogynist	catholic
venal	chimera	nebulous

Question 12

Dismissed by the establishment, professing nothing but disdain for the canon, and yet beloved by his followers who trumpet his _____ opinions, the raffish pundit is laughing all the way to the bank.

iconoclastic
blithe
inveterate
meretricious
meritless

Question 13

The 1966 opening of the relatively expansive Grace Memorial Bridge signaled a (i)_____ improvement in highway safety in the low country of South Carolina; the old bridge had been (ii)_____ narrow, creating a (iii)_____ driving experience for traders and tourists alike.

Blank (i)	Blank (ii)	Blank (iii)
prodigious	insufficiently	malodorous
subsidiary	meagerly	cantankerous
radiant	precariously	perilous

Question 14

Thornton explained that Sarah Grand's short story "The Tenor and the Boy" should be viewed as (i)_____ version of her popular novel _The Heavenly Twins_, for it was published years before the novel was completed. Unlike the novel's characters, who were drawn in rich detail, the short story contained mere (ii)_____ caricatures.

Blank (i)	Blank (ii)
a fallow	fractious
a parochial	dynamic
an inchoate	unbedizened

Question 15

One might sometimes wonder whether some of the stories passed down through generations are veritable or (i)_____; whether the heroes had such endless mettle or were, in their hearts, occasionally (ii)_____; and whether the denizens of the times described were really so (iii)_____, or were perhaps tinged with a bit of guile.

Blank (i)	Blank (ii)	Blank (iii)
heretical	pusillanimous	halcyon
jejune	arrant	ingenuous
apocryphal	insouciant	piquant

DRILL 7

Question 1

Although his latest project was relatively _____ —little more than a few basic plot points scribbled on a napkin—the veteran screenwriter easily sold the story to a major Hollywood studio.

undeveloped
polished
convoluted
prosaic
tortuous

Question 2

Anyone who assumes that all of California shares Los Angeles' sunny and temperate climate will be surprised by how _____ San Francisco's weather can be in June.

stimulating
inclement
balmy
appealing
duplicitous

Question 3

Possessing few natural resources upon its newly granted independence in 1863, Singapore remained economically _____ until an influx of industrialization and foreign investment took hold there.

powerful
prosperous
solvent
fortuitous
dubious

Question 4

Wealth and technology wrought by industrialization gave nations in the northern hemisphere strategic (i)_____. This included sophisticated weaponry that could easily overpower the more (ii)_____ arms held by the countries of the southern hemisphere.

Blank (i)	Blank (ii)
adoration	intricate
advantage	perilous
consequence	rudimentary

Question 5

Even though legislators claimed the Contagious Diseases Acts strengthened the nation, social purists argued the Acts _____ the nation's moral growth by encouraging licentious behavior.

advanced
ameliorated
hampered
supplanted
enhanced

Question 6

The new lecture hall's _____ design reflected the architect's minimalist influences.

posh
intricate
unadorned
refulgent
grandiose

Question 7

Though most famous for his musings on ethics, Bentham was also preoccupied with a much less (i)_____ topic: prison design. Bentham envisioned a central watchtower with a (ii)_____ view of the surrounding cells. Ingeniously, the windows were designed such that the prisoners never knew when they were being (iii)_____ and when the guards' gazes were elsewhere.

Blank (i)	Blank (ii)	Blank (iii)
esoteric	constricted	castigated
punitive	panoramic	scrutinized
quintessential	salubrious	exonerated

Question 8

The grave accusations made by the plaintiff were almost entirely (i)_____ the testimony of two witnesses. Therefore, when the court (ii)_____ the credentials of those witnesses, the plaintiff's case disintegrated, and the relevant claims were shown to be (iii)_____.

Blank (i)	Blank (ii)	Blank (iii)
subservient to	vindicated	facetious
isolated from	repudiated	unerring
dependent on	debated	specious

Question 9

Modern tennis fans have come to realize that, although quantum technological leaps in racquet technology have led to _____ increases in the speed and power with which players can hit the ball, this has not necessarily led to a more entertaining game.

innocuous
halcyon
malleable
commensurate
tractable

Question 10

Many Major League Baseball relief pitchers choose an electrifying theme song to play as they take the mound; the song _____ their fans and instills fear in their opponents.

eviscerates
enervates
assuages
innervates
pervades

Question 11

Emmet Ray, a fictional jazz guitarist in Woody Allen's film *Sweet and Lowdown*, is a paradoxical character; while he displays sophisticated musical artistry, in his dealings with other people he can only be called _____.

petulant
elegant
audacious
maladroit
multi-faceted

Question 12

The editorial, though intended to (i)_____ the current administration, inadvertently (ii)_____ several claims made against the regime suggested as a preferable alternative, effectively (iii)_____ any plans for a change in leadership.

Blank (i)	Blank (ii)	Blank (iii)
impugn	attenuated	politicizing
bolster	substantiated	metamorphosing
venerate	benighted	foreclosing

Question 13

Vervet monkeys, like most humans, are (i)_____, conducting most of their activities during the day. Their (ii)_____ behavior and desire for company shows us that humans are not the only species that values (iii)_____.

Blank (i)	Blank (ii)	Blank (iii)
quotidian	collaborative	litheness
circadian	gregarious	camaraderie
diurnal	egregious	fatuity

Question 14

A mathematician should not automatically reject theorems that might at first seem witless or juvenile; advanced degrees are not a license for (i)_____, nor do they (ii)_____ arrogance or egotism.

Blank (i)	Blank (ii)
haughtiness	sanction
puerility	dispel
substantiation	cultivate

Question 15

Bettelheim's (i)_____ of "Hansel and Gretel" is thorough and well-researched, but ultimately not compelling due to his (ii)_____ focus, which is severely constricted by his narrow worldview.

Blank (i)	Blank (ii)
incantation	parochial
exegesis	sweeping
relish	jaundiced

ANSWERS

Drill 1

1. E
2. initiative, strive
3. remote, corroboration
4. B
5. distinction between, interchangeably
6. B
7. anomalies, daunting, authoritative
8. C
9. E
10. A
11. despondency, elation, euphoric
12. glut, belied
13. pecuniary, panacea
14. B
15. timorous, precarious, suspect

Drill 2

1. A
2. D
3. chronically, agile
4. D
5. belligerent, corporeal, epithets
6. bucolic, cultural
7. C
8. glib, exacerbating, parlous
9. expatiate, petty, impending
10. esteem, approbation
11. inerrancy, doctrine
12. bellicose, diatribes, magnanimous
13. pilloried, deride
14. E
15. B

Drill 3

1. D
2. silences, falsely
3. C
4. tact, denigrating
5. E
6. precluded, pragmatic
7. B
8. umbrage, dross
9. deride, heretical, separate
10. D
11. apolitical, free from, subjective
12. execrable, an error to neglect, mitigate the effect
13. squandered, impugned
14. D
15. A

Drill 4

1. B
2. clandestine, obsolete
3. A
4. external, minutiae
5. D
6. complications, tarnish, assuage
7. zenith, feckless, temporal
8. C
9. profiteering, salutary
10. B
11. A
12. extemporaneous, germane
13. B
14. alacrity, chicanery, ardent
15. effusive, apposite

Drill 5

1. disappointing, garner, nigh
2. B
3. prestige, reaped
4. E
5. membrane, porous, permeate
6. D
7. duration, timorous, integral
8. E
9. B
10. anomalous, dissipating
11. C
12. E
13. A
14. dogmatic, checking
15. volatile, immutable, unfettered

Drill 6

1. C
2. B
3. oblivious, cognizant
4. C
5. A
6. proliferate, imminent
7. D
8. fallacious, denotation, distinct
9. tout, injudicious
10. D
11. erudite, paradigm, menial
12. A
13. prodigious, precariously, perilous
14. inchoate, unbedizened
15. apocryphal, pusillanimous, ingenuous

Drill 7

1. A
2. B
3. E
4. advantage, rudimentary
5. C
6. C
7. esoteric, panoramic, scrutinized
8. dependent, repudiated, specious
9. D
10. D
11. D
12. impugn, substantiated, foreclosing
13. diurnal, gregarious, camaraderie
14. haughtiness, sanction
15. cxegesis, parochial

EXPLANATIONS

Drill 1

1. **E** If you notice the same direction trigger *so too*, you can recycle the clue *personalities* for the blank. None of *initiations*, *implementations*, or *rationalizations* means *personalities*, so eliminate (A), (B), and (D). Although *aptitudes* means skills, which pets can have, it does not directly relate to the clue in the sentence, *personalities*. So eliminate (C), and select (E).

2. **initiative** and **strive**

    Lisa is *frustrated* by her husband's lack of something, so that something must be good. *Lassitude* is the quality of being *lazy or lacking in energy*, which is not a good quality. *Eloquence*, or *being skilled in the use of language* is a positive quality, but the lack of *eloquence* would not likely be something that a wife would find frustrating. *Initiative* means *ambition*, a positive quality for a person to have. To *motivate* a person who lacks *initiative*, one must encourage him to try to do things. To *mitigate* means *to make a problem better*, which isn't quite what you're looking for. To *invigorate* means *to give life to something*, and there's no indication in the sentence that the husband is expected to give life to anything. To *strive* means *to aim for*; a person with a lack of *initiative* should try to *aim for* things, so this word is a good fit for the blank.

3. **remote** and **corroboration**

    The astronomers have discovered objects *at the edges of the universe*, so you need a word that is consistent with that clue. *Paranormal* means *beyond the scope of scientific understanding*; it is usually used to describe supernatural things like aliens and ghosts. *Viscous* means *fluid* or *sticky*, so that word is definitely not consistent with the blank. *Remote* means *distant*, which would describe objects *at the edges of the universe*. The quasars have shown scientists something about *the existence of stars*, so blank (ii) must mean something like *proof*. *Distortion* means *changing*, so that word is not consistent with the blank. *Intuition* is a feeling that something is true, but not actual *proof*. *Corroboration* means *proof*, and so it is a good fit for blank (ii).

4. **B** With the opposite direction trigger *but in fact*, you can recycle the opposite of the descriptive clue *much less well-known*, by filling the blank with *well-known*. None of *contingent*, *cogent*, or *insistent* means *well-known*, so eliminate (C), (D), and (E). *Infamous* means *well-known*, but in a negative way, so eliminate (A). *Renowned* means *well-known*, so select (B).

5. **distinction between** and **interchangeably**

    For the first blank, the clues *difference* and *has become unimportant* require something like *difference between*. *Similarity of* and *usefulness of* do not mean *difference between*; *distinction between* does. For the second blank, the opposite-direction trigger *but* and the clue *difference* require something like similar. *Statistically* and *differentially* do not mean *similar,* but *interchangeably* does. Select *distinction between* and *interchangeably.*

6. **B** The clue is that Klemfuss *created Secretaries' Day*, so he must have appreciated the *value and significance of administrative assistants.* None of *proscribed, refuted, undermined,* or *admonished* means *appreciated,* so eliminate (A), (C), (D), and (E). Although *touted* does not—strictly speaking—mean *appreciated,* a person touts only something that is appreciated, so select (B).

7. **anomalies, daunting,** and **authoritative**

For the first blank, recycle the clue *differences.* Only *anomalies* means *differences.* The second blank relates how these differences affect the task of *literary scholars,* so a word like *difficult* or *challenging* would make sense. Only *daunting* makes sense. The third blank describes the type of texts that such *differences* would make so challenging, so a word that means *genuine* or *authentic* would make sense. Here, *authoritative* is the best fit.

8. **C** The clue is the CD is *similar* to the painting, so you can fill the blank with something like *reminds people of.* None of *obfuscates, disenchants,* or *sanctions* means *reminds people of,* so eliminate (B), (D), and (E). Although the designer of the CD may *admire* the painting, the CD itself does not. Moreover, *admires* does not mean *reminds people of. Evokes* means *reminds people of,* so eliminate (A) and select (C).

9. **E** Despite the use of the word *although,* the structure of this sentence, including the colon, makes clear that you need a word that goes in the same direction as the clue. Whether you look to *known* or the phrase after the colon (or both), the blank must mean something like *recognized.* None of *excepted, abrogated, incorporated,* or *criticized* means *recognized,* so eliminate (A), (B), (C), and (D). Someone who is positively *recognized* for something would be *canonized,* so select (E).

10. **A** With the opposite-direction trigger *though,* and the clue that Dan wanted *honest criticism,* the blank can mean something like *yes-men.* None of *pedants, benefactors, adversaries,* or *mavericks* means *yes-men,* so eliminate (B), (C), (D), and (E). *Sycophants* means *yes-men,* so select (A).

11. **despondency, elation,** and **euphoric**

The third blank has the clearest clue, so start there: the trigger *although* indicates that you need a word to contrast *disappointed,* so you need something like *happy.* Only *euphoric* means happy. The third blank also provides part of the clue for the first two blanks: they'll describe *a strange mix* of emotions, and they'll be parallel to *disappointed* and *euphoric.* For the first blank, only *despondency* matches *disappointed*; for the second blank, only *elation* matches *euphoric.*

12. **glut** and **belied**

The sentence states that *sequels* and *remakes* are *derivative,* and thus the article would be *decrying* their existence. Eliminate *dearth,* which means *scarcity.* Also eliminate *quality* as too neutral a word. *Glut* means *overabundance* and correctly reflects the clue word *flooding.* Next, a large quantity of sequels decades ago would *disprove* the *claim* at the end of the sentence. Eliminate *underscored* and *predicted* because neither one is supported. *Belied* means *disproved*, making *glut* and *belied* the final answers.

13. **pecuniary** and **panacea**

For the first blank, the information regarding the type of *resources* that were *expended* are the clues *financial albatross* and *bankrupted*. Thus, the first blank must mean something like *financial*. *Assiduous* and *wholesome* do not mean *financial*; *pecuniary* does. For the second blank, you learn that the drug is supposed to be *used to treat numerous physical and mental ailments*. Thus, the second blank must mean something like *cure-all*. *Sinecure* and *mendicant* do not mean *cure-all*, but *panacea* does. Thus, select *pecuniary* and *panacea*.

14. B   Recycle the clue that Sheila made what seemed like *bitter complaints*. Neither *waffle about, cater to*, nor *mince about* means to make *bitter complaints*, so eliminate (A), (C), and (E). You might have associated *grieve* with the word *grievance*, but it actually means *to mourn*, so eliminate (D). To *rail against* is to make *bitter complaints*, so select (B).

15. **timorous, precarious,** and **suspect**

Because the stress tests are *supposed to reassure* the investors, the first blank must describe someone in need of reassurance, so something like *scared* or *nervous* would make sense; *timorous* is the best match. The second blank describes financial institutions that are *distinguished from reliable* ones, so the word for that blank should contrast with *reliable*. *Precarious* offers the best contrast. Finally, the results are reported with a *lack of candor*, so the test results should be *dishonest* or *unreliable*. *Suspect* is the best choice.

Drill 2

1. A   Recycle the clue *bickering*. None of *laudations, affectations, procrastinations,* or *humor* means *bickering*, so eliminate (B), (C), (D), and (E). To *squabble* means to *bicker*, so select (A).

2. D   The clues that the *mayor* was involved in a *long trial* and as a result suffered *failing health* require that the blank mean something like *sick*. None of *distraught, exonerated, inspired,* or *vindicated* means *sick*, so eliminate (A), (B), (C), and (E). *Debilitated* means *sick*, so select (D).

3. **chronically** and **agile**

The sentence starts with the trigger word *Despite* to set up a contrast between the two parts of the sentence. Since the first part describes her poor physical condition and the second her *surprisingly* positive state, the first blank has to describe her arthritis in a negative way. *Mildly* and *sympathetically* would not present the arthritis negatively, so the best answer is *chronically*. Similarly, the clue to the second blank is *pleasant* and it implies that the dog is positively described. *Enervated* means *lacking energy*, and *acute* could means *perceptive*, which also does not make sense here. Thus the best answers are *chronically* and *agile*.

4. **D**   The clue that the goal is *to prevent breaking* the *shell* requires that the blank mean something like *strong*. None of *tenuous, pristine, permeable,* or *obtuse* mean *strong,* so eliminate (A), (B), (C), and (E). *Resilient* means *strong,* so select (D).

5.   **belligerent, corporeal,** and **epithets**

   Start with the third blank: you need something that can be yelled, and can't be stopped with handcuffs, so a word like *insults* would make sense in the blank. Only *epithets* means insults. The second blank should contrast with the third blank, and describe the type of violence that can be stopped with handcuffs. Hence, you need a word like *physical; corporeal* is the best fit. Finally, the first blank should mean something like *fighting,* since you know the two men are *handcuffed* and have been engaging in *physical violence. Belligerent* is the best choice.

6.   **bucolic** and **cultural**

   The sentence starts with the trigger word *Though*, signaling that the two parts of the sentence will be different. Since you know the town is *scenically beautiful*, the second blank means something else besides its appearance. Eliminate *attractive*, and eliminate *picaresque* because there is no clue that the town refers to an *adventure story. Cultural* makes the most sense for the meaning of the second blank. The first blank describes the *scenically beautiful town*, and must mean something similar to *attractive country* as a contrast to the city. Eliminate *sprawling* and *desolate*, neither of which is suggested by the clues. *Bucolic*, which means *pertaining to country pleasantness*, is the strongest fit. The best answers are *bucolic* and *a cultural*.

7. **C**   Recycle the clue *dominion*. None of *heterodoxy, methodology, impotence,* or *timorousness* means *dominion,* so eliminate (A), (B), (D), and (E). *Hegemony* means *dominion,* so select (C).

8.   **glib, exacerbating,** and **parlous**

   The clues for the first blank indicate that the *chairman's comments* made the people *even angrier;* you can eliminate *compassionate* and *solicitous*, because people would not be angered by *kind or helpful comments. Glib* is the best choice. For the second blank, you need something like *making worse*, because you know that the people are even angrier; *exacerbating* is the best fit. The third blank describes the situation that was made worse, so it must have already been *bad*. Only *parlous*, which means perilous, is sufficiently negative.

9.   **expatiate, petty,** and **impending**

   The clue to the last blank is *next month*, so the missing word must mean *coming* or *about to happen. Impending* is the best match, and neither of the two other choices is supported. For the first blank, the clue is that the memoir allows *distinguished figures* to tell us about *experiences and wisdom learned*, so the missing word must mean *write about. Extemporize* means *to improvise*, which is incorrect because Grant wrote an actual account, and *exagitate* is incorrect because there is no suggestion of his *stirring up or censuring. Expatiate*, which means *to write about in detail*, is the best fit. For the second blank, note the contrast between *the significant works of distinguished figures* and *the experience of a fly-by-night internet celebrity*. The missing word will mean *insignificant. Apocryphal* is incorrect because the writings are not necessarily *fictional*, and *eccentric* is incorrect because there's no context to support the experiences being *unusual*. That leaves *petty*, which fits the context of the sentence.

10.   **esteem** and **approbation**

For the first blank, the opposite-direction triggers *although* and *not* cancel each other out, so you can recycle the clue *honored*. Neither *decorum* nor *ennui* means *honor*, but *esteem* does. For the second blank, the semicolon trigger indicates than an explanation will be given about how Father's Day became *an honored tradition*. Ask yourself what was *required* from *prominent figures* before Americans *embraced the holiday*. The second blank must mean something like *praise*. Neither *opprobrium* nor *hyperbole* means *praise*, but *approbation* means *praise*. Thus, select *esteem* and *approbation*.

11.   **inerrancy** and **doctrine**

For the first blank, the clue is that the conservatives' belief deals with the *Scripture never being wrong*, suggesting the missing word means *perfection* or *infallibility. Fallacy* is the opposite of what you need, and *interpretation* also does not mean *infallibility*. That makes *inerrancy* the best answer for the first blank. For the second blank, the trigger word *However* signals a different interpretation of the same *belief*, the meaning of the missing word. *Erudition*, or *scholarly knowledge*, can be eliminated, and *centurion* is irrelevant to the clues and blank. The right answer is *doctrine*, which means *belief*.

12.   **bellicose, diatribes,** and **magnanimous**

First, find the story. Here is the funeral of a mean, judgmental man. The speaker respectfully finds nice things to say about him. For the first blank, look for things that go with *arrogant* and *bitterly critical*. Only *bellicose*, meaning *aggressive and hostile*, is sufficiently negative. The second blank describes the actions of the guy, so we need something along the same lines. Although *eulogies* belong at funerals, we need something bad. *Diatribes* works. The last sentence changes the direction by starting with *nevertheless* so we need something positive. Only *magnanimous* is positive.

13.   **pilloried** and **deride**

Start with the first blank because it is easier. The clue *disruptive child* tells you the mother probably *punished* the child. *Touted* would provide you with a sentence that was opposite in meaning and *calumniated* has a similar negative connotation, but it would not be appropriate. The second blank's clue *mock* can be recycled for the blank. *Laud* is opposite of *mock*, and *renege* simply doesn't make sense. Select *pilloried* and *deride*.

14. E   The same direction trigger provided by the colon and *indeed*, and the clue that some people *have never even seen a live chicken or cow* requires that the blank mean something like absence. None of *pith*, *dross*, *surfeit*, or *culture* means *absence*, so eliminate (A), (B), (C), and (D). *Dearth* does mean *absence*, so select (E).

15. B   The same direction trigger *as* and the clues *hoax* and *feigned* require that the blank mean something like *tricked*. None of *reconnoitered*, *lambasted*, *vitiated*, or *derided* means *tricked*, so eliminate (A), (C), (D), and (E). *Hoodwinked* does mean *tricked*, so select (B).

Drill 3

1. D   The same-direction semicolon and the clues that an aloe plant is an *excellent choice* for someone who lacks time for frequent *watering or careful maintenance* requires that the blank mean something like *thrive*. None of *facilitate*, *ingest*, *consume*, or *advance* means *thrive*, so eliminate (A), (B), (C), and (E). *Flourish* means *thrive*, so select (D).

2.   **silences** and **falsely**

         The word in the first blank gives a false impression about Howard's *underlying gregariousness*, so you need something that suggests he isn't sociable; hence, *silences* is the best choice. Since Howard is, underneath it all, gregarious, *new acquaintances* who *accurately* or *quickly* perceive him as taciturn are incorrect, so *falsely* is the best fit.

3. C   Recycle the clue *peaceful pasture* for the blank. None of *luminous*, *perennial*, *eclectic*, or *quiescent* means relating to a *peaceful pasture*, so eliminate (A), (B), (D), and (E). *Bucolic* does mean relating to a *peaceful pasture*, so select (C).

4.   **tact** and **denigrating**

         The first blank refers to what Jill doesn't have, so you need a word that means *politeness*. Only *tact* fits. The second blank refers to what Jill does without meaning to, so you need a word that means *insulting*. Only *denigrating* means *insulting*.

5. E   The same-direction trigger *and* as well as the clue *nothing but contempt* requires that the blank mean something like *disrespectfully*. None of *didactically*, *affably*, *jocularly*, or *morosely* means *disrespectfully*, so eliminate (A), (B), (C), and (D). *Disdainfully* does mean *disrespectfully*, so select (E).

6.   **precluded** and **pragmatic**

         The council member's strategy made *her opponent's attacks* impossible or useless, so you need a word for the first blank that means something like *made impossible*. Only *precluded* makes sense. The second blank is a description of the strategy in opposition to a less effective one, so a word like *effective* or *useful* would make sense. Only *pragmatic*, which means *practical*, fits.

7. **B** Lindsay is described as *hesitant* and *unsure*, and is weighing the conflicting motivations of health and convenience, so you need a word that means something like *hesitated* or *was unsure*. Only *vacillated* makes sense. Be careful of (C): to support *equivocated*, you would have to know that Lindsay had already spoken to guests about the issue.

8. **umbrage** and **dross**

Start with the second blank. You know from the second part of the sentence that *slush piles* are *unsolicited, soon-to-be-rejected manuscripts*, so the missing word is probably something like *unwanted material*. Only *dross* is sufficiently negative. For the first blank, since the agent is *arguing that several major authors were discovered in the pile*, he must not like the idea of the slush pile being called *dross*. The missing word, then, must mean something like *offense*. Only *umbrage* means *offense*.

9. **deride, heretical,** and **separate**

For the first blank, the opposite-direction trigger *while* and the contrast between the clues *modernist* and *traditional* require that the blank mean something like *criticize*. *Venerate* and *celebrate* do not mean *criticize*, but *deride* does. For the second blank, the clue *traditional* as well as the completed first blank require that the second blank mean something like *unorthodox*. *Dogmatic* and *axiomatic* do not mean *unorthodox*, but *heretical* does. For the third blank, the opposite direction trigger *while* and the clue *inherently related* require that the blank mean something like *distinct*. *Logical* and *intertwined* do not mean *distinct*, but *separate* does. Thus, select *deride*, *heretical*, and *separate*.

10. **D** To describe the *voice* of the novel, recycle any of the clues *unaffected*, *common*, or *everyday*. Only *a candid* makes sense.

11. **apolitical, free from,** and **subjective**

This is a tricky passage. It talks about the controversies that surround history. It seems that even old history can still get people riled up and there are bound to be opposing views. As always, pay attention to trigger words. The second sentence says *while*, which signals that blank (ii) must be different from *remains the subject of polarizing debates*. This is a change in direction, so one would think there would be only one view. So the second blank should say something like *past* or *over*. *Free from* works the best. Since everything is being argued, we need something negative or argumentative for the last blank. That knocks out *mellifluous* and *subjective*. The first blank speculates on whether or not historical arguments are ever over. *Apolitical* is the best stand-in for the end of arguments over history.

12. **execrable, an error to neglect,** and **mitigate the effects**

The first blank describes the *state of the city's public schools*; since the author is seeking *remedies*, something like *bad* would make sense in the blank. Only *execrable* means bad. The second sentence lists elements that will *play a vital role* in the remedy, but the trigger *while* suggests more needs to be done; for the second blank, only *an error to neglect* allows this meaning. The final sentence is an example to reinforce this idea, and the third blank describes what *talented teachers* would do to negative factors; only *mitigate the effects* makes sense.

13. **squandered** and **impugned**

For the first blank, the clues that Garlin has a *diminutive attention span* and *uncompleted projects* require a word that means something like *wasted*. *Evinced* and *burnished* do not mean *wasted*, but *squandered* does. For the second blank, the opposite-direction trigger *while* and the clue *venerating* require a strong word such as *scorned*. *Parried* and *defrauded* do not mean *scorned*, but *impugned* does. Thus, select *squandered* and *impugned*.

14. **D** The clues *origins* and the entire phrase following the comma require that the blank mean something like uncertain. None of *esoteric, ephemeral, apposite,* or *ubiquitous* means *uncertain,* so eliminate (A), (B), (C), and (E). *Nebulous* means *mysterious* which is close enough to *unknown,* so select (D).

15. **A** The clue *made concentrating difficult* requires that the blank mean something like *noisy.* None of *quiescent, rapacious, enervated,* or *antagonistic* means *noisy,* so eliminate (B), (C), (D), and (E). *Obstreperous* means *noisy,* so select (A).

Drill 4

1. **B** The same-direction semicolon trigger and the clue *bought tickets for all the shows* require that the blank mean something like *loved.* None of *abhorred, owned, loathed,* or *managed* means *loved,* so eliminate (A), (C), (D), and (E). *Cherished* means *loved,* so select (B).

2. **clandestine** and **obsolete**

The clue for the first blank is that the language was created so the criminals could *communicate without the authorities knowing what was going on.* Thus, the missing word must mean something like *secret.* Only *clandestine* fits. The clue for the second blank is that the language was *widely used by criminals five hundred years ago,* but the trigger *although* means you need a word that means the opposite of *widely used.* Only *obsolete* makes sense.

3. **A** Even if you do not know the words *philately* and *numismatist,* the clue is *new hobby,* with yet additional information provided by the opposite-direction time trigger *had already become* and associated clue *expert.* Therefore, the blank must mean something like *amateur.* None of *philanderer,*

mentor, *specialist*, or *eccentric* means *amateur*, so eliminate (B), (C), (D), and (E). *Dilettante* means *amateur*, so select (A).

4.   **external** and **minutiae**

Start with the second blank, which refers to little things inside the structures: *flower pots, sink fixtures, and working windows*. The word in the blank, then, must mean something like *details*. Of the choices, only *minutiae* makes sense. Now work the first blank: the trigger *while* suggests you need a word that means the opposite of *internal minutiae*. Here, *external* is the best fit. While *august* might be tempting, it's too strong for the context. While the structures are important, there isn't any indication that they're inspiring reverence.

5.   D   The same-direction semicolon trigger and the clues *arduous combat, two battles in two days,* and *subsequent defeat* require that the blank mean something like *exhaustion*. None of *bellicosity, pugnacity, pacification,* or *aggravation* means *exhaustion*, so eliminate (A), (B), (C), and (E). *Enervation* means *weakening*, so select (D).

6.   **complications, tarnish,** and **assuage**

For the first blank, you need a word that explains what happened during production. Audrey Hepburn *almost refused the part* and *the director had to make several compromises*, so a word like *problems* would make sense. Only *complications* fits. The second blank describes what Hepburn feared would happen to her image; if she nearly turned down the part because her *image* was *pristine*, she didn't want to *hurt* her image. Only *tarnish* can mean *hurt*. The last blank describes why the director made compromises for the censors: to *make them happy*. Only *assuage* makes sense.

7.   **zenith, feckless,** and **temporal**

The first blank refers to the state of papal power under Innocent; since *his immense personal prestige cowed* even kings, a word that means something like *high point* or *greatest period* would make sense in the blank. Only *zenith* works. The second blank refers to John of England. Both the trigger *from…to* and the *epithets* given to John indicate that you need a word that contrasts with *powerful*. Only *feckless*, which means *ineffective*, fits. The third blank needs to contrast with *spiritual*. Don't be fooled by the word *and*, which is part of the change direction trigger *tension between…and*. *Temporal* is the only choice that makes sense.

8.   C   The clue *ironically* indicates that the blank needs to mean the opposite *of exceeded the average in education, intellect, and experience*, so your answer could be anything that suggests *uneducated, unintelligent,* or *inexperienced*. Only *mediocrity* makes sense.

9.   **profiteering** and **salutary**

The sentence talks about books that make money from publishing other people's disasters. This is often what *profiteering* means. For the second blank, the clue *helping us to appreciate the humanity of people* requires a word meaning something like *helpful*. *Specious* and *sedulous* do not mean *helpful*, but *salutary* does. Thus, select *profiteering* and *salutary*.

10. **B** The opposite-direction trigger *while* and the opposite-direction time trigger *after the incident*, along with the clue *answered him truthfully*, require that the second blank mean something like *mislead*. None of *vituperate, illuminate, covet*, or *desiccate* means *mislead*, so eliminate (A), (C), (D), and (E). *Obfuscate* does mean *mislead*, so select (B).

11. **A** The words *unpopular* and *preferred* act as opposite-direction triggers. The clues *roundabout* and *loquaciousness* require that the blank mean something like *briefness*. None of *enlargement, garrulousness, gregariousness*, or *perspicacity* means *brevity*, so eliminate (B), (C), (D), and (E). *Succinctness* does mean *brevity*, so select (A).

12. **extemporaneous** and **germane**

The students will *have only a few minutes to prepare*, so you need a word for the first blank that means *improvised*. *Spurious* means *inauthentic*, and can be eliminated. *Contentious* means *tending to argue* and does not address the lack of time to prepare, so eliminate this choice. *Extemporaneous* means *with little or no preparation* and is the best fit and correct answer. For the second blank, you need a word that means *effectively on topic* because their remarks have to be effective though they might know very little about the topic. *Sanctimonious* means *showing moral superiority* and *seditious* means *inciting a rebellion*, so eliminate these choices. *Germane* means *relevant*, and is the best fit for the second blank.

13. **B** The opposite-direction trigger *although* and the clue *tenuous display of solidarity* indicate that the remainder of the sentence will explain that the solidarity is not heartfelt. Thus, the clue *incensed* requires that the blank mean something like *anger*. None of *camaraderie, adulation, facetiousness*, or *hubris* means *anger*, so eliminate (A), (C), (D), and (E). *Rancor* does mean *anger*, so select (B).

14. **alacrity, chicanery,** and **ardent**

The second-string quarterback doesn't seem to have played much, but is well known off the field for something *infamous* or *deceitful*. For the second blank, *chicanery* fits the bill nicely. For the first blank, we know he turned the tide of the game and did it in a manner that surprised everyone. *Alacrity* will work for this blank since we are told that his impact was immediate. And for the third blank, winning a decisive game is likely to win him some passionate fans, so *ardent* works well.

15. **effusive** and **apposite**

For the first blank, you need a word that means *expressing praise*, since the journalist is giving praise at the end of the sentence. *Effusive* means *unrestrained in expressing praise*; this is the best fit and correct answer. *Tentative* means *holding back* and is not a match, and *bombastic* means *pompous* and is also incorrect. Since the crime rate has dropped, you need a word that means *appropriate* for the second blank. *Specious* means *seeming true but actually false*; eliminate this choice. *Presumptuous* means *based on assumption*, and is incorrect given the proven drop in crime rate. *Apposite* means *appropriate*; this fits the context of the blank and is the correct answer.

Drill 5

1.   **disappointing, garner,** and **nigh**

Rich has a deadline approaching and needs some more time. The storm would have given him a good excuse, but it seems to have changed direction. Its shift, therefore, must have been *disappointing* to him. He planned to use the excuse to buy himself some more time, so *garner* works in the second blank. The third blank describes the deadline, which is approaching, so *nigh* works well.

2. B   The clues *stirring words* and *not enough* require that the blank mean something like *eloquent*. None of *deceptive, lengthy, crafty,* or *impromptu* means *eloquent,* so eliminate (A), (C), (D), and (E), and select (B).

3.   **prestige** and **reaped**

The two parts of the sentence need to refer to the same topic, so recycle the clue *respect* for the first blank. Only *prestige* means *respect.* For the second blank, the clue *decline* and the trigger *in contrast to* indicate that you need a word that means something like *increased.* Only *reaped* makes sense.

4. E   The clue *odious reminder* requires that the blank mean *rejected.* None of *placated, extolled, circumscribed,* or *tempered* means *rejected,* so eliminate (A), (B), (C), and (D). *Repudiated* does mean *rejected,* so select (E).

5.   **membrane, porous,** and **permeate**

For the first blank, you need a word for the tissue right on the inside of an eggshell. *Yolk* is the central part of the egg, so eliminate this choice. *Albumen* is the egg white, but this does not line the eggshell; eliminate this choice. *Membrane* is the word meaning the *tissue that separates parts of an organism*, and is the best fit. For the second blank, you need a word that states the membrane lets things get through. *Impermeable* means *blocks from passage*, the opposite of what you need. *Flexible* does not mean *allowing to pass through*, so eliminate this choice. *Porous* is the best choice. For the third blank, you need a word that means *enter*, and the correct choice, *permeate,* means exactly that. *Addle* means *to confuse* and *infect* means *to cause to become ill*, and neither choice fits the context of the third blank.

6. D   The same-direction trigger *too* and the clue *emotional coddling* (and the opposite-direction trigger *forgetting* and its clue *competitive environments*) require that the blank mean something like *leniently*. None of *aggressively, quixotically, fortuitously,* or *belligerently* means *leniently*, so eliminate (A), (B), (C), and (E). *Indulgently* does mean *leniently*, so select (D).

7. **duration, timorous,** and **integral**

   The second blank has the strongest clue, so start there. The people who sit *for only a few moments* are contrasted with the *bold* who *sit for several hours*, so you need a word that means *not bold*. Only *timorous* fits. Now go to the first blank: if some are described as sitting only briefly, and others for longer periods, then something that means *period of time* would make sense. Only *duration* means *period of time*. The third blank refers to the role the visitors play; since the visitors themselves are half of the performance, you might use a word like *necessary* to describe what kind of *components* they are. *Integral* is another word for necessary, so it's the best fit.

8. **E** The clues *repulsed by* and *calculated flattery* require that the blank mean something like *flattering*. None of *natty, profligate, rapacious,* nor *sententious* means *flattering*, so eliminate (A), (B), (C), and (D). *Obsequious* means *flattering*, so select (E).

9. **B** The same-direction trigger colon and the clues *tortuous* and *confound* require that the blank mean something like *complex*. None of *banal, elegiac, mundane,* or *panegyric* means *complex*, so eliminate (A), (C), (D), and (E). *Recondite* does mean *complex*, so select (B).

10. **anomalous** and **dissipating**

    For the first blank, the clue is the contrast established between *Bavaria* and *the rest of Europe*. Thus, the blank must mean something like *weird*. *Felicitous* and *querulous* do not mean *weird*, but *anomalous* does. For the second blank, the opposite-direction trigger *while* and the clue *gained steam* require a word meaning something like *diminishing*. *Weltering* and *forswearing* do not mean *diminishing*, but *dissipating* does. Thus, select *anomalous* and *dissipating*.

11. **C** The clues *lacking radio and satellite, significant challenges,* and *changes on the battlefield* require that the blank mean something like *information about*. None of *fortification, adulteration, accretion,* or *adumbration* of means *information*, so eliminate (A), (B), (D), and (E). *Appraisal* means *review* or *evaluation*, so (C) is the best answer.

12. **E** The trigger *while* indicates that the two parts of the sentence will disagree, and the opposition is expressed by *loses* and *increases*. Thus, the blank needs to mean *effectiveness* of a *persuasive message*. Only *cogency* conveys this sense of a *convincingly logical* message.

13. **A** The clue *ouster* requires that the blank mean something like *resignation*. None of *vacillation, castigation, asceticism,* or *misanthropy* means *resignation,* so eliminate (B), (C), (D), and (E). *Abnegation* means *resignation of the throne,* so select (A).

14. **dogmatic** and **checking**

    The first blank describes the thinking of scientists who *refused to* consider a process they can't explain, so a word like *rigid* or *limited* would make sense. Only *dogmatic* matches the meaning you need. The second blank describes the result of such limited thinking on *the advancement of science*, so you need a word that means something like *slowing* or *stopping*. Only *checking* fits the context.

15.   **volatile, immutable,** and **unfettered**

The third blank must be consistent with the clue *free expression. Circumscribed* means *restricted* and would disagree with *free expression. Jingoistic* means *extremely nationalistic* and has a negative connotation. *Unfettered* means *without restriction*, making it the best choice for the third blank. If *America will always* have a particular characteristic, then that characteristic must be *always true. Egregious* means *extremely bad*, and *autonomous* means *self-governing*, so neither of those words is a good fit for the blank. *Immutable* means *unchanging* and is your best choice. The trigger *even in* tells you that the first blank must go in a different direction from the second blank, and that you need a word that indicates *changing. Arcadian* means *peacefully rustic*, and *idiosyncratic* means *strange*; neither of these words means *changing* and both choices can be eliminated. *Volatile* means *prone to change*, and is a good contrast to *immutable*.

Drill 6

1.   **C**   Recycle the clue *remaining calm.* None of *impracticality, cynicism, zeal,* or *malevolence* means *remaining calm,* so eliminate (A), (B), (D), and (E). *Equanimity* means *remaining calm,* so select (C).

2.   **B**   The clue that Seth *did not enjoy activities that required effort to meet new people* requires that the blank mean something like *shy.* None of *extroverted, gregarious, lackluster,* or *jaded* means *shy,* so eliminate (A), (C), (D), and (E). *Introverted* means *shy,* so select (B).

3.   **oblivious** and **cognizant**

If Denise looks *distant*, it appears that she is *unaware* of her surroundings. *Truant* means *absent*, which makes no sense here, and *fetching* means *attractive*, which is also irrelevant. Her *distant look* makes her appear *oblivious*, or *unaware*. The word *actually* signals that the second blank must go in a different direction from the first, and must mean something such as *aware. Sedulous* means *hard-working*, which has nothing to do with being *aware. Insensible* means *unaware*, and is the opposite of what you're looking for. *Cognizant* means *aware*, and is the best fit for the second blank.

4.   **C**   The same-direction trigger *because* and the clue *sin* indicate that the blank means *sinful.* Only *iniquitous* means *sinful* and is the best answer.

5.   **A**   The clue *ridiculed*, as well as the idea of eating snacks while working out, requires that the blank mean something like *foolish.* None of *pithy, indolent, hackneyed,* or *precarious* means *foolish,* so eliminate (B), (C), (D), and (E). *Fatuous* means *foolish,* so select (A).

6.   **proliferate** and **imminent**

The clue *the economy turned around* and the trigger word *and* dictate that the blank, which refers to what happened to *jobs*, must mean something like *increase* or *become more common.* Only *proliferate* makes sense. Be careful with *aggrandize*—it means *to make something greater*, not *to become more numerous.* To agree with the clue *the good news would be quite transient,* the second blank has to mean something like *about to happen.* Only *imminent* fits.

7. **D** You are told the subject is new and doesn't yet feel comfortable. For the blank, you need something to support the notion that she is new. *Tyro* means a beginner, so it fits nicely.

8. **fallacious, denotation,** and **distinct**

    Veeder thinks something about synonyms, words that mean the same thing. Meaning for him seems to depend upon context and connotation as much as an actual dictionary definition, which would make the notion of synonyms difficult since there would always be external circumstances to consider. Therefore, we need something negative for the first blank at least. That knocks out *veracious. Maladaptive* doesn't make sense since nothing is adapting, so *fallacious* must work. For the second blank, we need things that contribute to the meanings of words. Only *denotation* works. And for the last blank, we need something that says that even synonyms are different. *Distinct* fits the bill.

9. **tout** and **injudicious**

    A politician *emphasizes* his virtues, and so the first blank must mean *emphasize.* To *enfeeble* is to *weaken,* the opposite of what you need. To *democratize* is to *make democratic,* and doesn't mean *emphasize.* To *tout* is to *emphasize the positive nature of something,* and is consistent with the context of the first blank. The clue after the colon refers to a negative consequence of the politicians' actions, so the second blank must be a negative word. *Apt* means *smart* and is a positive word you can eliminate. *Injudicious* and *ostentatious* are both negative words. *Injudicious* means *unwise* and *ostentatious* means *pretentiously showy. Injudicious* is a better fit for the blank: the problem with the politicians emphasizing their own virtues is that it is *ineffective and ill-advised.*

10. **D** The opposite-direction trigger *while* and the clue *might* require that the blank mean something like *inevitable.* None of *desultory, endemic, salient,* or *seminal* means *inevitable,* so eliminate (A), (B), (C), and (E). *Ineluctable* means *inevitable,* so select (D).

11. **erudite, paradigm,** and **menial**

    The first and third blanks have the clearest clues, so start with them. For the first blank, recycle the clue *well-educated;* only *erudite* makes sense. For the third blank, recycle the clue *mundane;* only *menial* fits. The second blank describes Dorothea, and if her marriage into a life of *mundane and menial needs* causes debate among Eliot scholars, then Dorothea must have been an example of a *well-educated, erudite* woman. Only *paradigm* means *example.*

12. **A** Here is a guy who no one in the establishment takes seriously and yet has an exuberant following. His opinions must not match with the mainstream. *Iconoclastic* is the best fit.

13. **prodigious**, **precariously**, and **perilous**

The clues are the same for the second and third blanks, so start there. The new bridge was an *improvement in highway safety*, so the old bridge must have been a *danger*; only *precariously* makes sense in the second blank, and only *perilous* makes sense in the third. The first blank describes the *improvement*; the old bridge had been *narrow*, and the new one was *relatively expansive*, so a word that means *big* would make sense. Only *prodigious* means big.

14. **inchoate** and **unbedizened**

The trigger word *unlike* and the clue *drawn with rich detail* require that the second blank mean *lacking detail*. *Dynamic* and *fractious* do not mean *lacking detail,* and can be eliminated. *Unbedizened* means *unadorned* and is a good fit for this blank. For the first blank, the clue *years before the novel was complete* and the information later on indicate that the first blank means *incomplete*. *Parochial* means *narrow-minded* and *fallow* means *inactive,* so both can be eliminated. *Inchoate* means *coming into existence* and is the best choice for the first blank.

15. **apocryphal**, **pusillanimous**, and **ingenuous**

Each blank is associated with the opposite direction trigger *or*. For the first blank, the clue *veritable* requires a word that means *untrue*. Only *apocryphal* makes sense. For the second blank, the clue *mettle* requires a word that means *cowardly*. Here, *pusillanimous* is the best fit. For the third blank, the clue *guile* requires a word meaning something such as *guileless*. Only *ingenuous* means guileless.

Drill 7

1. **A** The missing word refers to a *project*—in this case a screenwriter's story—which consists of *little more than a few basic plot points*. Therefore, the missing word might mean something like *incomplete*, so you can immediately eliminate (B). There is not enough information to suggest that the story is *convoluted, prosaic,* or *tortuous,* so eliminate (C), (D), and (E). *Undeveloped* means *incomplete*, so (A) is the best answer.

2. **B** The blank describes the weather in San Francisco. The transition *though* indicates that it is not *sunny* and *temperate*. *Inclement* works the best.

3. **E** From the clues in this sentence, you know that Singapore's independence was *newly granted* and that *industrialization and foreign investment* had not yet taken root. You need a word that means something like unstable or weak for the blank. Choices (A), (B), and (C) all go in the opposite direction of what you're looking for, so eliminate them. *Fortuitous* doesn't fit in the context of your clues, making *dubious* the best answer.

4. **advantage** and **rudimentary**

The clue to the second blank, *sophisticated weaponry that could easily overpower*, suggests a word that means *less sophisticated*. *Intricate* and *perilous* do not pertain to being *less sophisticated* and can be eliminated, leaving *rudimentary* as the correct answer. The northern nations could easily overpower the southern nations, and so they had an *upper hand*. *Advantage* is the only choice that means *upper hand* and is correct.

5. **C** While the *legislators claimed the Contagious Diseases Acts strengthened the nation*, the change-direction trigger *even though* shows that the social purists disagreed. You want a word similar to *harm* or *weaken* for the blank. *Hampered* is similar to harm and provides you with an equivalent sentence; *advanced* and *enhanced* go in the opposite direction, so eliminate (A) and (E). *Ameliorated* and *supplanted* don't make sense in the context of the sentence, so eliminate (B) and (D) and select (C).

6. **C** The hall's design was likely plain or functional, given the clue *minimalist influences*. Choices (A), (B), and (E) are easy eliminations, as they are clearly opposite in meaning. You can eliminate (D) if you know that *refulgent* is the opposite of *plain*. *Unadorned* is the best match.

7. **esoteric**, **panoramic**, and **scrutinized**

For the first blank, the sentence states that prisons are *less* something than *musing on ethics*. Thus, while a word like *theoretical* would make sense, *esoteric* is the best match. The second blank describes the view you would have from the center; *panoramic* makes the most sense. Finally, the third blank is contrasting with when the guards are looking *elsewhere*; thus, *scrutinized* is the best match.

8. **dependent**, **repudiated**, and **specious**

Start with the last blank because it is the easiest. The clue tells you that *the plaintiff's case disintegrated*. Therefore, the claims must have been shown to be false. *Facetious*, though somewhat negative, does not mean *false* but does not go far enough. *Unerring* goes in the opposite direction. *Specious* is the best match. The first blank is the easiest one to attempt next. The case fell apart when something happened to the witnesses' credentials, so a good phrase for the first blank—which described the role of the witnesses in the plaintiff's case—is *based on*. *Dependent* is the only match. If the plaintiff's claims were based on the witnesses, and the case fell apart, logically the witnesses must have been discredited somehow. A good word for the second blank—which describes what the court decided about the witnesses' credentials—is *denied*. *Vindicated* goes in the opposite direction. *Repudiated* is the best match.

9. **D** The sentence states that *increases in technology have led to increases in speed and power*. The blank, therefore, requires something along the lines of *similar* or *proportional*. Only *commensurate* fits. The answer is (D).

10. **D** Look for the clue in the strong adjective *electrifying*. The song must pump up the pitchers' fans. *Eviscerates* and *enervates* are the opposite of what you want, so eliminate (A) and (B). *Pervades* is unrelated to the clue, and *assuages* sounds like a possibility, but has nothing to do with excitement; eliminate (C) and (E). You're left with (D), *innervates*, which means *to pump up*.

11. **D** The blank refers to Emmet Ray's *paradoxical* character. The trigger *while* follows the clue, indicating that his *sophisticated musical artistry* is contrary to some other aspect of his personality. Look for a word that means unsophisticated, and use POE to eliminate (B) and (E). *Petulant* and *audacious* have appropriately negative meanings, but are unrelated to sophistication in the context of *artistry*. *Maladroit* means clumsy, so (D) is the best match.

12. **impugn, substantiated, and foreclosing**

The first blank refers to the intention of the editorial, which suggested a *preferable alternative* to the current administration; a good word to describe the editorial's intention toward the incumbents might be a word such as *attack* or *undermine*. Only *impugn* means attack. The second blank refers to *claims made against* the group that the editorial was trying to support; the actions were inadvertent, so a good word for the blank might be something like *supported* or *proved*. The only word that makes sense is *substantiated*. Since the editorial ended up damaging the interests of the preferable alternative, a good word for the third blank might be something like *stopping*. *Foreclosing* matches this meaning.

13. **diurnal, gregarious, and camaraderie**

The clue for the first blank is *most of their activities during the day*, and so that blank must describe such a pattern. *Quotidian* means *common* and *circadian* patterns *occur once per day*, but not specifically during the daytime. *Diurnal* is the best fit because it means *during the daytime*. The second blank needs to be consistent with the clue *desire for company*. *Collaborative* means *enjoys working with others* but not a *desire for company*, but a *gregarious* creature is *quite social* and seeks out company. *Egregious* means *extremely bad*, and does not match. The third blank must also describe something like *company*. *Litheness* means *grace and flexibility* and *fatuity* means *idiotic*, and neither one truly refers to having company. *Camaraderie* means *trusting friendship*, which is the most like *company* and makes it the best answer.

14. **haughtiness and sanction**

The first part of the sentence states that mathematicians should not be dismissive of theorems that seem beneath them. Someone who does this would be snobbish, so the first blank must mean something like *snobbishness*. *Puerility* means *immaturity* and *substantiation* means *proof*, so neither of those is a match, while *haughtiness* does mean *snobbishness*. If the *advanced degrees are not a license*, that means that they do not give someone permission to do something bad such as have arrogance or egotism. The second blank must mean something like *permit*. To *dispel* is to *push away*, which is almost the opposite of what you need here. To *cultivate* means to *foster*, which is not the same as *permit*. *Sanction* is the best answer because one of its standard definitions is *give permission*.

15. **exegesis** and **parochial**

Bettelheim has produced something that is *thorough* and *well-researched* concerning "Hansel and Gretel." The first blank must then mean *scholarly study*. An *incantation* is a *magical spell* and *relish* could mean *enjoyment*, but neither word pertains to being scholarly. An *exegesis* is a *critical explanation*, or *scholarly study*, and is correct. Bettelheim's focus is *severely constricted by his narrow worldview*, so it must be *narrow*. *Sweeping* can mean *vast*, the opposite of what you need. A *jaundiced* focus is one that is *affected by envy or bitterness*, and there is no support for this idea in the clues. *Parochial* means *provincial* or *narrow-minded*, making it a solid fit for the second blank.

Reading
Comprehension

INTRODUCTION

Reading Comp Versus Text Completions and Sentence Equivalence

On any computer-adaptive test (CAT), there are always trade-offs between speed and accuracy. Nowhere is this truer than Reading Comprehension (RC). Reading Comprehension is an open-book test. In theory, with unlimited time, you should never get an RC question wrong. The first step to improving performance on Reading Comprehension questions, therefore, is to find that time. By improving your speed and efficiency with Text Completion and Sentence Equivalence questions, you leave yourself more time to spend on Reading Comprehension. When you become a master of the other two question types, you free yourself up to relax and take your time on RC where time equals points.

Question Types

There are three types of questions you might see with Reading Comprehension:

1. Multiple Choice
2. Select All That Apply
3. Select In Passage

Multiple Choice

These are the standard, five-choice, multiple-choice questions we have been doing. There is only one correct answer choice and four wrong ones.

Select All That Apply

These are a variation of the old Roman numeral questions. Remember the ones that gave you three statements marked I, II, and III, and the answer choices that said, "I only," "I and II only," "I, II, and III"? These are the same, but without the answer choices. They will give you three statements, with a box next to each. You have to select all that apply. The process is the same. Find lead words and look for proof.

Select In Passage

In this case, ETS will ask you to select a sentence in the passage that makes a particular point, raises a question, provides proof, or some other function. These questions will appear primarily on short passages. If one appears on a longer passage, they will limit the scope to a particular paragraph. Again, the same rules apply. Pick a lead word. Put the question into your own words, and use Process of Elimination. To answer one of these, you will literally click on a particular sentence in the passage or paragraph.

How Much to Read

Reading Comprehension is the most time-intensive portion of the Verbal test. Deciding how much time to allocate to the passage is another way to pick up valuable time without sacrificing accuracy. The amount of time you devote will depend upon four primary factors. They are Difficulty Level, Length, Skill Set, and Number of Questions.

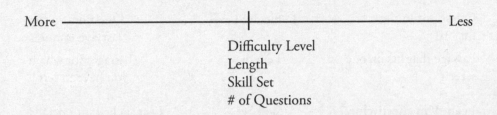

> RULES TO LIVE BY: You can always read more *IF* you have to, but you never want to read more *THAN* you have to.

Difficulty Level

There is an enormous range in the difficulty level of the different passages you will see. There is, however, no rule that says that you have to do the questions in the order in which they are given. If you come across a particularly impenetrable question—and you'll know pretty quickly if you do—just skip it and leave it for the end.

Length

Passages on the GRE come in two lengths: those that fit on a screen and those that force you to scroll. Scrolling is a nuisance. If the passage is so short that it fits on one screen, you might as well just read it. You'll probably end up reading the whole thing anyway.

Skill Set

Some people can skim; some cannot. Which are you? Can you skim quickly and still pick up the main idea of a passage? Or, when you skim, do you either miss the main idea or get sucked into the details? If you are inclined to get sucked in, you will get sucked in, and you shouldn't try to skim at all.

Number of Questions

The test will tell you how many questions are associated with a particular passage. If the next two or three questions are based upon the same passage, it's worth your time to read more of it.

More		Less
Questions in the first 10	Difficulty Level	Questions in the last five minutes
Passage that fits on one screen	Length	Passages for which you have to scroll
I can skim effectively	Skill Set	I get sucked into details and end up burning time
> 2 questions per passage	# of Questions	< 2 questions per passage

Strategy

You can always read more *if* you need to, but you don't ever want to read more *than* you have to in order to answer a particular question. If you see a short passage with two questions in the first 10, you should read the whole thing. If you see a long passage with one question in the last few minutes, and you have more questions to get to, just bubble in and move on. For anything else, you will need a moderated approach. One method is to read the first sentence of the passage, the first sentence of each additional paragraph, and the last sentence of the passage. This should be sufficient to get the GIST of the passage. Remember: If you need to read more, you always can.

Basic Question Approach

If you get a Reading Comprehension question wrong, it is for one of the three reasons. Either you misread something in the passage, misread the question, or misread one of the answer choices. The basic approach is designed to give some rigor to your interaction with each of these main components.

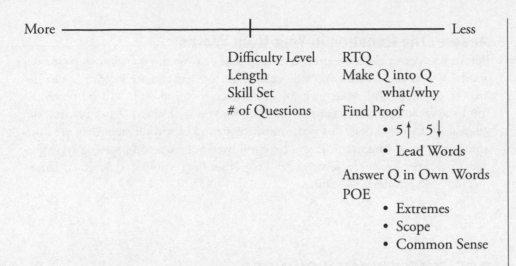

More ——————————————+—————————————— Less

Difficulty Level	RTQ
Length	Make Q into Q
Skill Set	what/why
# of Questions	Find Proof
	• 5↑ 5↓
	• Lead Words
	Answer Q in Own Words
	POE
	• Extremes
	• Scope
	• Common Sense

Read the Question (RTQ)

The first thing to do, naturally, is to read the question. Specifically, you should put your finger or pencil literally on the screen and read the question word for word. Misreading the question is one of the most common causes of errors. Reading with a pencil or finger, word for word, is a good habit, especially for strong readers who tend to skip over words without even noticing.

Turn the Question into a Question

After a few hours of testing, it is all too easy for the eyes to glaze over and to read without really comprehending. To ensure that the words aren't simply going in one eyeball and out the other, you should engage the question in a qualitative way. Most questions, you will notice, aren't really questions at all. They are incomplete sentences. The easiest way to own the question is to actually make it back into a question. The easiest way to do this is to simply start with the word "What" or "Why," and then to let the rest follow (any question-word will do, but the vast majority of questions either ask "What was stated in the passage?" or "Why was it said?").

5 Up, 5 Down

Never attempt to answer a question from memory. The minute you stop reading, you start forgetting. ETS counts on this and plays with the answer choices to change your recollection of the information. You must look at the information *in context*, but you don't have to read the whole paragraph. Choose a word from the question that will be easy to find in the passage, skim for it, and then read five lines above it to five lines below it. That should be sufficient to answer the question.

Answer the Question in Your Own Words

Before you get to the answer choices, stop and answer the question in your own words. When you do this, you will know exactly what you are looking for in the answer choices. With your own answer choice in mind, you will be protected from the tricks and traps that ETS has laid for you with theirs. After turning the question into a question, this is the most frequently blown-off step; they are both among the most important. If you have followed your question-solving strategies, one answer choice will look correct and the other four will look ridiculous. This is precisely the position you want.

POE: THE ANSWER CHOICES

There are three general characteristics that separate correct answers from incorrect ones. As you work through the drills, note these types whenever you see them. Over time you will develop an instinct for right versus wrong answers.

Extremes

ETS plays it safe. Correct answers are wishy-washy or very difficult to prove false. It is too easy to find exceptions to extreme answer choices. For this reason, they are almost never correct. Remember: To ETS it doesn't matter what the passages says. They don't write the passages, but they do write the questions and the answers. They can choose to word correct or incorrect answers any way they like. They choose to do it in a way that won't put them on the phone with dozens of experts in various fields who beg to differ with them.

Examples

(A)	Disproving the view that herbivores are less intelligent than carnivores	Can this even be done? *Prove* or *disprove* is a very extreme word.
(B)	Chaucer was the first English author to focus on society as a whole as well as on individual characters.	This is too definitive a statement for a subjective view.
(C)	The public is not interested in increasing its awareness of the advantages and disadvantages of nuclear fusion power.	Really? Says who? The whole of the public?

Scope

If you cannot physically put your finger on a specific word, line, phrase, or sentence that proves that your answer choice is correct, you cannot choose it. ETS loves to add to answer choices little bits and bobs that were never stated in the passage. If a passage is about a recent immigrant's first experience of America, ETS will widen the scope of an answer choice to include *all* immigrants. If the passage is about the existence of heavy metals on some planets, an incorrect answer choice will talk about all planets.

Examples

MAIN IDEA OF PASSAGE	OUT-OF-SCOPE ANSWER CHOICE
How new plant seeds got to Hawaii	1. Resolving a dispute about the adaptability of plant seeds to bird transport
	2. Refute the claim that Hawaiian flora evolved independently from flora in other parts of the world
	3. Why more varieties of plant seeds adapted to external rather than to internal bird transport

What's wrong with the answer choices?

1. *Resolving a dispute* is an awfully strong opening verb for this answer choice, but this answer choice is all about the nature of seeds, not about how seeds got to Hawaii. If the passage is about Hawaii, then the correct answer had better say "Hawaii."
2. The question is talking about Hawaii and seed transport, not about other parts of the world and evolution.
3. Again, this one is all about seeds and adaptation, not about Hawaii and transportation.

Common Sense

Many of the answer choices simply don't make any sense. Just because you see it on the GRE doesn't mean you have to take it seriously. Science passages may have answer choices that are highly illogical or physically impossible. Humanities passages may have answer choices that support different or even opposite views than those of the author, and certainly ones that ETS could never stand behind. And some answer choices are just downright ridiculous.

(A)	The public has been deliberately misinformed about the advantages and disadvantages of nuclear power.	The GRE is not your typical forum for exposing government cover-ups.
(B)	An interpretation of a novel should primarily consider those elements of novelistic construction of which the author of the novel was aware.	Unless someone can call up dead novelists from the grave, exactly how is the good critic to know which elements of novelistic construction the authors were aware of?
(C)	James, more than any other novelist, was aware of the difficulties of novelistic construction.	Extreme language aside, are there measurable degrees of awareness? Do we know how aware every novelist in history is or was? Is James really the Michael Jordan of Awareness of Novelistic Construction?

RULES TO LIVE BY: If you cannot physically put your finger on a specific word, line, phrase, or sentence that proves that your answer choice is correct, you cannot pick it.

POE: THE PROCESS

In general, you want to be doing, not thinking. Thinking gets you into trouble. The best way to tell if you are thinking rather than doing is to pay attention to your hands. If your hands are not moving, you are either spacing out, lost, or attempting to do work in your head—all are bad. The use of scratch paper, therefore, is as critical to the Verbal portion as it is to the math. Proper use of the scratch paper will help you stay on track, organize your thinking, and maintain an efficient, meticulous, and systematic approach.

The process of POE is, in essence, a two-pass approach. In the first pass, walk through the answer choices asking a simple question: Maybe or Gone? "Gone" refers to the answer choice that can be eliminated with confidence; "maybe" refers to everything else. This pass should take no more than 15 seconds. *You are not looking for the correct answer.* On this pass, you don't want to invest a lot of time in any one answer choice, because often the correct answer will be very clear, or you will be able to eliminate the other four. Remember that you have already found proof and answered the question in your own words. Correct and incorrect answer choices should leap out at you at this point. Only if you are left with two or three do you need to investigate further.

Make sure that you park your thinking on the page as you go; otherwise, you are doing two separate jobs. One is assessing the answer choices; the other is keeping track of what you've already decided about prior answer choices. This is confusing and inefficient. It is much better to simply park it on the page.

To do this you can use three basic symbols.

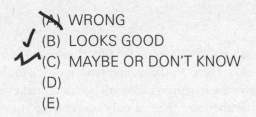

"Wrong" means that it is clearly wrong and therefore gone. You never need to spend any time on this answer choice again. "Maybe" simply means that it is possible or you're not sure. "Yes" means that it looks good. You are making these assessments through a combination of information you have acquired in the passage, and the three elimination techniques listed above. In the last 10 questions, you might even stop here if you have two "maybes" or a clear winner. In the first 10 questions, you must go back to the passage to find proof.

Here is what the two passes might look like on a short passage in the first 10 questions. In this case, you should have read the entire passage.

First Pass

First Pass

Main Idea:

Pros and cons of a unified assessment of the two halves of *Wuthering Heights*

Q: The author of the passage would be most likely to agree that an interpretation of a novel should

(A) not try to unite heterogeneous elements in the novel
Half of the passage is about why this is a good thing!

(B) not be inflexible in its treatment of the elements in the novel
Wording is ridiculous, but "be flexible," okay, that makes sense.

(C) not argue that the complex use of narrators or of timeshifts indicates a sophisticated structure
Umm. Not sure, it's got to stay in for now.

(D) concentrate on those recalcitrant elements of the novel that are outside the novel's main structure
No, the author definitely didn't prescribe what someone should or shouldn't concentrate on.

(E) primarily consider those elements of novelistic construction of which the author of the novel was aware
Common sense.

This first pass took about 15–20 seconds. You eliminated some obvious choices and got it down to two. Then, on the second pass, go back to the passage to check your proof. Paraphrase the remaining answer choices to make sure you are reading them correctly. Remember that there is only one correct answer. If you are absolutely sure that both are correct, you are misreading something. As usual, the correct answer is a clear, if awkward, paraphrase of something stated in the passage (the awkwardness is an obvious attempt to steer us away from this answer choice). The second choice is stated, but it's encouraged, not discouraged.

In the second pass, pay no attention to (A), (D), or (E) because they have already been eliminated. Occasionally you will end up eliminating all five; only in this case will you go back and reassess an answer choice you have already eliminated.

Second Pass

Second Pass

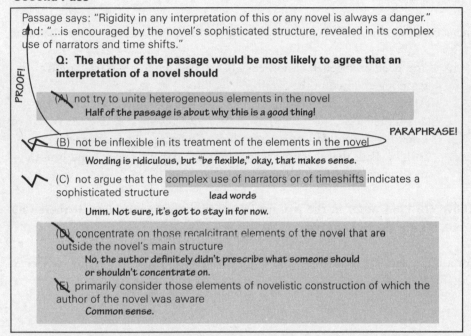

Passage says: "Rigidity in any interpretation of this or any novel is always a danger." and: "...is encouraged by the novel's sophisticated structure, revealed in its complex use of narrators and time shifts."

PROOF!

Q: The author of the passage would be most likely to agree that an interpretation of a novel should

(A) not try to unite heterogeneous elements in the novel
Half of the passage is about why this is a good thing!

PARAPHRASE!

(B) not be inflexible in its treatment of the elements in the novel
Wording is ridiculous, but "be flexible," okay, that makes sense.

(C) not argue that the complex use of narrators or of timeshifts indicates a sophisticated structure   lead words
Umm. Not sure, it's got to stay in for now.

(D) concentrate on those recalcitrant elements of the novel that are outside the novel's main structure
No, the author definitely didn't prescribe what someone should or shouldn't concentrate on.

(E) primarily consider those elements of novelistic construction of which the author of the novel was aware
Common sense.

SUMMARY

To sum up, read only as much as you have to and follow these five steps for all questions:

1. RTQ
2. Turn the Question into a Question
3. 5 up, 5 down
4. Answer the Question in Your Own Words
5. Process of Elimination

There are three things to keep in mind when working on Reading Comprehension:

1. You need only general knowledge of the passage to get started (don't get bogged down in the details).
2. Always answer the question in your own words before you look at the answer choices.
3. Look for reasons why an answer choice is wrong, not reasons why it is right. Park that thinking on your scratch paper. If your hand is not moving, you're stuck. Move on.

Above all: Find proof in the passage for every answer you select. If there's no proof, it's not the right answer.

For a more detailed description and more examples of these techniques, reference *Cracking the GRE*.

Reading
Comprehension
Drills

DRILL 1

Questions 1-2 refer to the following passage.

Little is known about the elusive section of the earth's atmosphere known as the mesosphere. Located between the stratosphere (the maximum altitude that airplanes can achieve) and the thermosphere (the minimum altitude of spacecraft), the mesosphere is poorly understood and little explored. The most significant feature of the mesosphere is the various tides and waves that propagate up from the troposphere and stratosphere. The dissipation of these waves is largely responsible for propelling the mesosphere around the globe. These wave patterns are further affected when gas particles in the mesosphere collide with meteoroids, producing spectacular explosions, which usually generate enough heat to consume the meteor before it can fall to earth. The conflagration leaves behind traces of iron and other metals and fuels the atmospheric tides radiating outward from the mesosphere.

Question 1

The author primarily describes the mesosphere as

- ○ destructive
- ○ opaque
- ○ unfamiliar
- ○ radiant
- ○ anarchic

Question 2

Consider each of the choices separately and select all that apply.

The passage suggests that the mesosphere is influenced by

- ☐ collisions with extraterrestrial debris
- ☐ vibrations from the troposphere
- ☐ oceanic tides

Questions 3-4 refer to the following passage.

Television programming is big business, with sales of interstitial advertising reaching billions of dollars annually. Advertising rates are determined by the viewership of the program in question, which has traditionally been determined by ACNielsen, part of The Nielsen Company. Nielsen wields an immoderate amount of industry clout considering its questionable methods of statistics gathering.

The Nielsen Company relies on selected households to catalog their television watching habits in "diaries." The ratings are then reported as a percentage that indicates the number of viewers watching a television program at a given time. The company has come under criticism for choosing residences that underreport daytime and late-night television viewing and for overrepresenting minorities in sample populations. Critics also point to the nonviable practice of measuring how many individuals are watching a given television set and of gauging how attentive the audience is to a program or its advertising.

Question 3

It can be inferred from the passage that the author considers the Nielsen Company's techniques

○ intentionally biased
○ dubious
○ worthless
○ unscrupulous
○ overly boastful

Question 4

Consider each of the choices separately and select all that apply.

Which of the following does the passage indicate is true of the household members who report their viewing habits?

☐ Because ratings are reported as a percentage, each household is counted only as one person.
☐ They are not always accurate when it comes to recording their viewing habits.
☐ The indirect influence they exert on advertising costs may not be based on all relevant factors.

Questions 5-8 refer to the following passage.

Although multi-organ transplants have become more common, scientists and surgeons continue to face the ineluctable obstacle of time. Current donor organ preservation times hover around five to six hours. Because of the complicated tissue-matching process, oftentimes organs are unable to reach their beneficiaries, wasting valuable, viable organs. However, scientists are hopeful that a certain substance, called the Hibernation Induction Trigger (HIT), will extend the life of a potential transplant organ.

HIT is an opiate-like substance found in the blood of hibernating animals. Previous experiments have shown that opioids act as an autoperfusion block, preventing blood from flowing through the lymphatic system to organs, a phenomenon known as ischemia. In a preliminary experiment, an infusion of plasma with the Delta opioid delayed hemorrhaging in certain laboratory animals. When this arresting of activity was applied to the transplantation of organs, physicians reported preservation times up to 15 hours, a more than two-fold increase over standard conservation.

Scientists have extrapolated from these findings, further identifying the opioid DADLE as integral to triggering the hibernation process. Infusing HIT-molecule-containing plasma from hibernating woodchucks into canine lungs increased preservation times more than three-fold from previous findings. This experiment suggests that, should a potential donor organ be infused with these trigger molecules before the organ is harvested, the organ would remain transplantable for up to 45 hours, greatly increasing the chance for doctors to find a suitable recipient.

Though these results are exciting, they do nothing to increase survival rates from an organ transplant operation, which currently hover at 60 percent over four years, because patients are still susceptible to infection and rejection. Scientists are a long way from declaring HIT-molecules a safe and consistent method of organ preservation. Still, other areas of science have taken an interest in this research. NASA, for example, is considering the implications of human hibernation for deep space travel.

Question 5

Which of the following can be inferred from the passage?

○ Ischemia is essential to the organ transplantation process.

○ The same process by which HIT induces hibernation might be applicable to donor organs.

○ The biggest obstacle facing physicians in the science of organ transplantation is the difficulty of matching suitable donors and recipients.

○ Additional time could be saved by computerizing the tissue-matching process.

○ HIT could also be administered to patients awaiting an organ transplant, thereby lengthening the amount of time they are eligible for surgery.

Question 6

Given the information in the passage about blocking autoperfusion, which of the following could also be true?

○ DADLE and HIT must be present in an organ at the same time in order for autoperfusion to be prevented for any length of time.

○ If scientists could circumvent the passage of blood through the lymphatic system, organs would cease to deteriorate.

○ Scientists are close to developing a method to induce production of HIT in a non-hibernating animal in a laboratory setting.

○ Administering HIT after transplantation is likely to lower the current rates of infection and organ rejection.

○ Isolating and infusing opioids may be the key to retarding the progression of decay in transplant organs.

The author refers to the experiment with the woodchuck in order to

○ illustrate successful preliminary experiments

○ suggest genetic similarity between species

○ warn that the findings are preliminary at best

○ explain why other scientists may be interested in the findings

○ suggest the feasibility of inter-species transplant

Select the sentence from the passage which suggests how the use of isolated HIT molecules, if they were to be approved for general use, would be limited.

Questions 9-11 refer to the following passage.

It might seem illogical that the development of modern currency rests on a scientific discovery, but the invention of the "touchstone" allowed ancient societies to create a standard by which valuable metals could be judged. In its most basic form, a touchstone is any dark, finely grained stone upon which soft metals leave traces. When rubbed, a process known as "probing," precious metal alloy cleaves to the stone, leaving a stripe. The color of the stripe (which reveals the percentage of its content that is base metal) can then be compared to a stripe of a known grade of standard alloy. Despite its primitiveness, this probing process allowed merchants to examine alloys quickly and with reasonable certainty. Though civilizations were using gold and silver currencies as early as 500 B.C., coins were easily forged or diluted with less valuable metals, such as tin or lead. The invention and popularization of the touchstone ensured that pure gold and silver could become a standard expression of value.

Question 9

The primary purpose of the passage is to

○ demonstrate that science can influence non-scientific progress

○ underline the touchstone's importance in the history of currency

○ explain how the touchstone is able to measure the purity of an alloy

○ explore the etymology of the word "touchstone"

○ refute an historical misconception

Question 10

The author's description of how coins were adulterated is included in the passage in order to

○ illustrate the historical precedent replaced by the invention

○ outline for the reader the chronology of the events in the passage

○ explain the larger importance of the details just provided

○ give the passage a cultural context

○ dismiss a misleading counterargument

Question 11

Consider each of the choices separately and select all that apply.

The passage indicates that the advances brought about by the probing process included

☐ an efficient means of ascertaining the purity of a metal

☐ a means by which governments could standardize currency values

☐ a measure of security against adulterated coins

Questions 12-15 refer to the following passage.

Women played a substantial role in the furthering of the Polish art song in the late eighteenth and early nineteenth centuries. One notable woman from this time period was Maria Szymanowska, who was both a concert pianist and a composer.

Szymanowska was a member of the Warsaw Music Society who contributed pieces to a cycle entitled Historical Songs. Her songs are by far the most creative and individualistic of the cycle. In addition, Szymanowska composed more than one hundred other pieces, mostly for the piano, including six romances.

Her songs most resemble French romances, and she also employs Polonaise rhythms in two of her songs. In all her works, the melodic line is technically superior. She employs idiomatic keyboard writing, wide chord-spacing, broad cantilenas, and interesting modulations. She also uses the most compelling registers of the instrument and pianistic keys. Her romances are on par with those of Beethoven, Schubert, and Mozart. In fact, Szymanowska was praised by her contemporaries, such as Schumann, who lauded her etudes. Her piano playing was frequently equated to that of Hummel, though Szymanowska's was said to be more ethereal. Thus, she is a progenitor of Chopin in both piano technique and composition.

Female contributors to the development of Polish music have been chiefly ignored. From the meager records which have been preserved, it is incontrovertible that Polish women were, in fact, playing, instructing, and writing music as early as the fifteenth century. However, patriarchal societal structures have precluded adequate documentation about, and preservation of, their work. Unless changes take place, human society will be made poorer for its inability to recognize the expertise and inventiveness of these women.

Question 12

Select the sentence in the third paragraph that gives evidence for the idea that Szymanowska's work laid the foundation for at least one future composer.

Question 13

The author's tone in the final sentence ("Unless changes . . . these women") is best described as

○ nostalgic
○ emphatic
○ dismissive
○ perplexed
○ didactic

Question 14

According to the passage, the musical contributions of Polish women have been neglected due to

- ○ an absence of any documentation of the efforts of female composers
- ○ improper preservation of musical scores produced by women
- ○ the male-dominated social order that has existed since at least the fifteenth century
- ○ society willfully ignoring the talent and hard work of female composers
- ○ the fact that people did not realize the genius and creativity of female composers

Question 15

Consider each of the choices separately and select all that apply.

Which of the following can be properly inferred from the passage?

- ☐ Szymanowska's advancement of the music of Polish art songs in spite of patriarchal pressure demonstrates her feminist tendencies.
- ☐ Szymanowska composed works beyond the genre of the Polonaise that are deserving of praise.
- ☐ Szymanowska's works that contributed to the development of Polish art song garnered a disproportionate amount of attention, considering that such compositions were only a small part of her repertoire.

DRILL 2

Questions 1-2 refer to the following passage.

Historically, sociologists have presumed that people will attribute certain characteristics to a member of a particular group when it is generally believed that most members of that group possess the characteristics in question. For sociologists Hepburn and Locksley, such social stereotyping has led to the broader question of whether people are cognizant of their own stereotyping behavior. Seemingly, if one knows that one holds a stereotypical notion such as "all members of a certain ethnic group are natural musicians," then one might also be aware that the notion that "a particular musician of that ethnic group is a great musician" is a corollary of that stereotype. However, people are most aware of their stereotyping when they have no information. When given information that conforms to their beliefs and the individual case observed, people become less aware of their tendency to stereotype and therefore more likely to engage in stereotyping.

Question 1

Which of the following best describes the function of the first sentence?

○ To present a criticism of Hepburn and Locksley's conceptualization of why individuals stereotype

○ To provide evidence to support Hepburn and Locksley's claims about the problems inherent with stereotyping

○ To provide the backdrop for Hepburn and Locksley's study

○ To provide an overview of a social phenomenon and its contributions to Hepburn and Locksley's area of inquiry

○ To provide a history of social stereotyping alongside Hepburn and Locksley's reservations about the practice

Question 2

The author of the passage is primarily concerned with

○ investigations into stereotyping and an awareness of stereotyping by individuals

○ an examination of the relative truths behind well-known stereotypes

○ an attempt to prove that stereotypes are a result of ignorance

○ a refutation of a broader question surrounding stereotypes

○ a detailed list of when individuals are likely to be aware that they are applying stereotypes

Questions 3-6 refer to the following passage.

The literature of the American West ranges from lowbrow entertainment to great works of fiction. The extremes are obvious enough, but the middle tends to blur. The dime-store Western never aspired to be anything but entertainment. James Fenimore Cooper and Willa Cather, however, used themes of westward expansion in works clearly intended as highbrow literature. The novels of modern writer Larry McMurtry broke new ground: He took the Western and created a great piece of fiction, without changing its fundamental genre appeal or its accessibility to the general reader.

As an example of his retooling of the Western genre, consider McMurtry's themes. While the Western myth is fundamentally about resettlement to new lands, McMurtry's novels combine elements of the Western myth with less traditional motifs: profound reluctance to face change, conflict between urbanization and the Western ideal, the importance of place, and the role of the land itself. While the traditional Western is rooted in the past, McMurtry's themes combine nostalgia for that past with a sense of emptiness in the present and hopelessness for the future.

Or consider McMurtry's treatment of character. The traditional Western formula depicts mainly masculine characters and portrays them as both heroic and human. In his novels, McMurtry creates strong female characters, transmuting the conventional plot of the trials and dangers of the frontier by folding in deeper ideological insights. Critics rightly credit his novels with reshaping the Western genre, praising his work and its meticulous attention to the Western *mise en scène* as a subversive but sincere tribute to the American West.

Question 3

Select the sentence that shows the author's view of McMurtry's treatment of gender.

Question 4

The author refers to James Fenimore Cooper and Willa Cather in order to suggest

○ that their works are examples of entertaining literature

○ that their literary achievements were no less impressive than those of McMurtry

○ that the themes of the Western genre could be employed in literature meant to appeal to a more sophisticated reader

○ that they were contemporaries of McMurtry

○ that the theme of westward expansion was a multicultural concept

Question 5

Consider each of the following answer choices separately and select all that apply.

According to the passage, the ideological undertones in McMurtry's novels stem from the

- ☐ introduction of strong female characters
- ☐ portrayal of the dangerous nature of the Western frontier
- ☐ subversive nature of the writing

Question 6

It can be inferred that the author regards McMurtry's treatment of characters with

- ◯ regret because McMurtry did not adhere to Western novelistic conventions
- ◯ concern that the characterizations altered the nature of the Western formula
- ◯ approval for the manner in which their inclusion transformed the Western genre
- ◯ puzzlement, because the characters seem insignificant to the plot
- ◯ enthusiasm, because the characters reform the conventionality of Western plots

Questions 7-10 refer to the following passage.

"Hydrothermal vent" is the term that scientists use to describe a crack in a planet's surface from which geothermally heated water emerges. Because these vents are common in places that are volcanically active, they are plentiful on Earth. While the most famous hydrothermal vent is probably the geyser at Yellowstone National Park in the United States, there are several different types of vents, existing both on land and underwater. Black Smokers, for instance, are a common type of submarine vent. The National Oceanic and Atmospheric Administration first discovered these in the vicinity of the Galapagos Islands in 1977. Underwater vents such as these form when water that has been heated by magma beneath the earth's crust exits through cracks in the ocean floor. Scientists are interested in these vents primarily for their ability to host biologically dense communities in areas that are otherwise hostile to life. Studies show that Chemosynthetic archaea, a life form similar to bacteria, allows these areas to support such diverse organisms as clams and shrimp. Black Smokers are also visually striking. Minerals in the water that emerge from the earth's crust crystallize around each vent to create their distinctive black chimney-like formations.

While on a vessel exploring the Atlantis Massif in the mid-Atlantic Ridge, scientists recently discovered a completely new kind of hydrothermal system, which they dubbed "Lost City." Here, a "forest" of white limestone pillars rises 180 feet above the sea floor. There are several important differences that distinguish the hydrothermal vents in Lost City from the more familiar Black Smokers. The heat and fluid flow at Lost City is driven by the intermingling of seawater and mantle rocks on the sea floor, rather than by hot magma. As these fluids mix with magnesium-rich sea water, they deposit calcium carbonate and magnesium hydroxide, thereby creating the stunning white structures of Lost City. The fluids here are also much cooler (less than 100 degrees Celsius) and are composed of substances and gases that are different from those of Black Smokers. For instance, the fluids here have high pH content and contain significant amounts of hydrogen and methane gas.

The discovery of Lost City is still a fairly recent one, and scientists currently have more questions than answers. However, they hope that the insights they gain from this study will provide information that will lead to a better understanding of some of the earliest hydrothermal systems on earth and the life they supported.

Question 7

The primary purpose of the passage is to

○ refute a well-established theory
○ describe a newly discovered natural phenomenon and compare it to another
○ explain how the study of a certain natural phenomenon has changed over time
○ evaluate opposing theories
○ reconsider a natural phenomenon in light of new discoveries

Question 8

Select the sentence that explains why Black Smokers have piqued the curiosity of biologists.

Question 9

Consider each of the following answer choices separately and select all that apply.

The passage suggests that the hydrothermal vents that constitute Lost City are different from Black Smokers in which of the following ways?

☐ Magma propels the heat and water of Black Smokers, whereas the vents at Lost City are driven by the merging of seawater and mantle rocks.

☐ Black Smoker vents release water that is much cooler than the water released at Lost City.

☐ Chemosynthetic archaea fosters many different life forms around Black Smokers but is not present at Lost City.

Question 10

Consider each of the following answer choices separately and select all that apply.

According to the passage, which of the following statements are true about Black Smokers?

☐ As water emerges from the vents, it deposits calcium carbonate.

☐ Black chimney-like structures form around each vent.

☐ Black Smokers host biologically dense communities.

Questions 11-12 refer to the following passage.

The paintings of Eugene Delacroix are as political, complex, tumultuous, and vivid as the life of Lord Byron, who inspired some of Delacroix's best works, such as *Greece Expiring on the Ruins of Missolonghi* and *Scène des massacres de Scio.* Simultaneously, the paintings boast an incredible mélange of the artistic traditions of prior masters and movements—such as a preoccupation with *terribilitas* from Michelangelo; a flair for color from Titian; and power, strength, and exuberance from Rubens—all underlain by the harmony and balance of classical artists and tinted with the Baroque. Delacroix combined eclectic elements and infused them with his own genius, creating a unique expression of Romanticism, and in so doing, inspired yet another style, Symbolism.

Question 11

Consider each of the following answer choices separately and select all that apply.

The passage suggests that which of the following are NOT unique elements of the paintings of Delacroix?

☐ A tint of the Baroque
☐ A preoccupation with *terribilitas*
☐ Diverse artistic traditions mixed with Delacroix's own acumen

Question 12

According to the passage, Delacroix's painting *Scène des massacres de Scio* was influenced by

○ *Greece Expiring on the Ruins of Missolonghi*
○ a mix of artistic traditions
○ the life of Lord Byron
○ prior masters and their movements
○ the Baroque period

Questions 13-15 refer to the following passage.

Sociobiologists, the most well known of whom is Edward O. Wilson, contend that there is a biological basis for the social behavior of animals, and they test their hypotheses through observation of animals in situations. Species studied have varied as widely as to encompass both termites and rhesus macaques. Sociobiologists further argue that students of human behavior cannot adequately account for the panoply of human nature through only such traditional variables as culture, ethnicity, and environment but must also include evolutionary processes. However, many scientists, notably Stephen Jay Gould and Richard Lewontin, have criticized this approach to the study of humans on a number of grounds: for example, that it is based on Eurocentric notions and that it is plagued by methodological problems. These detractors label it a pseudo-science because sociobiological theories are not falsifiable and thus, in this respect, are similar to alchemy or astrology.

Question 13

Consider each of the following answer choices separately and select all that apply.

It can be inferred that Gould and Lewontin might agree with which of the following statements about a sociobiological approach to the study of humans?

☐ Sociobiological theories cannot be proven false, and consequently they cannot be conclusively verified; thus, sociobiology is not a real science.

☐ When applied to the study of humans, sociobiology is problematic because it is rooted in a Western worldview and it does not comport with proper scientific methodology.

☐ Scientists cannot adequately explain human behavior through the consideration of cultural, ethnic, and environmental factors alone; therefore, they must resort to sociobiological explanations.

Question 14

The author mentions culture, ethnicity, and environment in order to

○ offer justification for a comparative study between termite colonies and rhesus macaques

○ assert that sociobiology is problematic because it is Eurocentric and beset by methodological complications

○ illustrate that sociobiology is an inappropriate method for studying humans

○ enumerate some variables that sociobiologists believe are insufficient in the study of humans and thus necessitate the addition of biological considerations

○ provide a comprehensive list of the factors that influence human behavior

Question 15

The primary purpose of the passage is to

○ offer praise for an influential scientific approach to the study of animal and human behavior

○ argue for a sociobiological approach to the study of human behavior

○ dispute a sociobiological approach to the study of human behavior

○ justify a sociobiological approach to the study of termite colonies and rhesus macaques

○ set forth an influential approach to the study of animal and human behavior and discuss some objections to this approach

DRILL 3

Questions 1-2 refer to the following passage.

In *The Federalist Number Ten*, James Madison forewarned against the dangers of factions—groups of people with a common interest adverse to the overall good of the nation, what today are referred to as "special interest groups." Madison described two hypothetical ways to check a faction: Either eliminate the causes or mitigate the effects of the faction. To eliminate the causes, the government would either have to make all people perfectly equal, an impossible goal, or take away people's liberty and thus defeat the purpose of having a republican form of government. Madison argued, alternatively, for ameliorating the effects of factions by enlarging the population of the country and thus diluting their influence. If there are a sufficient number of diverse peoples, it will be difficult for a majority to share a common interest at the same time.

Question 1

According to the passage, why does Madison believe it necessary to check a faction?

○ Madison considered factions to be detrimental to the common welfare.

○ Madison thought factions were a way to encourage population growth.

○ Madison relied on factions to support the republican style of government.

○ Madison accepted factions as a consequence of allowing people to participate in government.

○ Madison surmised that factions would likely be run by his political adversaries.

Question 2

Which of the following can be most correctly inferred from the passage?

○ Madison solved the problem of factions in the United States.

○ Madison thought that the best solution was to make all citizens equal.

○ Madison argued against a republican government in *The Federalist Number Ten*.

○ Madison analyzed the effects of increased population.

○ Madison considered more than one way to constrain factions.

Questions 3-4 refer to the following passage.

William Le Baron Jenney is considered the founder of the Chicago School of architecture, as well as the father of the American skyscraper. He served as an engineering officer during the Civil War but by 1868 was a practicing architect. His greatest accomplishments were his mammoth commercial buildings, including the Home Insurance Building in Chicago, which was one of the first buildings to use a metal skeleton. This structure, in fact, would become the archetypical American skyscraper design. Other notable accomplishments included his 16-story Manhattan Building, which was the first edifice ever to achieve that height, and the Horticultural Building, which was the largest botanical conservatory ever erected.

William Holabird also assisted in the evolution of the Chicago School, beginning as a draftsman for Jenney and then founding his own practice in 1880. Holabird invented the "Chicago window," which made buildings appear to be constructed of glass.

Question 3

Consider each of the following answer choices separately and select all that apply.

According to the passage, which of the following describe William Jenney?

☐ He served as an architect during the Civil War.

☐ He is credited with the development of a much-copied design for skyscrapers.

☐ He designed buildings in New York, as well as Chicago.

Question 4

The author mentions the "Chicago window" in order to

○ highlight a feature of glass buildings

○ strengthen the argument that Holabird developed the Chicago School

○ argue that Holabird was a better inventor than Jenney

○ provide an example of Holabird's contributions to the Chicago School

○ demonstrate the artistry of architecture

Questions 5-8 refer to the following passage.

"Solar wind" is the term scientists use to describe the stream of particles that the sun's corona constantly emits. These solar winds, which consist mainly of hydrogen and helium, are intensely hot, fully ionized plasma. Because of the corona's intense heat, these particles continuously escape the sun's gravitational attraction, flowing away from the sun at extreme velocities. Solar winds, though, are not without variation, because they contain faster and slower moving pockets. For instance, solar winds that originate from streamers are slower moving winds at approximately 300 km/second, as opposed to the winds that originate from corona holes and reach speeds of 800 km/second. As they flow away from the sun, tangential discontinuities and interplanetary shocks form, producing pressure variations. Moreover, researchers also know that solar winds are directly related to geomagnetic storms, auroras, and comets. It is these winds that cause comet tails to bend away from the sun, as Kepler accurately predicted in the early 1600s.

Studies have been done on the effect of solar winds on the planets in the solar system. While all the planets are surrounded by this hot, super-charged plasma, the Earth's magnetic field protects it from the solar wind by deflecting the particles. However, solar winds are responsible for the Earth's magnetosphere, and changes in their speed and direction strongly influence Earth's space environment. As the planet closest to the sun, Mercury endures the main impact of solar winds. If Mercury had an atmosphere, these winds would have stripped it away, leaving the planet bathed in radiation. Though Mars is much further from the sun than Mercury, solar winds have also greatly reduced its atmosphere. While Venus has a substantial atmosphere—100 times denser than ours—solar winds reduce its clouds. It is not just those planets nearest the sun which bear the effects of solar winds: The winds travel far beyond the limits of Pluto. Interestingly, while much is now known about solar winds, scientists still do not fully understand how the gases and particles in the sun's corona reach such high velocities.

Question 5

Consider each of the following answer choices separately and select all that apply.

According to the passage, which of the following is true of the effect of solar winds on the Earth?

☐ Though the Earth's magnetic field largely protects it from the full effects of solar winds, the winds have an impact on its magnetosphere and its space environment.

☐ Solar winds play a significant role in the development of auroras and geomagnetic storms.

☐ Because of the corona's intense heat, solar wind particles continuously escape the sun's gravitational attraction, flowing away from the corona at extremely high velocities and surrounding the Earth with hot, super-charged plasma.

Question 6

It can be inferred from the passage that the Earth's magnetic field acts to

○ absorb the particles blown by solar winds

○ incinerate the particles present in solar winds

○ assimilate the particles in solar winds into the Earth's atmosphere

○ divert the particles in solar winds from the Earth

○ re-orient the particles in solar winds toward a central collection point

The author most likely discusses Kepler's predictions in order to

○ illustrate the observable effect solar winds have had on other celestial objects

○ denounce Kepler's work as unreliable because the technology required to study solar winds directly has been developed only within the last century

○ describe more generally the first major contribution to the study of solar winds and the sun

○ disprove Kepler's theories on the motion of comets and auroras

○ establish a standard against which to compare the observations concerning the atmospheres of Mars and Mercury

Select the sentence that attempts to correct a possible misconception about the effects of solar winds.

Questions 9-10 refer to the following passage.

The American people have an incorrect understanding of what it means to be at war. At least, so argues T. H. Pickett in his conservative interpretation of American military history.

Pickett does present a wealth of examples, along with a refreshingly candid argument that America often goes to war for an abstract ideal such as democratization of societies, world peace, liberty, or freedom. For instance, the Spanish-American War of 1898 was ostensibly a consequence of national enthusiasm for the cause of Cuban liberty. And, more obviously, America's entry into World War I stemmed from a desire to "make the world safe for democracy." Although these observations are supportable, Pickett overstates the case when he argues that these abstract causes typically lead to a war hysteria in which American leadership can no longer enforce any measured policies.

Question 9

Consider each of the following answer choices separately and select all that apply.

It can be inferred from the description of Pickett's work that the author believes which of the following?

☐ The desire for tangible rewards is not always the primary reason that America enters into warfare.

☐ Democratization of a foreign country was a rationale for at least one war that America has waged.

☐ Pickett provides a large number of examples to bolster his case.

Question 10

Which of the following best states the author's main point?

○ Pickett's study overturned the conventional understanding of why America engages in warfare.

○ Pickett's study is valuable primarily because it provides a thorough understanding of the causes of American warfare.

○ The rationale for American warfare is well documented.

○ Pickett provides a cogent rationale for why America engages in warfare; however, he draws conclusions that the author does not fully support.

○ Pickett's analysis of American military history provides the definitive historical record of the period from the Spanish-American War to World War I.

Questions 11-12 refer to the following passage.

Though artist Chuck Close has devoted his life to portraiture, his paintings rarely comport with that genre's traditional purpose. His early photorealist images, which are created by overlaying a grid on a photograph and painstakingly copying the image cell by cell, are, to the naked eye, nearly undifferentiable from photographs. Furthermore, Close's emphasis is on the disembodied head itself, expressionless and devoid of any overt personality. He has never acceded to commissions, relying on both his own image and his friends as models. In 1988, a collapsed spinal artery caused almost total paralysis, but Close has continued to work. His freer paintings evince a natural extension of an augmented interest in the minute grid over the total work that predated his illness. This non-privileging of any particular part of the canvas finds its inspiration, oddly enough, in abstract expressionism, despite the apparent inconsonance of the two techniques.

Question 11

What is the author's intent when discussing Close's focus on the head of his subjects?

○ The author compares the artistic impact of photographs of heads to that of abstract photographs of the same head.

○ The author ruminates on what early experiences led to Close's focus on the head as a unifying theme in his work.

○ The author expounds upon how, by not accepting commissions, Close's work has remained free of commercial influences.

○ The author deconstructs the impact that Close's illness had on the content of his paintings.

○ The author believes that Close's approach of depicting the head but none of the personality of the subject is rare.

Question 12

Consider each of the following answer choices separately and select all that apply.

Which of the following statements are supported by the passage?

☐ Close's portraits are so realistic that they are sometimes mistaken for photographs.

☐ There are conceptual connections between Close's later work and other, apparently dissimilar works.

☐ Throughout his career as an artist, none of the portraits Close has painted have been done in exchange for money.

Questions 13-15 refer to the following passage.

The anti-foundationalist belief that there is no secure basis for knowledge was worked out philosophically in the somewhat wearisome tracts of Jacques Derrida. *Différance*, Derrida tells us, is the idea that any attempts to discuss universal features of human nature are merely products of local standards, often serving the vested interests of the status quo, and should rightly be dismantled and critiqued. Derrida was considered the originator of a profound challenge to the history of human thought. However, a century before Derrida, Darwin's theory of natural selection had made anti-foundationalism almost an inevitable consequence. From an evolutionary point of view, our understanding of the world depends on earlier and less-developed forms of understanding; meaning is continuously referred or deferred to other terms or experiences.

Question 13

Derrida's definition of "difference" suggests that he would most likely subscribe to which of the following beliefs?

○ The interests of the status quo always maintain local standards.

○ Ideas expressed by those who are part of the status quo do not necessarily represent a universally accepted truth.

○ Any attempts to discuss human nature serve the interests of the status quo.

○ The interests of the status quo should be critiqued and dismantled by those who are part of the status quo.

○ Ideas that are a product of local standards cannot contain elements of a universal truth.

Question 14

Select the sentence which states a position with which the author does NOT agree.

Question 15

The passage implies that which of the following beliefs is embraced by anti-foundationalists?

- ○ In many cases humans cannot be completely secure in thinking that they fully understand a given situation.
- ○ The meaning of an experience can best be understood outside the cultural context in which it occurs.
- ○ Those who are part of the status quo are best able to dismantle and critique society.
- ○ Derrida's work would not have been possible without the prior ruminations of Darwin a century earlier.
- ○ Darwin's faith in the status quo is sufficient grounds to develop universal truths about cultural experiences.

DRILL 4

Questions 1-2 refer to the following passage.

Some readers categorize Maxine Hong Kingston as a great Asian-American writer, a classification that is ultimately too narrow for her body of work. However, the subject matter of Kingston's novels and autobiographies espouses the Asian immigrant experience, as the following characters suggest: immigrant laborers in California and Hawaii, railroad laborers, and Chinese doctors. In natural harmony with her choice of subject matter are the personal sensibilities of a first-generation American writer who endeavors to explain her mother's alien sensibility and her relationship with her silent, angry father.

Kingston's Asian influences are present in another type of work, Chinese myths in the guise of "talk stories." A character in her novel *Tripmaster Monkey* is based on Sun Wu Kong, a mythical Chinese figure. In response to this work, Herbert Gold notes that the author "invigorates her novel with an avid personal perspective, doing what the novel is supposed to do—she brings us the news of the world and makes magic of it."

Question 1

Consider each of the following answer choices separately and select all that apply.

It can be inferred that Kingston uses "talk stories"

☐ to provide an outlet for critiques of her work

☐ as a way to present Chinese myths in her stories

☐ as a method of engaging children who are not yet reading on their own

Question 2

The author focuses on the content of Kingston's work primarily to

○ illustrate why one might be tempted to call Kingston an Asian-American author

○ assert why Kingston's work is difficult to categorize

○ explain why Kingston's work is thought by many to have universal appeal

○ illustrate how Kingston's work is affected by her parental influences

○ show what makes Kingston unique among Asian-American writers

Questions 3-6 refer to the following passage.

Préciosité, "preciousness," or the manifestation of the baroque in literature, is often dismissed as a "feminine concoction," mocked by Molière and thought to be ridiculous by modern standards. Preferring appearance to substance and excess to moderation, baroque expression is given to wild exaggeration and purple description. However, when one considers its historical context, the movement can be seen as a subtle rebellion by an otherwise powerless sex against its restrictive society.

Crippled and stunned from a series of religious wars, seventeenth-century France under Louis XIII was characterized by political intrigue and violence. Escaping the crude court, a group of cultured and educated ladies met to discuss—in a fantastically embellished and witty manner—literature, art, and philosophy. They rejected the predominant emphasis on vulgarity and sought the elevation of *l'éducation,* or "manners" they considered essential to society. More salons followed, and these *précieuses* (literally, "precious ones") produced works of literature that are still widely read, such as novels, essays, and poems that elevated the ideal of courtly, or Platonic, love with an emphasis on sensuality and scrupulous rules of behavior.

Though men scoffed at their wives' pretensions, baroque literature as a reaction to political instability reawakened French proclivities for cultural expression. When Louis XIV ascended to the throne in 1661, French society was primed for the reestablishment of the arts. Baroque ideals served important roles regarding the criticism of the political situation and the influence of cultural trends. Louis XIV's peace provoked the cultural pendulum to swing to the other direction, ushering in a neo-classical movement that elevated simplicity and minimalism. It is surely no coincidence that it was the performance of "Les Précieuses Ridicules" ("The Conceited Ladies"), Molière's play mocking *préciosité,* that first gained him wide acclaim and established him as the preeminent father of French theater.

Question 3

Consider each of the following answer choices separately and select all that apply.

Which of the following can be inferred based on the information in the passage?

☐ Literature can be a weapon of protest.

☐ Before the seventeenth century, the French expressed themselves through the arts.

☐ Literature was the only means of protest available to women in the seventeenth century.

Question 4

The primary purpose of the passage is to

○ demonstrate the importance of the role of a specific artistic movement to a culture

○ show that women had a greater influence on history than was previously thought

○ define and explain the origins of an obscure art form

○ correct a commonly held historical misconception about the origins of a literary movement

○ emphasize the influence of a nation's ruler on its arts and culture

Question 5

Consider each of the following answer choices separately and select all that apply.

The author suggests which of the following about how *préciosité* was viewed during the seventeenth century?

- ☐ It became the preferred method of communication for all members of French society.
- ☐ It was tolerated until Molière's popular play mocked it.
- ☐ Its importance as a cultural force was not understood.

Question 6

Select the sentence that most concisely describes the contrast between *préciosité* and the neo-classicism that followed it.

Questions 7-8 refer to the following passage.

The mid-nineteenth century witnessed two major wars on U.S. soil: the Mexican-American War and the Civil War. That Abraham Lincoln would commit the country to civil war appears to require little explanation, since he endorsed the abolition of slavery and the preservation of the young nation. However, Lincoln's disdain for the Mexican-American War, which was ostensibly fought to keep Texas in the Union, requires some examination. After all, Lincoln's swift military response to the Southern secessionists at the beginning of the Civil War illustrates that Lincoln would not shrink from battle if the war could ensure a united country. Perhaps Lincoln's resistance to the Mexican-American War can best be seen in light of his sincere belief that President Polk had overstepped his constitutional boundaries in declaring war against Mexico, a sovereign nation. In this light, it is perhaps ironic that Lincoln's own presidential legacy includes a greater centralization of federal government power.

Question 7

Consider each of the following answer choices separately and select all that apply.

According to the passage, which of the following is true of the Mexican-American War?

- ☐ Lincoln did not initiate the war.
- ☐ Lincoln would have disagreed with President Polk about whether it was justified by the codes of government.
- ☐ It was fought ostensibly to abolish slavery.

Question 8

Which of the following best describes the function of the sentence about Lincoln's swift military response in the passage?

- ○ It provides evidence that Lincoln generally supported wars.
- ○ It explains that Lincoln, despite his pacifist tendencies, was not convinced that the Mexican-American War effort was wrong.
- ○ It confirms that Lincoln's belief in the wisdom of entering a war was formulated on the basis of what is good for a united country.
- ○ It suggests that Lincoln's opinions on the Mexican-American War were not based on a belief in unification.
- ○ It illustrates that opponents of United States foreign policy within the federal government convinced Lincoln to enter the Civil War.

Questions 9-11 refer to the following passage.

The increasing pressure on American businesses to pursue cost-cutting measures will eventually lead to an increase in the outsourcing of business processes to venues with lower overhead, such as India. However, this shift may not provide the dramatic gains for American business that might have been expected by an enterprise with an ethos for change that is oriented to preserving bottom-line profits. The difficulty is that a significant portion of American society remains uncomfortable with shifting business tasks overseas. Therefore, American businesses will predominantly opt for outsourcing opportunities for repetitive tasks that can easily be brought back to the United States if necessary. Nevertheless, opportunities for Indian firms to get a larger piece of the pie seem certain to arise. The growing emphasis on bringing down the cost of back-office operations is bound to offer increasing scope for Indian firms to become involved in novel types of ever more complex business processes.

Question 9

Select the sentence in which the author specifies a characteristic of jobs likely to be outsourced.

Question 10

The primary purpose of the passage is to

○ present an overview of the different types of business opportunities available to Indian firms

○ present a reasoned prognosis of the business opportunities that may become available to Indian firms

○ present the trend toward outsourcing business operations as a model case of business operations in action

○ analyze how opportunities available to Indian firms were necessitated by an increasing number of American firms

○ analyze the use of cost-cutting measures as a substitute for outsourcing in the new American business climate

Question 11

Consider each of the following answer choices separately and select all that apply.

According the passage, despite the increasing pressure on American businesses to pursue cost-cutting measures, certain other factors preclude

☐ Indian firms' performing all of the business processes currently being performed onshore by American businesses

☐ American businesses committing to outsourcing jobs overseas

☐ Indian firms' outsourcing more complex tasks to American firms in order to create an interconnected hierarchy of business needs

Questions 12-15 refer to the following passage.

Scientists are growing increasingly concerned that coral, which grows abundantly in the circumtropical shallow waters near bodies of land, is evincing a paling, or bleaching effect. Though experts are still at odds over what has precipitated this event, most agree that it is a stress response to changes in habitat and water quality, including temperature variations and salination percentage, and predict a loss of 95 percent of existing coral populations.

An exemplary symbiotic entity, scleractinian coral lives harmoniously with vertebrates, invertebrates, and plants. Corals receive nutrients in two ways: by capturing planktonic organisms with nematocyst-capped tentacles and by resource-sharing and recycling with single-celled algae called zooxanthellae. These algae live within the polyps of the coral, using photosynthesis to increase (and thereby strengthen) coral calcification, and providing energy for coral growth. The zooxanthellae benefit from the relationship through protection from predators and a steady supply of necessary carbon dioxide. Interestingly, it is the zooxanthellae that provide coral with its brilliant coloration.

When coral loses its color, it is a sign that the single-celled algae are not able to thrive. Though not necessarily a sign of mortality, a pale, wan color indicates imminent danger and is considered a stress response. The zooxanthellate invertebrates lose their concentration of pigmentation or die altogether when stressed, turning translucent and allowing the slightly darker coral skeleton to show through the decaying tissue. Whether this response stems from anthropogenic pollutions such as overharvesting coral for the exotic travel market, overfishing coral waters, and increased water temperatures due to global warming, or from natural disturbances (storms, temperature extremes, and diseases), scientists fear for the future of the radiant corals. If zooxanthellate populations continue to decrease without recovery, their host corals will eventually follow suit, triggering a cascade of unanticipated biological events.

Question 12

It can be inferred from the passage that zooxanthellae are

○ able to use camouflage to blend into their surroundings
○ dependent on carbon dioxide
○ unable to live without coral hosts
○ considered parasitical to coral
○ unnecessary for the continued survival of coral

Question 13

The author attributes the pollution cited as being detrimental to coral to

○ overpopulation by large sea mammals, such as dolphins
○ activities of humans
○ purely accidental causes which cannot be influenced
○ overpopulation by photosynthetic archaebacteria
○ natural phenomena, such as changes in weather

Question 14

Select the sentence from the third paragraph that explains why zooxanthellae lose their coloration.

Question 15

It can be inferred from the passage that which of the following situations is a possible contributing factor to coral bleaching?

○ The proliferation of large-scale freight ships in circumtropical regions

○ Modern civilization's dependence on fossil fuels

○ Tourists' demand for coral souvenirs

○ Governmental apathy due to more pressing problems

○ Coral's unusual sensitivity to the vagaries of natural climate changes

DRILL 5

Questions 1-2 refer to the following passage.

Country music scholars generally overlook the role that African-Americans played in the formation of this genre. Typically, scholars trace the birth of country music to the recording sessions that record producer and talent scout Ralph Peer held in Bristol, Tennessee, in 1927. However, the origins of country music go back much further and owe a great deal to African-American musicians, some known and some anonymous and unheralded. The banjo, field hollers, and gospel music are examples of country genre staples that are rooted in the African-American experience. Moreover, some of the "stars" of country music learned their trade from African-American musicians. Rufus "Tee Tot" Payne, for instance, educated Hank Williams. In addition to jazz, gospel, and the blues, country music now clearly needs to be included in the list of musical genres that have an African-American lineage.

Question 1

Consider each of the following answer choices separately and select all that apply.

It can be inferred from the passage that the author would be most likely to agree with which of the following statements concerning the contributions of African-Americans to country music?

☐ Rufus "Tee Tot" Payne is responsible for teaching Hank Williams the banjo, field holler, and gospel.

☐ African-Americans were instrumental in developing country music and for teaching it to some of the well-known musicians in the field.

☐ Jazz music is commonly acknowledged to have African-American lineage.

Question 2

According to the passage, the "African-American experience" is crucial to country music because other previously established African-American genres

○ provided the instrumental and vocal basis for country music

○ were not as well developed as country music

○ preceded country music

○ weakened the popularity of country music

○ were more accepted and conventional than country music

Questions 3-4 refer to the following passage.

Face perception is the mind's ability to recognize and register another visage. It plays a significant role in social interactions. Through it we distinguish the familiar from the strange and formulate nuanced readings of people's moods and characters. However, controversy surrounds the process of face perception. Psychologists argue that it involves a series of stages: Individuals recognize physical features, make broad inferences regarding gender and age, and finally recall meaningful information regarding the face they perceive, such as a name. Cognitive neuroscientists, on the other hand, posit the idea that face perception works through analogy: The mind has an inherent ability to connect similar objects. While the exact process of face perception is still unclear, evidence suggests that it involves a specific set of skills and that the fusiform gyrus, a part of the brain, is necessary for it to occur.

Question 3

The author mentions cognitive neuroscientists in order to

○ provide a specific example of a general idea the author mentions in the preceding sentence

○ present one side in the debate surrounding the issue of how minds identify and understand faces

○ trace the development of scientific inquiry into the phenomenon of face perception

○ compare the process of face perception with the process of visual recognition more generally

○ reconcile two contradictory viewpoints

Question 4

What can be inferred from the use of the word "analogy" to describe face perception?

○ Cognitive neuroscientists believe face perception works via a process of comparison.

○ Psychologists believe face perception works via a process of dissemblance.

○ Cognitive neuroscientists believe face perception works via a process of analysis.

○ Psychologists believe face perception works via a process of resolving discrepancies.

○ Cognitive neuroscientists believe it works via contraposition.

Questions 5-8 refer to the following passage.

It has frequently been argued that freeing schools from the rigid rules, regulations, and statutes that have traditionally fettered them would have a revolutionary effect on academic achievement. For instance, it has been suggested that schools embodying this idea could develop more effective teaching methods that could then be replicated in other schools. Charter schools—public schools that operate under a contract, or "charter"—were given just such an opportunity beginning in 1991, when Minnesota passed the first charter school law. At that time, many critics warned of deleterious rather than beneficial effects that such freewheeling schools could have on the academic achievement of students. Thus, while public opinion differed concerning the social desirability of charter schools, most agreed that there would be a pronounced effect.

Surprisingly, educators who study educational reform now seriously question the degree to which charter schools have made an impact. They conclude that freedom from many of the policies and regulations affecting traditional public schools and the concomitant control over decisions that guide the day-to-day affairs of the school have not resulted in equally dramatic changes in students' academic performance. In some states, charter schools are less likely to meet state performance standards than traditional public schools. It is, however, impossible to know whether this difference is due to the performance of the schools, the prior achievement of the students, or some other factor.

Metrics for educational accountability have changed considerably in the past decade, moving increasingly to performance as measured by state mandated tests of individual student achievement. Fundamentally, however, the challenging conditions under which schools operate, be they traditional or charter, have changed little: the struggle for resources, low pay for teachers, accountability to multiple stakeholders, and the difficulty of meeting the educational requirements of children with special needs all persist.

Question 5

Which of the following statements best summarizes the main point of the passage?

- ○ Charter schools, despite their merits, fail to overcome the long-standing problems in public education.
- ○ Recent studies have shown that charter schools have had a revolutionary effect on student achievement.
- ○ Freeing schools from some of the restrictions that govern them has caused a change in education since 1991.
- ○ Charter schools have created a whole new way of educating children that did not previously exist.
- ○ Assessments of charter schools' performance have reinforced the position that rigid rules and regulations are stifling academic achievement.

Question 6

Select the sentence from the second paragraph that best explains why the author neither dismisses nor endorses the opinion of the critics of charter schools.

Question 7

In the last paragraph the author mentions all of the following as challenges faced by all schools EXCEPT

- ○ the difficulty of securing capital
- ○ the challenge of providing appropriate conditions for special-needs students
- ○ the necessity to answer to different interest groups
- ○ the manner in which student performance is measured
- ○ poor compensation for teachers

Question 8

Consider each of the following answer choices separately and select all that apply.

It can be inferred from the passage that the author would consider which of the following, if true, a likely indication of a fundamental alteration in education brought about by charter schools?

- ☐ Statistics show that the majority of children who attended charter schools in the 1990s are attending or have attended college.
- ☐ A national standard of academic performance, to which all students in every type of school must adhere, is created.
- ☐ A consistent score improvement in state-mandated tests has been achieved by children who attend charter schools, but not by those who attend traditional schools.

Questions 9-12 refer to the following passage.

Many scholars consider Marcel Proust's *Remembrance of Things Past* (1913–1927) a significant literary achievement. For instance, Harold Bloom states that it is "widely recognized as the major novel of the twentieth century." In addition to noting its length—it spans seven volumes and 3,200 pages—many commentaries have focused on Proust's treatment of two kinds of memory, involuntary and voluntary. Involuntary memory occurs through the stimulation of the senses, while voluntary memory is a deliberate effort to remember the past. For Proust, involuntary memories are superior because they contain the spirit of the past in a way that voluntary memories do not; the former are more vivid, and they have the power to erase the temporal distance between the present moment and past experiences. More recently, scholars such as André Benhaïm have explored the relationship between Proust's treatment of memory and his representation of France and French culture. According to Benhaïm, memory functions within this text to reconfigure both.

Proust describes France in ways that one would not expect. In his work, French cities are archaic and exotic. As a result, the narrator becomes a stranger to, or is estranged from, his homeland, and lives the life of an exile. For instance, when recalling his travels through the fictional French town of Balbec, he states, "These strangely ordinary and disdainfully familiar cathedrals cruelly stunned my unconsidered eyes and stabbed my homesick heart." Words such as "stun" and "stab" suggest the hostility the narrator feels from this French territory. Proust's suggestion of Middle Eastern influences further distorts the idea of a singular French experience. First, the town's name refers to the ancient city of Baalbek, located in what is now Lebanon. Second, Balbec is populated by Jewish residents. Proust is widely recognized as an icon of French literature and culture, but ultimately his mysterious representations of this place and its culture call into question the existence of a single Francophone literature or a single French identity.

Question 9

Consider each of the following answer choices separately and select all that apply.

It can be inferred that Benhaïm might agree with which of the following statements about the role of memory in *Remembrance of Things Past*?

☐ The study of memory in Proust's novel is the most important approach to this text and has led to valuable insights regarding the human condition.

☐ The study of Proust's exploration of memory is a useful starting place with which to consider other issues, such as French culture and traditions.

☐ While the study of memory in Proust's novel once yielded interesting insights into the workings of the human mind, new approaches to this text have proven more useful.

Question 10

The author uses the quotation from *Remembrance of Things Past* in order to

○ illustrate Proust's concept of involuntary memory

○ exemplify an assertion regarding the narrator's relationship to his homeland, which the author mentions in the preceding sentence

○ mark a turning point in the passage in which the author switches from describing life in France to exploring Proust's representation of it

○ bolster Proust's disdain for reliance on personal memories when returning to the locales of childhood

○ dissuade the reader from accepting Proust's characterizations of voluntary memory

Consider each of the following answer choices separately and select all that apply.

The passage refers to which of the following as a feature of the French town of Balbec, as Proust represents it?

☐ mausoleums
☐ itinerants
☐ churches

Select the sentence from the second paragraph in which the author summarizes Proust's description of France.

Questions 13-15 refer to the following passage.

According to scholars, the indigenous peoples of ancient Mesoamerica, specifically the Nahuas, developed a rich and complex philosophy comprising four interrelated and overlapping branches of knowledge: metaphysics, epistemology, theory of value, and aesthetics. At the core of their philosophy was *teotl,* which, rather than an immutable supernatural being like the Judaeo-Christian deity, was an ever-moving and ever-changing, self-producing sacred power that animated the universe and its contents. It was responsible for all things in nature—animals, rocks, rain, and so on—and permeated the details of everything. There was no distinction between teotl and the natural world; teotl was in every entity, and every entity was also teotl. Unlike Western philosophy, which fosters dichotomies, such as the personal versus the impersonal, that of the Nahuas posited a sacred power that was united with everything; it was both intrinsic and transcendent.

Question 13

The definition of "teotl" and its comparison to the Judaeo-Christian deity plays which of the following roles within the passage?

○ It compares a lesser-known idea to a more common one to further understanding.

○ It contrasts the sacred power of teotl with a more familiar object of veneration in order to illustrate that cultures often possess diverging narratives on the origins of the world and the organisms therein.

○ It provides an explanation of the origins of the cosmos according to some of the proponents of Western philosophy.

○ It bolsters the case for accepting an aboriginal explanation for the creation of the universe over a Western one.

○ It encourages further inquiry into a lesser known understanding of the world.

Consider each of the choices separately and select all that apply.

In writing this passage, the author most likely intended to

- ☐ explain the system of principles that guided the customs of an ancient group of people
- ☐ elaborate on a theoretical belief that is incongruous with other beliefs on a similar topic
- ☐ describe the fundamental ideology of a certain society

According to the passage, the ancient philosophy of the Nahua people is different from European-based philosophy in that

- ○ at the center of Nahua philosophy was a detached and unmoving deity, whereas Christianity is based on the notion of a dynamic, ever-flowing supernatural force
- ○ Nahua philosophy consisted of several interlocking concepts, whereas Western philosophy is composed only of dichotomies
- ○ Nahua philosophy was based on the notion that a vivifying and mutable force saturated all matter, whereas in Western religion there is little or no division between supernatural powers and the natural world
- ○ rather than promoting mutually exclusive but dependent binaries, Nahua philosophy fostered an integrated and holistic worldview
- ○ within Nahuas society there was not a strong sense of individualism, whereas in Western societies, worldviews based on dichotomies engender excessive concern for self

DRILL 6

Questions 1-2 refer to the following passage.

The wombat is a muscular quadruped, about 3 feet in length with a short tail. The animal, which is not a mythical creature but an Australian marsupial, has a name derived from the language of the native peoples of the Sydney area, the Eora aboriginals. Wombats are herbivores and leave cubic scats that are easily recognized. Because wombats are seldom seen, attributed to the fact that they are nocturnal, the scats provide crucial evidence regarding territory. This large, burrowing mammal is not related to the badger, whose habits are similar. In fact, the koala is the wombat's closest relative. The principal burrowing instrument of the latter is its incisors which, like those of other rodents with orange enamel, are never worn down. Burrows can be extensive and shared by more than one wombat, despite the generally solitary nature of the creature. Territories within the burrow are marked by scent, vocalizations, and aggressive displays.

Question 1

Consider each of the choices separately and select all that apply.

According to the passage, which of the following is NOT true regarding wombats and their territory?

☐ Scats are the only way to determine territorial limits of wombats.

☐ The question of how much territory a wombat covers is of interest to some people.

☐ Wombats are generally not territorial about the space they occupy within their burrows.

Question 2

The author states that the wombat is an Australian marsupial in order to

○ describe the role of stories about the wombat as part of the Eora's oral tradition

○ dispel the belief of some people that the wombat is not a real animal

○ create parallels between the Eora culture and the mythology of the ancient Greeks

○ contrast the behavior of wombats with that of other rodents

○ undermine the validity of research surrounding naming standards

Questions 3-4 refer to the following passage.

Theorists are divided about the cause of the Permian mass extinctions. Some hypothesize that the impact of a massive asteroid caused a sudden disappearance of species. However, a look at the carbon-isotope record suggests that existing plant communities were struck down and re-formed several times. To produce such a pattern would require a succession of asteroid strikes thousands of years apart. Other theorists have proposed that volcanic explosions raised the CO_2 levels, leading to intense global warming. One problem with this theory is that it cannot explain the massive marine extinctions at the end of the Permian period. A new theory posits that rising concentrations of toxic hydrogen sulfide in the world's oceans plus gradual oxygen depletions in the surface waters caused the extinctions. Fortunately, this theory is testable. If true, oceanic sediments from the Permian period would yield chemical evidence of a rise in hydrogen sulfide-consuming bacteria.

Question 3

The primary purpose of the passage is to

○ present several hypotheses concerning the cause of the Permian mass extinctions

○ discuss the strengths and weaknesses of the asteroid hypothesis of the Permian mass extinctions

○ propose that theories regarding the cause of the Permian mass extinctions be tested

○ argue that Permian mass extinctions could not have been caused by a volcanic explosion

○ describe one reason that a rise in hydrogen sulfide would cause massive marine extinctions

Question 4

Which of the following, if true, would most weaken the author's conclusion about the hydrogen sulfide theory?

○ The oceanic sediment is stable and not prone to catastrophic change.

○ Changes in the chemical composition of oceanic sediment have rendered the Permian period indistinguishable from earlier periods.

○ The oceanic sediments of the Permian period contain unusually high levels of carbon.

○ The oceanic sediments contain many chemicals more toxic than simple hydrogen sulfide.

○ The oceanic sediments can mask large populations of other types of bacteria.

Questions 5-6 refer to the following passage.

In her self-portraits, Frida Kahlo blends realism and fantasy to capture the psychological and physical pain she constantly endured as a result of the trolley car accident she experienced as a young woman. This self-representation sets her apart from her contemporaries, who were more interested in public forms of art, such as murals. This was the time of the Mexican revolution, after all, a period that fostered an interest in nationalistic themes.

The more well-known artists of this period included David Alfaro Siqueiros, Diego Rivera, Jose Clemente Orozco, and Juan O'Gorman. These figures dominated the Mexican art world in the 1920s and 1930s. Unlike her contemporaries, Kahlo's work did not achieve recognition until long after her death. In the late twentieth century, she became a feminist icon, a phenomenon attributable to the candor with which she portrayed issues relating to women.

Question 5

The purpose of the author's discussion of the Mexican revolution is to

○ provide a historical context for the reader to clarify what distinguished Kahlo's art from her contemporaries' art

○ discuss aspects of Mexican history, such as the revolution and nationalism, which were irrelevant to Kahlo's art

○ contrast the way male and female artists responded to a tumultuous time in Mexican history

○ explain why it was not until after Kahlo's death that her work received greater acknowledgment

○ highlight the differences between feminists and revolutionaries at the time that Kahlo was painting

Question 6

Consider each of the following answer choices separately and select all that apply.

Which of the following can be inferred from the passage about Kahlo's contemporaries:

☐ They never painted self-portraits.

☐ They received recognition for their work while they were still alive.

☐ They used their art as a form of political expression.

Questions 7-8 refer to the following passage.

The controversial concept of terraforming, or changing a planet's atmosphere to make it more habitable for humans, is still no more than a theoretical debate. However, the most recent data from two American Mars Rovers suggest that the terraforming of Mars may be more feasible than previously thought. The rovers found evidence of stratification patterns and cross bedding (indicating a history of sediment deposited by water) in rocks on the edges of craters, as well as chlorine and bromine, suggestive of a large body of salt water. If Mars once held water, it is possible that its atmosphere was at one time somewhat similar to Earth's. Even if this theory were true, however, scientists would have to prevent a recurrence of the desiccation of the Martian atmosphere once it is made habitable, as well as endeavor to preserve any extant life. Of course, until a reliable method of transporting humans to Mars is developed, any possibility of terraforming is mere conjecture.

Question 7

Consider each of the choices separately and select all that apply.

It can be inferred from the passage that the author would be most likely to agree with which of the following statements?

☐ Whether conditions on Mars are conducive to human habitation is not the only issue that limits realistic consideration of terraforming.

☐ If we terraform Mars, it will be important to think about the long-term effects of changing a planet's climate.

☐ It is highly likely, according to recent data, that there is, or was at one time, life on Mars.

Question 8

Which of the following statements, if true, would most likely make terraforming Mars more feasible?

○ Scientists have devised a technique to provide a layer of carbon dioxide in the Martian atmosphere, which would trap solar radiation and thus modify temperature.

○ Mars has stronger solar winds than does Earth, thus, making it difficult to retain atmospheric gases.

○ Mars' core has cooled faster than Earth's, and its temperature is much lower than Earth's.

○ Terraforming Mars is likely to have a galvanizing effect on Earth's governments.

○ Terraforming Mars is unlikely to disturb life on other planets, should it exist.

Questions 9-12 refer to the following passage.

The harshness and extreme unpopularity of the "war communism" system imposed in Russia from 1918 to 1921 led the Soviet leadership to adopt the New Economic Policy (NEP) in March of 1921. Under the NEP, the prodnalog system of tax in kind was begun, and a semi-market economy was allowed to develop alongside government control of what Lenin had called the "commanding heights industries." When the NEP was abandoned in 1927, the state declared it a failure as a result of several adverse events: the scissors crisis, the goods famine, and speculation by "NEPmen."

The scissors crisis of 1923 was caused by high industrial prices relative to agricultural prices. When these two sets of prices are graphed, the wide disparity resembles an open pair of scissors. The government had been spurring industry but felt that this price disparity had to be immediately addressed. To do so, it adopted policies favoring agriculture. There is some speculation by economists, however, that the scissors would have closed on their own.

The goods famine occurred at roughly the same time. Because of burgeoning industry, demand for industrial and consumer products skyrocketed. The state could not produce goods equal to demand, forcing prices up. In the midst of shortages, the state found itself in a losing contest with "NEPmen," small entrepreneurs who sold goods at prices often higher than those of the state. NEPmen were seen as capitalists who sought to return the Soviet state to its position as lapdog to the Western capitalist states. Since the state could not produce or profit as well as the NEPmen, it adopted measures to put the NEPmen out of business. By 1926, speculating on pricing was a crime. As a result, profits and incentives had fallen, and the speculation crisis was somewhat alleviated.

Question 9

Select the sentence from the third paragraph which describes an action undertaken by the Soviet government.

Question 10

The speculation by economists refers to which of the following beliefs?

- ○ The government's belief that the crisis would one day have ended, even if the government had not moved to support agriculture
- ○ Economists' belief that the government was mistaken in supporting agriculture over industry
- ○ Economists' belief that the scissors crisis could have been averted without government intervention
- ○ Economists' belief that the price disparity would have eventually resolved itself without action by the government
- ○ The government's belief that agricultural and industrial prices would have balanced each other, but not in time to stop a crisis from occurring

Question 11

Which of the following would make the most appropriate title for this passage?

- ○ The Fall of the New Economic Policy
- ○ An End to War Communism
- ○ Why the New Economic Policy Failed
- ○ Three Crises That Ended an Era
- ○ Soviet Economic Systems: an Overview

Question 12

Consider each of the choices separately and select all that apply.

It can be inferred from the passage that each of the following accurately represents the author's opinions EXCEPT

- ☐ NEPmen were like capitalists, who sought to earn their fortune at the expense of others and brought about the downfall of the NEP.
- ☐ The government was partially responsible for the goods famine, due to its inability to control supply and demand.
- ☐ The war communism system caused the scissors crisis by spurring agriculture prices.

Questions 13-16 refer to the following passage.

The determination of the age of KNM-ER 1470, a humanoid skull, would add greatly to our knowledge of mammalian evolution. Anthropologists originally dated the *habilis* skull at 3 million years old. This age seemed unlikely because it was older than the age of any known australophithecines, which are presumed to be the *habilis's* ancestor. Further attempts to date the skull have led to speculative results.

An elemental property of all living things is that they contain a certain portion of their carbon as the radioactive isotope carbon-14. Carbon-14 is created when solar radiation blasts nuclei in the upper atmosphere, in turn producing neutrons that bombard nitrogen-14 at lower altitudes, turning it into carbon-14. All living things maintain an equilibrium of carbon-14 as they exchange carbon with their surrounding atmosphere. Presuming the rate of production to be constant, the activity of a sample can be compared to the equilibrium activity of living matter, and thus the age can be calculated. However, carbon-14 decays at a half-life of 5,730 years, limiting age determinations to the order of 50,000 years. This time frame can be extended to perhaps 100,000 years using accelerator techniques. Even so, at these ages carbon dating is increasingly unreliable as a result of changes in the carbon-isotope mix. Over the last century, the burning of fossil fuels, which have no carbon-14 content, have had a diluting effect on the atmospheric carbon-14. As a countervailing effect, atmospheric testing of nuclear weapons in the 1950s may well have doubled the atmosphere's carbon-14 content.

Other radiometric dating methods, using relative concentrations of parent-daughter products in radio decay changes of other elements, such as argon, may prove to be of greater benefit for dating such ancient samples as *habilis*. However, the assumption that the decay rates of these isotopes have always been constant would first have to be substantiated.

Question 13

Consider each of the following answer choices separately and select all that apply.

The author suggests that the burning of fossil fuels has had which of the following effects on the efficacy of carbon dating techniques?

☐   It may increase the carbon-isotope mix of the object being dated.

☐   It may make items subjected to carbon dating appear to have died later than is the case.

☐   It may tilt the fragile equilibrium activity of living matter.

Question 14

The author first mentions the half-life of carbon in order to

○   provide a reason why carbon dating techniques fail to give an age for the *habilis* skull

○   explain the success of carbon dating techniques

○   illustrate the difference between carbon dating and other techniques

○   show the need for extending carbon dating results with accelerator techniques

○   illustrate the carbon equilibrium that all living things maintain

What can be inferred about the proposed solution mentioned in the final paragraph?

○   Continued experimentation with nuclear weapons could restore the expected carbon-14 content to the atmosphere to ensure accuracy of carbon dating.

○   Alternatives to fossil fuels should be pursued to prevent further interference with carbon dating procedures.

○   Decay rates of isotopes involved in radiometric methods need to be invariable.

○   Carbon-14 levels could be artificially restored to previous historical levels to allow an appropriate basis of comparison.

○   Appropriate technology to implement radiometric methods needs to be engineered.

Select the sentence in the passage in which the author raises a possible objection to proposed alternatives to carbon dating.

ANSWERS

Drill 1

1. C
2. A, B
3. B
4. B, C
5. B
6. E
7. A
8. This experiment suggests that, should a potential donor organ be infused....
9. B
10. C
11. A, C
12. Thus, she is a progenitor of Chopin....
13. B
14. C
15. B

Drill 2

1. C
2. A
3. In his novels, McMurtry creates strong female characters, transmuting....
4. C
5. A, C
6. C
7. B
8. Scientists are interested in these vents primarily for their ability to host....
9. A
10. B, C
11. A, B
12. C
13. A, B
14. D
15. E

Drill 3

1. A
2. E
3. B
4. D
5. A, B
6. D
7. A
8. It is not just those planets nearest the sun....
9. A, B, C
10. D
11. E
12. B
13. B
14. Derrida was considered the originator of a profound challenge....
15. A

Drill 4

1. B
2. A
3. A, B
4. A
5. C
6. Preferring appearance to substance and excess to moderation....
7. A, B
8. D
9. Therefore, American businesses will predominantly opt for outsourcing....
10. B
11. A, B
12. B
13. B
14. The zooxanthellate invertebrates lose their concentration of pigmentation....
15. C

Drill 5

1. B, C
2. A
3. B
4. A
5. A
6. It is, however, impossible to know whether this difference is due to....
7. D
8. C
9. B
10. B
11. C
12. In his work, French cities are archaic and exotic.
13. A
14. B, C
15. D

Drill 6

1. A, C
2. B
3. A
4. B
5. A
6. B, C
7. A, B
8. A
9. By 1926, speculating on pricing was a crime.
10. D
11. C
12. A, C
13. B
14. A
15. C
16. However, the assumption that the decay....

EXPLANATIONS

Drill 1

1. **C**   The passage describes the mesosphere as elusive, poorly understood, and little explored. The answer closest to this is (C), unfamiliar. Although the passage states that spectacular explosions can occur *within* the mesosphere, it does not say that the mesosphere itself is *destructive*. Choices (A), (B), (D), and (E) are never mentioned in the passage.

2. **A, B**   This question asks about things which could affect the mesosphere. According to the passage, the mesosphere is affected by *tides and waves that propagate up from the troposphere and stratosphere,* so (B) is correct. The mesosphere is also *further affected when gas particles in the mesosphere collide with meteoroids,* so (A) is also correct. Although the passage mentions tides, it does not specify that they are oceanic tides, so (C) is incorrect, and the answers are (A) and (B).

3. **B**   The author says the Nielsen Company has *questionable methods* and has *come under criticism*, and puts the word *diaries* in quotes as though to make fun of its methodology as quaint or clunky, so (B) is the best answer. There is no indication that Nielsen's bias is intentional, so eliminate (A). Choices (C) and (D) are extreme because the passage does not suggest that Nielsen's research is so bad as to be worthless or unscrupulous. The passage does not offer any information about Nielsen's opinion of itself, boastful or otherwise, so eliminate (E).

4. **B, C**   The passage says that the percentage *indicates the number of viewers watching,* so (A) is not correct. The passage says that residences *underreport daytime and late-night television viewing,* so (B) is true. Finally, the passage says that *gauging how attentive the audience is to…advertising* is a *nonviable practice.* Because the first paragraph says that *advertising rates are determined by the viewership,* (C) is true. Attentiveness would be another relevant factor.

5. **B**   The woodchuck example is provided to show that the same molecules that induce hibernation might have applications in organs being readied for transplants. Therefore, (B) is the best answer. There is no evidence that ischemia plays any role in the transplantation process, so (A) is incorrect. Choice (C) is too extreme; nothing is identified as the biggest obstacle. The passage does not comment on the feasibility of changing the tissue-matching process, so (D) is not a well-supported answer choice. The passage does not mention the effects of HIT on patients awaiting transplants, so (E) is wrong.

6. **E**   The passage describes an experiment wherein infusing opioids delayed decay, so (E) is true. Choice (B) is incorrect because the passage does not state that the lymphatic system is what causes organs to deteriorate. There is no information in the passage on when HIT will be produced in a lab, so (C) can be eliminated. Choice (D) extrapolates too far on the effects of HIT, and there is not enough information in the passage to support the relationship in (A).

7. **A** Choice (A) is the best answer because the author cites the experiment with woodchucks to give an example of a promising line of research. There is no suggestion of genetic similarity, so (B) is incorrect. Though the author does warn that the findings are preliminary, he/she does so in another context in the passage, which makes (C) wrong. Similarly, other areas of science are not mentioned in conjunction with this experiment, but rather later on in the passage, so (D) is incorrect. Though an interspecies infusion of HIT is mentioned, that is not the primary purpose of the woodchuck experiment, and (E) is incorrect as well.

8. **This experiment suggests that, should a potential donor organ be infused....**

The correct sentence indicates that the molecules must be infused *before* the organ is harvested; this is a limitation. If you chose the sentence in the last paragraph that includes the phrase *patients are still susceptible to infection and rejection*, you should realize that *infection and rejection* are not problems related to infusing HIT molecules, but rather of the transplant process itself. Also, the sentence after that one, which begins *scientists are still a long way...* mentions the limitation of safety and consistency, problems which the question specifically indicates are not what you should be looking for in the correct answer.

9. **B** The text is primarily concerned with showing the ancient origin of modern currency and underlines the touchstone's importance within this history; therefore, (B) is correct. Choice (A) is too broad—the passage is concerned only with currency, not science in general. Conversely, (C) is too narrow; the passage talks about the touchstone's historical importance, not just the science behind it. The passage does not discuss where the word came from, so (D) is incorrect. Choice (E) is also wrong because there is no historical misconception that needs to be cleared up.

10. **C** Choice (C) accurately describes the reason for including the details concerning the inclusion of lesser metals in early coins: it takes the details of how the touchstone works and shows why the touchstone was important for trade. The passage does not state how individuals previously tested metals, so (A) cannot be true. Choice (B) is also incorrect because the date given in the passage is of the earliest use of coins; it does not talk about the date of the touchstone. The purpose of the sentence is not to give a cultural context because the passage does not identify the cultures involved, so eliminate (D). There is no counterargument given, making (E) incorrect.

11. **A, C** Choices (A) and (C) are supported by the phrases *this probing process allowed merchants to examine alloys quickly and with reasonable certainty.* You know that the *certainty* referred to is about *adulterated coins* because the passage later mentions that *coins were easily forged or diluted.* Choice (B) is incorrect because although the passage does mention standardization, it does not mention specifically that it would be a function of the government.

12. **Thus, she is a progenitor of Chopin....**

A *progenitor* is a precursor or an ancestor, so the correct sentence tells you that Szymanowska's techniques and compositions came before and influenced those of Chopin. The other composers mentioned in the passage are either described as her contemporaries or given no chronological relationship to Szymanowska, so none of the other sentences that refer to composers can be supported.

13. B The author states *human society will be poorer for its inability to recognize the expertise and inventiveness of these women.* The author states this as a blunt fact. Choice (B), *emphatic,* is closest to this, as the author states, with emphasis, his opinion. The author does not wish for the past to return, so (A), *nostalgic,* is incorrect. The author is not *dismissive* of the musicians, but rather dislikes the fact that others have dismissed the musicians, so (C) is incorrect. The final sentence is unequivocal, so (D), *perplexed,* is incorrect. The author is not being instructive, so *didactic* is incorrect, and the answer is (B).

14. C Choice (A) describes a problem, but it is too extreme because some documentation must exist for people to know about Szymanowska's work. Choice (B) also describes a problem but is too specific—musical scores were never mentioned. Choice (C) provides a good paraphrase of the second and third sentences of the last paragraph and is, therefore, the best choice. Choice (D) is too extreme. If you chose (E), you probably were looking at the last line of the passage, which talks about the future, not about the past and present.

15. B Choice (A) is not supported. Although the passage does say that women's role in the development of Polish music was largely ignored, there's no indication that Szymanowska composed music to make a statement about feminism. Choice (B) is supported. All her pieces have *technically superior* elements, but only two are specified to have *Polonaise rhythms.* Choice (C) is not supported. The passage never specifies which of her over one hundred works were most highly praised, and more specific information is needed before a judgment of *disproportionate amount of attention* can be justified.

Drill 2

1. C The first sentence states that sociologists have historically held the view that individuals stereotype. The rest of the paragraph delves into Hepburn and Locksley's study, which investigates the extent to which people are aware of their own stereotyping behavior. Therefore, the first sentence provides the historical background for Hepburn and Locksley's study. The closest answer is therefore (C).

2. A The passage starts with a historical overview of stereotypes and then focuses on two investigators who look at the related issue of whether or not individuals are aware that they are applying stereotypes. Choice (A) sums this up the best. Choice (B) is out of scope. Choices (C) and (D) are too strong; it is neither an attempt to prove nor to refute anything. Choice (E) is too specific, and the passage doesn't contain any detailed lists.

3. **In his novels, McMurtry creates strong female characters, transmuting....**

   The third paragraph discusses the differences between *the traditional Western formula* and *McMurtry* in their treatment of character. The main difference this paragraph focuses on is that the traditional Westerns feature mostly male characters, whereas McMurtry focuses on female characters. The identified sentence says that McMurtry's creation of strong female characters folds in *deeper ideological insights*. This is a good thing, suggesting that the author views this practice with a positive eye. The final sentence may be tempting, but it conveys the opinion of critics, not necessarily the author, and it doesn't specifically address the issue of gender.

4.   **C**   In the first paragraph the author notes how Western literature ranges from lowbrow entertainment to great literature and offers the dime-store novel as an example of writing that is merely entertaining. At the other end of the spectrum, the author states that *James Fenimore Cooper and Willa Cather, however, used themes of westward expansion in works clearly intended as highbrow literature.* In other words, they wrote literature that expects the reader to be more sophisticated, so the best answer is (C). Choice (A) is incorrect, (B) and (D) are not discussed in the passage, and (E) is off the topic.

5.   **A, C**   McMurtry folds in *deeper ideological insights* by using *strong female characters*, so the female characters referenced in (A) definitely contribute to the ideological undertones. *Subversive* means *rebellious* or *going against the norm*; in this case, McMurtry's writing goes against the ideology of the traditional Western. The subversive differences in McMurtry's writing referenced throughout the passage are thus indicative of his ideology. The focus on the *dangerous nature of the Western frontier* is a characteristic of the traditional Western, not McMurtry's Westerns, so (B) is not an indication of the ideology of McMurtry's novels.

6.   **C**   In the last paragraph the author talks about McMurtry's use of characters, stating that *In his novels McMurtry creates strong female characters, transmuting the conventional plot of the trials and dangers of the frontier by folding in deeper ideological insights.* When referring to the critics, the author notes that they rightly credit his novels with reforming the Western genre. The use of the word *rightly* suggests that the author agrees with the critics, thereby making (C) the best answer.

7.   **B**   Choice (A) isn't supported in the text. Eliminate (C) because, while the passage suggests that the body of knowledge relating to hydrothermal vents is expanding due to a recent discovery, the author doesn't really look at how scientists study hydrothermal vents or mention how these studies might have changed. Choice (D) isn't supported in the passage. In (E), while the author discusses the discovery of a new natural phenomenon, the author doesn't reconsider or reevaluate previous studies on similar natural phenomenon. Choice (B) is the correct answer and is an accurate summary of the author's purpose over the course of the passage.

8.   **Scientists are interested in these vents primarily for their ability to host....**

To hone in on the correct sentence, use lead words to find the general part of the passage which likely holds the answer to the question. In this case, the words *Black Smokers* leads you to the first paragraph. The question asks you *why* the biologists' curiosity is piqued, so the sentence you are looking for is explanatory and refers to the value of the Black Smokers. The sentence beginning with *Scientists are interested…* is an answer to a *why* question, and you can make the link between *biologists* in the question and *biologically* in the sentence.

9. **A** The passage states that the heat and fluid flow at the Lost City is driven *by the intermingling of seawater and mantle rocks on the sea floor, rather than by hot magma.* This statement means that *the vents at Lost City are driven by the merging of seawater and mantle rocks.* The *rather than* indicates a comparison between Lost City and some other hydrothermal vents. The only other vents mentioned in this paragraph are the Black Smokers, so they must be driven by hot magma. Choice (B) is directly contradicted by the passage, which states that *the fluids here are much cooler,* referring to Lost City. *Chemosynthetic archaea* are mentioned only in paragraph one, and thus (C) is out of scope for a question about paragraph three.

10. **B, C** Choice (A) is a true statement from paragraph two, but it is a statement about the Lost City, while the question asks about the Black Smokers. *Black chimney-like formations* are mentioned in the last sentence of paragraph one, which discusses the Black Smokers, so you know that (B) is a true statement about the Black Smokers. Paragraph one also states that *scientists are interested in these vents primarily for their ability to host biologically dense communities in areas that are otherwise hostile to life.* Since the rest of this paragraph is talking about the Black Smokers, this statement must mean that Black Smokers do *host biologically dense communities,* supporting (C).

11. **A, B** Because this is a NOT question, you are looking to eliminate answer choices that are *unique elements* of Delacroix's work in the passage. You will find this statement: *Delacroix combined eclectic elements and infused them with his own genius, creating a unique expression of Romanticism.* Therefore *eclectic elements* and *own genius* are the ingredients in his *unique expression.* Eliminate (C), which paraphrases and reiterates this thought; you need a choice describing what is NOT unique. Choices (A) and (B) are also supported in the passage as elements that Delacroix borrowed from an entire period, in the case of (A), or from another artist, in the case of (B). Because he borrowed those elements, they are not *unique* and are correct answers.

12. **C** The painting *Scènes des massacres de Scio* is mentioned in the first sentence of the passage, introduced by the phrase *The paintings of Eugene Delacroix are as political, complex, tumultuous, and vivid as the life of Lord Byron, who inspired some of Delacroix's best works.* Therefore, Lord Byron inspired the painting in question, so (C) is correct. Choice (A) is a painting that was also inspired by Byron but is not the inspiration for the painting in the question. Choices (B), (D), and (E) are all mentioned elsewhere in the passage, but do not answer the question asked.

13. **A, B** Gould and Lewontin believe that sociobiology is flawed because it is Eurocentric and has methodological problems. *Western worldview* is another way of saying *Eurocentric*; coupled with *not comport with proper scientific methodology,* (B) is a paraphrase of Gould and Lewontin's position. *These detractors* (i.e., Gould and Lewontin) call sociobiology a *pseudo-science,* meaning a fake science, because it is not *falsifiable,* meaning that it cannot be proven false. This position is consistent with (A).

14. **D** The author discusses *culture, ethnicity, and environment* in relation to the justification offered by sociobiologists when applying sociobiology to humans. In their view, these factors don't adequately explain human behavior. Choice (D) is a good paraphrase of this justification. Choice (A) isn't supported in the passage. Choice (B) is Gould's and Lewontin's position on sociobiology. Choice (C) contradicts the sociobiologists' view. Choice (E) is incorrect because, although the list comprises some factors that influence human behavior, the author intends it to serve a greater purpose in the passage. In addition, it would be extreme to assert that the list is *comprehensive.*

15. **E** The author doesn't praise either side in the debate, so eliminate (A). Both (B) and (C) suggest that the author has a point of view, while the passage offers no indication as to which side the author may favor. Eliminate (D) because no such justification is made, and the thrust of the passage is on human, not animal, behavior. Choice (E) is an accurate summary of the entire passage because it takes into account both sociobiological theories and their critics in an impartial fashion.

Drill 3

1. **A** The reason for controlling factions is described in the opening sentence with Madison's claim that they are *adverse to the overall good of the nation*. Choice (A) is the best answer. Choices (B), (C), and (D) are not accurate based on the information in the passage. Since Madison never specifies exactly who will make up the factions, (E) is also incorrect.

2. **E** The passage discusses Madison's theories on constraining factions by controlling either their causes or effects. Choice (A) goes too far; the passage does not solve the problem. Choices (B) and (C) are contrary to the passage. Choice (D) is overly broad; the passage considers only one effect of increased population. Choice (E) is the best answer because it encompasses the scope of Madison's ideas in *The Federalist Number Ten*.

3. **B** One of Jenney's designs *would become the archetypical American skyscraper design*. An archetype is an original model from which many copies are made, lending support to (B). Jenney served as an *engineering officer* during the Civil War, not an architect, so (A) is incorrect. One of Jenney's buildings was called the *Manhattan Building*, but that does not necessarily mean that it was located in New York (in fact, the building is in Chicago), so (C) also lacks support.

4. **D** Choice (D) is the best answer. The *Chicago window* is a development of Holabird's; it is the only specific feature mentioned, so it must be significant. Choice (A) is partially correct, in that a feature is highlighted, but the buildings are not made of glass; they merely *appear* to be glass. Choice (B) says Holabird developed the Chicago School, but the passage says he helped Jenney do so. Choice (C) goes against the tone of the passage, which does not make that argument at all. Choice (E) is too broad to be the purpose of this small detail.

5. **A, B** Since *solar winds are directly related to geomagnetic storms, auroras, and comets*, and cause comet tails to bend in particular directions, they *play a significant role in the development of auroras and geomagnetic storms*, thus supporting (B). The second paragraph states both that the

Earth's magnetic field protects it from the solar winds, and that *solar winds are responsible for the Earth's magnetosphere, and changes in their speed and direction strongly influence Earth's space environment*, thus supporting (A). The first part of (C) is almost an exact reproduction of sentence 3, but that sentence doesn't say anything about *super-charged plasma*.

6. **D** The author uses the word *deflecting* to describe the action of Earth's magnetic field in the face of the solar winds. In other words, the earth's magnetic field protects the earth by turning aside the harmful, radiation-filled solar winds. Look for an answer choice that has a similar meaning. Eliminate (B) and (E) because they are not supported by the text. Eliminate (A) and (C), which contradict the passage. Choice (D) is the correct answer because the word *divert* is a synonym for the word *deflect*, and this action would provide the protection that is observed.

7. **A** Eliminate (B) because it is not supported by the text; the author makes no mention of the technology required for scientists to observe solar winds. Eliminate (C) for similar reasons; while Kepler made an accurate guess regarding comet tails and the reasons for which they bend away from the sun, one cannot infer that these observations constitute the first major contribution to the study of solar winds or the sun more generally. Choice (D) goes beyond the scope of the text in discussing Kepler's work, and (E) compares two different types of information. The correct answer is (A).

8. **It is not just those planets nearest the sun....**

   The credited response, the second sentence from the end of the passage, indicates that some people might be expected to believe solar winds affect only the innermost planets. If you were tempted by the sentence that begins *Solar winds, though, are not without variation*, be sure to read the question carefully. Like most of the first paragraph, that sentence focuses on the solar winds themselves, rather than their effects.

9. **A, B, C**

   Choice (A) is supported by the characterization of the argument that *America often goes to war for an abstract ideal* as *refreshingly candid*. Choice (B) is supported by the inclusion of *democratization of societies* in the list of such ideals, as well as by the examples of the Spanish-American War and World War I. Choice (C) is supported by the use of the phrase *wealth of examples* to describe the work.

10. **D** The topic of the passage is Pickett's interpretation of American military history. In the second paragraph, the author states that while Pickett's work provides a *refreshingly candid argument* of why America goes to war, he *overstates the case when he argues that these abstract causes typically lead to a war hysteria in which American leadership can no longer enforce any measured policies*. In other words, while the author believes that some of the ideas Pickett presents are correct, the author also notes that Pickett's conclusions cannot be fully supported. The best answer is therefore (D). All the other answers are outside the scope of the passage. Additionally, (B) and (E) are extreme.

11. **E** The author discusses the ways in which Close's ideas of portraiture differ from tradition, and Close's emphasis on a head without expression or personality is the opposite of traditional portraiture. Choice (E) best addresses this uncommon approach. Choices (A) and (B) are not suggested in the passage. There is not enough information to support (C), and (D) is only partially addressed late in the passage.

12. **B** Choice (A) can be eliminated because, while the text tells you that the paintings are *nearly indistinguishable from photographs*, there is nothing that says anyone is confused by the paintings. Choice (B) is correct because the passage says that Close's later work found inspiration from abstract expressionism. Choice (C) is incorrect because the passage never states whether Close has sold his works.

13. **B** The second sentence of the passage provides Derrida's description of the concept of *difference* and includes *attempts to discuss universal features of human nature are merely products of local standards*. Thus the answer needs to make clear that acceptance does not equate truth. This is best summarized in (B). The other answers all discuss some aspect of the status quo, but none sufficiently debunk it as the accepted standard.

14. **Derrida was considered the originator of a profound challenge....**

The credited response relates a view of Derrida as *the originator of* the anti-foundationalists' *profound challenge to the history of human thought*. The following sentences, though, put forth the view that the origin of anti-foundationalism is better traced to Darwin's theory of natural selection, which made the later movement *almost an inevitable consequence*.

15. **A** The author states that anti-foundationalists believe that *there is no secure basis for knowledge*. Therefore, (A) is correct. The author states that Derrida held the belief that *any attempts to discuss universal features of human nature are merely products of local standards*. In other words, meaning is understood within a cultural context; thus eliminate (B). Choice (C) misquotes the information in the passage. Though the passage talks about Darwin's work, almost making Derrida's inevitable, (D) is too extreme. Eliminate (E) because it does not address the question.

Drill 4

1. **B** The use of the word *guise* means that the *talk stories* are a way to convey other information, namely the myths of Kingston's cultural background. Choice (B) is the best answer because it paraphrases this point. Neither (A) nor (C) is mentioned in the passage.

2. **A** In the first paragraph, the author notes that some readers categorize Kingston as a great Asian-American writer. The author follows this statement by referencing examples in her writing that support the contention, so the best answer is (A). The other choices are not supported by the passage. In addition, (E) is extreme in its use of the word *unique*.

3. **A, B**   In the first paragraph, the movement is described as a *subtle rebellion,* so the author sees literature as something that can be used as a protest as stated in (A). Choice (B) also works because the text tells you that while *seventeenth-century France was characterized by political intrigue and violence,* it also tells you that that same instability *reawakened French proclivities for cultural expression* and that by the time Louis XIV took the throne, society was *primed for the reestablishment of the arts.* Therefore, prior to the unrest of the 17th century, the French had more involvement with the arts. Choice (C) can be eliminated because the wording is too strong and inclusive; literature was a form of protest available, but you do not know that it was the *only* form of protest.

4. **A**   The passage is primarily concerned with how *préciosité* paved the way for a resurgence of interest in the arts in 17th century France, which makes (A) the best answer. Though the passage does highlight the role of women in the Baroque movement, it does not attempt to make any larger statements about women in history; therefore, (B) is incorrect. The passage does define and explain the origins of a literary movement, but that is not the primary purpose, so eliminate (C). The primary purpose of the passage is not a discussion of how nations' rulers affect the arts, which makes (E) incorrect. Finally, (D) is not suggested in the passage.

5. **C**   Choice (A) can be eliminated because the text tells you that *préciosité* came from a group of *cultured and educated ladies,* not the entirety of French society. Choice (B) can also be eliminated because of phrases such as *men scoffed* and *often dismissed*, which indicate that *préciosité* was mocked before Molière wrote his play. Choice (C) is the only statement supported by the text, as the references to the mocking show that no one at the time truly understood the cultural importance of what was going on.

6.   **Preferring appearance to substance and excess to moderation....**

   While there are descriptions all throughout the text of both *préciosité* and neo-classicism, this sentence is the only one with the direct contrast. The passage tells you that the *préciosité* was *fantastically embellished and witty in manner,* and that the neo-classicism *elevated simplicity and minimalism.* However, it's only in the correct sentence from the first paragraph that the author directly contrasts the two styles.

7. **A, B**   The passage states that *President Polk had overstepped...against Mexico.* If Polk declared war against Mexico, then you know Lincoln did not start the war; (A) is supported by the passage. If Lincoln thought that Polk *overstepped his constitutional boundaries,* then that indicates Lincoln did not think that Polk's declaration of war was justified by the Constitution. This provides support for the disagreement referenced in (B). Choice (C) is not supported by the passage and can be eliminated: the Civil War, not the Mexican-American war, was *fought ostensibly to abolish slavery.*

8. **D**   It is important to read the lines within the context of the passage. Earlier in the passage the author informs you that Lincoln felt *disdain* for the Mexican-American War. The author notes that given Lincoln's willingness to fight the Civil War, this seeming inconsistency bears some explanation. The passage states that *Lincoln would not shrink from battle if the war could ensure a united country.*

Therefore, given that Lincoln supported the Civil War, you can assume that he had reasons for opposing the Mexican-American War on grounds other than unification. Therefore, the correct answer is (D).

9.   **Therefore, American businesses will predominantly opt for outsourcing....**

The author only once explains what type of jobs will be outsourced: *repetitive tasks that can easily be brought back to the United States.*

10. **B**   The author's purpose is sometimes presented at the end of the passage, as is the case with this passage, which ends with *[t]he growing emphasis on bringing down the cost of back office operations is bound to offer increasing scope for Indian firms to become involved in novel types of ever more complex business processes.* Choice (B) presents the best paraphrase of this statement. Choices (A) and (C) are too broad; (D) and (E) are not supported by the passage.

11. **A, B**   Be sure you understand what the question is asking: You need to look for what you can prove *isn't* going to happen in the text, despite the pressure to *pursue cost-cutting measures.* The passage states that *American society remains uncomfortable shifting business tasks overseas.* Therefore, the Indian firms would not perform all of the business processes, making (A) a valid answer. Choice (B) is also supported by the text, because American businesses *opt for outsourcing...tasks that can easily be brought back to the United States.* Choice (C) is not supported by the text, because India is not outsourcing tasks to American firms.

12. **B**   The zooxanthellae need carbon dioxide for their survival so (B) is correct. We know that the zooxanthellae benefit from their relationship with coral, but the passage never says that they couldn't live without coral, so (C) goes too far. Since the zooxanthellae are helpful to the coral, they cannot be *parasitical*, which rules out (D). The passage never says anything about *camouflage*, so (A) is out of scope. The last sentence of the passage says that *If zooxanthellate populations continue to decrease without recovery, their host corals will eventually follow suit...*, indicating that coral may die without zooxanthellae, so (E) is incorrect.

13. **B**   The pollutions referred to are described as *anthropogenic*; the root means that they are linked to humans. Thus (B) is the best answer. The pollutions are not linked to any other type of organism, so eliminate (A) and (D). Choice (C) is incorrect because overfishing and other such activities are not accidents. Choice (E) is wrong because the pollutions are not natural.

14. **The zooxanthellate invertebrates lose their concentration of pigmentation....**

Concentration of pigmentation is another way of saying *coloration*. The sentence states that the zooxanthellae *lose their concentration of pigmentation when stressed*, which provides an explanation for their loss of their coloration.

15. **C** The third paragraph lists a number of factors that contribute to coral bleaching, including *over-harvesting coral for the exotic travel market*. This supports the idea that tourist demand contributes to coral bleaching, thus making (C) the best answer. The passage says nothing about *freight ships, fossil fuels,* or *governmental apathy*, so (A), (B), and (D) can be eliminated. The third paragraph does suggest that coral is sensitive to natural climate changes, but it does not say that this sensitivity is *unusual* as stated in the answer, so (E) cannot be properly inferred from the passage.

Drill 5

1. **B, C** The passage states that the *origins of country music…owe a great deal to African-American musicians*, so that means that *African-Americans were instrumental in developing country music*; this supports the first part of (B). The passage also states that *some of the "stars" of country music learned their trade from African-American musicians*, implying that the African-American musicians taught them, completing the necessary support for (B). The last sentence of the passage states that *in addition to jazz,…country music now clearly needs to be included in the list of musical genres that have an African-American lineage*. This implies that jazz is already *commonly acknowledged* to arise from the *African-American lineage*, and this fact supports (C). Choice (A) is a trap answer; the passage says that Payne taught Williams, but it doesn't specify exactly what he taught him.

2. **A** The quote draws attention to the sentence naming some African-American musical traditions that shaped country music; thus, the answer needs to describe that relationship. Only (A) depicts this previous music as the source from which country music arose. There is nothing in the passage to support (B), (D), or (E). Choice (C) is true but does not answer the question.

3. **B** The sentence that details the possible stages of face perception is a more specific description of the psychologists' theory so eliminate (A). The author never provides the history described in (C) so it is also incorrect; he/she merely provides two arguments on the phenomenon. The author never discusses visual perception more generally; thus (D) goes beyond the scope of the passage. The author never reconciles the psychologists' and cognitive neuroscientists' views, so (E) is not supported. Choice (B) is the best match.

4. **A** *Analogy* describes the way cognitive neuroscientists believe the brain functions when confronted with faces. In the sentence that follows the word *analogy*, the author discusses the way in which brains have a natural ability to recognize things of the same character or quality. Eliminate (B) and (D) because they discuss psychologists. Choice (C) is too unspecific, and (E) leaves out the comparison factor. The best match is (A) because it addresses the matching that neuroscientists think is happening.

5. **A** When looking for the main idea, you need to consider the entire passage. In the first paragraph, the author states that some people had assumed that schools that were freed from rules and regulations (such as charter schools) would revolutionize education. In the second paragraph, the author states that those who study educational reform have found that charter schools did not in fact

have a revolutionary impact on education—either for better or worse—although students who attend charter schools sometimes do not seem to do as well academically. In the last paragraph, the author talks about the challenges that schools face in general, be they charter schools or traditional schools. Choice (A) gets closest to summarizing the entire passage. Choices (B) and (E) contradict the passage, (D) is too extreme, and (C) is not the whole point.

6. **It is, however, impossible to know whether this difference is due to....**

The critics, mentioned in the first paragraph, fear *deleterious rather than beneficial effects...on the academic achievement of students*. The second paragraph discusses academic outcomes of charter schools, so that is where you should look for the answer. The first two sentences of the paragraph discuss the amount of impact charter schools have had, but do not make specific mention of bad effects. The third sentence provides factual evidence for the critics, but does not give the author's opinion regarding this evidence. The final sentence of this paragraph is correct because in it, the author questions whether simply being a charter school is the reason that some schools do not meet state standards.

7. **D** At the end of the final paragraph, the author lists the challenges that schools face. Choices (A), (B), (C), and (E) are paraphrases of these points. While the paragraph does discuss how student performance is measured, this information is not presented as a particular challenge that schools face; thus (D) is the best answer.

8. **C** Choice (A) is not supported; although college attendance may seem like a useful measure of academic achievement, (A) provides no information about students from traditional schools for comparison. Choice (B) is likewise not supported. Although having a new standard might eventually allow relevant information to be gathered, the simple creation of such a standard would itself give no way to differentiate between students at the two types of schools. Choice (C) is supported because the author uses *state performance standards* to assess *academic performance* in the second paragraph.

9. **B** Choice (A) can be eliminated because the wording is too extreme. While the study of memory is important, there's no evidence that it's *the most important approach*. No other approach is mentioned in the text. Choice (B) works well because the text tells you Proust is "widely recognized as an icon of French culture and literature" and that "many commentaries have focused on Proust's treatment of... memory." Choice (C) can be eliminated because the second half of the answer cannot be supported. There is no evidence that studies on memory in Proust are no longer useful.

10. **B** The second paragraph focuses on Benhaïm's study of Proust's text. Because of Proust's mysterious and, at times, hostile representations of French cities, the narrator is turned into an exile in his homeland. The quotation illustrates this point using the narrator's perception of Balbec, which for him is strange and cruel. Choice (B) is the best match. Eliminate (A) because it uses information from the passage but doesn't answer the question. Eliminate (C) because the author never discusses

the realities of living in France. Choice (D) goes beyond the scope of the question, and (E) is unrelated to the quoted text.

11. C In the second paragraph, Proust describes *These strangely ordinary and disdainfully familiar cathedrals*. Choice (C) is the best answer because *churches* is another word for *cathedral*. You can eliminate (A) because the quote does not mention graves. Choice (B) could be attractive because the narrator is described as *a stranger to his homeland and living the life of an exile*, but Proust himself does not mention travelers as a feature of Balbec. Therefore, you can eliminate (B).

12.   **In his work, French cities are archaic and exotic.**

        In the sentence before, the author says that Proust *describes France in ways that one would not expect.*

13. A Eliminate (B); while the author compares the Judeo-Christian concept of god with the Nahuas' belief in the sacred power of *teotl*, the author never discusses any Christian stories that explain the beginnings of the world. *Teotl* is not a concept in Western philosophy, so eliminate (C). Though the author's definition of *teotl* makes a comparison, one isn't supported over the other, eliminating (D). While this definition may spark curiosity, the role of this statement is not to advocate action, so (E) is eliminated. Thus, the best answer is (A).

14. B, C The author spends the bulk of the passage discussing *teotl*, which is described as the *core of their philosophy*, so (C) is supported. Much of the passage also describes the ways in which the concept of *teotl* is distinct in nature from the concepts of Western philosophy, so (B) is supported. Choice (A) may seem like a logical inference, but the passage never explicitly discusses customs of the Nahuas, so (A) is not supported.

15. D Eliminate (A) because this answer clearly mixes up a couple of the central ideas in the passage. According to scholars, Nahua philosophy was complex and interrelated, but the author doesn't say that Western philosophy consists *only* of dichotomies, so eliminate (B) as this is an extreme answer. The first part of (C) is great, but the second part is very wrong; half bad is all bad, so eliminate it. Eliminate (E) because it is too extreme. Within the Nahuas' worldview, the supernatural force was united with the natural world, so (D) is the best match.

Drill 6

1. A, C The passage says that *scats provide crucial evidence regarding territory*. This phrase indicates that the issue of territory is worth studying, so you know that (B) is true. Choice (A), however, is phrased in too extreme a form to be supported by the passage; additionally, the final sentence says that *scent, vocalization, and aggressive displays* also mark territory. That last indicator of territory, *aggressive displays*, also tells you that (C) is not supported. Therefore, (A) and (C) are the credited responses.

2. B By saying that the wombat is not mythical, the passage suggests that someone must have thought that the wombat does not really exist; thus the correct answer is (B). This passage does not tie the

wombat to the Eora culture, nor does it extend that culture to any other civilization, thus eliminating (A) and (C). The passage also does not provide any contrast with other rodents, so (D) is incorrect. Eliminate (E) because, while the passage addresses the derivative of the wombat's name, it does not refer to naming standards.

3.   A   The right answer to a main idea question will cover the entire passage. This passage describes three theories for the cause of the Permian mass extinctions: asteroid impact, volcanic eruption, and rising concentrations of hydrogen sulfide in the earth's oceans. The first two of these theories are shown to be problematic. All you are told about the third theory is that it can be tested. The answer that best covers all three theories is (A).

4.   B   According to the passage, the hydrogen sulfide theory could be tested by checking *oceanic sediments from the Permian period* for evidence of the proliferation of certain bacteria. If, as (B) suggests, the Permian period can't be distinguished from earlier periods, then it will be impossible to test for an increase in bacteria from that period. Choice (A), if anything, would strengthen the author's argument by proving that the sediment is a reliable measure to use; (C), (D), and (E) are irrelevant to the question, because they mention substances *other than* hydrogen sulfide or *other types* of bacteria.

5.   A   Eliminate (B) because it is an extreme answer and not supported by the text. While Kahlo focused on self-representation, it is too much of a leap to infer that the Mexican revolution and/or nationalism were irrelevant to Kahlo's art. Eliminate (C) because it is too broad. This passage focuses on Kahlo and some of her male contemporaries, not female and male artists in general. The information about the war does not explain Kahlo's relative obscurity nor does it address issues of feminist beliefs, so eliminate (D) and (E). The correct answer is (A).

6.   B, C   Go back to the text to see what the passage tells you about Kahlo's contemporaries: while she was painting *self-portraits*, they were *more interested in public forms of art*. Choice (A) is too extreme: there's no support for them *never* painting self-portraits. Choice (B) is supported because the fact that Kahlo *did not achieve recognition until long after her death* made her *unlike her contemporaries*. Choice (C) is supported by the end of the first paragraph: her contemporaries' interest in *public forms of art* is explained by placing them in *the time of the Mexican revolution…a period that fostered an interest in nationalistic themes*.

7.   A, B   The final sentence of the passage indicates that transportation is a clear problem that limits consideration of terraforming to *mere conjecture*, so (A) is supported. Choice (B) is supported because the author is worried about the Martian atmosphere dehydrating again after the planet is made habitable. Choice (C), however, goes beyond the scope of the information presented in the passage: the previous existence of water and an atmosphere similar to that of Earth does not necessarily mean that Mars hosted life.

8. **A** One of the major obstacles to terraforming Mars as mentioned in the passage is the lack of a life-sustaining atmosphere; if the carbon dioxide layer were able to retain atmospheric heat, terraforming would be more feasible. Thus, (A) is the best answer. Choice (B) makes terraforming less feasible; without an atmosphere it would be inhospitable to man. Choice (C) makes terraforming neither more nor less likely—the point of terraforming is to change the environment. The passage is not concerned with governments on Earth, making (D) incorrect. Choice (E) is incorrect because the passage is not concerned with other planets.

9. **By 1926, speculating on pricing was a crime.**

   The question asks for a description of *an action undertaken by the Soviet government*. Most of the third paragraph details the actions of the NEPmen. The text, *The state could not produce consumer goods…* is incorrect because it does not describe an actual action by the Soviet government, but describes an action the government could not do: producing enough goods. The text, *Since the state could not produce or profit…* is incorrect because, although it says that the state *adopted measures*, it does not specify what those measure were. *By 1926, speculating on pricing was a crime* is the answer because it specifies the action the Soviet government took against the NEPmen: it made speculation a crime.

10. **D** Choices (A) and (E) can be eliminated, because the passage does not refer to the government's view. Choice (B) may look attractive, but the word *mistaken* is too strong. Choices (C) and (D) are quite similar, so compare them to each other. The only real problem is that (C) says the *crisis could have been averted*. The passage does not say the crisis was preventable. Choice (D) is the best answer.

11. **C** Choice (B) is too narrow because it refers only to the beginning of the passage. Choice (E) is too broad; only a few systems are mentioned and only one is the focus. Choices (A), (C), and (D) are similar, so compare them to one another. If you can't decide which one to choose, make a guess and move on. Choice (C) is best because it captures the real focus of the passage: *why* the NEP failed. Choice (D) is close, but the three crises ended a policy, not a whole era.

12. **A, C** Choice (A) is not supported by the text because the NEPmen were not solely responsible for the downfall of the NEP. Also, the question asks about the *author's opinions*, and the description given of the NEPmen is that of popular opinion, not necessarily the author. Choice (B) is supported by the text in the second paragraph stating that *the state could not produce or profit as well as the NEPmen*. Choice (C) is not supported by the text. Although all the words in the answer choice look familiar, nothing about the context of the answer choice is actually in the text. The *scissors crisis* was actually caused by the NEP, not war communism, and it was caused by the government's spurring of *industry*, not *agriculture*. The correct answers are (A) and (C).

13. **B** According to the passage, *the burning of fossil fuels, which have no carbon-14 content, has diluted the atmospheric carbon-14 content*. Since carbon dating works by comparing the percentage of carbon remaining in an ancient object to that found in living matter, you would need to have a consistent

ratio of carbon-14. Because the burning of fossil fuels has decreased that ratio, however, living matter that died prior to the burning of fossil fuels would have more carbon-14 content when it died, and would therefore appear to have died more recently. Choice (A) is the opposite of what you're looking for, so you can eliminate it. Choice (C) is not supported by the passage.

14. **A**   In the first paragraph, the author discusses the trouble that anthropologists have had in dating the *habilis* skull, which at first they thought to be 3 million years old. In the second paragraph, the author describes how carbon dating techniques work; objects are dated by the ratio of carbon-14 they possess. However, the author goes on to show that the half-life of carbon can date objects only up to 50,000 years old, or 100,000 years at most if accelerator techniques are used. This limitation suggests that carbon dating is unsuitable for providing the exact age of the *habilis* skull, making (A) the best answer. Choice (B) is actually the opposite of what the author suggests for the time frame being discussed. Choice (C) does not answer the question; while the difference is indeed highlighted, this answer ignores the *purpose* of the contrast. In (D), accelerator techniques would still not be adequate to date *habilis*. Choice (E) is off the mark; the half-life in itself does not *illustrate the equilibrium*.

15. **C**   The proposed solution comes at the end of the passage, where the author discusses radiometric dating methods, so the answer needs to address the requirements of this solution. There is an assumption in this method that the isotopes being measured decay at a consistent rate, and this issue is best addressed in (C). While (E) addresses radiometric methods, the author does not discuss the equipment involved in the process. The remaining answers do not cover this proposed solution.

16.   **However, the assumption that the decay....**

Be sure to read the question carefully: the author raises a number of *possible objections to carbon dating*, but only the final paragraph discusses *proposed alternatives*. The last sentence, the credited response, points out that these alternatives may have the same problem as the carbon dating: inconsistent decay rates.

Sentence
Equivalence

SENTENCE EQUIVALENCE

The directions for Sentence Equivalence read as follows: *Select the two answer choices that, when used to complete the sentence, fit the meaning of the sentence as a whole and produce completed sentences that are alike in meaning.*

In other words, figure out the story being told and pick the two words in the answer choices that complete the story in the same way. These are like Sentence Completion questions you might remember from the SAT or previous versions of the GRE, but you are picking two words rather than one for the same blank.

A word of warning on Sentence Equivalence: Beware of the answer choices. They will always fit grammatically into the sentence, and most of them will sound pretty attractive. Just remember that the answer choices represent ETS's "suggestions" for what to put in the blank. We don't like ETS's suggestions, we don't trust ETS's suggestions, and we don't want ETS's suggestions. The answer choices have been carefully selected and then tested on thousands of students for the sole purpose of messing with your head. The first step on Sentence Equivalence is always to cover up the answer choices. Literally put your hand on the screen, and don't let them pollute your thinking.

Think of the sentence itself as a mini Reading Comprehension passage. Before you do anything, find the main idea. Who is the passage talking about? What are you told about this person or thing? Once you have the story firmly in mind, come up with your own word for the blank, and eliminate the answer choices that don't match.

The Process

Step 1—Cover the answer choices.

Step 2—Find the story. Who is the main character? What are you told about the main character?

Step 3—Come up with your own word for the blank. Don't look at the answer choices. Force yourself to come up with your own word based upon the information in the passage.

Step 4—Use Process of Elimination (POE). Use your word to eliminate answer choices. Look at each answer choice and ask whether it matches your word. If not, get rid of it. If the answer is "I'm not sure," give it the maybe and move on. If the answer is yes, give it the check. Make sure that all of this work takes place on your scratch paper.

Finding the Clue

The "Clue" is that part of the sentence that tells you what to put in the blank. Every sentence must have one because it's the part of the sentence that tells you whether an answer choice is right or wrong. The clue is like an arrow that points only to right answers. Finding the clue is the key to coming up with your own word and eliminating wrong answers!

Triggers

Imagine a conversation that begins, "That's Frank. He won the lottery and now _____." Something good is going to go into that blank. Frank could be a millionaire, could be living on his own island, or could be a great collector of rare jeweled belt buckles. Whatever it is, this story is going to end happily.

Now consider this story: "That's Frank. He won the lottery but now _____." This story is going to end badly. Frank could be tied up in court for tax evasion, panhandling on the corner, or in a mental institution.

The only difference between these two stories is the words *but* and *and*. These are triggers. Here are some of the triggers that show up on the GRE most frequently.

but	in contrast
although (though, even though)	unfortunately
unless	heretofore
rather	thus
yet	and
despite	therefore
while	similarly
however	; *or* :

When it comes to Sentence Equivalence, remember these three things:

1. Invest your time in the sentence. Stick with the sentence until you find the story. Don't even think about looking at the answer choices until that story is crystal clear.

2. Your word is your filter. Come up with your own word for the blank and use it to eliminate answer choices. Actively identify and eliminate wrong answers. Keep your hand moving on your scratch paper. If it takes more than a few seconds to decide whether to keep or eliminate an answer choice, give it the maybe and move on. Note: If an answer choice has no synonym among the other answer choices, it's unlikely to be correct.

3. Mark and come back. If a sentence isn't making sense, or none of the answer choices look right, walk away. Don't keep forcing the sentence. You may have read something wrong. Do a few other questions to distract your brain, and then take a second look at it.

Sentence
Equivalence
Drills

DRILL 1

Question 1

Despite their initial fears, most environmentalists now concede that the artificial reefs have had a largely _____ effect on surrounding ecosystems.

- ☐ unfounded
- ☐ benign
- ☐ caustic
- ☐ interminable
- ☐ innocuous
- ☐ plaintive

Question 2

Scholarship reductions and player defections notwithstanding, the new coach applied himself to rebuilding the program with such _____ that the rest of the staff struggled to match his enthusiasm.

- ☐ cessation
- ☐ indifference
- ☐ rhetoric
- ☐ fervency
- ☐ heedlessness
- ☐ zeal

Question 3

After hours of practice and innumerable fruitless attempts to catch the balls, Allen was finally forced to admit that he wasn't sufficiently _____ to be a juggler.

- ☐ sedate
- ☐ lumbering
- ☐ dexterous
- ☐ implicit
- ☐ adroit
- ☐ awkward

Question 4

The cohesion of Alexander the Great's vast empire was _____; at his death, Alexander's lands were divided among his generals, Ptolemy, Seleucus, and Antigonus the One-Eyed.

- ☐ abiding
- ☐ precarious
- ☐ protracted
- ☐ redoubled
- ☐ renowned
- ☐ tenuous

Question 5

His wife's icy stare and aloof demeanor told Johann unequivocally that his propitiatory gifts had failed to _____ her.

- ☐ vilify
- ☐ garner
- ☐ exacerbate
- ☐ aggravate
- ☐ placate
- ☐ mollify

Question 6

By consuming _____ numbers of power bars, some athletes believe they will have proportionally greater amounts of endurance and strength because of the energy-producing ingredients these products claim to contain.

- ☐ scant
- ☐ furtive
- ☐ copious
- ☐ solvent
- ☐ measured
- ☐ profuse

Question 7

Proponents of small government bemoaned the passage of the comprehensive bill, which was signed into law by the president late last week and was _____ new regulations on the fishing industry.

- ☐ elucidated by
- ☐ rife with
- ☐ deficient in
- ☐ unencumbered by
- ☐ replete with
- ☐ exempted from

Question 8

The CEO's former employees started a blog that revealed the embarrassing quirks of their boss, an act which had _____ impact on the company's CEO.

- ☐ a virulent
- ☐ an assuaging
- ☐ a monumental
- ☐ a discomfiting
- ☐ a bolstering
- ☐ a mortifying

Question 9

The late Samuel Huntington was well known for his _____ opinions on relations among different cultures; many of his ideas are still passionately debated today.

- ☐ zealous
- ☐ pedantic
- ☐ polemical
- ☐ rhetorical
- ☐ divisive
- ☐ hegemonic

Question 10

The _____ plant life on the previously barren volcanic rock created by the Kilauea lava flow is strong evidence that humans, too, will one day be able to inhabit the area.

- ☐ incipient
- ☐ nascent
- ☐ waning
- ☐ fervent
- ☐ flagging
- ☐ static

Question 11

Regardless of the long-winded answers Michael consistently gave in class, his teachers remember him as a _____ student, rather than a garrulous one, because he generally kept to himself.

- ☐ taciturn
- ☐ voluble
- ☐ laconic
- ☐ querulous
- ☐ disinterested
- ☐ prolix

Question 12

For the cities in the foothills of the Rocky Mountains, where the shortage of rain often leaves wells and rivers empty, a winter without liberal snowfall will mean a _____ of the run-off that normally provides fresh water in the summer months.

- ☐ proliferation
- ☐ conduit
- ☐ paucity
- ☐ surfeit
- ☐ dearth
- ☐ burgeoning

Question 13

Despite her father's endeavors to placate his daughter every time she had a grievance, the young girl was simply _____ complainer, and so could always find something else that displeased her.

- ☐ an inveterate
- ☐ a lachrymose
- ☐ a plaintive
- ☐ an oblique
- ☐ a chronic
- ☐ an abysmal

Question 14

Retherford argued that modern viewers are so transfixed by the search for secret messages that even though Lisa del Giocondo, the model for Leonardo da Vinci's *Mona Lisa*, was regarded by all as _____, modern viewers are convinced that there is an enigma behind the celebrated smile.

- ☐ dulcet
- ☐ guileless
- ☐ comely
- ☐ facile
- ☐ inscrutable
- ☐ ingenuous

Question 15

Though the futurist conceded that Apple's iPhone was a revolutionary device, she was adamant that it would not be immune to the same forces that caused such previous "game changing" products as Ford's Model T and Sony's Walkman eventually to be considered _____.

- ☐ avant-garde
- ☐ electronic
- ☐ circuitous
- ☐ antediluvian
- ☐ superannuated
- ☐ radical

Question 16

The results of a survey of movie-goers gainsaid the scholar's claim that the filmmakers' intent would remain opaque to most viewers; it seems the metaphors employed were rather _____.

- ☐ perspicuous
- ☐ abstruse
- ☐ manifest
- ☐ aesthetic
- ☐ cryptic
- ☐ recalcitrant

Question 17

To call the area _____ was perhaps hyperbolic; while it was certainly quaint, the presence of mining equipment was decidedly imposing.

- ☐ germane
- ☐ gentrified
- ☐ inimical
- ☐ bucolic
- ☐ rancorous
- ☐ quiescent

Question 18

In an era in which mass media is but a thrall of its corporate masters, the amateurish _____ of commercials for local businesses provide a tonic for the slick homogeneity of most advertising.

- ☐ amalgamations
- ☐ eccentricities
- ☐ synergies
- ☐ conglomerations
- ☐ syllogisms
- ☐ idiosyncrasies

Question 19

Although he earned over two hundred million dollars during his career, the boxer's _____ spending and bad investments left him insolvent within a few years of retirement.

☐ parsimonious
☐ penurious
☐ perfidious
☐ prodigal
☐ profligate
☐ pugnacious

Question 20

When a Roman emperor visited a provincial city, an important part of the ceremony of *receptio* was the delivery of _____, in which a local poet or orator would lavish praise on the imperial visitor.

☐ a compendium
☐ an elegy
☐ an encomium
☐ a jeremiad
☐ a philippic
☐ a panegyric

DRILL 2

Question 1

Despite having steeled herself for the worst, the new band director was disheartened to hear the _____ sounds emanating from the freshman orchestra.

- ☐ arduous
- ☐ euphonious
- ☐ cacophonous
- ☐ ample
- ☐ discordant
- ☐ harmonious

Question 2

Bede, the author of *A History of the English Church and People*, was so widely _____ that he has been almost universally known as "The Venerable Bede" since the ninth century.

- ☐ defamed
- ☐ consoled
- ☐ revered
- ☐ esteemed
- ☐ mitigated
- ☐ reviled

Question 3

In addition to the detailed written regulations regarding play, a novice golfer must also learn the _____, but nonetheless important, rules of etiquette.

- ☐ implicit
- ☐ laconic
- ☐ express
- ☐ tacit
- ☐ reclusive
- ☐ manifest

Question 4

Based on the desire to restrict further water pollution, the Clean Water Act of 1972 began _____ enough, but opponents soon assailed the bill in the court system and discouraged those who had fought for its ratification.

- ☐ bleakly
- ☐ auspiciously
- ☐ unfavorably
- ☐ suspiciously
- ☐ promisingly
- ☐ ineffectually

Question 5

Jane Austen's novel, *Emma,* paints a comedy of errors that results when its heroine tries her hand at creating love matches, an effort which she attributes to her own _____ instead of a selfish need to meddle.

- ☐ gaiety
- ☐ benevolence
- ☐ elegance
- ☐ viscosity
- ☐ refinement
- ☐ magnanimity

Question 6

While interviewing for a job as a computer consultant, Robert consciously provided a _____ of references, knowing full well that he had few former employers who would be laudatory about his past projects.

- ☐ multitude
- ☐ array
- ☐ myriad
- ☐ potpourri
- ☐ paucity
- ☐ dearth

Question 7

While most of the tasks undertaken by the interns were undemanding, a fact that led to the flood of applicants for the positions each year, there was one _____ duty: cleaning out the garbage bins in the laboratory.

☐ unambiguous
☐ facile
☐ arduous
☐ onerous
☐ tenebrous
☐ lucid

Question 8

In an attempt to _____ voters to support her, the incumbent politician beguilingly greeted a room full of constituents and pledged to lower taxes—even though she had only ever done the opposite while in office.

☐ alienate
☐ abase
☐ inveigle
☐ eviscerate
☐ estrange
☐ entice

Question 9

After a series of storms, the once arid landscape became _____ for the first time in many months.

☐ innocuous
☐ barren
☐ verdant
☐ desolate
☐ bountiful
☐ limpid

Question 10

Although he received many visitors, the _____ old man shooed them away after only a few minutes.

☐ misanthropic
☐ curmudgeonly
☐ sarcastic
☐ chauvinistic
☐ garrulous
☐ affable

Question 11

Eileen used to be a picky eater; since a new complex of fine dining and ethnic restaurants opened in her neighborhood, however, she has turned into quite _____.

☐ a recluse
☐ a philistine
☐ an epicure
☐ a chauvinist
☐ a gourmand
☐ a vulgarian

Question 12

The SWAT team entered the dark building on high alert, their guns drawn and their night vision goggles on; each agent's eyes and ears were attuned to the slightest disturbance in the _____ recesses of the rooms.

☐ empty
☐ cacophonous
☐ stygian
☐ gloomy
☐ functional
☐ useful

Question 13

The man's desire to present a frugal picture to his friends and avoid being a labeled a _____ caused him to go to such an extreme that he ended up being called a Scrooge.

☐ a spendthrift
☐ a prodigal
☐ a miser
☐ a hedonist
☐ a skinflint
☐ an epicure

Question 14

The _____ pirate plundered every trade ship that came near his own ship; it was almost as if he could never loot or pillage enough to satisfy his craving for gold and jewels.

☐ raffish
☐ ebullient
☐ voracious
☐ showy
☐ rapacious
☐ effusive

Question 15

The homicide detectives didn't truly understand the _____ of the criminal until they found the secret hideout where he stored his instruments of torture and carried out his heinous acts.

☐ pulchritude
☐ enormity
☐ ingenuity
☐ iniquity
☐ canniness
☐ perfidy

Question 16

As portrayed in Livy's *Ab Urbe Condita,* Cincinnatus was the _____ of the Roman ideal of the farmer-soldier: invested with supreme dictatorial power while plowing his fields, he defeated the Aequi and the Sabines, resigned his title, and returned to his farm a scant sixteen days later.

☐ supplicant
☐ antithesis
☐ quintessence
☐ epitome
☐ contraposition
☐ veracity

Question 17

In contrast to the stark facades of their surviving ruins, medieval castles were depicted in contemporary tapestries as _____ with colorful banners and pennants.

☐ ablated
☐ attenuated
☐ bedizened
☐ caparisoned
☐ extirpated
☐ fomented

Question 18

The young minister was startled to learn that his parishioners considered him _____; he had been unaware that his message was being undermined by his sanctimonious and self-righteous tone.

☐ ingenuous
☐ moralistic
☐ punctilious
☐ salacious
☐ sententious
☐ unaffected

Many senior faculty members who were accustomed to being addressed in a more collegial and egalitarian manner were alienated by the _____ tone of the new department chair's introductory remarks.

- ☐ ignominious
- ☐ imperious
- ☐ peremptory
- ☐ propitious
- ☐ sanguine
- ☐ saturnine

Meant to demonstrate an air of sophistication and worldliness, the comments that Hannah made upon exiting the building served only to emphasize her _____ mentality and reinforce Mr. Hassan's conviction that her dismissal was justified because she was not yet mature enough for the corporate world.

- ☐ adroit
- ☐ venal
- ☐ puerile
- ☐ callow
- ☐ indolent
- ☐ mercernary

DRILL 3

Question 1

Sylvia Plath was not as _____ a poet as was her husband Ted Hughes, having produced just two volumes of poetry in her short lifespan.

- ☐ dejected
- ☐ celebrated
- ☐ satiric
- ☐ jubilant
- ☐ prolific
- ☐ fruitful

Question 2

The unfounded fear that some children, and even adults, have of the circus clown is rather ironic considering that he is meant to be _____ character who invokes laughter and enjoyment.

- ☐ an ace
- ☐ a surly
- ☐ a genial
- ☐ an artful
- ☐ a crackerjack
- ☐ an affable

Question 3

The photographer _____ posed the bride for her portrait, carefully adjusting each fold of her dress and each curl of her hair before taking the picture.

- ☐ meticulously
- ☐ frantically
- ☐ subversively
- ☐ hectically
- ☐ fastidiously
- ☐ hysterically

Question 4

After finishing the editing workshop, the writers found that they were able to give each other _____ comments, instead of the general and unhelpful suggestions they had been making beforehand.

- ☐ cursory
- ☐ derisive
- ☐ superficial
- ☐ amateurish
- ☐ critical
- ☐ constructive

Question 5

Many admirers of art _____ the beauty of Jackson Pollock's paintings, while others disparage the splatters of color as simplistic.

- ☐ defame
- ☐ overlook
- ☐ ignore
- ☐ commend
- ☐ underrate
- ☐ extol

Question 6

Expecting Tom to protest the poor grade on his psychology paper, the professor was disheartened when he _____ tossed it in his bag and left the room.

- ☐ gingerly
- ☐ flippantly
- ☐ timidly
- ☐ prudently
- ☐ thoughtlessly
- ☐ delicately

Question 7

The stock market having plunged drastically, the investor's _____ mood on the trading floor seemed incongruous.

- ☐ enervated
- ☐ sanguine
- ☐ inconsolable
- ☐ sardonic
- ☐ funereal
- ☐ buoyant

Question 8

Hundreds of _____ fans waited in line for hours at the comic book convention to talk to their favorite artists and buy limited-edition toy variants otherwise unavailable.

- ☐ staunch
- ☐ malodorous
- ☐ hirsute
- ☐ zealous
- ☐ noisome
- ☐ impecunious

Question 9

The group's final paper, replete with errors in spelling, diction, and idiom, showed every sign of having been given only _____ proofreading.

- ☐ an artless
- ☐ a cursory
- ☐ an extraneous
- ☐ a fastidious
- ☐ a meticulous
- ☐ a perfunctory

Question 10

Releasing a series of solo recordings, collaborating with such musicians as David Byrne and Robert Fripp, and producing artists from Devo to U2 made Brian Eno so _____ for a time that one music industry observer was moved to note that "Brian Eno is everywhere—like God, or salt."

- ☐ omnivorous
- ☐ ignoble
- ☐ fortuitous
- ☐ omnipresent
- ☐ odious
- ☐ ubiquitous

Question 11

Some of Dr. Seuss's most famous characters had _____ meanings that would be lost on his young readers until adulthood; the title character in *Yertle the Turtle,* for instance, was based on Hitler, and the imperiled Who people in *Horton Hears a Who* represented the citizens of post-World War II Japan.

- ☐ banal
- ☐ manifest
- ☐ oblique
- ☐ nascent
- ☐ allusive
- ☐ lucid

Question 12

Oblivious to the magnitude of his costly mistake, Whitman was unprepared to be _____ at so public a forum as the annual shareholder's meeting.

- ☐ censured
- ☐ excoriated
- ☐ instigated
- ☐ lauded
- ☐ repatriated
- ☐ extolled

Question 13

Because they were written to entertain both parents and children, *Looney Tunes* and *Merrie Melodies* served an unexpectedly _____ purpose: *vex, parry,* and *overture,* for example, are among the advanced vocabulary that the young audience could learn in context from *The Bugs Bunny Show.*

- ☐ didactic
- ☐ obfuscating
- ☐ edifying
- ☐ aggrandizing
- ☐ ephemeral
- ☐ mystifying

Question 14

Not known to go out of his way to get along with people, the reclusive author nonetheless managed to surprise the interviewer with his _____ comments.

- ☐ simpatico
- ☐ abstruse
- ☐ recondite
- ☐ splenetic
- ☐ winsome
- ☐ churlish

Question 15

The decision to continue the investigation was not so much about doubting the veracity of the witness's statement, which had been corroborated by other reliable interviews, as it was about a conviction that there was further evidence that could play a _____ role in the case.

- ☐ paramount
- ☐ negligible
- ☐ salient
- ☐ perjurious
- ☐ mendacious
- ☐ marginal

Question 16

Boycotting companies that engage in unethical behavior, such as promoting wars or violating privacy rights, can be an effective way to pressure corporations to stop inherently unacceptable behaviors; nonetheless, such demonstrations of consumer _____ can also have negative consequences including inflation and increased unemployment.

- ☐ endorsement
- ☐ ratification
- ☐ censure
- ☐ debilitation
- ☐ machinations
- ☐ disapprobation

Question 17

Instead of saying "killed" when reporting on war situations, the military often uses more anodyne phrases such as "neutralizing the target" or "collateral damage"; these attempts to gloss reality with _____ do nothing to alleviate the impact of the news.

- ☐ elucidation
- ☐ periphrasis
- ☐ prevarication
- ☐ circumlocutions
- ☐ hyperbole
- ☐ dysphemisms

Question 18

Truly understanding literary theory requires a greater academic investment than simply memorizing descriptions of aestheticism, deconstructionism, and post-modernism; one must also be willing to study philosophy, history, and society to develop an interdisciplinary _____ of how humans build meaning.

- ☐ discernment
- ☐ incognizance
- ☐ acumen
- ☐ somnolence
- ☐ nescience
- ☐ belletrism

Question 19

Many animals such as the poison dart frog, the tiger moth, and the black widow spider give predators advanced warning of their unpalatability or danger through aposematic warning signs, while other animals such as the harmless scarlet kingsnake simply mimic the bright colors of the _____ species to keep predators away.

- [ ] pernicious
- [ ] amicable
- [ ] comestible
- [ ] pulchritudinous
- [ ] deleterious
- [ ] esculent

Question 20

While some mummies, those of Egyptian pharaohs for example, were intentionally preserved with substances such as natron to dry out the bodies and prevent decomposition, others, such as the Tarim mummies found in present-day Xinjiang, China, were _____ naturally by the searing desert conditions.

- [ ] smelted
- [ ] disinterred
- [ ] espied
- [ ] vitiated
- [ ] exsiccated
- [ ] anhydrated

DRILL 4

Question 1

As the valedictorian of his graduating class, Thomas was tasked with delivering a(n) _____ speech, dutifully rehearsing in front of both his mirror and the cat.

- ☐ languid
- ☐ extended
- ☐ eloquent
- ☐ listless
- ☐ articulate
- ☐ enduring

Question 2

Worried that he had lost the support of his party, the prime minister forcefully _____ his controversial statement that healthcare would not be a priority.

- ☐ recanted
- ☐ affirmed
- ☐ validated
- ☐ overlooked
- ☐ disavowed
- ☐ ignored

Question 3

With recent advances in technology allowing for convenient online access to reading material, many forecasters expect to see hardcover book sales _____.

- ☐ multiply
- ☐ abate
- ☐ prevail
- ☐ assimilate
- ☐ dwindle
- ☐ appreciate

Question 4

Pulled over for speeding and nervous about receiving an unpleasant lecture, Natalie's fears were easily relieved by the _____ policeman.

- ☐ exacting
- ☐ affable
- ☐ atypical
- ☐ stringent
- ☐ sober
- ☐ genial

Question 5

Even among statisticians, who fully understand that true randomness includes repetition, there is often a misguided attempt to _____ one's chances of winning the lottery by declining to select numbers that have recently appeared on winning tickets.

- ☐ augment
- ☐ escalate
- ☐ divulge
- ☐ mitigate
- ☐ squander
- ☐ curtail

Question 6

"Out of sight, out of mind" is a useful _____ for those who cannot develop a logical argument to defend their failure to be concerned about poverty in foreign nations.

- ☐ fallacy
- ☐ allusion
- ☐ maxim
- ☐ query
- ☐ waiver
- ☐ proverb

Question 7

Although it initially seemed that the ideological gap between them was insurmountable—he believed in _____ while she believed in accumulating wealth, he in sensitivity toward others while she in self-interest—the marriage ultimately lasted 52 years until his death.

- ☐ largess
- ☐ avarice
- ☐ empathy
- ☐ parsimony
- ☐ cupidity
- ☐ philanthropy

Question 8

Those who criticized Coco Chanel's later clothing designs misjudged as _____ the style that generations of women to come would regard as the epitome of high fashion.

- ☐ defamatory
- ☐ prohibitive
- ☐ contrite
- ☐ mundane
- ☐ insipid
- ☐ exorbitant

Question 9

Since receiving a promotion to departmental chair, Brookstone has been even more prone to _____ against the university's administration, and consequently has lost several professional allies.

- ☐ approbations
- ☐ tirades
- ☐ diatribes
- ☐ precursors
- ☐ commendations
- ☐ canons

Question 10

Sergei's belief in astrology, a pseudoscience whose practitioners provide results that can never be conclusively proven or falsified, left him vulnerable to _____.

- ☐ censure
- ☐ chicanery
- ☐ vindication
- ☐ authentication
- ☐ wile
- ☐ vexation

Question 11

The _____ international aid agencies have toward selecting a fresh cause to champion approximately every five years is indicative of their desire to avoid apathy due to overexposure and, instead, continue to stimulate donor interest.

- ☐ ambivalence
- ☐ predilection
- ☐ affectation
- ☐ propensity
- ☐ wariness
- ☐ callousness

Question 12

Discussions about the use of high-fructose corn syrup as a sweetener lead to _____ among nutritionists, and the use of aspartame, which is also common, is just as controversial.

- ☐ discord
- ☐ concurrence
- ☐ gratification
- ☐ dissension
- ☐ veracity
- ☐ convergence

Question 13

Further recognition of the destructive effects of targeting fast food advertising at young children may lead to more efforts to _____ such tactics: there is already clear evidence that the necessary prohibitive regulations have widespread support.

- ☐ rally
- ☐ check
- ☐ embellish
- ☐ curb
- ☐ pirate
- ☐ muster

Question 14

Even though the judge personally found the law _____, his moral objection did not provide a legal basis on which to rule the law unconstitutional.

- ☐ anodyne
- ☐ abhorrent
- ☐ propitious
- ☐ permissible
- ☐ invidious
- ☐ salubrious

Question 15

Completely impenetrable to the layperson, the ancient text was _____ even to experts in the field.

- ☐ abstruse
- ☐ unequivocal
- ☐ opaque
- ☐ lucid
- ☐ incontrovertible
- ☐ obtuse

Question 16

The feudalism practiced by Carolingian rulers was still in its _____ stage; only later did features such as subinfeudation and the consequent necessity of designating a liege lord lead to the fully developed system familiar to students of the High Middle Ages.

- ☐ refractory
- ☐ byzantine
- ☐ nascent
- ☐ labyrinthine
- ☐ inchoate
- ☐ perfidious

Question 17

A key element of The Smiths' recognizable sound came from the tension between Morrissey's _____ lyrics and the cheerful, almost bouncy music composed by Johnny Marr.

- ☐ lubricious
- ☐ euphoric
- ☐ sanguine
- ☐ saturnine
- ☐ recondite
- ☐ lachrymose

Question 18

The bride was mortified to learn that her dress—which had appeared delicate, even _____, in the artificial light of the boutique— was nearly transparent in the bright sunlight of her outdoor wedding.

- ☐ ephemeral
- ☐ diaphanous
- ☐ ponderous
- ☐ mettlesome
- ☐ cumbersome
- ☐ gossamer

Question 19

The public's fascination with celebrities coupled with the innovations of the electronic age may inspire a new cadre of amateur "paparazzi": there are certainly indications that such a trend is _____.

- ☐ looming
- ☐ attenuating
- ☐ calumniating
- ☐ deliquescing
- ☐ flagging
- ☐ impending

Question 20

The doctor's real mistake, from the perspective of his _____ professional friends who quickly jilted him, was not that his choice of treatment was inappropriate, but rather that it was viscerally objectionable to the medical establishment.

- ☐ squeamish
- ☐ fickle
- ☐ staunch
- ☐ inconstant
- ☐ orthodox
- ☐ stodgy

DRILL 5

Question 1

By reordering the sentences in the problem and adding distracting figures, the professor successfully _____ a previously easy exam question and made it almost impossible to solve.

- ☐ engendered
- ☐ muddled
- ☐ interpreted
- ☐ erased
- ☐ obliterated
- ☐ obfuscated

Question 2

Because she always had the correct answers to life's difficult dilemmas, my grandmother was sought after for her _____ by family members and neighbors.

- ☐ duplicity
- ☐ wisdom
- ☐ bewilderment
- ☐ ignorance
- ☐ sagacity
- ☐ guile

Question 3

The _____ road, made what seemed like a short trip on a map much longer in reality; it twisted its way through mountains to get from one valley to another.

- ☐ abbreviated
- ☐ invigorating
- ☐ fleeting
- ☐ immense
- ☐ serpentine
- ☐ tortuous

Question 4

Classmates who had pre-judged Lucy as unaware were surprised when she made the _____ observation that their professor's missing coffee mug indicated that he had left for the day.

- ☐ asinine
- ☐ perceptive
- ☐ obtuse
- ☐ transparent
- ☐ astute
- ☐ lucid

Question 5

Madeline's guests all agreed that had it not been for the terrible weather, her wedding day, complete with white dress and three-tiered cake, would have been _____.

- ☐ urban
- ☐ divine
- ☐ excessive
- ☐ disproportionate
- ☐ idyllic
- ☐ rustic

Question 6

The Shakespeare scholar argued that in all of the playwright's 37 works, he had never written the part of _____ character, only relying on vibrant and colorful individuals to propel his stories forward.

- ☐ a pedestrian
- ☐ an original
- ☐ an imperial
- ☐ a domineering
- ☐ an extraordinary
- ☐ a mundane

Question 7

The intricate, complex photographic process of the daguerreotype contributed to the rapid development of numerous related processes, _____ that included tintypes and calotypes.

- ☐ a proliferation
- ☐ a stagnation
- ☐ a primogenitor
- ☐ an archetype
- ☐ an antiquity
- ☐ a burgeoning

Question 8

The athlete, once well respected for his work with the anti-drug programs, was scorned for his _____ nature when medical tests proved he'd been using steroids for years.

- ☐ esteemed
- ☐ felonious
- ☐ sanguine
- ☐ disingenuous
- ☐ buoyant
- ☐ duplicitous

Question 9

The protestors acknowledged the leader's appeal to _____ violence, and walked quietly in the funeral processions instead of throwing rocks at police officers.

- ☐ mollify
- ☐ abjure
- ☐ eschew
- ☐ condone
- ☐ glorify
- ☐ manifest

Question 10

Diecast truck manufacturers release limited edition models with obscure commercial advertising in order to _____ their trucks and ensure that certain items become dedicated collectibles instead of toys.

- ☐ rarefy
- ☐ circulate
- ☐ investigate
- ☐ subtilize
- ☐ spur
- ☐ incite

Question 11

The *phacellophora camtschatica*, which can grow up to two feet in diameter, is more commonly referred to as the Fried Egg jellyfish because of its white bell and cloudy yellow organs, which give its tentacles a _____, semi-transparent look.

- ☐ caustic
- ☐ resplendent
- ☐ natatory
- ☐ diaphanous
- ☐ calamitous
- ☐ gossamer

Question 12

Before the Clone Wars, the Jedi were a powerful peace-keeping force in the galaxy, but they were unable to avoid _____ after Palpatine called out Order 66, which reprogrammed every clone trooper to immediately assassinate his Jedi masters.

- ☐ decimation
- ☐ sovereignty
- ☐ annihilation
- ☐ ingenuity
- ☐ misrepresentation
- ☐ ascendancy

Question 13

Hollywood studios, usually guided by their penchant for hiring A-list movie stars, are rethinking their strategies in an economy more suited to hiring _____ actors who command far less per picture than their celebrity counterparts, who can cost studios upward of 15 or 20 million dollars for one movie.

- ☐ luminary
- ☐ renowned
- ☐ fledgling
- ☐ neoteric
- ☐ exorbitant
- ☐ iniquitous

Question 14

Joseph was never outwardly perturbed by bad news, and was known as the _____ of composure.

- ☐ quintessence
- ☐ bane
- ☐ rector
- ☐ epitome
- ☐ antithesis
- ☐ regent

Question 15

The president could not tolerate dissent from his views, and so he only appointed people to his cabinet who were more _____ than advisors.

- ☐ pundits
- ☐ sycophants
- ☐ cynics
- ☐ toadies
- ☐ partisans
- ☐ authoritarians

Question 16

The young poet feared that her career may have prematurely reached its _____ after reading the encomium with which her first publication was met.

- ☐ apogee
- ☐ auspice
- ☐ coda
- ☐ nadir
- ☐ perigee
- ☐ zenith

Question 17

The philosopher's arguments were so _____ that it was nearly impossible to follow the logic from his premises to his conclusion.

- ☐ rhetorical
- ☐ libertine
- ☐ labyrinthine
- ☐ unscrupulous
- ☐ byzantine
- ☐ decorous

Question 18

After his embezzlement was discovered, the CEO was _____ by board members, shareholders, and customers alike.

- ☐ cachinnated
- ☐ blandished
- ☐ upbraided
- ☐ approbated
- ☐ caviled
- ☐ lambasted

While the new bistro's service was absolutely punctilious, the cuisine was rather _____.

- ☐ obsequious
- ☐ quotidian
- ☐ distasteful
- ☐ pedestrian
- ☐ gustatory
- ☐ pedantic

After mispronouncing the name of the leader of an allied nation, the secretary was quite ashamed; she had never before heard such _____ levied against her as the leader's angry response.

- ☐ a laudation
- ☐ a dictum
- ☐ a panegyric
- ☐ an approbation
- ☐ an invective
- ☐ a vituperation

DRILL 6

Question 1

The con artist was so _____ that he most often left his victims feeling pleased that they had given him their money.

- ☐ innocuous
- ☐ crafty
- ☐ cunning
- ☐ maladroit
- ☐ discrete
- ☐ unskillful

Question 2

Although the book reveals some surprising information about the sharp-eyed Secret-Service employees, most people already know that such people are far more _____ than the average citizen.

- ☐ potent
- ☐ robust
- ☐ weary
- ☐ vulnerable
- ☐ vigilant
- ☐ mindful

Question 3

The _____ at the gala was not conducive to enjoyment; the presence of many direct political rivals filled the air with tension.

- ☐ decor
- ☐ discourse
- ☐ ambience
- ☐ etiquette
- ☐ atmosphere
- ☐ diversion

Question 4

It is generally assumed to be _____ to increase taxes on the middle class without a proportional increase on the taxes of the upper class as well.

- ☐ untenable
- ☐ sporadic
- ☐ indefensible
- ☐ subtle
- ☐ dignified
- ☐ pardonable

Question 5

It is difficult to provide _____ proof for the existence of ghosts and other spiritual beings that remain unseen by the majority of the population.

- ☐ indisputable
- ☐ daunting
- ☐ uncanny
- ☐ momentous
- ☐ skeptical
- ☐ demonstrable

Question 6

The politician insisted that he did not seek to enrich himself during the campaign, but the ethics committee concluded that he was motivated by _____.

- ☐ charity
- ☐ greed
- ☐ estrangement
- ☐ avarice
- ☐ compassion
- ☐ apprehension

Question 7

The calamitous event transformed the once unspoiled seascape into the very embodiment of _____.

- ☐ cataclysm
- ☐ conflict
- ☐ determination
- ☐ melancholy
- ☐ tenacity
- ☐ obliteration

Question 8

The company's new president immediately embarked upon a strategy of reorganization, but informed investors that these initial steps, while the most urgent and _____, would be just the first among many changes required to turn the company around.

- ☐ unappealing
- ☐ trivial
- ☐ paramount
- ☐ exigent
- ☐ dispassionate
- ☐ insipid

Question 9

Concerned about being assigned the job of analyzing a poem which might be esoteric in meaning, Erika was delighted to be given instead Roethke's "The Waking," the _____ of which she embraced.

- ☐ cadency
- ☐ ambiguity
- ☐ cogency
- ☐ melancholy
- ☐ lucidity
- ☐ opacity

Question 10

To highlight Albert Einstein's image as a _____ scholar, there is an exaggerated tale floating around that his request to shut a window was the first sentence he had uttered in five years.

- ☐ loquacious
- ☐ consummate
- ☐ reticent
- ☐ judicious
- ☐ laconic
- ☐ garrulous

Question 11

Concerned about the noxious effects of pesticides on local rivers, Tess petitioned her local farmers to employ _____ amount of the repellent.

- ☐ a capacious
- ☐ an abiding
- ☐ a nominal
- ☐ an enduring
- ☐ a negligible
- ☐ a profuse

Question 12

Despite his lack of education and somewhat obtuse demeanor, the night watchman was relied upon by many for his _____ advice on matters of love and romance.

- ☐ insightful
- ☐ jejune
- ☐ pragmatic
- ☐ vapid
- ☐ expedient
- ☐ perspicacious

Question 13

Because his work as a department store Santa Claus is inherently periodic, Emile had to _____ as many assignments as he could during his busy period to earn enough money to cover his expenses during the off season.

- ☐ rebuke
- ☐ amass
- ☐ eschew
- ☐ garner
- ☐ relinquish
- ☐ disseminate

Question 14

Throughout the mid-2000s, many corporations viewed internet applications such as personal email and social media as detractors from productivity; however, most businesses have now embraced the power of these applications not only to _____ productivity, but also further their brands in the marketplace.

- ☐ bolster
- ☐ engender
- ☐ vilipend
- ☐ buttress
- ☐ depreciate
- ☐ supplant

Question 15

Darryl argued that the poet's latest volume was ultimately _____, containing no new ideas; indeed containing nothing but overt drivel.

- ☐ platitudinous
- ☐ natty
- ☐ jejune
- ☐ labyrinthine
- ☐ lax
- ☐ amorphous

Question 16

In Jay Gatsby, Fitzgerald has created a conundrum of a character: as he grows progressively more flagrant in his spending and his lifestyle, Gatsby also becomes progressively more charming such that readers are forced to simultaneously admire and abhor his _____.

- ☐ ignominy
- ☐ dissipation
- ☐ repute
- ☐ volubility
- ☐ profligacy
- ☐ stature

Question 17

Animated and _____ by the ideals of the Enlightenment, the political unrest that began the French Revolution eventually erupted into anarchy.

- ☐ obliterated
- ☐ fomented
- ☐ galvanized
- ☐ paralleled
- ☐ exemplified
- ☐ extirpated

Question 18

A good editor must be able to quickly _____ excellent submissions from a pile of dross, distinguishing the best offerings from the worst in an efficient manner.

- ☐ consolidate
- ☐ integrate
- ☐ finagle
- ☐ intimate
- ☐ winnow
- ☐ sift

Question 19

In her recent book *Palmeriste: A Biography*, Sklar argues that Palmeriste was a connoisseur of many things, rather than a dilettante; Brand believes this is a _____ distinction, obscuring the more relevant question of where exactly he got all of his money.

- ☐ critical
- ☐ cardinal
- ☐ nice
- ☐ baleful
- ☐ minute
- ☐ feckless

Question 20

Because political theorists often rely on jargon, their writing sometimes seems _____ to the general public, who cannot understand a word of it.

- ☐ risible
- ☐ vapid
- ☐ opaque
- ☐ abstruse
- ☐ equivocal
- ☐ uncanny

DRILL 7

Question 1

By the third day of being sick with the flu, her feelings of _____ were so strong, all she could do was lie on the couch, unable even to get up to shower.

- ☐ vitality
- ☐ innuendo
- ☐ lethargy
- ☐ freshness
- ☐ hunger
- ☐ weariness

Question 2

When he fell into the pit of vipers, Jake was instantly _____ about the possibility of getting bitten by a poisonous snake.

- ☐ distressed
- ☐ apprehensive
- ☐ amazed
- ☐ ambivalent
- ☐ optimistic
- ☐ equivocal

Question 3

Jane was so passionately insistent on her assertions during the negotiation that her _____ tone was noted as the main reason her team prevailed.

- ☐ compromised
- ☐ adamant
- ☐ unusual
- ☐ unsteady
- ☐ unwavering
- ☐ vacillating

Question 4

When the 25 dogs and cats escaped for the third time that month, the mayor publicly expressed his _____ regarding the clear and ongoing mismanagement of the city kennel.

- ☐ discontentment
- ☐ approval
- ☐ contempt
- ☐ reverence
- ☐ joy
- ☐ lethargy

Question 5

The young employee was more _____ by his new assignment than he seemed to be, for his confusion was disguised by his confident smile.

- ☐ perturbed
- ☐ discomposed
- ☐ placated
- ☐ vilified
- ☐ conciliated
- ☐ belabored

Question 6

Compulsory math and science courses are _____ requirements for many liberal arts students whose minds are more attuned to philosophical debate.

- ☐ facile
- ☐ stupefying
- ☐ meticulous
- ☐ elementary
- ☐ grievous
- ☐ onerous

Question 7

As _____ a dancer as she was, at least in the opinion of the general public, her failure to have trained at the illustrious Kirov School of Ballet precluded her from achieving the coveted title of *prima ballerina assoluta*.

- ☐ perfunctory
- ☐ evanescent
- ☐ consummate
- ☐ fulsome
- ☐ noisome
- ☐ virtuoso

Question 8

After months of research, the degree candidate was confident in the validity of her thesis, but certain key errors in methodology left the review committee _____.

- ☐ persuaded
- ☐ mollified
- ☐ dubious
- ☐ irked
- ☐ convinced
- ☐ incredulous

Question 9

Because the discovery of the ancient letters _____ the historian's claims about the inhabitants of that time, the historian must reconsider the premises of his life's work.

- ☐ innervates
- ☐ belies
- ☐ corroborates
- ☐ controverts
- ☐ anticipates
- ☐ validates

Question 10

The theater critic made an appeal in his most recent review for playwrights to avoid _____ characters and situations, for he could not sit through one more trite play.

- ☐ judicious
- ☐ banal
- ☐ rapturous
- ☐ expedient
- ☐ entrancing
- ☐ pedestrian

Question 11

Consider the _____ of the nature of war, the outcome of which can hardly be considered favorable even for those who emerge victorious.

- ☐ enormity
- ☐ exposition
- ☐ bombast
- ☐ austerity
- ☐ depravity
- ☐ hegemony

Question 12

The legitimacy of a fledgling political party is highly dependent on the decorum of its members, since the _____ behavior of any one person can be used to disparage an entire movement.

- ☐ garrulous
- ☐ debauched
- ☐ reticent
- ☐ profligate
- ☐ cogent
- ☐ capricious

Question 13

Although typically quite lucid in his explanations of his theories, James used words that were so _____ that the students asked him to review yesterday's discussion in its entirety.

- ☐ realistic
- ☐ obvious
- ☐ abstruse
- ☐ benevolent
- ☐ obscure
- ☐ disparate

Question 14

The Renaissance, Dutch masters, Impressionists, and Cubist paintings were all installed in the same museum gallery with what seemed to be no consideration to the arrangement, but closer examination revealed that the _____ was actually arranged in alphabetical order of work title.

- ☐ jumble
- ☐ littoral
- ☐ chromatic
- ☐ gallimaufry
- ☐ melisma
- ☐ diatribe

Question 15

The halcyon days of the new administration belied the president's _____ journey to the White House.

- ☐ facile
- ☐ tortuous
- ☐ anfractuous
- ☐ imperial
- ☐ dexterous
- ☐ felicitous

Question 16

After being defeated in 2007, the Australian Liberal party needed to find a leader who could return them to power; they hope that the current leader, a _____ social conservative who leads the opposition on a number of issues, including stem cell research and carbon trading, and who wrote a book with the telling title *Battlelines*, may be the man for the job.

- ☐ compliant
- ☐ circumspect
- ☐ diffident
- ☐ pugnacious
- ☐ milquetoast
- ☐ disputatious

Question 17

The bill pushed through by the foreign government was touted as increasing transparency, professional integrity, and independence for the media; in reality, though, the bill was simply a way for the officials to protect their cronyism from the newspapers that had been _____ in their attempts to expose government corruption.

- ☐ assiduous
- ☐ lackadaisical
- ☐ perfunctory
- ☐ eschewed
- ☐ abjured
- ☐ sedulous

Question 18

The preening emperor loved to display sartorial splendor, and regularly gave great attention to the detail of his _____.

- ☐ panegyric
- ☐ raiment
- ☐ fetes
- ☐ caparison
- ☐ soirees
- ☐ oratory

Question 19

Though Marian thought her grandmother's hat was unquestionably _____, the young woman respected her elders enough to make no comment on her grandmother's fashion choices.

- ☐ iconoclastic
- ☐ imperious
- ☐ haughty
- ☐ gaudy
- ☐ garish
- ☐ heretical

Question 20

The more mature students in the dining hall quickly learned to avoid any table where Fred was sitting because he constantly interjected _____ remarks into every conversation going on nearby.

- ☐ puerile
- ☐ crude
- ☐ limpid
- ☐ inimical
- ☐ jejune
- ☐ insidious

ANSWERS

Drill 1

1. benign, innocuous
2. fervency, zeal
3. dexterous, adroit
4. precarious, tenuous
5. placate, mollify
6. copious, profuse
7. rife with, replete with
8. a discomfiting, a mortifying
9. polemical, divisive
10. incipient, nascent
11. taciturn, laconic
12. paucity, dearth
13. an inveterate, a chronic
14. guileless, ingenuous
15. antediluvian, superannuated
16. perspicuous, manifest
17. bucolic, quiescent
18. eccentricities, idiosyncrasies
19. prodigal, profligate
20. an encomium, a panegyric

Drill 2

1. cacophonous, discordant
2. revered, esteemed
3. implicit, tacit
4. auspiciously, promisingly
5. benevolence, magnanimity
6. paucity, dearth
7. arduous, onerous
8. inveigle, entice
9. verdant, bountiful
10. misanthropic, curmudgeonly
11. an epicure, a gourmand
12. stygian, gloomy
13. spendthrift, prodigal
14. voracious, rapacious
15. enormity, iniquity
16. quintessence, epitome
17. bedizened, caparisoned
18. moralistic, sententious
19. imperious, peremptory
20. puerile, callow

Drill 3

1. prolific, fruitful
2. a genial, an affable
3. meticulously, fastidiously
4. critical, constructive
5. commend, extol
6. flippantly, thoughtlessly
7. sanguine, buoyant
8. staunch, zealous
9. a cursory, a perfunctory
10. omnipresent, ubiquitous
11. oblique, allusive
12. censured, excoriated
13. didactic, edifying
14. splenetic, churlish
15. paramount, salient
16. censure, disapprobation
17. periphrasis, circumlocutions
18. discernment, acumen
19. pernicious, deleterious
20. exsiccated, anhydrated

Drill 4

1. eloquent, articulate
2. recanted, disavowed
3. abate, dwindle
4. affable, genial
5. augment, escalate
6. maxim, proverb
7. largess, philanthropy
8. mundane, insipid
9. tirades, diatribes
10. chicanery, wile
11. predilection, propensity
12. discord, dissension
13. check, curb
14. abhorrent, invidious
15. abstruse, opaque
16. nascent, inchoate
17. saturnine, lachrymose
18. diaphanous, gossamer
19. looming, impending
20. fickle, inconstant

Drill 5

1. muddled, obfuscated
2. wisdom, sagacity
3. serpentine, tortuous
4. perceptive, astute
5. divine, idyllic
6. a pedestrian, a mundane
7. a proliferation, a burgeoning
8. disingenuous, duplicitous
9. abjure, eschew
10. rarefy, subtilize
11. diaphanous, gossamer
12. decimation, annihilation
13. fledgling, neoteric
14. quintessence, epitome
15. sycophants, toadies
16. apogee, zenith
17. labyrinthine, byzantine
18. upbraided, lambasted
19. quotidian, pedestrian
20. an invective, a vituperation

Drill 6

1. crafty, cunning
2. vigilant, mindful
3. ambiance, atmosphere
4. untenable, indefensible
5. indisputable, demonstrable
6. greed, avarice
7. cataclysm, obliteration
8. paramount, exigent
9. cogency, lucidity
10. reticent, laconic
11. a nominal, a negligible
12. insightful, perspicacious
13. amass, garner
14. bolster, buttress
15. platitudinous, jejune
16. dissipation, profligacy
17. fomented, galvanized
18. winnow, sift
19. nice, minute
20. opaque, abstruse

Drill 7

1. lethargy, weariness
2. distressed, apprehensive
3. adamant, unwavering
4. discontentment, contempt
5. perturbed, discomposed
6. grievous, onerous
7. consummate, virtuoso
8. dubious, incredulous
9. belies, controverts
10. banal, pedestrian
11. enormity, depravity
12. debauched, profligate
13. abstruse, obscure
14. jumble, gallimaufry
15. tortuous, anfractuous
16. pugnacious, disputatious
17. assiduous, sedulous
18. raiment, caparison
19. gaudy, garish
20. puerile, jejune

EXPLANATIONS

Drill 1

1. **benign** and **innocuous**

    The trigger *despite* indicates that the reefs had not justified the environmentalist's *initial fears*, so you need a word such as *positive* or *harmless* in the blank. Neither *caustic* nor *interminable* means *positive* or *harmless*, so eliminate (C) and (D). Neither *unfounded*, which means *groundless*, nor *plaintive*, which means *mournful*, makes sense in the blank; eliminate (A) and (F). Both *benign* and *innocuous* can mean *harmless*, so (B) and (E) give you appropriate, equivalent sentences.

2. **fervency** and **zeal**

    Recycle the clue and put *enthusiasm* in the blank. Both *indifference* and *heedlessness* are nearly the opposite of what you are looking for, so eliminate (B) and (E). Neither *cessation*, which means *stoppage*, nor *rhetoric*, which is the art of effective or persuasive use of language, makes sense in the blank, so eliminate (A) and (C). Both *fervency* and *zeal* can mean *enthusiasm*, so (D) and (F) give you appropriate, equivalent sentences.

3. **dexterous** and **adroit**

    The clue *innumerable fruitless attempts* indicates that Allen lacked the crucial qualification to juggle, so a word that means something like *manually coordinated* will fit the blank. Both *lumbering* and *awkward* are nearly the opposite of what you're looking for, so eliminate (B) and (F). Neither *sedate*, which means *calm,* nor *implicit*, which means *implied,* makes sense in the blank, so eliminate (A) and (D). Both *dexterous* and *adroit* can mean *manually coordinated,* so (C) and (E) give you appropriate, equivalent sentences.

4. **precarious** and **tenuous**

    If Alexander's generals broke up his empire *after his death*, then its *cohesion* must have been *weak* or *short-lived*. Both *abiding* and *protracted* are nearly the opposite of what you're looking for, so eliminate (A) and (C). Neither *redoubled*, which means *made twice as great*, nor *renowned*, which means *famous,* makes sense in the blank, so eliminate (D) and (E). Both *precarious* and *tenuous* can mean *weak,* so (B) and (F) give you appropriate, equivalent sentences.

5. **placate** and **mollify**

    If you're comfortable with the meaning of *propitiatory*, you can recycle the verb *propitiate* into the blank; if not, the clue *icy stare and aloof demeanor* can tell you—like Johann—that the gifts didn't calm her anger. Both *exacerbate* and *aggravate* are nearly the opposite of what you're looking for, so eliminate (C) and (D). Neither *vilify*, which means *to speak ill of,* nor *garner*, which means *to amass or acquire,* makes sense in the blank, so eliminate (A) and (B). Both *placate* and *mollify* can mean *to calm,* so (E) and (F) give you appropriate, equivalent sentences.

6.   **copious** and **profuse**

If they believe the benefits of the *energy-producing ingredients* increase *proportionally,* the athletes would want to eat more of the energy bars, so you need a word that means something like *plentiful.* Both *scant* and *measured* are nearly the opposite of what you're looking for, so eliminate (A) and (E). Neither *furtive,* which means *stealthy,* nor *solvent,* which means *capable of paying debts,* makes sense in the blank, so eliminate (B) and (D). Both *copious* and *profuse* can mean *plentiful,* so (C) and (F) give you appropriate, equivalent sentences.

7.   **rife with** and **replete with**

The bill is described as *comprehensive* and has been *bemoaned* by *proponents of small government,* so something like *full of* would make sense in the blank. Both *deficient in* and *unencumbered by* are nearly the opposite of what you're looking for, so eliminate (C) and (D). Neither *elucidated by,* which means *clarified by,* nor *exempted from* makes sense in the blank, so eliminate (A) and (F). Both *rife with* and *replete with* mean *full of,* so (B) and (E) give you appropriate, equivalent sentences.

8.   **a discomfiting** and **a mortifying**

Recycle the clue *embarrassing* into the blank. Both *assuaging* and *bolstering* are nearly the opposite of what you're looking for, so eliminate (B) and (E). The impact may be *monumental,* but that answer choice isn't sufficiently negative, so eliminate (C); *virulent,* on the other hand is too strong, so eliminate (A). Both *discomfiting* and *mortifying* can mean *embarrassing,* so (D) and (F) give you appropriate, equivalent sentences.

9.   **polemical** and **divisive**

Samuel Huntington's ideas are *still passionately debated,* so they must be described as ideas that people are likely to disagree about. His opinions may well have been *pedantic* or *hegemonic,* but those words do not necessarily lead to disagreement. The same goes for *zealous,* which, in addition, is used to describe people, rather than their ideas. The correct answers are (C) and (E), since *polemical* means *arguing passionately,* and *divisive* means *causing a disagreement.*

10.   **incipient** and **nascent**

The sentence tells you that there was no plant life in the area before, based on the time trigger word *previously.* Furthermore, if humans will be able to live in the area some day, then you know that plant life being described must be alive and flourishing. This eliminates *static, waning,* and *flagging.* *Fervent* is used to describe human feelings or something that is very hot, so it does not work in this context. *Incipient* and *nascent* both mean that the plant life has recently come into being and are the correct answers.

11.   **taciturn** and **laconic**

You have multiple clues here: Michael *generally kept to himself,* rather than being *garrulous,* and the way his teachers remember him is *Regardless of* his *long-winded answers.* Thus, you'll need a word that means *quiet* or *not talkative* for the blank. Both *voluble* and *prolix* are nearly the opposite of what you're looking for, so eliminate (B) and (F). Neither *querulous* nor *disinterested* makes sense in the blank, so eliminate (D) and (E). Both *taciturn* and *laconic* mean *not talkative,* so (A) and (C) give you appropriate, equivalent sentences.

12.   **paucity** and **dearth**

The snow provides the fresh water so if there isn't much snowfall, the cities will be lacking water. Choices (A), (D), and (F) all have the opposite meaning and *proliferation* and *burgeoning* are not really words that could be used to describe *run-off* either. A *conduit* is a connector or pipe, which isn't appropriate for the blank, so eliminate (B). *Paucity* and *dearth* both indicate that something is lacking and are the correct choices.

13.   **an inveterate** and **a chronic**

The girl *could always find something else that displeased her,* which means that she must be a *habitual* complainer. Choices (B) and (C) are synonymous with each other, but nothing in the sentence supports the description of the complaints as *sad* or *mournful.* Neither *oblique* nor *abysmal* makes sense in the blank, so eliminate (D) and (F). Both *inveterate* and *chronic* mean *habitual,* so (A) and (E) give you appropriate, equivalent sentences.

14.   **guileless** and **ingenuous**

The different-direction trigger word to focus on here is *instead,* which tells you that the type of person she is should be different from one who has a secret. *Inscrutable* is similar in meaning to *an enigma behind the celebrated smile,* so (E) is incorrect. Lisa del Giocondo may well have been *dulcet* or *comely,* but there is no supporting evidence for these words in the sentence. Since you are looking for a word that refers to someone who doesn't keep secrets, (B), *guileless,* and (F), *ingenuous,* are the best answers.

15.   **antediluvian** and **superannuated**

The sentence contains the trigger word *Though,* indicating a shift in the meaning of the sentence. In the first part, the futurist *conceded* that the iPhone was *revolutionary;* thus the second part must mean that it was old-fashioned. Check the answers. Only *antediluvian* and *superannuated* mean *old-fashioned.* Choices (D) and (E) are the best answers.

16. **perspicuous** and **manifest**

Gainsaid means *contradicted*, so the words that will fill in the blank will roughly mean *transparent*. *Abstruse* and *cryptic* both mean *difficult to understand*, so eliminate (B) and (E). Neither *aesthetic*, which means *concerned with beauty*, nor *recalcitrant*, which means *resistant to authority*, fits the meaning you need; eliminate (D) and (F). Both *perspicuous* and *manifest* can mean *easily understood*, so (A) and (C) produce logical sentences with the same meaning.

17. **bucolic** and **quiescent**

Hyperbolic means *exaggerated*, so the correct answers will be words that mean something a bit more extreme than *quaint* and also contrast with the imposing presence of *mining equipment*. Choices (C) and (E) give you synonymous meanings, but nothing in the sentence supports the description of the area as *hateful*. Neither *germane* nor *gentrified* makes sense in the blank, so eliminate (A) and (B). Both *bucolic* and *quiescent* can mean *peaceful* or *pastoral*, which is a bit more extreme than *quaint*, so (D) and (F) give you appropriate, equivalent sentences.

18. **eccentricities** and **idiosyncrasies**

The sentence says that *local* commercials are a *tonic* or "cure" for *homogeneity* or "sameness," so a good word would be *quirks* or *individualities*. Check the answers. Both *eccentricities* and *idiosyncrasies* mean *quirks*. The best answers are (B) and (F).

19. **prodigal** and **profligate**

The *spending*, combined with *bad investments*, left the boxer *insolvent*, so you need something like *excessive* for the blank. Both *parsimonious* and *penurious* are nearly the opposite of what you're looking for, so eliminate (A) and (B). Neither *perfidious*, which means *disloyal*, nor *pugnacious*, which means *belligerent*, makes sense in the blank, so eliminate (C) and (F). Both *prodigal* and *profligate* can mean *excessive*, particularly in reference to *spending*, so (D) and (E) give you appropriate, equivalent sentences.

20. **an encomium** and **a panegyric**

Since the blank refers to something delivered by a *poet or orator* and meant to *lavish praise*, you need something like *poem of praise* or *speech of praise*. Three of the choices are the wrong kind of writing: both an *elegy* and a *jeremiad* express lamentation, and a *philippic* expresses condemnation, so eliminate (B), (D), and (E). A *compendium* is a brief summary, so eliminate (A). Both *encomium* and *panegyric* can mean *poem or speech of praise*, so (C) and (F) give you appropriate, equivalent sentences.

Drill 2

1.   **cacophonous** and **discordant**

   What she heard *disheartened* the band director—and this despite *having steeled herself for the worst*—so you need a word that means *bad-sounding.* Both *euphonious* and *harmonious* are nearly the opposite of what you're looking for, so eliminate (B) and (F). Neither *arduous*, which means *difficult,* nor *ample,* which means *sufficient,* makes sense in the blank, so eliminate (A) and (D). Both *cacophonous* and *discordant* can mean *bad-sounding,* so (C) and (E) give you appropriate, equivalent sentences.

2.   **revered** and **esteemed**

   All the sentence tells you about Bede is that he earned the epithet *venerable,* so something like *venerated* or *honored* would make sense in the blank. Both *defamed* and *reviled* are nearly the opposite of what you're looking for, so eliminate (A) and (F). Neither *consoled,* which means *gave comfort to,* nor *mitigated,* which means *made less severe,* makes sense in the blank, so eliminate (B) and (E). Both *revered* and *esteemed* can mean *honored,* so (C) and (D) give you appropriate, equivalent sentences.

3.   **implicit** and **tacit**

   The sentence contrasts the *rules of etiquette* with *the detailed written regulations regarding play,* so you need something like *vague* or *unwritten* for the blank. Both *express* and *manifest* are nearly the opposite of what you're looking for, so eliminate (C) and (F). Be careful about *laconic*: it means using few words, but not unspoken, so eliminate (B). *Reclusive,* which means *withdrawn from society,* doesn't make sense in the blank, so eliminate (E). Both *implicit* and *tacit* can mean *unwritten,* so (A) and (D) give you appropriate, equivalent sentences.

4.   **auspiciously** and **promisingly**

   The trigger word *but* is key in this sentence because it denotes a reversal over time. Since you are told that *those who had fought for its ratification* were *discouraged,* the word *but* tells you they were once encouraged. Therefore, *auspiciously* and *promisingly* fit the blank, as they tell the same story as encouraged. *Bleakly* and *unfavorably* tell the opposite story and are not correct. *Suspiciously* means distrustful and *ineffectually* means useless, so neither word fits the meaning of the blank.

5.   **benevolence** and **magnanimity**

   Instead of is a trigger that tells you that the word in the blank must mean the opposite of *a selfish need to meddle. Benevolence* and *magnanimity* both mean *showing good will toward others*, which is the opposite of selfishness. *Elegance* and *refinement* are synonyms that mean *gracious style,* which is not the opposite of selfishness. *Gaiety* means *happiness* and *viscosity* means *stickiness,* neither of which is the direct opposite of selfishness.

6. **paucity** and **dearth**

Since he had *few former employers who would be laudatory about his past projects*, Robert could not provide more than a *few* references. Both *dearth* and *paucity* can mean few, so (E) and (F) give you appropriate, equivalent sentences. Both *multitude* and *myriad* mean the opposite of what you're looking for, so eliminate (A) and (C). Likewise, *array* and *potpourri* are synonyms that mean assortment, so eliminate (B) and (D).

7. **arduous** and **onerous**

The trigger *while* indicates that most of the tasks, which are described as *undemanding*, differ from the one described in the blank; hence, you need a word like *demanding*. Both *arduous* and *onerous* can mean *demanding,* so (C) and (D) give you appropriate, equivalent sentences. Choices (A) and (F) give you synonymous meanings, but nothing in the sentence supports the description of the tasks as clear.

8. **inveigle** and **entice**

The blank describes what the politician is doing: she *beguilingly greeted a room full of constituents* to get their support, so a word like *convince* would make sense. Both *alienate* and *estrange* are nearly the opposite of what you're looking for, so eliminate (A) and (E). Neither *abase*, which means *to degrade,* nor *eviscerate*, which means *to gut,* makes sense in the blank, so eliminate (B) and (D). Both *inveigle* and *entice* can mean *convince,* so (C) and (F) give you appropriate, equivalent sentences.

9. **verdant** and **bountiful**

The time triggers *after* and *once* indicate that the *landscape* is no longer *arid*, so you need a word that means something like *not dry and lifeless.* Both *barren* and *desolate* are nearly the opposite of what you're looking for, so eliminate (B) and (D). Neither *innocuous*, which means *harmless,* nor *limpid*, which means *clear,* is supported by the sentence, so eliminate (A) and (F). Both *verdant* and *bountiful* can mean *not dry and lifeless,* so (C) and (E) give you appropriate, equivalent sentences.

10. **misanthropic** and **curmudgeonly**

The man's response to visitors was that he *shooed them away*, so you need a word that means something like *not social.* Both *garrulous* and *affable* are nearly the opposite of what you're looking for, so eliminate (E) and (F). Neither *sarcastic* nor *chauvinistic* is supported in the sentence, so eliminate (C) and (D). Both *misanthropic* and *curmudgeonly* can mean *not social,* so (A) and (B) give you appropriate, equivalent sentences.

11. **an epicure** and **a gourmand**

The time trigger *used to be* indicates that Eileen is no longer *a picky eater*, so you need a word that means something like *someone who is adventurous with food.* Both *philistine* and *vulgarian* are nearly the opposite of what you're looking for, so eliminate (B) and (F). Neither *recluse* nor *chauvinist* makes sense in the blank, so eliminate (A) and (D). Both *epicure* and *gourmand* can mean *someone who is adventurous with food*, so (C) and (E) give you appropriate, equivalent sentences.

12. **stygian** and **gloomy**

The blank describes the *recesses of the rooms*, so recycle the clue *dark*. Both *gloomy* and *stygian* can mean dark, so (C) and (D) give you appropriate, equivalent sentences. If you don't know *stygian*—it's the adjectival form of Styx, the river crossed to get to the Greek afterlife, and so literally means *dark as hell*—use your POE. Choices (E) and (F) are synonyms, but aren't supported by the sentence. The recesses may be *empty*, but, again, that can't be supported by the sentence; eliminate (A). *Cacophonous* means having a harsh or discordant sound, so (B) wouldn't make sense in a room where the agents' *ears were attuned to the slightest disturbance.*

13. **spendthrift** and **prodigal**

The text tells you that the man is *anxious to avoid* a label, so his actions must contrast with the label he is trying to avoid. He wants to *present a frugal picture*, so he must be saving money. Therefore, the missing word must mean something like *reckless spender*. Choices (C) and (E) could be attractive if you miss the contrast between the clue and the blank; these words mean *stingy person* and are opposite of what you need. Choices (D) and (F) are synonyms, but there aren't any clues in the sentence that indicate the man is seeking pleasure. That leaves (A) and (B), both of which mean *wasteful spender,* as the best answers.

14. **voracious** and **rapacious**

The clue here is that the pirate can't *satisfy his craving*, so you need a word like *insatiable* or *greedy* for the blank; *rapacious* and *voracious* give you appropriate, equivalent sentences. Both *ebullient* and *effusive* are nearly the opposite of what you're looking for, so eliminate (B) and (F). *Raffish* and *showy* could describe a pirate, but there's no context to support that pair of synonyms, so eliminate (A) and (D).

15. **enormity** and **iniquity**

The clue is that *the criminal carried out heinous acts*, so the blank describing the criminal must be something like *evil*. Both *enormity* and *iniquity* can mean evil, so (B) and (D) give you appropriate, equivalent sentences. Choices (C) and (E) give equivalent meanings, but the sentence doesn't support the characterization of the criminal as clever. Neither *pulchritude*, which means beauty, nor *perfidy*, which means disloyalty, makes sense in the blank, so eliminate (A) and (F).

16. **quintessence** and **epitome**

Since the text after the colon describes how Cincinnatus exemplified both halves of the farmer-soldier ideal, you might say he was a *perfect example* of that ideal. Both *antithesis* and *contraposition* are nearly the opposite of what you're looking for, so eliminate (B) and (E). Neither *supplicant* nor *veracity* makes sense in the blank, so eliminate (A) and (F). Both *quintessence* and *epitome* mean *perfect example*, so (C) and (D) give you appropriate, equivalent sentences.

17.   **bedizened** and **caparisoned**

The trigger *in contrast to* indicates that the *colorful* depictions of castles differ from *the stark facades of their surviving ruins*, so you need a word like *decorated* for the blank. Both *bedizened* and *caparisoned* can mean *decorated,* so (C) and (D) give you appropriate, equivalent sentences. Choices (A) and (B) would also give equivalent meanings, but nothing in the sentence suggests the castles were *weakened*. Neither *extirpated*, which means *exterminated,* nor *fomented*, which means *incited,* makes sense in the sentence, so eliminate (E) and (F).

18.   **moralistic** and **sententious**

Recycle the clue *sanctimonious and self-righteous* into the blank. Both *ingenuous* and *unaffected* are nearly the opposite of what you're looking for, so eliminate (A) and (F). Neither *punctilious*, which means *overly concerned with precise formalities,* nor *salacious*, which means *obscene,* is supported by any clues in the sentence, so eliminate (C) and (D). Both *moralistic* and *sententious* can mean *sanctimonious and self-righteous,* so (B) and (E) give you appropriate, equivalent sentences.

19.   **imperious** and **peremptory**

The blank refers to the tone of the chair's remarks, which offended people *accustomed to being addressed in a more collegial and egalitarian manner.* Thus, you need a word that means *non-collegial* or *non-egalitarian*; a simple word like *bossy* works well. Choices (D) and (E) give roughly synonymous meanings, but nothing in the sentence supports the idea that the speech was *optimistic*. Neither *ignominious*, which means *shameful,* nor *saturnine*, which means *gloomy,* makes sense in the blank, so eliminate (A) and (F). Both *imperious* and *peremptory* can mean *bossy,* so (B) and (C) give you appropriate, equivalent sentences.

20.   **puerile** and **callow**

Hannah's comments were *Meant to demonstrate an air of sophistication and worldliness,* but instead showed that *she was not yet mature enough for the corporate world,* so a word that means *unsophisticated* or *immature* would make sense in the blank. Choices (B) and (F) are roughly synonymous in meaning, but nothing in the sentence supports the description of Hannah as *corruptible* or *motivated by a desire for money*. Neither *adroit* nor *indolent* makes sense in the blank, so eliminate (A) and (E). Both *puerile* and *callow* mean *immature,* so (C) and (D) give you appropriate, equivalent sentences.

Drill 3

1.   **prolific** and **fruitful**

The clue here is that Plath *produced just two volumes*. This phrase, in addition to the comparison to the number of volumes her husband produced, tells you that she did not produce many. Remember that before the blank you have the trigger word *not*, so you need a word that means productive. Choices (A), (B), (C), and (D) are all adjectives that describe what Plath might or might not have been, but they do not fit the given clue. Choices (E) and (F) are correct because they are synonyms of *productive*.

2.   **a genial** and **an affable**

The clown *invokes laughter and enjoyment*, so he must represent a happy character. *Ace* and *cracker-jack* are synonyms that refer to someone with a certain talent, which may be true of the clown, but these answers are not supported by the clues. *Artful* may sound like an appropriate answer, but, in addition to meaning skilled, it can mean *sly* or *crafty*. None of these are the right definitions. *Surly* has the opposite connotation of *happy*, so the correct answers are (C) and (F), which both mean *friendly or pleasant*.

3.   **meticulously** and **fastidiously**

Recycle the clue *carefully* into the blank. Choices (B) and (D) can be eliminated; they give synonymous meanings, but nothing in the sentence supports the idea that the photographer was rushed. Neither *subversively*, which means *rebelliously*, nor *hysterically*, which means *characterized by irrationality due to uncontrollable emotion*, is supported by the sentence, so eliminate (C) and (F). Both *meticulously* and *fastidiously* can mean *carefully*, so (A) and (E) give you appropriate, equivalent sentences.

4.   **critical** and **constructive**

Before the workshop, the writers' comments were *general and unhelpful*; the time triggers in the sentence tell you that things were different *after finishing the editing workshop*, so you need a word like *specific* or *helpful* in the blank. Three of the choices—*cursory*, *superficial*, and *amateurish*—are nearly the opposite of what you're looking for, so eliminate (A), (C), and (D). *Derisive*, which means *scornful*, isn't supported by the sentence, so eliminate (B). Both *critical* and *constructive* can describe comments that are specific and helpful, so (E) and (F) give you appropriate, equivalent sentences.

5. **commend** and **extol**

The trigger *while* indicates that the *admirers* do the opposite of the *others*, who *disparage* it, so something like *praise* would make sense in the blank. Both *defame* and *underrate* are nearly the opposite of what you're looking for, so eliminate (A) and (E). Choices (B) and (C) give roughly synonymous meanings, but aren't supported by the sentence. Both *commend* and *extol* can mean *praise*, so (D) and (F) give you appropriate, equivalent sentences.

6. **flippantly** and **thoughtlessly**

The professor was *disheartened* because Tom didn't seem to care about his grade, so a word that means *without care* would make sense in the blank. Both *gingerly* and *delicately* are nearly the opposite of what you're looking for, so eliminate (A) and (F). Neither *timidly*, which means *fearfully*, nor *prudently*, which means *cautiously,* is supported by the sentence, so eliminate (C) and (D). Both *flippantly* and *thoughtlessly* can mean *without care*, so (B) and (E) give you appropriate, equivalent sentences.

7. **sanguine** and **buoyant**

The clue here is that the investor's mood *seemed incongruous* in light of the bad news about the stock market; since *incongruous* means *out of place*, you need a word like *happy* for the blank. Both *inconsolable* and *funereal* are nearly the opposite of what you're looking for, so eliminate (C) and (E). Neither *enervated*, which means *weakened*, nor *sardonic*, which means *mocking and derisive,* is supported by the sentence, so eliminate (A) and (D). Both *sanguine* and *buoyant* can mean *happy*, so (B) and (F) give you appropriate, equivalent sentences.

8. **staunch** and **zealous**

The blank describes fans who would wait *in line for hours* to *talk to artists* and buy *toy variants*, so a word like *devoted* would make sense. Choices (B) and (E) give roughly synonymous meanings, but nothing in the sentence supports the idea that the fans smelled bad. Neither *hirsute*, which means *hairy*, nor *impecunious*, which means *poor,* is supported by the sentence, so eliminate (C) and (F). Both *staunch* and *zealous* can mean *devoted,* so (A) and (D) give you appropriate, equivalent sentences.

9. **a cursory** and **a perfunctory**

The blank describes the kind of *proofreading* that would miss *errors in spelling, diction, and idiom*, so a word like *sloppy* or *hasty* would make sense—anything that suggests a lack of attention to detail. Both *fastidious* and *meticulous* are nearly the opposite of what you're looking for, so eliminate (D) and (E). Neither *artless*, which means *without guile*, nor *extraneous*, which means *irrelevant,* is supported by the sentence, so eliminate (A) and (C). Both *cursory* and *perfunctory* can mean *inattentive to detail,* so (B) and (F) give you appropriate, equivalent sentences.

10.   **omnipresent** and **ubiquitous**

Your word for the blank needs to reflect the idea that Eno is *everywhere,* so something like *common* or *prevalent* would make sense. Choices (B) and (E) give roughly synonymous meanings, but nothing in the sentence supports the idea that Eno is disreputable. Neither *omnivorous,* which means *eating all foods,* nor *fortuitous,* which means *accidental,* is supported by the sentence, so eliminate (A) and (C). Both *omnipresent* and *ubiquitous* mean *present everywhere*—like sodium and divine beings—so (D) and (F) give you appropriate, equivalent sentences.

11.   **oblique** and **allusive**

The blank describes the kind of *meanings* that don't become clear for years, so you need something like *hidden* or *unclear.* Both *manifest* and *lucid* are nearly the opposite of what you're looking for, so eliminate (B) and (F). Neither *banal,* which means *trite and commonplace,* nor *nascent,* which means *newly formed,* is supported by the sentence, so eliminate (A) and (D). Both *oblique* and *allusive* can mean *unclear,* so (C) and (E) give you appropriate, equivalent sentences.

12.   **censured** and **excoriated**

Having committed an expensive error, Whitman might reasonably expect to be *criticized* or *blamed.* Both *lauded* and *extolled* are nearly the opposite of what you're looking for, so eliminate (D) and (F). Neither *instigated,* which means *incited,* nor *repatriated,* which means *returned to one's land of citizenship,* is supported by the sentence, so eliminate (C) and (E). Both *censured* and *excoriated* can mean *criticized,* so (A) and (B) give you appropriate, equivalent sentences.

13.   **didactic** and **edifying**

The colon indicates that the *purpose* will agree with the information in the second part of the sentence, where *the young audience* is learning *advanced vocabulary*; a word that means something like *teaching* would make sense. Both *obfuscating* and *mystifying* are nearly the opposite of what you're looking for, so eliminate (B) and (F). Neither *aggrandizing,* which means *making larger or more powerful,* nor *ephemeral,* which means *short-lived,* is supported by the sentence, so eliminate (D) and (E). Both *didactic* and *edifying* can mean *intended to instruct,* so (A) and (C) give you appropriate, equivalent sentences.

14.   **splenetic** and **churlish**

The blank describes *comments* that were startling, despite the author's reputation as antisocial, so something that means *antisocial* or *unfriendly* would make sense. Both *simpatico* and *winsome* are nearly the opposite of what you're looking for, so eliminate (A) and (E). Choices (B) and (C) give synonymous meanings, but nothing in the sentence supports the idea that the author is hard to understand. Both *splenetic* and *churlish* can mean *unfriendly,* so (D) and (F) give you appropriate, equivalent sentences.

15. **paramount** and **salient**

The blank describes the *role* played by the kind of *evidence* that would justify a decision to continue the investigation, so a word that means something like *important* would make sense. Both *negligible* and *marginal* are nearly the opposite of what you're looking for, so eliminate (B) and (F). Choices (D) and (E) give roughly synonymous meanings as well, but nothing in the sentence supports the description of the *role* as dishonest. Both *paramount* and *salient* can mean *important,* so (A) and (C) give you appropriate, equivalent sentences.

16. **censure** and **disapprobation**

The blank describes what consumers demonstrate when *boycotting companies,* so a word like *disapproval* would make sense in the blank. Both *endorsement* and *ratification* are nearly the opposite of what you're looking for, so eliminate (A) and (B). Neither *debilitation,* which means *weakening,* nor *machinations,* which means *schemes,* is supported by the sentence, so eliminate (D) and (E). Both *censure* and *disapprobation* can mean *disapproval,* so (C) and (F) give you appropriate, equivalent sentences.

17. **periphrasis** and **circumlocutions**

The military is using *anodyne phrases* to *gloss reality,* so a word that means something like *euphemisms* or *unclear statements.* Both *elucidation* and *dysphemisms* are nearly the opposite of what you're looking for, so eliminate (A) and (F). Neither *prevarication,* which means *untruth,* nor *hyperbole,* which means *exaggeration,* is supported by the sentence, so eliminate (C) and (E). Both *periphrasis* and *circumlocutions* can mean *unclear statements,* so (B) and (D) give you appropriate, equivalent sentences.

18. **discernment** and **acumen**

The semicolon trigger indicates that the two parts of the sentence will agree, so recycle the clue *understanding* into the blank or use a simple word like *knowledge.* Both *incognizance* and *nescience* are the opposite of what you're looking for, so eliminate (B) and (E). Neither *somnolence,* which means *drowsiness,* nor *belletrism,* which means *engagement in the genre of literature known as belles-lettres,* is supported by the sentence, so eliminate (D) and (F). Both *discernment* and *acumen* can mean *understanding,* so (A) and (C) give you appropriate, equivalent sentences.

19. **pernicious** and **deleterious**

The sentence tells you that *animals give predators advanced warning of their danger,* so you know the bright colors are warning signs. The *while* trigger changes the direction of the second part of the sentence, which you can see with the mention of the *harmless scarlet kingsnake,* but then there's another contrast with the *simply mimic* phrase. This brings you back to the animals that are *unpalatable or dangerous.* You can recycle *dangerous* for the blank. Eliminate (B) right away, because if the animals are dangerous, they definitely aren't friendly. Choice (D) might initially look appealing, but it actually means *beautiful*. While the animals might be brightly colored, you're looking for something that means *dangerous*, so you can eliminate that answer. You're left with two sets of synonyms, (A) and (E) and (C) and (F). The words in the second set, (C) and (F), mean *edible*. If you missed one of the contrast triggers, you might be tempted to go with that pair, but because you have the two different changes of direction, you can eliminate them. That leaves *pernicious* and *deleterious* as the best answers.

20.   **exsiccated** and **anhydrated**

The topic of the text is mummification, which deals with *drying out the body* and *preventing decomposition*. There is a contrast, indicated by the *while* trigger, between the *Egyptian pharaoh* mummies and the *Tarim mummies*. The text tells you that the Egyptian mummies were *intentionally* preserved, so you can fill in the blank with something to indicate the Tarim mummies were *naturally preserved*. Choices (B) and (C) could be tempting, because the mummies were discovered, but that's not what the missing word means. Choice (A) has nothing to do with the context of the sentence, and (D) is the opposite of what you're looking for. Both *exsiccated* and *anhydrated* can mean *dried out*, so (E) and (F) give you appropriate, equivalent sentences.

Drill 4

1.   **eloquent** and **articulate**

To prepare for his speech, Thomas was *dutifully rehearsing*, your clue that the speech was well spoken. Synonyms for *well-spoken* are *eloquent* and *articulate*, which makes (C) and (E) your answers. *Languid* means *dull* and *listless* means *without energy;* both (A) and (D) are similar adjectives that Thomas would try to avoid. *Extended* means *long,* and as you have no clues that the speech should be long, (B) can be eliminated. Finally, *enduring* means *everlasting* and, while such a speech would be commendable, Thomas is more interested in the well-spoken aspect of his speech. Eliminate (F).

2.   **recanted** and **disavowed**

The prime minister was *worried that he had lost the support of his party*, so he needed to *forcefully* reverse *his controversial statement*. You're looking for a word that means *take back*. Both *recanted* and *disavowed* convey taking back a previous statement, and so (A) and (E) produce equivalent, appropriate sentences. *Affirmed* and *validated* are synonyms that mean *declared true*, which is the opposite of what you're looking for, and rules out (B) and (C). *Overlooked* and *ignored* are close in meaning, but (D) and (F) don't make sense in the given context.

3.   **abate** and **dwindle**

From the clues *convenient online access to reading material*, it is likely that *forecasters* would predict a *sales decrease*. Therefore, you are looking for words that mean *decrease*. *Multiply* and *appreciate* both mean to *increase,* so you can eliminate (A) and (F). *Prevail* means to *dominate,* which does not match the meaning you need, and *assimilate* means to *integrate and adjust to*, which may seem apt but does not fit the context of the blank or retain the meaning of the sentence: eliminate (C) and (D). *Abate* and *dwindle* mean to *decrease,* and so (B) and (E) produce equivalent, appropriate sentences.

4.   **affable** and **genial**

If Natalie was *nervous about receiving an unpleasant lecture* but her *fears were easily relieved*, then *the policeman* must have been the opposite of *unpleasant*. So you are looking for words that means *pleasant* or *friendly*. *Exacting* and *stringent* mean *meticulously demanding*, and so you can eliminate (A) and (D). *Atypical* means *nonconforming*, which does not retain the meaning of the sentence, and so (C) can be eliminated. *Sober* can mean *calm*; though the policeman may have also been calm, you're looking for words that mean *pleasant* or *friendly*, which also rules out (E). Furthermore, *sober* does not have a synonym among the other answer choices. Choices (B) and (F), *affable* and *genial*, can both mean *friendly,* and are the best answers.

5.   **augment** and **escalate**

The statisticians certainly hope to win the lottery and the change-direction trigger word *even* and the clue *misguided* signal that they are acting inappropriately, despite their knowledge. You want words that mean *increase*. *Mitigate* and *curtail* make a good synonym pair that means *to lessen*, which is contrary to what you need. *Squander* is what the statisticians might do with the money after they win it and *divulge,* meaning to *make known*, does not make sense in context. *Augment* and *escalate* both mean to *increase*, and so (A) and (B) give you appropriate, equivalent sentences.

6.   **maxim** and **proverb**

Since the people in the sentence *cannot develop a logical argument*, they might be offering a saying that would provide an excuse for their behavior. The word *saying* would be appropriate for the blank. *Fallacy* might seem like a suitable answer, but there aren't any clues in the sentence to prove that the statement is false. *Allusion* is a *reference to something*, a *query* is a *question*, and a *waiver* is the *relinquishment of something*. None of these words has the meaning of *saying*. *Maxim* and *proverb* are both *meaningful sayings*, and so (C) and (F) give you appropriate, equivalent sentences.

7.   **largess** and **philanthropy**

Both the description of the *ideological gap* as *insurmountable* and the trigger *while* tell you that the word for the blank needs to mean the opposite of *accumulating wealth*. Both *avarice* and *cupidity* are the opposite of what you're looking for, so eliminate (B) and (E). Neither *empathy*, which means the vicarious experience of another person's feelings, nor *parsimony*, which means frugality, is supported by the sentence, so eliminate (C) and (D). Both *largess* and *philanthropy* can refer to generosity with money, so (A) and (F) give you appropriate, equivalent sentences.

8. **mundane** and **insipid**

The critics *misjudged* the *designs*, so you know that the word in the blank must mean the opposite of *epitome of high fashion*. Choices (B) and (F) give roughly synonymous meanings, but nothing in the sentence supports the idea that the critics thought the designs were expensive. Neither *defamatory*, which means *libelous*, nor *contrite*, which means *remorseful*, is supported by the sentence, so eliminate (A) and (C). Both *mundane* and *insipid* can mean *uninspired* or *ordinary*, so (D) and (E) give you appropriate, equivalent sentences.

9. **tirades** and **diatribes**

Since Brookstone *has lost several professional allies*, and the blank describes something done *against the university's administration*, a word that means something like *attacks* or *opposition* would make sense. Both *approbations* and *commendations* are nearly the opposite of what you're looking for, so eliminate (A) and (E). Neither *precursors*, which means *predecessors*, nor *canons*, which means *accepted principles or rules*, is supported by the sentence, so eliminate (D) and (F). Both *tirades* and *diatribes* mean *angry speeches*, so (B) and (C) give you appropriate, equivalent sentences.

10. **chicanery** and **wile**

Since the information given by astrologers *can never be conclusively proven or falsified*, Sergei can't know whether it's true; thus, a word that means something like *trickery* or *deception* would make sense in the blank. Both *vindication* and *authentication* are nearly the opposite of what you're looking for, so eliminate (C) and (D). Neither *censure*, which means *criticism*, nor *vexation*, which means *anger*, is supported by the sentence, so eliminate (A) and (F). Both *chicanery* and *wile* can mean *trickery*, so (B) and (E) give you appropriate, equivalent sentences.

11. **predilection** and **propensity**

The sentence tells you that the selection of a *fresh cause* happens *every five years*, so the blank must refer to a word such as *habit* or *custom*. *Ambivalence* would indicate that the agencies are not sure about taking this action, and *callousness* indicate a lack of caring. *Wariness* would indicate that they are *hesitant* to change the cause. *Affectation* is tricky because it sounds similar to *affection*, which might make it sound like a good choice. However, *affectation* actually means *artificiality*, which is not the meaning you need. Choices (B) and (D) are both good substitutes for *custom*, and produce equivalent, appropriate sentences.

12. **discord** and **dissension**

Using the same-direction trigger *and...just as*, you know that the use of high-fructose corn syrup must also be *controversial*, the clue to the blank. You want a word that means *disagreement* or *debate*. Choices (B) and (F) are synonyms that imply *agreement* in this context, and should be eliminated. Choice (C) means *satisfaction* and (E) means *accuracy*; neither choice suggests *disagreement* or *debate* and should be eliminated. *Discord* and *dissension* both mean *disagreement* and so (A) and (D) produce equivalent, appropriate sentences.

13. **check** and **curb**

Following the colon, the regulations are described as *prohibitive* and receiving *widespread support*, the clues to the meaning of the blank. So the goal must be to *prohibit* or *reduce* such tactics. *Rally* and *muster* are synonyms that mean *to raise support for*, and *pirate* means *to use without authorization*. None of these means *prohibit* or *reduce*, so eliminate (A), (E), and (F). Choice (C) can mean *adorn* or *elaborate*, neither of which fits the context of the blank. This leaves (B) and (D): *check* and *curb* mean to *limit* and produce equivalent, appropriate sentences.

14. **abhorrent** and **invidious**

The blank is about the judge's personal opinion; the passage provides that the judge found the law morally objectionable (even though the judge could not rule the law unconstitutional). Thus, find two answers that mean *morally objectionable*. Choices (A), (C), and (F) provide the opposite meaning. Choice (D), while related to the fact that the judge did not rule the law unconstitutional, does not fit with the blank's description of the judge's personal opinion. Choices (B) and (E), *abhorrent* and *invidious,* work well.

15. **abstruse** and **opaque**

The structure of the sentence and the use of the word *even* provide that the ancient text, while not entirely impenetrable to experts, was nonetheless quite unclear. Thus, find two answers that mean quite unclear. Choices (B), (D), and (E) provide the opposite meaning; while the experts may not be as confused as the laypeople, they do struggle with the meaning. Choice (F), despite its resemblance in sound to (A), has a completely different meaning. Choices (A) and (C), *abstruse* and *opaque,* work well.

16. **nascent** and **inchoate**

The time trigger *only later* tells you that the earlier feudal system differed from the *fully developed* version that came later, so the word for the blank needs to mean *not fully developed*. Both *byzantine* and *labyrinthine* are nearly the opposite of what you're looking for, so eliminate (B) and (D). Neither *refractory*, which means *stubborn*, nor *perfidious*, which means *disloyal*, is supported by the sentence, so eliminate (A) and (F). Both *nascent* and *inchoate* can mean *not fully formed*, so (C) and (E) give you appropriate, equivalent sentences.

17. **saturnine** and **lachrymose**

The blank describes the kind of *lyrics* that would create a *tension* with *cheerful, almost bouncy music*, so a word that means something like *sad* would make sense. Both *euphoric* and *sanguine* are nearly the opposite of what you're looking for, so eliminate (B) and (C). Neither *lubricious*, which means *lewd,* nor *recondite*, which means *not widely known,* is supported by the sentence, so eliminate (A) and (E). Both *saturnine* and *lachrymose* mean *sad,* so (D) and (F) give you appropriate, equivalent sentences.

18.   **diaphanous** and **gossamer**

Recycle the clue *delicate* into the blank. Both *ponderous* and *cumbersome* are nearly the opposite of what you're looking for, so eliminate (C) and (E). Neither *ephemeral*, which means *short-lived*, nor *mettlesome*, which means *courageous*, is supported by the sentence, so eliminate (A) and (D). Both *diaphanous* and *gossamer* can mean *delicate*, so (B) and (F) give you appropriate, equivalent sentences. If you selected (A), be sure to distinguish *ephemeral* from *ethereal*, which would have been an appropriate answer choice.

19.   **looming** and **impending**

Since the *fascination with celebrities* and the *innovations of the electronic age may inspire* something to occur, you need a word that means *about to happen*. *Flagging* and *attenuating* mean *weakening*, so those words go in the opposite direction from the blank and (B) and (E) should be eliminated. *Calumniating*, (C), means *slandering*; while the new paparazzi may indeed be engaging in slander, that's not what the blank is talking about. *Deliquescing*, (D), means *becoming liquid*, and a trend can't do that. *Looming* and *impending* both mean *about to happen*, so those words are good fits for the blank, and (A) and (F) give you appropriate, equivalent sentences.

20.   **fickle** and **inconstant**

The blank must describe the doctor's friends, so look for the clue that gives information about those friends. The friends *quickly jilted him*, meaning that they dishonorably abandoned him. Friends who would do that are not very good friends, so you're looking for a word that means *not loyal*. *Squeamish* describes someone who becomes uncomfortable easily, usually around things that are unpleasant to the senses (blood, rodents, and other unpleasant things). While the friends may be *uncomfortable* in the doctor's presence, that's not why they abandoned him, and so you can eliminate (A). *Orthodox* and *stodgy* describe people who adhere rigidly to convention. These words, (E) and (F), describe the *medical establishment*, not the friends. A *staunch* ally is one who is loyal, so (C) yields the opposite of the blank. *Fickle* and *inconstant* both mean *disloyal*, and so they are good fits for the blank, and mean that (B) and (D) yield appropriate, equivalent sentences.

Drill 5

1.   **muddled** and **obfuscated**

To fill in the blank, you need to identify what the professor did to the exam question. Because he or she reordered the sentences and added distractions, he or she made the problem more confusing and unclear. *Muddled* and *obfuscated* are synonyms that mean *made obscure* or *unclear* and are therefore the correct choices. *Erased* and *obliterated* mean *to destroy* and do not describe what the professor did to the question. *Interpreted* means *made clear*, which is the opposite of what the professor did. *Engendered* is a nice vocabulary word but means *produced* or *caused*, which has nothing to do with making a previously created problem confusing.

2. **wisdom** and **sagacity**

To fill in the blank, you need to find a word that describes the *grandmother* who is described in the sentence as having *the correct answers to life's difficult dilemmas*. Therefore, you want to find words that also describe someone who has all the right answers. *Sagacity* means *acuteness of mental discernment,* or, more simply, *wisdom.* Meanwhile, *bewilderment* and *ignorance* are words describing someone who does not have all the right answers. *Duplicity* and *guile* are both words having to do with deceit and lying and are not traits of the *grandmother* suggested in the sentence.

3. **serpentine** and **tortuous**

The semicolon trigger tells you the two parts of the sentence agree; since the blank is describing the *road*, you need a word that means *twisted*. Both *abbreviated* and *fleeting* are nearly the opposite of what you're looking for, so eliminate them. Neither *invigorating*, which means *energizing,* nor *immense,* which means *huge,* is supported by the sentence. Both *serpentine* and *tortuous* can mean *twisted,* so these choices give you appropriate, equivalent sentences.

4. **perceptive** and **astute**

The blank describes the kind of *observation* that would surprise people who thought Lucy was unaware, so a word that means something like *sharp* or *observant* would make sense—anything that would show that Lucy was aware. Both *asinine* and *obtuse* are nearly the opposite of what you're looking for, so eliminate them. *Transparent* and *lucid* have roughly synonymous meanings, but an observation that was *clear* wouldn't have impressed her classmates. Both *perceptive* and *astute* can mean *observant* and give you appropriate, equivalent sentences.

5. **divine** and **idyllic**

The clues are that the *guests agreed* that *had the weather* NOT been *awful*; the implication is that Madeline's wedding was otherwise perfect. You are looking for a word that means *perfect*. Eliminate *urban*, which means *metropolitan* and has nothing to do with the meaning you need. Eliminate *excessive* and *disproportionate* as well. Though the wedding may have been *overdone* or *out of balance*, these are irrelevant to the clues. Finally, eliminate *rustic* which means *having country simplicity*. The best answers are *divine* and *idyllic*, both of which mean *perfect* and produce equivalent, appropriate sentences.

6. **a pedestrian** and **a mundane**

The clue is that Shakespeare was *only relying on vibrant and colorful individuals*, so the blank must be the opposite of *vibrant and colorful*. You need a word that means *ordinary*. Eliminate *original* and *extraordinary*, synonyms that have the opposite meaning of *ordinary*. Eliminate *imperial*, which means *regal*, and *domineering*, which means *authoritarian*; neither one relates to the context of the blank. *Pedestrian* and *mundane* both mean *common* or *ordinary* and produce equivalent, appropriate sentences.

7. **a proliferation** and **a burgeoning**

The last part of the sentence parallels the middle part. The clue to the blank is *the rapid development of numerous related processes*, so the missing word must mean *rapid development* or *expansion*. Eliminate *stagnation* since it is the opposite of what you're looking for. *Primogenitor*, *archetype*, and *antiquity* each seem applicable, but none of these choices stays in the scope of the meaning you need in the blank. Although the daguerreotype was the oldest photographic process, there's no context for *oldest* being the meaning of the blank and you can eliminate those three choices. That leaves *proliferation* and *burgeoning*, both of which can mean *rapid growth* and produce equivalent, appropriate sentences.

8. **disingenuous** and **duplicitous**

You know that the athlete used to be *well-respected* because of his work with *anti-drug programs*. The contrast is that he was working with *anti-drug programs* while *using steroids for years*, so a good word for the blank would be *hypocritical* or *dishonest*. *Sanguine* and *buoyant* can be eliminated because they are both positive and mean *optimistic*, and *esteemed* does not mean *dishonest* and is also incorrect. *Felonious* means *related to a crime*, and does not necessarily mean *dishonest*. *Disingenuous* and *duplicitous* are the best answers because they both mean *deceitful* and produce equivalent, appropriate sentences.

9. **abjure** and **eschew**

The clue *walked quietly instead of throwing rocks* indicates the leader must have asked the protestors to *stop* the violence. Eliminate *condone* and *glorify* because they both convey a sense of *support* or *approval* and are opposite of what you need in the blank. *Manifest* also doesn't work because it means *demonstrate*. *Mollify* means *soothe* and does not apply in this context. *Abjure* and *eschew* are synonyms that mean *to avoid or give up* and produce equivalent, appropriate sentences.

10. **rarefy** and **subtilize**

The manufacturers' goal is to *make certain items dedicated collectibles*, so they would do something to *make them more rare or special*. *Spur* and *incite* are synonyms that mean *activate*, but the blank refers to the trucks themselves and so you can eliminate these choices. *Investigate* can be eliminated because it means *examine* and doesn't match the needed meaning. *Circulate* is also irrelevant to the context of the blank. That leaves *rarefy* and *subtilize,* both of which mean *to make more rare* and produce equivalent, appropriate sentences.

11. **diaphanous** and **gossamer**

The important clues in this sentence are the words *cloudy* and *semi-transparent*, both of which describe the inner workings of the jellyfish. *Caustic* could be tempting because a jellyfish tentacle could definitely be burning, but there's no context for it. You can eliminate *calamitous* for the same reason. It seems logical, but isn't actually supported by the text. *Natatory* is connected to the sentence because jellyfish are aquatic creatures, but the blank is specifically describing the appearance of tentacles, not the jellyfish as a whole. *Resplendent* has nothing to do with the sentence. *Diaphanous* and *gossamer* both mean *loose, flowing, or see-through*, which is what you're looking for.

12. **decimation** and **annihilation**

The sentence tells you that the Jedi were a *powerful peace-keeping force*, but there's a contrast indicated by the *but* and the time trigger *before the Clone Wars*. That lets you know that something is going to happen that will challenge the Jedi's status. The sentence also tells you that *every clone trooper was reprogrammed to assassinate his Jedi master*. This lets you know that there was a massive attack against the Jedi. So you could fill in the missing word with something like *serious injury* or *really bad experience*. You can eliminate *sovereignty* and *ascendancy* because those are going in the wrong direction. They only connect with the *powerful Jedi* clue, not taking into account the contrast triggers. *Ingenuity* and *misrepresentation* have nothing to do with the sentence, so you can eliminate them. That leaves *decimation* and *annihilation*, both of which mean *completely destroy*.

13. **fledgling** and **neoteric**

The sentence tells you that the studios have a *penchant for hiring A-list movie stars*. Then it tells you those studios are *rethinking that strategy*, so you know the actors they're looking for now are not A-list. This is further supported with the clues that tell you the economy is not suited to *celebrities* who get paid *$15 to $20 million*, but to another kind of actor who *commands far less per picture*. So put something in the blank like *unknown* or *new*. You can eliminate *luminary* and *renowned* because those two answers would describe the A-list celebrities. *Exorbitant* also fits more with the A-listers because they're the ones who would be *expensive*. *Iniquitous* doesn't fit with anything in the sentence. That leaves *fledgling* and *neoteric*, both of which mean *new* or *just starting out*, which is what you're looking for.

14. **quintessence** and **epitome**

You need a word for the blank that means that Joseph was the *model* of composure. Both *quintessence* and *epitome* would mean he is a *perfect embodiment* of composure, so these choices produce equivalent sentences that make sense. *Bane* would mean he somehow *annoys* composure, and is incorrect. *Rector* would mean Joseph is the *priest or academic leader* of composure, and *antithesis* would mean he *proves the opposite* of composure. *Regent* would mean he is the *king ruling over* composure.

15. **sycophants** and **toadies**

Since the president *could not tolerate dissent from his views*, you need a word that means his cabinet members would always agree with him. *Pundits* and *authoritarians* would offer their own strong opinions, so eliminate them. *Cynics* would act *pessimistically* and *partisans* would be *biased*, but not necessarily all in the same direction as the president, so eliminate them. *Sycophants* and *toadies* are synonyms indicating that the members are *flatterers* or *yes-men*, and produce equivalent statements.

16. **apogee** and **zenith**

The clue to the blank is *encomium*, which means *a speech of high praise*. Since the poet is young and afraid that her career reached a premature point, the word in the blank must mean peak. *Apogee* and *zenith* both mean *highest point*, so these choices validly complete the sentence. An *auspice* means *good sign*, so eliminate it. *Coda* means a *concluding section* and does not fit this context. *Nadir* and *perigee* both mean *lowest point* and are the opposite of what you need.

17. **labyrinthine** and **byzantine**

The logic is hard to follow, so you need a word for the blank that means confusing or convoluted. Both *labyrinthine* and *byzantine* mean *twisting and turning like a maze,* so keep them. *Rhetorical* means *using a strong, formal writing style,* so eliminate it. *Libertine* and *unscrupulous* are roughly synonymous, and both mean *having lax moral standards,* so eliminate them. *Decorous* means *dignified or proper* and doesn't work with the sentence. Only *labyrinthine* and *byzantine* produce equivalent sentences.

18. **upbraided** and **lambasted**

The CEO took money, so you need a word for the blank that means the board members, shareholders, and customers *punished* him. *Cachinnated* means *laughed at* and *blandished* means *flattered,* so eliminate them. *Upbraided* means *censured,* and so does *lambasted,* so keep them. *Approbated* means *approved of,* and *caviled,* while close, means *to find fault with unnecessarily.* Only *upbraided* and *lambasted* produce appropriate, equivalent sentences.

19. **quotidian** and **pedestrian**

Since *punctilious* means *having very strong attention to detail, especially with etiquette,* this is a good thing to describe *service.* The word *while* tells you that you need something in the other direction for cuisine, so you need a word that means the food is *not too great. Obsequious* means *flattering;* eliminate it. Both *quotidian* and *pedestrian* mean *commonplace or boring,* so keep these choices. *Distasteful* could work, because it could mean *unpleasant tasting,* but there is no synonym for this word in the choices, and therefore no way to make the sentence equivalent with another one of the choices. *Gustatory* means *having to do with the sense of taste,* but is too broad. *Pedantic* is a synonym for *punctilious,* but we need the opposite, so eliminate it.

20. **an invective** and **a vituperation**

Recycle the clue *angry response* into the blank. Three of your choices—*laudation, panegyric,* and *approbation*—are nearly the opposite of what you're looking for, so eliminate them. A *dictum* is a formal or authoritative statement; that's not supported by the sentence. Both *invective* and *vituperation* can mean *a speech of anger,* and give you appropriate, equivalent sentences.

Drill 6

1. **crafty** and **cunning**

To describe a con artist who left his victims pleased to be victimized, you'd need a word that means something like *skillful* or *tricky*. Both *maladroit* and *unskillful* are nearly the opposite of what you're looking for, so eliminate them. Neither *innocuous*, which means *harmless,* nor *discrete*, which means *distinct,* is supported by the sentence. Both *crafty* and *cunning* can mean *tricky;* these words give you appropriate, equivalent sentences. If you were tempted by *discrete* because a good con artist would be able to keep a secret, be sure to distinguish *discrete* from *discreet.*

2. **vigilant** and **mindful**

Given the clue *most people already know,* you know that the way the Secret Service employees are described in the first part of the sentence—in this case *sharp-eyed*—is the same as the way they are described in the second part. Thus, *vigilant* and *mindful* are appropriate for the blank. *Robust* and *potent* are a synonym pair which means *strong,* which is not supported by the clue, although they may indeed be strong people. They may also be *vulnerable* in some ways, but this choice would be the opposite of the intended meaning. The same applies for *weary,* which means *tired.*

3. **ambiance** and **atmosphere**

The clue in this sentence is *filled the air with tension.* Both *ambience* and *atmosphere* refer to the environment of a place or situation. All of the wrong answer choices are words that may be associated with a gala, but they do not fit this clue. *Decor* refers to how the room was *decorated,* *discourse* means *conversation,* *etiquette* means *acting appropriately,* and *diversion* means *distraction.*

4. **untenable** and **indefensible**

The sentence suggests that it is *unfair* to tax the middle class unless the upper class is taxed as well. *Sporadic* means *occurring at random times,* *subtle* means *barely noticeable,* *dignified* means *expressing worthiness or honor,* and *pardonable* means *forgivable.* None of these fits the idea of *unfair.* Only *untenable* and *indefensible* come closest to *unfair* or *unable to be justified.*

5. **indisputable** and **demonstrable**

Since ghosts are described as *unseen by the majority*, it must be difficult to provide *visible* or *definite* proof. *Indisputable* and *demonstrable* both convey the meaning you want, and produce equivalent, appropriate sentences. *Momentous* means *important. Daunting* means *intimidating,* and *uncanny* means *mysterious. Skeptical* may be a good word to describe those who don't see the ghosts, but it can't describe the proof.

6. **greed** and **avarice**

The sentence tells us that the politician claimed that he did not seek to enrich himself. However, the trigger word *but* indicates that the blank will have the opposite meaning: he did attempt to enrich himself. *Greed* and *avarice* work in this context. *Charity* and *compassion* go in the wrong direction, as they describe what the politician claimed, and *estrangement* and *apprehension* have no relationship to the blank.

7. **cataclysm** and **obliteration**

The clues to the blank are that the seascape was once unspoiled before the *calamitous* event, which indicates that it is now *damaged*, the word you are looking for. *Cataclysm* and *obliteration* can be used to describe physical destruction and are the best answers. *Determination, melancholy,* and *tenacity* are used to describe people and don't mean damaged. *Conflict* does not provide a good substitute for destroyed or spoiled.

8. **paramount** and **exigent**

The blank is about the first steps taken as part of the strategy of organization. The clues indicate that these steps were among many *required* steps and were *urgent*. Thus, they were the *most immediate* of the required steps. *Paramount* and *exigent* indicate the immediacy and importance of the steps, and are correct. *Unappealing* does not reflect the clue, and *trivial* is the opposite of the word you need. There is no information in the sentence to support the remaining choices, *dispassionate* and *insipid*.

9. **cogency** and **lucidity**

Someone worried about having to analyze an *esoteric* poem would be *delighted* to get one that was clear or easily understood, so something like *clarity* would make sense in the blank. Both *ambiguity* and *opacity* are nearly the opposite of what you're looking for, so eliminate these. Neither *cadency*, which means *rhythm,* nor *melancholy*, which means *sadness,* is supported by the sentence, so eliminate both. Both *cogency* and *lucidity* can mean *clarity,* so these choices give you appropriate, equivalent sentences.

10. **reticent** and **laconic**

A story about Einstein not uttering a sentence *in five years* would emphasize his image as a *quiet* scholar. Both *loquacious* and *garrulous* are nearly the opposite of what you're looking for, so eliminate them. Neither *consummate*, which means *perfect,* nor *judicious*, which means *showing good judgment,* is supported by the sentence. Both *reticent* and *laconic* can mean *using few words,* so these choices give you appropriate, equivalent sentences.

11. **a nominal** and **a negligible**

Since Tess was worried about the pesticides' *noxious effects*, a word like *small* or *minimal* would make sense in the blank. Both *capacious* and *profuse* are nearly the opposite of what you're looking for, so eliminate them. *Abiding* and *enduring* give equivalent meanings as well, but *lasting effects* are what Tess is trying to avoid. Both *nominal* and *negligible* can mean small, so these choices give you appropriate, equivalent sentences.

12. **insightful** and **perspicacious**

The trigger word *despite* tells you that the first part of the sentence contrasts the second part. So, the blank will have a word that means the opposite of the clues *lack of education* and *obtuse*, such as *keenly smart. Perspicacious* and *insightful* mean observant or perceptive; these are the best choices. *Jejune* means *immature* and *vapid* means *dull,* but neither is the opposite of *obtuse. Pragmatic* means *practical* and *expedient* means *appropriate;* both words could describe good advice, but don't follow from the clue in this sentence.

13. **amass** and **garner**

You are told that Emile must *earn enough money to cover his expenses;* to do so he must work as much as he can during his busy season. Therefore, he must *acquire* as many *assignments* as he can. The best answer choices are *amass* and *garner. Rebuke* means to *reprimand* and *disseminate* means to *scatter.* Neither of these works with the sentence. Both *eschew* and *relinquish* are the opposite of what you need.

14. **bolster** and **buttress**

To fill in the blank, you need to determine what *these applications* are doing to *productivity* now. The trigger word *however* signals that the *applications* were *detractors from productivity,* but now have the opposite effect, such as *to help. Bolster* and *buttress* are synonyms that mean *to add support or improve,* both of which are the opposite of *detract* and produce equivalent, appropriate sentences. *Vilipend* and *depreciate* both mean *to reduce the value of* and are the opposite meaning of what you want. *Engender* means *to cause to happen* and *supplant* means *to replace*; neither word works with the clue or in the context of the blank.

15. **platitudinous** and **jejune**

The missing word must be consistent with the clues *no new ideas* and *containing nothing but overt drivel. Lax* and *amorphous* both mean *without precision or structure;* they're consistent with the end of the sentence, but not with this clue. *Natty* means *neat and tidy,* usually in reference to clothing, and does not reflect the clue. *Labyrinthine* means *unnecessarily complicated,* but the problem with the poetry is lack of freshness. *Platitudinous* and *jejune* both mean *trite or uninteresting* and produce equivalent, appropriate sentences.

16. **dissipation** and **profligacy**

The clue is that Gatsby *grows progressively more flagrant in his spending and his lifestyle*, so the word in the blank must mean something like *inclined to spend money unwisely*. *Ignominy* means *shame* and *volubility* means *talkativeness*, but nothing in the sentence indicates that he feels shame or talks incessantly. *Repute* and *stature* mean *fame*; though Gatsby is a famous character, the blank does not refer to his fame. *Dissipation* and *profligacy* can both mean *inclined to wastefulness*, and produce equivalent, appropriate sentences.

17. **fomented** and **galvanized**

The word in the blank must agree with *animated*, so anything that means *gave life to* will work—feel free to recycle *animated*. Both *obliterated* and *extirpated* are nearly the opposite of what you're looking for, so eliminate them. Neither *paralleled*, which means *was similar to*, nor *exemplified*, which means *were examples of*, is supported by the sentence. Both *fomented* and *galvanized* can mean *inspired*, so these choices give you appropriate, equivalent sentences.

18. **winnow** and **sift**

A good editor is interested in *distinguishing the best offerings from the worst in an efficient manner*, so your word for the blank needs to mean the same thing as *distinguish*. Both *consolidate* and *integrate* are nearly the opposite of what you're looking for, so eliminate them. Neither *finagle*, which means *to obtain by dishonest or indirect means*, nor *intimate*, which—as a verb—means *to insinuate*, is supported by the sentence. Both *winnow* and *sift* can mean *separate*, so these choices give you appropriate, equivalent sentences.

19. **nice** and **minute**

Brand believes that the distinction obscures a *more relevant question*, so the word in the blank must mean something consistent with *not relevant*. *Baleful* means *dangerous*, and *feckless* means *incompetent or irresponsible*, neither of which is close to *not relevant*. *Critical* and *cardinal* both mean *important*, so those words are the opposite of what you're looking for. The correct answers here rely on secondary definitions of the words *nice* and *minute*. Both of these words can be used to mean *so small as to be insignificant*.

20. **opaque** and **abstruse**

The word in the blank must be a characteristic of something written in *jargon* that makes the writing *difficult to understand* for *the general public*. *Risible* means *laughably absurd*, which is sometimes, but not always, a characteristic of jargony writing. *Vapid* means *boring*, which might also sometimes be true of this type of writing, but it does not mean *difficult to understand*. *Uncanny* means *strange* and *equivocal* means *having multiple meanings*, which is not the same as *difficult to understand*. *Opaque* and *abstruse* both mean *difficult to understand* and produce appropriate, equivalent sentences.

Drill 7

1.   **lethargy** and **weariness**

The clue is that she has been *sick for three days* and that she is *unable to get up*, so the missing word means *tiredness* or *exhaustion*. *Vitality* is the opposite of what you're looking for, and *innuendo* is irrelevant to the context of the blank; both choices can be eliminated. *Freshness* and *hunger* could be feelings following recovery from the flu, but do not mean *exhaustion*. *Lethargy* and *weariness*, both of which mean *lacking energy*, produce equivalent, appropriate statements.

2.   **distressed** and **apprehensive**

Jake would be *scared* by the *poisonous snake*. You can eliminate *amazed* and *optimistic* because they are positive words. *Ambivalent* and *equivocal* do not relate to *being scared*, and can be eliminated. *Distressed* and *apprehensive* are correct because both mean *worried or scared*.

3.   **adamant** and **unwavering**

The clue to the blank is *passionately insistent of her assertions*, signifying that a similar *tone* helped *her team prevail*. Recycle the clue and look for words that mean *passionately insistent*. *Compromised*, *unsteady*, and *vacillating* indicate that she would have an *insecure*, *impaired* or *unsure* tone, and can be eliminated. *Unusual* is incorrect because there is no clue that she had an *odd* tone. *Adamant* and *unwavering* both mean *unshakably determined* and produce equivalent, appropriate sentences.

4.   **discontentment** and **contempt**

The clue *clear and ongoing mismanagement of the city kennel* indicates that the mayor would have negative feelings of *disapproval*. *Approval, reverence,* and *joy* are positive words that do not complement the clue and should be eliminated. *Lethargy* means *lack of energy* and does not match the meaning you want. Only *discontentment* and *contempt* mean *disapproval* and produce equivalent, appropriate sentences.

5.   **perturbed** and **discomposed**

The employee's *confident smile* is hiding *confusion*, so something that means *confused* would make sense in the blank. Both *placated* and *conciliated* are nearly the opposite of what you're looking for, so eliminate them. Neither *vilified*, which means *defamed*, nor *belabored*, which means *excessively insisted upon,* is supported by the sentence either. Both *perturbed* and *discomposed* can mean *confused*, so these choices give you appropriate, equivalent sentences.

6.   **grievous** and **onerous**

Students who are *more attuned to philosophical debate* would find *math* and *science* to be *difficult* or a *burden*. Both *facile* and *elementary* are nearly the opposite of what you're looking for, so eliminate them. Neither *stupefying*, which means *perplexing*, nor *meticulous*, which means *attentive to detail,* is supported by the sentence. Both *grievous* and *onerous* can mean *a difficult burden,* so these choices give you appropriate, equivalent sentences.

7.   **consummate** and **virtuoso**

Although the fact that the ballerina didn't achieve a *coveted title* might suggest she wasn't a good dancer, the change-direction trigger—*at least in the opinion of the general public*—indicates that the word in the blank needs to mean something like *skillful.* Both *fulsome* and *noisome* are nearly the opposite of what you're looking for, so eliminate them. Neither *perfunctory,* which means *careless,* nor *evanescent,* which means *fleeting,* is supported by the sentence either. Both *consummate* and *virtuoso* can mean *extremely skilled,* so these choices give you appropriate, equivalent sentences.

8.   **dubious** and **incredulous**

The blank is about the review committee's opinion of the candidate's thesis, and the trigger word *but* indicates that the committee holds the opposite view of the candidate's view. The candidate is *confident* that the thesis is valid, so the blank means *not confident.* Correct choices *dubious* and *incredulous* mean *doubtful,* and produce equivalent, appropriate sentences. *Persuaded* and *convinced* represent the candidate's view, not the committee's view. *Mollified* means *soothed,* not *doubtful.* *Irked* means *annoyed* and goes beyond the context of the blank and is not supported.

9.   **belies** and **controverts**

The blank is about the effect of the letters on the historian's claims. The clue is *the historian must reconsider his life's work,* so the blank means *disproves.* *Belies* and *controverts* mean *makes false* and produce equivalent, appropriate sentences. *Corroborates* and *validates* both have the opposite meaning of *disproves,* and can be eliminated. *Innervates* and *anticipates* also do not mean *disprove* and are incorrect.

10.   **banal** and **pedestrian**

The blank is about what playwrights should avoid according to the critic, and the clue word *trite* signals the blank must mean *ordinary.* If you do not know the word *trite,* you nevertheless know that the blank must be negative from the phrase *could not sit through.* Correct choices *banal* and *pedestrian* mean *dull and ordinary,* and produce equivalent, appropriate sentences. *Rapturous* and *entrancing* are positive, and can be eliminated. *Judicious* means *in good judgment* and *expedient* means *conveniently practical,* and neither choice means *ordinary.*

11.   **enormity** and **depravity**

The first of two trigger words, *hardly,* tells you that the outcome of war is not *favorable,* the clue word. The other trigger is *even*; you would expect a good outcome for the victors, but this is not the case here and so the nature of war must be *very bad.* *Hegemony* relates to war but the clue does not support a word that means *domination.* *Austerity* means *strict* or *stern,* but is also not a match for the clue. *Bombast* refers to *pompous use of language*, and *exposition* means *a public display or discourse*. Both should be eliminated. The correct answers, *enormity* and *depravity*, mean *evil* or *baseness*.

12.   **debauched** and **profligate**

The behavior being described is used to *disparage* the movement, so it must be *inappropriate* behavior. *Reticent* means *reserved* or *shy*, so it is incorrect. *Garrulous* means *talkative* and *cogent* means *convincing*, but there are no clues to support these choices. *Capricious* is often used with a negative connotation and means *impulsive* or *unpredictable*. *Debauched* and *profligate* both mean *disregarding social or moral correctness*, which makes them the two best answers that produce equivalent, appropriate sentences.

13.   **abstruse** and **obscure**

The trigger word and clue *Although typically quite lucid in his explanations* signals that his explanation in yesterday's discussion was not very clear. So, you need words that mean *unclear* or *hard to understand*. *Realistic* means *reasonable* and *benevolent* means *kind-hearted*. The word *obvious* has the opposite meaning of the word you need. *Disparate* means *distinct*, which isn't correct because the sentence isn't comparing multiple items, so eliminate (F). Only correct answers *abstruse* and *obscure*, both of which mean *hard to grasp*, produce appropriate, equivalent sentences.

14.   **jumble** and **gallimaufry**

The clue is that first the paintings were *installed with no consideration to the arrangement* and then they were *actually arranged in alphabetical order*. The blank comes after the trigger word *but* and agrees with the first description. So, the missing word must mean something like *disorganized grouping*. *Chromatic* and *melisma* are similar in meaning, but do not pertain to a disorganized group; they can be eliminated. The paintings do not have anything to do with water or the beach, so you can eliminate *littoral*. *Diatribe* is also irrelevant to the meaning you need. *Jumble* and *gallimaufry* fit within the context of the sentence and both refer to a *random grouping of items*.

15.   **tortuous** and **anfractuous**

The word *belied* indicates a contrast between the current state of the administration, *halcyon days*, and the president's journey to the White House. Therefore, the missing words must mean the opposite of *peaceful* or *calm*; you need a word such as *rough* or *chaotic*. Eliminate *felicitous*, because that word agrees with *halcyon*. *Facile* and *dexterous* both convey *done easily with skill*, and can be eliminated. There is also no context to support a *domineering* journey, and thus *imperial* is incorrect. That leaves *tortuous* and *anfractuous*, both of which mean *twisted* or *not smooth* and produce equivalent, appropriate sentences.

16. **pugnacious** and **disputatious**

The blank describes a politician who *leads the opposition*, and whose martially themed book title is said to be *telling*, so a word that means something like *argumentative* or *belligerent* would make sense. Both *compliant* and *diffident* are nearly the opposite of what you're looking for, so eliminate them. Neither *circumspect*, which means cautious, nor *milquetoast*, which means timid, is supported by the sentence, so eliminate them as well. Both *pugnacious* and *disputatious* can mean *argumentative*, so these choices give you appropriate, equivalent sentences.

17. **assiduous** and **sedulous**

The blank describes the newspapers' *attempts to expose government corruption*; since the sentence suggests that the threat posed by the papers inspired the new law, a word that means something like *effective*, *thorough*, or *hard-working* would make sense. Both *lackadaisical* and *perfunctory* are nearly the opposite of what you're looking for, so eliminate them. *Eschewed* and *abjured* give roughly synonymous meanings, but aren't supported by the sentence. Both *assiduous* and *sedulous* can mean *hard-working*, so these choices give you appropriate, equivalent sentences.

18. **raiment** and **caparison**

The clue word *sartorial* means *relating to tailoring or clothing*, so the word in the blank must mean *clothing*. *Panegyric* and *oratory* both mean *speech*, so eliminate them. *Raiment* and *caparison* both mean *clothing*, making these choices correct. *Fetes* and *soirees* are both types of *parties*, so eliminate them.

19. **gaudy** and **garish**

Marian does not comment on her grandmother's hat out of respect, which means she dislikes the hat. You need a word that means *ugly or in poor taste*. *Iconoclastic* and *heretical* both mean *going against established beliefs*. This is too strong and does not describe a hat, so eliminate these choices. *Imperious* and *haughty* both mean *arrogant*, so eliminate these choices as well. *Gaudy* and *garish* both mean *showy and in poor taste*, and can be used to describe clothing, making these choices correct.

20. **puerile** and **jejune**

The *more mature* students did not want to sit at Fred's table because they did not like the remarks he made. The word in the blank must mean *immature*. *Puerile* and *jejune* both mean *childish and immature*, so these choices produce appropriate, equivalent sentences. *Crude* means *lacking tact*, which fits but there is no synonym for *crude* among the options. *Limpid* is positive and means *clear*, so it does not work in the sentence. *Inimical* means *hostile* and *insidious* means *stealthy or treacherous*, but neither word is supported by the sentence.

The Math Section

Plugging In

PLUGGING IN

Let's try a math problem.

> Anna goes into a candy store and purchases 4 pieces of candy that cost 60 cents each and gives the clerk 10 dollars. Let's assume this transaction takes place in a state, such as Oregon, that does not have sales tax. How much change will Anna receive?

The answer is $7.60. While a little arithmetic is required to solve this, the problem wasn't too difficult.

Unfortunately problems on the GRE are not typically that straightforward. On the GRE this problem might look like this.

> Anna goes into a candy store and purchases x pieces of candy that cost y cents each and gives the clerk z dollars. In terms of x, y, and z, how much change, in dollars, will Anna receive?

Now the problem is a bit more abstract and difficult. It will likely take longer to find the solution. And the solution many people provide is $z - xy$, which is incorrect.

Why is $z - xy$ is incorrect? When working through the version with numbers, multiply 4 by 60 to find the total cost is 240 cents, which naturally converts to 2.40 dollars. So when working through the version with variables, multiply x by y to find the total cost is xy cents and then convert that to dollars by dividing by 100, which equals $\frac{xy}{100}$. So the correct answer is $z - \frac{xy}{100}$.

Sure, now $z - \frac{xy}{100}$ makes sense but when in test-taking mode and the timer is ticking, it is often difficult to capture these types of details with algebra. Arithmetic is more efficient and lends itself to fewer errors. When working with numbers rather than variables, the problem tends to be easier and quicker. And we get more correct answers.

Plugging In is a technique used to convert a problem with variables into a problem with numbers, so speed and accuracy increases. On the GRE, when there are variables in the answer choices or question stem, you can often use this technique.

Let's try plugging in with this example.

Eleven years ago, Lauren was half as old as Mike will be in 4 years. If Mike is m years old now, how old is Lauren now in terms of m ?

○ $4m - 11$

○ $\frac{1}{2}(m+4)+11$

○ $\frac{1}{2}(m-11)$

○ $4m+\frac{11}{2}$

○ $2m - 7$

Step 1: Recognize the opportunity

There are variables in the answer choices and question stem.

Step 2: Set up your scratch paper

Write A, B, C, D, and E in a column on your scratch paper.

Step 3: Plug in an easy number (e.g., 2, 5, 10, 100) to one or more variables

The problem introduces Mike's age now as m years old. Let's say $m = 10$. Write this down on your scratch paper.

Step 4: Work through the problem

If Mike is now 10 years old, he will be 14 in 4 years. Eleven years ago from that, Lauren was 7. This means that Lauren is now 18 years old.

Step 5: Find the answer to the question. That's your target. Circle it.

The answer to the question is the target number. The question asks how old Lauren is now. So the target number is 18. Write it down and circle it.

Step 6: Check all your answer choices

Anywhere there is an m in the answer choices, Plug In 10. Look for an answer choice equal to 18, the target number.

(A) $4(10) - 11 = 29$. This does not equal 18. Eliminate.

(B) $\frac{1}{2}(10+4)+11=18$. This looks good, but when there are variables in the answer choices, check all answer choices.

(C) $\frac{1}{2}(10-11)=-\frac{1}{2}$. This does not equal 18. Eliminate.

(D) $4(10)+\frac{11}{2}=40+\frac{11}{2}$. This is much greater than 18. Eliminate.

(E) $2(10) - 7 = 13$. This does not equal 18. Eliminate.

Only one of the choices is 18. The answer is (B).

Here's what the scratch paper looks like:

A) $4(10) - 11 = 29$ $m = 20$ (18)

	Lauren	Mike
11 yrs ago	7	
now	18	10
in 4 yrs		14

B) $\frac{1}{2}(10 + 4) + 11 = 18$

C) $\frac{1}{2}(10 - 11) = -\frac{1}{2}$

D) $4(10) + \frac{11}{2} = 40 + \frac{11}{2}$

E) $2(10) - 7 = 13$

When there are variables in the answer choices and question stem, Plug In. For every problem, label the terms, circle the target number, and check all the answer choices. If more than one answer choice works, Plug In a new number, find the new target, and work with the remaining answer choices. This all happens on your scratch paper.

PLUGGING IN ON QUANTITATIVE COMPARISONS

Plugging In also works well for Quantitative Comparison questions with variables.

Let's try Plugging In on this problem.

> Wendy purchased n napkins and Juan purchased 2 fewer than half as many napkins as Wendy.
>
> | Quantity A | Quantity B |
> |---|---|
> | The number of napkins Juan purchased | $\dfrac{n-4}{2}$ |
>
> ○ Quantity A is greater.
> ○ Quantity B is greater.
> ○ The two quantities are equal.
> ○ The relationship cannot be determined from the information given.

Step 1: Recognize the opportunity

There are variables in the question stem and the quantities.

Step 2: Set up your scratch paper

Write A, B, C, and D horizontally on the scratch paper, with columns for Quantity A and Quantity B on either side, as shown on the scratch paper below.

Step 3: Plug In an easy number (according to the problem's restrictions)

Make n = 10. If n = 10, then Quantity A has the value 3 and Quantity B has the value 3. Write down these values on the scratch paper.

Step 4: Eliminate two of answers A, B, and C

In this case the two quantities are equal, so Quantity A isn't *always* greater than Quantity B and Quantity B isn't *always* greater than Quantity A. Eliminate A and B. Now determine whether the quantities are always equal.

Step 5: Repeat using FROZEN

After Plugging In an easy number, test out whether they are always equal by using trickier numbers. To know which tricky numbers to use, think of the acronym FROZEN. It stands for all the weird numbers that you might normally shy away from, or not think of, when Plugging In the first time: *Fractions*, *Repeats from the problem*, *One*, *Zero*, *Extreme numbers*, and *Negatives*. Start with *n* = 0. If *n* = 0, then Quantity A is –2 and Quantity B is –2. The quantities are still equal, so nothing can be eliminated. Next try an extreme number, such as *n* = 200. If *n* = 200, then Quantity A is 98 and Quantity B is 98. The quantities are still equal. After Plugging In several different weird numbers and getting the same relationship between the quantities, it appears that the quantities are *always* equal. The correct answer is (C).

Here's what the scratch paper looks like:

```
 A    A B ⓒ d    B
 3    n = 10      3
–2    n = 0      –2
98    n = 200    98
```

MUST BE

Plugging In more than once can also be helpful on other problems. When the question has the term "must be," that means the answer must always be true. Again determine if it is always true by Plugging In weird numbers until you narrow the answer choices down to one.

Let's try Plugging In on this one.

If $x < y < 0$, which of the following statements must be true?

○ The product of x and y is greater than 1.
○ The product of x and y is less than 1.
○ The product of x and y is greater than 0.
○ The product of x and y is less than 0.
○ The sum of x and y is less than –1.

Step 1: Recognize the opportunity

There are variables in the answer choices and question stem. Because the question states "must be," expect to Plug In more than once.

Step 2: Set up your scratch paper

Write A, B, C, D, and E vertically on the scratch paper. To the right, leave space for variables.

Step 3: Plug In an easy number (according to the problem's restrictions)

Plug In values that satisfy the condition of the question, such as $x = -3$ and $y = -2$.

Step 4: Eliminate incorrect answer choices

The product of -3 and -2 is 6. Choices (A) and (C) work, so keep them. Choices (B) and (D) don't work, so eliminate them. The sum of -3 and -2 is -5. Choice (E) works, so keep it as well.

Step 5: Repeat using FROZEN

Plug In again using FROZEN numbers to try to eliminate more answer choices. Try fractions, such as $x = -\frac{1}{2}$ and $y = -\frac{1}{4}$. The product of $-\frac{1}{2}$ and $-\frac{1}{4}$ is $\frac{1}{8}$. Choice (A) doesn't work, so eliminate it. Choice (C) works, so keep it. The sum of $-\frac{1}{2}$ and $-\frac{1}{4}$ is $-\frac{3}{4}$. Choice (E) doesn't work, so eliminate it. The only answer choice remaining is (C), which is the correct answer.

Here's what the scratch paper looks like:

	$x = -3$		$x = -\frac{1}{2}$
	$y = -2$		$y = -\frac{1}{4}$
~~A)~~	6	$\frac{1}{8}$	
~~B)~~	6		
Ⓒ)	6	$\frac{1}{8}$	
~~D)~~	6		
~~E)~~	-5	$-\frac{3}{4}$	

Step 1

Step 2

Step 3

Step 4

Step 5

STRATEGY SUMMARY

In all of these problems, variables are a trigger to Plug In. Here are the three kinds of Plugging In discussed in this section:

1. **Plugging In for Variables.** When there are variables in the answer choices, Plug In. Plug In a value for the variables, work through the problem, circle the target number, and check all answer choices.

2. **Quantitative Comparison Plug In.** When there are unknown values on Quantitative Comparison questions, set up for Plugging In. Use an easier number first and then go through FROZEN numbers until you are left with one answer choice.

3. **Must Be.** Put answer choices in a vertical column and leave space above to Plug In for a variety of variables. Remember to start with an easy number and then go through the FROZEN numbers until you are left with one answer choice.

For more on Plugging In, check our student-friendly guidebook, *Cracking the GRE*.

DRILL 1

Question 1

The profit from selling y units of a product is given by the formula $4y - 2$, where $y > 0$.

Quantity A	Quantity B
4 times the profit from selling y units	$16y - 4$

○ Quantity A is greater.
○ Quantity B is greater.
○ The two quantities are equal.
○ The relationship cannot be determined from the information given.

Question 2

J is the set of all fractions in the form of $\dfrac{a}{a^2}$, where $a \neq 0$.

Quantity A	Quantity B
Any member of set J	1

○ Quantity A is greater.
○ Quantity B is greater.
○ The two quantities are equal.
○ The relationship cannot be determined from the information given.

Question 3

$$x^3 = 27$$
$$y^2 = 16$$

Quantity A	Quantity B
x	y

○ Quantity A is greater.
○ Quantity B is greater.
○ The two quantities are equal.
○ The relationship cannot be determined from the information given.

Question 4

$$x > y > 0$$

Quantity A	Quantity B
$4x$	$5y$

○ Quantity A is greater.
○ Quantity B is greater.
○ The two quantities are equal.
○ The relationship cannot be determined from the information given.

Question 5

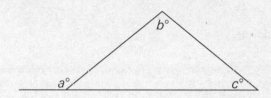

In the figure above, what is a in terms of b and c ?

○ $180 - b + c$
○ $180 + b + c$
○ $b + c$
○ $b + c - 180$
○ $b + c + 180$

Question 6

Quantity A	Quantity B
$3a^5$	$(3a)^5$

○ Quantity A is greater.
○ Quantity B is greater.
○ The two quantities are equal.
○ The relationship cannot be determined from the information given.

Question 7

3-D Printer A can print 10 Sheldon action figures in x hours, while 3-D Printer B can print 10 Sheldon action figures in $10 - x$ hours. x is an integer and $0 < x < 10$.

Quantity A	Quantity B
The number of action figures Printer B can produce in x hours	The number of hours it takes both machines working together to make 100 action figures

- ○ Quantity A is greater.
- ○ Quantity B is greater.
- ○ The two quantities are equal.
- ○ The relationship cannot be determined from the information given.

Question 8

$$0 < a < 3$$
$$-3 < b < 0$$

a and b are integers.

Quantity A	Quantity B
$a + b$	$a - b$

- ○ Quantity A is greater.
- ○ Quantity B is greater.
- ○ The two quantities are equal.
- ○ The relationship cannot be determined from the information given.

Question 9

$$0 < a < b < 1$$

Quantity A	Quantity B
0	$2(a - b)$

- ○ Quantity A is greater.
- ○ Quantity B is greater.
- ○ The two quantities are equal.
- ○ The relationship cannot be determined from the information given.

Question 10

Rachel, David, and Kristen decide to pool their money to buy a video game system. David contributes 4 dollars more than twice what Kristen does, and Kristen contributes 3 dollars less than Rachel does. If Rachel contributes r dollars, then how much does David contribute in terms of r ?

- ○ $\dfrac{r - 7}{2}$
- ○ $\dfrac{r - 2}{2}$
- ○ $\dfrac{2r + 7}{2}$
- ○ $2r - 2$
- ○ $2r + 7$

Question 11

If $x \neq 0$ and $y = \dfrac{x + 1}{x} - 1$, what is $\dfrac{1}{y}$?

- ○ x
- ○ $\dfrac{1}{x}$
- ○ $-x + 1$
- ○ $\dfrac{x + 1}{x - 1}$
- ○ $-(x + 1)$

Question 12

$$x < 0$$
$$y > x$$

Quantity A	Quantity B
x^2	y^3

○ Quantity A is greater.
○ Quantity B is greater.
○ The two quantities are equal.
○ The relationship cannot be determined
    from the information given.

Question 13

Quantity A	Quantity B
$x + y - 1$	$x - y + 1$

○ Quantity A is greater.
○ Quantity B is greater.
○ The two quantities are equal.
○ The relationship cannot be determined
    from the information given.

DRILL 2

Question 1

$$x > 1$$

Quantity A	Quantity B
$5^x + 1$	6^x

- ○ Quantity A is greater.
- ○ Quantity B is greater.
- ○ The two quantities are equal.
- ○ The relationship cannot be determined from the information given.

Question 2

At a crafts supply store, the price of a type of decorative string is c cents per foot. At this rate, what would be the price, in dollars, of y yards of this string?

- ○ $\dfrac{cy}{300}$
- ○ $\dfrac{100}{3cy}$
- ○ $\dfrac{3y}{100c}$
- ○ $\dfrac{3cy}{100}$
- ○ $\dfrac{300}{cy}$

Question 3

$$x^2 = |y|$$

Quantity A	Quantity B
$|x|$	y

- ○ Quantity A is greater.
- ○ Quantity B is greater.
- ○ The two quantities are equal.
- ○ The relationship cannot be determined from the information given.

Question 4

$$ab \neq 0$$

Quantity A	Quantity B
$\dfrac{a + b + c}{5}$	$\dfrac{1}{5ab} + \dfrac{c}{5}$

- ○ Quantity A is greater.
- ○ Quantity B is greater.
- ○ The two quantities are equal.
- ○ The relationship cannot be determined from the information given.

Question 5

If $D = \sqrt{C}$, where $C > 0$ and $C \neq 4$, then which of the following is equal to $\dfrac{D^2 - 4}{4C^{-1} - 1}$?

- ○ C
- ○ D
- ○ $C - D$
- ○ $-C$
- ○ $-D$

Question 6

If m is an odd integer, which of the following expresses the number of even integers between m and $2m$ inclusive?

- ○ $\dfrac{m}{2} + 1$
- ○ $\dfrac{m}{2} - 1$
- ○ $\dfrac{m + 1}{2}$
- ○ $\dfrac{m - 1}{2}$
- ○ $2m + 1$

Question 7

$$\frac{9}{5} = \frac{4}{5y}$$

Quantity A	Quantity B
$\dfrac{8}{9y}$	2

- ○ Quantity A is greater.
- ○ Quantity B is greater.
- ○ The two quantities are equal.
- ○ The relationship cannot be determined from the information given.

Question 8

$$x < 0 < y$$
x and y are integers.
$$w \neq 0$$

Quantity A	Quantity B
$-\dfrac{w}{x}$	$\dfrac{y}{w}$

- ○ Quantity A is greater.
- ○ Quantity B is greater.
- ○ The two quantities are equal.
- ○ The relationship cannot be determined from the information given.

Question 9

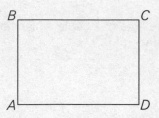

The length of rectangle *ABCD* is 60 percent of its width.

Quantity A	Quantity B
$\dfrac{1}{10}$ area of *ABCD*	The length of *ABCD*

- ○ Quantity A is greater.
- ○ Quantity B is greater.
- ○ The two quantities are equal.
- ○ The relationship cannot be determined from the information given.

Question 10

Two children named Peter and Wanda are playing a number game. If Peter's number z is 200 percent of Wanda's number, what is 20 percent of Wanda's number, in terms of z ?

- ○ $10z$

- ○ $2z$

- ○ $\dfrac{z}{5}$

- ○ $\dfrac{z}{10}$

- ○ $\dfrac{z}{20}$

Question 11

What is the area of a circle which has a circumference of x ?

- $\dfrac{x^2}{4\pi}$
- $\dfrac{x^2}{2\pi}$
- $\dfrac{x}{4\pi}$
- $\dfrac{x}{2\pi}$
- $2\sqrt{\pi x}$

Question 12

$$130 < x < 150$$

Quantity A	Quantity B
The greatest odd factor of x	The greatest even factor of x

- Quantity A is greater.
- Quantity B is greater.
- The two quantities are equal.
- The relationship cannot be determined from the information given.

DRILL 3

Question 1

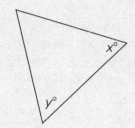

Quantity A	Quantity B
$358 - 2(x + y)$	$180 - (x + y)$

- ○ Quantity A is greater.
- ○ Quantity B is greater.
- ○ The two quantities are equal.
- ○ The relationship cannot be determined from the information given.

Question 2

$$pq \neq 0$$

Quantity A	Quantity B
$(p + q)^3$	$p^3 + q^3$

- ○ Quantity A is greater.
- ○ Quantity B is greater.
- ○ The two quantities are equal.
- ○ The relationship cannot be determined from the information given.

Question 3

$$D > E > 0$$

Quantity A	Quantity B
D^x	E^y

- ○ Quantity A is greater.
- ○ Quantity B is greater.
- ○ The two quantities are equal.
- ○ The relationship cannot be determined from the information given.

Question 4

Let x, y, and z be non-zero numbers such that the average (arithmetic mean) of x and twice y is equal to the average (arithmetic mean) of y and twice z. What is the average (arithmetic mean) of x and y ?

- ○ $\dfrac{z}{2}$
- ○ z
- ○ $2z$
- ○ $z - x$
- ○ $z - y$

Question 5

a, b, and c are consecutive even integers such that $a < b < c$ and $a + c \neq 0$.

Quantity A	Quantity B
$\dfrac{3}{a+c}$	$\dfrac{3}{2b+2}$

○ Quantity A is greater.
○ Quantity B is greater.
○ The two quantities are equal.
○ The relationship cannot be determined from the information given.

Question 6

$\dfrac{1}{r}$ of a circular pizza has been eaten. If the rest of the pizza is divided into m equal slices, then each of these slices is what fraction of the whole pizza?

○ $\dfrac{r}{rm}$

○ $\dfrac{r-1}{rm}$

○ $\dfrac{1}{m}$

○ $\dfrac{m-1}{rm}$

○ $\dfrac{m-r}{rm}$

Question 7

Quantity A	Quantity B
$(x + y)^2 - 2xy$	$x^2 + y^2$

○ Quantity A is greater.
○ Quantity B is greater.
○ The two quantities are equal.
○ The relationship cannot be determined from the information given.

Question 8

If $\dfrac{1}{x} < x < 0$, then which one of the following must be true?

○ $1 < x^2$

○ $x^2 < x$

○ $-1 < x^3 < 0$

○ $\dfrac{1}{x} > -1$

○ $x^3 < x$

Question 9

If $A = q - r$, $B = r - s$, and $C = q - s$, what is the value of $A - (B - C)$?

○ $-r$
○ 0
○ 1
○ $q + r$
○ $2(q - r)$

Question 10

If $ab > 0$ and $c \neq 0$, then which of the following must be positive?

○ abc

○ $-abc$

○ $a(-bc)^2$

○ $\dfrac{a}{b^2}$

○ a^3b^3

Question 11

If a factory produces cars at a rate of x cars per week, how many cars will two such factories produce in 24 hours?

○ $\dfrac{x}{7}$

○ $\dfrac{x}{24}$

○ $\dfrac{24x}{7}$

○ $\dfrac{2x}{7}$

○ $24x$

Question 12

If 7 orchids cost d dollars, then how much do 10 orchids cost, in dollars, at the same rate?

○ $70d$

○ $\dfrac{70}{d}$

○ $\dfrac{7}{10d}$

○ $\dfrac{10d}{7}$

○ $\dfrac{d}{70}$

DRILL 4

Question 1

Point A is located on a number line. If point A is between x and y, which are values on the same number line, and if $0 < x < y$, which of the following could represent the position of point A on the number line?

Indicate <u>all</u> possible values.

☐ $x + 1$
☐ $x - 1$
☐ $y + 1$
☐ $y - 1$
☐ $x + y$
☐ $x - y$
☐ $y - x$

Question 2

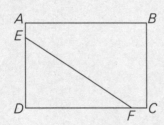

In the rectangle above, $AB = x$ feet, $BC = y$ feet, and $AE = FC = 2$ feet. What is the area of triangle DEF, in square feet?

○ $\dfrac{xy}{2} + 2$

○ $\dfrac{xy}{2} - x - y - 2$

○ $\dfrac{xy}{2} - x - y + 2$

○ $xy - 2x - 2y - 4$

○ $xy - 2x - 2y + 4$

Question 3

If integer a is divisible by both 3 and 14, which of the following must be true?

Indicate <u>all</u> such statements.

☐ a is divisible by 6
☐ a is equal to 42
☐ a is divisible by 21
☐ a is positive

Question 4

Points A and B are separated by 50 miles on a straight road. Cyclist A leaves point A, heading toward point B, at a constant speed of 15 miles per hour. At the same time, cyclist B leaves point B, traveling toward point A, at a constant speed of 10 miles per hour. How many minutes have elapsed when the two cyclists meet?

Question 5

If $x < y$ and $0 < x + y$, which of the following must be negative?

Indicate <u>all</u> possible values.

☐ $-x$
☐ $-y$
☐ $x - y$
☐ $(x - y)^2$
☐ $2x - y$

Question 6

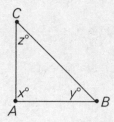

In the figure above, if x, y, and z are integers and $x < y + z$, then what is the greatest possible value of x ?

Question 7

If p is a negative even integer and q is a positive odd integer, which of the following must be true?

○ pq is a negative odd integer.

○ $\dfrac{p}{q}$ is a negative odd integer.

○ $p - q$ is a positive odd integer.

○ $p + q$ is a positive odd integer.

○ $q - p$ is a positive odd integer.

Question 8

If f is a fraction between -1 and 1, which of the following must be true?

Indicate <u>all</u> such answers.

☐ $f^7 < f^5$

☐ $f^6 - f^7 < f^4 - f^5$

☐ $f^6 + f^7 < f^5 + f^4$

☐ $(-f)^3 < f^3$

☐ $f^6 < f^4$

Question 9

At Pedantic Publishing Corporation, $\dfrac{1}{5}$ of the employees take the bus to work and $\dfrac{1}{3}$ drive to work. Of the employees who do not take the bus or drive to work, $\dfrac{1}{4}$ take the subway. If $\dfrac{1}{7}$ of the remaining employees ride a bicycle to work, and the rest walk, what fraction of the employees walks to work?

Question 10

If a is 60% of b, b is 40% of c, and c is 20% of d, then $6d$ is what percent of $20a$?

☐

Question 11

If $1 \leq n \leq 100$, and $\dfrac{n+7}{2}$ is a multiple of 4 but not a multiple of 3, then which of the following could be true?

Indicate <u>all</u> such statements.

☐ n is even
☐ n is odd
☐ n is prime
☐ n is a multiple of 3
☐ n is a multiple of 4

ANSWERS

Drill 1	Drill 2	Drill 3	Drill 4
1. B	1. B	1. D	1. A, D, G
2. D	2. D	2. D	2. C
3. D	3. D	3. D	3. A, C
4. D	4. D	4. B	4. 120
5. C	5. D	5. A	5. B, C
6. D	6. C	6. B	6. 89
7. D	7. C	7. C	7. E
8. B	8. D	8. C	8. B, C, E
9. A	9. D	9. E	9. $\dfrac{3}{10}$
10. D	10. D	10. E	10. 625
11. A	11. A	11. D	11. B, C, D
12. D	12. D	12. D	
13. D			

EXPLANATIONS
Drill 1

1. **B**   There are variables in the question stem and quantities, so Plug In. Start by Plugging In an easy value for y, such as 2. Quantity A is $4 \times 6 = 24$ and Quantity B is $16(2) - 4 = 28$. Quantity B is greater, so eliminate (A) and (C). Plug In more than once for Quant Comp problems, this time using a FROZEN number such as 1. Quantity A is $4 \times 2 = 8$ and Quantity B is $16 - 4 = 12$. Quantity B is still greater so eliminate (D). The correct answer is (B).

2. **D**   There are variables in the question stem, so Plug In a value for a, such as $a = 1$. Quantity A is equal to 1 and Quantity B is also 1. Both quantities are equal so eliminate (A) and (B). For Quant Comp problems, Plug In more than once using a FROZEN number such as Fractions. If you Plug In $a = \dfrac{1}{2}$, Quantity A is still 1. Plug In again, this time using a regular integer such as $a = 4$. If $a = 4$, then Quantity A is $\dfrac{1}{4}$. Since Quantity B is now greater than Quantity A, eliminate (C) and select (D).

3. **D**   This problem has variables in the question stem and quantities, so Plug In. This problem looks suspiciously simple. Clearly $x = 3$ and $y = 4$. Eliminate choices (A) and (C). However, remember to Plug In more than once using FROZEN numbers for Quant Comp problems. Plug In again. Because $y^2 = 16$ could represent either $y = 4$ or $y = -4$. If y equals -4, then Quantity A is greater. Eliminate (B) and the correct answer is (D).

4. **D**   This problem has variables in the question stem and quantities, so Plug In. Start by Plugging In easy numbers such as $x = 2$ and $y = 1$. Quantity A is greater, so eliminate (B) and (C). Now Plug In again using FROZEN numbers and try to get a different answer. Use extreme numbers such as $x = 100$ and $y = 101$. Quantity B is now greater, so eliminate (A) and the correct answer is (D).

5. **C**   Algebraically, both a and $b + c$ are equal to 180 minus the unnamed angle in the triangle. Like most relationships that involve both algebra and geometry, though, this is most easily seen by Plugging In values for the angles. If $a = 110$, for instance, the unnamed angle in the triangle is 70°. Plug In 60 for b, which means c is 50. Because a equals the sum of b and c, select (C).

6. **D**   There are variables in the quantities, so Plug In. Begin with something that impacts exponents in a unique way, such as 1. When $a = 1$, Quantity A is 3 and Quantity B is something greater than 3. Eliminate (A) and (C). Now Plug In again using FROZEN numbers. Try $a = 0$. In this case, both quantities are equal. Eliminate (B) and the correct answer is (D).

7. **D**   Use Rate Pies to organize the information. Draw a Rate Pie for Printer A and fill in 10 for the number of action figures and x for the number of hours. Divide to find that Printer A's rate is $\dfrac{10}{x}$.

       Then draw a Rate Pie for Printer B and fill in 10 for the number of action figures and $10 - x$ for the number of hours. Divide to find that Printer B's rate is $\dfrac{10}{10 - x}$.

To find Quantity A (the number of action figures Printer B can produce in x hours), draw another Rate Pie and write x for the number of hours and write $\frac{10}{10-x}$ for the rate. Multiply to get that the number of action figures produced is $\frac{10x}{10-x}$.

To find Quantity B (the number of hours required for both printers to make 100 action figures), draw another pie for the two machines working together. For the rate, combine their rates, and for the total use 100. Divide to find that the number of hours is $\frac{100}{\frac{10}{x}+\frac{10}{10-x}}$.

Since this is a quantitative comparison with variables, Plug In multiple times using FROZEN. Start with an easy number such as $x = 1$. In this case, Quantity A is $\frac{10}{9}$. Quantity B is

$\frac{100}{10+\frac{10}{9}} = \frac{100}{\frac{90}{9}+\frac{10}{9}} = \frac{100}{\frac{100}{9}} = 9$. Quantity B is greater here, so eliminate (A) and (C). Now consider FROZEN. Fractions are not allowed, there are no repeats, 1 has been used, 0 is not allowed, and negatives are not allowed. Try an extreme number such as $x = 9$, since that is the maximum x value.

In this case, Quantity A is $\frac{90}{1} = 90$. Quantity B is $\frac{100}{\frac{10}{9}+10} = 9$. Now Quantity A is greater, so eliminate (B). The correct answer is (D).

8. **B** There are variables in the question stem and quantities, so Plug In values for a and b that do not violate the restrictions of the problem. Try $a = 1$ and $b = -2$. In Quantity A, the sum is $1 + (-2) = -1$, and in Quantity B the difference is $1 - (-2) = 3$. Quantity B is greater, so eliminate (A) and (C). Plug In again using FROZEN numbers. There aren't many FROZEN numbers that can be used, so instead try $a = 2$ and $b = -1$. Quantity B is still greater, so eliminate (D) and the correct answer is (B).

9. **A** There are variables in the question stem and quantities, so Plug In values for a and b. If $a = \frac{1}{4}$ and $b = \frac{1}{2}$, then the value in Quantity B is $2\left(\frac{1}{4}-\frac{1}{2}\right) = 2\left(-\frac{1}{4}\right) = -\frac{1}{2}$. Quantity A is greater, so eliminate (B) and (C). Because b is greater than a, $(a - b)$ is negative, so any other allowable values for a and b produce the same results. Quantity A is greater than Quantity B, so the correct answer is (A).

10. **D** The answer choices contain variables, so Plug In. If $r = 6$, then Kristen contributes 3 dollars less than r, or \$3, and David contributes twice as much as Kristen plus 4 more, or $6 + 4 = 10, which is

the target number. Now Plug In 6 for *r* in the answer. Only (D) matches the target number of $10, as $2r - 2 = 2(6) - 2 = 12 - 2 = 10$. The correct answer is (D).

11.   **A**   There are variables in the question stem and answer choices, so Plug In values for *x* such as 2. When $x = 2$, *y* is $\frac{1}{2}$. The question asks to solve for $\frac{1}{y}$, so the target number is 2. Replace *x* with 2 in each of the answer choices to find that (A) is the only one that matches the target number. The correct answer is (A).

12.   **D**   Because this is a quantitative comparison with variables, Plug In multiple times using FROZEN. Start with easy numbers like $x = -1$ and $y = 1$. In this case, Quantity A is 1 and Quantity B is also 1. Because the two quantities are equal in this case, eliminate (A) and (B). Next try making both numbers negative, such as $x = -2$ and $y = -1$. In this case, Quantity A is 4 and Quantity B is −1. Since the two quantities are not equal with these numbers, eliminate (C). The correct answer is (D).

13.   **D**   There are variables in the quantities, so Plug In values for *x* and *y*, such as $x = 10$ and $y = 1$. Quantity A equals 10 and Quantity B equals 10. The quantities are equal, so eliminate (A) and (B). Plug In again using FROZEN numbers. Try repeats but do them in reverse, such as $x = 1$ and $y = 10$. Now Quantity A is 10, but Quantity B equals −8. The quantities are no longer equal, so eliminate (C) and the correct answer is (D).

Drill 2

1.   **B**   There are variables in the question stem and quantities, so Plug In a value for *x*, such as $x = 2$. In this case, Quantity A is 26 and Quantity B is 36. Eliminate (A) and (C). Now Plug In again using FROZEN numbers. Extreme numbers such as $x = 100$ result in a larger Quantity B than Quantity A. In fact, no matter what number is Plugged In for *x*, Quantity B is greater. The correct answer is (B).

2.   **D**   There are variables in the question stem and answer choices, so Plug In values such as $c = 100$ and $y = 2$. The price of the string is 100 cents (or 1 dollar) per foot. Therefore, the string is 3 dollars per yard, so the price of 2 yards is 6 dollars. Plug In $c = 100$ and $y = 2$ into the answer choices. The only answer that produces a value of 6 is (D). The correct answer is (D).

3.   **D**   There are variables in the question stem and quantities, so Plug In. Plug In a value for *x* that makes the calculation easy, such as $x = 2$. If $x = 2$, then $y = 4$. Quantity B is greater than Quantity A, so eliminate (A) and (C). Now Plug In again using FROZEN numbers. If $x = 1$, then $y = 1$, and the quantities are equal. Eliminate (B) and the correct answer is (D).

4. **D** There are variables in the question stem and answer choices, so Plug In. Plug In numbers that sum to a multiple of 5 such as $a = 2$, $b = 3$, and $c = 5$. With these numbers, Quantity A is 2 and Quantity B is $1\frac{1}{30}$. Eliminate (B) and (C). Plug In again using FROZEN numbers and try to make Quantity B greater. Try negative numbers such as $a = -2$, $b = -3$, and c is something much less, such as -20. Now Quantity A is 3 and Quantity B is $4\frac{1}{30}$, so eliminate (A). The correct answer is (D).

5. **D** This problem has variables in the problem and in the answer choices, so Plug In. Pick a perfect square for C other than 4, such as $C = 9$. Therefore, according to the problem's conditions, $D = 3$. Plug C and D into the expression to get $\frac{D^2 - 4}{4C^{-1} - 1} = \frac{3^2 - 4}{4 \times 9^{-1} - 1} = \frac{9 - 4}{\frac{4}{9} - 1}$. Replacing the 1 with $\frac{9}{9}$ makes subtracting fractions in the denominator that much easier. $\frac{9 - 4}{\frac{4}{9} - \frac{9}{9}} = \frac{5}{\frac{-5}{9}}$. Rewrite the fraction as $5 \div \left(\frac{-5}{9}\right) = 5 \times \left(\frac{9}{-5}\right)$. Canceling the 5s leaves -9, which is the target. Next Plug In the values for C and D into the answer choices. Choice (A) is 9, so eliminate it. Choice (B) is 3, so eliminate it. Choice (C) is $9 - 3 = 6$, so eliminate it. Choice (D) is -9, so keep it. Choice (E) is -3, so eliminate it. The correct answer is (D).

6. **C** There are variables in the question stem and answer choices, so Plug In. Try $m = 3$. Between 3 and 6 inclusive, there are two even integers, so 2 is the target number. Plug In 3 for m in the answer choices, looking for an answer choice that matches the target number. The only choice that matches is (C), which is the correct answer.

7. **C** Start by solving for the value of y, which appears in the equation $\frac{9}{5} = \frac{4}{5y}$ in the question stem. Cross multiply to produce $\frac{9(5y)}{5} = 4$; then reduce and divide to get $y = \frac{4}{9}$. Next, substitute this value for y into Quantity A to yield $\frac{8}{9\left(\frac{4}{9}\right)}$. Reduce and divide to find that Quantity A is equal to 2 and the two Quantities are equal. The correct answer is (C).

8. **D** There are variables in the question stem and quantities, so Plug In. Begin Plugging In with numbers that are easy to work with, such as $w = 1$, $x = -2$, and $y = 1$. With these numbers, Quantity A is $\frac{1}{2}$ and Quantity B is 1. Eliminate (A) and (C). Now Plug In again using FROZEN numbers, abiding by any restrictions given by the question stem. Following the

restrictions provided in the question stem for the values, try a negative number for w, such as $w = -1$, $x = -2$, and $y = 4$. Now, Quantity A is $-\frac{1}{2}$ and Quantity B is -4. Because $-\frac{1}{2}$ is greater than -4, eliminate (B). The correct answer is (D).

9. **D** First, try plugging in some easy numbers for the length and width that obey the restrictions, such as 6 and 10. The area of the rectangle is 60, so the two columns are equal. Eliminate (A) and (B). Now try plugging in different numbers, such as 12 and 20. This time, column A is greater, so the answer must be (D).

10. **D** There are variables in the question stem and answer choices, so Plug In. Plug In a value for z that is easy to work with, such as $z = 100$. If $z = 100$, then Wanda's number is 50 and 20 percent of 50 is 10. So, 10 is the target number. Plug In 100 for z in all the answer choices looking for one that equals 10. Choice (D) is the only choice that equals 10, so the correct answer is (D).

11. **A** There are variables in the question stem and answer choices, so Plug In. Because the variable x represents the circumference of the circle, pick a number to Plug In that makes it easy to solve for the radius, such as $x = 8\pi$. In this case, the radius of the circle is 4 and the area is 16π, which is the target number. Now Plug In 8π for x into all the answer choices looking for one that matches the target number. Choice (A) is the only answer choice that matches the target. The correct answer is (A).

12. **D** There is a variable in the question stem and in the quantities, so Plug In. The variable is any number between 130 and 150. The question asks about the greatest factors, so start by Plugging In the greatest integer which is 149. If x is 149, then the greatest odd factor of x is 149. However, there is no even factor of 149, so Quantity A is greater. Eliminate (B) and (C). Plug In again. If $x = 148$, then the greatest even factor is 148 and there is no odd factor, so Quantity B is greater. Eliminate (A). The correct answer is (D).

Drill 3

1. **D** There are variables in the figure and the quantities, so Plug In. The triangle has 2 angles labeled but not the third, so label the third angle of the triangle z. For this problem, it may be easier to Plug In for angle z. Plug In an easy number such as $z = 100$, which means $x + y = 80$. Quantity A calculates to 198 and Quantity B is 100. Eliminate (B) and (C). Now Plug In again using FROZEN numbers. Try an extreme number, such as $z = 2$. If $z = 2$, then Quantity A is 2 and Quantity B is also 2. Eliminate (A) and the correct answer is (D).

2. **D** There are variables in the question stem and quantities, so Plug In. Start with easy numbers for p and q such as $p = 1$ and $q = 2$. In this case, Quantity A is 27 and Quantity B is 9. Eliminate (B) and (C). Plug In again using FROZEN numbers. Try fractions such as $p = \frac{1}{2}$ and $q = \frac{1}{4}$. In this case, Quantity A is $\frac{27}{64}$ and Quantity B is $\frac{9}{64}$. Quantity A is still greater. Plug In one more time,

this time with negative numbers such as $p = -3$ and $q = -2$. Now, Quantity A is -125 and Quantity B is -35. Because -35 is greater than -125, Quantity B is greater than Quantity A. Eliminate (A). The correct answer is (D).

3. **D** As this problem has variables in a quantitative comparison, Plug In multiple times. Start with easy numbers such as $D = 2$, $E = 1$, $x = 2$, and $y = 2$. In this case, Quantity A is $2^2 = 4$, and Quantity B is $1^2 = 1$. Since Quantity A is greater in this case, eliminate (B) and (C). Now consider FROZEN numbers. Try using 0 for x and y and keeping $D = 2$ and $E = 1$. In this case, Quantity A is $2^0 = 1$, and Quantity B is $1^0 = 1$. Since the two quantities are equal in this case, eliminate (A). The correct answer is (D).

4. **B** There are variables in the question stem and answer choices, so Plug In making sure to follow the restrictions in the question stem. Plug In something simple, such as $x = 2$ and $y = 3$. Therefore, the average is 4, which is equal to the average of $y + 2z$. Plug In for y to solve that z is 2.5. The question asks for the average of x and y, which is also 2.5. The target number is 2.5. Plug In for the variables in the answer choices, looking for one that equals 2.5. The correct answer is (B).

5. **A** This is a quantitative comparison with variables, so Plug In multiple times. Start with easy numbers that fulfill the conditions stated in the problem, such as $a = 2$, $b = 4$, $c = 6$. In this case, Quantity A is $\frac{3}{8}$ and Quantity B is $\frac{3}{10}$. Quantity A is greater, so eliminate (B) and (C). Now consider FROZEN numbers. Fractions and 1 are not allowed, and repeats include 2 and 3. The number 2 has already been used and 3 is not allowed by the problem. Try zero because it is an even integer. Let $a = 0$, $b = 2$, and $c = 4$. In this case, Quantity A is $\frac{3}{4}$ and Quantity B is $\frac{3}{6} = \frac{1}{2}$. Quantity A is still greater. Now test extreme numbers such as $a = 20$, $b = 22$, and $c = 24$. In this case, Quantity A is $\frac{3}{44}$ and Quantity B is $\frac{3}{46}$. Quantity A is still greater. Next try negative numbers such as $a = -6$, $b = -4$, and $c = -2$. In this case, Quantity A is $\frac{3}{-6 + (-2)} = -\frac{3}{8}$ and Quantity B is $\frac{3}{-8 + 2} = \frac{3}{-6} = -\frac{1}{2}$. Quantity A is still greater. Since everything from FROZEN that is allowed by the problem has been used, choose (A). The correct answer is (A).

6. **B** There are variables in the question stem and answer choices, so Plug In. Start with easy numbers such as $r = 2$ and $m = 4$. If $\frac{1}{2}$ of the pizza has been eaten, and the remaining $\frac{1}{2}$ is divided into 4 equal slices, then each of those remaining pieces is $\frac{1}{8}$ of the whole pizza, which is the target number. Plug In 2 for r and 4 for m in the answer choices looking for one that matches the target answer. The correct answer is (B).

7. **C** There are variables in the quantities, so Plug In. However, first simplify as much as possible by recognizing the common quadratics. In Quantity A, $(x + y)^2 = x^2 + 2xy + y^2$. This means that $x^2 + 2xy + y^2 - 2xy = x^2 + y^2$. Thus, the two quantities are equal and the correct answer is (C). However, if the common quadratics were not noticed, then Plug In. If $x = 2$ and $y = 3$, then Quantity A equals $25 - 12 = 13$, and Quantity B equals $4 + 9 = 13$. Any set of values gives the same outcome, so the correct answer is (C).

8. **C** There are variables in the question stem and answer choices, so Plug In a value for x that satisfies all the conditions of the question such as $x = -\dfrac{1}{2}$. This question asks what must be true, so Plug In this value of x into the answer choices, eliminating any that are false. The only choice that is true is (C), which is the correct answer.

9. **E** There are variables in the question stem and answer choices, so Plug In. Try numbers that are easy to work with such as $q = 10$, $r = 5$, and $s = 2$. So, $A = 10 - 5 = 5$, $B = 5 - 2 = 3$, and $C = 10 - 2 = 8$. In this case, $A - (B - C) = 5 - (3 - 8) = 5 - (-5) = 10$. This is the target number, so Plug In for the answer choices to see if any match the target number. The correct answer is (E).

10. **E** With variables in the problem and in the answer choices, use Plugging In. Since the problem uses the words "must be," keep in mind the possibility of Plugging In more than once. Start with easy numbers that fit the conditions of the problem, such as $a = 1$, $b = 2$, and $c = 3$. In this case, (A) is 6, so keep it. Choice (B) is -6, so eliminate it. Choice (C) is $1(-6)^2 = 36$, so keep it. Choice (D) is $\dfrac{1}{4}$, so keep it. Choice (E) is $1(8) = 8$, so keep it. Now try a different type of number, such as negatives. Let $a = -1$, $b = -2$, and $c = -3$. In this case, (A) is -6, so eliminate it. Choice (C) is $-1(-6)^2 = -36$, so eliminate it. Choice (D) is $-\dfrac{1}{4}$, so eliminate it. Choice (E) is $(-1)(-8) = 8$, so keep it. The correct answer is (E).

11. **D** This problem has variables in the question and answer choices, so use Plugging In. Try $x = 14$ cars per week. 24 hours is 1 day and there are 7 days in a week. So 1 factory will produce $\dfrac{14}{7} = 2$ cars per day. Therefore, 2 factories will produce twice that many, or 4, cars per day, which is the target number. Plug 14 in for x for each of the answer choices and see which one(s) match the target. Choice (A) is 2, so eliminate it. Choice (B) is $\dfrac{14}{24} = \dfrac{7}{12}$, so eliminate it. Choice (C) is 48, so eliminate it. Choice (D) is 4, so keep it. Choice (E) is 336, so eliminate it. The correct answer is (D).

12. **D** There are variables in the question stem and answer choices, so Plug In a number for d such as $d = 14$. If $d = 14$, then 7 orchids cost 14 dollars. Since $14 \div 7 = 2$, one orchid must cost 2 dollars. If one orchid costs 2 dollars, then 10 orchids cost 20 dollars, so 20 is the target number. Plug In $d = 14$ for the answer choices. Choice (A) is 70×14, which is too great, so eliminate (A). Choice (B) is $70 \div 14$, which is also not equal to 20, so eliminate (B). Choice (C) is $7 \div 10 \times 14$, which is a fraction, and not equal to 20, so eliminate (C). Choice (D) is $140 \div 7 = 20$, which matches the

target number. Keep (D), but remember to check all five choices on Plugging In problems. Choice (E) is 14 ÷ 70, which is not equal to 20. Only (D) matches the target, so it is the correct answer.

Drill 4

1. **A, D, G**

   There are variables in the question stem and answer choices, so Plug In values for x and y. This question involves number lines, so draw a number line. Plug In $x = 4$ and $y = 10$. In this case, point A is on the number line between 4 and 10. Choice (A) is $4 + 1$, which equals 5. Since 5 is on the number line between 4 and 10, this works, so select (A). Choice (B) is $4 - 1$, which equals 3. This is not between 4 and 10. Eliminate (B). Choice (C) is $10 + 1$. Since 11 is not on the number line between 4 and 10, eliminate (C). Choice (D) is $10 - 1$. Since 9 is on the number line between 4 and 10, this works, so select (D). Choice (E) is $4 + 10$. Since 14 is not on the number line between 4 and 10, eliminate (E). Choice (F) is $4 - 10$. Since -6 is not on the number line between 4 and 10, eliminate (F). Choice (G) is $10 - 4$. Since 6 is on the number line between 4 and 10, it works. Select (G). The correct answer is (A), (D), and (G).

2. **C** There are variables in the question stem and answer choices, so Plug In values for x and y. If $x = 4$ and $y = 5$, then the sides of the triangle are 2 and 3. The area of a triangle is $\frac{1}{2}bh$, so the triangle has an area of 3, which is the target number. Plug In for each of the answer choices, looking for one that matches the target number. Only (C) matches the target, so the correct answer is (C).

3. **A, C** There are variables in the question stem and answer choices, so Plug In a value for a. If $a = -42$, then it is divisible by 6 and 21 but is not positive or equal to 42, so eliminate (B) and (D). If $a = 84$, it is still divisible by 3 and 14, as well as by 21 and 6. In fact, a is always divisible by 6 and 21, because the prime factors of 3 and 14 are 2, 3, and 7 and the distinct prime factors of 6 and 21 are also 2, 3, and 7. The correct answer is (A) and (C).

4. **120** Cyclists A and B start 50 miles apart and are heading at each other at 15 and 10 miles per hour, respectively. Use the distance formula, which is $d = r \times t$. The rates at which the two travel are different, so the distances they travel are different. However, since they start at the same time and meet at the same time, their times are the same. Therefore write both of the distance equations as follows:

   (1) $d_A = 15 \times t$,
   (2) $d_B = 10 \times t$.

   Since their distances together equals 50 miles, write another equation:

   (3) $d_A + d_B = 50$.

   There are three equations with three variables, so it is possible to solve for t. Plug equations (1) and (2) into (3), finding the following:

   $$15 \times t + 10 \times t = 50$$

   Now solve for t, finding $t = 2$. Their speeds were given in miles per hour, and the question asks for the answer in minutes, so convert hours to minutes, which results in 120 minutes, which is the correct answer.

5. **B, C** There are variables in the question stem and answer choices, so Plug In. Start with easy values such as $x = 2$ and $y = 3$. Plug In $x = 2$ and $y = 3$ into the answer choices and use process of elimination. Choice (A) is -2 and (B) is -3, so keep (A) and (B). Because $2 - 3 = -1$, keep (C). Choice (D) is the same as (C), but squared. Because $(-1)^2 = 1$, eliminate (D). Choice (E) is $2(2) - 3$, which equals 1, so eliminate (E). Because the problem says "must be," Plug In more than once to see if there are ways to eliminate any other answer choices. Try negative numbers. If $x = -2$ and $y = 3$, then $x + y = -2 + 3 = 1$, so the requirements of the problem are still met. In this case $-x$ is now positive 2, so eliminate (A). Choice (B) is still positive. In fact, even though x can be negative, y is always positive to make $0 < x + y$, so (B) is always correct. Choice (C) is $-2 - 3 = -5$. Because a greater number is being subtracted from a lesser number, (C) is always negative, so keep (C). The correct answer is (B) and (C).

6. **89** Since there are variables in the question stem and the figure, Plug In. Since all angles of a triangle add up to $180°$, $x + y + z = 180$. Since x is less than $y + z$, $180 - (y + z) < y + z$. This means that 180 is less than $2(y + z)$ and therefore, $y + z$ is greater than 90. Because the question is looking for the greatest value for x, select the least possible value of $y + z$ which is 91. If $y + z = 91$, then $x = 89$. Because x cannot be any larger, 89 is the correct answer.

7. **E** There are variables in the question stem and answer choices, so Plug In. Because this is a "must be" question, Plug In more than once. Start with $p = -2$ and $q = 3$. Eliminate (A), because $pq = -6$. Eliminate (B), because $\frac{p}{q} = -\frac{2}{3}$. Eliminate (C), because $p - q = -5$. Choices (D) and (E) both work, so use new values to test the remaining answers. Try $p = -4$ and $q = 1$. Now $p + q = -3$, so eliminate (D). The correct answer is (E).

8. **B, C, E**

There are variables in the question stem and answer choices, so Plug In. This is a "must be" question, so Plug In more than once. First, Plug In $f = \frac{1}{2}$. Plugging this value for f into the answer choices yields all correct answers, so choose a different number, such as $f = -\frac{1}{2}$. Eliminate (A) and (D). The correct answer is (B), (C), and (E).

9. $\dfrac{3}{10}$ Plug In for the total number of employees in the company. If there are 60 employees, then the number of employees who take the bus to work equals $60 \times \frac{1}{5} = 12$, and the number of employees who drive to work equals $60 \times \frac{1}{3} = 20$. Therefore, $60 - 12 - 20 = 28$ left who neither take the bus nor drive to work. $\frac{1}{4}$ of these employees take the subway, so there are $28 \times \frac{1}{4} = 7$ employees who

ride the subway. $28 - 7 = 21$, so there are 21 employees remaining. $\frac{1}{7}$ of those employees ride a bicycle, so there are $21 \times \frac{1}{7} = 3$ employees who ride a bicycle. $21 - 3 = 18$, so there are 18 employees who walk to work. $\frac{18}{60} = \frac{3}{10}$, which is the correct answer.

10. **625** There are variables in the question stem, so Plug In, keeping in mind the requirements of the problem. Meet the first requirement by making $a = 60$ and $b = 100$. Since b is 40% of c, $100 = \frac{40}{100} \times c$, and $c = 250$. Because c is 20% of d, $250 = \frac{20}{100} \times d$, and $d = 1,250$. Now use the values for the variables to translate the last part of the question into the equation $6(1,250) = \frac{x}{100} \times 20(60)$, which is $7,500 = \frac{x}{100} \times 1,200$. Therefore, $7,500 = 12x$, and $x = 625$. The correct answer is 625.

11. **B, C, D**

There are variables in the question stem and answer choices, so Plug In. Before Plugging In for n, assign a value that meets the requirement of the question that the fractional expression is a multiple of 4 but not 3. Set the equation equal to 4 and solve for n. Since $\frac{n+7}{2} = 4$, then $n = 1$. This makes (B) true. Plug In another value and solve for n again. If $\frac{n+7}{2} = 8$, then $n = 9$, so (D) is true. Note that $\frac{n+7}{2} \neq 12$, because 12 is a multiple of 3, so $n \neq 17$. Look for a pattern. The 3 values for what n can and can't be—1 and 9, but not 17—are enough to establish a pattern, which is increase by 8, but eliminate every third term. The rest of the list is thus 25 and 33, but not 41; 49 and 57, but not 65; 73 and 81, but not 89; and 97. Since 73 and 97 are both prime, (C) can be true as well. The correct answer is (B), (C), and (D).

PITA and
Hidden Plug In

PITA AND HIDDEN PLUG IN

Plugging In can also be applied to questions that just have numbers. While there are only numbers in the problem, they typically require an algebraic solution. But again with Plugging In, we can just do arithmetic and avoid the time-consuming and sometimes difficult algebra.

PITA (PLUGGING IN THE ANSWERS)

When there are numeric answer choices and the question asks for a specific value that is represented by the answer choices, we know one of the numbers has to be correct. We can Plug In the Answers until we find one that works. Since only one number can work, there is no need to try all of the answer choices. Stop once a number works with all of the information given in the problem.

Let's look at this example.

> Vicken, Roger, and Adam went to buy a $90 radio.
> If Roger agrees to pay twice as much as Adam,
> and Vicken agrees to pay three times as much as
> Adam, how much must Roger pay?
>
> ○ $10
> ○ $20
> ○ $30
> ○ $45
> ○ $65

Step 1: Recognize the opportunity
There are ways to know if a certain problem is a good candidate to Plug In the Answers:

- the question asks for a specific amount that the answer choices represent
- the question asks "how many" or "how much"
- it seems appropriate to write and solve an algebraic equation

In this case the question asks "**How much** must Roger pay?" and the answer choices represent that specific amount.

Step 2: List the answer choices on your scratch paper.
List $10, $20, $30, $45, and $65 in a vertical column.

Step 3: Label the answer choices

What do those numbers represent? The amount Roger pays. Label this first column Roger.

Step 4: Plug In (C)

Assume Roger pays $30.

Step 5: Work the problem in bite-sized pieces, making a new column for each new step

If Roger pays $30, then Adam pays $15. Make a column for Adam with $15 written under the column in the same row as (C). Vicken pays $45, so make a column for Vicken with $45 written under it.

Step 6: Use POE

Add up all three contributions to find a total of $90. The radio costs $90 so all the information fits together. Because on a multiple-choice problem only one answer choice works, when you Plug In the Answers and find a choice that works, you're done. The correct answer is (C). If this choice didn't work, then try another answer choice. If the amount is less than expected, try a greater value. If the amount is too great, try a lesser value.

Here's what the scratch paper looks like:

Roger	Adam	Vicken	Total
10			
20			
(30)	15	45	90
40			
65			

HIDDEN PLUG IN

If the question implies a variable, but does not explicitly detail the variable, Plugging In is still an option. This is a Hidden Plug In question. While these problems can be difficult, Plugging In makes the problems easier. Often the hardest part is identifying that Plugging In is an option.

Let's look at this example.

> Jacob eats $\frac{1}{5}$ of his daily caloric intake at breakfast and $\frac{4}{15}$ at lunch. If he eats $\frac{1}{2}$ of his remaining daily caloric intake by snacking, what portion of his daily caloric intake is left over for dinner?
>
>

Step 1: Recognize the opportunity

There are ways to know if a certain problem is a good candidate as a Hidden Plug In:

- the question asks for a fraction, ratio, or percent
- it seems appropriate to write and solve an algebraic equation
- the problem would be a lot easier if it gave one more value (Plug In a number for that value.)

This question asks for a portion and would be a lot easier to solve if we knew Jacob's daily caloric intake.

Step 2: Plug In an easy number (according to the problem's restrictions)

Plug In an amount for Jacob's daily caloric intake. Since there are fractions in the question pick a value that works well with 5, 15, and 2. Let's say Jacob's daily caloric intake is 30. It's okay if the numbers aren't very realistic. Make the numbers easy to work with.

Step 3: Work through the problem

If Jacob's daily caloric intake is 30, then he eats 6 calories for breakfast and 8 calories for lunch. Then 16 calories are remaining, so snacking accounts for 8 calories. This leaves 8 calories for dinner.

Step 4: Find the answer

The question asks what portion of his daily caloric intake is left over, which is 8 of 30 calories. The answer is $\frac{8}{30}$, which simplifies to $\frac{4}{15}$.

With the Plugging In techniques discussed in the last section, in addition to PITA and Hidden Plug In, almost any algebraic problem can be solved with a Plugging In strategy. For further examples of PITA and Hidden Plug Ins, check out our student-friendly guidebook, *Cracking the GRE*.

DRILL 1

Question 1

Alice buys a house to fix up and then resell. If the cost to fix it up is 25% of the price she paid for the house, and the total cost of the house and repairs is $140,000, how much did Alice pay for the house alone?

- ○ 102,000
- ○ 105,000
- ○ 110,000
- ○ 112,000
- ○ 175,000

Question 2

If 3 less than twice a certain number is equal to 2 more than 3 times the number, then 5 less than 5 times the number is

- ○ −30
- ○ −20
- ○ −5
- ○ 0
- ○ 20

Question 3

A sports league encourages collaboration by awarding 3 points for each goal scored without assistance and 5 points for each goal scored with assistance. A total of 48 points was scored by a team in a single game. Which of the following CANNOT be the number of goals scored without assistance by this team in this game?

- ○ 1
- ○ 6
- ○ 11
- ○ 12
- ○ 16

Question 4

Melinda and Shirley worked together to make hamburger patties. Shirley worked for 1 hour and 45 minutes and Melinda worked for 45 minutes. Melinda's hourly rate, however, is twice that of Shirley's. If together they earned a total of $48.75, what was Shirley's hourly rate?

- ○ $15
- ○ $20
- ○ $25
- ○ $30
- ○ $35

Question 5

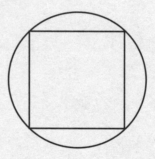

In the figure above, a square is inscribed in a circle. If the area of the circle is 16π, then what is the area of the square?

- ○ 16
- ○ 24
- ○ 28
- ○ 32
- ○ 64

Question 6

At a restaurant, all tips are added together to be split among the employees at the end of a shift. The 4 waiters combined get $\frac{2}{3}$ of the money, the manager receives $\frac{1}{4}$, and the busboy receives the remainder. If 1 waiter and the busboy together receive $30, how much money was earned in tips for the entire shift?

- ○ $90
- ○ $96
- ○ $108
- ○ $120
- ○ $180

Question 7

If $\dfrac{\sqrt{27}}{\sqrt{54}} \times \dfrac{\sqrt{x}}{\sqrt{6}} = \dfrac{1}{2}$, what is the value of x?

- ○ 2
- ○ 3
- ○ 4
- ○ 5
- ○ 7

Question 8

If n is positive, $\dfrac{n}{m} = 4$, and $mn = 9$, then $m =$

- ○ $\dfrac{1}{6}$
- ○ $\dfrac{2}{3}$
- ○ $\dfrac{3}{2}$
- ○ 6
- ○ $\dfrac{27}{2}$

Question 9

During a sale, the original price of a garment is lowered by 20%. Because the garment did not sell, its sale price was reduced by 10%. The final price of the garment could have been obtained with a single discount of what percent?

- ○ 22%
- ○ 25%
- ○ 28%
- ○ 30%
- ○ 32%

Question 10

At Betty's Bagels, it costs $1.40 less to buy a dozen bagels than to buy 12 individual bagels at their regular price. If Billy buys 56 bagels and spends an average of 90 cents per bagel with the discount, what is the regular price of one bagel?

- ○ $1.00
- ○ $1.40
- ○ $1.60
- ○ $2.20
- ○ $2.75

Question 11

A bookstore stocks $\frac{1}{5}$ of its books as fiction works and $\frac{1}{3}$ less than the fiction books as self-help books. What fraction of the total books are the fiction and self-help books?

- ○ $\frac{3}{5}$
- ○ $\frac{11}{30}$
- ○ $\frac{4}{15}$
- ○ $\frac{2}{15}$
- ○ $\frac{1}{3}$

Question 12

Reservoir A contains 450 million more gallons of water than does Reservoir B. If 100 million gallons of water were to be drained from Reservoir A into Reservoir B, then Reservoir A would contain twice as much water as would Reservoir B. How many million gallons of water does Reservoir A currently contain?

- ○ 500
- ○ 600
- ○ 700
- ○ 800
- ○ 900

Question 13

A bag contains 8 pennies, 3 nickels, and x dimes. If the probability of drawing a penny is between 0.3 and 0.6, which of the following represent possible numbers of dimes?

Indicate all possible values.

- ☐ 1
- ☐ 2
- ☐ 3
- ☐ 4
- ☐ 5
- ☐ 6
- ☐ 7
- ☐ 8

DRILL 2

Question 1

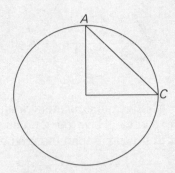

In the figure above, the length of chord AC is $4\sqrt{2}$. If the length of arc AC is equal to one-fourth of the circumference of the circle, what is the area of the circle?

- ○ 4π
- ○ 6π
- ○ 8π
- ○ 12π
- ○ 16π

Question 2

At a particular zoo, $\dfrac{2}{5}$ of all the animals are mammals, and $\dfrac{2}{3}$ of the mammals are allowed to interact directly with the public. If 24 mammals are allowed to interact directly with the public, how many animals in this zoo are NOT mammals?

- ○ 36
- ○ 48
- ○ 54
- ○ 60
- ○ 72

Question 3

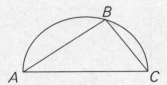

In the figure shown above, a right triangle is inscribed within a semicircle. If the length of line segment AB is 4 and the length of line segment BC is 3, what is the length of arc ABC?

- ○ $\dfrac{\pi}{2}$
- ○ $\dfrac{5\pi}{2}$
- ○ 5π
- ○ 10π
- ○ 25π

Question 4

What is the area of the square depicted below?

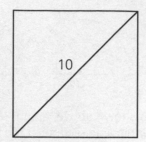

10

- ○ 20
- ○ 40
- ○ 50
- ○ 80
- ○ 100

Question 5

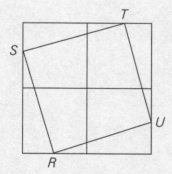

The figure above shows four adjacent small squares, forming one large square. The vertices of square *RSTU* are midpoints of the sides of the small squares. What is the ratio of the area of *RSTU* to the area of the large outer square?

- ○ $\dfrac{1}{2}$
- ○ $\dfrac{5}{9}$
- ○ $\dfrac{7}{12}$
- ○ $\dfrac{3}{5}$
- ○ $\dfrac{5}{8}$

Question 6

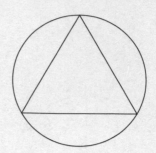

In the figure above, an equilateral triangle is inscribed in a circle. How many times greater is the area of the circle than the area of the triangle?

- ○ $\dfrac{\pi}{\sqrt{3}}$
- ○ $\dfrac{3\pi}{4}$
- ○ $\dfrac{4\pi}{3\sqrt{3}}$
- ○ 3
- ○ $\dfrac{2\pi}{\sqrt{3}}$

Question 7

If $\dfrac{(x+2)(x-5)}{(x-3)(x+4)} = 1$, then $x =$

- ○ –2
- ○ $-\dfrac{1}{2}$
- ○ 1
- ○ $\dfrac{1}{2}$
- ○ 2

Question 8

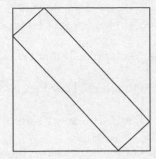

The figure above shows a rectangle inscribed within a square. How many times greater is the perimeter of the square than the perimeter of the inscribed rectangle?

- ○ $\sqrt{2}$
- ○ $\dfrac{2 + \sqrt{2}}{2}$
- ○ 2
- ○ $2\sqrt{2}$
- ○ $\dfrac{2\sqrt{2}}{2}$

Question 9

For which of the following values of x is $\dfrac{x^2}{4} + \dfrac{x}{2} - 4$ between 0 and 4 ?

Indicate all such values.

- ☐   1
- ☐   2
- ☐   3
- ☐   4
- ☐   5
- ☐   6

Question 10

At Alex's Burger Palace, customers can purchase 2 veggie burgers and 2 shakes for $6.50. Customers can also purchase 2 veggie burgers and 2 beef burgers for $7.00. Which of the following could be accurate assignments of price to food item?

Indicate all such assignments.

- ☐   veggie burger: $2.25, shake: $1.00
- ☐   veggie burger: $2.25, beef burger: $1.75
- ☐   veggie burger: $2.00, shake: $1.25
- ☐   beef burger: $1.50, shake: $1.25
- ☐   veggie burger: $2.25, shake: $1.25

Question 11

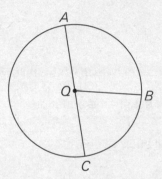

The radius of Circle Q is 8. If the length of arc ABC is greater than 26, which of the following could be the value of the sums of angles AQB and BQC ?

Indicate all such values.

- ☐   45°
- ☐   60°
- ☐   90°
- ☐   150°
- ☐   180°
- ☐   240°
- ☐   270°

Question 12

$$\frac{8x^{21} + 12x^{20} - 108x^{19} + \sqrt{36x^4}}{2x} = 3x$$

Which of the following values of x satisfy the equation above?

Indicate _all_ such values.

- ☐ -6
- ☐ -4.5
- ☐ -3
- ☐ 0
- ☐ 3
- ☐ 4.5
- ☐ 6

Question 13

If k is an integer, which of the following values of x satisfy the equation $\dfrac{81}{3^{\left(\frac{x}{2}\right)}} = k$?

Indicate _all_ such values.

- ☐ $x = 0$
- ☐ $x = 1$
- ☐ $x = 2$
- ☐ $x = 3$
- ☐ $x = 8$
- ☐ $x = 12$

Question 14

Two rectangular tiles are placed together to form a larger rectangle. The short side of Tile A is laid such that it is in contact with the long side of Tile B. The short side of Tile B is $\frac{2}{3}$ the length of its longer side. Tile A has a perimeter of 160 and an area of 1500. What is the length of the shorter side of Tile B?

- ○ 10
- ○ 20
- ○ 30
- ○ 40
- ○ 50

DRILL 3

Question 1

Shares of XYZ Co and ABC Corp are sold on a stock exchange that closes at 5 p.m. each day. At the close of business on Monday, shares of XYZ Co sold for half the price of shares of ABC Corp. On Tuesday and Wednesday, the price of shares of XYZ Co decreased at a rate of $\frac{1}{5}$ per day. During that same period, shares of ABC Corp increased at a rate of $\frac{1}{4}$ per day. At the close of business on Wednesday, the price of shares of ABC Corp was how many times greater, rounded to the nearest integer, than the price of shares of XYZ Co?

$\boxed{}$

Question 2

A model rocket takes off from an elevated launch pad which is 32 feet above the ground. The rocket's elevation is given by the equation $h(t) = -16t^2 + 64t + 32$, where $h(t)$ represents the height, in feet above ground, after t seconds. At which of the following times, in seconds, is the rocket's height 80 feet above ground?

Indicate all such values.

- ☐ 0.5
- ☐ 1
- ☐ 2
- ☐ 2.5
- ☐ 3
- ☐ 4

Question 3

If $a + b = 15$ and $2a - b = 6$, what is the value of b ?

- ○ 6
- ○ 7
- ○ 8
- ○ 9
- ○ 10

Question 4

If the area of a rectangle is 255 and the perimeter is 64, what is the length of its longer side?

- ○ 15
- ○ 17
- ○ 19
- ○ 21
- ○ 25

Question 5

Betty sold $\frac{3}{5}$ of her family's garage sale items. Ernest sold $\frac{1}{2}$ of the remaining items.

What fraction of the family's garage sale items did Ernest sell?

Question 6

In Seattle, the total rainfall in a certain year was 37 inches. From April to October of that year, the average rainfall was approximately 1.7 inches per month. What was the average rainfall, in inches, for the remaining months of the year?

- ○ 2
- ○ 3.1
- ○ 4
- ○ 5
- ○ 7.1

Question 7

The number 150 can be written as the product of three positive integers x, y, and z. x is equal to twice y, and z is a prime number. What is the value of z ?

- ○ 2
- ○ 3
- ○ 5
- ○ 10
- ○ 13

Question 8

If the expression $12x + 3 - (4 - 4x)$ is equal to an integer, which of the following CANNOT be a possible value for x ?

Indicate all such values.

- ☐ $-\dfrac{4}{3}$
- ☐ 0
- ☐ $\dfrac{3}{4}$
- ☐ $\dfrac{4}{3}$

Question 9

G is the sequence of numbers $g_1, g_2, g_3 \dots g_n$ such that each term following the first is one more than two times the preceding term. If $g_2 + g_4 = 30\dfrac{1}{2}$, what is the first term in G ?

- ○ $\dfrac{3}{4}$
- ○ 1
- ○ $\dfrac{3}{2}$
- ○ $\dfrac{9}{4}$
- ○ $\dfrac{7}{2}$

Question 10

Nelson bowled 4 games and scored an average (arithmetic mean) of 120 points. If his overall average for all 5 games is a multiple of 7, which of the following could be his score on the fifth game?

Indicate all such scores.

- ☐ 80
- ☐ 110
- ☐ 155
- ☐ 185

Question 11

Wendy, Yvonne, and Elizabeth are baking cookies for a bake sale. Wendy can bake all of the cookies in 10 hours, Yvonne can bake half of the cookies in 3 hours, and Elizabeth can bake a third of the cookies in 5 hours. If Wendy and Elizabeth bake for 2 hours, how many hours will it take Yvonne to finish baking the rest of the cookies?

- ○ 1.8
- ○ 2
- ○ 3
- ○ 3.6
- ○ 4

Question 12

Jackie is the manager of a sales department. She spends half of her monthly budget on base salaries. She spends another quarter of her budget on commissions, one-tenth of the budget on promotional items, one-twentieth on office supplies, one-twentieth on coffee and donuts for the team, and the remainder on the New Year's Eve party. What percentage of the budget is available for the party?

- ○ 5%
- ○ 8%
- ○ 10%
- ○ 15%
- ○ 20%

Question 13

Katherine drank 25 percent of her bottle of soda on the way to work, and drank another 3 ounces when she got there. The bottle now contains 60 percent of what it contained originally. How many ounces of soda did Katherine's bottle originally hold?

- ○ 4
- ○ 8
- ○ 10
- ○ 16
- ○ 20

Question 14

Brian spent $\frac{1}{4}$ of his paycheck to repair his car, and then paid the registration and insurance, which each cost $\frac{1}{3}$ of the remainder of his paycheck. If Brian had $0 before he was paid, and he now has $231 left, what was the amount of his paycheck?

- ○ $2,772
- ○ $1,622
- ○ $924
- ○ $870
- ○ $693

ANSWERS

Drill 1

1. D
2. A
3. D
4. A
5. D
6. D
7. B
8. C
9. C
10. A
11. E
12. B
13. C, D, E, F, G, H

Drill 2

1. E
2. C
3. B
4. C
5. E
6. C
7. D
8. A
9. D, E
10. A, C, D
11. F, G
12 B, E
13. A, C, E
14. C

Drill 3

1. 5
2. B, E
3. C
4. B
5. $\frac{1}{5}$
6. D
7. B
8. A, D
9. D
10. A, D
11. E
12. A
13. E
14. C

EXPLANATIONS
Drill 1

1. **D** This question has numbers in the answer choices, so Plug in the Answers starting with (C). 25% of $110,000 is $27,500, and $100,000 plus $27,500 equals $137,500. Since this is too small, choose a bigger number, such as (D), $112,000. In this case, 25% of $112,000 is $28,000, and $112,000 plus $28,000 is $140,000, which is the total stated in the problem, so (D) is the correct response.

2. **A** This question asks for a specific value and that value is represented by the answer choices, so Plug In the Answers. Start with (C) and carefully work through the problem, one step at a time. Choice (C) is –5. This number is "5 less" than "5 times the number," so first add 5 to –5. That yields 0. Then, 0 is "5 times the number" and the only number when multiplied by 5 that results in 0 is 0 itself. However, because "three less than two times" 0 is just 2(0) – 3, or –3, this value does not work because "two more than three times the number," is 3(0) + 2, or 2. Eliminate (C) and try another answer, such as (A), which is –30. You know that –30 is 5 less than the number, so add 5. That yields –25. Because –25 is five times the sought after number, the sought after number is –5 (because 5 × –5 = –25, so –25 is five times –5). Now check –5 in the first part of the question, which yields 2(–5) – 3 = –13. Because 3(–5) + 2 is also –13, the correct answer is (A).

3. **D** This question asks for the value that cannot work, so Plug In the Answers. Because this question is looking for the answer that cannot work, it is acceptable to start with (A). If 1 goal for 3 points is scored, then the team scored 45 points on unassisted goals (because the team had 48 points and 1 goal was worth 3 points, that leaves 48 – 3 = 45). To score 45 points, the team needs 9 assisted goals (9 goals at 5 points each gives us 9 × 5 = 45), so (A) cannot be correct. Try (B). If 6 goals for 3 points are scored, then there are 18 points scored on unassisted goals and 30 points remain to be accounted for. 30 points can be achieved by 6 goals scored with assistance, so (B) cannot be correct. Try (C). If 11 goals for 3 points are scored, there are 33 points scored and 15 left over, so that equals 3 goals scored without assistance, making (C) incorrect. Try (D). If 12 goals for 3 points are scored, then 36 points have been scored and there are 12 points remaining. This is not divisible by 5, so (D) does not work and is therefore the correct answer.

4. **A** The question asks for a specific value and that value is represented by the answer choices, so Plug In the Answers. Label the answer choices "Shirley's hourly." Assume Shirley's hourly is $25, which is (C); Melinda's hourly is twice that, or $50. Shirley worked at that rate for 1.75 hours and earned $43.76 (1.75 × 25 = 43.75). Melinda worked for 0.75 hour and earned $37.50 (0.75 × 50 = 37.50). The two together, therefore, earned $81.25, which is almost double what it should be. Eliminate (C), (D), and (E) and work with (A). If Shirley's hourly rate is $15 per hour, Melinda's hourly rate is $30 per hour. Shirley worked for 1.75 hours and earned $26.25, and Melinda worked for 0.75 hour and earned $22.50. Together they earned $48.75. Choice (A) is the correct answer.

5. **D** Since this question has numbers in the answer choices and the question asks for a specific quantity, use Plugging in the Answers starting with (C). If the area of the square is 28, then each side of the square is $\sqrt{28}$, which can be simplified to $2\sqrt{7}$. The radius of the circle is also half the diagonal of the square, so draw a radius line to one of the corners of the square and then a line from the center of the circle to the side of the square. This forms a right triangle with the radius as the hypotenuse and half of the side of the square as the other two sides. Half the side of the square in this case is $\sqrt{7}$, so using the Pythagorean Theorem results in $\left(\sqrt{7}\right)^2 + \left(\sqrt{7}\right)^2 = r^2$, or $7 + 7 = r^2$, and thus $14 = r^2$ and $r = \sqrt{14}$. The area of the circle is then 14π, which is too small. Eliminate (A), (B), and (C). Next try (D), 32. Each side of the square in this case is $\sqrt{32}$ or $4\sqrt{2}$. Half the side of the square in this case is $2\sqrt{2}$. This time the Pythagorean Theorem produces $\left(2\sqrt{2}\right)^2 + \left(2\sqrt{2}\right)^2 = r^2$ or $16 = r^2$, which means $r = 4$. The area is then 16π, so (D) is correct.

6. **D** This question asks for a specific value and that value is represented by the answer choices, so Plug In the Answers. Start with (C). If the total tips earned was $108, then the 4 waiters receive $72, which is $18 each. The manager receives $27 and the busboy receives $11. Therefore, one waiter and the busboy together receive $29. This is less than the $30 specified by the problem, so eliminate (C). Eliminate choices (A) and (B) as well because the number needs to be greater. Try (D). In (D), if the total earned in tips was $120, then the 4 waiters combined receive $\frac{2}{3}$ of $120, or $80. The manager receives $\frac{1}{4}$ of $120, or $30, and the busboy receives the remaining $10. Because 4 waiters received $80, and 1 waiter received $20, 1 waiter and the busboy together receive $30. The correct answer is (D).

7. **B** Since there are numbers in the answer choices, Plug In the Answers, starting with (C). However, first simplify the numbers on the left. $\sqrt{27}$ is the same as $\sqrt{9 \times 3}$, so pull out the $\sqrt{9}$ to find $3\sqrt{3}$ for the numerator. For the denominator, $\sqrt{54}$ is equal to $\sqrt{9 \times 6}$, which can be simplified to $3\sqrt{6}$. The 3 in the numerator and denominator cancel out, leaving $\frac{\sqrt{3}}{\sqrt{6}}$.
Next, Plug In (C), in which case the equation is $\frac{\sqrt{3}}{\sqrt{6}} \times \frac{\sqrt{4}}{\sqrt{6}} = \frac{1}{2}$. The $\sqrt{4}$ is 2, and the $\sqrt{6} \times \sqrt{6}$ in the denominator is equal to 6. This results in $\frac{\sqrt{3} \times 2}{6} = \frac{1}{2}$. In order for the fraction on the left to equal $\frac{1}{2}$, the numerator would need to be 3, but it's not, so eliminate (C). Since the left fraction is slightly greater than the right, try a smaller number such as (B), 3. Plugging in 3 yields $\frac{\sqrt{3}}{\sqrt{6}} \times \frac{\sqrt{3}}{\sqrt{6}} = \frac{1}{2}$. Since the numerators multiply to 3 and the denominators multiply to 6, the result on the left is $\frac{3}{6}$ or $\frac{1}{2}$, so (B) is the correct answer.

8. **C** The question asks for a specific value and that value is represented by the answer choices, so Plug In the Answers. The question asks for the value of m, so see which of the choices works in the problem. Start with (C), which is $\frac{3}{2}$. The problem states that $mn = 9$, so that means $\frac{3}{2}n = 9$. Solve to find that $n = 6$. The problem states that $\frac{n}{m} = 4$ so make sure this is true. Because $\frac{6}{\frac{3}{2}} = 6 \times \frac{2}{3}$, which is 4, this choice works. The correct answer is (C).

9. **C** This is a percent question with no specific values, so this is a Hidden Plug In question. The question mentions "the original price," but gives no actual number, so assume, since you're working with percents, that the original price of the garment is $100. After the first reduction, the sale price is $80. After the second reduction, the final price is $72. The total reduction from the original price is $28, which is 28% of the original price. The correct answer is (C).

10. **A** The question asks for a specific value and that value is represented by the answer choices, so Plug In the Answers. The answer choices represent the price of a bagel. Start with (A). If one bagel costs $1.00, then 56 bagels costs $56.00. Because there is a discount of $1.40 per dozen and there are 4 complete dozens in the order, the total discount is $5.60. Therefore, the actual price paid is $50.40, or an average of $0.90 per bagel. This matches the information in the problem. The correct answer is (A).

11. **E** This question asks for a fraction of an unknown total, so this is a Hidden Plug In question. Since 15 is a multiple of both 3 and 5, let's Plug In 15 for the total. So $\frac{1}{5}$ of 15 = 3 fiction books. Then $\frac{1}{3}$ of 3 is 1, so there's 1 fewer self-help than fiction, or 3 − 1 = 2 self-help books. Together, there are 3 + 2 = 5 fiction and self-help books out of 15 total books so $\frac{5}{15} = \frac{1}{3}$. The correct answer is (E).

12. **B** This question asks for a specific value and that value is represented by the answer choices, so Plug In the Answers. Start with (C). If Reservoir A contains 700 million gallons of water, then Reservoir B has 450 million gallons less, or 250 million gallons. When 100 million gallons are drained from Reservoir A to Reservoir B, then the reservoirs hold 600 million and 350 million gallons of water, respectively. The problem states that Reservoir A has twice the water that Reservoir B has, so this choice is incorrect. Eliminate (C). It is hard to tell if the number needs to be larger or smaller, so pick a direction. Try (B). If Reservoir A contains 600 million gallons of water, then Reservoir B has 450 million gallons less, or 150 million gallons. When 100 million gallons are drained from Reservoir A to Reservoir B, then the reservoirs hold 500 million and 250 million gallons of water, respectively. Because Reservoir A has twice the amount of water as Reservoir B, this is the appropriate relationship. The correct answer is (B).

13. C, D, E, F, G, H

This problem has one variable in the question and no variables in the answer choices, so Plugging In the Answers (PITA) is the ideal technique. The probability of something happening is the number of desired outcomes divided by the total number of possible outcomes. In this case, it is the number of pennies divided by the total number of coins in the bag. Because this is a "select all that apply" problem, there can be more than one right answer, so all answer choices need to be tested. Start with (A) rather than (C), and draw columns to stay organized.

Number of Dimes	Total Coins	Probability = Pennies/All coins	Correct?
A 1	8 + 3 + 1 = 12	8/12 = .66	Incorrect
B 2	8 + 3 + 2 = 13	8/13 = .62	Incorrect
C 3	8 + 3 + 3 = 14	8/14 = .57	Correct
D 4	8 + 3 + 4 = 15	8/15 = .53	Correct
E 5	8 + 3 + 5 = 16	8/16 = .5	Correct
F 6	8 + 3 + 6 = 17	8/17 = .47	Correct
G 7	8 + 3 + 7 = 18	8/18 = .44	Correct
H 8	8 + 3 + 8 = 19	8/19 = .42	Correct

Because (C), (D), (E), (F), (G), and (H) all produce probabilities between 0.3 and 0.6, they are the correct answer.

Drill 2

1. E   There are numbers in the answer choices, so Plug In the Answers. Start with (C) as usual. If 8π is the area and the area of a circle is πr^2, then r must be $\sqrt{8}$, which can be simplified to $2\sqrt{2}$. Since the arc is $\frac{1}{4}$ of the total circumference, then the corresponding central angle must be $\frac{1}{4}$ of the total number of degrees in the circle (360), or 90 degrees. Thus, this is a right triangle, and the Pythagorean Theorem can be used to find the chord, which is the hypotenuse. If the radii, and thus the legs of the triangle, are both $2\sqrt{2}$, then the hypotenuse, AC, is $\sqrt{(2\sqrt{2})^2 + (2\sqrt{2})^2}$ or $\sqrt{8+8} = \sqrt{16}$, which is 4. This is too low, so go up to the next answer, 12π. This time r is $\sqrt{12}$, or $2\sqrt{3}$, and the hypotenuse is thus $\sqrt{(2\sqrt{3})^2 + (2\sqrt{3})^2} = \sqrt{24}$, which reduces to $2\sqrt{6}$. This is still less than $4\sqrt{2}$, so the correct answer must be (E), in which the radius comes out to be 4 and the hypotenuse is $\sqrt{32} = 4\sqrt{2}$.

2. C   This question asks for a specific value and that value is represented by the answer choices, so Plug In the Answers. Start by Plugging In (C), 54, for the number of non-mammals. Now, use the information in the problem to find the number of mammals. According to the problem, 24 mammals are allowed to interact with the public, and this is $\frac{2}{3}$ of all the mammals. Thus, there is 36 total mammals in the zoo (because 24 is $\frac{2}{3}$ of 36). If there are 36 mammals and 54 non-mammals, then there are 90 animals in the zoo. Now, check this number against the information in the problem. The problem says that $\frac{2}{5}$ of all the animals are mammals and 36 is $\frac{2}{5}$ of 90. The correct answer is (C).

3. **B**   This question has numbers in the answers, so Plug In the Answers. Start with (C) as usual. Arc *ABC* represents half of the circumference of the circle. So, if half of the circumference is 5π, then the whole circumference is 10π. That makes the diameter, *AC*, 10. Since it is a right triangle and *AC* is the hypotenuse, and the other two sides are 4 and 3, $4^2 + 3^2$ should equal 10^2. However, $16 + 9$ does not equal 100. The diameter is way too high here, so the answer must be lower. Eliminate (D) and (E). Using (B) produces 5π for the whole circumference and thus a diameter of 5. Now $4^2 + 3^2$ does equal 5^2, so the correct answer is (B).

4. **C**   Since there are numbers in the answer choices and the question asks for a specific thing, Plug In the Answers. Start with (C) as usual. If the area is 50, then each side is $\sqrt{50}$, which is $5\sqrt{2}$. If each side is $5\sqrt{2}$, then using the Pythagorean Theorem, the diagonal is $\sqrt{\left(5\sqrt{2}\right)^2 + \left(5\sqrt{2}\right)^2}$, which equals $\sqrt{50 + 50} = \sqrt{100} = 10$. This matches the figure, so (C) is correct.

5. **E**   This is a Hidden Plug In question, so Plug In a value for the side of each smaller square. Make the side of each smaller square 4. To find the area of the square in the middle, determine the length of one of its sides. Get this by using the Pythagorean Theorem. There is a right triangle formed by the length of one smaller square plus half of the length of the adjacent square because points *R, S, T,* and *U* are all midpoints. So if the length of a side of a smaller square is 4, the legs are length 6 and 2. By the Pythagorean Theorem, the hypotenuse is $\sqrt{40}$. This is the length of one of the sides of the square in the middle. The area of this inner square is $\sqrt{40}$ squared, which is 40. Each side of the outer square is 8, so the area of the big square is $8^2 = 64$. The ratio of areas is $\frac{40}{64}$, which is equal to $\frac{5}{8}$. The correct answer is (E).

6. **C**   This is a Hidden Plug In question, so Plug In a value for the side of the equilateral triangle. Make each side of the equilateral triangle 6. To find the area of the triangle, draw in the height to create a 30-60-90 triangle with base 6 and height $3\sqrt{3}$. These values yield an area of $9\sqrt{3}$ for the triangle. To find the radius, draw lines from the center of the circle to each vertex of the triangle.

This creates two smaller 30-60-90 triangles. The side opposite the 60 degree angle is equal to 3. The hypotenuse of the smaller triangle is twice the length of the side opposite the 30 degree angle. This shorter side is equal to $\dfrac{3}{\sqrt{3}}$. The hypotenuse of the triangle is twice this value, or $\dfrac{6}{\sqrt{3}}$. This is equal to the radius of the circle, so the area of the circle is $\pi\,\dfrac{6}{\sqrt{3}}$ squared, or 12π. Finally, the ratio of the areas is $\dfrac{12\pi}{9\sqrt{3}}$. Reduce this to find the correct answer is (C).

7. **D** This question asks for a specific value and that value is represented by the answer choices, so Plug In the Answers. Start with (C), which is 1. The numerator of the fraction is (3)(–4) and the denominator of the fraction is (–2)(5). This doesn't equal 1. Eliminate (C). Try (D). The numerator of the fraction is (2.5)(–4.5) and the denominator of the fraction is (–2.5)(4.5). This does equal 1. The correct answer is (D).

8. **A** This is a Hidden Plug In question, so Plug In values for the length of the side of the square. Make the length of the side of the square 8. Also Plug In for the values of the sides of the small triangle. Plug In for the sides of the small triangles a number such as 2. The rest of the side is 6. The sides of the rectangle are the hypotenuses of the right triangles. The smaller right triangle is 2 by 2, so the hypotenuse is $2\sqrt{2}$. The larger triangle is 6 by 6, so the hypotenuse is $6\sqrt{2}$. Now, add up the sides to get the perimeters. The square is simply 8 + 8 + 8 + 8, which equals 32. The rectangle is $2\sqrt{2}$ + $2\sqrt{2}$ + $6\sqrt{2}$ + $6\sqrt{2}$, which is $16\sqrt{2}$. Because 32 is $\sqrt{2}$ times greater than $16\sqrt{2}$, (A) is the correct answer.

9. **D, E** This question asks for a specific value and that value is represented by the answer choices, so Plug In the Answers. Start with (C). If $x = 3$, then $\dfrac{3^2}{4} + \dfrac{3}{2} - 4 = \dfrac{9}{4} + \dfrac{6}{4} - \dfrac{16}{4} = -\dfrac{1}{4}$. This does not match the information in the problem, so eliminate (C). Because (C) is less than the value in the problem, also eliminate (A) and (B), as they make the final result even less. Try (D). If $x = 4$, then $\dfrac{4^2}{4} + \dfrac{4}{2} - 4 = 4 + 2 - 4 = 2$, so (D) is one of the correct answer choices. Check (E) next. If $x = 5$, then $\dfrac{5^2}{4} + \dfrac{5}{2} - 4 = \dfrac{25}{4} + \dfrac{10}{4} - \dfrac{16}{4} = \dfrac{19}{4} = 4\dfrac{3}{4}$. Keep (E). Because this choice is close to 5, (F) is too great. The correct answer is (D) and (E).

10. **A, C, D**

This question asks for a specific value and that value is represented by the answer choices, so Plug In the Answers. Because this is an All that Apply question, it is acceptable to start with (A). If the veggie burger costs $2.25 and the shake costs $1.50, then 2($2.25) + 2($1.00) = $6.50. Choice (A) works, so keep (A). Choice (B) does not work, since 2 veggie burgers and 2 beef burgers cost $7.00, but 2($2.25) + 2($1.75) = $8.00. Eliminate (B). Choice (C) works, since 2 veggie burgers and 2 shakes cost $6.50, and 2($2.00) + 2($1.25) = $6.50. Keep (C). Try (D). If 2 veggie burgers and 2 beef burgers cost $7.00, and beef burgers cost $1.50, then 2(veggie) + 2($1.50) = $7.00, and veggie burgers cost $2.00. This works with the other equation, since 2 veggie burgers and 2 shakes cost $6.50, and 2($2.00) + 2($1.25) = $6.50, so keep (D). Finally, (E) does not work, since 2 veggie burgers and 2 shakes cost $6.50, but 2($2.25) + 2($1.25) = $7.00. Eliminate (E). The correct answer is (A), (C), and (D).

11. **F, G** This question asks for a specific value and that value is represented by the answer choices, so Plug In the Answers. While it is customary to start Plugging In the answers with one of the middle choices, (E) looks easiest to solve because it is half the circle. Therefore, the circumference of the whole circle is 16π, which is about 50. Half the circle, then, is about 25. Since the length of the arc is greater than 26, (E) is not great enough, so eliminate (E) as well as (A), (B), (C), and (D). Choice (F) makes the sum of the angles represent $\frac{240}{360}$, or $\frac{2}{3}$, of the whole circle; $\frac{2}{3}$ of about 50 is easily greater than 26, so keep (F). Choice (G) is even greater, so (G) works as well. The correct answer is (F) and (G).

12. **B, E** This question asks you to determine which answer choice satisfies the equation, so check each answer choice individually. First, however, work on simplifying the exponents in the numerator. Multiply both sides of the equation by $2x$ to remove the denominator. Now, notice that the term under the radical can be simplified to $6x^2$, which is exactly what is on the other side of the equation. Cancel them to yield $8x^{21} + 12x^{20} - 108x^{19} = 0$. Factor out a 4 and x^{19} to yield $4x^{19}(2x^2 + 3x - 27) = 0$. While it may appear that $x = 0$ is an answer, if $x = 0$, then the denominator on the left side of the original equation is 0 and the fraction is undefined. So, $x = 0$ is not a solution to the problem. Eliminate (D). There is a quadratic equation, so factor the quadratic to $(2x + 9)(x - 3)$. The roots of this quadratic are -4.5 and 3, which are (B) and (E). Alternatively, use the values in the answer choices for x and see which answer choices satisfy the equation. The correct answer is (B) and (E).

13. **A, C, E**

There are numbers in the answer choices and the question asks for a specific thing, so use Plugging in the Answers. Because this is an "all that apply" problem, start with (A) and test all of the answer choices.

Plug In $x = 0$ to get $\frac{81}{3^0} = \frac{81}{1} = 81$, so choose (A) because it produces an integer value for k.

Plug In $x = 1$ to get $\frac{81}{3^{\frac{1}{2}}} = \frac{81}{\sqrt{3}}$. This does not produce an integer value for k, so eliminate (B).

Plug In $x = 2$ to get $\frac{81}{3^1} = \frac{81}{3} = 27$. This produces an integer value for k, so choose (C).

Plug In $x = 3$ to get $\frac{81}{3^{\frac{3}{2}}} = \frac{81}{\sqrt{3^3}} = \frac{81}{\sqrt{27}}$, which is not an integer, so eliminate (D).

Plug In $x = 8$ to get $\frac{81}{3^4} = \frac{81}{81} = 1$. This is an integer, so choose (E).

Plug In $x = 12$ to get $\dfrac{81}{3^6}$. Since $3^4 = 81$, 3^6 must be greater than 81. This expression must be less than 1, so it is not an integer. Eliminate (F). The correct answer is (A), (C), and (E).

14.   C   The presence of rectangles implies that this is a geometry problem, so first follow the steps for the basic approach to geometry. Draw and label the figure.

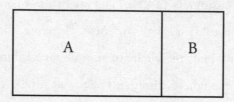

Write down relevant formulas. The area of a rectangle is $A = lw$, and its perimeter is $P = 2l + 2w$. To solve this problem directly would require some detailed algebra. There are no variables named in the problem or the answer choices, and the answers represent a defined object (the length). This problem is a good candidate for the Plugging in the Answers (PITA) strategy. Start with (C), plug it into the problem, and work through the question, making columns. If the short side of tile B is 20, the long side is 30 because 20 is $\dfrac{2}{3}$ of 30. This is also the short side of tile A. Since the area of A is 1500 and its shorter side is 30, use the area formula $A = lw$ to find that the other side is 50. The last remaining information is the perimeter of tile A. If the sides are 30 and 50, the perimeter is 160. This matches the information in the problem, so the correct answer is (C).

Drill 3

1.   5   This is a Hidden Plug In question, so Plug In a number for the starting share price of either stock that is divisible by 2, 4, and 5, such as 400. If XYZ Co sold on Monday for $400, then ABC Corp sold for $800. To calculate the price of XYZ Co on the next 2 days, $\dfrac{1}{5}$ of 400 is 80, so the price on Tuesday is $400 – $80 = $320; $\dfrac{1}{5}$ of 320 is 64, so the price at the close of business on Wednesday is $320 – $64 = $256. For ABC Corp, $\dfrac{1}{4}$ of 800 is 200, so the price on Tuesday is $800 + $200 = $1,000; $\dfrac{1}{4}$ of 1,000 is 250, so the price at the close of business on Wednesday is $1,000 + $250 = $1,250. Finally, divide the final price of ABC Corp by that of XYZ Co: 1,250 ÷ 256 equals about 4.88, which rounds to 5.

2. **B, E** This question asks for a specific value and that value is represented by the answer choices, so Plug In the Answers. Because this is an All That Apply question, it is acceptable to start with (A). For (A), Plug In 0.5 for t and solve for $h(t)$. The result is $h(0.5) = -16(0.5)^2 + 64(0.5) + 32 = -16(0.25) + 64(0.5) + 32 = -4 + 32 + 32 = 60$, so (A) does not work. Eliminate (A). Try (B), $h(1) = -16(1)^2 + 64(1) + 32 = -16 + 64 + 32 = 80$, so (B) works. Keep (B). Since this is an All That Apply question, check every answer choice. After checking every choice, find that (E) also yields 80: $h(0) = -16(3)^2 + 64(3) + 32 = -144 + 192 + 32 = 80$. The correct answer is (B) and (E).

3. **C** This question asks for a specific value and that value is represented by the answer choices, so Plug In the Answers. Since (C) represents the middle value of this range of answers, begin by Plugging In (C). If $b = 8$, then a is 7. Then, use that value for the second equation to find that $2 \times 7 = 14$. Because $14 - 8 = 6$, the value is equal to the problem. The correct answer is (C).

4. **B** There are numbers in the answer choices and the question asks for one specific thing, so Plug In the Answers. Label the answer choices as the longer side and start with (C) as usual. The area is length times width, so divide the area by 19 to get the shorter side. In this case, the shorter side is about 13.42. The problem states that the perimeter is 64. The formula for perimeter of a rectangle is $P = 2l + 2w$. With a width of 13.42 and a length of 19, the perimeter is 64.84. This is close, but not exactly right, so eliminate (C). It's unclear whether a greater or lesser number is needed, so try (B) next. 255 divided by 17 is 15, so the shorter side in this case is 15. With sides of 15 and 17, the perimeter is 64, so (B) is the correct answer.

5. $\frac{1}{5}$ This is a Hidden Plug In problem, so Plug In for the number of items. Plug In 10 items. That means Betty sold 6, and Ernest sold half of 4, or 2. The question asked for the *fraction* of items Ernest sold, so, Ernest sold $\frac{2}{10}$, or $\frac{1}{5}$.

6. **D** Simplify this question by using Average Pies to deal with the two steps of the problem. First, figure out how many total inches of rain fell in the 7 months from April to October. This results in 11.9, which can be rounded to 12 since the problem said "approximately." Next, subtract that total from 37 to find out how many remaining inches fell during the other 5 months. Finally, take those remaining 25 inches and divide by the remaining five months. The correct answer is (D).

7. **B** This problem has numbers in the answer choices and asks for one specific thing, so Plug In the Answers. Label the answer choices as z. To save time, first consider whether there are any answer choices that don't make sense with what the problem states. The problem states that z is a prime number. Choice (D), 10, is not a prime number, so eliminate it. The problem also indicates that z is a factor of 150. Choice (E), 13, is not a factor of 150, so eliminate it. Now start in the middle of the remaining options, with (B). If $z = 3$, determine what x and y must be. The problem indicates that x, y, and z multiply together to equal 150, so divide 150 by 3 to get 50. The value of xy must be equal to 50 in this case. Consider the factor pairs of 50: 1, 50; 2, 25; 5, 10. The problem states that x is equal to twice y. Thus, x must be 10 and y must be 5. This works, so the correct answer is (B).

8. **A, D**   This question asks for a specific value and that value is represented by the answer choices, so Plug In the Answers. Because this is an All That Apply question, it is acceptable to start with (A). Plug In the values in the answer choices for *x*. Choices (A) and (D) do not result in an integer while (B) and (C) do. The correct answer is (A) and (D).

9. **D**   This question asks for a specific value and that value is represented by the answer choices, so Plug In the Answers. Start with (C). If the first term is $\frac{3}{2}$, then one more than twice the previous term is 4, so that's g_2. Compute the rest of the sequence from there to find that $g_3 = 4 \times 2 + 1 = 9$; $g_4 = 9 \times 2 + 1 = 19$; and $g_2 + g_4 = 4 + 19 = 23$. This is less than indicated in the problem so eliminate (C). Eliminate (A) and (B) as well as they make the value even less. It is easier to double (E), so work with (E) next. If $g_1 = \frac{7}{2}$, then $g_2 = 8$, $g_3 = 17$, and $g_4 = 35$; now $g_2 + g_4 = 8 + 35 = 41$. This is too great, so eliminate (E). Because one answer choice must be correct, there is no need to check (D) as it has to be the correct answer. The correct answer is (D).

10. **A, D**   First, use an Average Pie. Multiply 4 by 120 and to find a total of 480 points for the first 4 games. Now, Plug In the Answers to figure out which answers give an overall average that is divisible by 7. Start with (A), because on All That Apply questions, there's no reason to start in the middle if many answers might work. Choice (A) yields $480 + 80 = 560$, and $560 \div 5 = 112$. That is divisible by 7. Choice (B) is $480 + 110 = 590$, and $590 \div 5 = 118$. This is not divisible by 7, so eliminate (B). Continue checking all the answer choices, looking for any that result in an integer divisible by 7. The correct answer is (A) and (D).

11. **E**   This is a Hidden Plug In question, so Plug In for the number of cookies. Choose a number that's divisible by all the numbers in the question, such as 30. That means that Wendy's rate is 3 cookies per hour. Yvonne can bake 15 cookies in 3 hours, or 5 per hour. Elizabeth can bake 10 cookies in 5 hours, or 2 per hour. If Wendy and Elizabeth bake together, they can make a total of 5 cookies in one hour. If they bake for 2 hours, they'll bake 10 cookies. For Yvonne to finish the baking on her own, she'll need to bake the 20 remaining cookies. At a rate of 5 cookies per hour, it takes her 4 hours to finish the job, so (E) is the correct answer.

12. **A**   There is no variable given, but there is a desire to create a complex equation to solve, so this must be a Hidden Plug In. The hidden variable is the budget, or *B*. Pick a number that is easily divisible by all of the denominators in the question. $80 works well. Half of that is spent on salaries, so $40. One quarter goes to commissions, which is $20. A tenth for promotional items, or $8, and a twentieth each on office supplies and coffee and donuts, which is $4 for each. $80 - 40 - 20 - 8 - 4 - 4 = 4$. $\frac{4}{80} = \frac{1}{20}$, which is 5%. The correct answer is (A).

13. E This question asks for a specific value and that value is represented by the answer choices, so Plug In the Answers. Normally the first choice to use is (C), but because 10 is not divisible by 4, (C) can be eliminated. Try (D). Subtract 25% from the original amount of 16 to yield 12. Subtracting 3 from 12 results in 9. Because 9 is 56.25% of 16, this number is not great enough, so eliminate (D). Choices (A) and (B) can also be eliminated because they make the value even less. The correct answer is (E).

Original	–25%	–3	% of original
4			
8			
10	yucky!		
16	12	9	56.25% — too small
20	15	12	60%

14. C The question asks for a specific value and the answer choices represent that value, so Plug In the Answers. Start with (C). If Brian's paycheck is $924, and he spends $\frac{1}{4}$ on the repair, then he spends $231, which leaves $693 left over. The insurance and registration each cost $\frac{1}{3}$ of the balance, or $231, so he spends another $462, leaving him with $693 – $462 = $231. This matches the information in the question, so (C) is correct.

Number Properties

NUMBER PROPERTIES

The language used in the math section of the GRE is very precise. It's important to be familiar with the math vocabulary and not make any assumptions. For example if a problem says x is a number, don't assume it is has to be a positive integer. Many mistakes on the math section are due to misreading the problem rather than not knowing the math concepts.

MATH VOCABULARY

Finding the correct answer rests on your knowledge of key math terms. The GRE is very precise with the language they use in a problem and rely on this precision to trip students up. Here is a list of common math terms tested on the GRE.

Term	Definition	Examples
Integer	a "whole" number that does not contain decimals, fractions, or radicals; can be positive, negative or zero	–500, 0, 1, 28
Positive	greater than zero	0.5, 25, $\frac{5}{3}$
Negative	less than zero	–72.3, $-\frac{7}{4}$, –2
Even	an integer divisible by two	–40, 0, 2
Odd	an integer not divisible by two	–41, 1, 3
Divisible	when a number divides into another number with nothing leftover	10 is divisible by 2, but not 3.
Remainder	the whole number "left over" when one number doesn't divide evenly into another number	When 10 is divided by 3, the remainder is 1.
Divisor	a number that divides into another number	In the statement "24 divided by 6," 6 is the divisor.
Sum	the result of adding	The sum of 3 and 4 is 7.
Difference	the result of subtracting	The difference between 7 and 2 is 5.
Product	the result of multiplying	The product of 5 and 7 is 35.
Quotient	the result of dividing	The quotient of 8 and 2 is 4.
Prime	a number that has exactly two factors—itself and 1; 1 is not considered prime since it has only one factor; negative numbers and zero are not prime	2, 3, 5, 7

Consecutive	In a row, usually ascending	1, 2, 3, 4; –3, –2, –1, 0
Digits	0–9; the numbers on a keyboard	1, 2, 3, 4, 5, 6, 7, 8, 9, 0
Distinct	different	2 and 3 are distinct; 6.25 and 6.26 are distinct; 4 and 4 are not distinct.

CALCULATING

On GRE problems with just numbers, it is possible to calculate the answer. But in many cases, it can be rather tedious and easy to make mistakes. If the calculations seem a bit cumbersome, there is often another way to solve the problem. Especially in the case of Quant Comp problems when you are comparing values, the solution is not always necessarily to determine the value of each quantity individually. Knowledge of the following patterns can help in determining the solutions without a lot of number crunching.

Multiplication	Division
negative × negative = positive	negative ÷ negative = positive
positive × positive = positive	positive ÷ positive = positive
negative × positive = negative	negative ÷ positive = negative
positive × negative = negative	positive ÷ negative = negative

Addition	Subtraction	Multiplication
even + even = even	even − even = even	even × even = even
odd + odd = even	odd − odd = even	odd × odd = odd
even + odd = odd	even − odd = odd	even × odd = even
odd + even = odd	odd − even = odd	odd × even = even

While memorizing these relationships can be helpful, they can be "remembered" by plugging in a couple easy numbers. For example, rediscover an even × odd = even by calculating 2 × 3 = 6. Then apply this relationship to the greater numbers in the problem and avoid the time-consuming calculations.

Rules of Divisibility

Divisibility is another area in which shortcuts can be used to save time-consuming calculations. Rather than dividing numbers all the way out, apply the following divisibility rules.

An integer is divisible by	Rule	Examples
2	It's even (i.e., it ends in 0, 2, 4, 6 or 8).	1,57<u>6</u>
3	Its digits add up to a multiple of 3.	8,532 8 + 5 + 3 + 2 = 18
4	Its last two digits are divisible by 4.	121,5<u>32</u> 32 ÷ 4 = 8
5	Its last digit is 5 or 0.	568,74<u>5</u> 32<u>0</u>
6	Apply the rules of 2 and 3.	55,740 It's even and 5 + 5 + 7 + 4 + 0 = 21
8	Its last three digits are divisible by 8.	345,862,<u>120</u> 120 ÷ 8 = 15
9	Its digits add up to a multiple of 9.	235,692 2 + 3 + 5 + 6 + 9 + 2 = 27
10	Its last digit is zero.	11,13<u>0</u>
12	Apply the rules of 3 and 4	3,552 3 + 5 + 5 + 2 = 15 and 52 ÷ 4 = 13

Some problems appear to require the rules of divisibility but seem to involve time-consuming calculations. Breaking numbers down to their most basic components, prime factors, can be helpful on these problems. Here's an example.

$$n = \frac{12^{11}}{x}$$

For the equation above, if n is an integer, which of the following could be a possible value of x ?

Indicate <u>all</u> such values.

☐   24

☐   36

☐ 2^{11}

☐ 2^{22}

☐ 3^{11}

☐ 3^{12}

☐   40

☐ 48^2

Expand the numbers out using prime factors. Think of the question as a fraction that can be reduced. The numerator is 12^{11} and the denominator is each of the choices. On the top is $(2 \times 2 \times 3)^{11} = (2^2 \times 3)^{11} = 2^{22} \times 3^{11}$. The first answer choice, 24, can be broken down into $2 \times 2 \times 2 \times 3$. Cancel each of the numbers on the bottom of the fraction with the equivalent number on the top, so 24 divides evenly into 12^{11}. Now try the other 7 answer choices.

36	Correct. This choice breaks down into $2 \times 2 \times 3 \times 3$. The two 2's and two 3's cancel out with numbers in the numerator.
2^{11}	Correct. The eleven 2's cancel out with the 2's in the numerator.
2^{22}	Correct. The twenty-two 2's cancel out with all the 2's in the numerator.
3^{11}	Correct. The eleven 3's cancel out with all the 3's in the numerator.
3^{12}	No. There is one 3 remaining in the denominator after the eleven 3's cancel out with all the 3's in the numerator.
40	No. This choice breaks down into $2 \times 2 \times 2 \times 5$. There is one 5 remaining in the denominator after the three 2's cancel out with the 2's in the numerator.
48^2	Correct. This choice breaks down into $(2 \times 2 \times 2 \times 2 \times 3)^2 = (2^4 \times 3)^2 = 2^8 \times 3^2$. The eight 2's and two 3's cancel out with numbers in the numerator.

When a division problem has numbers too great to calculate reasonably, use prime factors to figure out how many times one number divides evenly into the other.

ABSOLUTE VALUE

Absolute value is a number's distance from zero on the number line. It doesn't matter if you are moving in a positive or a negative direction. For example, $|4| = 4$ and $|-4| = 4$. Absolute value tends to show up on Quant Comp questions, because it's easy to forget about the negative solutions. For example in the equation $|x| = 4$, there are two solutions, both 4 and -4. Remember to Plug In both positive and negative numbers when you have a variable inside absolute value brackets.

PEMDAS

Many problems on the GRE require the correct application of the order of operations, and many of the wrong answers on these problems are the result of common mistakes.

Here's how it works.

P|E|MD|AS

- **P** stands for "parentheses." Solve inside the parentheses or other grouping symbols first.

- **E** stands for "exponents." Solve the exponents next.

- **M** stands for "multiplication" and **D** stands for "division." The arrow is meant to indicate that you do all the multiplication and division together in the same step, going from left to right. For example, $12 \times 6 \div 3 = 72 \div 3 = 24$.

- **A** stands for "addition" and **S** stands for "subtraction." Again, as the arrow indicates, you do all the addition and subtraction together in the same step, going left to right. For example, $12 - 6 + 3 = 6 + 3 = 9$.

For more practice and a more in-depth look at The Princeton Review math techniques, check out our student-friendly guidebook, *Cracking the GRE*.

DRILL 1

Question 1

3 and 5 are factors of x.

Quantity A	Quantity B
The remainder when x is divided by 10	6

- ○ Quantity A is greater.
- ○ Quantity B is greater.
- ○ The two quantities are equal.
- ○ The relationship cannot be determined from the information given.

Question 2

$$\frac{5 \times 5}{5 + 5} + \frac{5 \times 5}{5 + 5} =$$

- ○ 1
- ○ $\dfrac{5}{4}$
- ○ 2
- ○ $\dfrac{5}{2}$
- ○ 5

Question 3

$$\left|1 - 5\right| = \left|5 - m\right|$$

Quantity A	Quantity B
m	4

- ○ Quantity A is greater.
- ○ Quantity B is greater.
- ○ The two quantities are equal.
- ○ The relationship cannot be determined from the information given.

Question 4

x, y, and z are consecutive even integers.

Quantity A	Quantity B
xy	yz

- ○ Quantity A is greater.
- ○ Quantity B is greater.
- ○ The two quantities are equal.
- ○ The relationship cannot be determined from the information given.

Question 5

If $bc \neq 0$, and $3b + 2c = 18$, then which of the following is NOT a possible value of c ?

- ○ $5\dfrac{3}{5}$
- ○ 6
- ○ $8\dfrac{2}{5}$
- ○ 9
- ○ 12

Question 6

At the local grocery store, apples normally cost 40 cents each. During a recent sale, the price was reduced to 3 apples for a dollar. How much money would be saved by purchasing 30 apples at the sale price?

- ○ $1.00
- ○ $1.50
- ○ $2.00
- ○ $2.50
- ○ $3.00

Question 7

$$y < 0$$

Quantity A	Quantity B
$2y$	$20y$

- ○ Quantity A is greater.
- ○ Quantity B is greater.
- ○ The two quantities are equal.
- ○ The relationship cannot be determined from the information given.

Question 8

Which of the following could be the difference between two positive integers whose product is 28 ?

- ○ 1
- ○ 3
- ○ 4
- ○ 7
- ○ 14

Question 9

Set X consists of the positive multiples of 5, and set Y consists of the odd prime numbers less than 20. If set Z consists of every distinct integer less than 100 that is the product of one element from set X and one element from set Y, then set Z consists of how many elements?

- ○ 12
- ○ 14
- ○ 15
- ○ 16
- ○ 18

Question 10

$$\frac{u}{v}\left(\frac{x}{y+z}\right)$$

If the value of the expression above is to be doubled by halving exactly one of the five variables, which variable should be halved?

- ○ u
- ○ v
- ○ x
- ○ y
- ○ z

Question 11

$$m > 0, n > 0$$

Quantity A	Quantity B
$\dfrac{m}{mn}$	$\dfrac{n}{mn}$

○ Quantity A is greater.
○ Quantity B is greater.
○ The two quantities are equal.
○ The relationship cannot be determined from the information given.

Question 12

Which of the following is the best approximation of $\sqrt{\dfrac{(98.763)(0.49)^2}{(0.252)}}$?

○ $\dfrac{1}{4}$

○ $\dfrac{1}{2}$

○ 5

○ 10

○ 25

Question 13

Quantity A	Quantity B
Three times the sum of the prime numbers less than 10	The sum of the prime numbers between 20 and 30

○ Quantity A is greater.
○ Quantity B is greater.
○ The two quantities are equal.
○ The relationship cannot be determined from the information given.

Question 14

Tasha's favorite number can be written as $3^2 \times 17^2$.

Quantity A	Quantity B
The number of distinct positive divisors of Tasha's favorite number	9

○ Quantity A is greater.
○ Quantity B is greater.
○ The two quantities are equal.
○ The relationship cannot be determined from the information given.

DRILL 2

Question 1

If x is a positive integer greater than 1, which of the following has the greatest value?

- ○ $\dfrac{1}{x}$

- ○ $\dfrac{1}{x+1}$

- ○ $\dfrac{x}{x+1}$

- ○ $\dfrac{x}{\left(\dfrac{1}{x+1}\right)}$

- ○ $\dfrac{x}{\left(\dfrac{x}{x+1}\right)}$

Question 2

Which of the following CANNOT be the sum of two prime integers?

- ○ 7
- ○ 19
- ○ 23
- ○ 31
- ○ 43

Question 3

If r is an integer multiple of 8, then which of the following could NOT be divisible by r ?

- ○ 216
- ○ 384
- ○ 360
- ○ 416
- ○ 420

Question 4

If x, y, and z are consecutive even integers such that $x < y < z$ and $xyz = 960$, what is the value of z ?

Question 5

Which of the following integers has both 12 and 17 as factors?

- ○ 34
- ○ 84
- ○ 120
- ○ 204
- ○ 217

Question 6

f, g, and h are consecutive prime numbers such that $f < g < h$.

Quantity A	Quantity B
$f + g + h$	$3g$

○ Quantity A is greater.
○ Quantity B is greater.
○ The two quantities are equal.
○ The relationship cannot be determined from the information given.

Question 7

How many positive integers less than 20 are factors of 96 ?

○ 5
○ 6
○ 7
○ 8
○ 9

Question 8

If p and q are both positive odd integers, which of the following must be odd?

Indicate all such values.

☐ pq
☐ $2pq$
☐ $3pq$
☐ $pq + p^q$
☐ $p^q + q^p$

Question 9

If a and b are integers, $ab = -5$, and $a - b > 0$, which of the following must be true?

   I. $a > -1$
  II. b is odd
 III. $|a| = 5$

Indicate all such expressions.

○ I only
○ II only
○ I and II only
○ I and III only
○ I, II, and III

Question 10

$$y = |y|$$
$$y = -|y|$$

Quantity A	Quantity B
y	0

○ Quantity A is greater.
○ Quantity B is greater.
○ The two quantities are equal.
○ The relationship cannot be determined from the information given.

Question 11

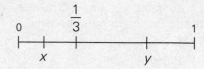

If x and y correspond to points on the number line shown above, which of the following statements must be true?

○ $x > y$

○ $\dfrac{1}{x} < \dfrac{1}{y}$

○ $\dfrac{1}{x} \times \dfrac{1}{y} > 9$

○ $xy < \dfrac{1}{3}$

○ $x + y > 1$

Question 12

n is a positive integer.

The remainder when $5n$ is divided by 4 is 3.

Quantity A	Quantity B
The remainder when $10n$ is divided by 4	2

○   Quantity A is greater.
○   Quantity B is greater.
○   The two quantities are equal.
○   The relationship cannot be determined from the information given.

Question 13

$$a < 0 < b$$

Quantity A	Quantity B
ab	$a + b$

○   Quantity A is greater.
○   Quantity B is greater.
○   The two quantities are equal.
○   The relationship cannot be determined from the information given.

DRILL 3

Question 1

When the number of people in an office is divided by 12, the remainder is 0. If $\frac{3}{2}$ times the number of people in the office is divided by 12, the remainder resulting from this operation is greater than 0, and therefore this remainder must be

○ 1
○ 2
○ 3
○ 5
○ 6

Question 2

a, *b*, and *c* are multiples of 15 and *a* < *b* < *c*

Quantity A	Quantity B
The remainder when *b* is divided by *c*	The remainder when (*b* + *c*) is divided by *a*

○ Quantity A is greater.
○ Quantity B is greater.
○ The two quantities are equal.
○ The relationship cannot be determined from the information given.

Question 3

Emma is 3 years older than Merrick, who is 8 years younger than Aliza. If Aliza is at least 25, which of the following could be Emma's age?

Indicate all such values.

☐ 12
☐ 15
☐ 17
☐ 20
☐ 25
☐ 29

Question 4

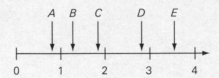

Note: Figure drawn to scale

If each letter on the number line above is the number that corresponds to the point below it, then which of the following is closest to *D* ÷ *A* ?

○ A
○ B
○ C
○ D
○ E

Question 5

Set *X* consists of all the even integers from 1 to 100, inclusive, and set *Y* consists of all the integers divisible by 5 from 1 to 100, exclusive. How many members of set *X* are not members of set *Y* ?

Question 6

If negative integer *a* is multiplied by *b* and the result is greater than 0 but less than |*a*|, then which of the following must be true of *b* ?

○ *b* > 1

○ 0 < *b* < 1

○ −1 < *b* < 0

○ *b* < *a*

○ |*b*| < *a*

Question 7

If r, s, and t are distinct even integers and r is also prime, which of the following must also be even?

- ○ $\dfrac{rs}{t}$
- ○ srt
- ○ $\dfrac{r}{t}s$
- ○ $\dfrac{1}{r}\left(\dfrac{t}{s}\right)$
- ○ $\dfrac{t}{s}r$

Question 8

What are the greatest and smallest positive differences between any of the factors of 210 ?

- ○ 103 and 1
- ○ 209 and 0
- ○ 210 and 1
- ○ 103 and 11
- ○ 209 and 1

Question 9

On Monday, Janice started training for a marathon and ran one mile that day. On Tuesday, Janice ran one mile more than she did on Monday. She continues this training process for 12 days. The sum of the total number of miles Janice ran has how many distinct prime factors?

[   ]

Question 10

Last year, Melania had a total of $20,000 invested in two mutual funds, Capital Growth Fund and Venture Index Fund. At the end of the year, she analyzed her investments and found that her earnings from her shares of Capital Growth Fund were three times half of her earnings on her investment in Venture Index Fund. If she earned a total of $1,250 from her investments in the two funds, and had three times as much money invested in Capital Growth Fund as in Venture Index Fund, what percent interest did Melania earn on her investment in Venture Index Fund? Remember:

percent interest $= \left(\dfrac{\text{earnings}}{\text{investment}}\right) \times 100$

- ○ 0.075%
- ○ 0.1%
- ○ 7.5%
- ○ 10%
- ○ 500%

Question 11

a is the product of 3 and the square root of 2, b is the product of 2 and the square root of 3, and c is the product of 2 and the square root of 6. If x is the square of the sum of a and b, y is the product of 6 and the difference of 5 and c, and z is the product of 2 squared and 3 squared, what is $\dfrac{xy}{z}$?

- ○   1
- ○ $30 - 12\sqrt{6}$
- ○   36
- ○ $30 + 12\sqrt{6}$
- ○   64

Question 12

The integer m is a multiple of 154, 250, and 264. Which of the following do <u>NOT</u> have to be factors of m ?

Indicate <u>all</u> such values.

- ☐   176
- ☐   242
- ☐   275
- ☐   924
- ☐   2,500
- ☐   7,000

Question 13

If when x is divided by z, the result is y remainder q, then which of the following must be true?

- ○ $z(y + q) = x$
- ○ $\dfrac{x}{z} - y = \dfrac{q}{z}$
- ○ $xz - q = y$
- ○ $\dfrac{x}{z} = y + q$
- ○ $\dfrac{x}{z} = yz + q$

DRILL 4

Question 1

If $x^a y^b z^c$ equals the product of 154 and 56, $z > y > x$, and $a > b > c$, then what is the value of $a^x b^y c^z$?

- ○ 1,024
- ○ 2,048
- ○ 8,624
- ○ 22,528
- ○ It cannot be determined from the information given.

Question 2

If $\left| -3x + 1 \right| < 7$, then which of the following represents all possible values of x?

- ○ $-2 < x$
- ○ $-2 < x < \dfrac{8}{3}$
- ○ $-2 \le x \le \dfrac{8}{3}$
- ○ $x < -2$, or $x > \dfrac{8}{3}$
- ○ $x \le -2$, or $x \ge \dfrac{8}{3}$

Question 3

What is the smallest common multiple of 160 and 240?

Question 4

When x is divided by 3, the remainder is 1. When x is divided by 7, the remainder is 2. How many positive integers less than 100 could be values for x?

Question 5

If j is a multiple of 12, and k is a multiple of 21, then jk must be a multiple of which of the following?

- ○ 8
- ○ 15
- ○ 22
- ○ 28
- ○ 35

Question 6

$$\frac{xz}{y} = 420$$

In the equation above, x is an integer with 3 distinct prime factors, and y is a positive integer with no prime factors. If z is a positive, non-prime number, what is the greatest possible value of z ?

$$\boxed{}$$

Question 7

If w is a non-positive integer, which of the following must be positive?

Indicate all such expressions.

- ☐ $-3w$
- ☐ $2w + 10$
- ☐ w^4
- ☐ w^0
- ☐ $-w + 0.5$

Question 8

Integers a and b are consecutive multiples of 6 such that $0 < a < b$. Integers x and y are consecutive multiples of 8 such that $0 < x < y$. In terms of a, b, x, and y, what is the ratio of the average of a and b to the average of x and y ?

- ○ $\dfrac{x + y}{a + b}$

- ○ $\dfrac{a + b}{x + y}$

- ○ $\dfrac{a + \dfrac{b}{4}}{y + \dfrac{x}{4}}$

- ○ $\dfrac{a + \dfrac{b}{4}}{y - \dfrac{x}{2}}$

- ○ $\dfrac{\dfrac{1}{2}(a + b)}{y + x}$

Question 9

If $\left|x^2y\right| = \left|(-w)z\right|$, then which of the following could be true?

Indicate all such expressions.

- ☐ $x^2 = wz$
- ☐ $\left|x^2y\right| = -\left|(-w)z\right|$
- ☐ $-(wz) = wz$
- ☐ $\left|-x^2\right| = \left|(-w)z\right|$
- ☐ $-w = z$
- ☐ $x^2 = -\left|y\right|$

Question 10

If p and x are non-negative numbers and y is a non-positive number, then which of the following must be true?

Indicate <u>all</u> such expressions.

☐ $px > xy$

☐ $px > 0$

☐ $pxy > -1$

☐ $pxy \leq 0$

☐ $px \neq y$

☐ $x \geq py$

Question 11

If $\dfrac{2}{3^x} < 0.02$, what is the least integer value of x ?

○   No such least value exists.

○   101

○   100

○   5

○   4

Question 12

If x is divisible by 78, which of the following must be divisible by x ?

Indicate <u>all</u> such expressions.

☐ $\dfrac{x}{78}$

☐ x

☐ $x + 78$

☐ $\dfrac{78}{x}$

☐ $78 - x$

☐ $78x$

☐ $78x + 78$

Question 13

$$\frac{2,100^2 \times 21^3 \times 49^{\frac{1}{2}}}{30^4 \times 3} = 7^x, \ x =$$

☐

ANSWERS

Drill 1	Drill 2	Drill 3	Drill 4
1. B	1. D	1. E	1. B
2. E	2. C	2. A	2. B
3. D	3. E	3. D, E, F	3. 480
4. D	4. 12	4. E	4. 4
5. D	5. D	5. 41	5. D
6. C	6. D	6. C	6. 14
7. A	7. D	7. B	7. D, E
8. B	8. A, C	8. E	8. B
9. B	9. C	9. 3	9. A, C, D, E
10. B	10. C	10. D	10. D, F
11. D	11. D	11. A	11. D
12. D	12. C	12. A, B, E	12. B, F
13. B	13. D	13. B	13. 6
14. C			

EXPLANATIONS
Drill 1

1. **B** Plug In a value that meets the given requirements; try $x = 15$. The remainder when 15 is divided by 10 is 5; Quantity B is greater, so eliminate (A) and (C). Any acceptable value of x gives the same outcome, so select (B).

2. **E** Find the value of each fraction by multiplying the numbers in the numerator and adding the numbers in the denominator. The value of each fraction is $\frac{25}{10} = \frac{5}{2}$. Add the two fractions: $\frac{5}{2} + \frac{5}{2} = \frac{10}{2} = 5$.

3. **D** Solve for m. If $|1-5| = |5-m|$, then $|-4| = |5-m|$, or $4 = |5-m|$. When you see absolute values, remember to consider both positive and negative solutions: $5 - m = 4$ or $5 - m = -4$, so m can equal 1 or 9, leaving you with (D) for the answer.

4. **D** Try Plugging In; one set of values that could work is $x = -2$, $y = 0$, and $z = 2$. In this case, both Quantity A and Quantity B have a value of 0. Eliminate (A) and (B). However, another set of values that could work is $x = -6$, $y = -4$, and $z = -2$. With this set of values, Quantity A has a value of 24 and Quantity B has a value of 8. Eliminate (C). You are left with (D) for the answer.

5. **D** This problem offers a good opportunity to Plug In the Answers—for simplicity's sake, start with the integers. If $c = 6$, (B), then $3b + 2(6) = 18$, so $3b + 12 = 18$, $3b = 6$, and $b = 2$. The only other requirement given is that $bc \neq 0$, so 6 is, in fact, a possible value of c. If $c = 9$, as in (D), then $3b + 2(9) = 18$, so $3b + 18 = 18$, $3b = 0$, and $b = 0$. A value of 0 for b would violate the given requirement, so 9 is NOT a possible value of c.

6. **C** 30 apples at 40 cents apiece cost $12. Buying 30 apples at 3 per dollar would cost $10. Therefore, the sale price is $2 less than the normal price.

7. **A** When $y = -1$, Quantity A is -2 and Quantity B is -20. Eliminate (B) and (C). Plug in another value for y. When $y = -100$, Quantity A is -200 and Quantity B is $-2,000$. Quantity A is always greater.

8. **B** The two positive integers must have a product of 28, so find the factor pairs of 28: 1 and 28, 2 and 14, and 4 and 7. Only (B) gives a possible difference: $7 - 4 = 3$.

9. **B** Solve this problem by brute force, but be systematic about it. Set Y has a finite number of elements, so list them out and start finding the products when those elements are multiplied by positive multiples of 5. Set $Y = \{3, 5, 7, 11, 13, 17, 19\}$, so multiplying by 5—the first positive multiple of 5—yields 15, 25, 35, 55, 65, 85, and 95; that's 7 elements for set Z thus far. Multiplying by 10—the next positive integer multiple of 5—yields 3 more products, 30, 50, and 70. Multiplying by 15 yields two new products, 45 and 75; multiplying by 20 yields only one new product, 60. That's a total of 13 elements for set Z so far. You already have 75 as a member of set Z, so multiplying by 25

yields no new products; multiplying by 30 yields the final new product, 90. Set Z thus consists of 14 elements: set Z = {15, 25, 30, 35, 45, 50, 55, 60, 65, 70, 75, 85, 90, 95}. If you got (E), you may have mistakenly included 2 as an element of set Y.

10. **B** Plug In values for the variables, such as u = 2, v = 4, x = 6, y = 8, and z = 10. With these values, the expression equals $\frac{1}{6}$. Try halving each of the values to find which one would change the value of the expression to $\frac{1}{3}$. Halving v to 2 works; the answer is (B).

11. **D** Time to Plug In! If you make m = 2 and n = 3, then Quantity A becomes $\frac{2}{2 \times 3} = \frac{1}{3}$, and Quantity B becomes $\frac{3}{2 \times 3} = \frac{1}{2}$. Quantity B is bigger; eliminate (A) and (C). However, if you make and n = 2, then the situation is reversed: Quantity A will be $\frac{1}{2}$, and Quantity B will be $\frac{1}{3}$. Eliminate (B); the answer must be (D).

12. **D** Try rounding your values before you calculate. The expression can be estimated as

$$\sqrt{\frac{(100)\left(\frac{1}{2}\right)^2}{\left(\frac{1}{4}\right)}} = \sqrt{\frac{100\left(\frac{1}{4}\right)}{\left(\frac{1}{4}\right)}} = \sqrt{\frac{25}{\left(\frac{1}{4}\right)}} = \sqrt{25 \times \frac{4}{1}} = \sqrt{100} = 10.$$

13. **B** The prime numbers less than 10 are 2, 3, 5, and 7—don't forget, 1 is not prime. Their sum is 17, and 3 × 17 = 51. The only prime numbers between 20 and 30 are 23 and 29, and their sum is 52. Quantity B is greater.

14. **C** It is easier to work with the factors of Tasha's favorite number, rather than with the number itself. Write out the number as 3 × 3 × 17 × 17 and make a list of the divisors—or factors—in pairs. The pairs are: 1 and 3 × 3 × 17 × 17, 3 and 3 × 17 × 17, 17 and 3 × 3 × 17, 3 × 3 and 17 × 17, and 3 × 17 and 3 × 17. The final pair contains only one *distinct* factor, giving you a total of 9 factors.

Drill 2

1. **D** Try Plugging In on this one. If x = 4, then choice (A) is $\frac{1}{4}$ or 0.25, choice (B) is $\frac{1}{5}$ or 0.2, (C) is $\frac{4}{5}$ or 0.8, (D) is $\frac{4}{\frac{1}{5}} = 4 \div \frac{1}{5} = 4 \times 5 = 20$, and (E) is $\frac{4}{\frac{4}{5}} = 4 \div \frac{4}{5} = 4 \times \frac{5}{4} = 5$. Choice (D) is the greatest.

2. **C** Rather than listing out all of the prime numbers up to 43, stay focused on the unique number, 2, the only even prime number. All of the choices are odd, and two odd numbers would yield an even sum, so you'll be able to eliminate answers only by adding 2 to an odd number. Each of the incorrect answers, therefore, is the sum of 2 and the previous prime number: Choice (A) is 2 + 5; (B) is 2 + 17; (D) is 2 + 29; and (E) is 2 + 41. The answer is (C).

3. E   Plug In a value for r: The first integer multiple of 8 is 8 itself. Only (E) fails to yield an integer: $\frac{420}{8} = 52.5$.

4. 12 Ballpark that 960 is about 1,000, which is $10 \times 10 \times 10$. Then test a set of consecutive even integers near 10, such as $10 \times 12 \times 14 = 1,680$. This product is too large. Try $8 \times 10 \times 12 = 960$, giving you $z = 12$.

5. D   Eliminate (A) and (E) because they are not divisible by 12. Eliminate (B) and (C) because they are not divisible by 17. That leaves (D), 204, which is divisible by both 12 and 17.

6. D   The intervals between consecutive prime numbers do not follow a consistent, predictable pattern. Prove it by Plugging In: try $f = 2$, $g = 3$, and $h = 5$. Now $f + g + h = 10$ and $3g = 9$. Quantity A is greater; eliminate (B) and (C). Now try $f = 7$, $g = 11$, and $h = 13$. This time, $f + g + h = 31$, and $3g = 33$. Quantity B is now greater. Eliminate (A), and you're left with (D).

7. D   The factors of 96 are 1, 2, 3, 4, 6, 8, 12, 16, 24, 32, 48, and 96. Eight of these numbers are less than 20.

8. A, C As soon as you see variables in the answer choices, set up your scratch paper to Plug In. Start with easy numbers like $p = 3$ and $q = 5$, and eliminate any answer choice that doesn't yield an odd result. Choice (A) is 15, so keep it. Choice (B) is 30, so eliminate (B). Choice (C) is 45, so keep it. Choice (D) is 258, and Choice (E) is 368, so you can eliminate both; if you recognize them as the sum of two odd numbers, you don't have to calculate either of them. It's a *must be* problem, so try another set of numbers in (A) and (C) to be sure; as long as p and q are both positive odd integers, (A) and (C) will always work.

9. C   If a and b are integers with a product of -5, then there are only 4 options: $a = 5$ and $b = -1$; $a = -5$ and $b = 1$; $a = 1$ and $b = -5$; and $a = -1$ and $b = 5$. The requirement that $a - b > 0$ eliminates the second and fourth options, leaving only $a = 5$ and $b = -1$ and $a = 1$ and $b = -5$. (I) and (II) are both true for these two cases and (III) is not true if $a = 1$, making (C) the answer.

10. C   The first equation tells you that y cannot be a negative number. The second equation tells you that y cannot be a positive number. Therefore, y must be 0.

11. D   Plug In values for x and y that fit the figure: try $x = \frac{1}{6}$ and $y = \frac{2}{3}$. Now, plug these numbers into each of the choices and use POE. Only (D) is correct: $\frac{1}{6} \times \frac{2}{3} = \frac{2}{18} = \frac{1}{9}$, which is less than $\frac{1}{3}$.

12. C   If the remainder is 3, then $5n$ must be 3 more than a multiple of 4, such as 4, 8, 12, or 16. Try adding 3 to these multiples to find a possible value for $5n$. $12 + 3$ yields 15 as a value for $5n$; $n = 3$. Quantity A is the remainder when 30 is divided by 4, or 2. Eliminate (A) and (B). Try a different number. If n is 7, then $5n$ is 35, which also has a remainder of 3 when divided by 4. In Quantity A, 70 divided by 4 has a remainder of 2. For any other numbers you try, (C) will be the answer.

13.   **D**   Plug In values for a and b. If $a = -2$ and $b = 2$, then Quantity B is greater. Eliminate (A) and (C). If $a = -\dfrac{1}{2}$ and $b = \dfrac{1}{4}$, then Quantity A is greater. Eliminate (B).

Drill 3

1.   **E**   The "must be" wording of the question is a trigger to use FROZEN and multiple Plug Ins may be required. Since the use of 1 is good in multiple Plug Ins, plug in 12 since $12 \div 12 = 1$ with a remainder of 0. $\dfrac{3}{2} \times 12 = 18$ and $18 \div 12 = 1$ with a remainder of 6. Next try a larger multiple of 12, say, 60. Then, $60 \div 12 = 5$ with a remainder of 0, $\dfrac{3}{2} \times 60 = 90$, and $90 \div 12 = 7$ with a remainder of 6. Both Plug Ins have disproven (A), (B), (C), and (D), and that is the goal in a "must be" question. Thus the answer is (E).

2.   **A**   Variables in Quant Comp are triggers for multiple Plug Ins so start with values that fit the conditions of the problem and see what answer choices can be eliminated. If $a = 15$, $b = 30$, and $c = 60$, Quantity A is 30 because c cannot divide into b even one time. Quantity B is 0 because 90 divided by 15 has no remainder. Eliminate (B) and (C). Try a new set of numbers to further narrow your choices. If $a = 30$, $b = 45$, and $c = 120$, Quantity A is 45, and Quantity B is 15. The answer is (A).

3.   **D, E, F**

   Since a minimum for Aliza's age is given, do the arithmetic using that as a starting point. If Aliza is 25, then Merrick is 17 and Emma is 20. Given that 25 was Aliza's minimum age, pick answers that make Emma 20 years or older; (D), (E), and (F) are all correct.

4.   **E**   Estimate that D is approximately 2.8 and A is approximately 0.8. So the answer is $2.8 \div 0.8$, or 3.5, which is closest to (E).

5.   **41**   Half of the integers from 1 to 100—inclusive—are even, so set X has 50 members. Set Y has 19 members, the integers divisible by 5 from 1 to 100 *exclusive*, so don't include 100. Of the 19 members of set Y, 9 are even and therefore, in set X. The 50 members of set X minus the 9 members that <u>are also in set Y</u> yields $50 - 9 = 41$ members.

6.   **C**   To solve this problem, Plug In for a and b, but don't forget your restrictions. If $a = -4$, then a value of $-\dfrac{1}{2}$ for b would yield a product greater than 0 but less than $|a|$. Only (C) works.

7.   **B**   Since this is a "must be" question with variables, use Plugging In to disprove answer choices until only one is left. r is both prime and even, so $r = 2$. Try $s = 6$ and $t = 8$ as easy numbers that fit the conditions. Plugging these numbers into (A), (C), (D), and (E) gives a fraction; fractions are neither even nor odd, so eliminate those choices. Also note that (A) and (C) are mathematically the same, and therefore neither can be your answer since this is not an "indicate all" question. Only (B) remains even.

8. **E**   First, list all of the factors of 210. The easiest way to do this is in pairs, starting with 1 and 210 (remember, the number itself is considered one of its factors). Count up from one and check to see if each number you count is a factor of 210.

| 1 and 210 | 3 and 70 | 7 and 3 | 14 and 15 |
| 2 and 105 | 5 and 42 | 10 and 21 | |

When you reach 14, you'll see that you'll just repeat 15 and 14 if you keep counting, so you know you're finished. The question asked for the greatest and smallest positive difference between any two factors. The way you listed the factors makes this easy because as you look down the list, the difference between factors decreases. So the greatest difference is between 210 and 1, and the smallest difference is between 14 and 15. The final answer is 209 and 1. Alternatively, you can use POE more aggressively here. Once you know 209 is a positive difference, eliminate (A), (C), and (D). Since 210 is not a perfect square, the other difference can't be 0 and must be 1 making (E) correct.

9. **3**   Adding the numbers together won't take long, but there is a shortcut to this problem. Match up the smallest number of miles (1) with the largest number of miles (12), and then the second smallest (2) with the second largest (11), and so on until all the numbers are matched up.

1	12
2	11
3	10
4	9
5	8
6	7

The sum of each of these 6 pairs is 13, which means you could multiply 13 by 6 = 78 to get the total number of miles. Next, find the prime factors of 78. We already know it's divisible by 13 and 6 (because we had multiplied those together to get 78). Given that 13 is prime, you now need to find the prime factors of 6, which are 2 and 3. All together we have 3 prime factors at the bottom of the prime factor tree, so that's our answer.

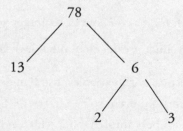

10. **D**   The question defines how to calculate percent interest, so focus on the two numbers that are involved: earnings and investment. Start by calculating the amount Melania had invested in each

fund. The question states that her total investment was $20,000 and she *had three times as much money invested in Capital Growth Fund as in Venture Index Fund,* so turn those words into math: $20,000 = (3 × *Venture*) + *Venture*. So Melania's investment in Venture was $5,000. Next, determine the amount she earned on each. Once again, turn the words into math: *earnings from her shares of Capital Growth Fund were three times half of her earnings on her investment in Venture Index Fund* and she earned a total of $1,250. Thus $1,250 = (3 × $\frac{1}{2}$ *VentureEarnings*) + *VentureEarnings*. Solving this shows she earned $500 on her investment in Venture. Putting these numbers into the percent interest formula given in the question yields $\left(\dfrac{500}{5,000}\right) \times 100 = 10$. Thus (D) is correct. Notice that (E) is the amount earned rather than the percent, and (B) is the answer as a decimal rather than a percent; both are trap answers.

11. **A** Let's translate this question, one step at a time.

$$a = 3\sqrt{2} \qquad b = 2\sqrt{3} \qquad c = 2\sqrt{6}$$

$$x = (3\sqrt{2} + 2\sqrt{3})^2 = (3\sqrt{2} + 2\sqrt{3})(3\sqrt{2} + 2\sqrt{3}) =$$

$$(9)(2) + 6\sqrt{6} + 6\sqrt{6} + (4)(3) = 18 + 12\sqrt{6} + 12 = 30 + 12\sqrt{6}$$

$$y = 6(5 - 2\sqrt{6}) = 30 - 12\sqrt{6}$$

$$z = 2^2 \times 3^2 = 6^2 = 36$$

$$\frac{xy}{z} = \frac{(30 + 12\sqrt{6})(30 - 12\sqrt{6})}{36} = \frac{900 + 360\sqrt{6} - 144(6)}{36} = \frac{900 - 864}{36} = \frac{36}{36} = 1$$

Did you recognize the common quadratics? Also, the product of *x* and *y* in the last chunk of the question contains one that could save you that intermediary step: $(x + y)(x - y) = x^2 - y^2$. Of course, it doesn't take too much longer to write out the math.

12. **A, B, E**

To solve this question, turn large numbers into small numbers by working with factors. The prime factors of 154 are 2, 7, and 11; the prime factors of 264 are 2, 2, 2, 3, and 11; and the prime factors of 250 are 2, 5, 5, and 5. The only numbers that must be a factor of *m* are those made up of factors contained in the other three numbers. You can't recount factors that overlap in the different numbers, so you know that *m* is made up of, at least, three 2's, one 3, three 5's, one 7, and one 11. Now check the answers. The prime factors of 176 are 2, 2, 2, 2, and 11, which is one 2 too many, so (A) is not a factor; since the question asks you to identify which choices are *not* factors, (A) is part of the credited response. The prime factors of 242 are 2, 11, and 11, which is one 11 too many, so (B) is also not a factor. The prime factors of 275 are 5, 5, and 11, so (C) is a factor. The prime factors of 924 are 2, 2, 3, 7, and 11, so (D) is a factor. The prime factors of 2,500 are 2, 2, 5, 5, 5, and 5, which is one 5 too many, so (E) is not a factor. And finally, the prime factors of 7,000 are 2, 2, 2, 5, 5, 5, and 7, so (F) is a factor. The correct answers are (A), (B), and (E).

13. **B** As soon as you see variables in the answer choices, set up your scratch paper to Plug In. If $x = 16$ and $z = 5$, then $16 \div 5 = 3$ remainder 1, so $y = 3$ and $q = 1$. Plug your values into the answer choices, and only (B) works: $\dfrac{16}{5} - 3 = \dfrac{1}{5}$.

Drill 4

1. **B** To solve this question, find the prime factors: the prime factors of 154 are 2, 7, and 11, and the prime factors of 56 are 2, 2, 2, and 7. Thus, the product of 154 and 56 will have the prime factors 2, 2, 2, 2, 7, 7, and 11, or $(2^4)(7^2)(11^1)$. Line up your bases and exponents with the inequalities, and you get $a = 4$, $b = 2$, and $c = 1$ for the bases, and $x = 2$, $y = 7$, $z = 11$ for the exponents. Now $a^x b^y c^z = (4^2)(2^7)(1^{11})$, which equals $16 \times 128 \times 1$, or 2,048. The correct answer is (B).

2. **B** You can Plug In or solve on this problem. To Plug In, choose a value that fits one of the answer choices, such as $x = 2$, which would fit in the range for (C). If $x = 2$, then $|-3x + 1| = 5$, which is true, so we can eliminate any answer choice that doesn't include $x = 2$: (A), (D), and (E). If $x = 2$ didn't make the inequality work, then we would eliminate any of the answer choices which included that value. Logically, it doesn't make sense that an inequality with a < sign would have a ≤ sign when it's been solved, but to be sure, check $x = -2$. In that case, $|-3x + 1| = 7$, and is not < 7, so the answer must be (B). If you solve this problem, remember that you have to solve both $-3x + 1 < 7$, and $-3x + 1 > 7$. Also remember that you must flip the sign any time you multiply or divide both sides of an inequality by a negative number.

3. **480** Make lists of the multiples for each number. Work on 240 first; then list the multiples of 160 until you find one on the list for 240.

240:	160:
240	160
480	320
720	480
960	

4. **4** To solve this question, write it out. Since there are fewer numbers that yield a remainder of 2 when divided by 7, start there. The first such number is 2, and thereafter they increase by 7; the rest of the list is thus 9, 16, 23, 30, 37, 44, 51, 58, 65, 72, 79, 86, and 93. Rather than list out all the numbers that yield a remainder of 1 when divided by 3, just select the numbers that meet the requirement from the list you already have: only 16, 37, 58, and 79 do, so there are 4 values for x.

5. **D** Plug in values for j and k. Since every number is a multiple of itself, go ahead and start with $j = 12$ and $k = 21$; jk is now 252. You can use your on-screen calculator to determine that, of the answer choices, only 28 divides evenly into 252. Choice (D) is correct. If more that one answer choice

divided in evenly after your first round of Plugging In, try again with a greater multiple and evaluate the answer choices you have not yet eliminated.

6. **14** There's only one positive integer with no prime factors, the number 1. Therefore, $y = 1$, and $xz = 420$. Create a prime factor tree to get the prime factors of 420: 2, 2, 3, 5, and 7. Pick 3 *distinct* values from that list that are the smallest (2, 3, and 5) and multiply them to find the smallest value of x since you are looking for the greatest value of z. One example is $2 \times 3 \times 5 = 30$, so $30z = 420$, and then $z = 14$. Confirm that 14 is not prime; then enter it in the field.

7. **D, E** Remember to Plug In multiple times for *must be* questions. First, use an easy number, such as –1, and try it in each choice:

   All of the answers are positive, so don't eliminate anything. Can we eliminate anything by making w smaller? A number such as –10 will allow us to eliminate (B), but everything else is still positive. But can $w = 0$? Non-positive just means the number can't be positive—it doesn't mean it can't be zero. Plugging in 0 eliminates (A) and (C) since 0 is not positive. This leaves (D) and (E).

8. **B** Variables in the problem and variables in the answer choices indicate you should Plug In. Start by picking easy values that meet the condition of the problem: $a = 6$, $b = 12$, $c = 8$, $d = 16$. The average of 6 and 12 is 9 and the average of 8 and 16 is 12, so the ratio of the averages is $\frac{9}{12} = \frac{3}{4}$. When these numbers are plugged into (A) and (E), they do not equal $\frac{3}{4}$, so eliminate both answer choices. However, (B), (C), and (D) all do equal $\frac{3}{4}$, so another round of Plugging In is necessary. Try something larger: $a = 24$, $b = 30$, $c = 80$, $d = 88$. The average of 24 and 30 is 27 and the average of 80 and 88 is 84, so the ratio of the averages is $\frac{27}{84} = \frac{9}{28}$. Plug the new numbers only into the remaining answer choices. Only (B) equals $\frac{9}{28}$, so eliminate (C) and (D). Be sure to solve for (C) and (D) again, because only by doing so can you be sure they do not equal (B) again this time.

9. **A, C, D, E**

   The best way to approach a *could be* question is to consider many different kinds of numbers to plug in that could work in the problem. We will have to Plug In a few times here, so let's start with easy numbers. For instance, let's try making every variable in the problem equal to 1. Immediately, (A) and (D) work. If we made $w = 1$ and $z = -1$, then (E) works as well. Try plugging in 0 for either w or z and (C) can also work. In the end, (B) and (F) are always going to have a positive value on the left side of the equation and a negative value on the right, and therefore will not be correct. An absolute value is *always* positive, so it can never equal something negative.

10. **D, F** As soon as you see variables in the answer choices, set up your scratch paper to Plug In. Start with easy numbers like $p = 2$, $x = 3$, and $y = -4$. Of the answer choices, all work except (C), which can be eliminated. Now plug in different numbers. Since the variables are described as *non-negative*

and *non-positive*, try making p, x, and y all 0. Now (A), (B), and (E) all yield false statements and can be eliminated. The correct answers are (D) and (F).

11. **D**   First, rewrite 0.02 as a fraction, $\frac{2}{100}$. For $\frac{2}{3^x}$ to be less than $\frac{2}{100}$, $3x$ must be greater than 100. Plugging In the Answers is the easiest way to get this right. Choice (E) is $3^4 = 81$ and the fraction is greater than 0.02; eliminate it. Choice (D) is $3^5 = 243$ and this makes the fraction less than 0.02. Therefore, the least value for x is 5. Be sure to answer what is asked. The inequality would be true if the denominator of $\frac{2}{3^x}$ were 101, which is (B); however, the question is asking for the least value of x, not of 3^x, so the correct answer is (D).

12. **B, F**   There are variables in the answer choices, so Plug In. Try $x = 78$. You can eliminate (A) and (D). Now try a weird number: 0 since $0 \times 78 = 0$. Eliminate (G). Try one more number: 156, which is 78×2. This time you can eliminate (C) and (E). A number is divisible by itself and a multiple of a number is divisible by that number, so the correct answers are (B) and (F).

13. **6**   Break down the left side of the equation into prime factors to make it easier to simplify. You should get

$$\frac{(3^2 \times 7^2 \times 2^4 \times 5^4) \times (3^3 \times 7^3) \times 7}{(2^4 \times 5^4 \times 3^4) \times 3} = 7^x$$

Then group all the like terms:

$$\frac{2^4 \times 3^5 \times 5^4 \times 7^6}{2^4 \times 3^5 \times 5^4} = 7^x$$

Everything cancels out on the left side except for 7^6, which makes 6 your answer.

Fractions, Decimals, and Percentages

FRACTIONS

You will see plenty of fractions on the GRE, but don't worry; everything you need to know about them you learned in second grade. You must be able to add, subtract, multiply, divide, and compare fractions. Here are the basics, with a couple of neat tricks thrown in.

Adding

In grade school, you learned to find the lowest common denominator. That still works. The Bowtie method is a convenient way to find the common denominator.

It looks like this.

$$10 = \quad\quad = 12$$
$$\frac{2}{3} \times \frac{4}{5} = \frac{10}{15} + \frac{12}{15} = \frac{22}{15}$$

Just multiply across the bottom to get your common denominator. Multiply on the diagonal to figure out your numerators and then add across the top. It works the same way for subtracting.

$$\frac{3}{8} \times \frac{1}{5} = \frac{15}{40} - \frac{8}{40} = \frac{7}{40}$$

Here's another helpful tip. If you have a fraction with addition or subtraction in the numerator, and a single number or variable in the denominator, you can split your original fraction into two separate fractions.

$$\frac{25+13}{19} = \frac{25}{19} + \frac{13}{19}$$

Comparing

The Bowtie method is also useful for comparing fractions; this comes in very handy on Quant Comp questions. Just multiply up on the diagonals to compare any two fractions. If you want to compare $\frac{5}{8}$ and $\frac{7}{12}$, for example, multiply 5 by 12 and 8 by 7, then compare. The larger number, 60, belongs to the larger fraction, $\frac{5}{8}$. Make sure you do this work on your scratch paper and not in your head.

$$\frac{5}{8} \text{ vs } \frac{7}{12} \qquad 60 = \frac{5}{8} \diagdown \frac{7}{12} = 56$$

Reducing

In general, get into the habit of reducing all fractions to their simplest forms; it will make your life easier. Before you do, however, have a quick look at the answer choices to make sure your fractions need to be reduced. You don't want to do more work than necessary.

Remember the following rules:

- Do not reduce across a +, −, or = sign. You can reduce individual fractions, but you cannot reduce the numerator of one fraction with the denominator of another, if +, −, or = signs are involved.

- When multiplying fractions, you can reduce anything, including the numerator of one fraction with the denominator of another.

- In $\frac{20}{36}$, you can take fours out of both, not sevens. This is shown with the factoring and cancellation of the twos.

$$\frac{20}{36} = \frac{\cancel{2} \times \cancel{2} \times 5}{\cancel{2} \times \cancel{2} \times 3 \times 3} = \frac{5}{3 \times 3} = \frac{5}{9}$$

Dividing a fraction by a fraction is the same thing as multiplying the first fraction by the reciprocal of the second fraction. You may be able to do this in your head, but don't. Take the extra two seconds to lay it out on your scratch paper. It won't take you much more time, and you're less likely to make a careless error.

$$\frac{\frac{1}{2}}{\frac{3}{4}} = \frac{1}{2} \div \frac{3}{4} = \frac{1}{\cancel{2}} \times \frac{\cancel{4}^2}{3} = \frac{2}{3}$$

DECIMALS

Occasionally ETS will give you a question in fractions and the answers in decimals, or one side of a Quant Comp in decimals and the other side in fractions. To convert a fraction to a decimal, use long division.

$$\frac{3}{7} = 7\overline{)3} = 7\overline{\smash{)}\begin{array}{r} 0.428 \\ 3.000 \\ \underline{2\ 8} \\ 20 \\ \underline{14} \\ 60 \\ \underline{56} \\ 4 \end{array}}$$

Make sure you check your answer choices and eliminate as you go, so you don't waste time doing extra work. You will rarely have to divide a fraction out to more than two decimal places.

Converting

When converting from a decimal to a fraction, think of the decimal point as a 1 that goes on the bottom of your new fraction; then count up the number of digits that come after the decimal point and add the same number of zeros after the 1.

$$0.42 = \frac{42}{100} \qquad\qquad 0.003 = \frac{3}{1,000}$$

Multiplying

When you multiply decimals, the answer must have the same number of decimal places as the total decimal places in the numbers you are multiplying. For example, if you multiply 0.4 by 0.2, the answer must have two places to the right of the decimal, because 0.4 and 0.2 have one decimal place each. The answer is 0.08. Just remember that when you multiply a decimal by a decimal, the answers will get pretty small pretty quickly.

Dividing

When you divide a decimal into a decimal, write it out as long division and convert the divisor into a whole number.

Since 0.003 is a very small number, it makes sense that it will go into 0.2751 (which is close to 0.3) nearly a hundred times. In fact, if you were Ballparking, you would notice that to get from 0.003 to a number close to 0.3 you would have to move your decimal point to the right two spaces. That is the same as multiplying by 100, so you would be looking for an answer choice that's close to 100. Because 0.2751 is a little bit less than 0.3, you want a number that's a little bit less than 100.

PERCENTAGES

How do you express $\frac{1}{2}$ as a percentage? 50 percent, right? How do you express $\frac{1}{2}$ as a decimal? 0.5, right? You may know that 25 percent, $\frac{1}{4}$, and 0.25 are all the same thing. They are all fractions and they all express a $\frac{part}{whole}$ relationship. The first tip for mastering percentages is realizing that they are really just fractions.

These are the most common fraction, decimal, and percentage equivalents; learn them, live them, love them.

Decimal	Fraction	Percentage
0.25	1/4	25%
0.5	1/2	50%
0.75	3/4	75%
1.0	4/4	100%
3.75	15/4	375%
0.33	1/3	33%
0.66	2/3	66%
1.0	3/3	100%
1.66	5/3	166%
0.2	1/5	20%
0.4	2/5	40%
0.6	3/5	60%
0.8	4/5	80%
1.0	5/5	100%
1.2	6/5	120%
2.4	12/5	240%
0.125	1/8	12.5%
0.250	2/8	25%
0.375	3/8	37.5%
0.5	4/8	50%
0.625	5/8	62.5%
0.75	6/8	75%
0.875	7/8	87.5%
1.0	8/8	100%
1.125	9/8	112.5%
2.5	20/8	250%

Memorize these fractions and be comfortable switching from one format to another, because when a question asks you for 75 percent, it may be easier to think of the percentage as $\frac{3}{4}$. When a Quant Comp asks you whether $\frac{4}{5}$ or $\frac{6}{8}$ is bigger, it may be easier to think of them as 80 percent and 75 percent.

Translating

Complicated percentages are often expressed as word problems rather than math problems. For example, "42 is what percent of 28"? This problem can be translated, word for word, into a single-variable equation.

Here's your translation guide.

Word	Symbol
percent	/100
of	* (times)
what	x, y, or z
is, are, was, were	=

Your translation is $42 = \dfrac{x}{100} \times 28$.

Stress-Free Tip Calculating

How often have you used this one? Your bill is $28.50. You want to tip 20 percent. You know that 10% = $2.85. Double it to get $5.70, and you have 20 percent. You want to leave only 15 percent? Okay, what is half of 10 percent? Let's call it $1.43. Add that back to the 10 percent, and you have $4.28, or 15 percent. You can do this with any number to quickly calculate exact percentages or to quickly Ballpark answers.

Number	Percentage
1,246	100%
124.6	10%
12.46	1%
62.3	5%
373.8 (10% × 3)	30%
398.72 (10% × 3 + 1% × 2)	32%

Part to Whole

The last, and perhaps most common, method of quickly calculating percentages is to set up a ratio of part to whole. Remember that the word percent simply means of 100, so 42 percent means 42 parts out of a total of 100.

$$\frac{\text{part}}{\text{whole}} = \frac{x}{100}$$

With this set-up, the variable could go anywhere. ETS might give you the percentage and ask you for the whole. For example, "42 is 60 percent of what"?

$$\frac{42}{x} = \frac{60}{100}$$

To solve, simply cross multiply: $4{,}200 = 60x$.

A question might ask you, "42 is what percent of 70"? In this case, the x goes over the 100.

$$\frac{42}{70} = \frac{x}{100}$$

Or a question might ask you, "What is 60 percent of 70"? In this case you know the percentage and the total, but not the part.

$$\frac{x}{70} = \frac{60}{100}$$

Cross multiply and you can solve. You can always put a percentage into this format.

For more practice and a more in-depth look at The Princeton Review math techniques, check out our student-friendly guidebook, *Cracking the GRE*.

DRILL 1

Question 1

$$3 \div \frac{6}{7} =$$

○ $\frac{36}{7}$

○ $\frac{2}{7}$

○ $2\frac{4}{7}$

○ 3

○ $3\frac{1}{2}$

Question 2

$$\frac{\frac{1}{5} - \frac{1}{2}}{\frac{1}{5} + \frac{1}{2}} =$$

○ -1

○ $-\frac{1}{2}$

○ $-\frac{3}{7}$

○ $\frac{6}{5}$

○ 2

Question 3

Quantity A	Quantity B
$\frac{15}{16} + \frac{1}{256}$	$1 - \frac{1}{64}$

○   Quantity A is greater.
○   Quantity B is greater.
○   The two quantities are equal.
○   The relationship cannot be determined from the information given.

Question 4

A deposit at a local bank earns between 2 percent and 5 percent simple interest in a year. If Shirley makes an initial deposit of $800 at the bank, which of the following could be the amount of money in her account at the end of one year?

○ $814
○ $820
○ $842
○ $848
○ $860

Question 5

Quantity A	Quantity B
The change in price of a pair of shoes marked down by 50%	The change in price of a pair of boots marked down by 30%

○   Quantity A is greater.
○   Quantity B is greater.
○   The two quantities are equal.
○   The relationship cannot be determined from the information given.

Question 6

Joey works at a clothing store and receives an employee discount of 10 percent off the regular price of any item. What is the regular price of an item that Joey purchases for $99 ?

- ○ $89.10
- ○ $108.90
- ○ $109.00
- ○ $109.90
- ○ $110.00

Question 7

Rohan began a savings account with a balance of $200. His current balance is $150.

Quantity A	Quantity B
The percent decrease from Rohan's original balance to his current balance	The percent increase that would return Rohan's current balance to his original balance

- ○ Quantity A is greater.
- ○ Quantity B is greater.
- ○ The two quantities are equal.
- ○ The relationship cannot be determined from the information given.

Question 8

If 20 percent of x is $5y$, and $y = 7$, what is 60 percent of x ?

- ○ 105
- ○ 115
- ○ 125
- ○ 145
- ○ 175

Question 9

$$\frac{1}{48} + \frac{1}{48} + \frac{1}{12} + \frac{1}{8} + \frac{1}{4} + \frac{1}{2} =$$

- ○ $\dfrac{49}{48}$
- ○ 1
- ○ $\dfrac{47}{48}$
- ○ $\dfrac{3}{4}$
- ○ $\dfrac{2}{3}$

Question 10

The Warm Muffin Bakery's cookie sales are always 60 percent of its muffin sales. What would be the increase in The Warm Muffin Bakery's cookie sales if its muffin sales increased from 10,000 to 20,000 ?

- ○ 10,000
- ○ 8,000
- ○ 6,000
- ○ 4,000
- ○ 2,000

Question 11

Quantity A	Quantity B
$\dfrac{7}{8} - 0.25$	$0.325 + \dfrac{1}{3}$

- ○ Quantity A is greater.
- ○ Quantity B is greater.
- ○ The two quantities are equal.
- ○ The relationship cannot be determined from the information given.

Question 12

Which of the following inequalities is true?

- ○ $\dfrac{1}{11} < 0.08 < \dfrac{1}{9}$
- ○ $\dfrac{1}{10} < 0.11 < \dfrac{1}{8}$
- ○ $\dfrac{1}{7} < 0.17 < \dfrac{1}{6}$
- ○ $\dfrac{1}{5} < 0.26 < \dfrac{1}{4}$
- ○ $\dfrac{1}{3} < 0.30 < \dfrac{1}{2}$

Question 13

Company A's output of 245 widgets per week is 35 percent of Company B's weekly widget output.

Quantity A	Quantity B
700	Company B's weekly widget output

- ○ Quantity A is greater.
- ○ Quantity B is greater.
- ○ The two quantities are equal.
- ○ The relationship cannot be determined from the information given.

Question 14

If $mn \neq 0$, $\dfrac{2+m}{mn} =$

- ○ $\dfrac{2}{m} + \dfrac{2}{mn}$
- ○ $2 + \dfrac{m}{mn}$
- ○ $\dfrac{2}{mn} + n$
- ○ $\dfrac{2}{mn} + \dfrac{1}{m}$
- ○ $\dfrac{2}{mn} + \dfrac{1}{n}$

DRILL 2

Question 1

A car with all available options costs $18,000, an increase of 20% from the base price of the car.

Quantity A	Quantity B
The base price of the car	$14,400

- ○ Quantity A is greater.
- ○ Quantity B is greater.
- ○ The two quantities are equal.
- ○ The relationship cannot be determined from the information given.

Question 2

What percent is equivalent to 0.0025 ?

- ○ $\frac{1}{25}$%
- ○ $\frac{1}{5}$%
- ○ $\frac{1}{4}$%
- ○ 4%
- ○ 5%

Question 3

Which of the following fractions is closest in value to $\frac{5}{8}$?

- ○ $\frac{2}{3}$
- ○ $\frac{3}{4}$
- ○ $\frac{7}{11}$
- ○ $\frac{19}{23}$
- ○ $\frac{23}{30}$

Question 4

A certain brand of imported cigars costs $30 for a box of 20; when bought individually, the cigars cost $2 each.

Quantity A	Quantity B
The percent saved when a box of cigars is purchased, rather than 20 individual cigars	$33\frac{1}{3}$

- ○ Quantity A is greater.
- ○ Quantity B is greater.
- ○ The two quantities are equal.
- ○ The relationship cannot be determined from the information given.

Question 5

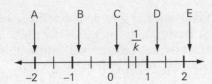

Which of the labeled coordinates on the number line above could represent the value of k?

- ○ A
- ○ B
- ○ C
- ○ D
- ○ E

Question 6

$(4 \times 100) + (6 \times 1,000) + (2 \times 1) + (3 \times 10) =$

- ○ 2,346
- ○ 4,632
- ○ 4,623
- ○ 6,324
- ○ 6,432

Question 7

What is the value of $\dfrac{3}{\left(\dfrac{3}{4}\right)} - \dfrac{\left(\dfrac{3}{2}\right)}{3}$?

- ○ $-\dfrac{7}{4}$

- ○ $-\dfrac{3}{4}$

- ○ 1

- ○ 2

- ○ $\dfrac{7}{2}$

Question 8

a is 40% of 45

18 is b% of 90

Quantity A	Quantity B
a	b

- ○ Quantity A is greater.
- ○ Quantity B is greater.
- ○ The two quantities are equal.
- ○ The relationship cannot be determined from the information given.

Question 9

$$\dfrac{\dfrac{x}{5} + \dfrac{x}{5} + \dfrac{x}{5} + \dfrac{x}{5}}{4} =$$

- ○ $16x$

- ○ $\dfrac{24x}{5}$

- ○ $4x$

- ○ $\dfrac{4x}{5}$

- ○ $\dfrac{x}{5}$

Question 10

$$n > 0$$

$$\frac{6n}{15}, 0.3n, \frac{19n}{50}, \frac{n}{4}$$

Quantity A	Quantity B
The positive difference between the greatest and least values above	Three times the positive difference between the two least values above

- ○ Quantity A is greater.
- ○ Quantity B is greater.
- ○ The two quantities are equal.
- ○ The relationship cannot be determined from the information given.

Question 11

Halfway through the season, Antonio's scoring average per game was 20% higher than David's. The two scored the same number of points in the second half of the season.

Quantity A	Quantity B
90% of Antonio's scoring average for the whole season	David's scoring average for the whole season

- ○ Quantity A is greater.
- ○ Quantity B is greater.
- ○ The two quantities are equal.
- ○ The relationship cannot be determined from the information given.

Question 12

The annual interest rate on a certain savings account increases from 1.25% to 1.5%. What percent increase in the annual interest rate does this change represent?

- ○ 0.2%
- ○ 0.25%
- ○ 0.167%
- ○ 20%
- ○ 25%

Question 13

Which of the following is equal to $\frac{1}{5}$ of the reciprocal of 0.004 percent?

- ○ 0.5
- ○ 50
- ○ 500
- ○ 5,000
- ○ 50,000

Question 14

Quantity A	Quantity B
The total value of 100 dollars after it is invested for m months at 8 percent simple annual interest	$100\left(1 + \dfrac{0.08}{m}\right)$ dollars

- ○ Quantity A is greater.
- ○ Quantity B is greater.
- ○ The two quantities are equal.
- ○ The relationship cannot be determined from the information given.

DRILL 3

Question 1

27 percent of p is 100.

p is q percent of 100.

Quantity A	Quantity B
q	400

○ Quantity A is greater.
○ Quantity B is greater.
○ The two quantities are equal.
○ The relationship cannot be determined from the information given.

Question 2

Which expression is equivalent to $\dfrac{1}{y - \dfrac{1}{y}} - y$?

○ $\dfrac{y^3 + y - 1}{y^2 - 1}$

○ $\dfrac{2y - y^3}{y^2 - 1}$

○ $\dfrac{-y^3}{y^2 - 1}$

○ $y^3 + y - 1$

○ $-y - 1$

Question 3

One cup of nuts that contains exactly half peanuts and half cashews is added to a bowl of nuts that is exactly one third peanuts, one third cashews, and one third almonds. This results in a three-cup mixture of nuts. What fraction of the new nut mixture is peanuts?

Question 4

Quantity A	Quantity B
16 percent of 83	83 percent of 16

○ Quantity A is greater.
○ Quantity B is greater.
○ The two quantities are equal.
○ The relationship cannot be determined from the information given.

Question 5

Leah wants to shrink her photos to fit a computer screen. Her photos currently have a width of 1,024 pixels and a height of 768 pixels. If she reduces the width to 800 pixels, then to what height, in pixels, must she reduce the photos to preserve the same ratio of width to height?

○ 1,066.7
○ 600
○ 576
○ 544
○ 500

Question 6

What is w if $\frac{1}{9}(w + 1) = \frac{1}{729}$?

Question 7

Maria removes $\frac{5}{6}$ of the cookies from a jar, and then Andrea removes $\frac{3}{5}$ of the remaining cookies from the same jar. Which of the following could NOT be the number of cookies originally in the jar?

Indicate all such values.

- ☐   6
- ☐   15
- ☐   30
- ☐   60
- ☐ 200
- ☐ 210
- ☐ 340

Question 8

If $.002x + .004y = 4$, what is the value of y in terms of x ?

- ○ $\dfrac{4 - 2x}{.04}$

- ○ $\dfrac{4000 - .002x}{.04}$

- ○ $4 - .5x$

- ○ $1000 - .5x$

- ○ $2(1000 - x)$

Question 9

What is the tenths digit of the quotient when thirty-five hundredths is divided by four thousandths?

Question 10

A group of freshmen, juniors, and seniors is going on a school trip. The number of seniors is 60% of the number of juniors, which is 50% of the number of freshmen. If there are at least 150 students on the trip, then which of the following could be the number of seniors?

Indicate all such values.

☐ 21
☐ 22
☐ 24
☐ 25
☐ 27

Question 11

Between the first day of May and the last day of June, the price per kilogram of Melange, a seasoning mix, first declined by 20 percent and then increased by 50 percent. During this same period, the price per liter of Blue, a spring water, first increased by 20 percent and then declined by 50 percent. If at the end of June, the prices were the same, then, at the beginning of May, the price per liter of Blue was what percent of the price per kilogram of Melange?

○   2
○   30
○   50
○ 100
○ 200

Question 12

A container is $\frac{4}{5}$ full. After 3 liters of its contents are poured out, the container is $\frac{3}{4}$ full. How many liters would need to be poured in to fill the container to capacity?

Question 13

The selling price of a house was decreased by 12 percent to $220,000. What was the original selling price of the house?

○ $193,600
○ $196,429
○ $221,200
○ $246,400
○ $250,000

DRILL 4

Question 1

In 2009, the price of an Econolux car increased by 10 percent from the 2008 price. In 2010, the price decreased by 5 percent and the car now costs between $18,000 and $19,800. Which of the following could be the 2008 price of an Econolux car?

Indicate all such values.

- ☐ $17,030
- ☐ $17,230
- ☐ $18,180
- ☐ $18,935
- ☐ $18,955
- ☐ $20,790

Question 2

$$\frac{(0.05)(0.5)}{(5)(0.005)} =$$

Question 3

Which of the following are greater than 1?

Indicate all such values.

- ☐ $\dfrac{4(3+0.07)}{11.092}$

- ☐ $\dfrac{\sqrt{82}-1.7^2}{\sqrt{34}}$

- ☐ $\dfrac{9978.4-0.0083}{101^2}$

- ☐ $\dfrac{\sqrt{143}\times\sqrt[3]{7}}{24.034}$

Question 4

If during a one-day period the Q train arrives at the station 30% less frequently than the B train, and the B train arrives 10% less frequently than the F train, then the Q train's frequency is what percent of the F train's frequency?

- ○ 27
- ○ 40
- ○ 60
- ○ 63
- ○ 90

Question 5

67.345×10^{15} is equivalent to which of the following?

Indicate all such values.

- ☐ 6.7345×1000^{13}
- ☐ 673.45×10^{16}
- ☐ 6.7345×10^{16}
- ☐ 67.345×100^{14}
- ☐ 0.0067345×10^{18}

Question 6

The sum $\dfrac{3}{10} + \dfrac{43}{100} + \dfrac{17}{1,000}$ is equivalent to which of the following sums?

- ○ $\dfrac{700}{1,000} + \dfrac{4}{10} + \dfrac{7}{100}$

- ○ $\dfrac{6}{10} + \dfrac{12}{100} + \dfrac{37}{1,000}$

- ○ $\dfrac{7}{100} + \dfrac{4}{10} + \dfrac{7}{1,000}$

- ○ $\dfrac{7}{100} + \dfrac{4}{1,000} + \dfrac{7}{10}$

- ○ $\dfrac{32}{100} + \dfrac{4}{10} + \dfrac{27}{1,000}$

Question 7

An investment club has had an average rate of return of 15% per year for the past 6 years. If Teresa invests $1,000 today and neither adds nor subtracts money from the club, how much will Teresa have invested after 5 years assuming that the rate of return does not change?

- ○ $1,000 + 1.15^5$
- ○ $1,000(1.15)^5$
- ○ $1,000 + 0.15$
- ○ $1,000(0.15)^5$
- ○ $1,000(5)^{0.15}$

Question 8

If $\dfrac{\left(x^{\frac{3}{2}}\right)^2}{x^6} = 8^{-1}$, then what is the value of x ?

$\boxed{}$

Question 9

Ben's music album sold $\dfrac{5}{6}$ the number of copies as Regina's album. If Regina's album sold at least 1,500 copies more than Ben's album, how many copies of Ben's album could have been sold?

Indicate all such values.

- ☐ 12,000
- ☐ 11,244
- ☐ 9,000
- ☐ 6,500
- ☐ 6,436
- ☐ 4,225

Question 10

Carmen wants to open a special savings account through her work. If Carmen invests $7,000 at 6 percent simple annual interest at the beginning of January, and no other money is added to or removed from the account, which of the following is true?

Indicate <u>all</u> such statements.

☐ At the end of April, Carmen will have earned $105 in interest.

☐ At the end of the year, Carmen will have earned $420 in interest.

☐ At the end of six months, Carmen will have earned $35 in interest.

☐ At the end of three months, Carmen will have $7,105 in the account.

Question 11

If each of three grocery stores receives $\frac{1}{4}$ of a farmer's potato crop, a farmer's market receives $\frac{1}{3}$ of the remaining, and a local fast food restaurant receives the remaining 200 pounds, how many pounds of potatoes were in the farmer's crop?

○   300
○   400
○   900
○   1,200
○   1,400

Question 12

The price of Mabel's car, without sales tax, is 12 percent more than the price of Rose's car, also without sales tax. Without sales taxes included, the combined price of both cars is $53,000. If sales tax is 5.20 percent, what is the cost of Mabel's car with sales tax included?

[   ]

Question 13

Evangeline must spend $\frac{3}{8}$ of her weekly salary on rent and $\frac{1}{6}$ of her remaining salary on food. Which of the following could be percentages of her weekly salary that Evangeline devotes to entertainment, while still enabling her to place $\frac{4}{9}$ of her salary into a savings account?

Indicate <u>all</u> such percentages.

☐   0.5%
☐   5.0%
☐   7.5%
☐   10.0%
☐   15.0%
☐   25.0%
☐   50.0%

ANSWERS

Drill 1

1. E
2. C
3. B
4. B
5. D
6. E
7. B
8. A
9. B
10. C
11. B
12. B
13. C
14. E

Drill 2

1. A
2. C
3. C
4. B
5. D
6. E
7. E
8. B
9. E
10. C
11. D
12. D
13. D
14. D

Drill 3

1. B
2. B
3. $\dfrac{7}{18}$
4. C
5. B
6. $-\dfrac{80}{81}$
7. A, B, E, G
8. D
9. 5
10. E
11. E
12. 15
13. E

Drill 4

1. B, C, D
2. 1
3. A, B
4. D
5. C
6. E
7. B
8. 2
9. A, C
10. B, D
11. D
12. 29,456
13. A, B, C

EXPLANATIONS
Drill 1

1. **E** When dividing by a fraction, flip the fraction and multiply: $3 \div \frac{6}{7} = 3 \times \frac{7}{6} = \frac{21}{6} = 3\frac{1}{2}$. Alternatively, you may estimate and realize that 3 divided by something slightly smaller than 1 must be slightly larger than 3.

2. **C** Use the Bowtie when adding or subtracting fractions: $\dfrac{\frac{1}{5}-\frac{1}{2}}{\frac{1}{5}+\frac{1}{2}} = \dfrac{\frac{2-5}{10}}{\frac{2+5}{10}} = \dfrac{-\frac{3}{10}}{\frac{7}{10}}$. Next, divide the fractions by flipping the numerator and denominator and multiplying: $\dfrac{-\frac{3}{10}}{\frac{7}{10}} = (-\frac{3}{10}) \times (\frac{10}{7}) = -\frac{3}{7}$.

3. **B** In Quantity A, $\frac{15}{16} + \frac{1}{256} = \frac{241}{256}$, and in Quantity B, $1 - \frac{1}{64} = \frac{63}{64}$. If you multiply the numerator and denominator of $\frac{63}{64}$ by 4, you obtain a common denominator: $\frac{63}{64} = \frac{252}{256}$. Clearly $\frac{252}{256} > \frac{241}{256}$, so Quantity B is greater.

4. **B** 5% of \$800 is \$40, thus, the maximum amount of money that could be in the account at the end of one year is \$840; eliminate (C), (D), and (E). Similarly, the minimum amount that could be in the account at the end of one year is \$800 plus 2% of \$800, or \$816; eliminate (A).

5. **D** Be careful! You're not given the original price of either the shoes or the boots, and because you can't assume they're the same price, try Plugging In a variety of values. If both quantities originally cost 10 dollars, then the change in price of the shoes in Quantity A is 5 dollars, and the change in price of the boots in Quantity B is 3 dollars; Quantity A is greater, so eliminate (B) and (C). If the boots in Quantity B originally cost 20 dollars, though, then the change in price is 6 dollars. Quantity B is now greater, so eliminate (A), and you're left with (D), the correct answer.

6. **E** With his employee discount, Joey purchases an item for 90% of its regular price, so 90% of the regular price of this item is equivalent to \$99 or $\frac{90}{100}x = 99$. Solve for x to find that the regular price is \$110.

7. **B** The percent change formula is $\frac{difference}{original} \times 100$. Remember that the "original" is the amount before the change. So, in Quantity A, the difference is $200 - 150 = 50$, and the original is 200, which

yields a 25% change. In Quantity B, the difference is also 50, but the number changes from 150 to 200, so the "original" is 150, which yields roughly a 33.3% change. Thus, Quantity B is greater.

8.   **A**   Begin by Plugging In 7 for y, so 20 percent of x is 35. You could go on to solve for x, but a shortcut would be to say that 60 percent of x is three times 20 percent of x, so multiply 35 by 3 to get 105.

9.   **B**   You have far too many fractions to add quickly with the Bowtie. Instead, convert all of the fractions to the common denominator of 48: $\frac{1}{48}+\frac{1}{48}+\frac{1}{12}+\frac{1}{8}+\frac{1}{4}+\frac{1}{2}=\frac{1+1+4+6+12+24}{48}=\frac{48}{48}=1$.

10.   **C**   If The Warm Muffin Bakery sells 10,000 muffins, it sells 6,000 cookies. If the Warm Muffin Bakery then sold 20,000 muffins, it would sell 12,000 cookies. The cookie sales would thus increase by 6,000.

11.   **B**   Convert the fractions to decimals. So $\frac{7}{8}=0.875$, making Quantity A 0.625. In Quantity B, $\frac{1}{3}$ is about 0.333, making Quantity B about 0.658. Quantity B is greater.

12.   **B**   Convert the fractions to decimals to see which inequality is correct. You can divide them out (remember, numerator divided by denominator), but it might help to have some common fraction/decimal equivalents memorized. Starting with (A), $\frac{1}{11}\approx 0.09$, so this inequality is not true. Convert the fractions in (B): 0.1 < 0.11 < 0.125; this inequality is true.

13.   **C**   Translate the question into a percent formula. So, "245 widgets per week is 35 percent of Company B's weekly widget output" means $245 = \frac{35}{100} \times B$. Try Plugging In Quantity A into this formula. Does $\frac{35}{100} \times 700 = 245$? Yes, so the quantities must be equal.

14.   **E**   Plug In for the variables. Let $m = 3$ and $n = 5$, and $\frac{2+3}{3\times 5}=\frac{5}{15}=\frac{1}{3}$. Only (E) works. Alternatively, you could manipulate the fractions: $\frac{2+m}{mn}=\frac{2}{mn}+\frac{m}{mn}=\frac{2}{mn}+\frac{1}{n}$.

Drill 2

1.   **A**   The question asks for a percent <u>increase</u> from the original price; be careful not to find 20% of $18,000, and reduce the higher total ($18,000) by that amount. Instead, you'll need to find the amount that yields the higher total, when increased by 20%, though, it's much easier to just increase the price in Quantity B and compare it to the total in the problem: 10% of $14,400 is $1,440, so 20% must be $2,880; adding this to the base price of $14,400 yields a total of $17,280. That's smaller than what you were looking for, so Quantity A is greater.

2. **C** Convert 0.0025 to a percent by sliding the decimal point two places to the right: 0.25%. Then convert 0.25 to a fraction to get $\frac{1}{4}$%.

3. **C** There are two ways to go about this problem. One is to use the Bowtie method to compare fractions. $\frac{2}{3}$ versus $\frac{5}{8}$ yields a 16 versus 15. Pretty close. $\frac{3}{4}$ versus $\frac{5}{8}$ yields 24 versus 20. Not as close, so eliminate it $\frac{7}{11}$ versus $\frac{5}{8}$ yields 56 versus 55, that's really close on a percentage basis because the numbers are bigger. Eliminate (A). $\frac{19}{25}$ versus $\frac{5}{8}$ yields 152 versus 115. Get rid of it. Choice (E) yields 18 versus 50. Get rid of it. Alternatively, you could also use long division, but if you do, there is no need to finish out the math for each answer. 5 divided by 8 = 0.625. $\frac{2}{3}$ = 0.66. Keep it. When you start to divide 3 by 4, the first number you see is a 7. Don't continue to divide, just eliminate it because 0.7 is farther from 0.625 than 0.66. Choice (C) yields 0.63, so keep it and eliminate (A). The answer for 19 divided by 23 begins with 0.8, so get rid of it. The answer to 23 divided by 30 begins with 0.7 so get rid of that too.

4. **B** Twenty cigars bought individually would cost $40, so apply the percent change formula—$\frac{difference}{original} \times 100$—to determine Quantity A. In this case, the difference is $10, and the original, because it's a percent decrease, is $40: $\frac{10}{40} \times 100 = 25$, so Quantity A is 25%. Quantity B is greater.

5. **D** Try Plugging In a possible value for $\frac{1}{k}$. If $\frac{1}{k} = \frac{3}{4}$, then $k = \frac{4}{3}$, which is closest to coordinate D.

6. **E** This question is really asking about place value. Start with the greatest place: the thousands. So, $6 \times 1,000$ means a 6 in the thousands place. Eliminate (A), (B), and (C). Next, 4×100 means the next digit should be 4. Eliminate (D), and select (E).

7. **E** To calculate this expression, break it into pieces: $\frac{3}{\left(\frac{3}{4}\right)} - \frac{\left(\frac{3}{2}\right)}{3} = 3 \div \frac{3}{4} - \frac{3}{2} \div 3 = 3 \times \frac{4}{3} - \frac{3}{2} \times \frac{1}{3} = 4 - \frac{1}{2} = \frac{7}{2}$.

8. **B** Solve each equation by translating into algebra. The first is $a = \frac{40}{100} \times 45$. Reduce and multiply to find $a = 18$. The second is $18 = \frac{b}{100} \times 90$. Multiply both sides by 100 and then divide by 90 to find $b = 20$. Quantity B is greater.

9. **E** Plug In a value for x: if $x = 20$, then the expression $\dfrac{\frac{20}{5}+\frac{20}{5}+\frac{20}{5}+\frac{20}{5}}{4}$ becomes

$\dfrac{4+4+4+4}{4}=\dfrac{16}{4}=4$. Now Plug in 20 for x in the answer choices; only (E) hits your target

answer of 4. Alternatively, you could factor the expression: $\dfrac{\frac{x}{5}+\frac{x}{5}+\frac{x}{5}+\frac{x}{5}}{4}=\dfrac{4\times\left(\frac{x}{5}\right)}{4}=\dfrac{x}{5}$.

10. **C** The first thing you need to do is to clean up these expressions. You have 15, 50, and 4 in the

denominators of three fractions, along with one decimal, so it is very difficult to compare values.

$\dfrac{6n}{15}$ can be reduced to $\dfrac{2n}{5}$, and $0.3n$ is the same as $\dfrac{3n}{10}$. Change your first expression from $\dfrac{2n}{5}$

to $\dfrac{4n}{10}$. The expression $\dfrac{19n}{50}$ is pretty close to $\dfrac{20n}{50}$ or $\dfrac{2n}{5}$, the first expression, but a bit smaller.

Because $\dfrac{n}{4}$ is clearly the smallest expression and you need concern yourself only with the smallest,

the second smallest, and the biggest, you can ignore $\dfrac{19n}{50}$. Convert $\dfrac{n}{4}$ to $\dfrac{5n}{20}$, and convert your

other expressions to 20ths as well. You now have $\dfrac{8n}{20},\dfrac{6n}{20}$, and $\dfrac{5n}{20}$. The difference between the

smallest and largest is $\dfrac{3n}{20}$. Three times the difference between the two smallest is also 3. The

answer is (C).

11. **D** Plug In some real numbers to compare quantities. For example, Plug In 10 for the number of
games in the season. For the first 5 games of the season, try an average of 10 points for David (for a
total of 50 points), which makes an average of 12 points for Antonio (for a total of 60 points). Next,
try a total of 0 points for each player for the second half of the season; now Antonio's average for
the season is 6 points, and David's is 5. Because 90% of 6 is 5.4, Quantity A is greater, so eliminate
(B) and (C). Finally, try a total of 100 points for each player for the second half of the season; now
Antonio has scored a total of 160 points in 10 games, for an average of 16 points, and David has
scored a total of 150 points in 10 games, for an average of 15 points. Because 90% of 16 is 14.4,
Quantity B is now greater, so eliminate (A), and you're left with (D).

12. **D** The percent change formula is $\dfrac{difference}{original}\times100$, so plugging the numbers from the problem into

the formula yields $\dfrac{0.25}{1.25}\times100 = \dfrac{25}{125}\times100 = \dfrac{1}{5}\times100 = 20$. If you selected (E), you may have

used the wrong value as the original. Remember, in a percent <u>increase</u>, the original number is the

<u>smaller</u> value.

13. **D** Solve this problem in chunks. To find the numerical value for 0.004 percent, divide by 100: $0.004 \div 100 = 0.00004$. The reciprocal of that is $\dfrac{1}{0.00004} = 25{,}000$. So $\dfrac{1}{5}$ of the result is $\dfrac{1}{5} \times 25{,}000 = 5{,}000$.

14. **D** Plug In values for m. When $m = 1$, Quantity B is larger. When $m = 12$, Quantity A is larger.

Drill 3

1. **B** To find exact values for p and q, apply percent translation: $\dfrac{27}{100} \times p = 100$, so $\dfrac{27p}{100} = 100$, $27p = 10{,}000$, and $p = 370.37$; p is q percent of 100, so $q = 370.37$ as well. Quantity B is greater.

   Alternatively, you could avoid the calculation altogether and Ballpark this one all the way through: 100 is more than 25% (or $\dfrac{1}{4}$) of p, so p must be less than 400—and so must q.

2. **B** This is a good problem for Plugging In. If $y = 2$, then the expression becomes equal to $-\dfrac{4}{3}$. Choice (B) is the only choice that gives you $-\dfrac{4}{3}$ when you replace y with 2.

3. $\dfrac{7}{18}$ The total mixture contains three cups, so the second bowl must contain two cups. This 2-cup bowl of nuts divided into even thirds consists of $\dfrac{2}{3}$ cups peanuts, $\dfrac{2}{3}$ cups cashews, and $\dfrac{2}{3}$ cups almonds. Combining this with the 1-cup mixture of $\dfrac{1}{2}$ cup peanuts and $\dfrac{1}{2}$ cup cashews results in $\dfrac{7}{6}$ cups peanuts in a 3-cup mixture. So, $\dfrac{\frac{7}{6}}{3} = \dfrac{7}{18}$ of the new nut mixture is peanuts.

4. **C** To find 16 percent of 83, multiply 83 by 0.16. To find 83 percent of 16, multiply 16 by 0.83. Both expressions yield 13.28, so (C) is correct.

5. **B** Set up a proportion so that the original ratio equals the final ratio: $\dfrac{1{,}024}{768} = \dfrac{800}{x}$. Cross multiply and then divide both sides by 1,024 to find $x = 600$.

6. $-\dfrac{80}{81}$ One easy way to solve this problem is to multiply both sides of the equation by 9, which gives you $(w + 1) = \dfrac{9}{729}$, or $(w + 1) = \dfrac{1}{81}$. Now subtract 1 from both sides to get $-\dfrac{80}{81}$.

7. **A, B, E, G**

   Anything that's a multiple of 30 will work here because of the two denominators of the two fractions in the question. Choices (C), (D), and (F) are all multiples of 30, but the remaining answers are not. You can also treat this as a PITA problem and try each answer. Take $\dfrac{5}{6}$ of each of the answer choices, and then take $\dfrac{3}{5}$ of what's left. Do you wind up with an integer? If so, eliminate it and keep working until you've tried every answer.

8. **D** Sure, you could use algebra here, but most likely you won't wind up with an answer that looks exactly like (D). Instead, try plugging in a value for x. Make x something easy such as 1,000, which makes $y = 500$. Plug $x = 1,000$ into each answer choice, and it turns out that only (D) gives you the correct value of 500.

9. **5** First, translate the English into math. Thirty-five hundredths is 0.35 and four thousandths is 0.004. Now, perform the calculation on your on-screen calculator to get 87.5; the first digit after the decimal point is the tenths digit, so the answer is 5.

10. **E** To solve this question, Plug In the answers as the number of seniors to determine whether the total number of students, seniors (S) + juniors (J) + freshmen (F), adds up to at least 150. Start with (C). If $S = 24$, then $24 = \dfrac{60}{100} J$ and $J = 40$; since $40 = 50\%$ of F, then $F = 80$; since the sum of the students is $24 + 40 + 80 = 144$, which is less than 150, try larger numbers and eliminate (A), (B), and (C). For (D), if $S = 25$, then $25 = \dfrac{60}{100} J$; thus, there are 41.67 juniors, which is incorrect since it is impossible to have a fraction of a student. For (E), if $S = 27$, then $27 = \dfrac{60}{100} J$; thus, $J = 45$; since $45 = 50\%$ of F, then $F = 90$; since $27 + 45 + 90 = 162$, which is at least 150, (E) is the only correct answer.

11. **E** Since the problem doesn't give you prices, Plug In; since the question involves percents, use 100. If the starting price for Melange was $100, then, after the 20% decrease, the price was $80; increase that by 50%, and the ending price was $120. Since the ending prices for Melange and Blue were the same, the ending price for Blue was also $120. Now, work backward to find the starting price for Blue. Declining by 50% is the same as being cut in half; if Blue was $120 after being cut in half, it must have been $240 before the decrease. Since that $240 was the result of a 20% increase, translate the question "240 is 120% of what?" to get the equation $240 = \dfrac{120}{100} \times x$; solve for x to get the starting price for Blue, $200. Finally, now that you have both starting prices, translate the question into $200 = \dfrac{x}{100} \times 100$, and solve for x to get your answer, 200.

12. **15** You know that the difference between $\dfrac{4}{5}$ and $\dfrac{3}{4}$ of the container is 3 liters, so set up the following equation to solve for the volume of the container:

$$\left(\frac{4}{5} - \frac{3}{4}\right)x = 3$$

$$\left(\frac{16}{20} - \frac{15}{20}\right)x = 3$$

$$\left(\frac{1}{20}\right)x = 3$$

$$x = 60$$

Since the container is still $\dfrac{3}{4}$ full, it has 45 liters in it. Therefore, you'll need to pour 15 liters in to fill it to capacity.

13.　E　Plug In The Answers. Subtract 12 percent from each answer choice to find the one that gives you 220,000. Start with (C):

$193,600

$196,429

$221,200 − .12(221,200) = 194,656

$246,400 − .12(246,400) = 216,832

$250,000 − .12(250,000) = 220,000

Drill 4

1.　B, C, D

It's useful to use PITA in this problem. Note that increasing something by 10 percent is the same as multiplying by 1.10, and decreasing something by 5 percent is the same as multiplying by 0.95. Definitely use your on-screen calculator on a problem like this. Because you are dealing with a range, it will save you time to work from the top down until you reach a correct answer; then work your way from the bottom up until you reach a correct answer. Each answer in between the smallest correct answer and the largest correct answer must also be correct.

2008	2009	2010	Between 18,000 and 19,800?
	×1.1	×.95	
$17,030	18,733	17,796	too small
$17,230	18,953	18,005	yes
$18,180			must also be correct
$18,935	20,828	19,787	yes
$18,955	20,851	19,808	too big
$20,790	22,869	21,726	too big

2.　1　Sometimes dealing with fractions is easier than dealing with decimals, and sometimes vice versa. Here are both methods. When multiplying decimals, first multiply the two numbers while ignoring the decimal points. Then, count the number of total digits or decimal places there were to the right of the decimal point, before you make the calculation. Finally, move the decimal point that many places to the left once you've done the multiplication. So first multiply while ignoring the decimal points. 5 × 5 = 25. Now, count the digits to the right of the decimal point in your original numbers. 0.05 has 2 digits to the right of the decimal point and 0.5 has 1 digit to the right of the decimal point. So that's 3 total places. Finally, take your calculation of 25 and move the decimal point 3 places to the left to get 0.025. Therefore, the numerator of the fraction is (0.05)(0.5) = 0.025. Computing similarly, the denominator of the fraction is (5)(0.005) = 0.025.

They equal the same thing, so the answer is 1.

When dealing with fractions, just remember that for each decimal place, you add another zero in the denominator of the fraction. So $0.05 = \dfrac{5}{100}$, because you put two zeroes on the bottom, one for each of the two digits to the right of the decimal point. Or, you could convert the decimals to fractions and then multiply:

$$\left(\frac{5}{100}\right)\left(\frac{5}{10}\right)=\frac{25}{1,000}$$

$$(5)\left(\frac{5}{1,000}\right)=\frac{25}{1,000}$$

Again, you get the same fractions in the numerator and in the denominator, so the answer is 1.

3. **A, B** You could use your on-screen calculator, but it would probably be faster to Ballpark on at least some of these—for example, think of $\sqrt{82}$ as slightly more than 9, or $\sqrt{34}$ as slightly less than 6. In order to figure out which fractions are greater than one, just figure out whether the numerator of the fraction is greater than the denominator:

$\dfrac{4(3+.07)}{11.092}$: numerator greater than 12, denominator less than 12, so (A) is greater than 1;

$\dfrac{\sqrt{82}-1.7^2}{\sqrt{34}}$: numerator greater than 6, denominator less than 6, because the square root of 36 is 6, the square root of something less than 36 must be less than 6, so (B) is greater than 1;

$\dfrac{9978.4-.0083}{101^2}$: numerator less than 10,000, denominator greater than 10,000, because 100 squared equals 10,000, so 101 squared must be greater than 10,000, so eliminate (C) as it's less than 1;

$\dfrac{\sqrt{143}\times\sqrt[3]{7}}{24.034}$: numerator is less than 24 because the square root of 143 is less than the square root

of 144 (12) and the cube root of 7 is less than the cube root of 8 (2), so the product must be less

than 12 × 2 (24); denominator is greater than 24 so eliminate (D), as it's less than 1.

4. **D** To solve this question Plug In. Since the question deals with percents, try 100. If the F train arrives 100 times per day, then the B will arrive 10% fewer times than 100: $B=(1-\frac{10}{100})F=(\frac{90}{100})100=90$ times, and the Q will arrive 30% fewer times than 90: $Q=(1-\frac{30}{100})B=(\frac{70}{100})90=63$ times.

Translating the question "the Q train's frequency is what percentage of the F train's" gives

$Q=(\frac{x}{100})F$ and thus $63=(\frac{x}{100})100$, which means that the Q's frequency is 63% of the F's. The

correct answer is (D).

5. **C** Start by converting the original number to conventional scientific notation. Typically, scientific notation is expressed with only one digit to the left of the decimal point in the first number, and then that number is multiplied by a power of 10. So you'll want to convert all the numbers into that format to best compare the answer choices.

Your original number: 67.345×10^{15}. Now convert to conventional scientific notation. Since you want to move the decimal point one space to the left, you'll increase the exponent by one. $67.345 \times 10^{15} = 6.7345 \times 10^{16}$.

Choice (A): The decimal point in the number is already in the right place, so just convert the number with the exponent. $1{,}000 = 10^3$ so replace 1,000 with 10^3 and you'll have $(10^3)^{13}$, which gives you $10^{(3 \times 13)}$ or 10^{39}. This number, 6.7345×10^{39}, is not equivalent to the original.

Choice (B): Since you want to move the decimal point two spaces to the left, increase the exponent by two. This number, 6.7345×10^{18}, is not equivalent to the original.

Choice (C): This is exactly what the original is, so this is equivalent to the original.

Choice (D): First, change 100^{14} to a power of 10 by replacing 100 with 10^2, giving you $(10^2)^{14}$ or $10^{(2 \times 14)}$ or 10^{28}. Next, move the decimal point one space to the left, so increase the exponent by one. $67.345 \times 10^{28} = 6.7345 \times 10^{29}$. This number is not equivalent to the original.

Choice (E): Move the decimal point three spaces to the right, so decrease the exponent by three. This number, 6.7345×10^{15}, is not equivalent to the original.

6. **E** To solve this question, convert the fractions into decimals and carefully add them. $\frac{3}{10} + \frac{43}{100} + \frac{17}{1000} = 0.3 + 0.43 + 0.017 = 0.747$; this is your target answer. Choice (A) equals $0.7 + 0.4 + 0.07 = 1.17$. Choice (B) equals $0.6 + 0.12 + 0.037 = 0.757$. Choice (C) equals $0.07 + 0.4 + 0.007 = 0.477$. Choice (D) equals $0.07 + 0.004 + 0.7 = 0.774$. Choice (E) equals $0.32 + 0.4 + 0.027 = 0.747$. The correct answer is (E).

7. **B** To solve this question, remember that the formula for finding the result of periodic increases at a certain rate is (Original Amount)$(1 + rate)^{\text{number of periods}}$. In this case, the final amount would be $1{,}000(1.15)^5$. The correct answer is (B). If you forgot the formula, you could calculate the final amount after 5 years, and then calculate all the answers for a match.

8. **2** To solve this question, remember the rules of exponents. When an exponent is outside a parentheses, it gets multiplied by any exponents inside the parentheses; thus $\left(x^{\frac{3}{2}}\right)^2 = x^3$. Next, since when two numbers of the same base are divided, the exponents are subtracted, x^3 divided by $x^6 = x^{3-6} = x^{-3}$. Finally, since a value raised to a negative exponent is equal to its reciprocal, but with

the exponent changed to positive, then $x^{-3} = \dfrac{1}{x^3} = 8^{-1} = \dfrac{1}{8}$ and thus $x^3 = 8$. Thus, $x = 2$, the correct answer.

9. **A, C**   To solve this question, Plug In the Answers. In (D), if Ben, B, sold 6,500 copies and $B = \dfrac{5}{6}R$, then $6,500 = \dfrac{5}{6}R$, so Regina, R, sold 7,800 copies, thus giving a difference of $7,800 - 6,500 = 1,300$. Since this is too small, eliminate (D), (E), and (F) and try larger numbers. In (C), if $B = 9,000$, then $9,000 = \dfrac{5}{6}R$, so $R = 10,800$, thus giving $10,800 - 9,000 = 1,800$; since this is bigger than 1,500, keep (C). In (B), if $B = 11,244$, then $11,244 = \dfrac{5}{6}R$, so $R = 13,492.8$ copies; eliminate (B), as it is impossible to sell a fraction of an album. In (A), if $B = 12,000$, then $12,000 = \dfrac{5}{6}R$, so $R = 14,400$ and $14,400 - 12,000 = 2,400$. Since this is bigger than 1,500, keep (A). The correct answers are (A) and (C).

10. **B, D**   To calculate the interest earned, multiply the original amount by the annual interest rate: in one year, Carmen will earn $\$7,000 \times 0.06 = \$420$ in interest, so (B) works. To calculate her interest for any part of the year, divide $\$420$ by the appropriate fraction of a year. At the end of April, $\dfrac{1}{3}$ of the year has passed, so Carmen will have earned $\dfrac{1}{3} \times \$420 = \$140$; eliminate (A). At the end of six months, Carmen will have earned $\dfrac{1}{2} \times \$420 = \$210$; eliminate (C). At the end of three months, $\dfrac{1}{4}$ of the year has passed, so Carmen has earned $\dfrac{1}{4} \times \$420 = \$105$; there will be a total of $\$7,000 + \$105 = \$7,105$ in the account, so (D) works.

11. **D**   Since you know there are 200 lbs remaining after the grocery stores and farmer's market get their shares, you cannot plug in your own number. So plug in the answers, and start with the middle (C):

Total	$-\dfrac{3}{4}$ to grocery stores	$\dfrac{1}{3}$ of remaining	remaining = 200?
300			
400			
900	225	75	150 too small
1,200	300	100	**200**
1,400			

12. **29,456**

First, set up two equations with two variables. Let m = the pre-tax cost of Mabel's car, and let r = the pre-tax cost of Rose's car. Equation one: Mabel's car cost 12% more than Rose's car: $m = (1.12)r$. Equation two: The combined price of their cars is $53,000: $m + r = 53,000$. Next, solve for the pre-tax price of each car by substituting $(1.12)r$ from equation one for m in equation two such that $(1.12)r + r = 53,000$. Now solve for r: $2.12r = 53,000$. Therefore, $r = 25,000$. Now substitute that back into equation two to calculate that $m = 28,000$. Lastly, since you're looking for the price of Mabel's car after sales tax, multiply 28,000 by 1.052 to find that $28,000 \times 1.052 = 29,456$.

13. **A, B, C**

The problem has percents in the answers and no real values in the question, so it's a Hidden Plug In; the hidden variable in this case is Evangeline's weekly salary. To find an easy number, try multiplying the denominators in the problem: $8 \times 6 \times 9 = 432$, so Evangeline makes $432 per week. Now work the problem in bite-sized pieces. She spends $\frac{3}{8}$ of $432, or $162, on rent, leaving her with $432 - $162 = $270. Of that, she spends $\frac{1}{6}$, or $45, on food, leaving her with $270 - $45 = $225. If she wants to put $\frac{4}{9}$ of her weekly salary, or $192, into a savings account, then she can spend only $225 - $192 = $33 on entertainment. Finally, use your on-screen calculator to determine that 33 is just over 7.6% of 432, so (A), (B), and (C) will all work.

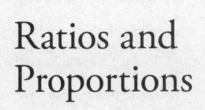

Ratios and Proportions

RATIOS AND PROPORTIONS

Much like averages, rates, and Quant Comp Plug Ins, ratios are all about organizing your information. That means recognizing when and how to effectively use your scratch paper.

Use a Ratio Box

A ratio is simply a fraction. Rather than expressing a part-to-whole relationship, it expresses the relationship between two parts. The two parts combined make up the whole. If you have a bag with 5 red marbles and 4 blue marbles, your ratio of red to blue is 5 : 4. Ratios can be expressed as fractions, so you can also express the relationship as $\frac{5}{4}$. Either way your total number of marbles is 9, because 5 plus 4 is 9.

You can keep the same ratio of red to blue marbles as long as you increase your total to a multiple of 9. If you had 27 marbles total, you would have 15 red and 12 blue, but your ratio would still be 5 : 4. To keep it straight, use a ratio box.

> The minute you see the word RATIO, draw a ratio box on your scratch paper.

Here's what the ratio box looks like.

Red Marbles	Blue Marbles	Total	
5	4	9	←———Ratio Total
×3	×3	×3	←———Multiplier
15	12	27	←———Actual Total

In this case you know that the ratio of red to blue marbles is 5 : 4, but the actual numbers of red and blue marbles are 15 and 12. $\frac{4}{9}$ of the marbles are blue, and approximately 55 percent ($\frac{5}{9}$) of the marbles are red. Unless a question asks for fractions of marbles, the actual total of marbles must be a multiple of nine.

As usual, ETS will give you just enough information to fill out the chart. The question may give you the actual number of marbles, the ratio of red to blue, and then ask you for the actual number of blue marbles. Alternatively, the question may ask you what the new ratio will be if the number of blue or red marbles is increased. A really tricky question may state that some blue ones have been added, give you the new ratio, and then ask you for the actual total of red ones. No matter what is asked, a ratio is still a ratio; the ratio box will organize the information you're given and help you get the information you need.

Ratio and Rates

Sometimes you will be given a simple ratio in the form of a rate. The question may tell you the number of widgets a factory can produce in an hour, the price of one gallon of gasoline, and the speed with which a silo fills with grain. You will then have to scale this rate up or down, depending on what is asked. Alternatively, you may have to find the number of widgets the factory will produce in 10 hours, the price of a 30 gallon tank of gasoline, or the percentage of the silo that will be filled in 2 hours. To solve these rate problems, set them up as proportions on your scratch paper, check your units, and label everything.

Example:

A digital scanner can scan five lines every second. If each line is one eightieth of an inch, how many minutes will it take to scan a 4½ inch photo?

$$\text{Lines} \atop \text{Inches} \quad \frac{80}{1} : \frac{x}{4.5} \quad x = 360 \text{ lines total}$$

$$\text{Lines} \atop \text{Seconds} \quad \frac{360}{x} : \frac{5}{1} \quad x = 72 \text{ seconds}$$

$$\text{Seconds} \atop \text{Minutes} \quad \frac{60}{1} : \frac{72}{x} \quad x = 1.2 \text{ minutes}$$

For more practice and a more in-depth look at The Princeton Review math techniques, check out our student-friendly guidebook, *Cracking the GRE*.

DRILL 1

Question 1

A certain recipe calls for 2 cups of sugar and $3\frac{1}{2}$ cups of flour. What is the ratio of sugar to flour in this recipe?

○ $\dfrac{3}{10}$

○ $\dfrac{2}{5}$

○ $\dfrac{4}{7}$

○ $\dfrac{4}{5}$

○ $\dfrac{6}{7}$

Question 2

CHARITABLE ANNUAL DONATIONS TO CHARITY GROUP X

Employees of Company:	Years 1990–2000		Years 1990–2010	
	Average (mean) annual donation per employee	Greatest single annual donation by an employee	Average (mean) annual donation per employee	Greatest single annual donation by an employee
A	24.3	1,000	34.6	1,000
B	18.2	500	40.2	500
C	45.5	300	45.5	2,000
D	34.6	2,000	34.6	2,000
E	34.7	1,000	32.4	1,000
F	150.3	2,000	100.8	2,000
G	23.7	500	23.7	500
H	34.7	500	34.7	1,000
I	74.5	5,000	80.2	5,000
J	85.6	3,000	85.6	3,000
K	126.7	5,000	104.4	5,000
L	234.4	3,000	234.4	3,000
M	422.4	400	455.2	2,000

What is the approximate ratio of Company F's average annual donation to charity group X for the period 1990–2000 to that for the period 1990–2010 ?

○   3 : 40
○   3 : 5
○   1 : 1
○   3 : 2
○   5 : 2

Question 3

If a certain vitamin pill has 400 milligrams of magnesium, then how many <u>grams</u> of magnesium are in a bottle of 500 vitamin pills? (1 gram = 1,000 milligrams)

- ○   20
- ○   200
- ○   2,000
- ○   20,000
- ○ 200,000

Question 4

If $a = \dfrac{1}{6}$ and $\dfrac{6}{7} = \dfrac{5}{b}$, what is the value of $a + b$?

- ○ $\dfrac{71}{210}$

- ○ 3

- ○ $\dfrac{187}{42}$

- ○ 6

- ○ $\dfrac{47}{6}$

Question 5

James can swim 750 yards in 10 minutes. If he swims at the same constant rate, how many minutes will it take him to swim 4.2 times this distance?

Question 6

b is a multiple of positive integer a.

Quantity A	Quantity B
The ratio of a to b	$\dfrac{1}{2}$

- ○ Quantity A is greater.
- ○ Quantity B is greater.
- ○ The two quantities are equal.
- ○ The relationship cannot be determined from the information given.

Question 7

Keri, Neill, and Rich use toilet paper in their apartment in a ratio of 3 : 2 : 2. Rich buys two cases of toilet paper online for everyone's use at 28 rolls per case, at an average (arithmetic mean) cost of $3.50/roll and with an additional $14 delivery charge. If they each contribute to the cost of the toilet paper in direct proportion to the amount they use, how much must Keri contribute?

Question 8

$$36a = 25b$$
$$ab \neq 0$$

Quantity A	Quantity B
$\dfrac{5}{6}$	$\dfrac{a}{b}$

- ○ Quantity A is greater.
- ○ Quantity B is greater.
- ○ The two quantities are equal.
- ○ The relationship cannot be determined from the information given.

Question 9

By volume, cranberry juice makes up 12.5 percent of Bee's punch and 25 percent of Flo's punch. If 3 liters of Bee's punch are mixed with 6 liters of Flo's punch, approximately what percent of the mixture, by volume, is cranberry juice?

- ○　6.25%
- ○　18.75%
- ○　20.83%
- ○　33.33%
- ○　50.00%

Question 10

At the beginning of the day, the ratio of cats to dogs at a boarding kennel was 10 to 11. Throughout the day, 4 dogs and 5 cats were admitted to the boarding kennel and no animals were released.

Quantity A	Quantity B
The number of cats in the boarding kennel at the end of the day	The number of dogs in the boarding kennel at the end of the day

- ○　Quantity A is greater.
- ○　Quantity B is greater.
- ○　The two quantities are equal.
- ○　The relationship cannot be determined from the information given.

Question 11

If $7(a - 1) = 17(b - 1)$, and a and b are both positive integers the product of which is greater than 1, then what is the least possible sum of a and b ?

- ○　2
- ○　7
- ○　17
- ○　24
- ○　26

Question 12

A machine works at a constant rate and produces a bolts in 15 minutes and b bolts in c hours.

Quantity A	Quantity B
b	$3ac$

- ○　Quantity A is greater.
- ○　Quantity B is greater.
- ○　The two quantities are equal.
- ○　The relationship cannot be determined from the information given.

Question 13

On a fishing trip, Robert caught salmon and halibut in a ratio of 4 : 5. If Robert caught 12 salmon, how many total fish did he catch?

☐

DRILL 2

Question 1

If a high school's varsity tennis team is made up of 24 juniors and seniors, which of the following could be the ratio of juniors to seniors on the team?

Indicate <u>all</u> such ratios.

- ☐   1 : 2
- ☐   1 : 3
- ☐   1 : 4
- ☐   1 : 5
- ☐   3 : 5
- ☐   3 : 8

Question 2

Ann wants to make cookies, but she has only 2 eggs and the recipe calls for 3. If the recipe calls for 3 cups of flour, 1 cup of sugar, and $\frac{1}{2}$ cup of butter, how many cups of butter does she need to use if she wants to keep the ratios of ingredients consistent with the original recipe, but using only 2 eggs?

Questions 3 and 4 refer to the following data.

Question 3

CHARITABLE ANNUAL DONATIONS TO CHARITY GROUP X

Employees of Company:	Years 1990–2000		Years 1990–2010	
	Average (mean) annual donation per employee	Greatest single annual donation by an employee	Average (mean) annual donation per employee	Greatest single annual donation by an employee
A	24.3	1,000	34.6	1,000
B	18.2	500	40.2	500
C	45.5	300	45.5	2,000
D	34.6	2,000	34.6	2,000
E	34.7	1,000	32.4	1,000
F	150.3	2,000	100.8	2,000
G	23.7	500	23.7	500
H	34.7	500	34.7	1,000
I	74.5	5,000	80.2	5,000
J	85.6	3,000	85.6	3,000
K	126.7	5,000	104.4	5,000
L	234.4	3,000	234.4	3,000
M	422.4	400	455.2	2,000

For any Company X listed in the chart to the left, let ΔX be defined as the difference between the mean annual donation of employees of Company X in the period 1990–2000 and that for the same company in the period 1990–2010. Which of the following is closest to the ratio of ΔM to ΔB ?

○ 2 to 1
○ 3 to 2
○ 1 to 1
○ 2 to 3
○ 1 to 2

Question 4

If Company A had, on average, 15 times as many employees in the period 1990–2010 as did Company K, then which of the following is closest to the ratio of the actual donations from Company A in 1990–2010 to the actual donations from Company K in the same period?

○ 1 : 3
○ 1 : 2
○ 3 : 1
○ 4 : 1
○ 5 : 1

Question 5

A jar contains only marbles of three different colors: red, green, and yellow. The red and green marbles are in a ratio of 2 : 5, and the yellow and red marbles are in a ratio of 5 : 6. Which of the following could be the total number of marbles?

Indicate all such numbers.

☐ 13
☐ 24
☐ 52
☐ 90
☐ 134
☐ 182

Question 6

If the ratio of b to c is 15 to 4, and the ratio of a to c is 3 to 7, then what is the ratio of a to b ?

○ $\dfrac{3}{35}$

○ $\dfrac{4}{35}$

○ $\dfrac{1}{5}$

○ $\dfrac{1}{4}$

○ $\dfrac{7}{15}$

Question 7

Jenny's factory produces gear shafts at the rate of 250 gear shafts per hour. She finds that she is short 3,000 gear shafts on an order that must be completed in the next 10 hours. By what percent must Jenny increase her rate of production, in gear shafts per hour, in order to complete the order on time?

[   ]

Question 8

In one day, Juan sends Keith three times as many messages as he sends Laurence, and Laurence sends Missy 4.5 times as many messages as he receives from Juan. If Missy receives 18 messages from Laurence, how many messages does Keith receive from Juan?

○ 3
○ 12
○ 16
○ 18
○ 56

Question 9

If the smallest angle of a triangle measures 45 degrees, which of the following could be the ratio of the three angles of the triangle?

Indicate all such ratios.

☐ 2 : 3 : 3
☐ 3 : 4 : 5
☐ 3 : 5 : 7
☐ 9 : 10 : 17
☐ 9 : 11 : 13
☐ 15 : 17 : 18

Question 10

If $\dfrac{a}{b} = \dfrac{11}{6}$ and $\dfrac{b}{c} = \dfrac{4}{3}$, then what is the ratio of a to c ?

Question 11

Mariko can knit 5 rows of a scarf in x minutes. If there are 100 rows in each foot of the scarf, how many hours, in terms of x and y, will it take Mariko to finish a scarf that is y feet long?

○ $\dfrac{xy}{3}$

○ $\dfrac{1,200}{xy}$

○ $1,200xy$

○ $\dfrac{3}{xy}$

○ $3xy$

Question 12

If Elier can bake c cakes in h hours, then at this rate how many hours will it take him to bake 777 cakes?

○ $777ch$

○ $\dfrac{777h}{c}$

○ $\dfrac{h}{777c}$

○ $\dfrac{777c}{h}$

○ $\dfrac{c}{777h}$

Question 13

A 60 ounce package of trail mix contains x ounces of raisins, $x + 8$ ounces of peanuts, and 32 ounces of granola. If the ratio of peanuts to granola is 9 : 16, what is the value of x ?

ANSWERS

Drill 1

1. C
2. D
3. B
4. D
5. 42
6. D
7. 90
8. A
9. C
10. D
11. E
12. A
13. 27

Drill 2

1. A, B, D, E
2. $\dfrac{1}{3}$
3. B
4. E
5. C, F
6. B
7. 20
8. B
9. A, B, D
10. $\dfrac{22}{9}$
11. A
12. B
13. 10

EXPLANATIONS
Drill 1

1. **C** A ratio is a part-to-part relationship, but it can be expressed and manipulated just like a fraction—

   in this case, $\dfrac{2}{3\frac{1}{2}}$. None of the answers have a fractional value in the denominator, so you need to

   find a multiplier that will get rid of the fraction. In this case, just doubling the entire ratio will do

   the trick: $\dfrac{2}{3\frac{1}{2}} \times \dfrac{2}{2} = \dfrac{4}{7}$.

2. **D** Read the chart carefully and then Ballpark. Company F's annual average donation was about 150 for 1990–2000 and about 100 for 1990–2010. Reduce 150 : 100 to 3 : 2.

3. **B** First, find that 400 milligrams × 500 pills = 200,000 milligrams total. Then, convert to grams by dividing by 1,000 to find the answer: 200 grams. When doing multiple conversions, be sure to label carefully and watch for arithmetic errors.

4. **D** Cross multiply to find the value of b, $\dfrac{35}{6}$. Then substitute in the values of a and b:
   $$a + b = \dfrac{1}{6} + \dfrac{35}{6} = \dfrac{36}{6} = 6$$

5. **42** To swim 4.2 times the original distance, James needs to swim for 4.2 times the original time. Multiply the original time of 10 minutes by 4.2 to get 42, the correct answer.

6. **D** Because you have variables, make your set-up on your scratch paper. Plug In different values for a and b. First, try $a = 2$ and $b = 4$: $\dfrac{2}{4}$ reduces to $\dfrac{1}{2}$, making the quantities equal. Eliminate (A) and (B). Next, try $a = 2$ and $b = 6$. The fraction $\dfrac{2}{6}$ reduces to $\dfrac{1}{3}$, which is less than $\dfrac{1}{2}$. Quantity B is now greater, so eliminate (C). You're left with (D).

7. **90** The three roommates spend a total of $210 on toilet paper. If you make your ratio box, you will see that your ratio total is 7 and your actual total is 210, so your multiplier is 30. Keri therefore needs to contribute $90.00 to the cost of the toilet paper.

8. **A** Divide both sides by b, and then divide both sides by 36 to find: $\dfrac{a}{b} = \dfrac{25}{36}$. Although $\dfrac{5}{6} \times \dfrac{5}{6} = \dfrac{25}{36}$, this does not mean that $\dfrac{25}{36}$ reduces to $\dfrac{5}{6}$. Use the Bowtie to compare the two fractions: 36 times 5 equals 180, while 6 times 25 equals 150. Since 180 is bigger, Quantity A is greater.

9.   C   Mathematically, take 12.5% of 3 liters to get $\frac{3}{8}$ liters of cranberry juice from Bee's punch. Then, take 25% of 6 liters to get $\frac{3}{2}$ liters of cranberry juice from Flo's punch. Add them together and you get that $\frac{3}{8} + \frac{3}{2} = \frac{15}{8}$ liters of the new mixture is cranberry juice. To calculate the percentage of the new mixture that is cranberry juice, first calculate that the new mixture is composed of $3 + 6 = 9$ liters of punch, and then divide $\frac{15}{8}$ by 9 to get that $\frac{15}{72}$, or 20.83%, of the new mixed punch is cranberry juice.

10.   D   Try Plugging In. If there are 10 cats at the beginning of the day, then there are 11 dogs; at the end of the day, there would be 15 cats and 15 dogs. In this case, Quantity A and Quantity B are equal. Eliminate (A) and (B). However, there could be 20 cats and 22 dogs at the beginning of the day; then there would be 25 cats and 26 dogs at the end of the day. In that situation, Quantity B is greater; eliminate (C). Only (D) remains.

11.   E   To solve this problem, systematically Plug In values for a and b until you arrive at the right answer. The question tells you that a and b are both positive integers, and you're looking for the least possible sum of a and b, so begin by Plugging In the smallest positive numbers. You could start with either a or b, but since b is being multiplied by a larger number, b itself is definitely the smaller of a and b, so Plug In for b.

Could $b = 1$? If $b = 1$, then $17(b - 1) = 0$. Solving for a, this would mean that $7(a - 1) = 0$, and therefore $a = 1$ as well. However, this cannot be the final solution because the problem tells you that $ab > 1$ and in this case $ab = 1$. So $b \neq 1$. Continue Plugging In.

Could $b = 2$? If $b = 2$, then $17(b - 1) = 17$. Solving for a, this would mean that $7(a - 1) = 17$, and therefore $a = \frac{24}{7}$. However, this cannot be the solution because the problem tells you that a must be an integer. So $b \neq 2$. Continue Plugging In.

Could $b = 3$? If $b = 3$, then $17(b - 1) = 34$. Solving for a, this would mean that $7(a - 1) = 34$, and therefore $a = \frac{41}{7}$. However, this cannot be the solution because the problem tells you that a must be an integer. So $b \neq 3$. Continue Plugging In.

Could $b = 4$? If $b = 4$, then $17(b - 1) = 51$. Solving for a, this would mean that $7(a - 1) = 51$, and therefore $a = \frac{58}{7}$. However, this cannot be the solution because the problem tells you that a must be an integer. So $b \neq 4$. Continue Plugging In.

This may seem like a lot of work, but it's easier than thinking conceptually about the number theory principles that are required to get to the solution.

Could $b = 5$? If $b = 5$, then $17(b - 1) = 68$. Solving for a, this would mean that $7(a - 1) = 68$, and therefore $a = \dfrac{75}{7}$. However, this cannot be the solution because the problem tells you that a must be an integer. So $b \neq 5$. Continue Plugging In.

Could $b = 6$? If $b = 6$, then $17(b - 1) = 85$. Solving for a, this would mean that $7(a - 1) = 85$, and therefore $a = \dfrac{92}{7}$. However, this cannot be the solution because the problem tells you that a must be an integer. So $b \neq 6$. Continue Plugging In.

Could $b = 7$? If $b = 7$, then $17(b - 1) = 102$. Solving for a, this would mean that $7(a - 1) = 102$, and therefore $a = \dfrac{109}{7}$. However, this cannot be the solution because the problem tells you that a must be an integer. So $b \neq 7$. Continue Plugging In.

Could $b = 8$? If $b = 8$, then $17(b - 1) = 119$. Solving for a, this would mean that $7(a - 1) = 119$, and therefore $a = \dfrac{126}{7}$, which can be reduced to $a = 18$. You've found it. The final answer, therefore, is that $b = 8$, $a = 18$, and therefore the smallest possible sum of $a + b$ is $18 + 8 = 26$.

12. **A** Plug In values. If $a = 5$ and $c = 1$, then $b = 20$. In that situation, Quantity A is larger; eliminate (B) and (C). Plug In again to see if this is always the case. If $a = 100$ and $c = 2$, then $b = 800$. Quantity A is still larger. There isn't anything else you can try that would change the values, so (A) is the best answer.

13. **27** Make a ratio box and fill in what you know: the ratio and the total number of salmon. You then can add $4 + 5$ in the ratio row to find the total number of fish (9), and use that information in the salmon column to find the multiplier. $4 \times m = 12$. So the multiplier is 3. Fill in the same multiplier across the middle row. Multiply down the total column (9×3) to figure out the actual total number of fish, which is 27.

Salmon	Halibut	Total
4	5	9
3	3	3
12	15	27

Drill 2

1. **A, B, D, E**

   Set up your ratio box. The number given is the actual total number of players, so put 24 there. Then start Plugging In the Answers into your ratio row to see which could work. The ratio of 1 : 2 in (A) would yield a ratio total of 3; this works with a multiplier of 8, so you know (A) works. Choice (B) gives a ratio total of 4, which would work with a multiplier of 6; (B) works. Choice (C), however, gives a ratio total of 5; since 24 isn't a multiple of 5, it would yield a fractional multiplier, and thus fractional juniors and seniors. Eliminate (C). Choices (D) and (E) would work with multipliers of 4 and 3, respectively. Choice (F) yields a ratio total of 11, which will again yield a fractional multiplier, so eliminate (F).

2. $\dfrac{1}{3}$

   Set up a ratio box. Put the recipe's original ratio of ingredients in the top row. Then put 2 eggs in the "actual" row. This makes your multiplier $\dfrac{2}{3}$. Fill out the rest of the ratio box to determine the number of cups of butter.

	Flour	Sugar	Butter	Eggs	Total
Ratio	3	1	$\dfrac{1}{2}$	3	
Multiplier	$\dfrac{2}{3}$	$\dfrac{2}{3}$	$\dfrac{2}{3}$	$\dfrac{2}{3}$	
Actual	2	$\dfrac{2}{3}$	$\dfrac{1}{3}$	2	

3. **B**

   According to the given definition, ΔM is $455.2 - 422.4 = 32.8$, and ΔB is $40.2 - 18.2 = 22$. Round ΔM to 33, and the ratio of ΔM to ΔB is 33 to 22, which reduces to 3 to 2. Choice (B) is correct.

4. **E**

   To simplify this problem, ignore the chart column about the greatest single employee donation and plug in easy values for the number of employees for each company. Try 15 employees for Company A and 1 employee for Company K. Now you have a total donation of $15 \times 34.6 = 519$ per year from Company A, and a total donation of 104.4 per year from the single employee of Company K. The ratio is thus 519 : 104.4, which reduces almost exactly to 5 : 1, so (E) is correct. If you selected (A), you may have solved for the averages rather than the actual amount of the donations; if you selected (D), you may have solved for the period 1990–2000.

5. **C, F**   Since red is common to the given ratios, you'll want to multiply the red : green ratio by 3 so that red is 6 in both. Now you can put it all together in one ratio—red : green : yellow = 6 : 15 : 5. More importantly, you can put them in one Ratio Box:

Red	Green	Yellow	Total
6	15	5	26

No need to finish the rest of the Ratio Box—you have all you need. Look for answer choices that are multiples of 26. Only (C) and (F) work.

6. **B**   When you need to compare ratios, think of the ratios as fractions that need common denominators. The value of c in each ratio will need to become 28, and the other values will need to change accordingly. That will make $b : c = 105 : 28$ after multiplying the original values by 7, and $a : c = 12 : 28$ after multiplying the original values by 4. This means $a : b = 12 : 105$. Simplify, and you get $4 : 35$.

7. **20**   Jenny must complete 3,000 gear shafts in 10 hours, which is a rate of 300 gear shafts per hour. Percent change is $\left(\dfrac{difference}{original}\right) \times 100$. In this case, the difference is 50 and the original is 250, so the percent change is $\left(\dfrac{50}{250}\right) \times 100 = 20$. The question asks for percent increase, so be sure to enter 20, and not 0.2.

8. **B**   It's an algebra question with numbers for answer choices, so set up your scratch paper to Plug In the Answers. The answers represent the number of messages Keith receives from Juan, so label them K, or something similar, and give yourself columns for L, which is $K \div 3$, and M, which is $4.5 \times L$. Start with (C). If $K = 16$, then L is a fraction; since you cannot send a fractional message, eliminate (C)—and go ahead and eliminate (E), since it's also not divisible by 3. Next, try (B), since it's the middle of the remaining 3 answer choices. If $K = 12$, then $L = 4$ and $M = 18$. That's the correct number of messages for Missy, so (B) is correct.

9. **A, B, D**

    For each choice, use a ratio box. The first part of each ratio represents 45 degrees. For (A), the multiplier will be 45 divided by 2, or 22.5. The ratio adds up to 8 (2 + 3 + 3), so check that 8 × 22.5 = 180. It does, so (A) works. For (B), based on a ratio number of 3 representing 45 degrees, the multiplier is 15. The ratio numbers add up to 12, and 12 × 15 = 180, so this choice works as well. Using this approach, (C) does not work: the multiplier is again 15, but 15 × 15 does not equal 180. Choice (D) works, with a multiplier of 5: 5 × 36 = 180. When you test the remaining two choices, neither one produces the 180 degrees you need for the triangle, so eliminate them.

10. $\dfrac{22}{9}$ The common element between both proportions is *b*, so that's what you'll want to start with. However, the numerical value of *b* does not match from proportion to proportion, so you'll essentially want to find a common multiple for both values of *b*. Both 4 and 6 are factors of 12, so use 12 as your common multiple. For the first proportion, you'll need to double it in order to make $b = 12$. When you do so, $a = 22$. For the second proportion, you'll need to triple it to make $b = 12$. Therefore, $c = 9$. Now that the two proportions have the same value for *b*, you know that $a : c$ equals $22 : 9$, which can be written as a fraction. Alternatively, you can think of the ratios as fractions and simply multiply them together. Because $\dfrac{a}{b} \times \dfrac{b}{c} = \dfrac{a}{c}$, you can multiply $\dfrac{11}{6} \times \dfrac{4}{3}$ to get your answer, $\dfrac{44}{18}$, which reduces to $\dfrac{22}{9}$.

11.   **A**   As soon as you see variables in the answer choices, set up your scratch paper to Plug In. Start with $x = 5$, so it takes 1 minute to knit 1 row. Now make $y = 2$. A scarf 2 feet long means Mariko has to knit 200 rows, which will take 200 minutes; since the problem asks how many *hours* it will take, your target answer is $\dfrac{200}{60} = 3\dfrac{1}{3}$. Now plug your values into the answer choices; only (A) hits your target. Choices (C) and (E) are clearly too small, and (D) is a fraction, so you may not have to calculate all the choices.

12.   **B**   Plug In for *c* and *h*. Let's say Elier can bake 14 cakes in 2 hours; this makes $c = 14$ and $h = 2$. That means he can bake 7 cakes per hour. At this rate, it will take him 111 hours to bake 777 cakes. Circle 111 as your target number. When you Plug In your values, (A) and (D) are way too big. Choices (C) and (E) are way too small. Using your calculator, you can determine that (B) matches.

13.   **10**   Here's the ratio box you can set up. From the ratio with the granola and the actual ounces of granola provided, you can solve for the multiplier, which is 2.

Raisins	Peanuts	Granola	Total
?	9	16	30
2	2	2	2
x	x + 8	32	60

Multiplying vertically in the peanuts column, the number of peanuts is 18. You have $18 = x + 8$, so $x = 10$.

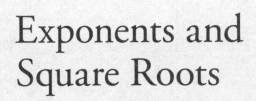

Exponents and
Square Roots

EXPONENTS AND SQUARE ROOTS

For some reason, exponents and square roots always look scary; maybe it's the funny little symbols. ETS has a real gift for making them look challenging, but they are all based on the same set of basic rules.

EXPONENTS

If you see a^2, it simply means $a \times a$. If you see a^3, it means $a \times a \times a$, and so on. Hence, the golden rule of exponents is

> When in doubt, expand it out.

x^2 times x^3 equals x^5, because

$$x^2 \cdot x^3 = (x \cdot x) \cdot (x \cdot x \cdot x) = x^{2+3} = x^5$$

When multiplying exponent expressions and those expression have the same base, simply add the exponents.

You can continue this logic when you are dividing exponent expressions that have the same base.

$\dfrac{x^2}{x^3}$ equals $\dfrac{1}{x}$, because expanding out and canceling leaves you with only one x in the divisor.

$$\frac{x^2}{x^3} = \frac{x \cdot x}{x \cdot x \cdot x} = \frac{\cancel{x} \cdot \cancel{x}}{\cancel{x} \cdot \cancel{x} \cdot x} = \frac{1}{x} = x^{2-3} = x^{-1}$$

When dividing exponent expressions and those expression have the same base, simply subtract the exponents. Thus, x^{2-3} equals x^{-1} which is the same thing as $\dfrac{1}{x}$.

There's one more rule to know. What happens if you raise an exponent expression to another power?

$$\left(x^2\right)^3 = (x \cdot x)(x \cdot x)(x \cdot x) = x^{2 \cdot 3} = x^6$$

When you raise a number with a power to another power, simply multiply the exponents.

The one thing to remember with an exponent outside of a parenthesis is that the exponent applies to everything inside the parenthesis. Thus: $\left(\dfrac{2}{5}\right)^2 = \dfrac{4}{25}$, and $(4x)^2 = 16x^2$.

Adding and Subtracting Large Exponents

If you see a problem that asks you to add or subtract large exponents, look for an opportunity to factor. This is particularly true on Quant Comp problems. Often, you don't need to solve; you just need to make the two columns look similar.

Here's an example:

Quantity A	Quantity B
$\dfrac{3^{30} - 3^{28}}{2^3}$	3^{28}

Quantity A involves the subtraction of two large exponent expressions. Quantity B has a large exponent expression suspiciously similar to the ones in Quantity A. When a question like this appears, you know two things right away. First, you will never be asked to figure out the actual value of 3^{30}. The answer to this problem will come from knowledge and manipulation, not from calculation. Second, the number in Quantity B is a clue: 3^{28} exists in both columns. Your strategy is to isolate the information that is the same in both columns and examine the information that is different.

> When large exponent expressions are added or subtracted, look for opportunities to factor.

Start by trying to isolate the 3^{28} in Quantity A.

Here's what happens:

$$\frac{3^{30} - 3^{28}}{2^3} = \frac{3^{28}(3^2 - 1)}{2^3} = \frac{3^{28}(9 - 1)}{2^3} = \frac{3^{28}(\cancel{8})}{\cancel{8}} = 3^{28}$$

When you factor 3^{28} out of the expression in the numerator, you are left with 3^2 minus 1. This you can solve; it equals 8. Low and behold, there is also an 8 in the denominator, and now you know you're getting somewhere. The 8's cancel out and you're left with 3^{28} in both columns; thus, the answer is (C), because the two quantities are equal.

Exponent Rules

Here are some other things to keep in mind about exponents.

- Any nonzero number raised to the power zero equals one.
- Any number raised to the power of 1 is equal to itself.
- The result of a negative number raised to an even power is positive.
- The result of a negative number raised to an odd power is negative.
- The result when numbers between zero and one (fractions) are raised to powers is less than the original number. The higher the power, the smaller the result.

SQUARE ROOTS

Square roots are the same thing as exponents, but in reverse. Rather than making things exponentially larger, square roots make them exponentially smaller. There's not much you can do with square roots. You can add them or subtract them only when the roots are the same; thus $\sqrt{3} + \sqrt{3} = 2\sqrt{3}$, because now there are two of them. When the roots are different, though, you can't add or subtract them.

When you are multiplying square roots, you can combine things under a single radical.

$$\sqrt{4} \times \sqrt{16} = \sqrt{4 \times 16} = \sqrt{64} = 8$$

You can also combine when dividing.

$$\frac{\sqrt{64}}{\sqrt{4}} = \sqrt{\frac{64}{4}} = \sqrt{16} = 4$$

Remember that even if the number under a square root sign is not a perfect square, it doesn't mean that there aren't some perfect squares in there. For example, the square root of 12 is not an integer but 12 is a product of three and four. The square root of 3 is not an integer so it must stay under the radical. Four is a perfect square, though; you can take its square root and write that outside the radical.

$$\sqrt{12} = \sqrt{3 \times 4} = \sqrt{3} \times \sqrt{4} = \sqrt{3} \times 2 = 2\sqrt{3}$$

Remember that $2\sqrt{3}$ means two times the square root of three.

Negative Squares

There is one tricky thing about square roots: negative numbers. When you square 3, you get 9, but when you square −3, you also get 9. That means that when you're going in the other direction, you have two possible answers. Thus, if you're told that $x^2 = 9$, then $x = \pm 3$. However, the square root of a number is defined as the positive root only, so $\sqrt{9}$ equals 3, <u>not</u> ±3.

A square root is always positive: for instance, $\sqrt{25}$ = +5. However, if a variable is squared, then you will have two solutions, one positive and one negative. For instance, if $x^2 = 25$, then there are two possible solutions for x: $x = 5$, or $x = -5$, because both $(5)^2 = 25$ and $(-5)^2 = 25$. So, remember that if a question has a variable to the 2nd power, there will be two possible answers.

For more practice and a more in-depth look at The Princeton Review math techniques, check out our student-friendly guidebook, *Cracking the GRE*.

DRILL 1

Question 1

$$a < 0$$

Quantity A	Quantity B
a^2	$2a$

- ○ Quantity A is greater.
- ○ Quantity B is greater.
- ○ The two quantities are equal.
- ○ The relationship cannot be determined from the information given.

Question 2

$$8z^4 = 128$$

Quantity A	Quantity B
2	z

- ○ Quantity A is greater.
- ○ Quantity B is greater.
- ○ The two quantities are equal.
- ○ The relationship cannot be determined from the information given.

Question 3

If $(3^2)^a = 81$, what is the value of a ?

- ○ 1
- ○ 2
- ○ 3
- ○ 4
- ○ 5

Question 4

Quantity A	Quantity B
$x + y$	$(x + y)^2$

- ○ Quantity A is greater.
- ○ Quantity B is greater.
- ○ The two quantities are equal.
- ○ The relationship cannot be determined from the information given.

Question 5

Quantity A	Quantity B
$\dfrac{5^{15}}{5^5}$	$\dfrac{5^{18}}{5^6}$

- ○ Quantity A is greater.
- ○ Quantity B is greater.
- ○ The two quantities are equal.
- ○ The relationship cannot be determined from the information given.

Question 6

$$x > 0$$

Quantity A	Quantity B
$\left(\dfrac{1}{3}\right)^x$	$\left(-\dfrac{1}{2}\right)^x$

- ○ Quantity A is greater.
- ○ Quantity B is greater.
- ○ The two quantities are equal.
- ○ The relationship cannot be determined from the information given.

Question 7

$$\sqrt{405} \times \sqrt{75} \times 3^{-2} =$$

- ○ 15
- ○ $5\sqrt{15}$
- ○ $9\sqrt{5}$
- ○ $9\sqrt{15}$
- ○ $45\sqrt{15}$

DRILL 2

Question 1

$$y > 0$$

Quantity A	Quantity B
$\left(\dfrac{2}{y}\right)^3$	$\left(\dfrac{3}{y}\right)^2$

○ Quantity A is greater.
○ Quantity B is greater.
○ The two quantities are equal.
○ The relationship cannot be determined from the information given.

Question 2

$$\dfrac{9^4 - 3^5}{6^5} =$$

○ $\dfrac{1}{6^6}$

○ $\dfrac{9}{6^5}$

○ -1

○ $\dfrac{13}{16}$

○ $\dfrac{27}{32}$

Question 3

Quantity A	Quantity B
$(x^3 + 1)^2$	x^6

○ Quantity A is greater.
○ Quantity B is greater.
○ The two quantities are equal.
○ The relationship cannot be determined from the information given.

Question 4

$$\left(\sqrt{5} + \sqrt{7}\right)^2 =$$

○ 12
○ $12 + 2\sqrt{3}$
○ $12 + 4\sqrt{3}$
○ $12 + \sqrt{35}$
○ $12 + 2\sqrt{35}$

Question 5

If $\sqrt{x} = 4$, then $x^2 =$

○ 2
○ 4
○ 8
○ 16
○ 256

Question 6

What is the value of $x^2 - 1$ when $9^{x+1} = 27^{x-1}$?

$$\boxed{}$$

Question 7

Quantity A	Quantity B
$(y - x)^7$	$(y - x)^2$

○ Quantity A is greater.
○ Quantity B is greater.
○ The two quantities are equal.
○ The relationship cannot be determined from the information given.

Question 8

If $(2^k)(2^m) = 16$ and $(3^k)(27^m) = 81$, what is the value of k ?

○ 0
○ 1
○ 2
○ 3
○ 4

DRILL 3

Question 1

If $-1 < a < 0$, $q = a - 1$, $r = a^2$, and $s = a^3$, then which of the following is true?

- ○ $q < r < s$
- ○ $q < s < r$
- ○ $r < q < s$
- ○ $s < q < r$
- ○ $s < r < q$

Question 2

$$\sqrt{10y} = 5$$
$$z^4 = 81$$

Quantity A	Quantity B
z	y

- ○ Quantity A is greater.
- ○ Quantity B is greater.
- ○ The two quantities are equal.
- ○ The relationship cannot be determined from the information given.

Question 3

If $x \geq 0$, then $\sqrt{0.49x^{16}} =$

- ○ $0.07x^8$
- ○ $0.07x^4$
- ○ $0.7x^{14}$
- ○ $0.7x^8$
- ○ $0.7x^4$

Question 4

$$0 > d > e$$

Quantity A	Quantity B
de	$\sqrt{de}$

- ○ Quantity A is greater.
- ○ Quantity B is greater.
- ○ The two quantities are equal.
- ○ The relationship cannot be determined from the information given.

Question 5

If $m > 0$ and $n > 0$, which of the following is equivalent to $\left(\dfrac{nm}{m^2}\right)\left(\sqrt{\dfrac{m^2}{n}}\right)$?

- ○ $\sqrt{n}$
- ○ $\dfrac{nm}{\sqrt{n}}$
- ○ $\dfrac{m^2}{n}$
- ○ $\dfrac{n^2}{m}$
- ○ $\dfrac{1}{nm}$

Question 6

Which of the following is equivalent to
$\dfrac{2 - \sqrt{3}}{2 + \sqrt{3}}$?

○ $-\dfrac{1}{5}$

○ -1

○ $\dfrac{4\sqrt{3} - 1}{7}$

○ $4\sqrt{3} - 7$

○ $7 - 4\sqrt{3}$

Question 7

$$-1 < m < 1$$

Quantity A	Quantity B
0	m^{20}

○ Quantity A is greater.
○ Quantity B is greater.
○ The two quantities are equal.
○ The relationship cannot be determined from the information given.

Question 8

$$ab = 12$$
$$b^2 = 16$$

Quantity A	Quantity B
a	b

○ Quantity A is greater.
○ Quantity B is greater.
○ The two quantities are equal.
○ The relationship cannot be determined from the information given.

DRILL 4

Question 1

$$(x + y)(x - y) = 0$$
$$xy \neq 0$$

Quantity A	Quantity B
$6\sqrt{\dfrac{19}{2x^2}}$	$\sqrt{\dfrac{342}{y^2}}$

○ Quantity A is greater.
○ Quantity B is greater.
○ The two quantities are equal.
○ The relationship cannot be determined from the information given.

Question 2

If $x < 1$, then 1^x could equal

○   0

○ $\dfrac{1}{4}$

○ $\dfrac{1}{2}$

○   1

○ $1\dfrac{1}{2}$

Question 3

$$\dfrac{2^{-3}\sqrt{3 + \left(\sqrt[3]{64}\right) + \sqrt{81}}}{2^{-2}} =$$

[   ]

Question 4

$$\dfrac{x}{12} = \left(2^{-5}\right)\left(4^{\frac{1}{2}}\right)$$

$$\dfrac{\boxed{}}{\boxed{}}$$

Question 5

If $\dfrac{8^r}{4^s} = 2^t$, then what is r in terms of s and t ?

○ $s + t + 1$

○ $s + t + 5$

○ $\dfrac{2s + t}{3}$

○ $\dfrac{2st}{3}$

○ $\dfrac{s}{2} + \dfrac{t}{4}$

Question 6

What is the value of y if $9^3 = 3^{2y+5}$?

Question 7

$(\sqrt{245} - \sqrt{75})^2 =$

- ○ $170 - 5\sqrt{8}$
- ○ $170 - 70\sqrt{15}$
- ○ $320 - 70\sqrt{15}$
- ○ $318 - 35\sqrt{15}$
- ○ 170

Question 8

If $x^2 - x\sqrt{2} + 3x\sqrt{3} = \sqrt{54}$ then $x =$

Indicate <u>all</u> such values.

- ☐ $-\sqrt{2}$
- ☐ $-3\sqrt{2}$
- ☐ $-3\sqrt{3}$
- ☐ $\sqrt{2}$

Question 9

$$\frac{6\sqrt[3]{24} - 3\sqrt[3]{24}}{\sqrt[3]{3}} =$$

DRILL 5

Question 1

$$y \neq 0$$

Quantity A	Quantity B
$-\dfrac{y^3}{2}$	$\dfrac{y^2}{2}$

- ○ Quantity A is greater.
- ○ Quantity B is greater.
- ○ The two quantities are equal.
- ○ The relationship cannot be determined from the information given.

Question 2

$$(\sqrt[3]{64} + \sqrt[3]{x})^2 = 36$$

For the equation shown above, what is the value of x ?

- ○ 6
- ○ 7
- ○ 8
- ○ 12
- ○ 14

Question 3

Which of the following is equivalent to 17,640 ?

Indicate all such expressions.

- ☐ $2^3 \times 3^2 \times 5 \times 7^2$
- ☐ $2^3 \times 3^2 \times 7^2 \times 11$
- ☐ $\left(2 \times 3 \times 7\right)^2 \times 10$
- ☐ $5 \times 7 \times 7 \times 8 \times 9$
- ☐ $7 \times 7 \times 8 \times 9 \times 11$

Question 4

If $\sqrt[3]{x + 3} = 4$, $x =$

Question 5

If $pq \neq 0$, and $\dfrac{1}{p} = \sqrt{q}$, what is the value of p ?

- ○ q
- ○ $\sqrt{q}$
- ○ $\dfrac{\sqrt{q}}{q}$
- ○ $\dfrac{1}{q}$
- ○ $\dfrac{1}{q^2}$

Question 6

If j is a nonzero integer, which of the following must be greater than j ?

Indicate all such values.

- ☐ j^{-2}
- ☐ j^{-1}
- ☐ j^0
- ☐ j^2
- ☐ j^3
- ☐ j^4

Question 7

$$\left(\sqrt{23} - 1\right)\left(\sqrt{23} + 1\right)\left(\sqrt{22} - 1\right)\left(\sqrt{22} + 1\right) =$$

$$\boxed{}$$

Question 8

$$\frac{81^3 - 27^3}{3^7} =$$

$$\boxed{}$$

Question 9

For which of the following values of x is $\dfrac{4^x}{x^4}$ an integer?

Indicate all such values.

- ☐ 2
- ☐ 3
- ☐ 4
- ☐ 5
- ☐ 6
- ☐ 7
- ☐ 8

Question 10

$$s > 0$$

$$s^2 + p^2 = 35$$
$$s^2 - p^2 = 15$$

What is the value of s ?

$$\boxed{}$$

ANSWERS

Drill 1	Drill 2	Drill 3	Drill 4	Drill 5
1. A	1. D	1. B	1. C	1. D
2. D	2. D	2. D	2. D	2. C
3. B	3. D	3. D	3. 2	3. A, C, D
4. D	4. E	4. D	4. $\dfrac{3}{4}$	4. 61
5. B	5. E	5. A	5. C	5. C
6. D	6. 24	6. E	6. $\dfrac{1}{2}$	6. D, F
7. B	7. D	7. D	7. C	7. 462
	8. E	8. D	8. C, D	8. 234
			9. 6	9. A, C, G
				10. 5

EXPLANATIONS
Drill 1

1. **A** Try Plugging In. If $a = -3$, then Quantity A is $(-3)^2 = 9$ and Quantity B is $2(-3) = -6$. Eliminate (B) and (C). Notice that Quantity A must always be positive because the result when any nonzero number is raised to an even power is positive. Quantity B must be negative because a positive times a negative is always negative. Thus, Quantity A must always be greater.

2. **D** Look at the Quantities you have to choose from and realize that all you need to do is solve for z. Divide both sides of the equation by 8 to find that $z^4 = 16$. Try the number in Quantity A to see whether $2^4 = 16$. It does, so 2 is a correct answer. Eliminate (A) and (B) and it appears that the answer is (C). However, remember that any negative number raised to an even exponent results in a positive number so $-2 \times -2 \times -2 \times -2 = 16$ as well. As the two quantities are now equal, eliminate (C). So, the answer to this question is actually answer (D).

3. **B** The most effective way to solve the equation $(3^2)^a = 81$ is to realize that 3 is a prime number that is also a prime factor of 81. Since $81 = 3 \times 3 \times 3 \times 3$, you know that $3^4 = 81$. Now, rewrite the equation as $(3^2)^a = 3^4$. When you raise a number with an exponent to another power you multiply the exponents. So $3^{2a} = 3^4$. As the bases are the same, you set the exponents equal: $2a = 4$ and $a = 2$. The answer is (B).

4. **D** Plug In! If $x = 2$ and $y = 3$, then Quantity A is 5 and Quantity B is 25. Quantity B is greater, so eliminate (A) and (C). Next, make x and y both 0. Both Quantities A and B are now 0; thus, they are equal. Eliminate (B), and you're left with (D).

5. **B** Simplify each of the expressions by subtracting the exponents. You get 5^{10} in Quantity A and 5^{12} in Quantity B. Quantity B is greater.

6. **D** Evaluate the relationship between the quantities by Plugging In values for x. If $x = 2$, then Quantity A is $\frac{1}{9}$ and Quantity B is $\frac{1}{4}$; Quantity B is greater, so eliminate (A) and (C). Now, if $x = 3$, then Quantity A is $\frac{1}{27}$ and Quantity B is $-\frac{1}{8}$; Quantity A is now greater, so eliminate (B), and you're left with (D).

7. **B** Try to simplify these expressions one at a time. To find the square root of a number that is not a perfect square, we need to simplify the number. To do so, try to find a factor of the number that is also a perfect square. 405 can be factored into 3×135, 5×81, 9×45, and 15×27. The factor pair that is easiest to work with is 5 and 81 because 81 is a perfect square, so $\sqrt{405} = \sqrt{81 \times 5}$. Simplify and you get $\sqrt{81 \times 5} = 9\sqrt{5}$. Do the same for $\sqrt{75}$ so, $\sqrt{75} = \sqrt{25 \times 3} = 5\sqrt{3}$. Lastly, $3^{-2} = \frac{1}{9}$, so the whole expression now looks like $\frac{9\sqrt{5} \times 5\sqrt{3}}{9} = \frac{45\sqrt{15}}{9} = 5\sqrt{15}$, (B).

Drill 2

1. **D** Plug In values for y. If $y = 1$, then Quantity A is 8 and Quantity B is 9. In this case, Quantity B is greater, so eliminate (A) and (C). If $y = \dfrac{1}{2}$, then Quantity A is 64 and Quantity B is 36; eliminate (B). You are left with (D).

2. **D** The numbers are large enough in this problem that trying to do them on your calculator will result in some messy fractions, so try to manipulate the exponents using the rules. Try to find a common base. $9^4 - 3^5$ can be manipulated to $(3^2)^4 - 3^5$; also, 6^5 can be manipulated to $3^5 \times 2^5$. Combining the newly manipulated exponents leaves an equation of $\dfrac{\left(3^2\right)^4 - 3^5}{3^5 \times 2^5}$. When you raise an exponent to a power, you multiply the numbers together so $\dfrac{\left(3^2\right)^4 - 3^5}{3^5 \times 2^5}$ becomes $\dfrac{3^8 - 3^5}{3^5 \times 2^5}$. When there are no more rules that you can follow, start looking for ways to factor. $\dfrac{\left(3^2\right)^4 - 3^5}{3^5 \times 2^5}$ becomes $\dfrac{3^5\left(3^3 - 1\right)}{3^5 \times 2^5}$. Now cancel out the 3^5 to yield $\dfrac{3^3 - 1}{2^5}$. These numbers are now small enough to calculate out. $\dfrac{3^3 - 1}{2^5} = \dfrac{27 - 1}{32} = \dfrac{26}{32} = \dfrac{13}{16}$, or answer (D).

3. **D** Plug In a value for x; you're dealing with exponents, so keep your numbers small. If $x = 0$, then Quantity A is greater, so eliminate (B) and (C). If $x = -1$, though, then Quantity A is 0 and Quantity B is 1. Quantity B is now greater, so eliminate (A), and you're left with (D).

4. **E** You could use the common quadratic pattern $(x + y)^2 = x^2 + 2xy + y^2$. So, $\left(\sqrt{5} + \sqrt{7}\right)^2 = \left(\sqrt{5}\right)^2 + 2\sqrt{5 + 7} + \left(\sqrt{7}\right)^2 = 5 + 2\sqrt{35} + 7 = 12 + 2\sqrt{35}$. The answer is (E).

5. **E** First, square both sides of the equation to get $x = 16$. Then, square both sides of the equation again to get $x^2 = 256$. The answer is (E).

6. **24** Start by expressing both terms in the original equation as powers of 3: $9^{x+1} = 27^{x-1}$ becomes $\left(3^2\right)^{x+1} = \left(3^3\right)^{x-1}$. To raise a power to another power, multiply the exponents, so the equation becomes $3^{2x+2} = 3^{3x-3}$. Now that the bases are the same, set the exponents equal to each other and solve for x: $2x + 2 = 3x - 3$, so $x = 5$. Finally, remember to enter the correct value. The problem asks for $x^2 - 1$, so $5^2 - 1 = 25 - 1 = 24$.

7. **D** Try Plugging In values for x and y. If $x = 1$ and $y = 3$, then Quantity A is 2^7 and Quantity B is 2^2. Quantity A is greater, so eliminate (B) and (C). Then try $x = 1$ and $y = 1$; now both quantities are equal, so eliminate (A) and select (D).

8. E   This question can be solved with Plugging in the Answers. Start by labeling the answer choices as k. Next, rewrite the equation $(2^k)(2^m) = 16$ as $2^{(k+m)} = 16$. This defines $k + m$ as 4 since $2^4 = 16$. Start by putting (C) into the first equation. If $k = 2$, then $m = 2$. However, m cannot be 2 since 27^2 is far greater than 81. Eliminate (C). Since m needs to be lower, eliminate (A) and (B), which would make m even greater. Plug In (D). When $k = 3$, $m = 1$. The second equation is then $(3^3)(27^1) = 81$. However, this statement is not true since 3^3 is 27, and 27×27 does not equal 81. Eliminate (D). Plug In (E). When $k = 4$, $m = 0$. This time, the second equation is $(3^4)(27^0) = 81$, which is true since $3^4 = 81$ and $27^0 = 1$. Choice (E) is correct.

Drill 3

1. B   Plug In to solve this one, but don't forget the restrictions. If $a = -\dfrac{1}{2}$, then $q = -\dfrac{3}{2}$, $r = \dfrac{1}{4}$, and $s = -\dfrac{1}{8}$. Only (B) lists the values in the correct order.

2. D   To find y, square both sides of the given equation: if $\sqrt{10y} = 5$, then $\left(\sqrt{10y}\right)^2 = 5^2$, so $10y = 25$, and $y = 2.5$. To find z, do the opposite and take the square root of both sides of the given equation: if $z^4 = 81$, then $\sqrt{z^4} = \sqrt{81}$, so $z^2 = 9$, and either $z = 3$, in which case you can eliminate (B) and (C), or $z = -3$, in which case you can now eliminate (A). The answer is (D).

3. D   The term under the radical is a product, so you can separate the number and the variable $\sqrt{0.49x^{16}} = \sqrt{0.49} \times \sqrt{x^{16}}$. Just as the square root of 49 is 7, $\sqrt{0.49} = 0.7$; eliminate (A) and (B). Next convert $\sqrt{x^{16}}$ to $\sqrt{\left(x^8\right)^2}$; the radical and the outer exponent cancel out, and you're left with x^8. Select (D).

4. D   To solve this one, Plug In for d and e, but don't forget the restriction: $0 > d > e$. First, make $d = -2$ and $e = -8$; Quantity A is 16, and Quantity B is $\sqrt{16} = 4$. Quantity A is greater, so eliminate (B) and (C). Next, make $d = -\dfrac{1}{8}$ and $e = -\dfrac{1}{2}$; now, Quantity A is $\dfrac{1}{16}$, and Quantity B is $\sqrt{\dfrac{1}{16}} = \dfrac{1}{4}$. Quantity B is now greater, so eliminate (A), and you're left with (D).

5. A   Plug In $m = 2$ and $n = 4$, so $\dfrac{2 \times 4}{2^2}\sqrt{\dfrac{2^2}{4}} = \dfrac{8}{4}\sqrt{\dfrac{4}{4}} = 2\sqrt{\dfrac{1}{1}} = 2$, your target answer. When you plug in the values you chose for m and n for every answer, only (A) works.

6. E   You cannot have a square root in the denominator of a fraction. To rationalize (get rid of the root sign in the denominator), multiply the numerator and denominator by $2 - \sqrt{3}$:

$\dfrac{\left(2 - \sqrt{3}\right)\left(2 - \sqrt{3}\right)}{\left(2 + \sqrt{3}\right)\left(2 - \sqrt{3}\right)} = \dfrac{4 - 4\sqrt{3} + 3}{4 - 3} = \dfrac{7 - 4\sqrt{3}}{1}$. Choice (E) is correct.

7. **D** This could be a good opportunity to Plug In, though the relatively large exponent would require a calculator. However, even without a calculator, this problem is solvable with some basic knowledge of exponents. The inequality indicates that m is a fraction or 0 and could be negative, positive, or neither. If m is positive, Quantity B is greater since a positive fraction raised to any exponent will always be positive and therefore greater than zero. Eliminate (A) and (C). It is possible, however, for m to equal zero. Zero raised to the power of 20 is still zero. Eliminate (B). Choice (D) is correct.

8. **D** Start by using the second equation to find the values for b, and then use the first equation to find the corresponding value for a. In the equation $b^2 = 16$, b could be 4, then a is 3; Quantity B is greater, so eliminate (A) and (C). However, b could also be -4, in which case a is -3; Quantity A is now greater, so eliminate (B), and you're left with (D).

Drill 4

1. **C** If $(x + y)(x - y) = 0$ and $xy \neq 0$, then either $x + y = 0$ or $x - y = 0$; hence, $x = y$ or $x = -y$. Plug In values for x and y to simplify the comparison. Try making both x and y equal to 2. Now Quantity A is $6\sqrt{\dfrac{19}{2(2)^2}}$, or $6\sqrt{\dfrac{19}{2^3}}$; Quantity B is $\sqrt{\dfrac{342}{4}}$. At this point, manipulate Quantity B to make it look like Quantity A. Since Quantity A contains 19, test 19 as a factor of 342 in Quantity B: $\sqrt{\dfrac{342}{4}} = \sqrt{\dfrac{19 \times 9 \times 2}{2^2}}$; multiplying by $\dfrac{2}{2}$ under the radical yields $\sqrt{\dfrac{19 \times 9 \times 2 \times 2}{2^2 \times 2}}$, or $\sqrt{\dfrac{19 \times 36}{2^3}}$. Moving the perfect square 36 outside the radical yields $6\sqrt{\dfrac{19}{2^3}}$. The quantities are equal, so the correct answer is (C).

2. **D** From the restriction in this problem, x could equal a positive fraction, 0, or any negative number. If you raise 1 to any power, it remains equal to 1. This also applies if x equals 0, because any non-zero number raised to the 0 power equals 1. Therefore, the only possible correct answer is (D).

3. **2** There is a lot going on in this problem so remember to just start rearranging the roots and exponents one step at a time. $\dfrac{2^{-3}\sqrt{3 + \left(\sqrt[3]{64}\right) + \sqrt{81}}}{2^{-2}} = \dfrac{\left(\dfrac{1}{8}\right)\sqrt{3 + \left(\sqrt[3]{64}\right) + \sqrt{81}}}{2^{-2}}$. Now work with the numerator first. $\sqrt{3 + \left(\sqrt[3]{64}\right) + \sqrt{81}} = \sqrt{3 + 4 + 9} = \sqrt{16} = 4$. The fraction now looks like $\dfrac{\left(\dfrac{1}{8}\right)4}{2^{-2}}$. Now look at the denominator. $2^{-2} = \dfrac{1}{4}$, so the whole equation is now $\dfrac{\left(\dfrac{1}{8}\right)4}{\dfrac{1}{4}} = \dfrac{\dfrac{1}{2}}{\dfrac{1}{4}}$. When there is a fraction in the denominator, remember to simplify so, $\dfrac{\dfrac{1}{2}}{\dfrac{1}{4}} = \dfrac{1}{2} \times \dfrac{4}{1} = 2$.

4. $\dfrac{3}{4}$ Remember that a negative exponent means to write the reciprocal. Thus, $2^{-5} = \dfrac{1}{2^5}$. A fractional

exponent asks you to find the root, so $4^{\frac{1}{2}} = \sqrt{4} = 2$. Therefore, the initial equation can be rewrit-

ten as $\dfrac{x}{12} = \dfrac{1}{2^5} \times 2$, or $\dfrac{x}{12} = \dfrac{1}{2^4}$. Simplifying again, $\dfrac{x}{12} = \dfrac{1}{16}$. Multiply both sides by 12 to find

that $x = \dfrac{12}{16} = \dfrac{3}{4}$, the final answer.

5. C If you're extremely comfortable working with exponents, start by converting everything to the

same base so you can use the basic exponent rules: $\dfrac{8^r}{4^s} = \dfrac{(2^3)^r}{(2^2)^s} = \dfrac{2^{3r}}{2^{2s}} = 2^{3r-2s}$. Thus $2^{3r-2s} = 2^t$, and

$3r - 2s = t$; solve for r, and $r = \dfrac{2s+t}{3}$. Alternately, you could dispense with all the algebra and Plug

In numbers to make the equation true: if $r = 2$ and $s = 3$, for instance, $\dfrac{64}{64} = 2^t$, so $t = 0$. Plug your

values for s and t into the answers, and only (C) hits your target answer of 2.

6. $\dfrac{1}{2}$ When working with exponents, everything must have the same base. Express 9 as 3^2. Now the
equation is $(3^2)^3 = 3^{2y+5}$. When raising a power to another power, you multiply the exponents. This
gives you $3^6 = 3^{2y+5}$. The bases are the same, so now you can set the exponents equal to each other
and solve for y: $6 = 2y + 5$. The correct answer is $\dfrac{1}{2}$.

7. C This problem is simplified when you recognize that this is actually a common quadratic equation of
the formula $x^2 - y^2 = x^2 - 2xy + y^2$. Therefore $\left(\sqrt{245} - \sqrt{75}\right)^2 = 245 - 2\left(\sqrt{245}\right)\left(\sqrt{75}\right) + 75$ simplifies to $320 - 2(\sqrt{245})(\sqrt{75})$. Rather than multiplying $(\sqrt{245})(\sqrt{75})$, check to see if these large
numbers simplify to the multiples of perfect squares. As is usually the case on the GRE, they do.
$\sqrt{245} = \sqrt{5 \times 49} = 7\sqrt{5}$ and $\sqrt{75} = \sqrt{3 \times 25} = 5\sqrt{3}$, so $2(\sqrt{245})(\sqrt{75}) = 2(7\sqrt{5})(5\sqrt{3}) = 70(\sqrt{15})$.
Therefore, $(\sqrt{245} - \sqrt{75})^2 = 320 - 70\sqrt{15}$.

8. C, D Try Plugging In each of the answers rather than solving the quadratic:

$x = -\sqrt{2}$ $\left(-\sqrt{2}\right)^2 - (-\sqrt{2})\sqrt{2} + 3(-\sqrt{2})\sqrt{3} = 2 + 2 - 3\sqrt{6} \neq \sqrt{54}$

$x = -3\sqrt{2}$ $(-3\sqrt{2})^2 - (-3\sqrt{2})\sqrt{2} + 3(-3\sqrt{2})\sqrt{3} = 9 \times 2 + 3 \times 2 - 9\sqrt{6} = 24 - 9\sqrt{6} \neq \sqrt{54}$

$x = -3\sqrt{3}$ $\left(-3\sqrt{3}\right)^2 - (-3\sqrt{3})\sqrt{2} + 3(-3\sqrt{3})\sqrt{3} = 9 \times 3 + 3\sqrt{6} - 9 \times 3 = \sqrt{54}$

$x = \sqrt{2}$ $(\sqrt{2})^2 - (\sqrt{2})\sqrt{2} + 3(\sqrt{2})\sqrt{3} = 2 - 2 + 3\sqrt{6} = \sqrt{54}$

9. **6** The first step is to subtract $3\sqrt[3]{24}$ from $6\sqrt[3]{24}$. That leaves $3\sqrt[3]{24}$ as the numerator of this expression. Next, divide $3\sqrt[3]{24}$ by $\sqrt[3]{3}$. This can be rewritten as $3\sqrt[3]{\dfrac{24}{3}}$. The fraction inside the radical is reduced to 8, so the expression can now be read as $3\sqrt[3]{8}$. The cube root of 8 is 2, so the final step is to multiply 3 by 2. The correct answer is 6.

Drill 5

1. **D** Plug In for y. If $y = 2$, then in Quantity A you have $-\dfrac{2^3}{2} = -4$, and in Quantity B you have $\dfrac{2^2}{2} = 2$. In this case, Quantity B is greater than Quantity A, so you can eliminate (A) and (C). Plug In again using $y = -2$: in Quantity A you have $-\dfrac{(-2)^3}{2} = 4$, and in Quantity B you have $\dfrac{(-2)^2}{2} = 2$. In this case, Quantity A is greater, so you can eliminate (B). The correct answer is therefore (D).

2. **C** Plug In the answers to solve this equation. Start with (C). If you plug in 8 for x, you will find that $(4 + 2)^2 = 36$. This statement is true and (C) is the correct answer. Alternatively you could have realized that (C) was the only answer that was a perfect cube, making it the only possible answer.

3. **A, C, D**

   Based on the answer choices, it looks like you're being asked to find the prime factors of 17,640 and then rewrite them in a few different ways. Instead of starting there, though, take a look at the number you're being asked to factor. Clearly, it's a multiple of 10. And if it's a multiple of 10, then, whatever else might factor in, a 5 and a 2 have to show up somewhere. Eliminate (B) and (E), neither of which contains a 5. From there, look for an opportunity to use the on-screen calculator easily: choice (D) shouldn't be too hard to multiply (as there are no exponents) and works out to 17,640. Expand out the 8 ($2 \times 2 \times 2$) and the 9 (3×3) of (D) to compare to (A). They are equivalent. Finally, you may either use the on-screen calculator to check (C), or simply compare it to (A) (they've combined a 2 and a 5, and compressed the remaining numbers since they all have the same power). In either case, you should get that it also works out to 17,640.

4. **61** Raise both sides of the equation to the third power, and you'll have $x + 3 = 64$, so $x = 61$.

5. **C** As soon as you see variables in the answer choices, set up your scratch paper to Plug In. Start with the number under the radical: if $q = 4$, then $\dfrac{1}{p} = 2$, and p, which is also your target answer, is $\dfrac{1}{2}$. Plug 4 into the answers for q, and only (C) is $\dfrac{1}{2}$.

6. **D, F** As soon as you see variables in the answer choices, set up your scratch paper to Plug In. Start with an easy number like $j = 2$; (A) and (B) are fractions and (C) is 1, so eliminate all three. Next, try a number like $j = -2$; now (E) is -8, so eliminate it. Try more numbers if time permits; (D) and (F) will always work.

7. **462** You can try to hammer this out on your calculator, but it's a lot easier to use the common quadratic $(x - y)(x + y) = x^2 - y^2$. Start with the first 2 terms: $\left(\sqrt{23} - 1\right)\left(\sqrt{23} + 1\right) = \left(\sqrt{23}\right)^2 - 1^2$, or $23 - 1 = 22$. For the last 2 terms, $\left(\sqrt{22} - 1\right)\left(\sqrt{22} + 1\right) = \left(\sqrt{22}\right)^2 - 1^2$, or $22 - 1 = 21$. The whole expression, then, equals $21 \times 22 = 462$. If you don't recognize the common quadratic, you can get the same product by FOILing the first 2 terms and the last 2 terms separately and multiplying the results.

8. **234** Rewrite the numerator in terms of powers of 3. Since $81 = 3^4$, then $81^3 = (3^4)^3$, or 3^{12}. Since $27 = 3^3$, then $27^3 = (3^3)^3$, or 3^9. Therefore, you can rewrite the entire numerator as $\dfrac{3^{12} - 3^9}{3^7}$. Now you can factor the numerator so that you get $\dfrac{3^9(3^3 - 1)}{3^7} = 3^2(26) = 234$.

9. **A, C, G**

    This algebra question has numbers for answer choices, so set up your scratch paper to Plug In the Answers and look for an integer answer. If $x = 2$, then $\dfrac{4^2}{2^4} = \dfrac{16}{16}$, so (A) works. If $x = 3$, then $\dfrac{4^3}{3^4} = \dfrac{64}{81}$, so eliminate (B). If $x = 4$, then $\dfrac{4^4}{4^4} = 1$, so (C) works. If $x = 5$, then $\dfrac{4^5}{5^4}$ isn't an integer, since the 5's in the denominator cannot be canceled; eliminate (D). Likewise in (E), $\dfrac{4^6}{6^4}$ isn't an integer, because each of the 6's in the denominator has a 2 you can cancel, but a 3 you cannot cancel. Eliminate (E) as well as (F), since it too is not an integer. Finally, $\dfrac{4^8}{8^4}$ is an integer: expand it out $\dfrac{4 \times 4 \times 4 \times 4 \times 4 \times 4 \times 4 \times 4}{8 \times 8 \times 8 \times 8} = \dfrac{4 \times 4 \times 4 \times 4 \times 4 \times 4 \times 4 \times 4}{4 \times 2 \times 4 \times 2 \times 4 \times 2 \times 4 \times 2}$ which cancels down to all 1's and 2's. Choices (A), (C), and (G) are correct.

10. **5** On simultaneous equation questions, look for ways to add or subtract the equations in order to eliminate one of the variables. Since the question asks for the value of s, the goal is to eliminate p. The top equation contains a positive p^2, while the bottom equation contains a negative p^2. Therefore, adding the equations together by like terms will eliminate the variable p. The two s^2 values combine to equal $2s^2$. The two p^2 values will be eliminated. The two integers, 35 and 15, combine to equal 50. At this point, the single equation can be read as $2s^2 = 50$. Dividing both sides by 2 yields $s^2 = 25$. Without the problem noting that $s > 0$, s could either be positive 5 or negative 5. However, this designation makes it clear that the correct answer is 5.

Lines and Angles

LINES AND ANGLES

This is Geometry 101. Before you get to shapes, such as circles and triangles, you must first have a solid grasp of lines, intersecting lines, parallel lines, and degree measurements.

There are a couple of key concepts you need to know.

- There are 180 degrees in a straight line.
- A perpendicular line forms a right angle.
- When two lines intersect, four angles are formed.
- Opposite angles are equal.

PARALLEL LINES

Line and angle questions will often involve parallel lines. Never assume two lines are parallel, no matter what they show you, unless you are told they are parallel or you can prove it.

> When two parallel lines are intersected by a third line, two kinds of angles are formed, big ones and small ones. All big angles are equal, all small angles are equal, and any big angle plus any small angle will add up to 180 degrees.

On all geometry problems, use your scratch paper and follow these five steps.

Step 1: Draw your shape

In some cases the test will give you a shape, which you may or may not be able to trust, or it will give you a word problem and leave it up to you to envision the shape. As with every other part of the test, getting your hand moving is an important first step to entering the problem. Get your shape down on your scratch paper so that you can begin working with it there. On Quant Comp questions involving geometry, instead of Plugging In more than once, you may have to draw your shape more than once.

Step 2: Fill in what you know

Whether you are given the shape or not, you will be given a certain amount of information regarding the shape, such as the measure of some angles, lengths of some sides, or volume. Fill in what you know.

Step 3: Make deductions

If you are given two angles of a triangle, find the third. If you are given the radius of a circle, find the area. Often this will be the entire problem. Geometry on the GRE is all about finding the missing piece of information. You will be given just enough information to find the piece that is missing.

Step 4: Write down relevant formulas

If step three didn't get you the answer, you must still be missing a piece of information. Writing down the formula is a way to organize your information and to tell you what is missing. When you write your formulas down, fill in the information you have directly underneath the relevant part of the formula. It seems simple, but this way you can't make a mistake, and finding the missing piece of information becomes a simple case of solving for *x*.

Step 5: Drop heights/draw lines

If you're still stuck, you may need to manipulate or subdivide your shapes. If you have triangles, draw in the height. Have you created a 30-60-90? A 45-45-90? Or a Pythagorean triple? Try subdividing the shape or, if it's a three-dimensional figure, dashing in the hidden lines.

For more practice and a more in-depth look at The Princeton Review math techniques, check out our student-friendly guidebook, *Cracking the GRE*.

DRILL 1

Question 1

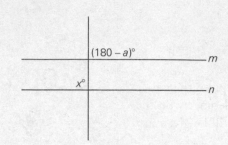

$m \parallel n$

Quantity A	Quantity B
a	90

○ Quantity A is greater.
○ Quantity B is greater.
○ The two quantities are equal.
○ The relationship cannot be determined
  from the information given.

Question 2

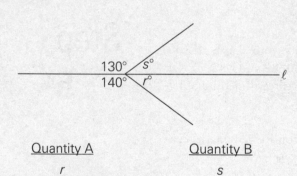

Quantity A	Quantity B
r	s

○ Quantity A is greater.
○ Quantity B is greater.
○ The two quantities are equal.
○ The relationship cannot be determined
  from the information given.

Question 3

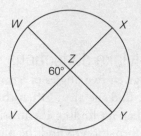

If Z is the center of the circle above, then
what is the sum of the measures of $\angle WZX$
and $\angle VZY$?

○ 60°
○ 120°
○ 220°
○ 240°
○ 280°

Question 4

In the figure above, c is $\frac{4}{5}$ of d. What is the
value of c ?

○ 72
○ 80
○ 100
○ 108
○ 120

Question 5

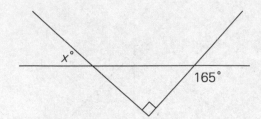

In the figure above, what is the value of *x* ?

- ○   15
- ○   55
- ○   65
- ○   75
- ○   115

Question 6

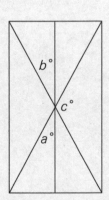

Quantity A	Quantity B
a + *b*	180 − *c*

- ○   Quantity A is greater.
- ○   Quantity B is greater.
- ○   The two quantities are equal.
- ○   The relationship cannot be determined
    from the information given.

Question 7

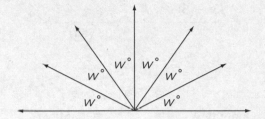

In the figure above, what is the value of *w* ?

- ○   10
- ○   15
- ○   30
- ○   45
- ○   60

Question 8

What is the area of a regular six-sided figure
with side length 8 ?

- ○   64
- ○ $64\sqrt{3}$
- ○   78
- ○ $78\sqrt{3}$
- ○ $96\sqrt{3}$

Question 9

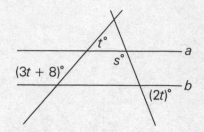

$a \parallel b$

Quantity A	Quantity B
95	s

○ Quantity A is greater.
○ Quantity B is greater.
○ The two quantities are equal.
○ The relationship cannot be determined
   from the information given.

Question 10

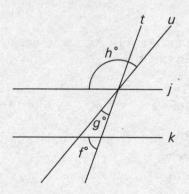

In the figure above, line j is parallel to line k. If $h = 130$ and $f = 70$, then $g =$

○ 10
○ 20
○ 30
○ 60
○ 80

Question 11

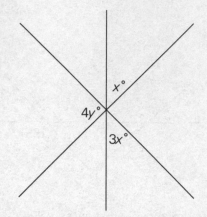

In the figure above, if $5x = 4y$ then what is the value of y ?

○ 25
○ 50
○ 60
○ 80
○ 100

Question 12

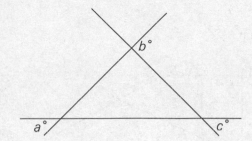

Quantity A   Quantity B
  $a + c$ b

○   Quantity A is greater.
○   Quantity B is greater.
○   The two quantities are equal.
○   The relationship cannot be determined
     from the information given.

Question 13

A regular polygon with n sides has interior
angles that measure p degrees each. The
value of p when $n = 8$ is how much greater
than the value of p when $n = 6$?

[   ]

Question 14

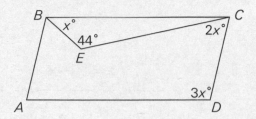

In the figure above, if AD is parallel to BC,
then $\angle ADC =$

○   11°
○   22°
○   33°
○   46°
○   134°

DRILL 2

Question 1

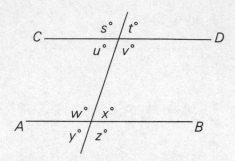

In the figure above, *AB* is parallel to *CD*. Which of the following must be equal to *s* ?

Indicate <u>all</u> such values.

- [ ] *t*
- [ ] *u*
- [ ] *v*
- [ ] *w*
- [ ] *x*
- [ ] *y*
- [ ] *z*

Question 2

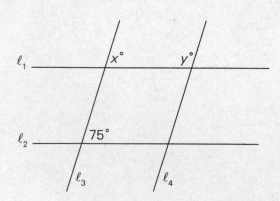

In the figure above, $\ell_1 \parallel \ell_2$ and $\ell_3 \parallel \ell_4$. What is the value of $x + y$?

Question 3

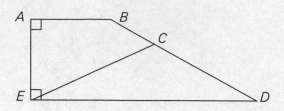

If $\angle ABC = 150°$ and $\triangle CED$ is isosceles, what is the value of $\angle CED$, in degrees?

Question 4

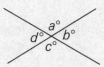

If $30 < a < 64$, which of the following could be the value of $b + d$?

Indicate <u>all</u> such values.

- [ ] 32
- [ ] 108
- [ ] 147
- [ ] 232
- [ ] 247
- [ ] 289
- [ ] 328

Question 5

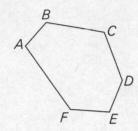

In the hexagon above, $\angle A = 101°$, $\angle E = 111°$, and all other angles are equal. What is the measure of $\angle F$?

○   82°
○   106°
○   120°
○   127°
○   222°

Question 6

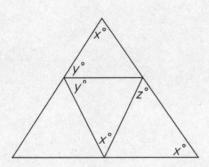

In the figure above, what is the sum of x and y in terms of z ?

○ $z + 90$

○ $\dfrac{z}{2} + 90$

○ $180 - 2z$

○ $180 - \dfrac{z}{2}$

○ $z + 180$

Question 7

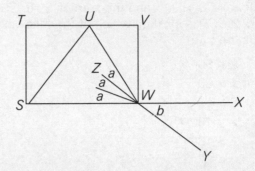

<u>Note:</u> Figure not drawn to scale

In the figure above, $STVW$ is a square. SX and YZ intersect at point W, and UW is twice as long as UV. What is the value of b ?

○   20°
○   40°
○   60°
○   120°
○   180°

Question 8

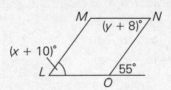

<u>Note:</u> Figure not drawn to scale

If $LMNO$ is a parallelogram, what is the value of $x + y$?

○   75
○   92
○   110
○   128
○   150

Question 9

A and B are the endpoints of a line segment. Segment AB is crossed through point C by another line segment with endpoints D and E. If ∠ACD > 90°, and the sum of ∠ACE and ∠BCD is x°, then which of the following must be true?

○ x < 90
○ x > 90
○ 90 < x < 180
○ x < 180
○ x > 180

Question 10

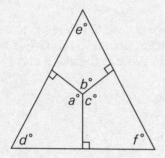

In the figure above a + b + f =

○ 180 + (c + d + e)
○ 360 − (c + d + e)
○ 360 + (c + d − e)
○ 540 − (c + d + e)
○ 540 − (c + d − e)

Question 11

If a regular polygon has x angles each measuring q degrees, then what is the value of q ?

○ $\dfrac{180(x-3)}{x}$

○ $180(x-3) + 180$

○ $\dfrac{30x + 180}{x}$

○ $\dfrac{180(x-2)}{x}$

○ $\dfrac{360}{x} - 10x$

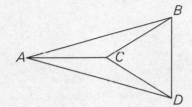

Triangles *ABC, ACD,* and *ABD* are all isosceles triangles. Point *E* (not shown) is the midpoint of $\overline{BD}$. If the ratio of the length of $\overline{CE}$ to the length of $\overline{BC}$ is equal to $\sqrt{3}$: 2, then what is the measure, in degrees, of ∠*CAD* ?

○   10
○   15
○   30
○   45
○   60

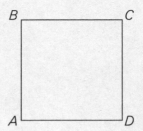

ABCD is a square. Point *E* (not shown) is the midpoint of $\overline{BC}$, and point *F* (not shown) is the midpoint of $\overline{CD}$. A triangle is inscribed in the square by connecting points *A, E,* and *F.* Which of the following <u>must</u> be true?

Indicate <u>all</u> such values.

☐   ∠ *CEF* = 45°
☐   ∠ *FEA* > 45°
☐   ∠ *EFA* < 90°
☐   ∠ *FAD* = 30°
☐   ∠ *AEB* = 60°
☐   ∠ *AFD* = 45°

ANSWERS

Drill 1

1. D
2. B
3. D
4. B
5. D
6. C
7. C
8. E
9. A
10. B
11. A
12. C
13. 15
14. C

Drill 2

1. C, D, G
2. 180
3. 30°
4. E, F
5. D
6. B
7. B
8. B
9. D
10. D
11. D
12. B
13. A, B, C

EXPLANATIONS
Drill 1

1. **D**   A line that cuts through two parallel lines creates big angles (bigger than 90°), small angles (smaller than 90°), or if the intersecting line is perpendicular to the two parallel lines, four 90° angles. Any big angle plus any small angle equals 180°. In the figure, *x appears to be* a 90 degree angle and $(180 - a)$ *appears to be* a 90 degree angle. So $x + (180° - a) = 180°$, or $x = a$. But in fact, because you can't trust the figure, you don't know whether *x* is really a big, small, or 90° angle. The answer is (D).

2. **B**   Remember that a straight line measures 180°. Therefore, $s + 130 = 180$ and $s = 50$. Likewise, $r + 140 = 180$. So, $r = 40$.

3. **D**   Because $\angle WZX$ forms a line with a 60° angle, it must be $180° - 60° = 120°$; $\angle WZX$ and $\angle VZY$ are vertical angles, so $\angle VZY$ must be 120° as well. The sum of the measures of $\angle WZX$ and $\angle VZY$ is $120° + 120° = 240°$.

4. **B**   The sum of *c* and *d* is 180, so you know that $\frac{4}{5}d + d = 180$. Solve this equation: $d = 100$. If $d = 100$, then $c = 80$. The answer is (B).

5. **D**   Remember that a straight line measures 180°. Therefore, the angle inside the triangle next to the 165° angle measures $180° - 165° = 15°$. A triangle contains 180° and a right angle measures 90°. The third angle in the triangle must measure $180° - (90° + 15°) = 75°$. Vertical angles are equal, so $x = 75$. The answer is (D).

6. **C**   Plug In your own numbers, choosing easy values for the angle measures. If $a = 40$ and $b = 60$, then the angle in between them must measure 80° to complete the 180° in a straight line. That angle and the angle measuring $c°$ are vertical, so $c = 80$ as well. Both quantities then equal 100; eliminate (A) and (B). Try a new pair of numbers for *b* and *c*, and you will realize that plugging in any values yields the same result, making (C) the answer.

7. **C**   There are 180° in a straight line. The straight line is divided into six equal angles in this figure, so $180° \div 6 = 30°$.

8. **E** The total number of degrees in the interior of a polygon of n sides is given by $(n - 2)180 = (6 - 2)180 = 720$. A regular polygon is one in which the sides and angles are all equal. Dividing $720°$ by 6 gives you $120°$ for each interior angle. Now draw the six-sided figure and a point in its center. Connecting the center to each vertex divides the figure into six equal triangles. These segments from the center to each vertex are all of equal length, so the triangles are isosceles. These segments also bisect each of the interior angles, so the base angles of these triangles each measure $60°$. Thus, the remaining angle in each triangle (near the center of the figure) also measures $60°$, and therefore these triangles are equilateral, with sides of length 8. The area of an equilateral triangle of side x is $\dfrac{x^2 \sqrt{3}}{4} = \dfrac{8^2 \sqrt{3}}{4} = 16\sqrt{3}$. Multiplying the area of each triangle by 6 gives you $96\sqrt{3}$; the answer is (E).

9. **A** First, solve for t: lines a and b are parallel, so $(3t + 8) + t = 180$; $4t + 8 = 180$. Solve this equation to find that $4t = 172$ and $t = 43$. Lines a and b are parallel. Because $2t$ is a small angle and s is a big angle, you know that $2t + s = 180$. So $2(43) + s = 180$. Solve to find that $86 + s = 180$ and $s = 94$. Quantity A is greater.

10. **B** Note that a triangle is formed by the intersection of lines t, u, and k. Since the three angles of the triangle will add up to 180 degrees, you can find the value of angle h by subtracting the value of the other two angles from 180. To find the bottom left angle of the triangle, note that because line j is parallel to line k, all of the large and small angles formed by the intersection of those two lines with line u will be the same. One of the large angles is f, which is equal to 130; thus, all of the large angles are equal to 130 and all of the small angles are equal to $180 - 130$, or 50. Since the bottom left angle of the triangle is one of the small angles, it is equal to 50. To find the bottom right angle of the triangle, note that it is complementary with angle g; since $g = 70$, the bottom right angle is equal to $180 - 70$, or 110. Therefore, angle h is equal to $180 - 50 - 110 = 20$. The correct answer is (B).

11. **A** The angle between the ones marked $x°$ and $3x°$ is vertical to the one that measures $4y°$. These three angles form a straight line, so $x + 4y + 3x = 180$. Since $4y = 5x$, $x + 5x + 3x = 180$. Solve to find that $9x = 180$ and $x = 20$. Therefore $4y = 5x = 100$; $y = 25$.

12. **C** Plug In values for the unknown angles. When $a = 60$ and $b = 130$, the angle vertical to a also measures $60°$, and the angle adjacent to b within the triangle must measure $180° - 130° = 50°$. The sum of the angles in a triangle is $180°$. Therefore, the remaining angle measures $180° - 60° - 50° = 70°$. Angle c is vertical to the $70°$ angle, so $c = 70$. Quantity A is $60 + 70 = 130$ and Quantity B is 130; the quantities are equal. Eliminate (A) and (B). Plugging In a second set of numbers will show you that any set of numbers yields the same result, so the answer is (C). Alternatively, you could use algebra to determine that the three angles in the triangle measure $a°$, $(180 - b)°$, and $c°$. Therefore, $a + (180 - b) + c = 180$. Subtract 180 from each side of this equation and add b to each side; $a + c = b$. The quantities are equal.

13. **15** The formula for the total interior angles of a polygon with n sides is $(n - 2)180$, so the interior angles of an 8-sided polygon total $6 \times 180 = 1{,}080°$. Since it's a regular polygon, divide that total by the 8 angles to determine that $p = 135$ when $n = 8$. For the 6-sided polygon, the total of the interior angles is $4 \times 180 = 720°$, and each angle is $720 \div 6 = 120$. Thus $p = 120$ when $n = 6$, and $135 - 120 = 15$.

14. **C** Use the laws of parallel lines to fill in the diagram. $\angle ADC + \angle DCE + \angle BCE = 180°$ because lines AD and BC are parallel. $\angle BCE = 180° - x° - 44°$. Therefore, $3x + 2x + 180 - x - 44 = 180$. Solving for x gives you 11, and $\angle ADC = 33°$.

Drill 2

1. **C, D, G**

    Remember that when a line intersects two parallel lines, it makes large and small angles; all of the large angles are equal, as are all of the small ones. In this case, s is equal to the other large angle measures: v, w, and z. Choices (C), (D), and (G) work.

2. **180** You don't actually have to do any math for this question. When parallel lines intersect, any big angle plus any small angle is $180°$; since x is a small angle and y is a big angle, the sum must be 180. However, you could also use the rules regarding opposite and corresponding angles, or the parallelogram rules, with the $75°$ in the corner. In this case, $x = 75$ and $y = 105$, so $75 + 105 = 180$.

3. **30°** The interior angles of a quadrilateral add up to $360°$. Angle $A = 90°$, angle $B = 150°$, and Angle $E = 90°$. So, $90° + 150° + $ angle $D + 90° = 360°$. Therefore, angle $D = 30°$. Since triangle CED is isosceles we know that $\angle CED$ is equal to angle D. Therefore, $\angle CED = 30°$.

4. **E, F** Because they are supplementary angles, $a + b = 180$. So subtract the range of values for a from 180 to get $116 < b < 150$. You know that b and d are equal, so double b to get $232 < b + d < 300$. Only (E) and (F) fall within this range. (You could also Plug In the Answers on this question.)

5. **D** The total number of degrees in the interior of a polygon of n sides is given by the equation $(n - 2)180$. Therefore, the number of degrees in a hexagon can be calculated as $(6 - 2)180 = 720$. Subtract the two known angles, leaving you with $508°$ for the four remaining angles. Since the remaining angles are equal, each angle is $508 \div 4 = 127°$.

6. **B** It's a geometry problem with variables in the answer choices, so draw the figure and set up your scratch paper to Plug In. Try $x = 60$ and $y = 70$; the missing angle in the small triangle on top is now 50°, as is the missing angle in the small triangle in the middle. Since z combines with the 2 angles you just found to form a line, $2(50) + z = 180$, and $z = 80$. The problem asked for the sum of x and y, so plug 80 in for z to all the answers and look for your target answer of 130. Only (B) works.

7. **B** The question is asking for a specific amount and there are no variables in the answer choices, so PITA. Starting with (C), $b = 60$. By vertical angles, $b = 2a$, so $a = 30$. If $a = 30$, then $\angle SWU = 90$. This won't work because all four angles of a square equal 90° and $\angle SWU$ must be smaller than 90. Eliminate (C), (D), and (E). Try a smaller value, such as in (B). Now $b = 40$ which means $a = 20$, $\angle SWU = 60$ and $\angle UWV$ is 30°. A right triangle in which the hypotenuse is twice one of the sides is a 30-60-90 triangle. That means that triangle UWV is a 30-60-90 triangle in which $\angle VUW$ is 60° and $\angle UWV$ is 30°. Per our calculations, that's what $\angle UWV$ is supposed to be, so the correct answer is (B).

8. **B** Note that angle LON is complementary with the angle measuring 55 degrees, and therefore angle LON is equal to $180 - 55$, or 125 degrees. Since $LMNO$ is a parallelogram, both large angles will be equal, and so each will measure 125 degrees, and both smaller angles will be complementary to the large angles, and will each measure 55 degrees. Since the problem asks for $x + y$, note that the two smaller angles must add up to 110, creating the equation $(x + 10) + (y + 8) = 110$, which simplifies to $x + y = 92$. The correct answer is (B).

9. **D** Since the problem does not provide a diagram, draw one for yourself; be sure line segments $\overline{AB}$ and $\overline{DE}$ intersect at C such that angle ACD is larger than 90 degrees. Note that angles ACD and BCE are equal, and both larger than 90 degrees, and that the remaining two angles (angles BCD and ACE) are both smaller than 90 degrees. If x equals the sum of the two smaller angles, x must always be less than 180 degrees, and so the correct answer is (D). If you wish, you can Plug In numbers to test each answer choice; if you plug in 100 degrees for angle ACD, the larger angles will total 200, and the smaller angles will total 160 degrees, allowing you to eliminate (A) and (E); next, if you plug in a much larger number such as 170 degrees for angle ACD, the larger angles will total 340, and the smaller angles will total 20 degrees, allowing you to eliminate (B) and (C) and verify that (D) is correct.

10. **D** The triangle is split into 3 quadrilaterals. Each of the quadrilaterals includes two 90° angles. The interior angles of any quadrilateral add up to 360°. Therefore, $b + e = 180$, $a + d = 180$, and $c + f = 180$. By adding all of these pairs together we get $a + b + c + d + e + f = 540$. Because we want only $a + b + f$, we need to subtract the angles we do not want, which is $540 - (c + d + e)$, or (D).

11. **D** To solve this question, Plug In some easy values for the variables. For example, if the polygon were a square, then $x = 4$. Since each angle would equal 90, $q = 90$, your target answer. Check all the answers by Plugging In $x = 4$. Only $\dfrac{180(4-2)}{4} = 90$, so (D) is correct.

12. **B** Redraw the figure and add point E and line segment AC. Because the ratio between $\overline{CE}$ and $\overline{BC}$ is $\sqrt{3}$: 2, triangle BCE is a 30-60-90 triangle, with the 60 degree angle opposite $\overline{CE}$, the 90 degree angle opposite $\overline{BC}$, and the 30 degree angle opposite $\overline{BE}$. From this information, you can fill in the remaining angles: triangle CDE is also a 30-60-90 triangle, and angle DCE is 30 degrees; angle ACD is complementary to angle DCE and is 150 degrees; and since triangle ACD is isosceles, the remaining angles total 30 degrees, and measure 15 degrees each. The correct answer is (B).

13. **A, B, C**

    Redraw the figure and add line segments *AE, AF,* and *EF.* Note that, because E and F are midpoints of the sides of the square, triangle ECF is a 45-45-90 triangle, so angles CEF and EFC are both 45 degrees. Also, note that line segments AE and AF have the same length, which means that angles AEF and EFA are congruent. Since the question asks which answer choices *must be true,* check to see if each answer choice could be false by Plugging In values for each answer. Choice (A) is correct, because angle CEF is equal to 45 degrees. For (B), if angle FEA is equal to 45 degrees, angle BEA will equal 90 degrees, which is impossible. Therefore, angle FEA must be greater than 45 degrees, so (B) is correct. For (C), if angle EFA is equal to 90 degrees, angle AEF would also equal 90 degrees, which is impossible, so (C) is correct. For (D), if angle FAD is 30 degrees, triangle AFD would be a 30-60-90 triangle and the ratio of line segment DF to line segment AD would be 1 to $\sqrt{3}$, but the ratio is 1 to 2, and so (D) is incorrect. For (E), if angle AEB is 60 degrees, triangle AEB would be a 30-60-90 triangle and the ratio of line segment BE to line segment AB would be 1 to $\sqrt{3}$, but the ratio is 1 to 2, and so (E) is incorrect. For (F), if angle AFD is equal to 45 degrees, then triangle AFD would be a 45-45-90 triangle and line segments AD and DF would be equal, but they are not, so (F) is incorrect. Choices (A), (B), (C) are each correct.

Triangles

TRIANGLES

Triangles on the GRE are suspicious. They are suspicious because of their tendency to fall into one of two categories: special right triangles and Pythagorean triples. Luckily, this also makes them suspiciously easy.

Triangles have sides, angles, and heights. The angles of any triangle will always add up to 180°. This means that if you have two angles, you can always figure out the third. If two angles of a triangle are equal (isosceles triangles) then the sides opposite those angles will also be equal. The same is true of the reverse; if the sides are equal, then the angles opposite those sides will be too. The height of a triangle is the line (not necessarily shown) from any point perpendicular to the side opposite that point. The height of a triangle is not necessarily drawn on a figure. Here are some examples.

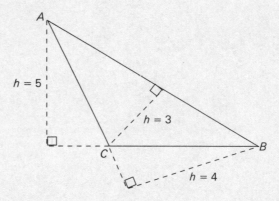

Note: The height is the dashed line.

In this case, if you use side *CB* as your base, your height will be five. If you use side *AC* as your base, your height will be four. You can use any side of a triangle as a base.

RIGHT TRIANGLES

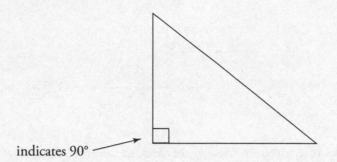

indicates 90°

A right triangle means that one of the angles in a triangle is 90°. This will be noted on the figure. Never assume an angle is 90° unless you're told it is or you can prove it. The side opposite the 90° angle is called the hypotenuse. On right triangles, you can apply the Pythagorean Theorem, which states that $a^2 + b^2 = c^2$ where c^2 is the hypotenuse. This means that the sum of the squares of the two shorter sides will always be equal to the square of the longest side. If you are given the length of any two sides of a right triangle, you can always find the third. Don't forget to Ballpark and eliminate before you spend time figuring out the square root of one of the sides.

SPECIAL RIGHT TRIANGLES

Remember that the GRE is not a test of your ability to be a calculator. Rarely will you have to actually apply the Pythagorean Theorem to find the third side of a triangle. More often, right triangles will turn out to be one of three common types called special right triangles. Because of this, be suspicious. When you see that a triangle has a right angle, start looking for clues that it is a special right triangle. Once you see it, the problem will go much faster.

30-60-90 Triangles

Take an equilateral triangle and fold it in half. The angle at the top has been bisected (cut in half). What was a 60° angle is now a 30° angle. The angles on the sides have not been touched; they are still 60°. The base of your triangle will be cut in half, and the angles where your fold hits the base will be 90°.

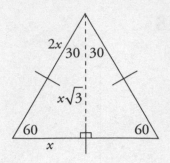

As the angles of a 30-60-90 triangle are fixed, so too is the ratio of its sides. If the short side—the one that was cut in half when you cut the equilateral triangle in half—is x, then the longest side—the untouched one—will be $2x$. The middle side—the height of your equilateral triangle—is $x\sqrt{3}$. It's easy to get lost on a 30-60-90 triangle. Just remember that the longest side, $2x$, is opposite the 90° angle. If you see a right triangle pop up on a question and you see a $\sqrt{3}$ in the answer choices, look for this triangle. It is because of this triangle that you always know the area of an equilateral triangle because you always know the height.

Isosceles Right Triangles

When you cut a square in half on the diagonal, you create an isosceles right triangle. The untouched angles remain 90°. The other two angles have been bisected by the hypotenuse and are opposite the equal sides of the square. These angles are both 45°. If the two equal sides of this triangle have a side length of x, then the long side, the diagonal of the square, has a side length of $x\sqrt{2}$. This means that you always know the length of the diagonal of a square. Like the 30-60-90 triangle, if you know the length of one side, you know the length of the other two.

Remember that $\sqrt{2}$ is 1.4 (or Valentine's Day, 2/14) and $\sqrt{3}$ is 1.7 (St. Patrick's Day, 3/17). $\sqrt{2}$ is less than one and a half and $\sqrt{3}$ is less than two. This will help enormously with Ballparking. Also, so that you don't get confused, a 30-60-90 triangle has three different sides and three different angles, and the length of the middle side is $\sqrt{3}$. A right isosceles triangle has only two different side lengths and two different angles; the length of the longest side is the length of one of the equal sides times $\sqrt{2}$.

Pythagorean Triples

Some right triangles have whole numbers for all three sides. These are called Pythagorean triples. On a 3-4-5 triangle, for example, three squared is nine and four squared is 16, so they add to 25. If you double this triangle, you get a 6-8-10. The other most common Pythagorean triple is a 5-12-13.

When you see a right triangle, be suspicious

If you see a $\sqrt{3}$ or $\sqrt{2}$ anywhere in the problem, you know what you're looking for. If you see any of the numbers above (3, 4, 5, 6, 8, 10, 12, or 13), be very suspicious. If you see them paired with any of the other numbers, you most likely have your answer. Spotting a Pythagorean triple will save you lots of time—you won't have to do any calculating.

Step 1: Draw your shape

In some cases the test will give you a shape, which you may or may not be able to trust, or it will give you a word problem and leave it up to you to envision the shape. As with every other part of the test, getting your hand moving is an important first step to solving the problem. Get your shape down on your scratch paper so that you can begin working with it there. On Quant Comp questions involving geometry, instead of Plugging In more than once, you may have to draw your shape more than once.

Step 2: Fill in what you know

Whether you are given the shape or not, you will be given a certain amount of information regarding your shape such as the measure of some angles, lengths of some sides, or volume. Fill in what you know.

Step 3: Make deductions

If you are given two angles of a triangle, find the third. You are given the radius of a circle, find the area. Often this will be the entire problem. Geometry on the GRE is all about finding the missing piece of information. You will be given just enough information to find the piece that is missing.

Step 4: Write down relevant formulas

If step three didn't get you the answer, you must still be missing a piece of information. Writing down the formula is a way of both organizing your information and telling you what is missing. When you write your formulas down, fill in the information you have directly underneath the relevant part of the formula. It seems simple, but this way you can't make a mistake and finding the missing piece of information becomes a simple case of solving for x.

Step 5: Drop heights/draw lines

If you're still stuck, you may need to manipulate or subdivide your shapes. If you have triangles, draw in the height. Have you created a 30-60-90? A 45-45-90? Or a Pythagorean triple? Try subdividing the shape or, if it's a three-dimensional figure, dashing in the hidden lines.

For more practice and a more in-depth look at The Princeton Review math techniques, check out our student-friendly guidebook, *Cracking the GRE*.

DRILL 1

Question 1

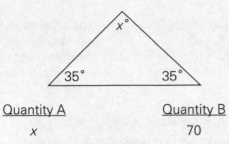

Quantity A	Quantity B
x	70

○ Quantity A is greater.
○ Quantity B is greater.
○ The two quantities are equal.
○ The relationship cannot be determined
  from the information given.

Question 2

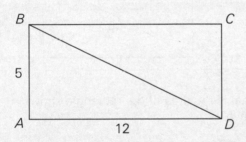

In the figure above, if *ABCD* is a rectangle,
then what is the perimeter of △*BCD* ?

○ 30
○ 32
○ 34
○ 40
○ 44

Question 3

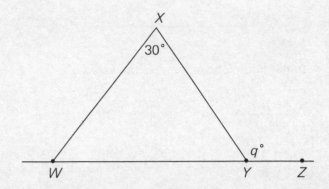

Note: Figure not drawn to scale

In the figure above, *WX* = *XY* and points *W*, *Y*,
and *Z* lie on the same line. What is the value
of *q* ? (Disregard the degree symbol when
entering the answer.)

Question 4

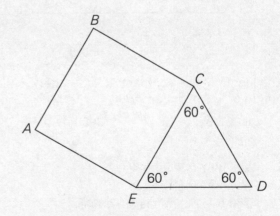

In square *ABCE, AB* = 4.

Quantity A	Quantity B
24	The perimeter of polygon *ABCDE*

○ Quantity A is greater.
○ Quantity B is greater.
○ The two quantities are equal.
○ The relationship cannot be determined
  from the information given.

Question 5

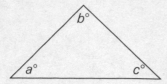

In the figure above, what is the value of

$\dfrac{a + b + c}{30}$?

- ○ 4
- ○ 6
- ○ 8
- ○ 10
- ○ 16

Question 6

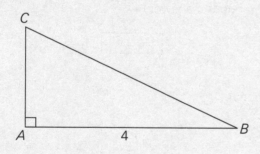

The length of line segment AC is $\dfrac{3}{4}$ the length of line segment AB.

Quantity A	Quantity B
BC	6

- ○ Quantity A is greater.
- ○ Quantity B is greater.
- ○ The two quantities are equal.
- ○ The relationship cannot be determined from the information given.

Question 7

A ship captain sails 500 miles due south and then 1,200 miles due east.

Quantity A	Quantity B
1,350 miles	The minimum number of miles the captain must sail to return to his original position

- ○ Quantity A is greater.
- ○ Quantity B is greater.
- ○ The two quantities are equal.
- ○ The relationship cannot be determined from the information given.

Question 8

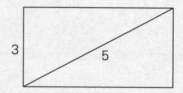

What is the area of the rectangle shown above?

- ○ 4
- ○ 6
- ○ 8
- ○ 10
- ○ 12

Question 9

In triangle *ABC*, side *AB* has a length of 12, and side *BC* has a length of 5.

Quantity A	Quantity B
The length of side *AC*	7

○ Quantity A is greater.
○ Quantity B is greater.
○ The two quantities are equal.
○ The relationship cannot be determined from the information given.

Question 10

A hiker left her tent and traveled due east for 5 miles, then traveled due south for 24 miles, then due east for 5 miles, arriving at a hut. What is the shortest possible distance from her tent to the hut?

○ 13
○ 20
○ 26
○ 28
○ 29

Question 11

The length of two sides of a triangle are 4 and 8. Which of the following is a possible length for the third side of the triangle?

Indicate all such values.

☐ 3
☐ 4
☐ 5
☐ 6
☐ 7
☐ 8
☐ 12

Question 12

Triangle *ABC* is not equilateral, and ∠*ABC* = 60 degrees.

Quantity A	Quantity B
The measure of the angle opposite the shortest side of the triangle	60

○ Quantity A is greater.
○ Quantity B is greater.
○ The two quantities are equal.
○ The relationship cannot be determined from the information given.

Question 13

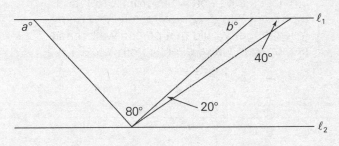

$\ell_1 \parallel \ell_2$

Quantity A	Quantity B
$a + b$	200

○ Quantity A is greater.
○ Quantity B is greater.
○ The two quantities are equal.
○ The relationship cannot be determined from the information given.

Question 14

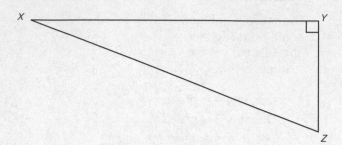

Points *X, Y,* and *Z* lie on a map as shown in the diagram. The distance from *X* to *Y* is 13 miles and the distance from *Y* to *Z* is 5 miles. If a person walks from *X* to *Y,* and then from *Y* to *Z,* approximately how many miles longer would that person walk than a person who walks directly from *X* to *Z* ?

- ○ 2
- ○ 3
- ○ 4
- ○ 5
- ○ 6

Question 15

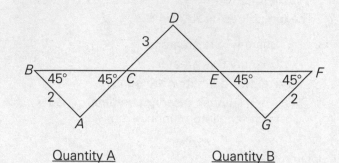

Quantity A	Quantity B
BF	$7\sqrt{2}$

- ○ Quantity A is greater.
- ○ Quantity B is greater.
- ○ The two quantities are equal.
- ○ The relationship cannot be determined from the information given.

DRILL 2

Question 1

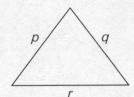

Quantity A	Quantity B
r	$p + q - 1$

- ○ Quantity A is greater.
- ○ Quantity B is greater.
- ○ The two quantities are equal.
- ○ The relationship cannot be determined from the information given.

Question 2

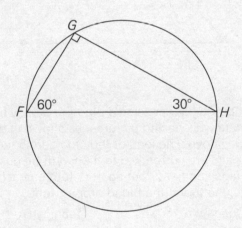

In the figure above, $FG = 4$, and FH is a diameter of the circle. What is the area of the circle?

- ○ 4π
- ○ 8π
- ○ 12π
- ○ 16π
- ○ 20π

Question 3

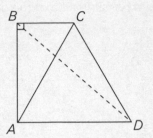

Quantity A	Quantity B
$(BC)^2 + (BA)^2$	$(BD)^2$

- ○ Quantity A is greater.
- ○ Quantity B is greater.
- ○ The two quantities are equal.
- ○ The relationship cannot be determined from the information given.

Question 4

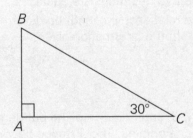

If the area of the above triangle is $8\sqrt{3}$, what is the length of side AB ?

- ○ 3
- ○ 4
- ○ $4\sqrt{3}$
- ○ $6\sqrt{3}$
- ○ $8\sqrt{3}$

Question 5

Mei is building a garden in the shape of an isosceles triangle with one side of 10. If the perimeter of the garden is 32, which of the following is a possible area of the garden?

- ○ 32
- ○ 48
- ○ 50
- ○ 60
- ○ 64

Question 6

Quantity A	Quantity B
The area of an equilateral triangle with a side length of 4	The area of an isosceles right triangle with a hypotenuse of $4\sqrt{2}$

- ○ Quantity A is greater.
- ○ Quantity B is greater.
- ○ The two quantities are equal.
- ○ The relationship cannot be determined from the information given.

Question 7

Towns A, B, and C lie in a plane but do not lie on a straight line. The distance between Towns A and B is 40 miles, and the distance between Towns A and C is 110 miles.

Quantity A	Quantity B
The distance between Towns B and C	60 miles

- ○ Quantity A is greater.
- ○ Quantity B is greater.
- ○ The two quantities are equal.
- ○ The relationship cannot be determined from the information given.

Question 8

Point A is both in the interior of triangle B and on line C. If A, B, and C are in the same plane, in how many places does line C intersect triangle B?

- ○ Zero
- ○ One
- ○ Two
- ○ Three
- ○ Five

Question 9

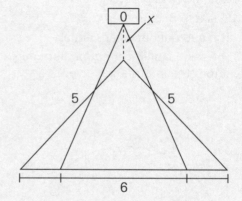

A photographer is using a bipod to steady his camera while taking pictures, as shown in the figure above. The legs of the bipod are 5 feet long and are currently 6 feet apart. If he pulls the legs another 2 feet apart (1 foot on each side), the top of the bipod drops x feet.

Quantity A	Quantity B
1	x

- ○ Quantity A is greater.
- ○ Quantity B is greater.
- ○ The two quantities are equal.
- ○ The relationship cannot be determined from the information given.

Question 10

If triangle ABC is equilateral and side AB has a length of s, then what is the area of triangle ABC in terms of s?

○ $\dfrac{s^2}{4}\sqrt{3}$

○ $\dfrac{s^2}{2}\sqrt{3}$

○ $\dfrac{s^2}{2}\sqrt{2}$

○ $s\sqrt{3}$

○ $s\sqrt{2}$

Question 11

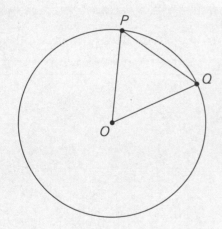

In the figure above, equilateral triangle OPQ is inscribed in the central angle of the circle and has perimeter 18. What is the area of circle O?

○ 6π
○ 12π
○ 18π
○ 36π
○ 72π

Question 12

Quantity A	Quantity B
The length of the side of a square with diagonal $\sqrt{50}$	The height of an equilateral triangle with side 6

○ Quantity A is greater.
○ Quantity B is greater.
○ The two quantities are equal.
○ The relationship cannot be determined from the information given.

Question 13

In a triangle, one angle is twice as large as the smallest angle, and another angle is three times as large as the smallest angle. What is the measure of the largest angle?

○ $30°$
○ $45°$
○ $60°$
○ $75°$
○ $90°$

Question 14

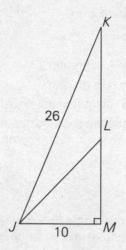

The area of △*JKL* is 65.

Quantity A	Quantity B
KL	*LM*

○ Quantity A is greater.
○ Quantity B is greater.
○ The two quantities are equal.
○ The relationship cannot be determined
   from the information given.

Question 15

Given four rods of length 1 meter, 3 meters, 5 meters, and 7 meters, how many different triangles can be made using one rod for each side?

○ 6
○ 4
○ 3
○ 2
○ 1

DRILL 3

Question 1

How much greater, in square inches, is the area of a square with a diagonal of 8 inches than the area of a square with a diagonal of 4 inches?

- ○   4
- ○   24
- ○   32
- ○   48
- ○   96

Question 2

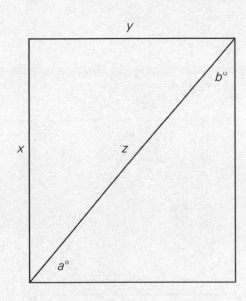

In the rectangle above, $a - b > b - a$.

Quantity A	Quantity B
$z^2 - 2x^2$	0

- ○   Quantity A is greater.
- ○   Quantity B is greater.
- ○   The two quantities are equal.
- ○   The relationship cannot be determined from the information given.

Question 3

The image of a star is projected onto a planetarium wall by a projector that sits atop a vertical 4-foot stand. If the projector is directed 30 degrees above the horizontal, and the image appears 16 feet above the level floor of the planetarium, then, in feet, how far is the projector from the wall?

- ○ $12\sqrt{2}$
- ○ $12\sqrt{3}$
- ○ $16\sqrt{2}$
- ○ $16\sqrt{3}$
- ○ 24

Question 4

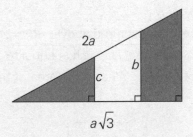

What is the area of the shaded region in the figure above, in terms of a, b, and c ?

- ○ $\sqrt{3}\left(a^2 + b^2 + c^2\right)$
- ○ $\dfrac{\sqrt{3}}{2}\left(a^2 - b^2 - c^2\right)$
- ○ $\dfrac{\sqrt{3}}{2}(a^2 - b^2 + c^2)$
- ○ $\dfrac{\sqrt{3}}{2}\left(a^2 + b^2 - c^2\right)$
- ○ $\dfrac{\sqrt{3}}{2}\left(a^2 + b^2 + c^2\right)$

Question 5

A boat travels due east for 3 kilometers, makes a right turn and heads due south for 12 kilometers, and finally makes a left turn and travels due east again for 6 more kilometers. What is the length, in km, of the shortest distance between the boat's starting and ending locations?

Question 6

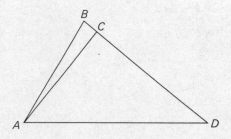

In triangle ABD pictured above, $\overline{AC} = 4$ and is perpendicular to $\overline{BD}$, which is equal to 125% the length of $\overline{AC}$. What is the area of triangle ABD ?

Question 7

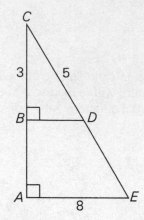

If BC is 3, CD is 5, and AE is 8, what is DE ?

○   3
○   4
○   5
○   6
○   10

Question 8

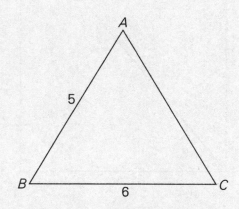

$\triangle ABC$ above is an isosceles triangle in which $AB = AC$. What is the area of $\triangle ABC$?

○   30
○   24
○   20
○   15
○   12

Question 9

A triangle has sides measuring 7 cm and 12 cm. Which of the following are possible values for the perimeter of the triangle?

Indicate <u>all</u> possible values.

- ☐ 22 cm
- ☐ 24 cm
- ☐ 26 cm
- ☐ 28 cm
- ☐ 30 cm
- ☐ 34 cm
- ☐ 38 cm

Question 10

In right triangle *LMN*, the ratio of the longest side to the shortest side is 5 to 3. If the area of *LMN* is between 50 and 150, which of the following could be the length of the shortest side?

Indicate <u>all</u> possible values.

- ☐ 3
- ☐ 6
- ☐ 9
- ☐ 12
- ☐ 15
- ☐ 18

Question 11

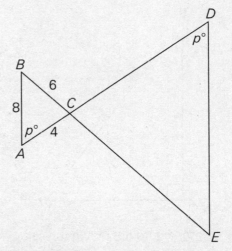

Note: Figure not drawn to scale

Which of the following are possible side lengths of triangle *CDE* ?

Indicate <u>all</u> such values.

- ☐ 2, 3, and 4
- ☐ 6, 8, and 10
- ☐ 6, 8, and 14
- ☐ 8, 12, and 16
- ☐ 12, 15, and 20
- ☐ 16, 24, and 32
- ☐ 16, 24, and 40

Question 12

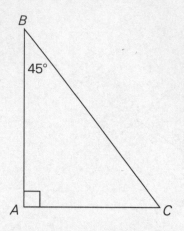

Note: Figure not drawn to scale

In the figure above, $BC = 8$. What is the area of triangle ABC ?

Question 13

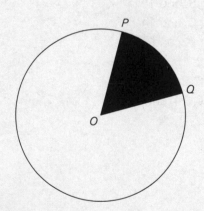

The circle above has center O and circumference 12π. If $\angle POQ = 30°$, what is the area of the unshaded region?

- ○ 3π
- ○ 6π
- ○ 30π
- ○ 33π
- ○ 36π

Question 14

Point A lies on the line given by the equation $12y = 5x + 50$ at the point $(2, s)$. Point B lies on the same line at the point $(t, 15)$. What is the distance from A to B ?

Question 15

Floyd is planting a garden in a triangular plot. One side of the plot measures $5\sqrt{3}$, and a second side measures $7\sqrt{11}$. Which of the following are possible values for the third side of the garden?

Indicate all such values.

- ☐ $6\sqrt{2}$
- ☐ $8\sqrt{3}$
- ☐ $11\sqrt{5}$
- ☐ $17\sqrt{3}$
- ☐ $26\sqrt{2}$
- ☐ $17\sqrt{7}$

ANSWERS

Drill 1		Drill 2		Drill 3	
1.	A	1.	D	1.	B
2.	A	2.	D	2.	B
3.	105	3.	D	3.	B
4.	A	4.	B	4.	C
5.	B	5.	B	5.	15
6.	B	6.	B	6.	10
7.	A	7.	A	7.	C
8.	E	8.	C	8.	E
9.	A	9.	C	9.	C, D, E, F
10.	C	10.	A	10.	C, D
11.	C, D, E, F	11.	D	11.	A, D, F
12.	B	12.	B	12	16
13.	C	13.	E	13.	D
14.	C	14.	A	14.	26
15.	C	15.	E	15.	C, D

EXPLANATIONS
Drill 1

1. **A** The interior angles of a triangle add up to 180°; therefore, $x = 110$.

2. **A** In a rectangle, opposite sides are equal, and each angle measures 90 degrees. Triangle *ABD* is a 5-12-13 right triangle, so $BD = 13$. Furthermore, $BC = 12$, and $CD = 5$. To find the perimeter of any figure, add the lengths of the sides. In this case, $5 + 12 + 13 = 30$, so the answer is (A).

3. **105** There are 180 degrees in both a straight line and a triangle. In the figure, $\angle XWY$ and $\angle XYW$ are congruent and their measures add up to $180° - 30° = 150°$, so each angle measures 75°. A straight line measures 180°, so $q = 180 - 75 = 105$.

4. **A** $\triangle CDE$ has equal angles, so it is equilateral. *ABCE* is also equilateral, as are all squares. To find the perimeter of any figure, add up all of the side lengths on the outside of the figure. In this case, 5 equal segments of length 4 result in a perimeter of 20, so Quantity A is greater.

5. **B** All three angles of the triangle add up to 180°, and 30 goes into 180 six times. The answer is (B).

6. **B** *AC* has a length of 3, so you can use Pythagorean Theorem, or recognize the Pythagorean triple, to find that *BC* has a length of 5. The answer is (B).

7. **A** Draw a right triangle representing the captain's route so far and the path back to his starting point:

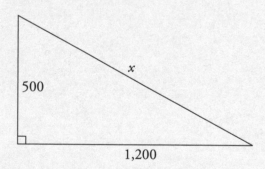

A right triangle with legs of 500 and 1,200 is a multiple of the familiar 5-12-13 triangle, so the hypotenuse—and the number of miles the captain must sail to return to his original position—is 1,300. The answer is (A).

8. **E** Recognize the 3-4-5 triple or use the Pythagorean Theorem to find that the missing side length of the rectangle is 4. The area of the rectangle is $bh = 3 \times 4 = 12$, so the answer is (E).

9. **A** The Third Side Rule states that the third side in any triangle must be shorter than the sum of, and longer than the difference between, the other two sides. Hence, the third side of this triangle must be greater than 7, and less than 17. Quantity A is greater.

10. C First, draw the picture (see below). Notice that this makes two right triangles, each with legs of 5 and 12. Either recognize the 5-12-13 triple or use the Pythagorean Theorem to see that the distance is 13 + 13 = 26.

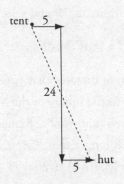

11. **C, D, E, F**

The Third Side Rule states that the third side of any triangle must be greater than the difference between the other two sides and less than the sum of the other two sides. Therefore, the third side of the triangle in the question must be between 4 and 12, and you can eliminate any choices outside this range. The only choices in this range are 5, 6, 7, and 8, the correct answers.

12. B The smallest angle in a triangle is always opposite the shortest side. If angle ABC is 60 degrees, the other two angles total 180° − 60° = 120°. Since the triangle isn't equilateral, the remaining two angles cannot both be 60°. Therefore, the smaller angle must be less than 60°, and Quantity B is greater.

13. C Start by finding the remaining angles of the triangle on the right: if the two small angles add up to 20° + 40° = 60°, then the unmarked angle must be 120°, and b must be 60. The remaining angle in the triangle on the left must be 40°, and a must be 140. So Quantity A is 140 + 60 = 200; the quantities are equal.

14. C Use the Pythagorean Theorem to find the length of path XZ: $5^2 + 13^2 = c^2$. So XZ is approximately 14 miles. John walks 18 miles, and James walks 14 miles, so the answer is (C).

15. C Although the figure may look complex, it's really just three 45-45-90 triangles attached end-to-end; BF is the sum of the long sides of the three triangles. If $AB = 2$, then $AC = 2$, and $BC = 2\sqrt{2}$; similarly, EG and FG are 2, and $EF = 2\sqrt{2}$. Two of the angles in triangle DCE are vertical angles with 45° angles in the other two triangles, so it must be a 45-45-90 triangle also—the legs are each 3, so $CE = 3\sqrt{2}$. So $BF = 2\sqrt{2} + 2\sqrt{2} + 3\sqrt{2} = 7\sqrt{2}$; the quantities are equal.

Drill 2

1. **D** According to the Third Side Rule, *r* must be less than the sum of *p* and *q*. Plug In to test if *r* is less than *p* + *q* – 1. Let *p* = 5 and *q* = 4. If *r* = 2, Quantity A is 2 and Quantity B is 8; Quantity B is greater, so eliminate (A) and (C). However, a value of 8 for *r* would also satisfy the Third Side Rule; now the quantities are equal, so eliminate (B) and select (D).

2. **D** This is a 30-60-90 triangle, so *FH* = 8. If the diameter is 8, then the radius is 4, so the area is 16π.

3. **D** Although the Pythagorean Theorem dictates that $(BC)^2 + (BA)^2$—the sum of the squares of two sides of a right triangle—is equal to the square of the hypotenuse, or $(CA)^2$, there's no way to determine the relationship between $(CA)^2$ and $(BD)^2$. Remember, figures are not drawn to scale on the GRE. Although it looks like *BD* is longer than *CA*, it's possible to redraw the figure so that either segment is longer; try varying the length of *AD*.

4. **B** Plug In the Answers, and be sure to note that this is a 30-60-90 triangle. In (B), if *AB* is 4 and *AC* is $4\sqrt{3}$, then the area is $\frac{1}{2}(4)\left(4\sqrt{3}\right) = 8\sqrt{3}$. So the answer is (B).

5. **B** If the triangle is isosceles, it must have two equal sides; thus, the triangle could have sides of 10, 10, and 12 or sides of 10, 11, and 11. To find one of the possible areas, draw out a 10-10-12 triangle. With the height drawn in, it should look like this:

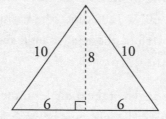

Note that the big triangle divides nicely into two of the familiar 6-8-10 triangles; you now have a triangle with a base of 12 and a height of 8, so the area is $\frac{1}{2}$ × 12 × 8 = 48. The answer is (B).

6. **B** In Quantity A, an equilateral triangle with a side length of 4 has a base of 4 and a height of $2\sqrt{3}$: remember, an equilateral triangle cut in half yields two 30-60-90 triangles. Thus, the triangle has an area of $\frac{1}{2} \times 4 \times 2\sqrt{3}$, or $4\sqrt{3}$. Remember that $\sqrt{3}$ is approximately 1.7, so $4\sqrt{3}$ is about 6.8. In Quantity B, "isosceles right triangle" means 45-45-90, so a long side of $4\sqrt{2}$ yields a base and a height both equal to 4, and an area of $\frac{1}{2} \times 4 \times 4$, or 8. Quantity B is greater.

7.　**A**　If the towns do not lie on a straight line, they must lie on a triangle; Quantity A represents the third side of the triangle. According to the Third Side Rule, this side must be greater than the difference, and less than the sum, of the other two sides. Thus, Quantity A lies between 110 – 40 = 70 miles and 110 + 40 = 150 miles, but is always greater than 60 miles; the answer is (A).

8.　**C**　Draw a triangle with a point inside. Draw a line through the point to see how many places the line intersects with the triangle. There are many ways to draw the line, but each way intersects the triangle at two points.

9.　**C**　Split the initial triangle into two right triangles. The figure should look like this:

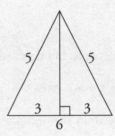

The smaller triangles are the familiar 3-4-5 triangles, with a height of 4. When the photographer pulls the legs another 2 feet apart, your figure looks like this:

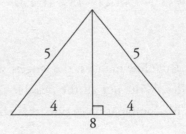

Again, the smaller triangles are 3-4-5 triangles, but now the height is 3. Because x is the change in the triangle's height, $x = 1$, so the quantities are equal.

10.　**A**　First, draw the figure and write out the area formula for triangles, $A = \frac{1}{2}bh$. Then, plug in a number for s; try $s = 6$. In order to find the height of an equilateral triangle, you need to draw an altitude from the top vertex down the middle to the opposite base, creating two 30-60-90 right triangles. The height of this equilateral triangle is $3\sqrt{3}$, so the area formula is $\frac{1}{2} \times (6) \times (3\sqrt{3}) = 9\sqrt{3}$. Now plug 6 in for s in the answer choices. Eliminate (C) and (E) because they have the wrong root. Of the remaining answers, only (A) yields the target answer of $9\sqrt{3}$: $\frac{s^2}{4}\sqrt{3} = \frac{36}{4}\sqrt{3} = 9\sqrt{3}$.

11. **D** The triangle is equilateral, so dividing the perimeter by 3 gives you the length of 6 for each side. Angle *POQ* is the central angle of the circle, so sides *OP* and *OQ* are also radii of the circle. Thus, the area of the circle is $\pi r^2 = \pi 6^2 = 36\pi$, so the answer is (D).

12. **B** A square cut in half from corner to corner yields two 45-45-90 triangles, so a diagonal of $\sqrt{50}$ —also known as $5\sqrt{2}$—gives a side of 5. The height of an equilateral triangle splits it into two 30-60-90 triangles, so a side of 6 gives a height of $3\sqrt{3}$. To compare, express both sides as square roots: 5 is equal to $\sqrt{25}$, and $3\sqrt{3}$ is equal to $\sqrt{27}$. Quantity B is greater.

13. **E** If *x* is the measure of the smallest angle, then the other two angles are 2*x* and 3*x*. The sum of the angles is 180°, so *x* + 2*x* + 3*x* = 180. Solve the equation to find *x* = 30, which means the largest angle measures 90°.

14. **A** Triangle *JKM* is the familiar 5-12-13 triple, but doubled, so *KM* = 24. *KL* may look the same length as *LM*, but remember that figures are not drawn to scale. In any triangle, the height is always measured perpendicular to the base from the opposite vertex. If you use *KL* as the base, then the height of triangle *JKL* is the length of *JM*, 10. You are given the area of triangle *JKL*, so plug all the information you know into the area formula for triangles: $A = \frac{1}{2}bh$; $65 = \frac{1}{2}(KL)(10)$; $KL = 13$. Subtracting *KL* from *KM* gives you *LM*: 24 – 13 = 11; *LM* = 11. Quantity A is 13, and Quantity B is 11, so the answer is (A).

15. **E** According to the Third Side Rule for triangles, the longest side of a triangle must be shorter than the sum of the other two sides. Write out all the possible combinations of sides: 1, 3, 5; 1, 3, 7; 3, 5, 7; 1, 5, 7. The only possible combination of sides that obeys the Third Side Rule is 3, 5, 7.

Drill 3

1. **B** Draw your own figures. The diagonal of a square creates 45-45-90 triangles with sides in the ratio of $x : x : x\sqrt{2}$. So, the larger square has a diagonal of $x\sqrt{2} = 8$. Divide by $\sqrt{2}$ to find the side length, $\frac{8}{\sqrt{2}}$. The area is $\left(\frac{8}{\sqrt{2}}\right)^2 = 32$. The smaller square has a diagonal of $x\sqrt{2} = 4$. Divide by $\sqrt{2}$ to find the side length, $\frac{4}{\sqrt{2}}$. The area is $\left(\frac{4}{\sqrt{2}}\right)^2 = 8$. The area of the larger square is 32 – 8 = 24 greater than that of the smaller square.

2. **B** To solve this question, first manipulate the statement given to you. Add *a* to both sides of the inequality and add *b* to both sides of the inequality to get 2*a* > 2*b*. Dividing both sides by 2 will give you *a* > *b*. Now, since you have variables, recognize that you can Plug In. Since you know this

figure is a rectangle and you therefore have right triangles, any numbers you must plug in must satisfy the Pythagorean Theorem. One of the easier sets of numbers to plug in for a and b is 60 for a and 30 for b since you know the 30-60-90 triangle relationship. If a is 60 and b is 30, then you can use $y = 1$, $x = \sqrt{3}$, and $z = 2$ (be careful with the x and y and how the triangle is drawn to make sure you get your relationship set up correctly). Using these numbers, Quantity A is $2^2 - 2\left(\sqrt{3}^2\right) = 4 - (2)(3) = 4 - 6 = -2$. Quantity B is greater so you can eliminate (A) and (C). You will need to Plug In again. For your next Plug In, think about what would happen if a and b were equal. If $a = 45$ and $b = 45$, then you can use $x = 1$, $y = 1$, and $z = \sqrt{2}$. Quantity A then becomes $\sqrt{2}^2 - (2)(1^2) = 2 - 2 = 0$. In this case, Quantity A and B would be equal, but since you cannot actually have a and b be equal due to the constraint, then Quantity A will always have to be negative and Quantity B will therefore always be greater. You can prove this by Plugging In a couple more times.

3. **B**   Draw your figure as a right triangle atop a rectangle. The hypotenuse represents the path of the image on the wall, and the rectangle's dimensions represent the height of the stand and its distance from the wall. It should look like this:

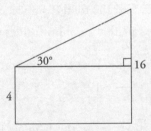

The triangle on top is a 30-60-90 triangle with a side opposite the 30 degree angle of 12; so the side across from the 60 degree angle is $12\sqrt{3}$, so the answer is (B).

4. **C**   The ratio of the given leg to the hypotenuse is $\sqrt{3}$ to 2 in the largest right triangle, so it is a 30-60-90 triangle, and the length of the other leg must be a. The smaller two triangles also contain 90 degree angles, and all three triangles share the left vertex angle, making all three triangles similar with proportional sides. So, the horizontal leg of the smallest triangle is $c\sqrt{3}$, and the horizontal leg of the medium-sized triangle is $b\sqrt{3}$. To find the area of the shaded region, find the area of the large triangle, subtract the area of the medium-sized one, and add back the area of the smallest one. Plug In values: $a = 8$, $b = 4$, $c = 2$. The area of the large triangle becomes $\frac{1}{2}\left(8\sqrt{3}\right)(8) = 32\sqrt{3}$.

The area of the medium triangle becomes $\frac{1}{2}\left(4\sqrt{3}\right)(4) = 8\sqrt{3}$. The area of the smallest triangle becomes $\frac{1}{2}\left(2\sqrt{3}\right)(2) = 2\sqrt{3}$. The shaded area is then $32\sqrt{3} - 8\sqrt{3} + 2\sqrt{3} = 26\sqrt{3}$. When you plug in the three values into each answer, only (C) hits your target, making it the correct answer.

5. 15 To solve this question, picture a triangle:

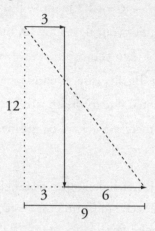

Since the boat travels a total of 3 + 6 = 9 kilometers east, and a total of 12 kilometers south, we can use the Pythagorean Theorem to find the total distance. Since $a^2 + b^2 = c^2$, then $9^2 + 12^2 = c^2$, and $81 + 144 = 225 = c^2$. Taking the square root of both sides gives that $c = 15$, the correct answer.

6. 10 To solve this question, label everything. First label angle ACD as a right angle. Next, label $\overline{AC}$ = 4. If $\overline{BD}$ = 125% of $\overline{AC}$, then $\overline{BD} = \frac{125}{100} \times 4 = \frac{5}{4} \times 4 = 5$. Since $\overline{AC}$ and $\overline{BD}$ are perpendicular, $\overline{BD}$ can be the base and $\overline{AC}$ can be the height. The formula for the area of a triangle is Area = $\frac{1}{2}bh$. So, the area here equals $\frac{1}{2} \times 5 \times 4 = 10$, and the correct answer is 10.

7. C This question is testing similar triangles. Do you recognize the 3-4-5 triangles? Triangle BCD is a 3-4-5 triangle, and triangle ACE is too, but it's a similar triangle—a 6-8-10 triangle. That means that CE is 10, which leaves 5 left over for DE.

8. E To find the area of this triangle, you must drop a line segment to make the height. If you call the midpoint of BC point X, you know that BX is equal to 3. If you see that this makes a right triangle with a side of 3 and a hypotenuse of 5, you can use the 3-4-5 triangle rule to get 4 for the height. Otherwise, use the Pythagorean Theorem. After you find the height of 4, use the formula for area of a triangle: Area = $\frac{1}{2}bh = \frac{1}{2}(6)(4) = 12$.

9. **C, D, E, F**

The Third Side Rule tells you that the third side must be more than the difference of the two other sides and less than their sum. Therefore, the third side must be greater than 5 and less than 19. The two known sides already add up to 19. If you add this to the range for the third side, the perimeter of the triangle is then between 24 and 38 centimeters. Choices (C), (D), (E), and (F) are correct.

10. **C, D** Draw and label the figure, and then set up your scratch paper to plug in the answers. For a given short side, use the 5 : 3 ratio to find the long side, and use either the Pythagorean Theorem or multiples of the familiar 3-4-5 triangles to determine the middle side; since *LMN* is a right triangle, the two shorter sides can be used as base and height to find the area. Start with (C). If the short side is 9, the middle side is 12 and the area becomes 54; this choice is correct, but just barely, and if you try smaller values you will fall out of the area's range. Eliminate (B) and (A). In (D), the short and middle sides are 12 and, 16 and the area is 96; this choice is correct. In (E), the short and middle sides are 15 and 20, and the area is 150. This is not in the area's range of 50 to 150, so eliminate it as well as (F), which would produce an even larger area. The correct answers are (C) and (D).

11. **A, D, F**

Triangles *ABC* and *CDE* are similar triangles: the angles where the triangles meet are equal, as are the angles marked p^o, so the remaining angles must be equal as well. Since similar triangles have proportional sides, any answer choice in the ratio of 4 : 6 : 8 will work. Choice (A) is 4 : 6 : 8 cut in half, so (A) works; remember the figure isn't drawn to scale, so don't worry about making *CDE* smaller than *ABC*. Choices (D) and (F) are 4 : 6 : 8 multiplied by 2 and 4, respectively, so both work as well. None of the remaining choices work.

12. **16** According to the information given, this must be a 45-45-90 isosceles right triangle, and the relationship between the sides can be written as $x : x : x\sqrt{2}$. That means that $BC = x\sqrt{2}$, or $8 = x\sqrt{2}$.

Solving for *x*, you get $x = \dfrac{8}{\sqrt{2}}$, so each of the legs of the triangle is equal to $\dfrac{8}{\sqrt{2}}$. The formula for the

area of a triangle is $A = \dfrac{1}{2}(base) \times (height)$, so the area of this triangle is $\dfrac{1}{2}\left(\dfrac{8}{\sqrt{2}}\right)\left(\dfrac{8}{\sqrt{2}}\right) = \dfrac{64}{4} = 16$.

13. **D** First, find the radius of the circle. The formula for circumference is $C = 2\pi r$. Put in the given circumference to get $12\pi = 2\pi r$ and then divide each side by 2π to get $r = 6$. Next, find the area of the whole circle by using the area formula. Area $= \pi r^2 = 36\pi$. If $\angle POQ = 30°$, then the shaded area must be $\dfrac{1}{12}$ of the whole area of the circle $\left(\dfrac{30}{360} = \dfrac{1}{12}\right)$, which means that the shaded area is therefore $\dfrac{1}{12}(36\pi)$ or 3π. Since you are looking for the unshaded area, subtract 3π from the whole area of 36π to get 33π.

14. **26** First, use the equation of the line to find points A and B. For point A, put 2 in for x and solve for y: $12y = 5(2) + 50$. So, $12y = 60$ and $y = 5$. Point A is therefore $(2, 5)$. For Point B, put 15 in for y and solve for x: $12(15) = 5x + 50$. So, $180 = 5x + 50$, which means that $130 = 5x$ and $x = 26$. So, point B is therefore $(26, 15)$. To find the distance between the 2 points, create a right triangle and use the Pythagorean Theorem to get the hypotenuse. The lengths of the 2 legs of the triangle will be 24 and 10. So, $24^2 + 10^2 = c^2$. Therefore, $676 = c^2$ and $c = 26$ (or you could recognize a 5-12-13 triangle doubled).

15. **C, D** First, use the calculator to determine values for $5\sqrt{3}$ and $7\sqrt{11}$: the first is approximately 8.66, and the second is approximately 23.22. The third side of a triangle must be greater than the difference of the other two sides and less than the sum of the other two sides; hence, the third side of the garden must measure between 14.56 and 31.88. Calculating for the value of the roots, you will find that only (C) and (D) fall within this range.

Circles

CIRCLES

Make sure you're familiar with the terms for the different parts of a circle.

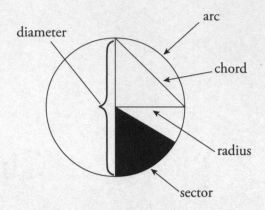

The primary circle formulas involve radius, diameter, circumference, and area.

$$diameter = 2 \times radius$$

$$circumference = 2\pi \times radius = \pi \times diameter$$

$$area = \pi \times radius^2$$

With these three formulas and information about just one part of the circle (radius, diameter, circumference, or area), the other three parts can be calculated. Write the formulas down on your scratch paper and fill in the information provided in the problem. This highlights what additional information is needed to answer the question.

Pi, or π, equals 3.14159… but on the GRE, you can often set π equal to 3. Check the answer choices before converting π to 3, however. Often, the answer choices are written in terms of π.

Some GRE circle problems focus on a portion of the circle, such as the length of an arc or the area of a sector. The angles, arcs, and areas of a circle are all proportional, so the following relationship can be used to find the missing information.

$$\frac{part}{whole} = \frac{central\ angle}{360°} = \frac{arc}{circumference} = \frac{area\ of\ sector}{area\ of\ circle}$$

If a circle is divided into a quarter, the central angle (the angle which has its vertex at the center of the circle) is 90°. Since the central angle is $\frac{1}{4}$ of the circle, the resulting arc is $\frac{1}{4}$ of the circumference, and the resulting sector is $\frac{1}{4}$ of the area of the circle.

Apply this three-step approach to geometry problems with circles.

Step 1: Draw the figure on your scratch paper

In some cases the test gives you a shape, which you may or may not be able to trust, and in others it gives you a word problem and leaves it up to you to envision the shape. As with every other part of the test, getting your hand moving is an important first step to entering the problem. Get the shape down on your scratch paper so that you can begin working it there. On Quant Comp questions involving geometry, instead of Plugging In more than once, you may have to draw your shape more than once.

Step 2: Label any information from the problem on the figure

Whether you are given the shape or not, you are given a certain amount of information regarding the shape such as the measure of some angles, lengths of some sides, areas of some sides, or volume. Put that information in the figure.

Step 3: Write down any formulas you need

Writing down the formula is a way of both organizing information and making clear what is missing. When you write formulas down, fill in the information you have directly underneath the relevant part of the formula. It seems simple, but this way you can't make a mistake. Finding the missing piece of information to solve a problem can sometimes become a simple case of solving for *x*.

Often, you will see circles in combination with other shapes. If you don't immediately see the correct path to the solutions, look for the radius. Everything about a circle derives from there. It is possible that you will see a circle inscribed on a coordinate plane. The same rules apply. Use right triangles to find the end points of as many radii as you need to check the answer choices.

For more practice and a further look at The Princeton Review math techniques, check out our student-friendly guidebook, *Cracking the GRE*.

DRILL 1

Question 1

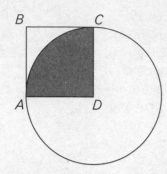

ABCD is a square with side length 2 and D is the center of the circle.

Quantity A	Quantity B
The area of the shaded region	π

- ○ Quantity A is greater.
- ○ Quantity B is greater.
- ○ The two quantities are equal.
- ○ The relationship cannot be determined from the information given.

Question 2

What is the degree measure of the smaller angle formed by the hands of a circular clock when it is 10:00 am?

Question 3

The area of the circle C is 9π.

Quantity A	Quantity B
The radius of the circle C	6

- ○ Quantity A is greater.
- ○ Quantity B is greater.
- ○ The two quantities are equal.
- ○ The relationship cannot be determined from the information given.

Question 4

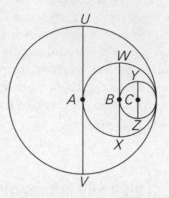

Line segments UV, WX, and YZ are diameters of the circles with centers A, B, and C, respectively. If YZ = 2, then what is the area of the circle with center A ?

- ○ 4π
- ○ 8π
- ○ 9π
- ○ 16π
- ○ 64π

Question 5

Quantity A	Quantity B
The circumference of a circle with a diameter of 6	The circumference of a circle with a radius of 12

- ○ Quantity A is greater.
- ○ Quantity B is greater.
- ○ The two quantities are equal.
- ○ The relationship cannot be determined from the information given.

Question 6

Quantity A	Quantity B
Four times the area of a circle with a circumference of 4π	The circumference of a circle with an area of 64π

- ○ Quantity A is greater.
- ○ Quantity B is greater.
- ○ The two quantities are equal.
- ○ The relationship cannot be determined from the information given.

Question 7

An office needs to buy circular pizzas for 20 employees. If each pizza is cut into equal slices, and each slice has a central angle of 40°, what is the minimum number of pizzas that need to be ordered so that each employee gets at least two slices of pizza?

```
┌──────────┐
│          │
└──────────┘
```

Question 8

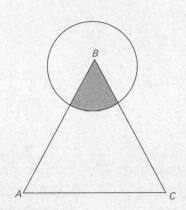

Triangle *ABC* is an equilateral triangle. If the circle with center *B* has a diameter of 6, then what is the area of the shaded region?

- ○ π
- ○ $\dfrac{3\pi}{2}$
- ○ 2π
- ○ 6π
- ○ 9π

Question 9

A circle with center *C* has a radius of 6.

Quantity A	Quantity B
The ratio of the circumference of circle *C* to the radius of circle *C*	Half the diameter of circle *C*

- ○ Quantity A is greater.
- ○ Quantity B is greater.
- ○ The two quantities are equal.
- ○ The relationship cannot be determined from the information given.

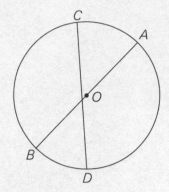

O is the center of the circle above.

Quantity A	Quantity B
Length of line segment AB	Length of line segment CD

○ Quantity A is greater.
○ Quantity B is greater.
○ The two quantities are equal.
○ The relationship cannot be determined from the information given.

Question 11

A circle with a radius of 3 is inscribed in a square

Quantity A	Quantity B
9	The area outside the circle but inside the square

○ Quantity A is greater.
○ Quantity B is greater.
○ The two quantities are equal.
○ The relationship cannot be determined from the information given.

Question 12

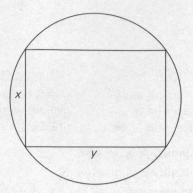

In the figure above, a rectangle is inscribed in a circle. Lengths x and y are both integers such that $x + y = 10$, and $1 < x < y$. Which of the following are possible values for the diameter of the circle?

Indicate all such values.

☐ $\sqrt{10}$
☐ $\sqrt{2}$
☐ $2\sqrt{13}$
☐ $\sqrt{58}$
☐ $\sqrt{69}$
☐ $2\sqrt{17}$
☐ 10

Question 13

The height of a right circular cylinder is increased by p percent and the radius is decreased by p percent.

Quantity A	Quantity B
The volume of the cylinder if $p = 10$	The volume of the cylinder if $p = 20$

○ Quantity A is greater.
○ Quantity B is greater.
○ The two quantities are equal.
○ The relationship cannot be determined from the information given.

Question 14

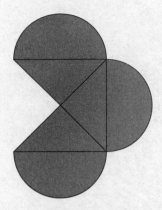

The diameters of the semicircles above are
8, and the diameter of the semicircle on the
right is perpendicular to those of the other
two semicircles. What is the total area of the
shaded region?

- ○ $12\pi + 64$
- ○ $24\pi + 12$
- ○ $24\pi + 48$
- ○ $32\pi + 48$
- ○ $32\pi + 64$

Question 15

Quantity A	Quantity B
The area of a square with a perimeter of p	The area of a circle with a circumference of p

- ○ Quantity A is greater.
- ○ Quantity B is greater.
- ○ The two quantities are equal.
- ○ The relationship cannot be determined from the information given.

Question 16

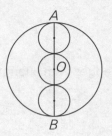

Line AB passes through the center of circle
O and through the centers of each of the 3
identical smaller circles. Each circle touches
two other circles at exactly one point each.

Quantity A	Quantity B
The circumference of circle O	The sum of the circumferences of the 3 smaller circles

- ○ Quantity A is greater.
- ○ Quantity B is greater.
- ○ The two quantities are equal.
- ○ The relationship cannot be determined from the information given.

DRILL 2

Question 1

A square has edges with a length of 12 inches.

Quantity A	Quantity B
24π	The area of the largest circle that can fit inside the square

○ Quantity A is greater.
○ Quantity B is greater.
○ The two quantities are equal.
○ The relationship cannot be determined from the information given.

Question 2

A circle with a circumference of 12π is divided into three sectors with areas having a ratio of 3 : 4 : 5. What is the area of the largest sector?

○ 6π
○ 9π
○ 12π
○ 15π
○ 18π

Question 3

A circle is inscribed in a square with area 36. What is the area of the circle, rounded to the nearest integer?

[ ]

Question 4

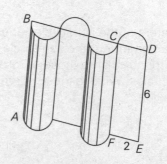

Rectangle *FCDE* has a length of 6 and a width of 2. Two right cylinders have been bisected into four identical half-cylinders, which intersect rectangle *ABDE* as shown. If each of the half-cylinders has the same radius, what is the combined volume of the four half-cylinders?

○ 6π
○ 9π
○ 12π
○ 18π
○ 21π

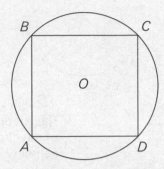

Inscribed square *ABCD* has a side length of 4. What is the area of the circle with center *O* ?

○ 2π
○ 4π
○ 6π
○ 8π
○ 10π

Question 6

If the diameter of circle *A* is eight times that of circle *B*, what is the ratio of the area of circle *A* to the area of circle *B* ?

○   4 : 1
○   8 : 1
○   16 : 1
○   32 : 1
○   64 : 1

Question 7

On a rectangular coordinate plane, a circle centered at (0, 0) is inscribed within a square with adjacent vertices at $(0, -2\sqrt{2})$ and $(2\sqrt{2}, 0)$. What is the area of the region, rounded to the nearest tenth, that is inside the square but outside the circle?

Question 8

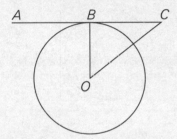

Line segment *AC* is tangent to the circle with center *O*, and *CO* = 5.

Quantity A	Quantity B
Circumference of the circle	10π

○   Quantity A is greater.
○   Quantity B is greater.
○   The two quantities are equal.
○   The relationship cannot be determined from the information given.

Question 9

The area of Circle C is x times the area of Circle B, which is x times the area of Circle A.

Quantity A	Quantity B
The ratio of the radius of Circle A to the radius of Circle C	$\dfrac{1}{x}$

○ Quantity A is greater.
○ Quantity B is greater.
○ The two quantities are equal.
○ The relationship cannot be determined from the information given.

Question 10

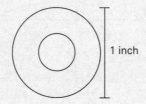

In the figure above, if the area of the smaller circular region is $\dfrac{1}{2}$ the area of the larger circular region, then the diameter of the larger circle is how many inches longer than the diameter of the smaller circle?

○ $\sqrt{2}-1$

○ $\dfrac{1}{2}$

○ $\dfrac{\sqrt{2}}{2}$

○ $\dfrac{2-\sqrt{2}}{2}$

○ $\sqrt{2}$

Question 11

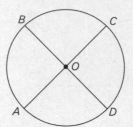

Quantity A	Quantity B
$AC + BD$	The circumference of the circle with center O

○ Quantity A is greater.
○ Quantity B is greater.
○ The two quantities are equal.
○ The relationship cannot be determined from the information given.

Question 12

Points A, B, and C lie in that order along the circumference of a circle with center O. A second circle with center M has a radius one-third as long as that of the circle with center O. If the area of sector $OABC$ is equal to the area of the circle with center M, then what is the degree measure of $\angle AOC$?

[   ]

Question 13

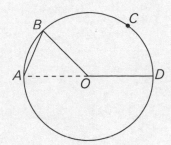

No line segment with endpoints on the circle with center O is longer than line segment AD.

$$OB = AB = 3$$

Quantity A	Quantity B
The area of sector $OBCD$	9

○ Quantity A is greater.
○ Quantity B is greater.
○ The two quantities are equal.
○ The relationship cannot be determined from the information given.

Question 14

An interior designer decides to accent a wall with an evenly spaced row of stenciled circles. The wall is 31 feet 6 inches long, and each stenciled circle has an area of 36π square inches. If the designer wants to leave a space of x inches between each circle and at either end of the row, with no space left over, and x must be an integer, then what is the greatest possible number of circles that the designer can use?

```
┌─────────────┐
│             │
└─────────────┘
```

Question 15

$\dfrac{1}{r}$ of a circular pizza has been eaten. If the rest of the pizza is divided into m equal slices, then each of these slices is what fraction of the whole pizza?

○ $\dfrac{r}{m}$

○ $\dfrac{r-1}{rm}$

○ $\dfrac{1}{m}$

○ $\dfrac{m-1}{m}$

○ $\dfrac{m-r}{m}$

Question 16

A single slice cut from the center of a circular pizza has an edge length (from the center of the pizza to the edge of the crust) of 5″, has an arc length of 1.25π″, and weighs 4 ounces. If a serving weighs 8 ounces, then, to the nearest integer, what is the largest number of servings that six 6″ diameter pizzas can yield? (Note that servings must weigh 8 ounces, but they do not need to be equal in shape.)

○ 1
○ 4
○ 6
○ 8
○ 9

ANSWERS

Drill 1

1. C
2. 60
3. B
4. D
5. B
6. C
7. 5
8. B
9. A
10. A
11. A
12. C, D, F
13. A
14. C
15. B
16. C

Drill 2

1. B
2. D
3. 28
4. C
5. D
6. E
7. 3.4
8. B
9. C
10. D
11. B
12. 40
13. A
14. 29
15. B
16. D

EXPLANATIONS
Drill 1

1. **C** The side length of the square is the radius of the circle, so the area of the circle is $\pi r^2 = 4\pi$. Central angle *CDA* measures 90 degrees because *ABCD* is a square. 90 degrees represents $\frac{90}{360} = \frac{1}{4}$ of the circle, so the area of the shaded region will be $\frac{1}{4}$ of the area of the circle, π. The quantities are equal.

2. **60** The clock is a circle of 360 degrees, and the 12 numbers create 12 equal intervals around the clock. Therefore, each interval between two consecutive numbers must equal $\frac{1}{12}$ of 360 degrees and therefore be equal to 30 degrees. At 10:00, the two hands are two numbers apart, and create an angle of 60 degrees.

3. **B** The formula for the area of a circle is πr^2, where *r* is the radius of the circle. If you set this formula equal to the area of circle *C*, you get $\pi r^2 = 9\pi$. Dividing by π on both sides of the equation yields $r^2 = 9$, and taking the square root of both sides results in $r = 3$. The radius of circle *C* is 3, giving you (B) for the answer.

4. **D** All diameters in a circle are of equal length. Draw a horizontal diameter in the smallest circle; it must be 2 units long. This diameter is also the radius of the circle with center *B*, whose diameter must therefore be 4 units long. Draw this diameter horizontally, and you realize that it is also the radius of the circle with center *A*, whose area is $\pi r^2 = 16\pi$.

5. **B** The circumference of a circle with a diameter of 6 is $\pi d = 6\pi$. The circumference of a circle with a radius of 12 is $2\pi r = 24\pi$, so (B) is larger.

6. **C** For this problem, use the circle formulas—Area = πr^2 and Circumference = $2\pi r$—and do the problem one step at a time. For Quantity A, a circle with a circumference of 4π yields $4\pi = 2\pi r$, so $2r = 4$, and $r = 2$; thus, the area of the circle is $2^2\pi$, or 4π, and 4 times that is 16π. For Quantity B, a circle with an area of 64π yields $64\pi = \pi r^2$, so $r^2 = 64$, and $r = 8$; thus, the circumference of the circle is $2(8)\pi$, or 16π. The quantities are equal.

7. **5** First, determine the number of slices that will satisfy the question: there are 20 employees that need at least two slices each, so you need a total of at least 40 slices. Next, determine how many slices each pizza has: each slice has a central angle of 40° out of 360°, so each pizza has $\frac{360}{40} = 9$ slices. Since 4 pizzas would provide only 36 slices, you need one more pizza, so 5 is the correct response.

8. **B** If the diameter of the circle is 6, then the radius is 3. The area of a circle is πr^2, so the area of the circle is 9π. Since ABC is an equilateral triangle, the degree measure of the shaded area must be $60°$ and the shaded area must be therefore $\frac{1}{6}$ of the area of the whole circle. $\frac{1}{6}$ of 9π is $\frac{3\pi}{2}$.

9. **A** For Quantity A, the circumference of C is $2\pi r = 2\pi(6) = 12\pi$; the radius is 6. So, the ratio is $\frac{12\pi}{6} = 2\pi$. For Quantity B, half the diameter is the same as the radius, 6. Ballpark that 2π is a little more than 6, making Quantity A greater.

10. **A** Notice that chord AB goes through the center of the circle. Thus, AB is a diameter; a diameter is the longest chord in a circle. Chord CD does not go through the center of the circle, so AB must be longer than CD.

11. **A** To find the area outside the circle but inside the square, you will need to find the area of the square and subtract the area of the circle. Since the radius is 3, the diameter of the circle will be 6, which will also be the length of the side of the square. The area of the square is therefore 36. The area of the circle is $\pi r^2 = 9\pi$. So, the area in Quantity B is $36 - 9\pi$. Since π is a little bit more than 3, you will be subtracting more than 27 from 36, which will therefore be less than 9.

12. **C, D, F**

   Consider all the possible different integer pairs for the dimensions of the rectangle. You cannot try the integer pair of 1 and 9 or 5 and 5, because you know that $x < y$. If the rectangle has sides of 4 and 6, you can solve for the diagonal (equal to the circle's diameter) with the Pythagorean Theorem, which gives you $\sqrt{52}$ or $2\sqrt{13}$, (C). If the rectangle has sides of 3 and 7, the diagonal is $\sqrt{58}$, (D). If the rectangle has sides of 2 and 8, the diagonal is $\sqrt{68}$, or $2\sqrt{17}$, (F).

13. **A** Plug In for the height and radius of the cylinder. Try $r = 10$ and $h = 20$. In Quantity A, h becomes 22 and r becomes 9. Now, find the volume. $V = \pi r^2 h = \pi(9^2)(22) = 1{,}782\pi$. In Quantity B, h becomes 24 and r becomes 8, so $V = \pi r^2 h = \pi(8^2)(24) = 1{,}536\pi$. Quantity A is larger, so the answer is (A).

14. **C** Draw a fourth triangle and semicircle, and you can see that the figure shown represents $1\frac{1}{2}$ circles and $\frac{3}{4}$ of a square. Because the three diameters are perpendicular and congruent, they represent three sides of a square; the isosceles right triangles shown constitute three of the four triangles in the completed square. The area of a circle with diameter of 8 (and radius of 4) is $\pi r^2 = 16\pi$. $1\frac{1}{2}$ times this area is 24π. Eliminate (A), (D), and (E) because they do not contain 24π. The diameter of each semicircle is the length of the side of the square. The area of the entire square would be $s^2 = 8^2 = 64$. $\frac{3}{4}$ of this area is 48. Adding the two areas together gives you the expression in (C).

15. **B** Plug In a value for p. If $p = 8$, then the side of the square is 2 and the area is 4. If the circumference of the circle is 8, then the radius is $\dfrac{4}{\pi}$, and the area is $\dfrac{16}{\pi}$—approximately 5. Quantity B is larger. Plug in another value for p and you will find that Quantity B remains larger.

16. **C** Start by Plugging In a radius for the smaller circles; try $r = 2$. The circumference of each circle is $2\pi r = 4\pi$, and the sum of all three circumferences is 12π. Because the diameter of circle O is equal to the sum of the 3 shorter diameters, the diameter of circle O is $4 + 4 + 4 = 12$, its radius is 6, and its circumference is 12π, so the quantities are equal.

Drill 2

1. **B** For Quantity B, the side of the square is the same length as the diameter of the circle. The diameter is twice the radius, so the radius is 6. Plug this into the formula for area: $A = \pi r^2$ to find that $A = 36\pi$. Quantity B is greater.

2. **D** The diameter of the circle is 12, so the radius is 6, and the area is 36π. The total number of parts in the ratio is $3 + 4 + 5 = 12$, so each part covers an area of $\dfrac{36\pi}{12} = 3\pi$. The largest ratio part is 5 times this amount, or 15π.

3. **28** First, draw the circle inside a square. Because the square has an area of 36, each side is 6. This means that the diameter of the circle is 6 and the radius is 3. Using the circle area formula, the answer is 9π, which rounds down to 28.

4. **C** The four identical half-cylinders combined form two complete cylinders. Each of these cylinders has a diameter of 2 and a height of 6, equivalent to the width and height, respectively, of rectangle $FCDE$. Thus, the radius of each cylinder is 1, and the volume of each cylinder is $V = \pi r^2 h$, or $V = \pi(1^2)(6)$, which simplifies to 6π. The volume of the two complete cylinders, then, is 12π, and the answer is (C).

5. **D** Draw in either diagonal of the square, which also is the diameter of the circle. You have now created two isosceles right triangles, so the length of the diagonal/diameter is $4\sqrt{2}$, and the radius is $2\sqrt{2}$. The area of the circle is $\pi\left(2\sqrt{2}\right)^2 = 8\pi$.

6. **E** Plug In 4 for circle B's diameter; thus circle A's diameter is 32. The radius of B is 2, and the radius of A is 16; circle B has an area of 4π and circle A has an area of 256π. The ratio is $256\pi : 4\pi$, which reduces to $64 : 1$.

7. **3.4** First, draw and label the figure. Each of the triangles formed by the origin and the two vertices has legs of $2\sqrt{2}$ and $2\sqrt{2}$. Since each one is an isosceles right triangle—in other words, a 45-45-90 triangle—the sides are in the ratio $x : x : x\sqrt{2}$, and the long side of each is $2\sqrt{2} \times \sqrt{2} = 4$. The long side of a triangle is also the side of the square, so the area of the square is 16. Since the side of the square is the same as the diameter of the circle, the diameter is 4, the radius is 2, and the area of the circle is 4π. The area inside the square but outside the circle, then, is $16 - 4\pi$; use an approximation for π to get $16 - (4 \times 3.14) = 3.44$. Rounded to the nearest tenth, the answer is 3.4.

8. **B** A tangent to a circle forms a right angle with a radius drawn to the point of tangency. If CO is the hypotenuse of $\triangle OBC$, then you know that the legs of the right triangle must be shorter than 5. Since OB is the radius of the circle, you know that the radius of the circle must be less than 5, so the circumference must be less than 10π.

9. **C** Try Plugging In 5 for x. If circle A has an area of 9π, it has a radius of 3. Circle B then has an area of $9\pi \times 5 = 45\pi$. Circle C has an area of $45\pi \times 5 = 225\pi$, with a radius of 15. Therefore, the ratio of circle A's radius of 3 to circle C's radius of 15 is $1 : 5$ or $1 : x$. Alternatively, note that circle C's area is the area of circle A times x^2, making the ratio of the areas $1 : x^2$. The ratio of the radii should be the square root of this ratio, because area is πr^2, giving you the ratio $1 : x$. Both solution methods prove that the quantities are equal.

10. **D** The diameter of the larger circle, in inches, is 1, so the radius is $\frac{1}{2}$. Therefore, the area of the larger circle is $\pi\left(\frac{1}{2}\right)^2 = \frac{\pi}{4}$, and the area of the smaller circle is half this area, $\frac{\pi}{8}$. Setting this amount equal to the area formula allows you to determine the radius of the smaller circle: $\pi r^2 = \frac{\pi}{8}; r = \frac{\sqrt{2}}{4}$. Therefore, the diameter is $\frac{\sqrt{2}}{2}$. Subtract this amount from 1 (the diameter of the larger circle): $1 - \frac{\sqrt{2}}{2} = \frac{2 - \sqrt{2}}{2}$.

11. **B** Plug in a value for the radius of the circle, say $r = 2$, making the diameter 4; $\overline{AD}$ and $\overline{BC}$ are both diameters of the circle, so Quantity A is 8. The circumference of the circle is $4\pi \approx 12$, so Quantity B is greater.

12. **40** Draw and label the figures, and then set up your scratch paper to Plug In. If circle O has a radius of 6, then it has an area of $\pi r^2 = 36\pi$; circle M, then, has a radius of 2 and an area of 4π. If sector $OABC$ has an area of 4π out of a total area of 36π, then the sector takes up $\frac{4\pi}{36\pi} = \frac{1}{9}$ of the entire circle, and the measure of $\angle AOC$ is equal to $\frac{1}{9}$ of 360°. The correct answer is thus $\frac{1}{9} \times 360 = 40$.

13. **A** Note that *AD* must be a diameter because it is the longest possible line segment crossing the circle. *OB* and *OA* (draw it in) are both radii, and therefore equal in length (3), and both of them are equal to *AB*. Therefore, triangle *ABO* is equilateral, and the measure of ∠*AOB* is 60°. The central angle for sector *OBCD* is 120° (the supplement to 60°), making this sector's area $\frac{1}{3}$ the area of the circle: $\frac{1}{3}3^2\pi = 3\pi$. Because π is slightly greater than 3, 3π is slightly greater than 9, giving you (A) for the answer.

14. **29** Draw a rough sketch of the wall, the circles, and the spaces. Notice that you need to include a space of *x* inches after every circle, plus add one space of *x* inches at the beginning before the first circle, so that the number of spaces of length *x* inches is one more than the number of circles. Since the area of each circle is 36π, the radius of each circle is 6 inches, and the diameter of each circle is 12 inches. Convert the length of the wall into inches: 31 × 12 = 372 inches, plus the extra 6 inches equals 378 inches. You know that the wall is covered in a certain number of circles plus a number of spaces equal to one more than the number of circles. If *n* represents the number of circles, then the distance covered by the circles can be represented as 12*n*, and the distance covered by the spaces can be represented as *x*(*n* + 1). So, the total length can be represented by 12*n* + *x*(*n* + 1) = 378. Since the question tells us that *x* must be an integer, and that you need the greatest possible number of circles, you need the smallest possible integer value of *x* that works. Rather than trying to simplify this equation algebraically, simply Plug In values for *x* to see if they work. If *x* = 0, then 12*n* = 378, and 378 divided by 12 is not an integer; since the number of circles must have an integer value, *x* cannot equal 0. If *x* = 1, then the equation becomes 12*n* + *n* + 1 = 378, and 13*n* = 377, leading to *n* = 29, and therefore 1 is the smallest possible value of *x* that works with the problem, and 29 is the greatest number of circles the designer can use.

15. **B** To solve this one, Plug In for *r* and *m*: try *r* = 2 and *m* = 4. If $\frac{1}{2}$ of the pizza has been eaten, and the remaining $\frac{1}{2}$ is divided into 4 equal slices, then each of those remaining pieces is $\frac{1}{8}$ of the whole pizza. Now Plug In 2 for *r* and 4 for *m* in the answer choices; only (B) hits your target answer of $\frac{1}{8}$.

16. **D** The original slice is cut from a pizza with a diameter of 10, and therefore a circumference of 10π. This slice represents $\frac{1.25\pi}{10\pi} = \frac{1}{8}$ of the circumference and therefore $\frac{1}{8}$ of the area, $\frac{25\pi}{8}$, which weighs 4 ounces. A serving weighs 8 ounces, which covers double the area, $\frac{25\pi}{4}$. The area of the six pizzas is $(6)\pi 3^2 = 54\pi$. Dividing this by the area of one serving gives you the total number of servings that the six pizzas represent: $\frac{54\pi}{\left(\frac{25\pi}{4}\right)} = 8\frac{16}{25} = 8.64$. The six pizzas yield 8 servings.

Quadrilaterals and
Polygons

QUADRILATERALS AND POLYGONS

Questions involving quadrilaterals and polygons are not very common on the GRE. Most problems that do involve quadrilaterals ask about the degree measurements of the angles in the quadrilateral, the perimeter of the quadrilateral, or the area of the quadrilateral. Most questions that involve polygons ask about the degree measurements of the angles in the polygon.

QUADRILATERALS

Quadrilaterals are four-sided figures and include rectangles, squares, and parallelograms. The degree measurements of the four angles inside any quadrilateral add up to 360°. This means that if the degree measurements of three angles are known, the degree measurement of the fourth can always be found.

Rectangles

A rectangle is a quadrilateral constructed from two sets of equal, parallel lines that are perpendicular to each other. This information will be noted on the figure or in the question. However, never assume an angle is 90° unless you're told it is or you can prove it. A diagonal line drawn between two opposite corners of a rectangle splits the rectangle into two right triangles.

The perimeter of a rectangle is just the sum of the lengths of its four sides. Given that a rectangle has sides of length l and width w, the formula for the perimeter of a rectangle is $P = 2l + 2w$, and the formula for the area of a rectangle is $A = lw$.

Squares

A square is a rectangle with four equal sides. The diagonal of a square splits it into two 45° : 45° : 90°, or isosceles, triangles.

The perimeter of a square is the sum of the lengths of its four sides. Given that a square has sides of length s, the formula for the perimeter of a square is $P = 4s$, and the formula for the area of a square is $A = s^2$.

Parallelograms

A parallelogram is a quadrilateral constructed from two sets of equal, parallel lines. Therefore, there are also two sets of equal angles. The perimeter of a parallelogram is just the sum of the lengths of its four sides.

The height of a parallelogram is a line drawn perpendicular from one side of the parallelogram to the opposite, parallel side. This line is not necessarily shown on any given figure and you likely need to draw it for parallelogram problems. The base of a parallelogram is the side of the parallelogram perpendicular to the height. Given that a parallelogram has base b and height h, the formula for the area of a parallelogram is $A = bh$.

Trapezoids

A trapezoid is a quadrilateral constructed from one set of unequal parallel lines. The perimeter of a trapezoid is just the sum of the lengths of its four sides.

The parallel sides of a trapezoid are called the bases. The height of a trapezoid is a line drawn perpendicular to the bases. Much like the height of a parallelogram, the height of a trapezoid is not necessarily shown on any given figure and you likely need to draw it for trapezoid problems. The area of a trapezoid is equal to the average of the bases multiplied by the height. Thus, given that a trapezoid has bases b_1 and b_2 and height h, the formula for the area of a trapezoid is $A = \frac{1}{2}(b_1 + b_2)h$.

POLYGONS

A polygon is a figure with any number of sides. While triangles and quadrilaterals are polygons, with their own sets of special rules, the GRE tests only two rules for polygons of five or more sides. First, a regular polygon has sides of equal lengths and equal angles. Second, the sum of the degree measurements of the angles in an n-sided polygon is found by $180(n - 2)$. For example, the degree measurements of the angles of a hexagon ($n = 6$) is $180(6 - 2) = 180(4) = 720°$.

THE BASIC APPROACH

The five-step approach to geometry problems applies to quadrilaterals and polygons.

Step 1: Draw the figure on your scratch paper

In some cases, the GRE provides a shape, which you may or may not be able to trust, or a word problem that leaves it up to you to envision the shape. As with every other part of the test, getting your hand moving is an important first step to entering the problem. Draw the shape on your scratch paper so that you can begin working with it there. On Quant Comp questions involving geometry, instead of Plugging In more than once, you may have to draw your shape more than once.

Step 2: Label any information from the problem on the figure

Whether you are given the shape or not, you will be given a certain amount of information regarding the shape, such as the measure of some angles, lengths of some sides, or volume. Write down any information provided to you about the figure on the figure itself, on its appropriate place on the figure.

Step 3: Write down any formulas you need

Writing down the formula is a way to organize your information and give you a hint as to what information is missing that is needed to solve the problem. When you write formulas down, fill in the information you have directly underneath the relevant part of the formula. It seems simple but writing down formulas makes it easier to avoid mistakes and find the missing pieces of information. By writing down the formulas, solving geometry problems sometimes becomes as simple as solving for a missing variable.

For more practice with The Princeton Review's math techniques, check out our student-friendly guidebook, *Cracking the GRE*.

DRILL 1

Question 1

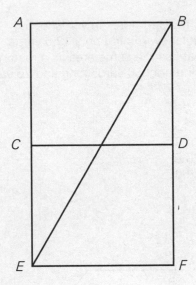

In the figure above, squares *ABCD* and *CDEF* have sides of length 7.

Quantity A	Quantity B
49	The area of triangle *ABE*

○ Quantity A is greater.
○ Quantity B is greater.
○ The two quantities are equal.
○ The relationship cannot be determined from the information given.

Question 2

A certain rectangle that is divided into two squares has an area of 128.

Quantity A	Quantity B
8	The length of the side of one of the squares

○ Quantity A is greater.
○ Quantity B is greater.
○ The two quantities are equal.
○ The relationship cannot be determined from the information given.

Question 3

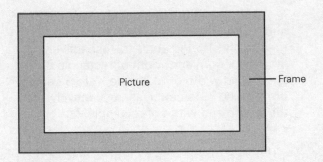

The figure above represents a rectangular picture with a frame around it. The picture is 12 inches long and 6 inches high. The frame is uniformly 2 inches wide, and its edges meet at right angles. What is the area of the frame, in square inches?

○ 40
○ 72
○ 88
○ 112
○ 160

Question 4

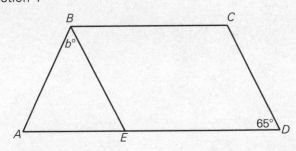

BCDE is a parallelogram and *AB = BE*.

Quantity A	Quantity B
65	*b*

○ Quantity A is greater.
○ Quantity B is greater.
○ The two quantities are equal.
○ The relationship cannot be determined from the information given.

Question 5

X, Y, and Z are three rectangles. The length and width of rectangle X are 15 percent greater and 15 percent less, respectively, than the length and width of rectangle Z. The length and width of rectangle Y are 5 percent greater and 5 percent less, respectively, than the length and width of rectangle Z.

Quantity A	Quantity B
The area of rectangle X	The area of rectangle Y

○   Quantity A is greater.
○   Quantity B is greater.
○   The two quantities are equal.
○   The relationship cannot be determined from the information given.

Question 6

If the perimeter of a rectangle is 44 and its area is 112, what is the length of each of the longer sides?

○   18
○   14
○   10
○   8
○   6

Question 7

What is the perimeter, in yards, of a rectangular swimming pool 12.5 yards wide that has the same area as a rectangular swimming pool 50 yards long and 25 yards wide?

○   75
○   113
○   150
○   225
○   1,250

Question 8

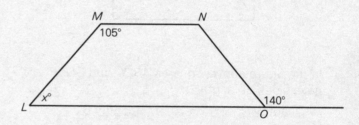

LMNO is a trapezoid.

Quantity A	Quantity B
x	40

○   Quantity A is greater.
○   Quantity B is greater.
○   The two quantities are equal.
○   The relationship cannot be determined from the information given.

Question 9

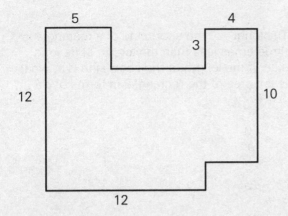

If all lines meet at right angles, what is the area of the region shown above?

Question 10

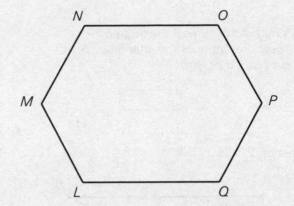

In the figure above, *LMNOPQ* is a regular hexagon. If *OP* = 4, then what is the length of *MP* ?

○ $2\sqrt{3}$
○   4
○ $4\sqrt{2}$
○ $4\sqrt{3}$
○   8

DRILL 2

Question 1

What is the sum of the degree measurements of the interior angles of a 12-sided polygon?

Question 2

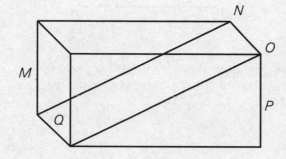

In the rectangular solid above, $MQ = 3$, $PQ = 12$, and $OP = 5$. What is the area of rectangle $MNOQ$?

Question 3

The length of the short side of a rectangle is three times less than the length of its long side. If the length of the short side is a, what is the area of the rectangle, in terms of a ?

- ○ $\dfrac{a^2}{9}$
- ○ $\dfrac{a^2}{3}$
- ○ $3a$
- ○ a^2
- ○ $3a^2$

Question 4

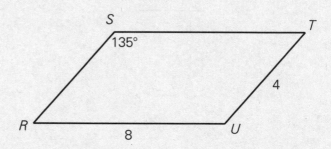

In the figure above, $RSTU$ is a parallelogram.

Quantity A	Quantity B
32	The area of parallelogram $RSTU$

- ○ Quantity A is greater.
- ○ Quantity B is greater.
- ○ The two quantities are equal.
- ○ The relationship cannot be determined from the information given.

Question 5

What is the degree measurement of each interior angle in a regular hexagon?

$$\boxed{}$$

Question 6

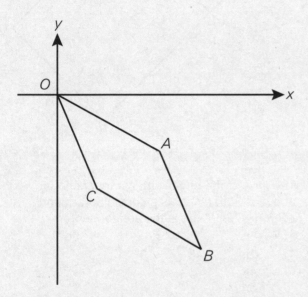

Parallelogram *ABCO* lies in the *xy*-plane, as shown in the figure above. The coordinates of point *A* are (7, −5) and the coordinates of point *B* are (10, −12). What are the coordinates of point *C* ?

- ○ (2, −6)
- ○ (3, −7)
- ○ (3, −17)
- ○ (4, −7)
- ○ (5, −17)

Question 7

If a circle with an area of 12π is inscribed in a rectangle, what is the area of the rectangle?

- ○ $2\sqrt{3}$
- ○ 12
- ○ 36
- ○ 48
- ○ 144

Question 8

What is the length of a diagonal of a rectangle that has length 4 and perimeter 14 ?

$$\boxed{}$$

Question 9

Rectangle *R* has a perimeter of 12.

Quantity A	Quantity B
The area of rectangle *R*	10

○ Quantity A is greater.
○ Quantity B is greater.
○ The two quantities are equal.
○ The relationship cannot be determined
    from the information given.

Question 10

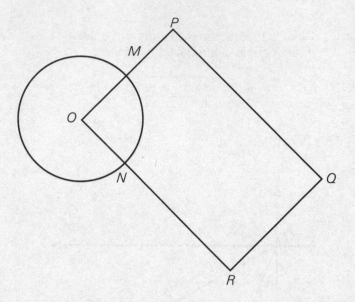

The area of the circle with center *O* shown above is 20π. *OPQR* is a parallelogram and ∠*OPQ* = 72°. What is the area of sector *MNO* ?

○ 2π
○ 4π
○ 5π
○ 6π
○ 10π

ANSWERS

Drill 1

1. C
2. C
3. C
4. A
5. B
6. B
7. D
8. A
9. 163
10. E

Drill 2

1. 1,800
2. 39
3. E
4. A
5. 120
6. B
7. D
8. 5
9. B
10. D

EXPLANATIONS

Drill 1

1. **C** This question provides a figure, so draw the shape. The question stem states that squares *ABCD* and *CDEF* have sides of length 7, so *AB*, *CD*, and *EF* are 7, and *AE* and *BF* are 14. The question asks for the area of triangle *ABE*. The formula for the area of a triangle is $A = \frac{1}{2}bh$. *AB* is the base of the triangle and *AE* is the height. Thus, the area of triangle *ABE* is $A = \frac{1}{2} \times 7 \times 14 = 49$. The correct answer is (C).

2. **C** The question describes a figure, so draw the shape, a rectangle constructed from two squares. Since this is a Quant Comp problem with an unknown in one quantity and an actual value in the other, PITA. Plug In the 8 from Quantity A as the side of each square. The formula for the area of a square is $A = s^2$, so each square has an area of $A = 8^2 = 64$ and the rectangle has an area of $2 \times 64 = 128$, which matches the information in the question stem. The two quantities are equal, so eliminate (A) and (B). Now, Plug In again using FROZEN keeping in mind the restriction of the question that the area of the rectangle is 128. Try to determine whether there is any other value for the side of each square that yields the same area for the rectangle. Each square is half of the rectangle, which means that each square has an area of 64. Thus, no side length other than 8 is possible for the squares, so (C) is correct.

3. **C** This question provides a figure, so draw the shape. The question asks about the area of a shaded region, so use the formula *Shaded Area = Total Area – Unshaded Area*. The total area is the area of the frame and picture together. Since the picture is 12 inches long and the frame is 2 inches on the left side and 2 inches on the right side, the total length of the frame is 12 + 2 + 2 = 16 inches. Likewise, the picture is 6 inches tall and the frame is 2 inches on the top and 2 inches on the bottom, so the total height of the frame is 6 + 2 + 2 = 10 inches. The total area is the area of a rectangle, and the formula for the area of a rectangle is $A = lw$. Therefore, the total area is $A = 16 \times 10 = 160$ square inches.

    The unshaded area is a rectangle with a length of 12 inches and a height of 6 inches, so the unshaded area is $A = 12 \times 6 = 72$ square inches. The area of the frame is *Shaded Area* = 160 – 72 = 88 square inches. The correct answer is (C).

4. **A** The question asks about the relationship between angles in a parallelogram. The opposite angles of a parallelogram are equal, so $\angle CDE = \angle CBE = 65°$. The sum of the angles of any quadrilateral is 360°, so the sum of the degree measurements of the other two angles is 360 – 65 – 65 = 230°. The other two angles are equal because they are opposite angles of a parallelogram, so $\angle BED = \angle BCD$ = 230 ÷ 2 = 115°. $\angle AEB$ and $\angle BED$ form a straight line, so the sum of their degree measurements

is 180° and $\angle AEB = 180 - 115 = 65°$. Since $AB = BE$, triangle ABE is an isosceles triangle and $\angle AEB = \angle BAE = 65°$. The sum of the degree measurements of these two angles is 130°. Because the sum of the degree measurements of the angles of a triangle is 180°, $\angle ABE = 180 - 130 = 50°$ and $b = 50$. Quantity A is greater, so the correct answer is (A).

5. **B** The question asks about percentages and does not give a starting number, so this is a Hidden Plug In question. Since both rectangles X and Y are compared to rectangle Z, Plug In 100 for the length and width of rectangle Z. Then, the length and width of rectangle X are 115 and 85, respectively, and the length and width of rectangle Y are 105 and 95, respectively. Since the question asks about the area of rectangles X and Y, use the formula for the area of a rectangle: $A = lw$. The area of rectangle X is $A = 115 \times 85 = 9,775$, and the area of rectangle Y is $A = 105 \times 95 = 9,975$. The area of rectangle Y is greater, so the correct answer is (B).

6. **B** The answer choices represent the information directly asked for by the question, and the question could be solved by writing and solving equations, so Plug in the Answers. The answer choices represent the length of the longer sides of a rectangle with a perimeter of 44 and area 112. Start with (C), 10.

The formula for the perimeter of a rectangle is $P = 2l + 2w$. If $l = 10$, then the perimeter is $44 = 2 \times 10 + 2w$, or $44 = 20 + 2w$. Subtract 20 from each side of the equation to yield $24 = 2w$. Divide each side of the equation by 2 to yield $w = 24 \div 2 = 12$. This yields a width greater than the length, so eliminate choice (C), as well as (D) and (E), as these answer choices will also yield a width greater than the length. Try (B).

If $l = 14$, then the perimeter is $44 = 2 \times 14 + 2w$, or $44 = 28 + 2w$. Subtract 28 from each side of the equation to yield $16 = 2w$. Divide each side of the equation by 2 to yield $w = 16 \div 2 = 8$. The formula for the area of a rectangle is $A = lw$, so the area of the rectangle is $A = 14 \times 8 = 112$. This matches the condition in the question, so the correct answer is (B).

7. **D** The question provides the area of a rectangle, so use the formula $A = lw$ for the area of a rectangle. The area of the 50-yard by 25-yard pool is $A = 50 \times 25 = 1,250$ square yards. Since the 12.5-yard-wide pool has the same area, $1,250 = l \times 12.5$. Divide each side of the equation by 12.5 to yield $l = 1,250 \div 12.5 = 100$ yards. The perimeter of a rectangle is found by the formula $P = 2l + 2w$, or $P = 2 \times 100 + 2 \times 12.5 = 200 + 25 = 225$ yards. The correct answer is (D).

8. **A** The question provides a figure, so draw the shape. A trapezoid is constructed from one set of parallel lines. In trapezoid $LMNO$, MN and LO are parallel. LM is a line that intersects two parallel lines, forming big angles and small angles. $\angle LMN$ is a big angle and $\angle MLO$ is a small angle. The sum of the degree measurements of a big angle and a small angle is 180°, so $x = 180 - 105 = 75°$. Quantity A is greater, and the answer is (A).

9. **163** The question provides a figure, so draw and label the shape. Draw a line down from the vertical line with length 3 in the upper right of the figure, forming a rectangle to the right of the line with length 4 and width 10. The formula for the area of a rectangle is $A = lw$, so the area of that

rectangle is $A = 4 \times 10 = 40$. To the left of the added line is a 12 by 12 square with a rectangular area missing from it. The formula for the area of a square is $A = s^2$, so the area of the whole square is $A = 12^2 = 144$. The width of the missing rectangle is 3. The length of the missing rectangle plus the horizontal line with length 5 in the upper left of the figure is equal to the side of the square, so the length of the missing rectangle is $12 - 5 = 7$. The area of the missing rectangle is thus $A = 7 \times 3 = 21$. Therefore, the area of the shape to the left of the added line is the area of the whole square minus the area of the missing rectangle, or $144 - 21 = 123$. Add the area of this shape to the area of the rectangle to the right of the added line to yield that the total area is $123 + 40 = 163$.

10. **E** The question provides a figure, so draw the shape. A regular hexagon has sides of equal length and interior angles of equal degree measurement. The sum of the degree measurements of the angles in a polygon with n sides is $180(n - 2)$, so the sum of the degree measurements of the angles in a hexagon is $180(6 - 2) = 180 \times 4 = 720°$. Each angle is thus $720 \div 6 = 120°$. The line MP bisects the interior angles LMN and OPQ, so $\angle LMP = \angle PML = 120 \div 2 = 60°$. Draw the lines LO and NQ, creating six triangles, each with a base equal to one side of the hexagon. The triangle with base LM has two angles of 60°, $\angle LMP$ and $\angle OLM$. Since the sum of the degree measurements of the angles in a triangle is 180°, the third angle of the triangle with base LM is $180 - 60 - 60 = 60°$, and the triangle is equilateral. $LM = OP$, so each side of the triangle is 4. All six triangles formed by the sides of the hexagon and lines LO, MP, and NQ are thus equilateral triangles with sides of 4. MP is the length of two sides of the triangles, so $MP = 2 \times 4 = 8$. The correct answer is (E).

Drill 2

1. **1,800** The question asks about the sum of the degree measurements of the interior angles of a polygon, which is given by $180(n - 2)$ where n is the number of sides of the polygon. Since the question states that the polygon has 12 sides, the sum of the degree measurements of the interior angles is $180(12 - 2) = 180 \times 10 = 1,800°$. The correct answer is 1,800.

2. **39** This question provides a figure, so draw the shape and label the known sides. So, $MQ = 3$, $PQ = 12$, and $OP = 5$. The question asks about the area of a rectangle, which is found from the formula $A = lw$. OQ is the length of rectangle $MNOQ$ and MQ is the width. OQ is the hypotenuse of right triangle OPQ, with legs of 5 and 12. The hypotenuse of a right triangle with legs of 5 and 12 is 13 since 5-12-13 is a Pythagorean triple. Rectangle $MNOQ$ thus has length 13 and width 3, so the area is $A = 13 \times 3 = 39$. The correct answer is 39.

3. **E** There are variables in the question and answer choices, so Plug In a value for a, such as $a = 2$. If $a = 2$, then the long side is three times greater, or $3 \times 2 = 6$. The formula for the area of a rectangle is $A = lw$, or $A = 2 \times 6 = 12$. Plug In $a = 2$ to the answer choices, looking for one that is equal to 12. Choice (A) is $\frac{2^2}{9} = \frac{4}{9}$, so eliminate (A). Choice (B) is $\frac{2^2}{3} = \frac{4}{3}$, so eliminate (B). Choice (C) is

$3 \times 2 = 6$, so eliminate (C). Choice (D) is $2^2 = 4$, so eliminate (D). Choice (E) is $3 \times 2^2 = 3 \times 4 = 12$, so keep (E). The correct answer is (E).

4. **A** The question provides a figure, so draw the shape. The question stem is about the area of a parallelogram, the formula for which is $A = bh$. The base of the parallelogram is 8 and the height is a line drawn perpendicular to the base. Draw the height from point U to create a right triangle with vertices at T and U. The hypotenuse of this triangle is 4 and the height is one of the legs. Since the length of a leg of a right triangle is always less than the length of the hypotenuse of a right triangle, the height of the parallelogram is less than 4. Therefore, the area of the parallelogram is less than $A = 8 \times 4 = 32$. The correct answer is (A).

5. **120** The question asks about the interior angles of a polygon. The sum of the degree measurements of the angles in a polygon of n sides is $180(n - 2)$. A hexagon has 6 sides, so $n = 6$ and the sum of the degree measurements of the angles is $180(6 - 2) = 180 \times 4 = 720°$. Each angle is equal in a regular polygon, so each angle of a hexagon is $720 \div 6 = 120°$. The correct answer is 120°.

6. **B** The question provides a figure, so draw the shape and label the points. Label A (7, –5) and B (10, –12). A parallelogram is constructed from two sets of parallel lines, so CO is parallel to AB. Parallel lines have the same slope, and the formula for slope is $Slope = \dfrac{y_2 - y_1}{x_2 - x_1}$. If A is the first point and B is the second point, the slope of AB is $Slope = \dfrac{-12 - (-5)}{10 - 7} = \dfrac{-12 + 5}{3} = \dfrac{-7}{3}$. The slope of CO is also $\dfrac{-7}{3}$ and point O is the origin, which has coordinates (0, 0). Thus, if C has coordinates of (x, y), the coordinates can be found from the slope equation, or $\dfrac{-7}{3} = \dfrac{y - 0}{x - 0} = \dfrac{y}{x}$.

The coordinates of point C are then (3, –7), and the correct answer is (B).

7. **D** The answer choices represent the information directly asked for by the question, and the question could be solved by writing and solving equations, so Plug in the Answers. The answer choices represent the area of a rectangle with a circle inscribed in it. In order for the circle to be inscribed in a rectangle, the rectangle has to be a square. Start with (C), an area of 36.

The formula for the area of the square is $A = s^2$. If the area is 36, then $36 = s^2$. Take the square root of each side of the equation to yield $s = 6$. The side of the square is equal to the diameter of the inscribed circle, so the radius of the circle is $6 \div 2 = 3$. The formula for the area of a circle is $A = \pi r^2$, so the area of the circle is $A = \pi(3)^2 = 9\pi$. This is less than the 12π area specified by the question, so eliminate (C), as well as (A) and (B), as these answer choices make the area even less. Try (D).

If the area of the square is 48, then $48 = s^2$. Take the square root of each side of the equation to yield $s = \sqrt{48} = \sqrt{16 \times 3} = 4\sqrt{3}$. Since the side of the square is equal to the diameter of the inscribed circle, the radius of the circle is $4\sqrt{3} \div 2 = 2\sqrt{3}$. The area of the circle is thus $A = \pi\left(2\sqrt{3}\right)^2 = \pi \times 4 \times 3 = 12\pi$, which matches the condition in the question. The correct answer is (D).

8. **5** The question describes a figure, so draw and label the shape. Draw a rectangle and the diagonal of the rectangle, and label one side 4. The question provides a perimeter, and the formula for the perimeter of a rectangle is $P = 2l + 2w$. Since the length of the rectangle is 4 and the perimeter is 14, $14 = 2 \times 4 + 2w$, or $14 = 8 + 2w$. Subtract 8 from each side of the equation to yield $6 = 2w$. Divide each side of the equation by 2 to find that the width of the rectangle is $w = 6 \div 2 = 3$. The diagonal of the rectangle is the hypotenuse of a right triangle with legs equal to the length and width of the rectangle. Since the length and width of the rectangle are 4 and 3, respectively, the legs of the right triangle are also 4 and 3. The hypotenuse of the triangle is 5, because 3-4-5 is a Pythagorean triple. The hypotenuse of the right triangle is also the diagonal of the rectangle, so the correct answer is 5.

9. **B** This question is a Quant Comp with an unknown value, so Plug In more than once. A square is a type of rectangle, so begin by determining the sides if rectangle R is a square. The formula for the perimeter of a square is $P = 4s$, so $12 = 4s$. Divide each side of the equation by 4 to yield that the sides of the square are $s = 12 \div 4 = 3$. The area of a square is found by the formula $A = s^2$, so the area of the square is $A = 3^2 = 9$. Quantity B is greater than Quantity A, so eliminate (A) and (C). Next, Plug In values for the sides that would make them as different as possible from a square, such as sides of 1 and 5. The perimeter of a rectangle is found by the formula $P = 2l + 2w$, so the perimeter of the rectangle is $P = 2 \times 1 + 2 \times 5 = 2 + 10 = 12$, which matches the condition in the question stem. The formula for the area of a rectangle is $A = lw$, so the area of the rectangle is $A = 1 \times 5 = 5$. Quantity B is still greater than Quantity A, and making the rectangle not a square reduced the area, so the greatest area is 9. The correct answer is (B).

10. **D** The question provides a figure, so draw the shape and label $\angle OPQ$ as 72°. The angles opposite one another in a parallelogram are equal, so label $\angle ORQ$ as 72°. The sum of the angles in a parallelogram is 360°, so the sum of the remaining two angles in the parallelogram, $\angle POR$ and $\angle PQR$, is $360 - 72 - 72 = 216°$. Since these two angles are opposite one another in the parallelogram, they have equal angle measurements of $216 \div 2 = 108°$. $\angle POR$ is the central angle of sector MNO. Since the question asks about the area of a sector, use the equation $\dfrac{area\ sector}{area\ circle} = \dfrac{angle}{360°}$, or $\dfrac{area\ sector}{20\pi} = \dfrac{108°}{360°}$. Divide the numerator and denominator of the right side of the equation by 36 to yield $\dfrac{area\ sector}{20\pi} = \dfrac{3}{10}$. Multiply each side of the equation by 20π to yield $area\ sector = 20\pi \times \dfrac{3}{10} = 6\pi$. The correct answer is (D).

3-D Figures

3-D FIGURES

Three-dimensional figures on the GRE involve the same fundamental geometry that you will see elsewhere on the test. They just offer ETS new ways to combine the usual circles, triangles, and quadrilaterals. The five-step approach remains the same.

Step 1: Draw your shape

In some cases the test will give you a shape, which you may or may not be able to trust, and in others it will give you a word problem and leave it up to you to envision the shape. As with every other part of the test, getting your hand moving is an important first step to entering the problem. Get your shape down on your scratch paper so that you can begin working with it there. On Quantitative Comparison questions involving geometry, instead of Plugging In more than once, you may have to draw your shape more than once.

Step 2: Fill in what you know

Whether you are given the shape or not, you will be given a certain amount of information regarding your shape such as the measure of some angles, lengths of some sides, or volume. Put that information in the figure.

Step 3: Make deductions

If you are given two angles of a triangle, find the third. If you are given the radius of a circle, find the area. Often this will be the entire problem. Geometry on the GRE is all about finding the missing piece of information. You will be given just enough information to find the piece that is missing.

Step 4: Write down relevant formulas

If step three didn't get you the answer, you must still be missing a piece of information. Writing down the formula is a way of both organizing your information and telling you what is missing. When you write your formulas down, fill in the information you have directly underneath the relevant part of the formula. It seems simple, but this way you can't make a mistake. Finding the missing piece of information becomes a simple case of solving for x.

Step 5: Drop heights/draw lines

If you're still stuck, you may need to manipulate or subdivide your shapes. If you have triangles, draw in the height. Have you created a 30-60-90? A 45-45-90? Or a Pythagorean triple? Try subdividing the shape or, if it's a three dimensional figure, dashing in the hidden lines.

FORMULAS

There are only three formulas that you need to know for three-dimensional figures. The volume of a rectangular solid is length times width times height. Remember that it has six sides should you need to know how to find the surface area. The formula for a right cylinder is easy to remember. Just take the area of the circle and multiply it by the height, pi times radius squared times height. You might occasionally need to know the super Pythagorean Theorem, which is $a^2 \times b^2 \times c^2 = d^2$. This is used to find the diagonal distance between the farthest two vertices of a rectangular solid, but check to see if there is a Pythagorean triple involved before you end up calculating large numbers.

Pythagorean triples show up just as frequently on three-dimensional solids as they do on triangle questions.

For more practice and a more in-depth look at The Princeton Review math techniques, check out our student-friendly guidebook, *Cracking the GRE*.

DRILL 1

Question 1

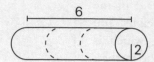

A right circular cylinder with a radius of 2 feet and a length of 6 feet is cut into three pieces of equal length. What is the volume, in cubic feet, of each of the three pieces?

- ○ 2π
- ○ 3π
- ○ 8π
- ○ 12π
- ○ 24π

Question 2

Quantity A	Quantity B
Three times the total surface area of a cube with edge length of 1 centimeter	The total surface area of a cube with edge length of 3 centimeters

- ○ Quantity A is greater.
- ○ Quantity B is greater.
- ○ The two quantities are equal.
- ○ The relationship cannot be determined from the information given.

Question 3

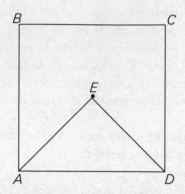

E is the center of square $ABCD$.

$$AB = 8$$

Quantity A	Quantity B
AE	4

- ○ Quantity A is greater.
- ○ Quantity B is greater.
- ○ The two quantities are equal.
- ○ The relationship cannot be determined from the information given.

Question 4

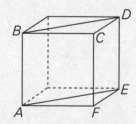

Each edge of the cube shown above has length n. What is the perimeter, in terms of n, of quadrilateral $ABDE$?

- ○ $2n(1 + \sqrt{2})$
- ○ $n\sqrt{2}$
- ○ $4n\sqrt{2}$
- ○ $4n$
- ○ $2n^2$

Question 5

ABCG and CDEF are squares with the same area that touch at point C. ∠BCD is a right angle.

Quantity A	Quantity B
3 times the length of AB	The length of AE

- ○ Quantity A is greater.
- ○ Quantity B is greater.
- ○ The two quantities are equal.
- ○ The relationship cannot be determined from the information given.

Question 6

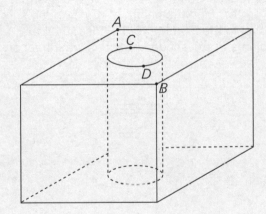

The figure above is a cube with edges of length 9. Points C and D lie on diagonal AB such that points A, C, D, and B are equally spaced. As shown, a right circular cylindrical hole is cut out of the cube so that segment CD is a diameter of the top of the hole. What is the volume of the resulting figure?

- ○ 729 − 162
- ○ $729 - \dfrac{81\pi}{2}$
- ○ 729 − 81π
- ○ 729 − 9π
- ○ 729

Question 7

What is the total surface area of a cube with a volume of 512 ?

- ○ 384
- ○ 320
- ○ 256
- ○ 152
- ○ 48

Question 8

The total surface area of a cube is 54.

Quantity A	Quantity B
The length of a diagonal of one face of the cube	3

- ○ Quantity A is greater.
- ○ Quantity B is greater.
- ○ The two quantities are equal.
- ○ The relationship cannot be determined from the information given.

Question 9

Cube C has an edge of 4 and cube D has an edge of 5.

Quantity A	Quantity B
The ratio of cube C's total surface area to its volume	The ratio of cube D's total surface area to its volume

- ○ Quantity A is greater.
- ○ Quantity B is greater.
- ○ The two quantities are equal.
- ○ The relationship cannot be determined from the information given.

Question 10

A certain building is a rectangular solid with a square base of side length of 25 meters and a volume of 13,000 cubic meters. What is the volume, in cubic meters, of a building that has a square base with a side of 75 meters and the same height as the other building?

- ○ 1,444.4
- ○ 4,333.3
- ○ 39,000
- ○ 117,000
- ○ 351,000

Question 11

Marty has a right circular cylindrical pool of diameter 12 feet and his neighbor, Rusty, has a right circular cylindrical pool of diameter 18 feet. If the depths of the pools are equal, then the volume of water in Rusty's pool is how many times that in Marty's pool?

- ○ 1.5
- ○ 2.25
- ○ 2.5
- ○ 4
- ○ 4.25

Question 12

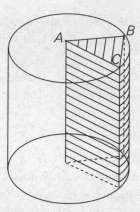

A is the center of the top face of the right circular cylinder in the figure above. If the degree measure of $\angle BAC$ is four times that of $\angle ACB$, and the height of the cylinder is equal to the diameter of its base, then the volume of the shaded region is what fraction of the volume of the entire cylinder?

Question 13

Jack is storing a rectangular box inside a cylindrical container. The container has a volume of 980π cubic inches and a height of 20 inches. Which of the following dimensions could the box have in order to fit inside the cylinder?

Indicate all such values.

- ☐ 3 inches by 6 inches by 12 inches
- ☐ 6 inches by 9 inches by 15 inches
- ☐ 10 inches by 10 inches by 10 inches
- ☐ 8 inches by 9 inches by 16 inches
- ☐ 11 inches by 15 inches by 18 inches
- ☐ 9 inches by 9 inches by 20 inches

DRILL 2

Question 1

The Pranger Metal Company makes solid cylindrical steel rods by melting down blocks of steel and pouring the melted steel into molds. Each cylindrical rod has a diameter of 14 inches and a height of 8 inches, and the dimensions of each steel block are 2 feet by 12 feet by 15 feet. If no steel is lost in the production process, how many complete cylinders can be made from a single block of steel?

Question 2

What is the surface area of a right rectangular cylinder with a radius of r and a height that is 1.5 times its diameter?

- ○ $6\pi r^2 + 4\pi r$
- ○ $7\pi r^2$
- ○ $8\pi r^2$
- ○ $3\pi r^3 + 2\pi r^2$
- ○ $3\pi r^3 + 4\pi r$

Question 3

If the volume of a cube equals 64, what is the surface area of the cube?

Question 4

The diagonal of the face of a cube is less than $10\sqrt{2}$ cm. Which of the following could be the volume of the cube?

Indicate all such values.

- ☐ 27 cm^3
- ☐ 64 cm^3
- ☐ 125 cm^3
- ☐ 476 cm^3
- ☐ 729 cm^3
- ☐ 1,000 cm^3

Question 5

To pack her books, Rebekka requires a cube-shaped box with a volume of at least 2 cubic feet. Which of the following amounts could be the length of the edge of her box, in feet?

Indicate all such values.

- ☐ 1.1
- ☐ 1.2
- ☐ 1.3
- ☐ 1.4
- ☐ 1.5

Question 6

Emily must ship a cylinder-shaped gift with a height of 11 inches and a volume of 176π cubic inches. What is the volume, in cubic inches, of the smallest rectangular box which can contain this cylinder?

Question 7

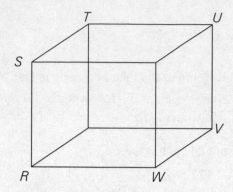

In the rectangular solid above, $RW = VW = UV = 7.5$. Which of the following statements must be true ?

Indicate all such statements.

☐ The surface area of the rectangular solid is 421.875

☐ The volume of the rectangular solid is 337.5

☐ SV (not shown) = UV

☐ The distance from T to W is 12.99

Question 8

A rectangular shipping container has dimensions of 23 feet by 29 feet by 37 feet. What is the longest distance between any two corners of the container, rounded to the nearest foot?

○ 41
○ 43
○ 44
○ 47
○ 52

Question 9

What is the surface area, in square inches, of a box that measures 29 inches by 37 inches by 47 inches?

☐

Question 10

If the volume of a cube is 125, then the total area of 2 of its faces is

○ 20
○ 25
○ 40
○ 50
○ 75

Question 11

An empty, cube-shaped swimming pool is filled part way with x cubic feet of water. It is then filled the rest of the way with y cubic feet of chlorine. Which of the following, in feet, expresses the depth of the swimming pool?

○ $x + y$

○ $\dfrac{x + y}{3}$

○ $\sqrt[3]{x + y}$

○ $(x + y)^3$

○ $\dfrac{\sqrt[3]{x + y}}{3}$

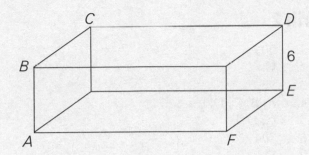

The volume of the rectangular solid above is 720. If $AF = 15$, which of the following is closest to the distance from C to F ?

○　6
○　8
○　12
○　15
○　18

Question 13

A cylindrical object has a volume of 332.75π cubic inches, and its height is equal to its diameter. What is the radius of the object?

☐

Question 14

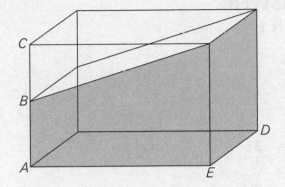

Note: Figure not drawn to scale

In the rectangular solid depicted above, $AC = 6$, $AE = 8$, $DE = 5$, and $BC > AB > 2$. Which of the following could be possible values for the volume of the shaded area?

Indicate all such values.

☐　60
☐　70
☐　150
☐　170
☐　180
☐　240

ANSWERS
Drill 1

1. C
2. B
3. A
4. A
5. A
6. B
7. A
8. A
9. A
10. D
11. B
12. $\dfrac{1}{3}$
13. A, B, D, F

Drill 2

1. 505
2. C
3. 96
4. A, B, C, D, E
5. C, D, E
6. 704
7. D
8. E
9. 8,350
10. D
11. C
12. E
13. 5.5
14. D

EXPLANATIONS
Drill 1

1. **C** The answer asks for $\frac{1}{3}$ of the whole volume, so begin by dividing the height of the trunk by 3 to find the volume of one of the sections of the trunk: $\frac{6 \text{ ft}}{3}$ = 2ft. The volume formula for a cylinder is: $V = \pi r^2 h = \pi \times 2^2 \times 2 = 8\pi$.

2. **B** Three times the surface area of a cube with edge length of 1 cm is three times the area of each square face times the number of faces: $3 \times (1 \text{ cm} \times 1 \text{ cm}) \times 6$ faces = 18 cm². The surface area of a cube with edge length of 3 cm is (3 cm × 3 cm) × 6 faces = 54 cm². Quantity B is greater.

3. **A** The diagonal of a square is always longer than its side, so half a diagonal—segment AE—must be longer than half a side. Half the length of a side of this square is 4. Therefore, AE is larger than 4.

4. **A** Plug In a value for n: try $n = 3$. If each edge of the cube is 3, $AB = DE = 3$, and because the diagonal of a square forms two 45-45-90 triangles, $BD = AE = 3\sqrt{2}$. The total perimeter is $3 + 3 + 3\sqrt{2} + 3\sqrt{2} = 6 + 6\sqrt{2}$. Now Plug In 3 for n in the answer choices; only (A) hits your target.

5. **A** Draw it! You should end up with two squares oriented the same way touching at C. The squares have the same area, so their sides must be the same length. Plug In a side length for the squares to simplify the comparison—try 2. A square cut in half along its diagonal yields a pair of 45-45-90 triangles, so these two squares with sides of 2 each have diagonals of $2\sqrt{2}$. Diagonals AC and CE connect to form segment AE. Quantity A is $3 \times 2 = 6$, and Quantity B is $2\sqrt{2} + 2\sqrt{2} = 4\sqrt{2} \approx 4(1.4) = 5.6$. Quantity A is greater.

6. **B** You will be subtracting the volume of the cylinder from that of the cube, so the answer will contain π; eliminate choices (A) and (E). To find the volume of the figure, start with the volume of the cube: $V = s^3 = 9^3 = 729$. The formula for volume of a cylinder is $V = \pi r^2 h$. The cylinder runs the length of the cube, so its height is the same as the length of the cube's edge, 9. Next, find the radius. The length of diagonal AB is $9\sqrt{2}$ (remember your special triangles—this is a 45-45-90 triangle!). The points between A and B are equally spaced, so the length of CD, the circle's diameter, is $\frac{1}{3}$ the length of AB, $3\sqrt{2}$. The radius is 1/2 the diameter, or $\frac{3\sqrt{2}}{2}$. Plug the radius and the height into the formula: $V = \pi r^2 h = \pi \left(\frac{3\sqrt{2}}{2} \right)^2 (9) = \frac{81\pi}{2}$. Subtract this from the cube's volume for a final answer of $729 - \frac{81\pi}{2}$.

7. **A** First, write out your formulas and draw a figure. The volume of a cube is $V = s^3 = 512$, giving you $s = 8$. The surface area of a cube is 6 times the area of each square face of the cube ($SA = 6s^2$); therefore, $6 \times 8^2 = 384$.

8. **A** The surface area of a cube is 6 times the area of each square face of the cube ($SA = 6s^2$), or $54 = 6s^2$. So each side is 3. The diagonal of the square forms the hypotenuse of a right triangle. Remember that the hypotenuse of a right triangle is always longer than either leg. Therefore, the diagonal is larger than 3.

9. **A** A cube has 6 identical faces, each with an area of s^2, so the surface area of a cube is $6s^2$; the volume of a cube is s^3. Quantity A is $\dfrac{6 \times 4^2}{4^3} = \dfrac{6}{4}$, and Quantity B is $\dfrac{6 \times 5^2}{5^3} = \dfrac{6}{5}$. Quantity A is greater.

10. **D** First, eliminate (A) and (B) because the volume must increase when the side of the square base increases. Next, set up a proportion using the square base of the prism: $\dfrac{13,000}{25^2} = \dfrac{x}{75^2}$. Finally, cross multiply and solve for x to get (D).

11. **B** Try Plugging In a value for the depth, 2 feet. Note that the radii are half the given diameters. Therefore, the volume of water held by Marty's pool is $V = \pi r^2 h = \pi(6)^2(2) = 72\pi$ and the volume of water held by Rusty's pool is $V = \pi r^2 h = \pi (9)^2(2) = 162\pi$. Dividing 162π by 72π yields 2.25.

12. $\dfrac{1}{3}$ First, find the angle measures. Since AC and AB are radii of the circle, the triangle they form along with BC must be isosceles. Let the small angles, $\angle ACB$ and $\angle ABC$, be x, which makes $\angle BAC$ equal to $4x$; now $4x + x + x = 180$, so $x = 30$ and $\angle BAC$ must be 120°. At this point, you're essentially done: though there's other information in the problem about diameters and heights and so on, it's all unnecessary. Since $\angle BAC$ represents $\dfrac{120}{360}$, or $\dfrac{1}{3}$, of the circular base, the shaded region represents the same fraction of the entire cylinder.

13. **A, B, D, F**

First, find the dimensions of the cylinder. Because the cylinder's height is 20 and its volume is 980π, and $V = \pi r^2 h$, $980\pi = \pi (r^2)(20)$, and $r = 7$. The diameter of the cylinder is 14. Because the end of the cylinder is a circle with a diameter of 14, the largest box that could fit in the cylinder would have a square base with a diagonal of 14. Using the Pythagorean Theorem, you can find that the length and the width of the largest possible box equal 14 divided by $\sqrt{2}$, or approximately 9.90. Therefore, the box's length and width must each be less than 10, and its height may be up to 20. Choices (A), (B), (D), and (F) match these criteria and work as the dimensions of the box.

Drill 2

1. **505** To find the number of cylinders that can be made from one block of steel, divide the volume of the block by the volume of a cylinder. Start by converting the dimensions of the block into inches: each steel block is 24 inches by 144 inches by 180 inches, so the volume is $24 \times 144 \times 180 = 622{,}080$. The formula for the volume of a cylinder is $V = \pi r^2 h$, so the volume of each cylinder is $\pi \times 7^2 \times 8 = 1{,}230.88$. Finally, $622{,}080 \div 1{,}230.88 = 505.395$; the problem asked for complete cylinders, so the correct answer is 505.

2. **C** It's a geometry problem with variables in the answer choices, so draw the figure and set up your scratch paper to Plug In. Plug In an easy number like $r = 5$; label the radius 5 and the height 15, which is 1.5 times your diameter of 10. The surface area of a cylinder is made up of 3 smaller areas: 2 identical circular bases on top and bottom, and a rectangle that's the height of the cylinder on one side and the circumference of the base on the other. If $r = 5$, then the area of each base is 25π, or 50π for the 2 of them. The rectangle is $15 \times 10\pi = 150\pi$, so the total surface area is 200π, your target answer. Plug 5 in for r in the answers, and only (C) matches your target answer of 200π.

3. **96** Use the formula for the volume of a cube to find the length of each side: $V = s^3$, so $64 = s^3$, and $s = 4$. To find the surface area of a cube, find the area of each face of the cube and multiply by 6: each side is 4, so each face has an area of $4 \times 4 = 16$, and the total surface area of the cube is $16 \times 6 = 96$.

4. **A, B, C, D, E**

   If the diagonal were exactly $10\sqrt{2}$, then the side of the cube would be 10. Because the diagonal is less than $10\sqrt{2}$, each side is less than 10. Therefore, the volume must be less than 10^3, or 1,000. Any value less than 1,000 is correct.

5. **C, D, E**

   Plug In the answers to your on-screen calculator. When cubed, (A) and (B) are less than 2 cubic feet, so you can eliminate those since the question is asking for a box that has a volume of AT LEAST 2 cubic feet. Choice (C), (D), and (E) are correct because they produce volumes over 2 cubic feet.

6. **704** Because the cylinder's height is 11 and its volume is 176π, and $V = \pi r^2 h$, $176\pi = \pi(r^2)(11)$, and $r = 4$. The diameter of the cylinder is 8. The box will need a length of 8 and a width of 8 to accommodate the base of the cylinder, and a height of 11. The volume of the smallest box will equal $8 \times 8 \times 11$, or 704.

7. **D** Because all the edges are equal, the figure is a cube. The formula for the surface area of a cube is $6s^2$, where s is a side of the cube. Thus, the surface area of the solid is 337.5; eliminate choice (A). The formula for the volume of a cube is s^3, so the volume of the cube is 421.875; eliminate (B). SV is a diagonal of the cube. The formula for the diagonal of a box is $a^2 + b^2 + c^2 = d^2$, where a, b, and c are the sides of the box and d is the diagonal. Thus, SV is 12.99 and does not equal UV. Eliminate (C). TW is also a diagonal of the cube, so its length is 12.99. The only correct answer is (D).

8.   **E**   Draw a rectangular box. The longest distance between any two corners is going to be the box's three-dimensional diagonal from a bottom corner to the top corner furthest away. You can solve this problem by using the Super Pythagorean Theorem $a^2 + b^2 + c^2 = d^2$. Substituting the values, you get $23^2 + 29^2 + 37^2 = 2{,}739 = d^2$. The square root is a little more than 52.

9. **8,350** Calculate the surface area of each side of the box. Two sides are each $29 \times 37 \times 2 = 1{,}073$ square inches. Two other sides are $29 \times 47 \times 2 = 2{,}726$ square inches. The last two sides are $37 \times 47 \times 2 = 3{,}478$ square inches. The sum of the six sides is 8,350.

10.   **D**   The volume formula for a cube is $V = s^3$, so a volume of 125 yields a side of 5. One face, therefore, has an area of 25, and the total area of 2 faces is 50. If you selected (C), you may have found the perimeter rather than the area. If you selected (B), you may have forgotten to find the total for 2 faces, and if you selected (A), you may have done both.

11.   **C**   Use Plugging In to solve the problem. The swimming pool has a total volume of $(x + y)$. You're trying to find the depth, or one side of the cube. Choose easy numbers. It helps to start with the depth, which is your target. If the depth is 2, then the total volume has to be 2^3, or 8. You could choose $x = 7$ and $y = 1$, but really you only use $x + y$ in the answers, so all you need is $x + y = 8$. Now Plug In to find your target in the choices. Choice (A) = 8, which doesn't match. Choice (B) is a fraction, which doesn't match. Choice (C) is $\sqrt[3]{8}$, which does equal 2, so keep it. Choice (D) is 8^3, which doesn't match. Choice (E) is $\dfrac{2}{3}$, which doesn't match.

12.   **E**   The distance from C to F is the diagonal of the box, so use the Super Pythagorean Theorem: $a^2 + b^2 + c^2 = d^2$, where a, b, and c are the sides of the box and d is the longest diagonal. You have the length and height of the box, so use the volume formula to find the width: $720 = (15)(6)w$, so the width is 8. Now plug your numbers into the formula: $15^2 + 8^2 + 6^2 = d^2$, so $325 = d^2$, and $d = 18.03$.

13.   **5.5**   The volume of a cylinder $= \pi r^2 h$. Since the height equals the diameter: $332.75\pi = \pi(r^2)(2r)$. Solving for r gives you 5.5 as the final answer.

14.   **D**   First, find the volume of the entire box, which equals $6 \times 8 \times 5 = 240$. Solve for the volume of the three-dimensional triangular shape on top and subtract it from the total volume to find the volume of the shaded part. The triangular shape has known dimensions of 8 by 5. The third dimension ranges based on the length of BC, with $3 < BC < 4$ because BC has to be bigger than AB. Therefore, the triangular shape's volume falls between one-half of $8 \times 5 \times 3 = 60$ and one-half of $8 \times 5 \times 4 = 80$. The shaded area's volume falls between $240 - 80 = 160$ and $240 - 60 = 180$. Only (D) works.

Charts and Graphs

CHARTS AND GRAPHS

The first step on a Charts and Graphs question is to get familiar with the data. You will often be given two or occasionally even three charts full of information. Just like in a Reading Comprehension question, you may have to scroll down to get to the second chart. **Make sure that you always scroll down to see if there is a second chart.** The questions would be pretty confusing if you missed a whole chart.

Pay careful attention to footnotes, parentheses, and small print. They almost always include information you will need to read the chart or to answer a question. Take note of the units as well. You won't need them when you calculate, but you will almost certainly see wrong answer choices that provide the right numbers with the wrong decimal points. If the chart gives you information in thousands or in millions make sure to count your zeros.

THE MATH

The math involved in chart questions is pretty fundamental. Typically it involves fractions, percentages, addition, multiplication, and subtraction. The addition, subtraction, and multiplication will be made more difficult by including large numbers with lots of zeros (information given in thousands, for example), answer choices expressed in scientific notation, or information taken from multiple charts.

Ballpark Before You Calculate

Remember that the answer choices are part of the question. As you go through these drills, note the range in numbers given in your answer choices. The highest answer choices could be double or even five times the size of the smallest answer choice. These questions are ripe for Ballparking. In fact, they are even designed for it. While you will have to do more actual calculating on charts questions than anywhere else on the test, you should never have to calculate all five answer choices; in fact, rarely will you have to calculate more than two. When ETS asks you to find approximately some piece of information, what they're really saying is, "It's okay to Ballpark." If there is a large value range in the answer choices, you should be able to eliminate at least two if not three answer choices by Ballparking, leaving you with only two close answer choices to calculate.

Percent Change

There is one formula to keep in mind for Chart questions. That is the percentage change formula. If a question asks you to find the percentage increase, or percentage decrease, the formula is difference/original × 100. For example, a question may give you the sales figures for company X for the years 1972 through 1986. The question may then ask you which period had the greatest percentage increase in sales. The answer choices will say 1979 to 1980, 1982 to 1983, and so on. At least one answer choice will have a percentage decrease. You can eliminate that. One or two others will have very small increases, so you can eliminate those. The remaining answer choices may have the exact, or very close, numerical increases, but differing totals. You should realize that the same numerical increase on a smaller total will yield a greater percentage increase (if you increase the total by one, from five to six, that is a 20 percent increase, but if you increase the total by one from ten to eleven, that is only a 10 percent increase). If you have to calculate, use the percentage change formula. If the sales total in 1982 was 5.4 million and the sales total in 1983 was 6.8 million, then the difference was 1.4 million. Divide that by the original of 5.4 million and you get approximately .26. Multiply this by one hundred and you're left with a percentage increase of 26 percent. If you don't want to do the long division, reduce your fraction to +/– ¼ and look for answer choices about 25 percent.

SCRATCH PAPER

As always, scratch paper is key. **Label everything.** Not only will you be dealing with multiple pieces of information, but you may be able to use information you found for one question on another question based upon the same chart. Because you will be doing some calculating, that scratch paper can get messy and confusing. Block out some clean space to do your work and label every number you put down. This becomes especially important if you need to check your units. Wrong answers on Charts problems can often be directly traced to sloppy scratch paper and unlabeled information. Don't be messy.

For more practice and a more in-depth look at The Princeton Review math techniques, check out our student-friendly guidebook, *Cracking the GRE.*

DRILL 1

Questions 1-3 refer to the following data.

NEW AND REFURBISHED YACHT SALES OF COMPANY *J*, 1994 TO 2004 AND MEDIAN SALE PRICE FOR SELECTED YEARS

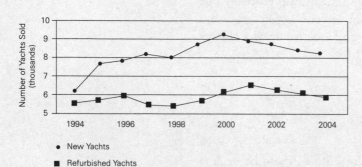

- ● New Yachts
- ■ Refurbished Yachts

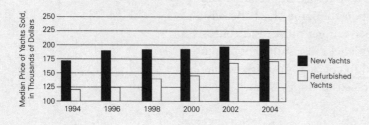

Question 1

According to the graph, which of the following could be the number of refurbished yachts sold in 1996?

- ○ 7,750
- ○ 5,900
- ○ 5,590
- ○ 5,400
- ○ 5,390

Question 2

In which of the following years did Company *J* sell more refurbished yachts than in the previous year, but fewer new yachts than in the previous year?

- ○ 1995
- ○ 1997
- ○ 1999
- ○ 2001
- ○ 2003

Question 3

In the year when the median price of new yachts sold by Company *J* was closest to the median price of refurbished yachts sold by Company *J*, how many thousand refurbished yachts did the company sell?

- ○ 6.3
- ○ 6.7
- ○ 7.9
- ○ 8.3
- ○ 8.7

Questions 4-6 refer to the following data.

TOTAL BUDGET FOR THE CITY OF SPRINGFIELD
1992 AND 1998

INCOME SOURCES (IN THOUSANDS OF DOLLARS)

EXPENDITURES (IN THOUSANDS OF DOLLARS)

1992 Total: 433

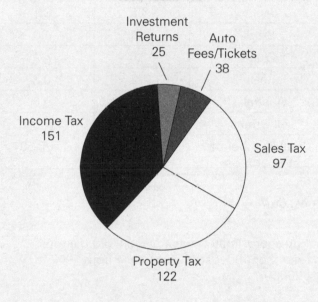

Investment Returns 25

Auto Fees/Tickets 38

Income Tax 151

Sales Tax 97

Property Tax 122

1992 Total: 433

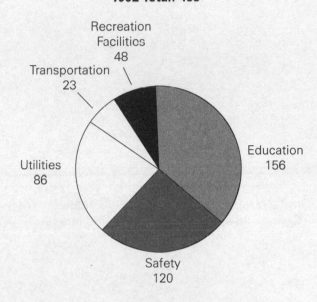

Recreation Facilities 48

Transportation 23

Utilities 86

Education 156

Safety 120

1998 Total: 532

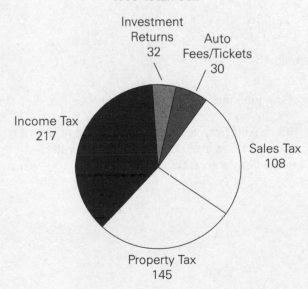

Investment Returns 32

Auto Fees/Tickets 30

Income Tax 217

Sales Tax 108

Property Tax 145

1998 Total: 532

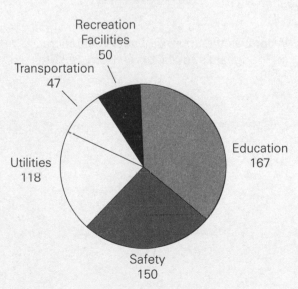

Recreation Facilities 50

Transportation 47

Utilities 118

Education 167

Safety 150

Question 4

In 1998, the amount that the city of Springfield spent on safety was how many times the amount the city spent on recreation facilities?

○ $2\frac{1}{4}$

○ $2\frac{2}{5}$

○ 3

○ $3\frac{1}{4}$

○ $3\frac{1}{2}$

Question 5

In 1992, approximately what percent of Springfield's income came from income tax?

○ 50%
○ 45%
○ 40%
○ 35%
○ 30%

Question 6

What was the approximate percent increase in Springfield's total income from 1992 to 1998 ?

○ 19%
○ 23%
○ 36%
○ 42%
○ 48%

Questions 7-8 refer to the following data.

AIRLINE DEPARTURES BY COUNTRY IN 2002 AND 2008

Country	2002 (percent)	2008 (percent)
United States	24.2	31.1
United Kingdom	10.8	9.5
France	9.1	5.0
Germany	5.5	6.2
Japan	4.3	3.1
Brazil	3.1	4.0
China	2.0	7.7
Spain	1.2	0.3
Australia	0.8	0.6
All Others	39.0	32.5
Total Number of Departures	12,050,205	18,205,301

Question 7

By approximately what percent did the total number of departures increase from 2002 to 2008 ?

○ 33%
○ 50%
○ 66%
○ 133%
○ 150%

Question 8

If the nine individually listed countries (excluding those characterized as "All Others") are ranked from highest to lowest by number of departures in 2002, how many countries ranked lower in 2008 than in 2002 ?

[   ]

Questions 9-12 refer to the following data.

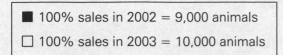

HAPPY PUPPY PET DEPOT SALES
BY PERCENT OF TOTAL ANNUAL SALES

■ 100% sales in 2002 = 9,000 animals

□ 100% sales in 2003 = 10,000 animals

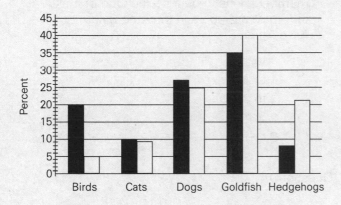

Question 9

In 2002, how many categories of animals individually accounted for more than 20% of the depot's annual sales?

Question 10

From 2002 to 2003, what was the increase in the total number of goldfish sold?

- ○ 5
- ○ 70
- ○ 225
- ○ 850
- ○ 1,380

Question 11

By approximately what percent did total cat sales change from 2002 to 2003 ?

- ○ 0%
- ○ 1%
- ○ 2%
- ○ 5%
- ○ 9%

Question 12

The total sales at Happy Puppy Pet Depot is calculated by adding the sales from Store A to those from Store B. Both stores sold an equal number of pets in 2002. If the sales of pets in Store A increased by 34% in 2003, by approximately what percent did sales decrease in Store B during the same year?

- ○ 12%
- ○ 34%
- ○ 42%
- ○ 66%
- ○ 97%

Questions 13-15 refer to the following data.

MEMBERSHIP OF THE NORTH COUNTY AUTO MECHANICS AND AUTO SALES ASSOCIATIONS IN 2012

Auto Mechanics Association		Auto Sales Association
	Gender	
345	Male	500
464	Female	400
809	Total	900
	Age	
23	Youngest	25
68	Oldest	72
34	Average	44
	Number of Children	
125	0	209
223	1	126
204	2	98
117	3	85
54	4	132
52	5	128
34	6 or more	122
	Highest Education Level	
129	Some High School	185
286	High School Graduate	419
307	College Graduate	202
87	Advanced Degrees	94

Question 13

If 50 of the male members of the Auto Sales Association were replaced by 50 female members, what would be the ratio of male to female members in the Auto Sales Association ?

○ 1 to 1
○ 1 to 2
○ 1 to 3
○ 2 to 1
○ 3 to 1

Question 14

If 92 members of the Auto Sales Association were females with 5 children, how many members of the Auto Sales Association were males who did not have 5 children?

```
                    
```

Question 15

If all the members of the Auto Mechanics Association who held advanced degrees and all the members of the Auto Mechanics Association who had at least 5 children voted for a measure, how many more votes were needed to gain a majority?

○ 173
○ 344
○ 556
○ 636
○ It cannot be determined from the information given.

DRILL 2

Questions 1-3 refer to the following data.

NUMBER OF BOOKS SOLD BY BOOK STORE X IN 2005 LISTED BY MAJOR CATEGORY AND TARGET AUDIENCE

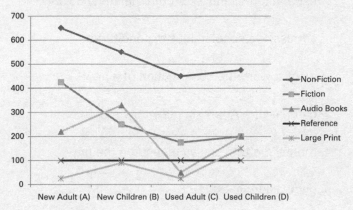

NUMBER OF NONFICTION BOOKS SOLD BY BOOK STORE X IN 2005

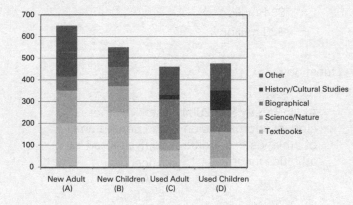

Question 1

For which major category of books is the number sold most nearly the same for each of the four groups?

○ Nonfiction
○ Fiction
○ Audio Books
○ Reference
○ Large Print

Question 2

Approximately how many Used Adult Science/Nature books did Book Store X sell in 2005 ?

○ 50
○ 70
○ 90
○ 110
○ 150

Question 3

Which of the following correctly lists the number of audio books sold for each of the four groups from greatest to least?

○ D, B, A, C
○ B, A, D, C
○ A, D, B, C
○ A, C, B, D
○ D, A, C, B

Questions 4-6 refer to the following data.

INCOME AND EXPENDITURES AT UNIVERSITY *F* IN 2004

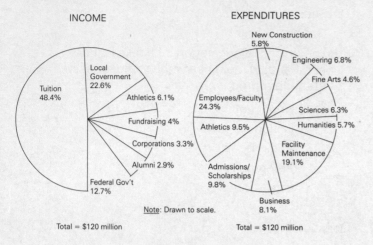

INCOME

EXPENDITURES

Note: Drawn to scale.

Total = $120 million

Total = $120 million

Question 4

University *F*'s expenditures in which of the following categories were most nearly equal to $5.4 million in 2004 ?

- ○ Fine Arts
- ○ Facility Maintenance
- ○ Humanities
- ○ Athletics
- ○ Business

Question 5

In 2004, $\frac{1}{2}$ of University *F*'s new construction expenditures, $\frac{1}{4}$ of its facility maintenance expenditures, and $\frac{3}{5}$ of both the athletics and admissions/scholarships expenditures went toward the construction of a new gymnasium. Approximately how much money did University *F* spend on the new gymnasium in 2004 ?

- ○ $13 million
- ○ $18 million
- ○ $20 million
- ○ $24 million
- ○ $30 million

Question 6

At University *F* in 2004, what was the closest approximation of the percentage of athletics expenditures NOT covered by athletics income?

- ○ 32%
- ○ 36%
- ○ 42%
- ○ 56%
- ○ 64%

Questions 7-8 refer to the following data.

AVERAGE TEMPERATURE HIGHS AND LOWS FOR CITY X

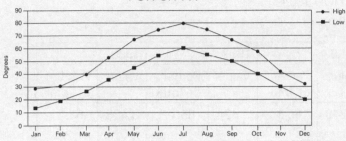

AVERAGE MONTHLY RAINFALL FOR CITIES X AND Y

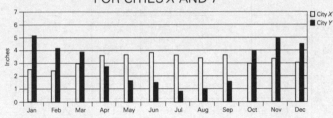

Questions 9-10 refer to the following data.

U.S. ENERGY SOURCES, 1979 AND 2004

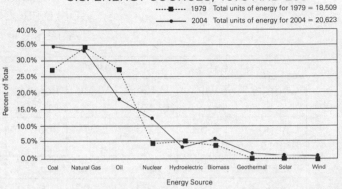

Question 7

During how many of the months in which City Y's average rainfall exceeded 3 inches was City X's average low temperature greater than or equal to 30 degrees?

- ○ One
- ○ Two
- ○ Three
- ○ Four
- ○ All

Question 8

The "monthly midpoint" is calculated by taking the average (arithmetic mean) of a month's average high and low. Which of the following is the average monthly midpoint in City X for the 3-month period from July to September?

- ○ 55.3
- ○ 60.0
- ○ 64.7
- ○ 69.3
- ○ 74.0

Question 9

What is the approximate ratio of total units of energy used from oil in 1979 to total units of energy used from oil in 2004 ?

- ○ $\dfrac{55}{1}$
- ○ $\dfrac{35}{1}$
- ○ $\dfrac{11}{7}$
- ○ $\dfrac{25}{18}$
- ○ $\dfrac{9}{10}$

Question 10

Which of the following can be inferred from the graphs?

Indicate all such statements.

- ☐ The number of nuclear power plants increased between 1979 and 2004.
- ☐ The percent of total energy used from oil, coal, and natural gas sources was greater in 2004 than the percent of total energy used from the same sources in 1979.
- ☐ The amount of energy used from hydroelectric sources in 2004 was less than one fourth the amount of energy used from hydroelectric sources in 1979.

Questions 11-13 refer to the following data.

PRODUCTION OF GOLF EQUIPMENT AND SUPPLIES
WORLD PRODUCTION 1994-1998
(values are in millions of dollars)

Country	1994 Value	1994 Percent of Total	1995 Value	1995 Percent of Total	1996 Value	1996 Percent of Total	1997 Value	1997 Percent of Total	1998 Value	1998 Percent of Total
United States	2,691	62.3	2,975	63.7	3,248	65.1	3,424	65.1	3,438	63.2
Japan	678	15.7	752	16.1	793	15.9	831	15.8	876	16.1
South Korea	376	8.7	383	8.2	384	7.7	426	8.1	457	8.4
Germany	177	4.1	159	3.4	180	3.6	179	3.4	201	3.7
Great Britain	125	2.9	140	3.0	135	2.7	153	2.9	169	3.1
Canada	125	2.9	103	2.2	105	2.1	100	1.9	125	2.3
Argentina	99	2.3	103	2.2	95	1.9	100	1.9	114	2.1
Other Countries	49	1.1	55	1.2	50	1.0	47	0.9	60	1.1
Total	4,320	100	4,670	100	4,990	100	5,260	100	5,440	100

UNITED STATES PRODUCTION

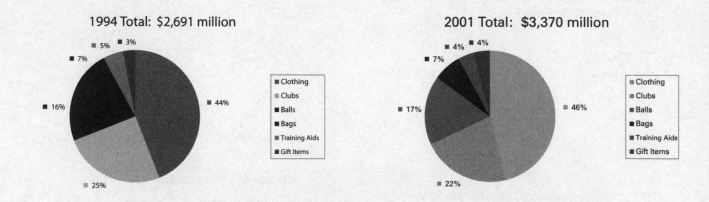

1994 Total: $2,691 million

2001 Total: $3,370 million

Clothing, Clubs, Balls, Bags, Training Aids, Gift Items

In 1994, the value of clubs produced in the United States was approximately what percent of the value of golf equipment and supplies produced in the world?

○   33%
○   25%
○   16%
○   13%
○   9%

In 1994, the total production for golf equipment and supplies from which country was nearest in value to the combined production of balls, bags, and gift items in the United States in the same year?

○   Japan
○   North Korea
○   Germany
○   Great Britain
○   Canada

From 1996 to 1998, the value of golf equipment and supplies produced by South Korea increased by approximately what percent?

○   1%
○   7%
○   16%
○   19%
○   27%

Questions 14-15 refer to the following data.

HONEY PRODUCTION IN REGION *Z*: 1980 TO 1986

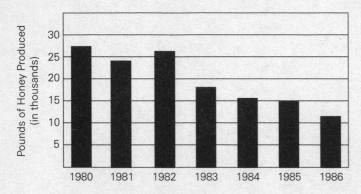

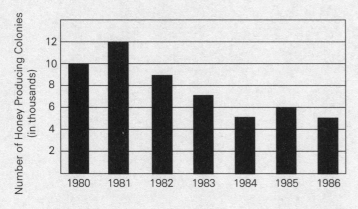

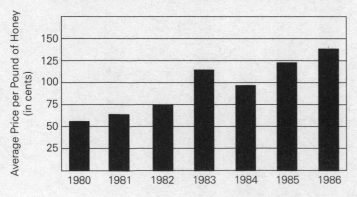

Question 14

What was the approximate value, in dollars, of the honey produced in Region *Z* in 1985 ?

- ○ 19,000
- ○ 15,000
- ○ 6,000
- ○ 580
- ○ 124

Question 15

By approximately what percentage did the number of colonies in Region *Z* decrease from the year with the highest number to that with the lowest number?

- ○ 140%
- ○ 60%
- ○ 40%
- ○ 30%
- ○ 7%

DRILL 3

Questions 1-3 refer to the following data.

2002 AIRPLANE INVENTORY FOR AIRLINES *A* AND *B*
BY YEAR OF PURCHASE
(as a percent of the 2002 inventory)

Airline *A*	Airline *B*
Total 2002 inventory: 250	Total 2002 inventory: 450

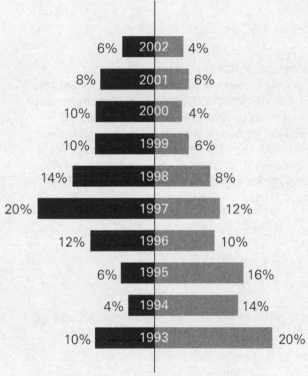

6%	2002	4%
8%	2001	6%
10%	2000	4%
10%	1999	6%
14%	1998	8%
20%	1997	12%
12%	1996	10%
6%	1995	16%
4%	1994	14%
10%	1993	20%

Question 1

What was the total number of inventoried airplanes purchased by both airlines from 1997 to 1999 ?

- ○ 110
- ○ 117
- ○ 175
- ○ 227
- ○ 315

Question 2

In 1994, Airline *A* bought 25 airplanes. All of these airplanes either remained in Airline *A*'s inventory or were sold to another airline. What percent of these airplanes was sold to another airline?

- ○ 4%
- ○ 10%
- ○ 40%
- ○ 60%
- ○ 90%

Question 3

Which of the following can be inferred from the graph?

Indicate <u>all</u> such statements.

- ☐ Airline *A* had fewer customers than Airline *B* over the period shown.
- ☐ In 2002, Airline *B*'s inventory of planes purchased in 1993 was twice that purchased by Airline *A* in the same year.
- ☐ If all airplanes were purchased new, then the median age of an airplane in Airline *B*'s inventory in 2002 was greater than that of an airplane in Airline *A*'s inventory in 2002.

Questions 4-6 refer to the following data.

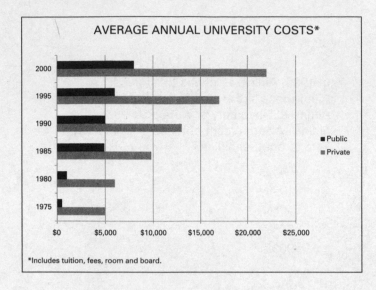

AVERAGE ANNUAL UNIVERSITY COSTS*

■ Public
■ Private

*Includes tuition, fees, room and board.

Question 4

In 2005, the ratio of the average annual cost to attend a private university to the average annual cost to attend a public university was the same as it was in 1990. If the average annual cost to attend a public university in 2005 was $11,000, what was the average annual cost to attend private university in that year, to the nearest $1,000 ?

○ $18,000
○ $24,000
○ $29,000
○ $32,000
○ $34,000

Question 5

By approximately what percent did the average annual cost to attend a private university increase from 1980 to 2000 ?

○   27%
○   73%
○   138%
○   267%
○   367%

Question 6

The average annual cost to attend a private university increased at a constant rate from 1995 to 2000, and 2.5 million students attended private universities in 1998. If 2 million students attended private universities in 1990, then by approximately what percent did the total dollar amount spent on private universities increase from 1990 to 1998?

○   25%
○   30%
○   55%
○   70%
○   90%

Questions 7-8 refer to the following data.

The following charts represent April 2011 plant sales at the Friendly Nursery.

Sales by Growth Pattern

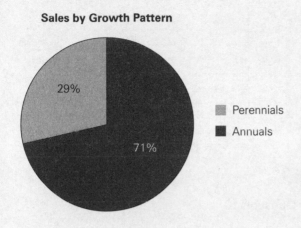

- Perennials
- Annuals

Sales of Annuals by Plant Type

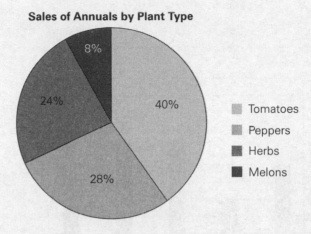

- Tomatoes
- Peppers
- Herbs
- Melons

Question 7

Which of the following is most nearly the percent of plants sold at Friendly Nursery in April 2011 that were herbs?

- ○ 70%
- ○ 40%
- ○ 24%
- ○ 17%
- ○ 8%

Question 8

In April 2011 there were four varieties of tomatoes available at Friendly Nursery: Red Giants, Mortgage Lifters, Beefsteaks and Sun Golds. If 1,000 plants were sold, which of the following could be the number of Beefsteak tomato plants sold?

Indicate all such values.

- ☐ .1
- ☐ 42
- ☐ 246
- ☐ 312
- ☐ 580

Question 9 refers to the following data.

HAPPY PUPPY PET DEPOT SALES
BY PERCENT OF TOTAL ANNUAL SALES

■ 100% sales in 2002 = 9,000 animals
□ 100% sales in 2003 = 10,000 animals

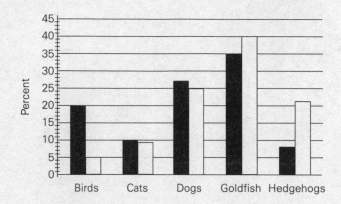

Question 9

If Happy Puppy Pet Depot saw the same percentage increase in total number of animals sold from 2003 to 2004 as it did from 2002 to 2003, how many animals, to the nearest integer, did the store sell in 2004 ?

Question 10 refers to the following data.

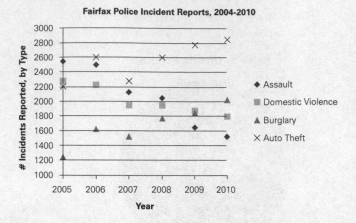

Question 10

For how many of the years shown in the graph was the number of reported nonviolent crimes (burglary and auto theft) greater than the number of reported violent crimes (assault and domestic violence)?

○ None
○ One
○ Two
○ Three
○ Four

Question 11 refers to the following data.

AVERAGE TEMPERATURE HIGHS AND LOWS FOR CITY X

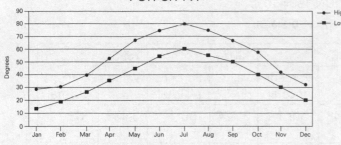

AVERAGE MONTHLY RAINFALL FOR CITIES X AND Y

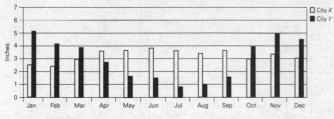

Question 11

For which of the following months does the average monthly high temperature for City X fall within one standard deviation of the average annual high temperature?

Indicate all such months.

☐ January
☐ March
☐ May
☐ July
☐ September
☐ November

Question 12 refers to the following data.

HONEY PRODUCTION IN REGION Z: 1980 TO 1986

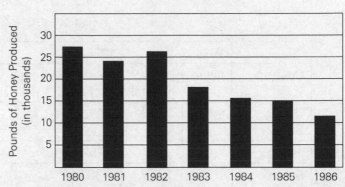

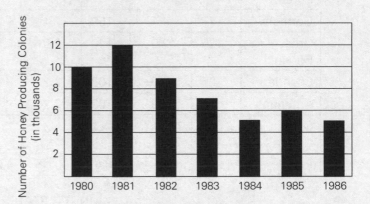

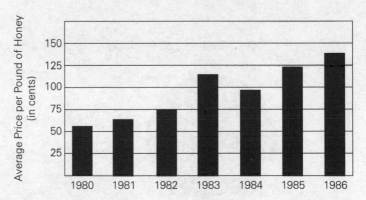

Question 12

For what year depicted in the graphs was the percent decrease from the previous year of the number of honey producing colonies most similar to the average percent increase of the average price of a pound of honey for the six-year period?

Question 13 refers to the following data.

PRODUCTION OF GOLF EQUIPMENT AND SUPPLIES
WORLD PRODUCTION 1994-1998
(values are in millions of dollars)

Country	1994 Value	1994 Percent of Total	1995 Value	1995 Percent of Total	1996 Value	1996 Percent of Total	1997 Value	1997 Percent of Total	1998 Value	1998 Percent of Total
United States	2,691	62.3	2,975	63.7	3,248	65.1	3,424	65.1	3,438	63.2
Japan	678	15.7	752	16.1	793	15.9	831	15.8	876	16.1
South Korea	376	8.7	383	8.2	384	7.7	426	8.1	457	8.4
Germany	177	4.1	159	3.4	180	3.6	179	3.4	201	3.7
Great Britain	125	2.9	140	3.0	135	2.7	153	2.9	169	3.1
Canada	125	2.9	103	2.2	105	2.1	100	1.9	125	2.3
Argentina	99	2.3	103	2.2	95	1.9	100	1.9	114	2.1
Other Countries	49	1.1	55	1.2	50	1.0	47	0.9	60	1.1
Total	4,320	100	4,670	100	4,990	100	5,260	100	5,440	100

UNITED STATES PRODUCTION

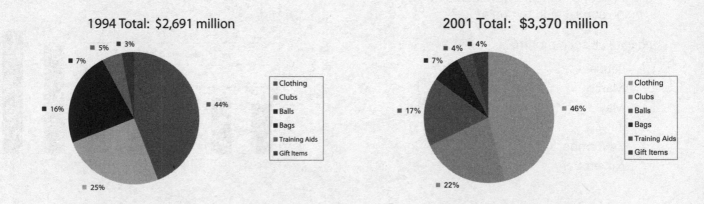

1994 Total: $2,691 million

2001 Total: $3,370 million

Legend: Clothing, Clubs, Balls, Bags, Training Aids, Gift Items

Question 13

Golf equipment manufacturing in the United States experienced the same percent growth rate from 2001 to 2008 as it did from 1994 to 2001. If the shares of golf supplies production made up of bags, balls and training aids each increased anywhere from one to five percentage points from 2001 to 2008, which of the following could be the sum of the value of bags, balls and training aids produced in the United States in 2008, in millions of dollars?

Indicate all such sums.

- ☐ 1,550
- ☐ 1,627
- ☐ 1,855
- ☐ 2,197
- ☐ 2,339

Question 14 refers to the following data.

Tree	Number of Trees	Average (arithmetic mean) diameter	Standard Deviation of Diameter
Oak	64	58	11.2
Maple	50	42	7.4
Hickory	12	17	9.6
Ash	8	39	14.5
Birch	7	25	12.0

Question 14

How many maple trees had a diameter greater than 49.4 cm ?

┌─────────┐
│   │
└─────────┘

DRILL 4

Questions 1-3 refer to the following data.

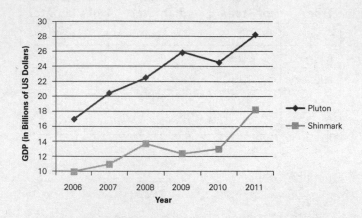

Question 1

Approximately what was the percentage growth of Pluton's GDP from 2010 to 2011 ?

- ○   4%
- ○   15%
- ○   25%
- ○   40%
- ○   115%

Question 2

In which year was the change from the prior year of the combined GDP of the two countries the least?

[   ]

Question 3

Shinmark spends $\frac{1}{2}$ of its GDP on military expenditures, while Pluton spends $\frac{1}{4}$ of its GDP on military expenditures. For which years does Shinmark's military spending exceed Pluton's?

Indicate all such years.

- ☐   2006
- ☐   2007
- ☐   2008
- ☐   2009
- ☐   2010
- ☐   2011

Question 4 refers to the following data.

U.S. ENERGY SOURCES, 1979 AND 2004

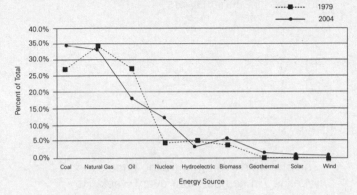

Legend:
- ----■---- 1979
- ——●—— 2004

Question 4

The population of the U.S. grew by 29% between 1979 and 2004, during which time per capita energy consumption doubled. If average per capita energy used from coal was 25 MBTUs in 1979, which of the following are in the range of per capita energy, measured in MBTUs, provided by a single fossil fuel (coal, natural gas or oil) in 2004 ?

Indicate all such values.

- ☐ 12
- ☐ 25
- ☐ 37
- ☐ 41
- ☐ 61
- ☐ 79

Question 5 refers to the following data.

AIRLINE DEPARTURES BY COUNTRY IN 2002 AND 2008

Country	2002 (percent)	2008 (percent)
United States	24.2	31.1
United Kingdom	10.8	9.5
France	9.1	5.0
Germany	5.5	6.2
Japan	4.3	3.1
Brazil	3.1	4.0
China	2.0	7.7
Spain	1.2	0.3
Australia	0.8	0.6
All Others	39.0	32.5
Total Number of Departures	12,050,205	18,205,301

Question 5

To the nearest percent, what was the percentage increase for the country that experienced the greatest percent increase in number of departures between 2002 and 2008 ?

☐

Questions 6-9 refer to the following data.

The following graph is a training log for a triathlete. It documents the number of hours she trained each week at each of three disciplines over a four-week period.

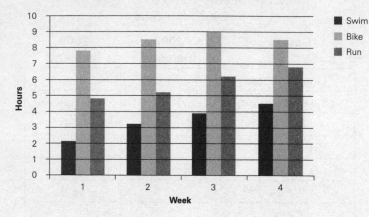

Question 6

The athlete's trainer recommends that the ratio of hours she spends biking to hours she spends swimming be between 2 : 1 and 3 : 1. For which of the following weeks did the athlete meet this recommendation?

Indicate <u>all</u> such weeks.

- ☐ Week 1
- ☐ Week 2
- ☐ Week 3
- ☐ Week 4

Question 7

The athlete aims to spend between 12 and 16 percent of her weekly training time swimming. For which of the weeks does her swimming fall within that range?

Indicate <u>all</u> such answers.

- ☐ 1
- ☐ 2
- ☐ 3
- ☐ 4

Question 8

The athlete's average running pace every week is 7 miles per hour every week. How many miles did she run in week 2 ?

- ○ 0.7
- ○ 5.1
- ○ 36.4
- ○ 44.6
- ○ 161.0

Question 9

In week 5, the athlete plans to decrease her training time in each sport by 10% to 20% of the hours she trained in week 4. Which of the following are possible numbers of hours she could bike in week 5 ?

Indicate <u>all</u> such values.

- ☐ 3.9
- ☐ 5.6
- ☐ 7.2
- ☐ 9.8
- ☐ 16.6
- ☐ 22.8

Question 10 refers to the following data.

SALES OF SCIENCE/NATURE BOOKS BY CATEGORY

	2004	2005	2006
New Adult Books	140	150	160
Used Adult Books	65	70	90
New Children's Books	130	120	110
Used Children's Books	105	120	135

Question 10

If, for the year 2005, technology book sales represented one-third of new adult science/nature book sales, 50% of used adult science/nature book sales, and $\frac{1}{10}$ of all children's science/nature book sales, how many technology books were sold in 2005?

```
┌─────────┐
│         │
└─────────┘
```

Questions 11-12 refer to the following data.

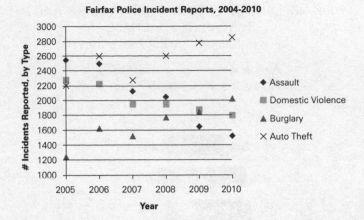

Question 11

The number of assaults reported in Fairfax dropped every year from 2004 to 2010. For which year(s) was the rate of decrease greater than it had been the previous year?

Indicate all such years.

- ☐ 2006
- ☐ 2007
- ☐ 2008
- ☐ 2009
- ☐ 2010

Question 12

Total crime incidents reported in Fairfax decreased by 25% from 2005 to 2010. For which of the crime categories presented in the graph was the percent change from 2005 to 2010 greater than the percent change of all crimes reported?

Indicate all such categories.

- ☐ Assault
- ☐ Domestic violence
- ☐ Burglary
- ☐ Auto theft
- ☐ None of the above

Question 13 refers to the following data.

2002 AIRPLANE INVENTORY FOR AIRLINES *A* AND *B*
BY YEAR OF PURCHASE
(as a percent of the 2002 inventory)

Airline *A*	Airline *B*
Total 2002 inventory: 250	Total 2002 inventory: 450

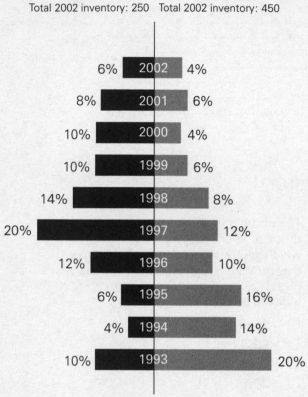

	Year	
6%	2002	4%
8%	2001	6%
10%	2000	4%
10%	1999	6%
14%	1998	8%
20%	1997	12%
12%	1996	10%
6%	1995	16%
4%	1994	14%
10%	1993	20%

Question 14 refers to the following data.

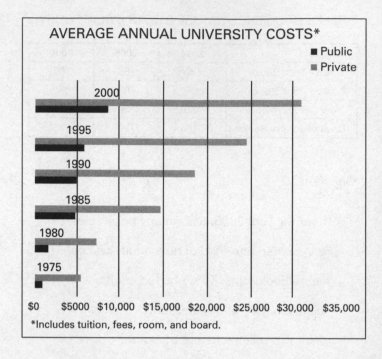

AVERAGE ANNUAL UNIVERSITY COSTS*
■ Public
■ Private

*Includes tuition, fees, room, and board.

Question 13

New regulations go into effect in 2003 that require all planes in inventory to be newer than ten years old. Each year following 2002, both airlines need to sell the planes the regulations force them to eliminate from inventory, and then use the proceeds of those sales to increase their inventory by 10% (rounded down because they are unable to buy fractions of planes). What is the combined number of planes owned by the two companies following their sales and purchases in 2004?

Question 14

The Great American Scholar (GAS) Grants cover 100% of students' tuition but no other expenses. In 1995, 4,000 GAS Grants were awarded, of which between $\frac{1}{4}$ and $\frac{1}{3}$ were mandated to go to public university students. In 1995, 50% of public university students' costs went to tuition, while 85% of private university students' costs went to tuition. Which of the following are possible total dollar values of all GAS Grants awarded in 1995?

Indicate <u>all</u> such answers.

☐ $35,500,000
☐ $42,000,000
☐ $57,000,000
☐ $64,000,000
☐ $72,000,000
☐ $96,000,000

ANSWERS

Drill 1

1. B
2. D
3. A
4. C
5. D
6. B
7. B
8. 3
9. 2
10. D
11. A
12. A
13. A
14. 464
15. E

Drill 2

1. D
2. A
3. B
4. A
5. D
6. B
7. B
8. C
9. D
10. B, C
11. C
12. A
13. D
14. A
15. B

Drill 3

1. D
2. D
3. C
4. C
5. D
6. E
7. D
8. A, B, C
9. 11,111
10. D
11. B, C, E, F
12. 1982
13. C, D
14. 8

Drill 4

1. B
2. 2010
3. A, B, C, E, F
4. C, D, E
5. 285
6. B, C
7. A
8. C
9. C
10. 109
11. B, D
12. A, C, D
13. 626
14. D

EXPLANATIONS
Drill 1

1. **B** Be sure you've identified the correct chart, the correct year, and the correct data line: use the chart showing the number of yachts sold, the data line showing refurbished yachts, and the information for 1996. The data point for 1996 lies just below 6,000, so select (B). If you selected (A), you may have used the data line showing information for new yachts; if you selected (C), (D), or (E), you may have used information from the wrong year.

2. **D** Because the number of new yachts sold by Company *J* was always greater than the number of refurbished yachts it sold, a decrease in the former and an increase in the latter results in the two data lines coming closer together. Only the year 2001 shows the correct pattern and both of the proper changes: the number of refurbished yachts sold increased from about 6,200 to about 6,500, and the number of new yachts sold decreased from about 9,300 to about 8,800. The answer is (D).

3. **A** First, use the median price chart to determine that 2002 was the year when the median prices of new and refurbished yachts were most similar. Next, use the data line for refurbished yachts in the other chart to determine that the number of yachts sold by Company *J* that year was less than halfway from 6,000 to 7,000; only (A) falls in the acceptable range.

4. **C** In 1998, Springfield spent $150,000 on safety and $50,000 on recreation facilities; hence, the city spent three times as much on safety as on recreation facilities. If you selected (B), you may have used the wrong chart.

5. **D** In 1992, Springfield collected $151,000 from income tax out of its total income of $433,000; $\dfrac{\$151,000}{\$433,000}$ is slightly greater than $\dfrac{1}{3}$, so select (D).

6. **B** The percent change formula is $\dfrac{difference}{original} \times 100$, so, $\dfrac{532-433}{433} \times 100 = \dfrac{99}{433} \times 100$, or slightly less than a quarter (25%). The answer is (B).

7. **B** Round the values and use the percent change formula to approximate the answer; ignore the millions, because they are in both numbers. The percent change formula is $\dfrac{difference}{original} \times 100$, so $\dfrac{18-12}{12} \times 100 = 50\%$.

8. **3** The chart already ranks the countries in order in 2002. In 2008, the rankings were: US—1st; UK—2nd; France—5th; Germany—4th; Japan—7th; Brazil—6th; China—3rd; Spain—9th; and Australia—8th. Only three countries—France, Japan, and Spain—ranked lower in 2008 than they did in 2002, making the answer 3.

9. **2** In 2002, only dogs and goldfish each accounted for *more* than 20% of the store's total sales.

10. **D** The number of goldfish sold in 2002 was 35% of 9,000, or 3,150 goldfish. The number of goldfish in 2003 was 40% of 10,000, or 4,000. To find the difference, simply subtract: 4,000 − 3,150 = 850.

11. **A** Total cat sales in 2002 can be calculated as 10% of 9,000, or 900 total cats. In 2003, the figure is 9% of 10,000, or 900 total cats. Therefore, the same number of cats was sold in both years. The answer is (A).

12. **A** Store A and Store B both sold an equal number of pets in 2002, meaning both sold 4,500 animals.

If the total number of pets sold by Store A then increases by 34%, Store A sold 6,030 animals in

2003. The total number of animals sold in 2003 was 10,000, meaning store B sold only 3,970 pets.

Use the percent change formula: $\dfrac{4500-3970}{4500} \times 100$ to get (A).

13. **A** If 50 male members were replaced by 50 female members, there would be 450 male members and 450 female members. The ratio would be 1 to 1.

14. **464** Use the second column of the chart. There are 128 total men and women with 5 children, and you are given 92 women with 5 children. Subtract to find 36 men with 5 children. To find the total number of men who did not have 5 children, take the total number of all men (500) and subtract the number with 5 children (36). The answer is 464 men who did not have 5 children.

15. **E** There is not enough information given to answer this question since some or none of the members who hold advanced degrees could also have 5 or more children.

Drill 2

1. **D** Use the first graph. Find the line that is the straightest across the four groups, thus, the line with the smallest range. Notice that the Reference line shows about 100 for each of the 4 groups. The answer is (D).

2. **A** Use the second graph. The section of the Used Adult bar for Science/Nature (grey portion) starts at approximately 70 and ends at approximately 120. So, the number of Science/Nature books is approximately 120 − 70 = 50, (A).

3. **B** Use the first chart. There were approximately 220 New Adult (A) audio books, 330 New Children's (B) audio books, 50 Used Adult (C), and 200 Used Children's (D) audio books. Putting these in order from greatest to least gives you: (B) 330, (A) 220, (D) 200, (C) 50, choice (B).

4. **A** Be sure to Ballpark this one: 10% of $120 million is $12 million, so 5% would be $6 million. Hence, you're looking for something just less than 5%. Of the options given, Fine Arts comes closest.

5. D Ballpark this one: $\frac{1}{2}$ of the university's New Construction expenditures is about 3%, $\frac{1}{4}$ of the Facility Maintenance expenditures is about 5%, and $\frac{3}{5}$ each of the Athletics and Admissions/Scholarships expenditures adds up to about 12%. That's a total of 3% + 5% + 12% = 20%, and 20% of $120 million is $24 million, so the answer is (D).

6. B Athletic expenditures were 9.5%, while income was 6.1%; the difference, the part of athletic expenditures NOT covered by athletic income, is 3.4%, and $\frac{3.4}{9.5}$ can be Ballparked to about $\frac{3.5}{10}$, or about 35%.

7. B First, look on the bar chart to figure out in which months City Y had an average rainfall greater than 3 inches and then apply that information to the temperature chart. According to the bar chart, the only months that City Y had an average rainfall exceeding 3 inches were January, February, March, October, November, and December. According to the line chart, in only two of those months did City X's average lows exceed 30 degrees: October and November.

8. C This is a multi-step problem, so you should take it one step at a time. First, determine the monthly midpoint for each month. The high in July is 78, and the low is 59, so the monthly midpoint is 78 + 59 = 137, and 137 ÷ 2 = 68.5. Similarly, the midpoint for August is 76 + 57 = 133, and 133 ÷ 2 = 66.5. September's midpoint is 68 + 50 = 118, and 118 ÷ 2 = 59. The average of the three midpoints is 59 + 66.5 + 68.5 = 194. 194 ÷ 3 = 64.7, (C).

9. D For 1979, find 27.5% of 18,509, which is approximately 5,090. For 2004, find 17.5% of 20,623, which is approximately 3,609. Round the numbers and reduce the ratio: $\frac{5,000}{3,600} = \frac{25}{18}$, (D).

10. B, C Choice (A) is incorrect; the graph gives no information on the number of power plants constructed. Choice (B) is correct. In 1979, coal and oil were each 26% and natural gas was 34% of total energy used, for a total of 68%. In 2004, coal was 34%, natural gas was 33%, and oil was 18% of total energy used, for a total of 85%. For (C), the amount of energy used from hydroelectric sources in 1979 is approximately 925 units and the amount for 2004 is approximately 203 units. You calculate these figures by using the different totals for each year and the percentage of total energy represented on the graph by hydroelectric energy. 203 is less than one fourth of 925, and thus (C) is valid.

11. C Avoid the temptation to work this problem in dollars—you can save considerable effort by dealing directly with the percentages. The pie chart for 1994 shows that clubs made up 25% of the total U.S. production, and the table shows that the United States accounted for 62.3% of the total world production; 25% (or $\frac{1}{4}$) of 62.3% is 15.575%, which is closest to (C), 16%.

12.   **A**   Avoid the temptation to work this problem in dollars. You can save considerable effort by dealing directly with the percentages. Start by adding the appropriate percentages from the pie chart for 1994: 16% (balls) + 7% (bags) + 3% (gift items) = 26%. Next, find what percentage that is of world production. Since the United States has 62.3% of world production, balls, bags, and gift items represent 26% of 62.3%, or 16.2% of world production. Finally, find the value in the chart that is nearest 16.2%—Japan, at 15.7%, is the closest.

13.   **D**   For this problem, be sure to get the correct dollar values from the chart and to use the percent change formula: $\dfrac{difference}{original} \times 100$. Because the increase was from $384 million in 1996 to $457 million in 1998, the difference is $73 million; $\dfrac{73}{384} \times 100$ reduces to 19.01%. The answer is (D). If you got (C), you may have mistakenly used the ending value, $457 million, in place of the original value.

14.   **A**   Since the problem asks for the approximate value of Region Z's honey production in 1985, you'll need to use the first and third graphs. The first graph tells you that there were about 15,000 pounds of honey produced that year, and the third graph tells you that each pound was worth just less than 125 cents, so try 120 cents—or, since the answer needs to be in dollars, $1.20: 15,000 pounds × $1.20 per pound = $18,000. The closest answer is (A).

15.   **B**   Use the graph to estimate your starting values and then use the percent change formula, which is $\dfrac{difference}{original} \times 100$. The largest number of colonies—about 12,000—was in 1981, while 1984 and 1986 appear to be tied for lowest at about 5,000 colonies. Since all values are in the thousands, simplify by calling your values 12 and 5: $\dfrac{12-5}{12} \times 100 = \dfrac{7}{12} \times 100$, which is approximately 60%. As always, watch out for trap answers: if you selected (A), you may have set the original value to 5 instead of 12.

Drill 3

1.   **D**   From 1997 to 1999, Airline A bought 44% of its 250 airplanes, or 110 airplanes. In the same time period, Airline B bought 26% of its 450 airplanes, or 117 airplanes. The sum of 110 and 117 is 227 airplanes, (D).

2.   **D**   The 2002 inventory at Airline A shows that 4% was purchased in 1994. The actual number in inventory is 4% of 250, or 10 airplanes. Of the 25 airplanes purchased, 15 must have been sold. Use percent translation to translate the question into algebra: "15 is what percent of 25" becomes $15 = \dfrac{x}{100} \times 25$. Solving for x gives you 60, (D).

3.   C   Although Airline *A* has fewer airplanes than does Airline *B*, you have no information about each airline's customers; (A) is incorrect. While the percent of airplanes purchased by Airline *B* is twice as large as that purchased by Airline *A*, the actual number of airplanes purchased by Airline *B* is approximately four times as large as those for Airline *A*, not twice as large. So, (B) is incorrect. To evaluate (C), you need to find the median airplane age for each airline. To do that, you need to add the percents in each column year by year until you get to 50%, which will be the median age. The airplane with the median age for Airline *A* was purchased in 1997. For Airline *B*, the median is between 1995 and 1996, making the median age for the airplanes in Airline *B*'s inventory older. This validates (C), the only correct answer.

4.   C   The private : public ratio in 1990 was about $\frac{13}{5}$. Setting the ratios equal for the two years (setting up a proportion) gives you: $\frac{13}{5} = \frac{x}{11,000}$. The private cost is approximately $29,000, so the answer is (C).

5.   D   The cost increases from about $6,000 to $22,000. Use the percent change formula to find the percent increase: $\frac{16,000}{6,000} \times 100 \approx 267\%$, so the answer is (D).

6.   E   The average cost of a private university in 1995 was $17,000, and the cost in 2000 was $22,000, as you discovered in the previous question. The increase over the 5-year period was $5,000. If the average cost increased at a constant rate, then the increase was $1,000 per year. The 3-year increase from 1995 to 1998 was therefore $3,000, putting the average cost for a private university at $20,000 in 1998. To find the total cost for that year, multiply the average cost per student by the number of students: ($20,000)(2.5 million) = $50 billion. Similarly, in 1990, the total dollar amount spent on private universities was ($13,000)(2 million) = $26 billion. The billions cancel out of the percent change formula, giving you $\frac{24}{26} \times 100 \approx 92\%$, which is the closest to (E).

7.   D   One way to answer this question is to assign numerical values to the percentages given in the graphs. You can choose any numbers to work with and get the same answer, but since the graphs give percentages, choosing 100 total plants sold will make things easy. If total plants sold were 100, 71 were annuals. Of those 71 annuals, the second graph says that 24% were herbs. 24% × 71 = 17.04. Since you started with 100 total plants, $\frac{17.04}{100} = 17.04\%$. Choice (D) is nearest 17.04%, so it is the best answer. Alternatively, you could just work with the percentages. 24% of 71% (0.24 × 0.71) is 17.04%, which is nearest (D).

8. **A, B, C**

    1,000 plants were sold, and from the first graph, you know that 71% of them, or 710, were annuals. Looking at the second graph, 40% of the 710 annuals, or 284, were tomatoes. Of those, any, all, or none could have been Beefsteaks—you don't know anything about that. So any number between 0 and 284 will work, making (A), (B), and (C) the correct answer.

9. **11,111** The key here is recognizing that the same *percentage increase* does not equal the same *total increase of items*. To find the percentage increase from 2002 to 2003, use the percentage change formula:

    $$\% \ change = \frac{X_{present} - X_{past}}{X_{past}} \times 100$$

    Plugging in 10,000 for $X_{present}$ and 9,000 for X_{past}, you find an 11.1111% increase for 2002 to 2003. Since the problem said the percent increase was the same, find the increase in number of animals sold from 2003 to 2004: 11.1111% × 10,000 = 1111.11 more animals in 2004. Adding that to the number sold in 2003 (10,000) yields 11,111.11 in 2004, which rounded to the nearest integer is 11,111.

10. **D** Before you add the number of violent and nonviolent crimes for each year, look at the chart to see if any of the years are so obvious that you don't have to do the calculation. For 2009 and 2010, nonviolent crimes are clearly greater; for 2005, violent crimes are clearly greater. In 2006, there were about 4,700 violent crimes and 4,200 nonviolent crimes. In 2007, there were about 4,100 violent crimes and 3,800 nonviolent crimes. And in 2008, there were about 4,400 nonviolent crimes and 4,000 violent crimes. So for each of the years 2008, 2009, and 2010, there were more nonviolent than violent crimes. The correct answer is (D).

11. **B, C, E, F**

    One standard deviation captures 68% of the data points, or 34% in each direction from the mean. For this question, that means that 68% of the months of the year will have average high temperatures within one standard deviation of the annual average high temperature. 12 × 68% = 8.16, so 8 months will be within one standard deviation. Standard deviation assumes a "normal" (balanced on the high and low ends) distribution, so the 2 months with the greatest average monthly high temperature and the 2 with the lowest average monthly high temperature will fall outside of one standard deviation. To answer the question, use POE to eliminate the 2 most extreme months on each end. (Note that you don't have to calculate anything to find the correct answers.) It is clear that January has the lowest average high temperature, so eliminate (A). February probably comes next, but it doesn't matter since neither it nor December is an answer choice. November is definitely not one of the two months with the lowest average high temperatures, so (F) is in. July has the highest average high temperature, so eliminate (D). Whether June or August is second doesn't matter for us because neither is an answer choice, but that means March, May, September, and November all make the cut.

12. **1982** The question asks you to determine the overall average percent increase in the price per pound of honey (the 3rd chart) and then compare that to each year's annual percent decrease in the number of honey producing colonies (the 2nd chart) to find the most similar percentage. So begin by first calculating the average percent increase in the price per pound of honey. In 1980, the average price per pound of honey is about 55 cents. In 1986, the average price per pound of honey is about 140 cents. So to calculate the average yearly increase, you'll use the percent change formula to find the total increase, and then divide that number by 6 to find the average annual increase over the 6-year period. The percent increase formula is $\% \ increase = \frac{X_{higher} - X_{lower}}{X_{lower}} \times 100$, so in this case the overall percent increase is $\frac{140 - 55}{55} \times 100 = \frac{85}{55} \times 100 \approx 155\%$. To find the average percent increase, divide that by 6. Therefore, $\frac{155}{6} \approx 26$. So there was an average annual increase of 26% over the 6-year period. Now, use the 2nd chart to find which percent decrease in the number of colonies is closest to 26%. You'll notice that there are only 4 years that show a decrease from the previous year: 1982, 1983, 1984, and 1986. So use the percent decrease formula: $\% \ increase = \frac{X_{higher} - X_{lower}}{X_{higher}} \times 100$.

1982: Shows a decrease from 12,000 to 9,000, so 25%. That's close.

1983: Shows a decrease from 9,000 to 7,000, so about 22%.

1984: Shows a decrease from 7,000 to 5,000, so about 29%.

1986: Shows a decrease from 6,000 to 5,000, so about 17%.

Therefore, 1982, at 25%, is the closest and the best answer.

13. **C, D** First, find the total U.S. production of golf goods in 2008. Calculate the percent change from 1994 to 2001 using the percent change formula:

$$\% \ change = \frac{X_{present} - X_{past}}{X_{past}} \times 100$$

with values of 3,770 for $X_{present}$ and 2,691 for X_{past}. The percent change from 1994 to 2001 was 40.1%. Multiply the 2001 value by 40.1% and add that to the original value to find the 2008 production value of 5,282. Next, figure out the percentage of 2008 production that could be from balls, bags, and training aids. In 2001, those three categories together made up 17% + 7% + 4% = 28%

of production. If each category's share of total production increased between one and five percentage points, the minimum the three categories together could have grown is 3%, and the maximum they could have grown is 15%. So, the minimum percent of production they represent in 2008 is 28% + 3% = 31%, and the maximum is 28% + 15% = 43%. The minimum production value they represent then is 31% × 5,282 = 1,637, and the maximum is 43% × 5282 = 2,271. Choices (C) and (D) are the only answers that fall in that range.

14. **8** On each side of the mean, 34% of individuals fall within one, an additional 14% of individuals fall within two, and the final 2% of individuals fall within three standard deviations. 49.4 cm is exactly one standard deviation above the mean maple tree diameter. Therefore, 16% of the maple trees will have a diameter larger than 49.4. Therefore, 16% × 50 trees = 8 trees.

Drill 4

1. **B** Remember the percent change formula:

$$\% \ change = \frac{X_{present} - X_{past}}{X_{past}} \times 100$$

All the values are in billions, so you can ignore all the zeroes and just use the smaller numbers from the graph. In this case, X_{past} is Pluton's 2010 GDP, or about 24.5, and $X_{present}$ is Pluton's 2011 GDP, or about 28.2. Plug those into the percent change formula and use your on-screen calculator to get an answer of 15.1%, making (B) the best answer.

2. **2010** The question asks you to sum the two countries' GDPs for each year and determine the year in which the change from the year prior was the least. Rather than determining the GDP for each country for each year and adding and subtracting, glance at the graph and see if any years stand out as having significantly less increase than the others. In 2010, Pluton's GDP shrank by about $1.5 billion and Shinmark's grew by $0.5 billion, for a net decrease of about $1 billion. In no other year was there a combined decrease, so 2010 must be the correct answer.

3. **A, B, C, E, F**

   You could calculate and compare $\frac{1}{2}$ of Shinmark's GDP to $\frac{1}{4}$ of Pluton's for each year. Alternatively, multiply both of the fractions by 4 to make the numbers easier to deal with; compare twice Shinmark's GDP to all of Pluton's. Looking at the graph, the only year that twice Shinmark's GDP isn't greater than Pluton's is 2009, so for all the other years, Shinmark's military spending exceeds Pluton's.

4. **C, D, E**

Ignore the population growth: the question is asked in *per capita* terms, so it's asking about the population as a whole. Coal production was 25 in 1979, when, according to the graph, coal represented 27% of energy; since 25 is 27% of 92.6, the total energy was 92.6 in 1979, and double that, or 185.2, in 2004. The lower end of the range is oil, at about 17%, and 17% of 185.2 is about 31.5; the upper end of the range is coal, at about 34%, or about 63. Choices (C), (D), and (E) fall within the range.

5. **285**   By inspecting the departures for all the countries in the table, China by far has the greatest increase in percentage of total number of departures. While no other country has even doubled its departure percentage, China has nearly quadrupled its percentage. Once you notice that, you need to remember the percentage change formula:

$$\% \ change = \frac{X_{present} - X_{past}}{X_{past}} \times 100$$

Then you can just plug in 2.0 for X_{past} and 7.7 for $X_{present}$ and find the correct answer: 285.

6. **B, C** To solve this question take each answer one at a time. For week 1, the ratio of biking to swimming was almost 8 to a little over 2; let's call it 7.8 : 2.1 or 8 : 2, which falls outside the range. For week 2, the ratio was 8.5 : 3.2, which falls within the range. For week 3, the ratio is 9 : 3.9, which is definitely within the range. For week 4, the ratio is 8.5 : 4.5, which is close, but outside the range.

7. **A**   To determine the percent of training time dedicated to swimming, divide the time spent swimming by the total training time and multiply by 100. For example, in week 1, the athlete swims 2.1 hours and trains a total of 14.7 hours, so she spent a little over 14% of her training time swimming. Week 2, swimming represents about 19%; week 3, 20%; and week 4, 23%. Week 1 is the only week for which swimming represents between 12 and 16% of total training time, so (A) is the correct answer.

8. **C**   Remember that Rate = Distance / Time. Since you are solving for distance, rearrange to get Distance = Rate × Time. In this case Rate = 7 miles per hour, and from the graph, Time = 5.2 hours. 7 × 5.2 = 36.4.

9. **C**   You can determine what hours make a 10–20% decrease by calculating 10% and 20% of the original value and subtracting, or, to save time, just calculate 90% and 80% of the original value. She biked 8.5 hours in week 4. 80% × 8.5 = 6.8, and 90% × 8.5 = 7.7, so any number of hours between 6.8 and 7.7 will be acceptable. Choice (C) is the only answer that falls in that range.

10. **109** First, to find the number of technology books in each category, you need to multiply the percentages or fractions by the total numbers of books sold for each respective category of science/nature books. Then add all those together to find the correct answer. For new adult, $\frac{1}{3} \times 150 = 50$. For used adult, $0.50 \times 70 = 35$. For new children's, $\frac{1}{10} \times 120 = 12$. For used children's, $\frac{1}{10} \times 120 = 12$. The final answer is $50 + 35 + 12 + 12 = 109$.

11. **B, D** Rather than calculating, think in terms of the slope of the line connecting successive data points for assault. A greater rate of increase means a more sharply sloping downward line: the line from 2006 to 2007 is steeper than the one from 2005 to 2006, so (B) is correct, and the line from 2008 to 2009 is steeper than the one from 2007 to 2008, so (D) is also correct. For all the other years, the decrease in assaults is less than the previous year, so only (B) and (D) are correct.

12. **A, C, D**

    To find the percent change, use the percent change formula, $\frac{\text{difference}}{\text{original}} \times 100$, and be sure to use the values for 2005 as the original. Assaults changed by 40%, burglary changed by 62%, and auto theft changed by 30%, so (A), (C), and (D) are correct. Only domestic violence, which changed 21%, didn't change more than 25%.

13. **626** You have to calculate the number of planes each company sells and buys for 2003 and 2004 in order to calculate the total number of planes in 2004. In 2003, each company sells the planes they bought 10 years prior to 1993. For A, $250 \times 10\% = 25$ planes removed; for B, $450 \times 20\% = 90$ planes removed. In 2003, A has only 225, so they add 10%, or 22 new planes, for a new total of 247, and B has 360 left, so they add 36 for a new total of 396. In 2004, they sell the old planes they bought in 1994: for A, $250 \times 4\% = 10$ planes; for B, $450 \times 14\% = 63$ planes. Now A has $247 - 10 = 237$, so they add 23 for a 2004 total of 260. B now has $396 - 63 = 333$, so they add 33 for a 2004 total of 366. Add the two numbers together to get $260 + 366 = 626$ planes in 2004.

14. **D** The grants cover only tuition, so you first need to find the costs of tuition for public and private university students in 1995. From the graph, a public student's average total costs were about $6,000 and the question says that 50% of that went to tuition, or about $3,000. For private students, average total costs were about $24,500 and 85% went to tuition, or about $20,825. Now multiply those average tuition costs by the number of students in each university type that got a grant to get the total dollars awarded. Between $\frac{1}{4}$ and $\frac{1}{3}$ of the 4,000 awardees were public university students, which equates to 1,000 to 1,333 students. The

remaining 2,667 to 3,000 awardees, then, were private university students. Based on the information provided, private university tuition is higher than public university tuition, so the high end of the total grant range will occur when the maximum number of private university students and the minimum number of public university students are awarded the grants: (3,000 private students × $20,825/student) + (1,000 public students × $3,000/student) = $65.48 million. The low end of the range will occur when the maximum number of public university students and the minimum number of private university students are awarded the grants: (2,667 private students × $20,825/student) + (1,333 public students × $3,000/student) = $59.54 million. The only answer choice that falls between $59.54 million and $65.48 million is (D).

Linear Equations and Inequalities

LINEAR EQUATIONS AND INEQUALITIES

Linear equations are simply problems that require manipulating the equations and solving for x. In a general sense, your job is to get all the numbers on one side and all the letters on the other. Whatever you do to one side, you must do to the other so that they remain equal. You can subtract a number from both sides. You can divide both sides by a variable so that it disappears from one side and its reciprocal shows up on the other.

As you are manipulating your equations, make sure that you aren't doing more work than you have to. If the question asks for the value of $3x$, you don't need to know the value of x, only $3x$. If you are asked for the value of $2x + 2y$, you may not need to know the actual value of either x or y—just manipulate the equation into a $2x + 2y$ format.

If you have a >, <, ≥, or ≤ sign, the processes remain exactly the same with one exception: if you multiply or divide by a negative number, you must reverse the sign.

USE PLUGGING IN

Don't forget that you can always Plug In if you're given the right conditions. If you have variables in the answer choices, Plug In. If it is a Quant Comp, this means making your set-up. If it is a problem-solving question, you must write down your answer choices, label your terms, circle your target number, and check all of your answer choices.

If you see the phrase "how much," "how many," or "what is the value of," you can plug in the answer choices. Label your first column—assume choice (C) to be the correct answer choice—and work though the problem in bite-sized pieces, making a new answer choice for every step.

SIMULTANEOUS EQUATIONS

You may also see simultaneous equations. This means that you have two equations with two variables or three equations with three variables. To get rid of one variable, you simply stack the equations, line up the variables and either add or subtract the equations. Your goal is to nullify one variable so that you can solve for the other.

Example:

$$2x + 3y = 12$$
$$+ \quad x - 3y = 3$$
$$\overline{3x = 15}$$
$$x = 5$$

When you add these two equations, the y's cancel out and you're left with only x's. If you're not sure whether to add or subtract, don't worry, just try one. If it doesn't work, try the other. Sometimes you may have to manipulate an equation a bit in order to make sure that one variable cancels out. For example, if you were to add

$$2x + 3y = 12$$

$$x - y = 3$$

...you wouldn't get very far. However, if you multiply the second equation by three (remember that whatever you do on one side of the equal sign you must do on the other), you can get the y's to cancel out.

$$2x + 3y = 12 \qquad 2x + 3y = 12$$
$$3(x - y = 3) = + \quad 3x - 3y = 9$$
$$\overline{5x = 21}$$
$$x = \frac{21}{5}$$

For more practice and a more in-depth look at The Princeton Review math techniques, check out our student-friendly guidebook, *Cracking the GRE*.

DRILL 1

Question 1

If $4c + 6 = 26$, then what is the value of $3c - 2$?

- ○ $-\dfrac{1}{2}$
- ○ 4
- ○ 5
- ○ 13
- ○ 22

Question 2

Quantity A	Quantity B
$\dfrac{3k - 12j}{9}$	$\dfrac{k - 4j}{3}$

- ○ Quantity A is greater.
- ○ Quantity B is greater.
- ○ The two quantities are equal.
- ○ The relationship cannot be determined from the information given.

Question 3

What is the value of $(n - 5)(m + 5)$ when $n = -5$ and $m = 5$?

- ○ −100
- ○ −10
- ○ 0
- ○ 10
- ○ 100

Question 4

$$\frac{2}{3}y = \frac{1}{8}$$

Quantity A	Quantity B
y	$\dfrac{1}{12}$

- ○ Quantity A is greater.
- ○ Quantity B is greater.
- ○ The two quantities are equal.
- ○ The relationship cannot be determined from the information given.

Question 5

$$7a + 8 = 8a - 24$$

Quantity A	Quantity B
a	24

- ○ Quantity A is greater.
- ○ Quantity B is greater.
- ○ The two quantities are equal.
- ○ The relationship cannot be determined from the information given.

Question 6

If x does not equal 0 or 1, the expression

$$\dfrac{\dfrac{1}{x} - 1}{\dfrac{1}{x}}$$ is equivalent to which of the following?

○ $\dfrac{x}{x-1}$

○ $x - 1$

○ -1

○ $1 - x$

○ 1

Question 7

$$0 < a < b < 1$$

Quantity A	Quantity B
0	$2(a - b)$

○ Quantity A is greater.
○ Quantity B is greater.
○ The two quantities are equal.
○ The relationship cannot be determined from the information given.

Question 8

If $a \geq 30$ and $b \leq 15$, then which of the following must be true?

○ $a - b \leq 45$
○ $a - b \leq 15$
○ $a - b \geq 15$
○ $a + b \leq 45$
○ $a + b \geq 45$

Question 9

The product of the reciprocal of a certain positive integer and 16,000 is equal to the result of moving the decimal point of the original number three places to the right. What is the original number?

Question 10

If $5(x - 3) > 2(x + 9)$, which of the following describes all possible values of x ?

○ $x < -8$
○ $x > -2$
○ $x < 2$
○ $x > 4$
○ $x > 11$

Question 11

If $\dfrac{7 + 2x}{6 + y} = \dfrac{7}{3}$, then $6x - 7y =$

○ -7
○ 7
○ 21
○ 63
○ It cannot be determined from the information given.

Question 12

$$2 < 3a - 7 < 14$$
$$19 < 5b + 9 < 34$$

Quantity A	Quantity B
$\dfrac{a}{b}$	$\dfrac{7}{2}$

- ○ Quantity A is greater.
- ○ Quantity B is greater.
- ○ The two quantities are equal.
- ○ The relationship cannot be determined from the information given.

Question 13

If $a = 3b + 2$, then, in terms of a, what is the value of b ?

- ○ $b = \dfrac{a}{3} - \dfrac{2}{3}$
- ○ $b = \dfrac{a}{3} + \dfrac{2}{3}$
- ○ $b = \dfrac{a}{3} - 2$
- ○ $b = a - \dfrac{2}{3}$
- ○ $b = a + \dfrac{2}{3}$

Question 14

If 25 percent of a is b, and 20 percent of b is c, then a is what percent of c ?

- ○   0.5
- ○   5
- ○   20
- ○   200
- ○   2,000

Question 15

If $\dfrac{1}{2x} + \dfrac{2}{x} = \dfrac{5}{8}$, what is the value of x ?

- ○   2
- ○   3
- ○   4
- ○   7
- ○   8

Question 16

Sally bought chocolate chip cookies at x dollars per box and oatmeal cookies at y dollars per box. Two boxes of chocolate chip cookies cost 6 dollars less than 4 boxes of oatmeal cookies and 2 boxes of oatmeal cookies cost 3 dollars more than a box of chocolate chip cookies.

Quantity A	Quantity B
x	y

- ○ Quantity A is greater.
- ○ Quantity B is greater.
- ○ The two quantities are equal.
- ○ The relationship cannot be determined from the information given.

DRILL 2

Question 1

If $z = 3x$, $y = 4z$ and $xy \neq 0$, then what is the value of $\dfrac{xy}{z^2}$?

○   12

○ $\dfrac{4}{3}$

○   1

○ $\dfrac{3}{4}$

○ $\dfrac{1}{12}$

Question 2

A family buys a home with a value of v dollars. After 10 years, the value of the home has increased by x percent. After another 10 years, the value of the home has increased by an additional y percent from the value at 10 years. What is the value of the home, in dollars, 20 years after the family bought it?

○ $\left(v + \dfrac{vx}{100}\right)\left(1 + \dfrac{y}{100}\right)$

○ $v + \dfrac{x}{100} + \dfrac{y}{100}$

○ $v + \dfrac{xy}{100}$

○ $v + \dfrac{vx}{100} + \dfrac{vy}{100}$

○ $v + x + y$

Question 3

If both p and q are odd integers and $q > 0$, which of the following must be odd?

○ $(p - 2)^{q + 2}$
○ $p^q + 1$
○ $(p - 1)^q$
○ $p^q + q^p$
○ $(p + 1)^{q - 1}$

Question 4

$-1 < a - b < 10$, with b an integer such that $-3 \leq b \leq 1$. What most accurately describes the range of a^2 ?

○ $-16 < a^2 < 11$
○ $-4 < a^2 < 11$
○ $0 < a^2 < 16$
○ $0 < a^2 < 121$
○ $16 < a^2 < 121$

Question 5

If $3x + 5y = 34$ and $7x - 5y = -4$, then what is the value of y ?

$$\boxed{}$$

Question 6

If $\dfrac{x}{y} = 2$, and if x is 75% of z and z is 175%

of w, then what is w in terms of y ?

- ○ $\dfrac{21}{32}y$
- ○ $\dfrac{20}{21}y$
- ○ $\dfrac{32}{21}y$
- ○ $\dfrac{32}{9}y$
- ○ $\dfrac{21}{8}y$

Question 7

If integer x is greater than -3 and less than 7, and integer y is less than -2 and greater than -10, then which of the following expresses all possible values of xy ?

- ○ $-14 > xy > -30$
- ○ $18 \geq xy \geq -54$
- ○ $30 \geq xy \geq -14$
- ○ $-30 > xy > -70$
- ○ $30 > xy > -70$

Question 8

$$5a + 2b = 18$$
$$20a - 8b = 48$$

Quantity A	Quantity B
a	$7(b + 2)^0$

- ○ Quantity A is greater.
- ○ Quantity B is greater.
- ○ The two quantities are equal.
- ○ The relationship cannot be determined from the information given.

Question 9

If $a - c = 17$, $b - a = 12$ and $2a + b + 3c = 7$, then what is the value of $a + b + c$?

- ○ 2
- ○ 6
- ○ 9
- ○ 12
- ○ 18

Question 10

If $-4 \leq a \leq 9$, and $-3 \leq b \leq 2$, then what is the greatest possible value of $a - b$?

Question 11

If m and n are positive integers such that $m > n$ and $mn = 300$, what is the least possible value of $m - n$?

Question 12

If $m - n > 3$, then which of the following must be true?

Indicate <u>all</u> such statements.

- ☐ m is an integer
- ☐ n is an integer
- ☐ $m > n$
- ☐ $m + n > 0$
- ☐ $m - n > 0$
- ☐ $m \times n > 0$
- ☐ $m \div n > 0$

Question 13

All of the students in a certain class are either 7 or 8 years old. 80 percent of the students are boys and 25 percent of the girls are 8 years old. If there are an equal number of 7 year olds and 8 year olds, what percent of the students in the class are boys who are 7 years old?

$$\boxed{}$$

Question 14

If $-12 < x < -2$ and $3 < y < 6$, which of the following could equal xy?

Indicate <u>all</u> such values.

- ☐ -36
- ☐ -27
- ☐ -14.5
- ☐ -6
- ☐ -1.5
- ☐ 0
- ☐ 1.5

ANSWERS

Drill 1

1. D
2. C
3. A
4. A
5. A
6. D
7. A
8. C
9. 4
10. E
11. C
12. B
13. A
14. E
15. C
16. D

Drill 2

1. B
2. A
3. A
4. D
5. 5
6. C
7. E
8. B
9. E
10. 12
11. 5
12. C, E
13. 35
14. A, B, C

EXPLANATIONS
Drill 1

1. **D** When solving algebraically, be careful to perform the same operation on both sides of the equation: $4c + 6 = 26$, so subtract 6 from both sides to find $4c = 20$ and $c = 5$. Therefore, $3c - 2 = (3 \times 5) - 2 = 13$.

2. **C** You can find the two quantities to be equal by plugging in values for k and j: if $k = 2$ and $j = 3$, then Quantity A is $\dfrac{3(2) - 12(3)}{9}$, or $-\dfrac{30}{9}$, which can be reduced to $-\dfrac{10}{3}$; Quantity B is $\dfrac{2 - 4(3)}{3}$, or $-\dfrac{10}{3}$. Algebraically, try factoring and canceling a 3 out of the numerator of Quantity A: $\dfrac{3k - 12j}{9} = \dfrac{3(k - 4j)}{3 \times 3} = \dfrac{k - 4j}{3}$.

3. **A** Start by substituting the given values for the variables in the equation. You'll be left with $(-5 - 5)(5 + 5)$, which simplifies to $(-10)(10)$, or -100.

4. **A** Solve the given equation by multiplying both sides of the equation by $\dfrac{3}{2}$. You get a value of $\dfrac{3}{16}$ for y. Then use the Bowtie method to compare the fractions in the quantities; the fraction in Quantity A is greater.

5. **A** To solve this single-variable equation, you'll just need to isolate the variable. First, add 24 to both sides to yield $7a + 32 = 8a$. Then subtract $7a$ from both sides to yield $32 = a$. Quantity A is greater.

6. **D** Since there are variables in the question and answer choices, Plug In for x. Try $x = 3$. This gives you $\dfrac{\frac{1}{3} - 1}{\frac{1}{3}} = \dfrac{-\frac{2}{3}}{\frac{1}{3}} = -\dfrac{2}{3} \times \dfrac{3}{1} = -2$. This is your target number. Plug it into all of the answer choices.

   Only (D) works.

7. **A** You know that b is greater than a, so $(a - b)$ will always be negative, and Quantity A will always be greater. Alternatively, you can solve this one by plugging in values for a and b. Try making $a = \dfrac{1}{4}$ and $b = \dfrac{1}{2}$: the value in Quantity B is now $2\left(\dfrac{1}{4} - \dfrac{1}{2}\right) = 2\left(-\dfrac{1}{4}\right) = -\dfrac{1}{2}$. If you plug in again a couple of times, Quantity A will continue to be greater.

8. **C** Solve this "must be" problem by Plugging In values for a and b. Starting with the simplest allowable values, $a = 30$ and $b = 15$, does not eliminate any answer choices. Next, try $a = 100$ and $b = 0$; now (A), (B), and (D) can be eliminated. Finally, try $a = 30$ and $b = -30$; now (E) can be eliminated, leaving only (C), which is the correct answer.

9.　4　Translate the information in the question into an algebraic equation. The question refers to a *certain positive integer*. Call that integer n. The *reciprocal* of that number is $\frac{1}{n}$. The word *product* refers to multiplication, so the product of $\frac{1}{n}$ and 16,000 is $\frac{1}{n} \times 16{,}000 = \frac{1}{n} \times \frac{16{,}000}{1} = \frac{16{,}000}{n}$. This product is equal to the result of moving the decimal point of the original number three places to the right. Moving a decimal three places to the right is equivalent to multiplying by 10^3, which is 1,000. Therefore, the information in the question translates to $\frac{16{,}000}{n} = 1{,}000n$. The question asks for the original number, so solve for n. Multiply both sides by n to get to get $16{,}000 = 1{,}000n^2$. Divide both sides by 1,000 to get $16 = n^2$. Take the square root of both sides to get $n = \pm 4$. Since the question says the answer is a positive integer, the answer is 4.

10.　E　The question asks for all possible values of x, so isolate x. Start by distributing on both sides of the inequality. Distribute the 5 on the left side to get $5x - 15$ and the 2 on the right side to get $2x + 18$, so the inequality is $5x - 15 > 2x + 18$. Subtract $2x$ from both sides to get $3x - 15 > 18$. Add 15 to both sides to get $3x > 33$. Divide both sides by 3 to get $x > 11$, which is (E).

11.　C　The question provides a rational equation, so cross multiply to get $3(7 + 2x) = 7(6 + y)$. Distribute the 3 on the left side and the 7 on the right side to get $21 + 6x = 42 + 7y$. The question asks for $6x - 7y$, so get all the variables on one side of the equation. Subtract $7y$ from both sides to get $21 + 6x - 7y = 42$. Subtract 21 from both sides to get $6x - 7y = 21$, which is (C).

12.　B　Simplify the inequalities in the question. Add 7 to all three parts of the first inequality to yield $9 < 3a < 21$. Divide all three parts by 3 to get $3 < a < 7$. Subtract 9 from all three parts of the second inequality to get $10 < 5b < 25$. Divide all three parts by 5 to get $2 < b < 5$. Determine the possible values of Quantity A by dividing the endpoints of the ranges of a by the endpoints of the ranges of b. These quotients are $\frac{3}{2}$, $\frac{3}{5}$, $\frac{7}{2}$, and $\frac{7}{5}$. The least of the quotients is $\frac{3}{5}$, and the greatest of the quotients is $\frac{7}{2}$. Therefore $\frac{3}{5} < \frac{a}{b} < \frac{7}{2}$. Since $\frac{a}{b}$ must be less than $\frac{7}{2}$, Quantity B is always greater, so the answer is (B).

13.　A　The problem has variables, so Plug In. Pick a number for b. If $b = 2$, then $a = 8$. The question asks for b, so the target is 2. Plug 8 in for a in the answer choices looking for 2. The only answer choice that will work is (A).

14.	E	This is a percent question, so use translation. Remember that the word *is* translates to *equals*, the word *what* translates to a variable, the word *percent* translates to $\frac{}{100}$, and the word *of* translates to *times*. Because the variables are given in terms of each other, Plug In. Because it is a percent question, Plug In $c = 100$. The phrase *20 percent of b is c* translates to $\frac{20}{100} \times b = c$. Substitute $c = 100$ to get $\frac{20}{100} \times b = 100$. Reduce the fraction on the left side to get $\frac{1}{5} \times b = 100$. Multiply both sides by 5 to get $b = 500$. The phrase *25 percent of a is b* translates to $\frac{25}{100} \times a = b$. Substitute $b = 500$ to get $\frac{25}{100} \times a = 500$. Reduce the fraction on the left side to get $\frac{1}{4} \times a = 500$. Multiply both sides by 4 to get $a = 2,000$. Translate the question *a is what percent of c* to get $a = \frac{x}{100} \times c$. Substitute $a = 2,000$ and $c = 100$ to get $2,000 = \frac{x}{100} \times 100$. Simplify the right side to get $2,000 = x$, so the answer is (E).

15.	C	Plug In the Answers starting with (C). Choice (C) yields $\frac{1}{8} + \frac{2}{4} = \frac{1}{8} + \frac{4}{8} = \frac{5}{8}$, so it's the correct answer.

16.	D	Translate the information given into equations. Two boxes of chocolate chip cookies cost 6 dollars less than 4 boxes of oatmeal cookies translates to $2x = 4y - 6$ and 2 boxes of oatmeal cookies cost 3 dollars more than a box of chocolate chip cookies translates to $2y = x + 3$. If you rearrange the two equations, you will get $2x = 4y - 6$ and $x = 2y - 3$. Now, notice that the first equation is a multiple of the second equation, which means that you have 2 variables and only 1 equation, so you cannot solve.

Drill 2

1.	B	You have variables in the answers, so Plug In. If $x = 2$, then $z = 6$ and $y = 24$. So, $\frac{xy}{z^2} = \frac{(2)(24)}{6^2} = \frac{48}{36} = \frac{4}{3}$. The correct answer is (B).

2.	A	There are variables in the question stem and answer choices, so this is a Plugging In problem. Because the question involves percents, Plug In $v = 100$ to make the value of the home $100. After 10 years, the value of the home increased by x%. Plug In $x = 20$. Since 20% of $100 is $20, the new value of the home is $100 + $20 = $120. After another 10 years, the value of the home increases by an additional y%. Pick an easy number for y such as $y = 10$. Since 10% of

$120 is $\frac{10}{100} \times \$120 = \frac{\$1,200}{100} = \$12$, the new value of the home is $120 + $12 = $132. The question asks for the value of the home 20 years after the family bought it, so the target is 132.

Plug $v = 100$, $x = 20$, and $y = 10$ into all the answer choices, looking for one that equals 132.

Choice (A) is $\left(100 + \frac{100 \times 20}{100}\right)\left(1 + \frac{10}{100}\right) = (100 + 20)\left(1 + \frac{1}{10}\right) = 120(1.1) = 132$, which matches the target, so keep (A). Choice (B) is $100 + \frac{20}{100} + \frac{10}{100} = 100 + 0.2 + 0.1 = 100.3$, so eliminate (B). Choice (C) is $100 + \frac{20 \times 10}{100} = 100 + \frac{200}{100} = 100 + 2 = 102$, so eliminate (C). Choice (D) is $100 + \frac{100 \times 20}{100} + \frac{100 \times 10}{100} = 100 + 20 + 10 = 130$, so eliminate (D). Choice (E) is $100 + 20 + 10$ = 130, so eliminate (E). The correct answer is (A).

3. **A** The question says *must be,* so Plug In. The question says that p and q are odd integers, so Plug In $p = 3$ and $q = 5$ into the answer choices and eliminate any that are not odd. Choice (A) is $(3 - 2)^{5+2} = 1^7 = 1$, which is odd, so keep (A). Choice (B) is $3^5 + 1 = 243 + 1 = 244$, which is even, so eliminate (B). Choice (C) is $(3 - 1)^5 = 2^5 = 32$, which is even, so eliminate (C). Choice (D) is $3^5 + 5^3 = 243 + 125 = 368$, which is even, so eliminate (D). Choice (E) is $(3 + 1)^{5-1} = 4^4 = 256$, which is even, so eliminate (E). The correct answer is (A).

4. **D** If a range of values for a can be found, then the range of values for a^2 can be found. Start by testing the end values of b, -3, and 1. Plug In -3 for b in the first given inequality and then solve for a. You will find that $-4 < a < 7$. Plugging In $b = 1$ will give you $0 < a < 11$. Combining the 2 ranges gives you the full range of a, which is $-4 < a < 11$. However, the question is looking for the range of a^2, not a. a^2 must always be positive and since $a < 11$, a^2 must be less than 121, which means $0 < a^2 < 121$; the answer is (D).

5. **5** There are simultaneous equations, so stack and add. The coefficients on the y terms in each equation are the same, so there is no need to multiply either equation by a constant before adding. Stack the equations to get

$$
\begin{array}{r}
3x + 5y = 34 \\
+\ 7x - 5y = -4 \\
\hline
10x \quad\ \ = 30
\end{array}
$$

Divide both sides by 10 to get $x = 3$. However, the question asks for the value of y, so substitute $x = 3$ into either of the original equations. Use the first. $3(3) + 5y = 34$. Simplify the left side to get $9 + 5y = 34$. Subtract 9 from both sides to get $5y = 25$. Divide both sides by 5 to get $y = 5$. The correct answer is 5.

6. **C** Since the question involves variables, Plug In. To find some good numbers to Plug In, translate the statements. If x is 75% of z, then $x = \dfrac{75}{100}z = \dfrac{3}{4}z$ and if z is 175% of w, then $z = \dfrac{175}{100}w = \dfrac{7}{4}w$. Notice you are dividing by 4 a couple times, so try $w = 16$. If $w = 16$, then $z = 28$, $x = 21$, and $y = \dfrac{21}{2}$. The question is asking for w, so the target is 16. Plug $y = \dfrac{21}{2}$ into the answer choices and only (C) will match the target.

7. **E** To solve this question, first translate the statements into inequalities. x is greater than –3 and less than 7 translates to $-3 < x < 7$ and y is less than –2 and greater than –10 translates to $-10 < y < -2$. The best way to test out all the possible solutions of xy is to multiply out the different combinations of the endpoints of x and y together and put them all on a number line. So, $(-3)(-10) = 30$, $(-3)(-2) = 6$, $(7)(-10) = -70$, and $(7)(-2) = -14$. Arranging these numbers in order gives you 30, 6, –14, –70. So, that means that xy can have values between 30 and –70, which is answer (E).

8. **B** The question involves simultaneous equations, so stack and add. However, first note what the two quantities are. Quantity A is a, and Quantity B is $7(b + 2)^0$. For Quantity B, any number raised to the 0th power is 1, so $7(b + 2)^0 = 7(1) = 7$. Therefore, there is no need to find the value of b. To find a, stack and add, but first, get the coefficients on b to have the same absolute value, so the b terms will cancel. Multiply both sides of the first equation by 4 to get $20a + 8b = 72$. Stack the two equations and add

$$\begin{array}{r} 20a + 8b = 72 \\ + \underline{20a - 8b = 48} \\ 40a = 120 \end{array}$$

Divide both sides by 40 to get $a = 3$. Since Quantity A is 3 and Quantity B is 7, Quantity B is greater. The correct answer is (B).

9. **E** Start by rearranging the equations to line up the variables and stacking the equations:

$a - c = 17$
$-a + b = 12$
$2a + b + 3c = 7$

Now, add all 3 equations to get $2a + 2b + 2c = 36$. Divide each side of the equation by 2 to get $a + b + c = 18$, (E).

10. **12** You are being asked to subtract the a and b terms. Be careful that you don't just combine the largest value of a with the largest value of b to get $a - b = 9 - 2 = 7$, the wrong answer. When you combine inequalities, you have to make four calculations to check the four possibilities. Subtract the smallest values of a and b: $-4 - (-3) = -1$. Subtract the largest values of a and b: $9 - 2 = 7$. Subtract the smallest value of a and the largest value of b: $-4 - 2 = -6$. Subtract the largest value of a and the smallest value of *b*: 9 − (−3) = 12. Of the four possible values above, the greatest possible value is 12.

11. 5   The question asks for the least possible value of *m* − *n*, so find the possible values of *m* and *n*. Since *mn* = 300, *m* and *n* are a pair of factors of 300. Find the pairs of factors by starting with 1 and 300. Find the other factors by working toward the middle. Since 2 × 150 = 300, 2 and 150 are a pair of factors. Since 3 × 100 = 300, 3 and 100 are a pair of factors. Since 4 × 75 = 300, 4 and 75 are a pair of factors. Since 5 × 60 = 300, 5 and 60 are factors. Since 6 × 50 = 300, 6 and 50 are a pair of factors. 7, 8, and 9 are not factors. Since 10 × 30 = 300, 10 and 30 are a pair of factors. 11 is not a factor. Since 12 × 25 = 300, 12 and 25 are a pair of factors. 13 and 14 are not factors. Since 15 × 20 = 300, 15 and 20 are a pair of factors. 16, 17, 18, and 19 are not factors. Since 20 is already on the list, there are no more factors. To find the least possible value of *m* − *n*, find the pair of factors that have the least difference. These are 15 and 20. Since *m* > *n*, let *m* = 20 and *n* = 15. Therefore, *m* − *n* = 20 − 15 = 5. The correct answer is 5.

12. C, E   Try Plugging In values for *m* and *n* into the inequality in the question. If *m* = 5 and *n* = 1, both numbers are integers, so (A) and (B) work as do all of the other choices. But what if *m* and *n* are negative decimals, say −2.3 and −6.3? Then (A) and (B) don't work, since neither number is an integer; eliminate them. Choice (C) still works. Choice (D) is out, since the sum of the two numbers is negative, but the difference is positive, leaving (E) in. Choices (F) and (G) also still work. However, by switching *m* to a positive value, such as 5, and keeping *n* negative, you can knock out (F) and (G). Only (C) and (E) will work no matter what numbers you plug in.

13. 35   You have a percentage of an unknown total, so this question is a Hidden Plug In. Pick a number for the total number of students. Since the question is dealing with percentages, pick 100 for the total number of students in the class. Since 80% of the students are boys, that means that there are 80 boys and 20 girls. And since there are an equal number of 7 year olds and 8 year olds, that means that 50 students are 7 years old and 50 students are 8 years old. If 25% of the girls are 8 years old, then that means that there are five 8-year-old girls and therefore there are fifteen 7-year-old girls. If there are fifteen 7-year-old girls, then there must be thirty-five 7-year-old boys. Since there were 100 total students to begin with, 35% of the class is boys who are 7 years old. Alternatively, you can employ the group grid:

	Boys	Girls	Total
7	35	15	50
8	45	5	50
Total	80	20	100

14. A, B, C

The lower boundary for *xy* is −12 × 6, or −72, and the upper boundary is −2 × 3 = −6. Any values between −72 and −6 work. Be careful about (D): the value has to be greater than −6, so −6 itself doesn't count.

Quadratic Equations

QUADRATIC EQUATIONS

You probably remember FOIL (First Outer Inner Last) from high school and you may also remember how to find the roots of an equation. On the GRE, there are really only three quadric equation formats that you will see.

Memorize these equations:

$$(x + y)^2 = x^2 + 2xy + y^2$$

$$(x - y)^2 = x^2 - 2xy + y^2$$

$$(x + y)(x - y) = x^2 - y^2$$

Each of the above expressions has two states—the factored state and the squared state. When you see an expression in one state, rewrite it in the other state. Typically these questions will be about manipulating equations, not about solving for x. If the equations don't match one of these three formats, see if you can factor numbers or variables out of them until they do.

Naturally, the minute you see a quadratic equation, either on a Quantitative Comparison or a problem-solving question, if you see variables in the question and variables in the answer choices, you can always Plug In. Use your Plug In setup for Quant Comp and Plug In more than once. On problem-solving questions, make sure you have labeled the terms, circled a target number, and checked all of the answer choices.

For more practice and a more in-depth look at The Princeton Review math techniques, check out our student-friendly guidebook, *Cracking the GRE*.

DRILL 1

Question 1

Quantity A	Quantity B
$(3p + 1)(3p - 1)$	$9p^2$

- ○ Quantity A is greater.
- ○ Quantity B is greater.
- ○ The two quantities are equal.
- ○ The relationship cannot be determined from the information given.

Question 2

$$a > 0$$

Quantity A	Quantity B
$(a + 2)(3a + 6)$	$(3a + 2)(a + 6)$

- ○ Quantity A is greater.
- ○ Quantity B is greater.
- ○ The two quantities are equal.
- ○ The relationship cannot be determined from the information given.

Question 3

Quantity A	Quantity B
$3^2 - 2^2$	$(3 - 2)(3 + 2)$

- ○ Quantity A is greater.
- ○ Quantity B is greater.
- ○ The two quantities are equal.
- ○ The relationship cannot be determined from the information given.

Question 4

If $(2x + 2)^2 = 0$, then $x =$

☐

Question 5

$$a > 0$$

Quantity A	Quantity B
$(-a - 10)(10 + a)$	10

- ○ Quantity A is greater.
- ○ Quantity B is greater.
- ○ The two quantities are equal.
- ○ The relationship cannot be determined from the information given.

Question 6

$$(y - 1)(y + 5) = 0$$

Quantity A	Quantity B
y	3

- ○ Quantity A is greater.
- ○ Quantity B is greater.
- ○ The two quantities are equal.
- ○ The relationship cannot be determined from the information given.

Question 7

If $m > 0$ and $3m^2 + 12m - 15 = 0$, then $m =$

☐

Question 8

If the difference between two numbers is 4, then which of the following would be sufficient to determine the value of each of the numbers?

Indicate all such values.

☐ The sum of the numbers is 4.
☐ The difference between the squares of the numbers is 16.
☐ The square of the difference between the numbers is 16.
☐ The sum of the squares of the numbers is greater than 8.
☐ Twice the greater number is 8.
☐ The smaller of the two numbers is less than 8.
☐ The product of the two numbers is 0, and neither of the numbers is negative.

Question 9

A rectangle is formed by increasing two opposite sides of a square of side length x by y units, and decreasing the two remaining sides of the square by y units. What is the area of the rectangle?

○ $4x$
○ $4x - 2y$
○ $x^2 - 2y$
○ $x^2 + 2y$
○ $x^2 - y^2$

Question 10

The net profit that Ann makes from selling x pillows is given by the expression $x^2 - 2x - 288$.

Quantity A	Quantity B
The number of pillows that Ann must sell for her net profit to be zero	20

○ Quantity A is greater.
○ Quantity B is greater.
○ The two quantities are equal.
○ The relationship cannot be determined from the information given.

Question 11

What is the greatest value of x for which $(3x - 2)(x + 1) = 0$?

○ -1

○ $-\dfrac{2}{3}$

○ $\dfrac{2}{3}$

○ 1

○ 2

Question 12

$$x^2 = y^2 + 1 \text{ and } y \neq 0.$$

Quantity A	Quantity B
x^4	$y^4 + 1$

○ Quantity A is greater.
○ Quantity B is greater.
○ The two quantities are equal.
○ The relationship cannot be determined from the information given.

DRILL 2

Question 1

The solutions of $x^2 + x - 20 = 0$ are

Indicate <u>all</u> such solutions.

- ☐ −5
- ☐ −4
- ☐ −2
- ☐ −1
- ☐ 4
- ☐ 5
- ☐ 10
- ☐ 20

Question 2

If x is positive and y is 1 more than the square of x, then what is the value of x in terms of y ?

- ○ $y^2 - 1$
- ○ $y^2 + 1$
- ○ $\sqrt{y} - 1$
- ○ $\sqrt{y - 1}$
- ○ $\sqrt{y + 1}$

Question 3

$$x^2 - 49 = 0$$

Quantity A	Quantity B
$x^2 - 7x$	$-7x + 49$

- ○ Quantity A is greater.
- ○ Quantity B is greater.
- ○ The two quantities are equal.
- ○ The relationship cannot be determined from the information given.

Question 4

For $x \neq -2$ and $x \neq -4$, $\dfrac{x}{x + 4} + \dfrac{-3}{x + 2} =$

- ○ $\dfrac{x^2 - x - 12}{(x + 4)(x + 2)}$
- ○ $\dfrac{-3x}{(x + 4)(x + 2)}$
- ○ $\dfrac{x - 3}{2x + 6}$
- ○ $\dfrac{1}{x + 4}$
- ○ -2

Question 5

$$a \neq -b$$

Quantity A	Quantity B
$\dfrac{6a^2 + 12ab + 6b^2}{a + b}$	$6(a + b)$

- ○ Quantity A is greater.
- ○ Quantity B is greater.
- ○ The two quantities are equal.
- ○ The relationship cannot be determined from the information given.

Question 6

Quantity A	Quantity B
$(141)^2 - (28)^2$	$(141 - 28)^2$

- ○ Quantity A is greater.
- ○ Quantity B is greater.
- ○ The two quantities are equal.
- ○ The relationship cannot be determined from the information given.

Question 7

$(-x + y)(-y + x) =$

- ○ $x^2 - y^2$
- ○ $y^2 - x^2$
- ○ 0
- ○ $-(x - y)^2$
- ○ $(y - x)^2$

Question 8

$$x \geq 0$$
$$y \geq 0$$

Quantity A	Quantity B
$\sqrt{x^{12}} - y$	$\left(x^3 + \sqrt{y}\right)\left(x^3 - \sqrt{y}\right)$

- ○   Quantity A is greater.
- ○   Quantity B is greater.
- ○   The two quantities are equal.
- ○   The relationship cannot be determined from the information given.

Question 9

Quantity A	Quantity B
$(s + t)^2$	$s^2 + t^2$

- ○   Quantity A is greater.
- ○   Quantity B is greater.
- ○   The two quantities are equal.
- ○   The relationship cannot be determined from the information given.

Question 10

$$x^2 - 2xy + y^2 = 0 \text{ and } y = \frac{9}{x}$$

Quantity A	Quantity B
y	3

- ○   Quantity A is greater.
- ○   Quantity B is greater.
- ○   The two quantities are equal.
- ○   The relationship cannot be determined from the information given.

Question 11

What is the sum of the roots of the equation $2x^2 - 4x = 6$?

Question 12

If $y = x^2 - 32x + 256$, then what is the least possible value of y ?

- ○   256
- ○   32
- ○   16
- ○   8
- ○   0

ANSWERS

Drill 1

1. B
2. B
3. C
4. −1
5. B
6. B
7. 1
8. A, B, E, G
9. E
10. B
11. C
12. A

Drill 2

1. A, E
2. D
3. C
4. A
5. C
6. A
7. D
8. C
9. D
10. D
11. 2
12. E

EXPLANATIONS
Drill 1

1. **B**   Evaluate the relationship between the quantities by Plugging In values for p: try $p = 2$. Quantity A is $7 \times 5 = 35$, and Quantity B is $9 \times 4 = 36$; Quantity B is greater, so eliminate (A) and (C). Any value gives the same outcome, so select (B). Algebraically, you could either FOIL Quantity A or recognize the common quadratics—either way, Quantity A simplifies to $9p^2 - 1$, which is always exactly 1 less than Quantity B.

2. **B**   Try FOILing. For Quantity A, you get $3a^2 + 6a + 6a + 12$, or $3a^2 + 12a + 12$. For Quantity B, you get $3a^2 + 18a + 2a + 12$, or $3a^2 + 20a + 12$. Remember to compare, not calculate. Notice that the only difference between the quantities is that between $20a$ and $12a$. Because a is positive, $20a$ must be greater than $12a$; thus, Quantity B will always be greater. You could also solve this problem using Plug In, which would give the same result.

3. **C**   This is one of the common quadratic equations: $(3 - 2)(3 + 2) = 3^2 - 2^2$. The answer is (C). If you don't recognize the common quadratic, you can just do the arithmetic and discover that $9 - 4 = (1)(5)$.

4. **−1**   Take the square root of both sides to begin solving this polynomial. So, $2x + 2 = 0$. Solve for x and enter in −1 as the final answer.

5. **B**   FOIL out Quantity A to find $-10a - a^2 - 100 - 10a$, or $-a^2 - 20a - 100$. Anything other than zero to an even power is positive, so $-a^2$ is negative. A negative number minus a positive number ($20a$) will remain negative. A negative minus 100 will be even more negative. So, Quantity A must be negative, and it must be less than Quantity B. The answer is (B). Alternatively, Plugging In a few positive values for a will give you, in the parentheses, (negative) times (positive) = negative for Quantity A.

6. **B**   If $(y - 1)(y + 5) = 0$, $(y - 1) = 0$ or $(y + 5) = 0$. So, y could be 1 or −5. Thus, Quantity B is greater.

7. **1**   Factor the quadratic equation: $3(m + 5)(m - 1) = 0$. Only the first factor gives a positive result: if $3m - 3 = 0$, then $m = 1$.

8. **A, B, E, G**

    Translate the question and answer choices into algebra. You are given that $x - y = 4$. Choice (A) tells you that $x + y = 4$, and you can solve these equations simultaneously by stacking them and adding to get $2x = 8$, $x = 4$ and $y = 0$. Choice (A) is sufficient and correct. Choice (B) tells you that $x^2 - y^2 = 16$, and can be factored: $x^2 - y^2 = (x + y)(x - y) = 16$. You are given that $(x - y) = 4$, so $(x + y)$ must also equal 4 and for that to happen, $x = 4$ and $y = 0$. Choice (B) is also sufficient and correct. Choice (C) states $(x - y)^2 = 16$. This is simply the result of squaring what you were already given and you have no way to determine what the values of x and y are, making this choice insufficient and incorrect. Choices (D) and (F) are inequalities, which means there will be multiple numbers that can work with the criteria given; eliminate both choices. Choice (E) tells you that the greater number is 4. Since $x - y = 4$, that now means the smaller number must be 0, making (E) sufficient and correct. Finally, (G) states $xy = 0$, so at least one of the numbers must be 0. Since you were also given $x - y = 4$ and that neither number is negative, this means the other number must be 4. Choice (G) is sufficient and correct.

9. **E** The dimensions of the new rectangle will be $x + y$ and $x - y$. To find the area of the rectangle, multiply the length by the width: $(x + y)(x - y) = x^2 - y^2$. The answer is (E). Or, you can just Plug In values for x and y.

10. **B** Set the expression equal to zero and then factor it. You are looking for factors of 288 that have a difference of 2. So find the integer factor pairs, starting with 1: 1 and 288; 2 and 144; 3 and 96; 4 and 72; 6 and 48; 8 and 36; 9 and 32; 12 and 24; 16 and 18. The last pair you found works, so the factored form of your equation is $(x - 18)(x + 16) = 0$. The solutions are 18 and −16, but obviously Ann cannot sell a negative number of pillows. The answer is (B).

11. **C** The expression on the left side of the equation will equal zero when either $(3x - 2) = 0$ or $(x + 1) = 0$. Solving these equations yields $x = \dfrac{2}{3}$ or $x = -1$. The question asks you for the greatest value of x, so the answer is (C).

12. **A** Because there are variables, you can use the Plug In technique. Plugging In 2 for y gives you $x^2 = 5$ in the given equation and 17 for Quantity B. Squaring this gives you $x^4 = 25$ for Quantity A, which is therefore larger. Plugging In any other number gives the same result. Alternatively, doing algebra by squaring both sides of the given equation reveals Quantity A: $x^4 = (y^2 + 1)(y^2 + 1) = y^4 + 2y^2 + 1$. The only difference between Quantities A and B is the $2y^2$ in Quantity A. Because the square of any number will always be positive, $2y^2$ is positive, and Quantity A will always therefore be larger. The answer is (A).

Drill 2

1. **A, E** Factoring this quadratic equation gives you $(x + 5)(x - 4) = 0$. For the first solution, $x + 5 = 0$, or $x = -5$. For the second solution, $x - 4 = 0$, or $x = 4$. Alternatively, you can PITA to determine which values will satisfy the equation.

2. **D** Variables in the answer choices indicate that Plug In is a good technique to use. Plug In $x = 4$, so $y = 17$. Now Plug In 17 into the answers to see which gives you 4. Only (D) does.

3. **C** Remember that when a variable is squared, it yields a positive and a negative solution; hence, $x^2 - 49 = 0$ means that $x^2 = 49$ and $x = \pm 7$. If $x = 7$, then both quantities are equal to zero. If $x = -7$, then both quantities are equal to 98. The answer is (C).

4. **A** Plug In $x = 2$, and the original expression turns into $\dfrac{2}{6} + \dfrac{-3}{4} = \dfrac{1}{3} - \dfrac{3}{4} = -\dfrac{5}{12}$, using the Bowtie.

Now Plug In 2 for x in the answer choices to see which equals $-\dfrac{5}{12}$. Only (A) does.

5. **C** Whenever you see exponents, think common quadratics. If you factor the 6 out of the numerator in Quantity A, you get $6(a^2 + 2ab + b^2)$, which includes a common quadratic $(a + b)^2$. Then you can cancel $(a + b)$ from both the numerator and the denominator; Quantity A is really just $6(a + b)$. The quantities are equal.

6. **A** Don't do the arithmetic! These are common quadratic patterns. It's not important that $x = 141$ and $y = 28$; Quantity A is $x^2 - y^2 = (x + y)(x - y)$, and Quantity B is $(x - y)(x - y)$. Since $(x - y)$ is a positive number, you can simply compare the remaining factors after it is removed from both quantities. Since x and y are positive, $(x + y)$ is greater than the remaining $(x - y)$ in Quantity B, and the answer is (A).

7. **D** Factor out -1 from the parentheses on the left and rearrange the expression in the parentheses on the right to get $-1(x - y)(x - y) = -(x - y)^2$. The answer is (D). Because there are variables in the answer choices, you could also Plug In numbers for x and y to find the answer.

8. **C** In Quantity A, $\sqrt{x^{12}} - y = \sqrt{\left(x^6\right)^2} - y = x^6 - y$. In Quantity B, you may recognize one of the common quadratics: $(a + b)(a - b) = a^2 - b^2$. If not, FOIL; either way, Quantity B is $x^6 - y$. Thus, the two quantities are equal.

9. **D** The best approach here is to Plug In. First, try $s = 2$ and $t = 3$: Quantity A is $(2 + 3)^2 = 5^2 = 25$, and Quantity B is $2^2 + 3^2 = 4 + 9 = 13$. Quantity A is greater, so eliminate (B) and (C). Next, make s and t both 0. Now Quantity A is $(0)^2 = 0$, and Quantity B is $0^2 + 0^2 = 0$. Now the two quantities are equal, so eliminate (A), and you're left with (D).

10. **D** Factor the quadratic expression to get $(x - y)(x - y) = 0$; $x - y$ must equal 0, so you know that $x = y$. Thus, $y = \dfrac{9}{y}$, $y^2 = 9$, and $y = 3$ or -3, eliminate (A), (B) and (C). The answer is (D).

11. **2** First, rearrange the equation to $2x^2 - 4x - 6 = 0$. Then, factor out a 2 to make the equation $2(x^2 - 2x - 3) = 0$. Now, factor to get $2(x - 3)(x + 1) = 0$. So, the two roots (or solutions) to the equation are $x = 3$ and $x = -1$. The sum of 3 and -1 is 2.

12. **E** First, factor the quadratic equation: $x^2 - 32x + 256 = (x - 16)^2$. Any quantity squared is either positive or zero. To minimize the expression $(x - 16)^2$ and the value of y, let $x = 16$, so that $y = 0$. The answer is (E).

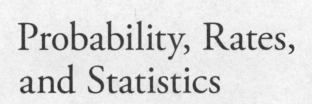

Probability, Rates, and Statistics

PROBABILITY, RATES, AND STATISTICS

The key to mastering these kinds of arithmetic questions is to learn simple, effective ways to organize your information. ETS will always give you just enough information to figure out the one piece that is missing. A good set-up will help you fill in the missing pieces quickly and easily.

Once you understand how the set-ups work, you need only train yourself to recognize the opportunity and use them. Think of words such as *average* and *probability* as triggers that provoke a very specific action. Sensitize yourself to these words and once you see them, before you've even finished reading the question, start making your set-up.

MEAN

Known to ETS as *arithmetic mean* and to the rest of us as *average,* these problems can be time-consuming if you don't know what you're doing, but will unravel easily when you do. For example, to find the average of five, seven, and nine, add the three numbers together and divide by three. Thus, averages consist of three parts, the average, the number of things, and the total. The minute you see the word *average* in a problem, draw an Average Pie.

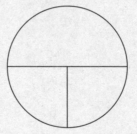

When you see the word **AVERAGE** make a pie on your scratch paper. If you see the word **AVERAGE** again, make another pie.

If ETS were to give a list of numbers and ask for the average, it would be too easy. While ETS will always give you two out of the three pieces, they probably won't be the pieces you expect. It may give you the average and the total and ask for the number of things, or it may give the average and the number of things and ask for the total.

Fill in the information you have.

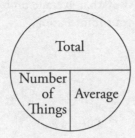

If you have the number of things and the total, you will divide to get the average. If you have the average and the total, you will divide to get the number of things. If you have the number of things and the average, simply multiply to get the total.

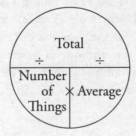

If asked to find the average of five, seven, and nine, your scratch paper would look like the image shown below.

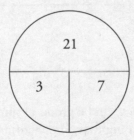

Of course, it's not usually quite that simple. ETS may give you the average of one group, the total of a second, and then ask for the average of both combined. Just make sure that you draw a new pie every time you see the word *average*. Work the problem through in bite-sized pieces, read with your finger, and make sure your hand is moving on the scratch paper.

RATE

Rate problems work the same way that average problems do. In fact, you can use the same method to organize your information.

This is what a Rate Pie looks like.

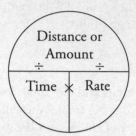

The first thing you do when you see a rate problem is to make your Rate Pie. ETS will always give you two of the three pieces of information. You will have to find the third. If you're asked for time, divide the distance or amount by the rate. If you're asked for rate, divide the distance or amount by the time, and if you're asked for distance or amount, multiply the time by the rate. Make sure to keep an eye on your units. You may be given a rate in miles per hour but asked for a number of minutes.

> The way to prevent units errors is to use your scratch paper and label everything.

MEDIAN

When you see the word *median,* find a group of numbers and put them in order. Median, like the median on a highway, simply means the number in the middle. It's not a difficult concept, so there are only two ways ETS can try to mess you up. The most common trick is to give you numbers out of order. Your first step must always be to put the numbers in order on your scratch paper.

> When you see the word **MEDIAN**, find a group of numbers and put them in order.

The second trick they may try is to give you an even number of numbers. In this case, the median will be the average of the two numbers in the middle. In the case of 2, 2, 3, 4, 5, 5, 5, 6, 7, 7, 120, 345, 607, the median is 5. In the case of 2, 2, 3, 4, 5, 5, 5, 6, 7, 7, 120, 345, 607, 1250, the median is 5.5.

MODE AND RANGE

Mode means the number that comes up most often. The mode of the set {4, 6, 6, 13, 14, 21} is 6. The *range* is the difference between the highest number and the lowest. In this case it is 17, or 21 – 4. Rarely will you see a problem testing mode by itself. It is more likely to come up in connection with mean, median, and/or standard deviation.

STANDARD DEVIATION

There are not a lot of standard deviation questions in the question pool, so they don't come up that often. However, because they might come up, you need to know how to handle them. But don't worry, on the GRE, ETS sticks to the basics. You will never need to know how to calculate standard deviation. You will only be asked about percentages of people or things that fall a few standard deviations from the norm.

Imagine you measured the weight of all apples picked at Orchard *X*. Suppose the average weight of an apple is 6 ounces. As you can imagine, the vast majority of those apples will weigh somewhere close to 6 ounces. A much smaller number will be about 7.5 ounces, and you may even get a few that are heavier than eight ounces. The weight of these apples is likely to follow a *normal distribution*, which means that if you graphed the number of apples at each weight on a bar graph, you would end up with a *bell curve*.

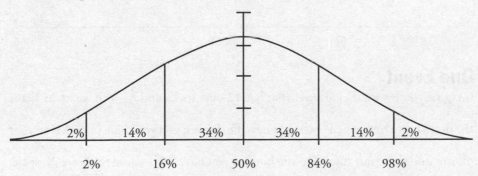

This chart is the bell curve. It will never change. Memorize the numbers 34, 14, and 2.

> The minute you see the words **STANDARD DEVIATION**, or **NORMAL DISTRIBUTION**, draw your bell curve and fill in the percentages.

On this curve, the mean, the median, and the mode are all the same. It makes sense, right? The average weight of our apples is also the most common weight and falls in the middle of the pack. If the apples have a standard deviation of 1.25 ounces, 34 percent of the apples picked in the orchard weigh between 6 and 7.25 ounces, 14 percent weigh between 7.25 and 8.5, and only 2 percent weigh more than 8.5 ounces. As you move from one percentage group to another, you are moving one standard deviation from the norm. If you're asked "What percentage of apples weighs more or less than two standard deviations from the norm?" the answer will be 4 percent.

PROBABILITY

Probability, on the GRE, can be defined as $\dfrac{\text{the \# of things you want}}{\text{the \# of things you could get}}$. It's a fraction and the number of things you could get is the total. The minute you see the word *probability*, make your divisor line and find your total. Once you've done this, you are already half way to the answer.

> The minute you see the word **PROBABILITY**, make your divisor line on your scratch paper and find your total.

One Event

Imagine you have a sock drawer that has 12 blue socks and 8 green socks. What is the probability that, when you reach into the drawer, you get a blue sock? Make your divisor and find your total. On the bottom you have 20 because there are 20 socks you could get. On top you have 12 because there are twelve socks (blue) that you want. The probability is $\dfrac{12}{20}$ or $\dfrac{3}{5}$. The probability of getting a green sock is $\dfrac{8}{20}$ or $\dfrac{2}{5}$. The probability of getting any sock is 20 things you want over 20 things you could get, or 1. The probability of getting a ham and cheese sandwich is, we hope, 0 ($\frac{0 \text{ things you want}}{20 \text{ things you could get}}$). It is important to note that probability is always between 1 and 0. The chance that something will happen added to the chance that it won't happen will always add up to 1.

Two Events

If two events are to occur, the probability of them both happening is equal to the probability of the first happening multiplied by the probability of the second happening. This makes sense because a fraction times a fraction equals a smaller fraction. If you have a very low probability of one event occurring and a very low probability of a second event happening, the odds of them both happening will be even lower. The probability of getting a green sock in the drawer above is $\frac{2}{5}$. The probability of getting a green sock the second time is $\frac{7}{19}$, because there are seven green socks left, after you've removed the first one, and 19 socks left in the drawer. The probability of getting a green sock both times is $\frac{2}{5} \times \frac{7}{19}$, or $\frac{14}{95}$.

One of Two Events

Imagine you now have five purple socks in your drawer. If you are asked to find the probability of getting a purple **OR** a green sock, you have to add the probabilities. With 12 blue socks, 8 green socks, and 5 purple socks, your new total is 25. You have an $\frac{8}{25}$ chance of getting a green sock and a $\frac{5}{25}$ chance of getting a purple one. The chance of getting one or the other is $\frac{5}{25} + \frac{8}{25}$ or $\frac{13}{25}$.

At Least One Event

The one last wrinkle to look at is what happens if you are asked to find the probability of *at least* one event happening. When rolling dice, for example, what is the probability that you roll 1 *at least* once out of three rolls? This will get complicated because at least once means that the event could occur once, twice, or even three times. That's more calculating than you want to do. Instead, when asked to find at least one, find the probability that none will occur and subtract it from 1. This will leave you with at least one. In this case, the chances of not rolling a one on the first roll are $\frac{5}{6}$. The chances on the second and third rolls are the same. Therefore the chances of not rolling a one go down with each additional roll, but only by a little bit because you have a very strong possibility that it will not happen. The chances that you will not roll a 1 in your first three rolls are $\frac{5}{6} \times \frac{5}{6} \times \frac{5}{6}$, or $\frac{125}{216}$. The chances that you will roll at least one 1, therefore are $\frac{91}{216}$ (216 − 125 = 91).

For more practice and a more in-depth look at math techniques, check out our student-friendly guidebook, *Cracking the GRE*.

DRILL 1

Question 1

In terms of *y*, what is the average (arithmetic mean) of 4*y* and 22 ?

○ $4y + 22$
○ $4y + 11$
○ $4y - 22$
○ $2y + 11$
○ $2y + 22$

Question 2

Quantity A	Quantity B
The average (arithmetic mean) of 14, 22, and 48	The average of 12, 22, and 50

○   Quantity A is greater.
○   Quantity B is greater.
○   The two quantities are equal.
○   The relationship cannot be determined from the information given.

Question 3

2, 3, 5, 7

Quantity A	Quantity B
The average (arithmetic mean) of the numbers above	The median of the numbers above

○   Quantity A is greater.
○   Quantity B is greater.
○   The two quantities are equal.
○   The relationship cannot be determined from the information given.

Question 4

Susan travels by car at an average speed of 50 miles per hour for 4 hours and then at an average speed of 20 miles per hour for 2 hours. What is her average speed, in miles per hour, for the entire 6-hour trip?

○   25
○   30
○   35
○   40
○   45

Question 5

Liz owns 2 green T-shirts, 4 blue T-shirts, and 5 red T-shirts.

Quantity A	Quantity B
The probability that Liz randomly selects a blue T-shirt	$\dfrac{2}{5}$

- ○ Quantity A is greater.
- ○ Quantity B is greater.
- ○ The two quantities are equal.
- ○ The relationship cannot be determined from the information given.

Question 6

A rope is cut into five pieces of differing lengths. After the rope is cut, the length of the longest piece is twice the average length of the five cut pieces and is four times the length of the shortest piece.

Quantity A	Quantity B
The median length of the five cut pieces	The average length of the five cut pieces

- ○ Quantity A is greater.
- ○ Quantity B is greater.
- ○ The two quantities are equal.
- ○ The relationship cannot be determined from the information given.

Question 7

For which of the following values of x is the mode of $2x$, $x + 5$, $3x - 2$, $5x - 7$, and $4x$ equal to 4 ?

- ○ 2
- ○ 3
- ○ 4
- ○ 5
- ○ 7

Question 8

A hat contains 18 raffle tickets, numbered 1 through 18. If two raffle tickets are chosen at random from the hat, what is the probability that both tickets are even numbers?

- ○ $\dfrac{2}{9}$
- ○ $\dfrac{4}{17}$
- ○ $\dfrac{1}{4}$
- ○ $\dfrac{1}{2}$
- ○ $\dfrac{33}{34}$

Question 9

Set P and set Q contain the same number of terms. The average of set P is greater than the average of set Q, and the range of set P is equal to the range of set Q.

Quantity A	Quantity B
The median of set of P	The median of set Q

○ Quantity A is greater.

○ Quantity B is greater.

○ The two quantities are equal.

○ The relationship cannot be determined from the information given.

Question 10

The average (arithmetic mean) number of passengers on a subway car is 60. If the number of passengers on a car has a normal distribution with a standard deviation of 20, approximately what percent of subway cars carries more than 80 passengers?

○ 16%

○ 48%

○ 68%

○ 88%

○ 98%

Question 11

If the average (arithmetic mean) of 10, 12, n, and n is greater than 25, what is the least possible value of integer n ?

○ 38

○ 39

○ 40

○ 41

○ 42

DRILL 2

Question 1

$$\{12, 5, 3, 4, 8, 10, 4, 2, 5, 1, 4, x, y\}$$

In Set P above, the sum of x and y is 10.

Quantity A	Quantity B
The median of set of P	The mode of set P

- ○ Quantity A is greater.
- ○ Quantity B is greater.
- ○ The two quantities are equal.
- ○ The relationship cannot be determined from the information given.

Question 2

Three machines A, B, and C, working together at their respective constant rates, can do a certain job in 4 hours. Machines B and C, working together at their respective constant rates, can do the same job in 5 hours. Machines A and B, working together at their respective constant rates, can do the same job in 10 hours.

Quantity A	Quantity B
The number of hours required by Machine A working alone at its constant rate to complete the job.	The number of hours required by Machine B working alone at its constant rate to complete the job.

- ○ Quantity A is greater.
- ○ Quantity B is greater.
- ○ The two quantities are equal.
- ○ The relationship cannot be determined from the information given.

Question 3

If the probability that the first event will occur is $\dfrac{1}{4}$, and the probability that the second event will occur is $\dfrac{1}{\sqrt{x + 2}}$, then what is the probability that both events will occur?

- ○ $\dfrac{\sqrt{x + 2}}{4x + 8}$
- ○ $\dfrac{\sqrt{x + 2}}{4}$
- ○ $\dfrac{\sqrt{x + 2}}{16x + 32}$
- ○ $\dfrac{4}{\sqrt{x + 2}}$
- ○ $4\sqrt{x + 2}$

Question 4

Five numbers in a set are arranged from least to greatest. If the median of the first two numbers is 13 and the average (arithmetic mean) of the remaining numbers is 23, what is the average of the entire set?

Question 5

A bag contains 12 marbles: 5 of the marbles are red, 3 are green, and the rest are blue.

Quantity A	Quantity B
The probability of consecutively choosing two red marbles and a green marble without replacement	The probability of consecutively choosing a red and two blue marbles with replacement

- ○ Quantity A is greater.
- ○ Quantity B is greater.
- ○ The two quantities are equal.
- ○ The relationship cannot be determined from the information given.

Question 6

If the average (arithmetic mean) of 31, 41, and p is between 29 and 47, inclusive, what is the least possible value of $(p - 7)^2$?

☐

Question 7

Water flows into a 25-liter bucket through a hose and out through a hole in the bottom of the bucket. The rate of flow through the hose is 1 liter per minute. If the bucket is filled to capacity in 40 minutes, at what rate, in liters per minute, was water flowing out of the bucket through the hole?

- ○ $\dfrac{3}{8}$
- ○ $\dfrac{3}{5}$
- ○ $\dfrac{5}{8}$
- ○ $\dfrac{8}{5}$
- ○ $\dfrac{13}{8}$

Question 8

A pair of fair, six-sided dice is tossed twice. What is the probability that the first toss gives a total of either 7 or 11 and the second toss gives a total of 7 ?

- ○ $\dfrac{1}{27}$
- ○ $\dfrac{1}{18}$
- ○ $\dfrac{1}{9}$
- ○ $\dfrac{1}{6}$
- ○ $\dfrac{7}{18}$

Question 9

A photocopier can copy r pages per hour. How many pages can it copy in s seconds?

- ◯ $\dfrac{rs}{60}$
- ◯ $\dfrac{r}{60s}$
- ◯ $\dfrac{s}{3,600r}$
- ◯ $\dfrac{rs}{3,600}$
- ◯ $3,600rs$

Question 10

Quantity A	Quantity B
The average (arithmetic mean) cost per hinge for 16 hinges that cost a total of $2p$ cents	The average cost per hinge for 4 hinges that cost a total of $\dfrac{p}{2}$ cents

- ◯ Quantity A is greater.
- ◯ Quantity B is greater.
- ◯ The two quantities are equal.
- ◯ The relationship cannot be determined from the information given.

Question 11

In both rural and urban areas of country G, the average annual number of holidays taken by citizens is 8, and the annual number of holidays follows a normal distribution. In rural areas, 2% of the citizens take more than 12 holidays per year. In urban areas, 2% of the citizens take more than 16 holidays per year. How much greater is the standard deviation of the annual number of holidays taken by urban citizens than that of rural citizens?

$$\boxed{}$$

Question 12

Three fair, six-sided dice are rolled simultaneously. What is the probability that exactly two of the dice will come up as the same number?

- ◯ $\dfrac{5}{12}$
- ◯ $\dfrac{11}{24}$
- ◯ $\dfrac{25}{54}$
- ◯ $\dfrac{13}{27}$
- ◯ $\dfrac{1}{2}$

DRILL 3

Question 1

There are 32 students in Jamie's eighth-grade class. Each student took a 50-point test; the class average (arithmetic mean) was 82% correct. The teacher has assigned one 4-point, extra-credit question. How many students will need to answer the extra-credit question correctly in order to bring the class average to 86% correct?

○ 15
○ 16
○ 17
○ 22
○ 32

Question 2

Vinay and Phil are driving in separate cars to Los Angeles, both leaving from the same place and traveling along the same route. If Vinay leaves at 1 a.m. and travels at 40 miles per hour, and Phil leaves at 5 a.m. and travels at 50 miles per hour, at what time does Phil catch up to Vinay?

○ 1 p.m.
○ 5 p.m.
○ 7 p.m.
○ 9 p.m.
○ 11 p.m.

Question 3

A set of six numbers consists of $x, x + 3,$ $x + 5, x + 7, x + 11,$ and $x + 13$. What is the median of this set, in terms of x ?

○ $x + 5$
○ $x + 6$
○ $x + 6.5$
○ $3x + 8$
○ $6x + 39$

Question 4

Damon rolls three fair, six-sided dice. What is the probability that his total is greater than 16 ?

Question 5

Eric and Hyde apply for different jobs at companies A and B, and the decisions to make job offers are completely independent of one another. The probability that Eric receives a job offer from company A is 0.4, and the probability that he receives a job offer from company B is 0.2. The probability that Hyde receives a job offer from company A is 0.2, and the probability that he receives a job offer from company B is 0.25. Which of the following values lie between the probability that Eric receives a job offer from exactly one company and the probability that Hyde does not receive a job offer from either company?

Indicate all such values.

☐ .47
☐ .51
☐ .55
☐ .59
☐ .63

Question 6

Set A = {y, 4, 7, 8}
Set B = {2y, 1, 3}

If the average (arithmetic mean) of set A above is 2 less than the average of set B, what is the value of y ?

$$\boxed{}$$

Question 7

List A: −7, −4, −1, 0, 5, 8, 10, 10, 13, 21

In List A above, if positive integer x is subtracted from the 3 greatest numbers in the list and x is added to the 3 least even numbers in the list, which of the following is true ?

Indicate all such values.

☐ The average (arithmetic mean) of the list increases by x.
☐ The average of the list decreases by x.
☐ The average of the list stays the same.
☐ There is no mode in the new set.
☐ The standard deviation of the list stays the same.
☐ The median of the list stays the same.
☐ The median of the list increases by x.

Question 8

Alejandra took five Spanish quizzes and scored a total of 227 points. Nigel took the same quizzes and scored a total of 189. What is the difference between Alejandra's average (arithmetic mean) score and Nigel's average score?

$$\boxed{}$$

Question 9

Which of the following could be the median for a set of integers {97, 98, 56, x, 86}, given that 20 < x < 80 ?

Indicate all such values.

☐ 71
☐ 86
☐ 91.5
☐ 97
☐ 397.5

Question 10

There are 40 marbles in a jar. Of the marbles in the jar, $\frac{1}{5}$ of the marbles are blue, $\frac{1}{4}$ of the remaining marbles are red, and 10 marbles are green. If a marble is selected at random, then what is the probability that the marble will not be blue, red, or green?

$$\boxed{}$$
$$\boxed{}$$

Question 11

During a sales contest at a local electronics store, 65 employees sold a total of $91,000 worth of merchandise. If the standard deviation of sales among those employees was $130 and the sales were normally distributed, what percentage of employees sold $1,270 or more worth of merchandise?

- ○ 28%
- ○ 50%
- ○ 65%
- ○ 84%
- ○ 98%

Question 12

On the most recent test in stats class, Jamal scored x points and Raya scored 73 points. If the average (arithmetic mean) of Cliff and Raya's scores is 79 points, and the average of Jamal and Cliff's scores is 89, then $x =$

$$\boxed{}$$

DRILL 4

Question 1

The distribution of the number of minutes a person spends on hold while waiting to speak with a certain customer service representative has a standard deviation of 4 minutes. A total of 20 phone calls are made to the customer service representative, and the total number of minutes on hold is 480 minutes. Which of the following numbers of minutes of time on hold are within 1 standard deviation of the mean of the distribution?

Indicate <u>all</u> such numbers.

☐ 16 minutes
☐ 18 minutes
☐ 21 minutes
☐ 24 minutes
☐ 27 minutes

Question 2

Jeff and Ali race each other at the Tentleytown Speedway. Ali's car travels at 300 feet per second, and Jeff's car travels at 250 feet per second. If one lap around the track is 3,000 feet long, and each car travels at a constant rate, how many laps will it take Ali to pass Jeff?

○ 1
○ 5
○ 6
○ 10
○ 60

Question 3

With its drainage valve closed, a fountain can be filled in 4 hours by pumping water through its inlet pipe. After turning off water from the inlet pipe, the fountain can be drained in 9 hours. How many hours will it take to fill the empty fountain using its inlet pipe if the drainage valve is left open?

[____]

Question 4

For a set consisting of five consecutive integers, which of the following changes the average (arithmetic mean) of the set without changing the median?

Indicate <u>all</u> such statements.

☐ Multiplying each of the numbers in the set by 6
☐ Adding 10 to each of the numbers in the set
☐ Subtracting 3.5 from each of the numbers in the set
☐ Adding 8.2 to the 2 largest numbers and subtracting 8.2 from the 3 smallest numbers in the set
☐ Adding 0.5 to the 2 largest and to the 2 smallest numbers in the set
☐ Dividing each of the numbers in the set by 2

Question 5

Paul is able to grade p essays every half hour, and Sarah is able to grade s essays every hour. If Paul and Sarah work together grading essays for h hours, then in terms of p, s, and h, how many essays do they grade?

Indicate all such amounts.

☐ $\dfrac{p + s}{h}$

☐ $\dfrac{3p + s}{h}$

☐ $h(p + s)$

☐ $2h(p + s)$

☐ $h(2p + s)$

☐ $h(p + 2s)$

☐ $2hp + hs$

Question 6

If the average (arithmetic mean) of 5 numbers is 36 and the average of four of those numbers is 34, then what is the value of the fifth number?

○   2
○   34
○   35
○   36
○   44

Question 7

Noah's contracting company builds road at a rate of 1 mile per week, except during the rainy season which lasts for 14 weeks, when that rate drops to $\dfrac{1}{2}$ mile per week. If Noah is hired to build 11 miles of road, and his company begins construction 5 weeks before the start of the rainy season, how many weeks will it take Noah's company to complete the contract?

┌──────────┐
│   │
└──────────┘

Question 8

At 10 a.m., Kelso leaves his parents' house traveling at a constant rate of 42 miles per hour. At 10:30 a.m., Kelso's parents leave their home traveling along the same route as Kelso at a constant speed of 48 miles per hour. When Kelso is between 6 and 9 miles ahead of his parents, which of the following distances, in miles, could represent the distance that Kelso has traveled from his parents' house?

Indicate all such distances.

- ☐ 91
- ☐ 101
- ☐ 111
- ☐ 121
- ☐ 131
- ☐ 141

Question 9

Two cyclists, A and B, are 145 miles apart on a straight road. At 1:30 p.m., cyclist A begins riding at a constant speed of 20 miles per hour toward cyclist B. At 2:00 p.m., cyclist B begins riding toward cyclist A at a constant speed. At 5:00 p.m., they meet. What is cyclist B's rate of speed, in miles per hour?

[_____]

Question 10

A shipment of 12 microwave ovens contains 3 defective units. Wilhelm receives 3 microwave ovens from this shipment. What is the probability that at least one of the units Wilhelm receives is defective?

- ○ $\dfrac{1}{4}$
- ○ $\dfrac{9}{55}$
- ○ $\dfrac{21}{55}$
- ○ $\dfrac{27}{55}$
- ○ $\dfrac{34}{55}$

Question 11

Victor is walking at a constant rate of 1 mile every 17 minutes. Sarah is walking at a constant rate of 1 mile every 14 minutes. If they are 10 miles apart and are approaching each other along a straight road, how many hours will it take them to meet, rounded to the nearest hundredth?

[_____]

ANSWERS

Drill 1	Drill 2	Drill 3	Drill 4
1. D	1. D	1. B	1. C, D, E
2. C	2. C	2. D	2. C
3. A	3. A	3. B	3. 7.2
4. D	4. 19	4. $\dfrac{1}{54}$	4. E
5. B	5. B		5. E, G
6. B	6. 64	5. A, B, C, D	6. E
7. A	7. A	6. 13	7. 17
8. B	8. A	7. C	8. C, D
9. D	9. D	8. 7.6	9. 25
10. A	10. C	9. B	10. E
11. C	11. 2		11. 1.28
	12. A	10. $\dfrac{14}{40}$	
		11 D	
		12. 93	

EXPLANATIONS
Drill 1

1. **D** To find the average, add up the values and divide by 2: $\frac{4y+22}{2} = \frac{2(2y+11)}{2} = 2y+11$. You can also Plug In on this one. If $y = 3$, then $\frac{4(3)+22}{2} = 17$, your target number. Only (D) hits the target.

2. **C** The average is the sum divided by the number of items. Both ask for the average of three numbers. The sum of the three numbers in both quantities is 84, so their averages must be equal.

3. **A** The mean is found by dividing the sum of the elements by the number of elements. In this case, $2 + 3 + 5 + 7 = 17$, and $17 \div 4 = 4.25$, the mean. The median is the middle number, or, if the list contains an even number of elements, the average of the middle two elements (when they are arranged in increasing order). In this case, the average of 3 and 5 is 4. Quantity A is greater than Quantity B.

4. **D** Use the given averages to figure out Susan's total distance: 4 hours at an average speed of 50 miles per hour is a total of 200 miles, and 2 hours at an average speed of 20 miles per hour is a total of 40 miles. Susan goes a total of 240 miles in 6 hours; thus, her average speed is $\frac{240 \text{ miles}}{6 \text{ hours}}$, or 40 miles per hour. The answer is (D).

5. **B** To calculate the probability, divide the part by the whole: $\frac{\text{blue shirts}}{\text{total shirts}} = \frac{4}{11}$. Choice (B) is correct because $\frac{4}{11} < \frac{4}{10}$ (which is simply $\frac{2}{5}$ multiplied by 2).

6. **B** This question asks for the average of an unknown quantity, so look for information to put into the Average Pie and Plug In for the unknown quantity. The question states that the rope will be cut into 5 pieces, so choose a value that is easy to divide by 5. Plug In 100 for the length of the uncut rope. Entering 100 for the total in the Average Pie and 5 for the number of pieces, we find the average length of the 5 pieces of rope is 20 and thus in this case Quantity B is 20.

    The question states that the length of the longest piece of rope is twice the average length of the cut pieces, so the longest cut piece is 20×2, or 40. The problem also says that the longest piece is four times the length of the smallest piece, so the shortest piece is $\frac{1}{4}(40)$, or 10.

    The question doesn't say anything about the size of the three middle pieces, but the sum of the lengths of the five pieces adds up to the length of the uncut rope, 100. The lengths of the shortest and longest pieces sum up to $10 + 40 = 50$, so by subtracting this value from the length of the uncut rope, the sum of the lengths of the middle three pieces can be found by doing $100 - 50 = 50$.

    Quantity A asks for the median length of the 5 pieces, so put the pieces in order.

    10, unknown, unknown, unknown, 40

The lengths of the three middle pieces are unknown, so Plug In for their lengths, keeping in mind that each length is greater than 10, the length of the shortest piece, and less than 40, the length of the longest piece. The sum of their lengths is equal to 50.

If the three middle pieces have lengths of 15, 17, 18, the five pieces will have lengths of 10, 15, 17, 18, 40, and the median length of the five pieces is 17. Quantity B is greater than Quantity A, so eliminate (A) and (C).

Plug In a second time using FROZEN, and try extreme values with the second shortest piece being very close to 10 and the middle piece and the second largest piece being very close together. If the pieces have lengths 10.01, 19.99, and 20, the five pieces will have lengths of 10, 10.01, 19.99, 20, and 40, and the median length of the five pieces is 19.99. Quantity B is still greater than Quantity A. The correct answer is (B).

7. **A** Remember that mode means the number that appears "most often." Plug In the Answers. For (C), if $x = 4$, then the numbers become: 8, 9, 10, 13, 16. For a list of numbers to have a mode, there has to be at least two of one of the numbers. So this list has no mode; eliminate (C). For (A), if $x = 2$, then the numbers become 4, 7, 4, 3, 8. Because 4 appears twice, 4 is the mode—the answer is (A).

8. **B** Think of this problem as if you're pulling out an even ticket and then another even ticket. So, for the first ticket there are 9 possible evens out of 18 total, so the probability that the first ticket is even is $\frac{9}{18}$. Now you have one fewer even ticket in the hat. So there are 8 evens out of 17 total tickets for the second ticket; thus, the probability is $\frac{8}{17}$. You want an even AND an even, so multiply: $\frac{9}{18} \times \frac{8}{17} = \frac{4}{17}$. The answer is (B).

9. **D** This question has unknown quantities and asks about averages, so Plug In and use the Average Pie.

Try set P = {5, 10, 15} and set Q = {3, 8, 13}. The range of set P is $15 - 5 = 10$, and the range of set Q is $13 - 3 = 10$. The average of set P is $\frac{5 + 10 + 15}{3} = \frac{30}{3} = 10$, and the average of set Q is $\frac{3 + 8 + 13}{3} = \frac{24}{3} = 8$, so these sets are consistent with the information given in the question. The median of set P is 10, and the median of set Q is 8. Quantity A is greater than Quantity B in this case, so eliminate (B) and (C).

Now try to find a set in which the median of set Q is greater than the median of set P. Try set P = {0, 5, 10, 15, 20} and set Q = {0, 2, 11, 12, 20}. The range of set P is $20 - 0 = 20$, which is equivalent to the range of set Q, $20 - 0 = 20$. The average of set P is equal to 10, and the average of set Q is equal to 9, so these sets are consistent with the information given in the question. The median of set P is 10, while the median of set Q is 11. Quantity B is greater than Quantity A in this case, so eliminate (A). The correct answer is (D).

10.   A   Adding the standard deviation (20) to the mean (60) gives you the number of passengers in a car that carries exactly one standard deviation above the mean number of passengers (80). The first standard deviation above the mean represents 34% of the population in a normal distribution, and a further 50% falls below the mean, so 84% of the cars will carry 80 people or fewer. Subtracting this from the entire population (100%) gives you the percent of cars that carry greater than 80: 100% − 84% = 16%. The answer is (A).

11.   C   To find the average, divide the total by the number of values. So, $\frac{10+12+n+n}{4} > 25$. Multiply both sides of the inequality by 4 and then subtract 22 (10 + 12) to find $2n > 78$. Divide by 2 to find $n > 39$. So, n is NOT 39; it is the least integer greater than 39, which is 40. Alternatively, you could Plug In the answers starting with (A) because the question asks for the least possible value. If $n = 38$ or 39, then the average is not greater than 25. If $n = 40$, the average is greater than 25. The answer is (C).

Drill 2

1.   D   This Quantitative Comparison question has variables, so recognize the opportunity to Plug In multiple times. The question also asks about a median and a mode of the set, so order the terms in the set.

The ordering of the known terms in the set yields {1, 2, 3, 4, 4, 4, 5, 5, 8, 10, 12}. Now consider x and y. The question states that the sum of x and y is equal to 10. Plug In $x = 3$ and $y = 7$. Using these values, set P is {1, 2, 3, 3, 4, 4, 4, 5, 5, 7, 8, 10, 12}. The median of this set, the seventh term, is 4 and the mode, the most frequently occurring term, is also 4. Quantity A and Quantity B are equal in this case, so eliminate (A) and (B).

Plug In again using FROZEN. This time try fractions. For example, make $x = 4\frac{1}{2}$ and $y = 5\frac{1}{2}$. In this case, P is {1, 2, 3, 4, 4, 4, $4\frac{1}{2}$, 5, 5, $5\frac{1}{2}$, 8, 10, 12}. In this case, the median is $4\frac{1}{2}$, but the mode is 4. The median and the mode are not equal, so eliminate (C). The correct answer is (D).

2.   C   This question involves rates and does not say what the job is, so set up a Rate Pie and Plug In the number of parts required to complete the job.

Plug In 20 parts as the number of parts required to complete the job. The question states that working together, Machines A, B, and C finish the job in 4 hours. Enter the number of hours and the parts required to complete the job into a Rate Pie to find that Machines A, B, and C produce

$\frac{20}{4} = 5$ parts per hour when working together. The question says that working together Machines

B and C finish the job in 5 hours. Enter the number of hours and the parts required to complete

the job into a Rate Pie to find that working together Machines B and C produce $\frac{20}{5} = 4$ parts per

hour when working together. Subtract these rates from one another to find the rate of Machine A,

5 − 4 = 1 part per hour. Enter the rate of Machine A and the number of parts required to complete

the job into a Rate Pie to find Quantity A, the number of hours Machine A requires to complete

the job when working alone. The number of hours required by Machine A to complete the job is

$\frac{20}{1} = 20$ hours.

The question states that working together, Machines A and B finish the job in 10 hours. Enter the

number of hours and the parts required to complete the job into a Rate Pie to find that Machines

A and B produce $\frac{20}{10} = 2$ parts per hour when working together. Subtract the rate of Machine

A from the rate of Machines A and B when they work together to find the rate of Machine B.

Machine B produces 2 − 1 = 1 part per hour. Enter the rate of Machine B and the number of parts

required to complete the job into a Rate Pie to find Quantity B, the number of hours Machine B

requires to complete the job when working alone. The number of hours required by Machine B to

complete the job is $\frac{20}{1} = 20$ hours. Quantities A and B are the same, so eliminate (A) and (B).

Now, change the number of parts required to complete the job to 40. Working together,

Machines A, B, and C produce $\frac{40}{4} = 10$ parts per hour. Working together, Machines B and C pro-

duce $\frac{40}{5} = 8$ parts per hour. Subtract these rates from one another to find the rate of Machine A.

Machine A produces 10 − 8 = 2 parts per hour. Enter this rate and the number of parts required to

complete the job to find Quantity A, the number of hours Machine A requires to complete the job

when working alone. The number of hours required by Machine A to complete the job is $\frac{40}{2} = 20$

hours.

Working together, Machines A and B produce $\frac{40}{10} = 4$ parts per hour. Machine B produces

4 − 2 = 2 parts per hour. Enter the rate of Machine B and the number of parts required to complete

the job into a Rate Pie to find Quantity B, the number of hours Machine B requires to complete the job when working alone. The number of hours required by Machine B to complete the job is $\frac{40}{2} = 20$ hours.

Again, Quantities A and B are the same, so the correct answer is (C).

3. A   Plug In to make this problem much simpler. If you plug in $x = 2$, then the probability for the second event is $\frac{1}{\sqrt{4}} = \frac{1}{2}$. Now, because this is an "and" probability problem, you multiply the two probabilities together to find the target answer: $\frac{1}{4} \times \frac{1}{2} = \frac{1}{8}$. Choice (A) is the only one that works: $\frac{\sqrt{2+2}}{4(2)+8} = \frac{2}{16} = \frac{1}{8}$.

4. 19 Take the problem a piece at a time. If a set has only two numbers, the median is the average of those two numbers. Set up Average Pies for each of the first two averages. For the first one, two numbers that average 13 total to 26. For the second average, three numbers that average 23, so they must have a total of 69. Set up one final Average Pie for all five numbers: 5 numbers total 95. Solve for the average, and you should get 19 from 95 ÷ 5.

5. B   Quantity A asks for the probability "without replacement," so that means you have to take into account that there will be one marble less in the total after each draw. The probability of first choosing a red marble is $\frac{5}{12}$, a second red marble is $\frac{4}{11}$, and then a green marble is $\frac{3}{10}$. This is an "and" probability problem, so you have to multiply the probability of each event together: $\frac{5}{12} \times \frac{4}{11} \times \frac{3}{10} = \frac{60}{1,320} = \frac{1}{22}$. For Quantity B, you do the same thing, but the total stays the same for each draw: $\frac{5}{12} \times \frac{4}{12} \times \frac{4}{12} = \frac{80}{1,728} = \frac{5}{108}$. Quantity B is greater.

6. 64 To find the least possible value of p, work with the lowest possible average, 29. Draw an Average Pie. You have 3 values with an average of 29, so your total is $3 \times 29 = 87$. Now you know that $31 + 41 + p = 87$, so $p = 15$, and $(p - 7)^2 = 64$.

7. A   Remember that *amount = rate × time*. So, 25 liters = *rate* × 40 minutes. The rate was $\frac{25\,\text{liters}}{40\,\text{minutes}} = \frac{5}{8}$ liters/min. The net rate at which the bucket is filling is the difference between the hose's rate and the leaking rate. So, (1 liter/min) – (leaking rate) = $\frac{5}{8}$. Solve for the leaking rate to find the leaking rate is $\frac{3}{8}$ liters/min; the answer is (A).

8.   A   There are a total of $6^2 = 36$ possibilities for each toss. There are a total of 8 ways we can get a total of

7 or 11 on the first toss: 6 ways to get a total of 7—(1, 6), (2, 5), (3, 4), (4, 3), (5, 2), or (6, 1)—plus

2 ways to get a total of 11—(5, 6) or (6, 5). Therefore, the probability of getting a total of either 7 or

11 on the first toss is $\frac{8}{36} = \frac{2}{9}$. The probability of getting a total of 7 on the second toss is $\frac{6}{36} = \frac{1}{6}$,

so the probability that both of these independent events occur is the product $\frac{2}{9} \times \frac{1}{6} = \frac{1}{27}$, (A).

9.   D   Try Plugging In a number for s that divides easily by 60, such as 7,200. So, if $s = 7,200$ seconds,
that's 120 minutes or 2 hours. Plug In a nice number for r such as 5. So, if the copier makes 5
pages per hour for 2 hours, your target is 10 pages. Plug $s = 7,200$ and $r = 5$ into the answers. Ballpark: Choice (A) is too large, (B) too small, (C) too small, and (E) far too large. Only (D) yields
your target of 10.

10. C   Plug In a value for p. Try $p = 16$: in Quantity A, then 16 hinges cost a total of 32 cents, for an average cost of 2 cents per hinge; in Quantity B, 4 hinges cost a total of 8 cents, for, again, an average
cost of 2 cents per hinge. The quantities are equal, so eliminate (A) and (B). Any value for p will
yield the same results: the quantities will always equal; the answer is (C).

11. 2   Draw two bell curves: one for rural areas, and one for urban areas. The three standard deviations above the mean each represent 34%, 14% and 2% of the population, respectively. The mean
in both cases is 8. In rural areas, 2% of the citizens take more than 12 holidays a year, so 12 is
two standard deviations above 8; the standard deviation is thus the difference between 8 and 12
divided by 2, or 2. In urban areas, similarly, the standard deviation is 16 − 8 divided by 2, or 4.
The difference between the two standard deviations is thus 4 − 2 = 2.

12. A   There are a total of $6^3 = 216$ total possible rolls for the three dice. First figure out the probability
of getting exactly two 1's. There are $5 \times 3 = 15$ ways this could happen: 112, 113, 114, 115, 116;
121, 131, 141, 151, 161; or 211, 311, 411, 511, 611. You could repeat this list of 15 possibilities in
the obvious way for exactly two 2's, exactly two 3's, and so on. Thus, the total number of favorable
rolls is $6 \times 15 = 90$. Because there are 216 possible rolls, 90 of which are favorable, the probability
of getting exactly two of the three dice to show the same number is $\frac{90}{216} = \frac{5}{12}$, (A).

Drill 3

1.   B   If the class average is 82% on a 50-point test, the average score was 41 points out of 50. Use the

Average Pie to find the sum of the class's scores: (41)(32) = 1,312. To reach a class average of 86%,

each student will need to average 43 points out of 50 points. Use the Average Pie to find the

desired sum of the class's scores: (43)(32) = 1,376. The difference is 1,376 − 1,312 = 64, so the class needs to make up 64 points; $\frac{64}{4}=16$, so 16 students need to answer the extra credit question correctly. The answer is (B). Alternatively, notice that the class's average needs to increase by 4%, or 2 points on average for a 50-question test. But the extra credit is worth 4 points, so to average half of a 4-point increase, only half the students (16) need to get the extra credit correct.

2. **D** Before Phil leaves, Vinay has traveled for 4 hours; the rate formula is *distance = rate × time*, so Vinay has gone 40 miles per hour × 4 hours = 160 miles. Upon leaving, Phil is gaining on Vinay at a rate of 10 miles per hour, because he travels 10 more miles per hour than Vinay. Now your equation is 160 miles = 10 miles per hour × *time*, so *time* = 16 hours. Phil left at 5 a.m., so he'll catch up to Vinay at 9 p.m., so the answer is (D).

3. **B** Since there are variables in the answer choices, try Plugging In 2 for *x*. Your two middle numbers are now 7 and 9, and the median is their average, 8. Circle 8 as your target answer. After you check all the choices, only (B) matches.

4. $\frac{1}{54}$ First, figure out how many different results Damon can get. Each die has 6 sides, so the total number of possible outcomes is 6 × 6 × 6 = 216. Now count out how many of those outcomes total more than 16. There are 3 ways to roll a 17—5, 6, and 6; 6, 5, and 6; and 6, 6, and 5—and 1 way to roll an 18—three 6's. The probability is thus $\frac{4}{216}$, which reduces to $\frac{1}{54}$.

5. **A, B, C, D**

This question asks for the probabilities between Eric receiving one job offer and Hyde not receiving a job offer. To figure out the probability that Eric receives one job offer, calculate the probability that Eric receives a job offer from company A but not from company B and add it to the probability that Eric does not receives a job offer from company A but does receive a job offer from company B. The probability that Eric receives a job offer from company A is 0.4, so the probability that he does not receive a job offer from company A is 1 – 0.4 = 0.6. The probability that Eric receives a job offer from company B is 0.2, so the probability that he does not receive a job offer from company B is 1 – 0.2 = 0.8. To figure out the probability that Eric receives a job offer from company A but does not receive a job offer from company B, multiply the individual probabilities together to get 0.4 × 0.8 = 0.32. Likewise, the probability that Eric does not receive a job offer from company A but does receive a job offer from company B is 0.6 × 0.2 = 0.12. Find the probability that Eric receives exactly one job offer by adding the probabilities together to get 0.32 + 0.12 = 0.44.

Now, find the probability that Hyde does not receive a job offer. To find the probability that Hyde does not receive a job offer from either company, multiple the probabilities that he does not receive a job offer from each company together. The probability that Hyde receives a job offer from company A is 0.2, so the probability that he does not receive a job offer from company A is 1 – 0.2 = 0.8, and the probability that he receives a job offer from company B is 0.25, so the probability that he does not receive a job offer from company B is 1 – 0.25 = 0.75. The probability that Hyde receives neither of the offers is 0.8 × 0.75 = 0.6.

Look for answers that are between 0.44 and 0.6. The correct answer is (A), (B), (C), and (D).

6. **13** The question asks about averages, so look for information to put into an Average Pie. Enter the sum of the terms in set A and the number of terms in set A into an Average Pie to find that the average of set A is $\dfrac{y+4+7+8}{4}=\dfrac{19+y}{4}$. Enter the sum of the terms in set B and the number of terms in set B into another Average Pie to find that the average of set B is $\dfrac{2y+1+3}{3}=\dfrac{2y+4}{3}$.

The question states that the average of set A is 2 less than the average of set B, so $\dfrac{19+y}{4}=\dfrac{2y+4}{3}-2$.

To simplify the right side of the equation above, express 2 as $\dfrac{6}{3}$ and combine the fractions to yield $\dfrac{2y+4}{3}-\dfrac{6}{3}=\dfrac{2y+4-6}{3}=\dfrac{2y-2}{3}$. So the equation $\dfrac{19+y}{4}=\dfrac{2y+4}{3}-2$ is expressed as $\dfrac{19+y}{4}=\dfrac{2y-2}{3}$. Now, cross multiply to yield 3(19 + y) = 4(2y – 2). Distribute to produce 57 + 3y = 8y – 8. Then, add 8 to both sides and subtract 3y from both sides of the equation to yield 65 = 5y.

Divide both sides by 5 to solve to find that y = 13. The correct answer is 13.

7. **C** There are variables in the answer choices, so Plug In. Try x = 3. Now write out your new set of numbers. Since you are subtracting 3 and adding 3 the same number of times, the sum and average stay the same, so eliminate (A) and (B). The median decreases by 0.5, so eliminate (F) and (G). There are now two modes in the set, so eliminate (D). The distance of the numbers from the mean changes in the new set, so the standard deviation is not the same. Eliminate (E). The correct answer is (C).

8. **7.6** Alejandra's average equals 227 ÷ 5 = 45.4. Nigel's average equals 189 ÷ 5 = 37.8. The difference is 7.6.

9. **B** First place the known values from the question in order: 56, 86, 97, 98. From the restriction, you know that x can be placed in only two slots: first (before 56) and second (between 56 and 86). In both cases, the middle number of the full set is 86, making (B) the only correct choice.

10. $\dfrac{14}{40}$ First figure out how many marbles of each color are in the jar. For blue, $\dfrac{1}{5}$ of 40 is 8, so there are 8 blue marbles and 32 other marbles. For red, $\dfrac{1}{4}$ of 32 is 8, so there are 8 red marbles and 24

marbles that are neither red nor blue. As there are 10 green marbles, there are 14 marbles left that are not green, red, or blue. Thus, the probability of selecting one of those marbles is $\frac{14}{40}$. If you answered $\frac{26}{40}$, you found the probability that the selected marble will be blue, red, or green. If you answered $\frac{12}{40}$, for the red marbles you perhaps found $\frac{1}{4}$ of 40 (the total marbles) rather than $\frac{1}{4}$ of 32 (the remaining marbles after blue) in the original calculation.

11. D   Set up your standard bell curve with the proper percentage markers of 2%, 16%, 34% on each side of the central average line. Use an Average Pie to find the average sales amount in dollars; you should get $91,000 \div 65 = 1,400$ as the average. Note that at the 50% mark, and then note the amounts at each deviation above and below the average by adding or subtracting the given standard deviation of $130. Once you've filled in the curve, look for $1,270 from the question. It is at the 16% mark, indicating that less than 16% of employees sold under $1,270 worth of merchandise. Therefore, the other 84% of employees were able to sell $1,270 or more worth of merchandise, making (D) the correct answer.

12. 93   Use the Average Pie. Consider Cliff and Raya's average first. There are 2 of them, and their average is 79, so multiply 2×79 to get their total of 158. Call Cliff's score c, and $c + 73 = 158$, so $c = 85$. Now repeat the process with Jamal and Cliff's average: 2 people with an average of 89, so $2 \times 89 = 178$ total points. Therefore, $x + 85 = 178$, and x is 93.

Drill 4

1. C, D, E

This question asks for the number of minutes that are within 1 standard deviation of the mean of the distribution. The question does not state the mean, so start by setting up an Average Pie to figure out the average number of minutes a person spends on hold. Enter the total number of minutes on hold and the number of phone calls into the Average Pie to find the average number of minutes a person spends on hold. The average number of minutes a person spends on hold is $\frac{480}{20} = 24$ minutes.

To figure out the maximum number of minutes that are within 1 standard deviation of the mean, add the standard deviation to the average, $24 + 4 = 28$ minutes.

To figure out the minimum number of minutes that are within 1 standard deviation of the mean, subtract the standard deviation from the average, $24 - 4 = 20$ minutes. Therefore, all times between 20 and 28 minutes are within 1 standard deviation of the mean. The correct answer is (C), (D), and (E).

2. **C** Use the Rate Pie. Ali is traveling 50 feet per second faster than Jeff is traveling. Therefore, that is the rate at which she is effectively gaining ground on him. Put that in the lower-right segment of the Rate Pie. We want to know how long it will take her to gain 3,000 feet on him. Put 3,000 in the top section of the Rate Pie. Now you can see that dividing $\frac{3,000}{50}$ will fill in the last segment of the Rate Pie, telling you how long it takes Ali to do so is 60 seconds. Be aware that (E) is an incorrect partial answer. Now you need to find out how many feet Ali will travel in 60 seconds, by multiplying 60 seconds × 300 feet per second, which equals 18,000 feet. Divide 18,000 feet by the length of one lap, or 3,000 feet, and you'll find that it will take Ali 6 laps to overtake Jeff.

3. **7.2** The question asks about rates, and the size of the fountain is unknown, so look for information to put into a Rate Pie and Plug In for the volume of the fountain. Because the fountain takes 4 hours to fill and 9 hours to drain, make the volume of the fountain a multiple of both 4 and 9. Since 4 × 9 = 36, choose 36 cubic units for the volume of the fountain.

   The question states that with the drainage valve closed, the fountain fills in 4 hours. Enter 36 for the volume or "amount" of the fountain and 4 hours for the time into a Rate Pie to find the rate at which water enters the fountain. The fountain fills at a rate of $\frac{36}{4} = 9$ cubic units per hour.

   The question states that with the inlet shut off, the fountain drains in 9 hours. Enter 36 for the volume of the fountain and 9 hours for the time into a Rate Pie to find the rate at which water drains from the fountain. The fountain drains at a rate of $\frac{36}{9} = 4$ cubic units per hour.

   The question asks how long it takes to fill the fountain if the drainage valve is left open. To figure out how quickly the fountain fills with the drainage valve open, subtract the drainage rate from the filling rate. The fountain fills at a rate of 9 cubic units per hour − 4 cubic units per hour = 5 cubic units per hour when the drainage valve is left open. Enter this rate and the volume of the fountain into a Rate Pie to find the number of hours it takes to fill the fountain when the drainage valve is open. It takes $\frac{36}{5} = 7.2$ hours to fill the fountain when the drainage valve is open. The correct answer is 7.2.

4. **E** Start by Plugging In a set of consecutive integers that encompasses the full spectrum of integers, such as −2, −1, 0, 1, 2. The average and median of the set are both 0. In any set of consecutive integers, the average will always equal the median. Performing the operations in (A), (B), (C), and (F) results in sets of numbers that are still consecutive. Thus, while in (B), (C), and (F) the averages

change, the medians also change to those same values. Eliminate (B), (C), and (F). In (A), neither the average nor the median changes, so you can eliminate it as well. For (D), the new average is –1.64 and the new median is –8.2. Again, both values change, so you can eliminate (D). In (E), the new average is 0.4, but the median hasn't changed; (E) works.

5. **E, G** Plug In numbers for *p*, *s*, and *h*, such as 2, 3, and 4, respectively. If Paul can grade 2 essays every half hour, then in 4 hours, he will grade 16 essays. If Sarah can grade 3 essays every hour, then in 4 hours, she will grade 12 essays. Thus, Paul and Sarah will grade a total of 28 essays. Now, plug your numbers into each answer choice. Choices (E) and (G) result in 28. If you Plugged In and (F) also worked, you picked the same number for Paul and Sarah. If you picked (C), you didn't notice that Paul grades *p* essays every half hour, not every hour.

6. **E** Use the Average Pie to solve each part of the problem. If the average of 5 numbers is 36, then the sum of those numbers is 180. If the average of four of the numbers is 34, then the sum of those numbers is 136.

If five numbers add up to 180 and four of those five numbers add up to 136, then the fifth number is the difference between those two sums: 180 – 136 = 44. If you picked (A), you found the difference between the two averages, not the fifth number. If you picked (C), you found the average of the averages. If you picked either (B) or (D), you re-solved for the average after determining the sum.

7. **17** Use the Rate Pie to organize your work. For the first 5 weeks, Noah's company builds 1 mile per week. Therefore, they build 5 miles of road before the start of the rainy season. Once the rainy season begins, they have 6 miles of road left to build. This number is the "work," and goes in the top of the Rate Pie. The rate, $\frac{1}{2}$ mile per week, goes in the lower left segment of the Rate Pie. Divide 6 by $\frac{1}{2}$, and you'll get the total amount of time, or 12 weeks, at that rate. Therefore, it will take a total of 17 weeks for Noah's company to build the road.

8. **C, D** This question asks about rates, so look for information to put into a Rate Pie. The question asks how far Kelso is from his parents' house. The question provides Kelso's speed, so the quantity needed to determine Kelso's distance is the time Kelso travels.

Begin by figuring out how far Kelso travels before his parents leave their house. The question says that Kelso travels at a constant rate of 42 miles per hour and that he leaves his parents' house at 10 am. The question also states that Kelso's parents leave their home at 10:30 a.m., so Kelso travels for 0.5 hour before his parents start moving. Enter 42 miles per hour and 0.5 hour into a Rate Pie to find the distance Kelso travels before his parents leave. Kelso is $42 \times 0.5 = 21$ miles from his parents' house when his parents start traveling.

Next, find how quickly Kelso's parents are catching up to him. The question states that Kelso is traveling 42 miles per hour and his parents are traveling 48 miles per hour. To find this rate, find the distance between Kelso and his parents at 11:30 (1 hour after his parents leave). Put 42 miles per hour and 1.5 hours into a Rate Pie to determine how far Kelso is from his parents' house at 11:30 a.m. At 11:30 a.m., Kelso is $42 \times 1.5 = 63$ miles from his parents' house. Put 48 miles per hour and 1 hour into a Rate Pie to figure out how far Kelso's parents are from their house at 11:30 a.m. At 11:30 a.m., Kelso's parents are $48 \times 1 = 48$ miles from their home. The distance between Kelso and his parents at 11:30 a.m. is $63 - 48$ miles $= 15$ miles. Kelso was 21 miles ahead of his parents at 10:30 a.m., so Kelso's parents get $21 - 15 = 6$ miles closer to Kelso in 1 hour. Enter 6 miles and 1 hour into a Rate Pie, to find that Kelso's parents are catching up to him at a rate of 6 miles per hour. (When two objects travel in the same direction, subtract the two rates from one another to figure out the closing rate. In this case, 48 miles per hour – 42 miles per hour = 6 miles per hour.)

The question asks how far Kelso is from his parents' house when Kelso is between 6 and 9 miles ahead of his parents. If Kelso is 9 miles ahead of his parents, Kelso's parents are $21 - 9 = 12$ miles closer to him than they were at 10:30 a.m. Enter 12 miles and a rate of 6 miles per hour into a Rate Pie to find how long Kelso and his parents have both been driving. Kelso is 9 miles ahead of his parents after they have both been driving for $12 \div 6 = 2$ hours. 2 hours after 10:30 a.m. is 12:30 p.m.

If Kelso is 6 miles ahead of his parents, Kelso's parents are $21 - 6 = 15$ miles closer to him than they were at 10:30 a.m. Enter 15 miles and a rate of 6 miles per hour into a Rate Pie to find how long Kelso and his parents have both been driving. Kelso is 6 miles ahead of his parents after they have both been driving for $15 \div 6 = 2.5$ hours. 2.5 hours after 10:30 a.m. is 1:00 p.m.

The question asks for possible distances between Kelso and his parents' house when Kelso is between 6 and 9 miles ahead of his parents. Kelso is between 6 and 9 miles ahead of his parents between 12:30 p.m. and 1:00 p.m. These times are between 2.5 and 3 hours after he leaves his parents' house at 10 a.m. Enter Kelso's rate, 42 miles per hour, and 2.5 hours into a Rate Pie to find the minimum distance Kelso travels from his parents' house. The minimum distance is $42 \times 2.5 = 105$ miles. Enter 42 miles per hour and 3 hours into a Rate Pie to find the maximum distance Kelso travels from his parents' house. The maximum distance is $42 \times 3 = 126$ miles.

The correct answer is (C) and (D).

9. 25 Cyclist *A* rode for 3.5 hours at 20 miles per hour, so she traveled 20 × 3.5 = 70 miles. Cyclist *B* then, must have traveled 145 – 70 = 75 miles. Since cyclist *B* left at 2:00, she rode for 3 hours, giving her a speed of 75 ÷ 3 = 25 miles per hour.

10. E This question asks for the probability that Wilhelm receives at least 1 defective unit. The general approach to finding the probability of something happening "at least once" is to find the probability that it doesn't not happen and subtract that probability from 1, which is the sum of all possible outcomes. In this question, the probability that Wilhelm receives at least 1 defective unit is equal to 1 – the probability he receives no defective units.

If Wilhelm receives 0 defective units, then each unit selected for his order is a good unit. There are 12 total units and 3 defective units in the shipment, so there are 12 total units – 3 defective units = 9 good units in the shipment. To find the probability that Wilhelm receives 3 good units, multiply the individual probabilities of selecting a good unit for his order together. For his first unit, he has a $\frac{9}{12}$ chance of it being good. For the second unit, this probability is $\frac{8}{11}$ because the first unit is no longer available. Then the third unit has a $\frac{7}{10}$ chance of being good. Multiply these probabilities to get $\left(\frac{9}{12}\right) \times \left(\frac{8}{11}\right) \times \left(\frac{7}{10}\right) = \left(\frac{3}{4}\right) \times \left(\frac{8}{11}\right) \times \left(\frac{7}{10}\right) = \left(\frac{168}{440}\right) = \left(\frac{21}{55}\right)$.

Remember the question asks for the probability that Wilhelm receives at least 1 defective unit, not the probability that he receives 3 good units. To find the probability that Wilhelm receives at least 1 defective unit, subtract the probability that Wilhelm receives 3 good units from 1. The probability that Wilhelm receives at least one defective unit is $1 - \left(\frac{21}{55}\right) = \frac{34}{55}$, and the correct answer is (E).

11. 1.28 First, find the two people's rates in terms of miles per hour (mph). Victor's rate equals distance over time, or 1 mile over $\frac{17}{60}$ hours, which equals approximately 3.529 mph. Calculating Sarah's speed using the same steps gives you her rate, 4.286 mph. When added, the two rates become their combined rate of 7.815 mph. When you divide 10 miles by 7.815, the answer is approximately 1.28 hours until they meet.

Groups, Sequences, and Functions

GROUPS, SEQUENCES, AND FUNCTIONS

None of these concepts shows up very frequently on the test. Therefore, if you have only a limited amount of time to prepare, spend it on Plugging In, geometry, exponents and square roots, and other concepts that you are guaranteed to see. As a general rule, the more questions on a particular subject that are in this book, the more likely those questions are to show up on your test.

Groups

There are two kinds of group problems on the GRE. Both include overlapping groups. Because of this, you have to be careful so that you don't confuse one for the other. As usual, once you recognize the type, use the appropriate set-up on your scratch paper, and organize your information, the solutions end up being a matter of simple arithmetic.

The first type of group problem you will recognize because it will include the words NEITHER and BOTH.

Example:

> Of the 60 employees of company X, 22 have laptops, and 52 have desktop computers. If 12 of the employees have neither laptops nor desk tops, how many employees have both?

Once you recognize the type of problem, use the formula

$$\text{Total} = \text{Group 1} + \text{Group 2} + \text{Neither} - \text{Both}$$

So, $60 = 22 + 52 + 12 - x$. $x = 26$.

The first type includes two overlapping groups and a population that might belong to one, the other, neither, or both. The second type actually involves four overlapping groups and a population that can belong to any two of the groups at one time. There is no option for NEITHER in this type of group problem.

Example:

> Of the 60 employees at company X, 25 use Macs and 35 use PCs. Four-fifths of the Mac users are in the graphics department and there are 40 people in the graphics department total, how many of the non-graphics employees use a PC?

To solve these problems, just get your pencil on your scratch paper and organize your information in a grid.

	Mac	PC	Total
Graphics	20	20	40
Non-Graphics	5	(15)	20
Total	25	35	60

Sequences

Sequence questions are really all about pattern recognition. You will recognize them because they will ask you specifically about a sequence of numbers, as in, "Each term in the sequence above is twice the previous term minus one. What is the value of the sixth term in the sequence?" or because they will involve a number that is too big to calculate, as in, "What is the value of the tens digit of $5^{26} - 6$?"

In both cases you will find the phrase, "What is the value of?" This is a sure tip-off that you can Plug In the answer choices. As always, when you see this phrase, label your first column, assume choice (C) to be the correct answer, and work though the problem in bite-sized pieces making a new answer choice for every step.

It may be the case that this problem is really a simple matter of following directions. If that is the case, you will have to go through multiple steps to get to the correct answer. Make sure you work slowly, carefully, methodically, and, above all, do your work on your scratch paper.

In the second case, you will never be asked to calculate 5^{26}. The question contains the phrase, "What is the value of...," but there is still no way to calculate a number of that size, even with the answer choices. Therefore, there must be a pattern. Begin to calculate the sequence, starting from the lowest term and working up. When the pattern emerges, figure out how often it repeats itself (Every third term? Every fourth term? Every fifth?). If the pattern repeats itself every fourth term, then the value of the ones digit on the eighth term will be the same as the one on the fourth term. It will be the same, as well, on the twelfth, the sixteenth, the twentieth, the fortieth, and the forty-fourth. To find the value on the twenty-sixth term, just find the value on the twenty-fourth term and count up two.

Functions

If you see a strange symbol on the GRE (it could be a star, a clover, a letter of the Greek alphabet), it doesn't mean that math has changed since you left high school and they've rewritten all of the textbooks. It just means that you are seeing a rare functions question. The symbol will be attached to a variable and an equal sign. It acts like a series of instructions and tells you what to do in generic terms.

Example:

If $x \heartsuit y = \left(\dfrac{x + y}{4} \right)^2$ for all integers x and y, then $10 \heartsuit 6 =$

As crazy as it looks, all this problem is telling you to do is Plug In a 10 every time you see an x and a 6 every time you see a y in the equation, $\left(\dfrac{x + y}{4} \right)^2$. Use your scratch paper, be meticulous, and follow directions. It's not upper-level math, just basic arithmetic with weird-looking symbols.

For more practice and a more in-depth look at The Princeton Review math techniques, check out our student-friendly guidebook, *Cracking the GRE*.

DRILL 1

Question 1

If the function f is defined by $f(x) = 2x + 5$, what is the value of $f(4)$?

- ○ 17
- ○ 15
- ○ 13
- ○ 11
- ○ 9

Question 2

Let the "par" of a rectangle be defined as one half the area of that rectangle.

Quantity A	Quantity B
The par of a rectangle with a perimeter of 24 and a length of 2	11

- ○ Quantity A is greater.
- ○ Quantity B is greater.
- ○ The two quantities are equal.
- ○ The relationship cannot be determined from the information given.

Question 3

$$3, 4.5, 6, 7.5, \ldots$$

Each term in the sequence above is formed by adding the positive number k to the preceding term.

Quantity A	Quantity B
The eighth term in the sequence above	14

- ○ Quantity A is greater.
- ○ Quantity B is greater.
- ○ The two quantities are equal.
- ○ The relationship cannot be determined from the information given.

Question 4

The operation denoted by the symbol $\rightarrow$ is defined for all real numbers a and b as $a \rightarrow b = a\sqrt{b}$. What is the value of $3 \rightarrow \left(2 \rightarrow 4\right)$?

- ○ $\dfrac{1}{4}$
- ○ 4
- ○ 6
- ○ $6\sqrt{2}$
- ○ 12

Question 5

Each of the even-numbered terms in a certain sequence is formed by multiplying the preceding term by −1. Each of the odd-numbered terms in the sequence is formed by adding 3 to the preceding term. If the first term in the sequence is 3, then what is the 168th term?

- ○ −3
- ○ −1
- ○ 0
- ○ 1
- ○ 3

Question 6

Quantity A	Quantity B
The sum of all the even integers from 18 to 36 inclusive	The sum of all the even integers from 22 to 38 inclusive

- ○ Quantity A is greater.
- ○ Quantity B is greater.
- ○ The two quantities are equal.
- ○ The relationship cannot be determined from the information given.

Question 7

A club of 65 people includes only standard members and gold members. Of the club's 30 gold members, 18 are men. Exactly 20 women are standard members.

Quantity A	Quantity B
The number of standard members who are men	13

- ○ Quantity A is greater.
- ○ Quantity B is greater.
- ○ The two quantities are equal.
- ○ The relationship cannot be determined from the information given.

Question 8

Mary is building a pyramid out of stacked rows of soup cans. When completed, the top row of the pyramid contains a single soup can, and each row below the top row contains 6 more cans than the one above it. If the completed pyramid contains 16 rows, then how many soup cans did Mary use to build it?

- ○ 91
- ○ 96
- ○ 728
- ○ 732
- ○ 736

Question 9

The sequence of numbers $S = \{s_1, s_2, s_3, \ldots\}$ is defined by $s_1 = 2$, $s_2 = 10$, and $s_n = s_{n-1}^{s_{n-2}}$ for each positive integer n greater than or equal to 3. For example, $s_3 = 10^2$. What is the greatest value of n for which s_n has 2,000 or fewer digits?

- ○ 100
- ○ 20
- ○ 5
- ○ 4
- ○ 3

Question 10

The "pluck" of a circle is defined as the area of the circle divided by π. What is the pluck of a circle with radius 5 ?

DRILL 2

Question 1

a is the sum of the second and third positive integer multiples of a.

Quantity A	Quantity B
<u>5</u>	15

- ○ Quantity A is greater.
- ○ Quantity B is greater.
- ○ The two quantities are equal.
- ○ The relationship cannot be determined from the information given.

Question 2

A certain vent releases steam every 20 minutes. If the vent releases steam at 6:25 p.m., which of the following could be a time at which the vent releases steam?

- ○ 9:15 p.m.
- ○ 10:40 p.m.
- ○ 11:00 p.m.
- ○ 12:20 p.m.
- ○ 1:05 a.m.

Question 3

For all nonzero integers l and m, let the operation § be defined by $l \, \S \, m = -\left| \dfrac{l + m}{lm} \right|$.

Quantity A	Quantity B
$3 \, \S \, \dfrac{3}{2}$	-1

- ○ Quantity A is greater.
- ○ Quantity B is greater.
- ○ The two quantities are equal.
- ○ The relationship cannot be determined from the information given.

Question 4

There are 30 students in Mr. Peterson's gym class. 14 of them play basketball, 13 play baseball, and 9 play neither basketball nor baseball.

Quantity A	Quantity B
The number of students who play both basketball and baseball	6

- ○ Quantity A is greater.
- ○ Quantity B is greater.
- ○ The two quantities are equal.
- ○ The relationship cannot be determined from the information given.

Question 5

In a regular n-sided polygon, the degree measure of each angle is $\dfrac{(n - 2)180°}{n}$. The degree measure of an angle in a regular 10-sided polygon is how much greater than the degree measure of an angle in a regular 6-sided polygon?

$$\boxed{}$$

Question 6

For all real numbers a and b, the operation $\oplus$ is defined by $a \oplus b = 2a - b$. What is the absolute value of the difference between $(3 \oplus 1) \oplus 2$ and $6 \oplus 3$?

$$\boxed{}$$

Question 7

Starting with the third term, each term in Sequence S is one-half the sum of the previous 2 terms. If the first 2 terms of Sequence S are 64 and 32, respectively, and the nth term is the first non-integer term of Sequence S, then $n =$

☐

Question 8

Quantity A	Quantity B
The units digit of 7^{29}	The units digit of 3^{27}

○ Quantity A is greater.
○ Quantity B is greater.
○ The two quantities are equal.
○ The relationship cannot be determined from the information given.

Question 9

Of the employees at a company, 60 percent were men and, of these, $\frac{1}{10}$ were still employed after a recent corporate restructuring. If the number of women who were still employed after the restructuring was five times the number of men who were employed after it, what percent of the women were still employed after the restructuring?

○   6%
○   20%
○   30%
○   50%
○   75%

Question 10

If q is even, then $\#q = -2$;
If q is odd, then $\#q = -4$.
a and b are integers such that $b - 3$ is odd.

Quantity A	Quantity B
$\#(6a)$	$\#b$

○ Quantity A is greater.
○ Quantity B is greater.
○ The two quantities are equal.
○ The relationship cannot be determined from the information given.

Question 11

Three digits have been removed from each of the following numbers. If $n = 25$, which of the numbers is equal to $(3)(2^{n-1})$?

○   47, _ _6, _23
○   47, _ _6, _32
○   49, _ _2, _64
○   49, _ _2, _36
○   50, _ _1, _48

ANSWERS

Drill 1

1. C
2. B
3. B
4. C
5. C
6. C
7. A
8. E
9. D
10. 25

Drill 2

1. A
2. E
3. E
4. C
5. 24
6. 1
7. 8
8. C
9. E
10. C
11. E

EXPLANATIONS
Drill 1

1. **C**   If $f(x) = 2x + 5$, then $f(4) = 2(4) + 5 = 13$.

2. **B**   Draw it. The rectangle in Quantity A has a length of 2 and a perimeter of 24. $P = 2l + 2w$, so $24 = 4 + 2w$. Solve for the width by subtracting 4 from both sides and then dividing by 2 giving a width of 10. The area of this rectangle is $lw = (2)(10) = 20$, and the "par" is one half that, or 10. Quantity B is greater.

3. **B**   Notice that each term in the sequence is 1.5 greater than the last (i.e., $k = 1.5$). So the second term is $3 + 1.5 = 4.5$, the third term is $4.5 + 1.5 = 6$, and so forth. So the fifth term is $7.5 + 1.5 = 9$, the sixth term is $9 + 1.5 = 10.5$, the seventh term is $10.5 + 1.5 = 12$, and finally, the eighth term is $12 + 1.5 = 13.5$. So, Quantity A is 13.5, and the answer is (B). Another way to attack this problem is to use the sequence formula of $3 + 1.5(n - 1)$, where the 3 is the first term, the 1.5 is the increase, and you are looking for the nth term. So, the eighth term is $3 + 1.5(8 - 1) = 13.5$.

4. **C**   To follow the order of operations, first evaluate the expression in parentheses.
    $3 \rightarrow (2 \rightarrow 4) = 3 \rightarrow 2\sqrt{4} = 3 \rightarrow 4 = 3\sqrt{4} = 6$. The answer is (C).

5. **C**   Write out sequences until you see the pattern. The second term in the sequence is $3(-1) = -3$. Adding 3 gives you the third term, 0. Multiplying by -1 gives you the fourth term, also 0. Adding 3 gives you 3, the fifth term. So the sequence repeats every four terms: 3, -3, 0, 0, 3, -3, 0, 0, and so forth. Dividing 168 by 4 gives you a remainder of zero, and the fourth, eighth, twelfth, and every other nth term where n is a multiple of 4 (including the 168th term) will all be the same value, 0. The answer is (C).

6. **C**   Even if you know the summation formula, you can avoid time-consuming calculations by disregarding the numbers that are common to both sums—the even integers from 22 to 36, inclusive. That leaves $18 + 20 = 38$ as the sum of the unique terms in Quantity A, and 38 as the only unique term in Quantity B. The quantities are equal.

7. **A**   Set up a group grid and fill in what you have:

	Men	Women	Total
Standard		20	
Gold	18		30
Total			65

Use this to find that there are $65 - 30 = 35$ total standard members. So there are $35 - 20 = 15$ standard male members, thus, Quantity A is 15. The answer is (A).

8. **E** The top row contains 1 can, the second row contains $1 + 1(6) = 7$ cans, the third row contains $1 + 2(6) = 13$ cans, and so forth, so that the sixteenth row contains $1 + 15(6) = 91$ cans. But you need to find the total number of cans, which is $1 + 7 + 13 +...+ 79 + 85 + 91$. Notice that adding the first and last term in the sequence gives you 92. Adding the second and second to last term also gives you 92: as you move to the next term at the beginning of the sequence, you are adding 6, while as you move to the previous term at the end of the sequence, you are subtracting 6, so the sum will remain constant. Thus, for each pair of rows, the sum is 92. Sixteen rows represents eight pairs of rows, so the total number of cans is $(8)(92) = 736$. The answer is (E).

9. **D** Decoding the definition of the sequence tells you that, to find the value of each term, you take the previous term, and raise it to the power of the term before it. You know $s_3 = 10^2 = 100$, $s_4 = \left(10^2\right)^{10} = 10^{20}$, and $s_5 = \left(10^{20}\right)^{100} = 10^{2000}$. So s_4 is the digit 1 followed by twenty zeroes, which is a total of 21 digits, and s_5 is the digit 1 followed by 2,000 zeroes, for a total of 2,001 digits. So the fourth term is the one that meets the condition set forth in the question, and the answer is (D).

10. **25** Ignore the unfamiliar terminology and follow directions. The area of a circle with radius 5 is $\pi r^2 = 5^2 \pi = 25\pi$. Dividing the area by π gives you 25.

Drill 2

1. **A** The second positive integer multiple of 5 is 10. The third positive integer multiple of 5 is 15. The sum of 10 and 15 is 25, so Quantity A is greater.

2. **E** List out the times until you figure out the pattern. The vent releases steam at 6:25 PM and then 20 minutes later at 6:45 PM, then 7:05 PM, then 7:25 PM. So the pattern is that steam is released at 5, 25, and 45 minutes after the hour. Only (E) fits the pattern.

3. **C** When a problem gives you a relationship signified by an unfamiliar symbol, just plug in the given values into the given "function" and solve. If $l \S\ m = -\left|\dfrac{l+m}{lm}\right|$, then $3\S\dfrac{3}{2} = -\left|\dfrac{3+\dfrac{3}{2}}{3\left(\dfrac{3}{2}\right)}\right| = -\left|\dfrac{\dfrac{9}{2}}{\dfrac{9}{2}}\right| = -|1| = -1$.

    The quantities are equal, so select (C).

4. **C** Use the group formula and fill in what you know. *Total = Group 1 + Group 2 − Both + Neither* becomes $30 = 14 + 13 - Both + 9$. So *Both* = 6, and the answer is (C).

5. 24   Find the measure of an angle in a regular 10-sided polygon by plugging 10 into the given formula: $\frac{(10-2)180°}{10} = 144°$. Then do the same for a regular 6-sided polygon by plugging 6 into the given formula: $\frac{(6-2)180°}{6} = 120°$. Finally, $144 - 120 = 24$.

6. 1   To follow the order of operations, first evaluate the expression in parentheses: $3 \oplus 1 = 2(3) - 1 = 5$, so now the first function can be written as $5 \oplus 2 = 2(5) - 2 = 8$. Next, rewrite the second function so that you have $6 \oplus 3 = 2(6) - 3 = 9$. Finally, $|8 - 9| = |-1| = 1$, so the answer is 1.

7. 8   Use brute force to solve this one. Write down the 2 given terms, find half the sum of the previous 2 terms, and repeat the process until you have a non-integer. When you work it out, Sequence S should begin 64, 32, 48, 40, 44, 42, 43, 42.5; the first non-integer term is the 8th term, so $n = 8$.

8. C   To find the pattern in each sequence, write out the units digit of the first few terms in the sequence. The pattern for the units digit of powers of 7 is 7, 9, 3, 1. The pattern for the units digit of powers of 3 is 3, 9, 7, 1. For both numbers, 1 repeats as the units digit every 4 powers, so the 4th power will have a units digit of 1, as will the 8th, the 12th, and so on. Because 28 is a multiple of 4, you know that 7^{28} will have a units digit of 1. So moving forward one in the pattern, 7^{29} will have a units digit of 7. Similarly, 3^{28} will have a units digit of 1, so moving backward one in the pattern, 3^{27} must have a units digit of 7. The quantities are equal, so the answer is (C).

9. E   Set up a group grid and, because you are dealing with percents and fractions, Plug In 100 for the total number of employees at the company. There will be 60 men, of whom 6 are still employed after the restructuring. Subtracting 60 from 100 gives you 40, the total number of women. Five times the 6 men who are still employed gives you 30, the number of women still employed. After filling in this information, the group grid looks like the figure below.

	Still employed	No longer employed	Total
Men	6		60
Women	30		40
Total			100

There are 30 women, but the question asks you what percent this represents of the total number of women. 30 out of 40 is 75 percent, so the answer is (E).

10. **C** Rather than trying to remember a bunch of rules about even and odd numbers, Plug In for a and b. If a is 2, then $6a$ is 12, and #12 = –2. Because $b - 3$ is odd, make $b = 6$, and #b = –2 as well. The two quantities are equal, so eliminate (A) and (B). Any set of values gives the same outcome, so select (C).

11. **E** As you have seen, the units digits of powers often follow patterns. The units digits of the powers of 2 are 2, 4, 6, 8, 2, 4, 6, 8, and so on. The pattern repeats every 4 terms. For this equation, $n = 25$, so you first need the units digit of 2^{n-1} or 2^{24}. Since 24 is a multiple of 4, 2^{24} will have a units digit of 6. Multiplying that number by 3 will give a value that has a units digit of 8. The only answer that fits the pattern is (E).

Combinations and Permutations

COMBINATIONS AND PERMUTATIONS

You will recognize these problems because they will ask you about the number of possible combinations, arrangements, groups, or ways to order a number of things or people. You may be asked about toppings on a salad, members in a group or on a committee, children in a line, or runners in a race.

For combinations and permutations, there are only two possible numbers you can generate, a big one and a small one. The big one happens when order matters, the small one happens when order does not matter.

Example 1

Supposed you are asked for the number of different ways eight runners come in first, second, or third in a race. The first step is to make slots on your scratch paper. You are looking at the runners in first, second, or third place; therefore you need three slots.

_ _ _

Before the race starts, everyone is a winner, or at least a potential winner, so there are eight possible runners who could come in first place. Once one runner comes in first, there are seven potential runners left who could come in second place, and six left for third place.

<u>8</u> <u>7</u> <u>6</u>

To figure out the number of ways eight runners could finish first, second, and third in a race, simply multiply all three numbers. Order, in the case of runners in a race, is highly significant. If Tom comes in first place, Jenny in second, and Alicia in third, that is one arrangement, but if Alicia comes in first, Tom in second, and Jenny in third, it counts as a new arrangement. There are 336 possible arrangements ($8 \times 7 \times 6 = 336$).

Example 2

Now imagine that you are asked to find the number of different ways eight senators can be arranged on a three-person committee. There are three seats on the committee so you need three slots. The problem begins the same way. There are eight potential senators for the first slot, seven for the second, and six left for the third.

<u>8</u> <u>7</u> <u>6</u>

As opposed to the situation of the runners in a race, however, order, in this case, does not matter. A committee made up of Ross, LB, and Shirley or a committee made up of LB, Shirley, and Ross is the same committee. The larger number counts each of these committees separately. You need a way to get rid of all of these committees of the same three people that you've counted just because they are in a different order. The way to do this is to divide by the factorial of the number of slots. It sounds complicated, but in reality, all you have to do is count down the number of slots in the divisor.

$$\frac{8\,7\,6}{3\,2\,1}$$

Before you multiply, reduce your fractions. You will always be able to reduce all of the numbers in the denominator. The three and the two each go evenly into the six once, so you are simply left with 56 (8 × 7). There are 56 different committees that can be made from a group of eight senators.

SUMMARY

That's it. It doesn't have to be anymore complicated than that. There are two numbers you can produce, a bigger one and a smaller one. The bigger number happens when order matters. In this case, just figure out the number of slots, fill in the numbers, and multiply across the top. The smaller number happens when order doesn't matter. In this case, figure out the number of slots, fill in the numbers on the top and count down the number of slots on the bottom; then reduce and multiply whatever remains.

Occasionally, if you are doing really well, they will give you some rules for your slots. For example, you might have three boys and four girls lining up for gym class. The question may ask you how many different ways they can be arranged in a line, but might stipulate that there must be a girl in first and last place. In this case, the approach is the same, just start with the slots that have the rules—we call these the restricted slots.

There are seven slots total because there will be seven children in the line. The first slot must be a girl, so there are four potential girls for that slot. The last slot must be a girl too, so there are three girls left who can stand last in line. The second slot is wide open. There are six children—three boys and two remaining girls—who are available for the second slot, five for the third, four for the fourth, and so on.

Your scratch paper will look like this.

$$\underline{4\,6\,5\,4\,3\,2\,3}$$

Because order matters and every different arrangement of students must be counted separately, you want the bigger number. Simply multiply across the top, and you are done. There are 8,640 different ways three boys and four girls can be arranged in a line with a girl at the head of the line and the back.

For more practice and a more in-depth look at The Princeton Review math techniques, check out our student-friendly guidebook, *Cracking the GRE*.

DRILL 1

Question 1

A club consists of 8 women and 8 men. The club has a president and a vice president and no club member can hold more than one position.

Quantity A	Quantity B
The number of possible assignments such that a woman is president and a man is vice president	The number of possible assignments such that both the president and vice president are women

- ○ Quantity A is greater.
- ○ Quantity B is greater.
- ○ The two quantities are equal.
- ○ The relationship cannot be determined from the information given.

Question 2

Given an alphabet of 26 letters, with 21 consonants, and 5 vowels, how many three-letter combinations are there such that a vowel is the middle letter and a consonant is the last letter?

- ○ 60
- ○ 546
- ○ 2,520
- ○ 2,730
- ○ 4,784

Question 3

Sydney has five blouses, twelve pairs of dress pants, ten pairs of shoes, and three hats in her closet.

Quantity A	Quantity B
$(5^2)(2^3)(3^2)$	The number of possible outfits if Sydney wears one blouse, one pair of dress pants, one pair of shoes, and one hat from her closet.

- ○ Quantity A is greater.
- ○ Quantity B is greater.
- ○ The two quantities are equal.
- ○ The relationship cannot be determined from the information given.

Question 4

Jose's Catering Service offers six different entrees and offers event menus that consist of one to six of these different entrees.

Quantity A	Quantity B
The number of possible menus that consist of two different entrees	The number of possible menus that consist of four different entrees

- ○ Quantity A is greater.
- ○ Quantity B is greater.
- ○ The two quantities are equal.
- ○ The relationship cannot be determined from the information given.

Question 5

A certain password must contain 3 distinct digits followed by 2 distinct capital letters. Given ten digits and 26 capital letters, how many different passwords are possible?

[   ]

Question 6

At least three students from a group of five student government members are required to meet with the university president annually, per the school's charter. How many different seating arrangements are possible for the student representatives at the meeting?

- ○ 60
- ○ 120
- ○ 243
- ○ 300
- ○ 360

Question 7

Geoff is setting up an aquarium and must choose 4 of 6 different fish and 2 of 3 different plants. How many different combinations of fish and plants can Geoff choose?

- ○ 8
- ○ 12
- ○ 18
- ○ 45
- ○ 90

Question 8

Ten players from the Southern Conference are chosen for an all-star basketball game. If a basketball team requires five starters, then how many possible starting combinations can the coach of the Southern Conference create?

- ○ 25
- ○ 50
- ○ 120
- ○ 252
- ○ 30,240

Question 9

If nine people are available to form a committee, what is the ratio of the number of different two-person committees to the number of different six-person committees that can be formed from this group?

- ○ 1 : 4
- ○ 2 : 7
- ○ 3 : 7
- ○ 7 : 3
- ○ 7 : 2

Question 10

Six students compete in a table tennis tournament. Each student plays each of the other students four times. What is the total number of games played in the tournament?

[   ]

Question 11

A four-person leadership committee is to be chosen from a student council that consists of seven juniors and five seniors.

Quantity A	Quantity B
The number of different leadership committees that include 3 seniors and 1 junior	75

○ Quantity A is greater.
○ Quantity B is greater.
○ The two quantities are equal.
○ The relationship cannot be determined from the information given.

Question 12

Maren is directing a play that contains four female roles and two male roles. Six women and five men show up for the auditions.

Quantity A	Quantity B
150	The number of different casting arrangements Maren could create from those who auditioned

○ Quantity A is greater.
○ Quantity B is greater.
○ The two quantities are equal.
○ The relationship cannot be determined from the information given.

Question 13

Depending on the night, a pizza restaurant offers anywhere from seven to nine different choices of toppings. Sam wants a pizza with three toppings. Which of the following could be the number of different ways that Sam can order his pizza with three different toppings?

Indicate all such values.

☐ 35
☐ 42
☐ 56
☐ 84
☐ 210
☐ 252
☐ 504

Question 14

Depending on the day, an ice cream shop offers seven to nine possible ice cream flavors and three to four possible sauces. A Deluxe Sundae consists of two different types of ice cream and two different sauces. Which of the following could be the number of different Deluxe Sundaes that a customer can order?

Indicate all such values.

☐ 36
☐ 54
☐ 84
☐ 216
☐ 432
☐ 864

DRILL 2

Question 1

Six state governors meet at an annual convention. They line up in random order to pose for a photograph. If the governors of Alaska and Hawaii are among the six governors, how many different ways can the governors line up for the picture so that these two governors are adjacent?

- ○ 5
- ○ 10
- ○ 120
- ○ 240
- ○ 720

Question 2

If Jeff has four movies, and must choose to watch either 1, 2, or 3 different movies, which of the following represents a possible number of different arrangements of movies that Jeff could watch?

Indicate all such values.

- ☐ 4
- ☐ 6
- ☐ 7
- ☐ 9
- ☐ 12
- ☐ 24

Question 3

Jess has nine different statues and chooses three to arrange in a row in a display. How many different arrangements can she make?

Question 4

Of a group of 10 PTA members, a committee will be selected that has 1 president and 3 other members. How many different committees could be selected?

Question 5

Esteban's restaurant offers a lunch special. A customer can order a platter consisting of four different small dishes from a selection of twelve choices. How many different platters can a customer create?

- ○ 24
- ○ 144
- ○ 495
- ○ 11,880
- ○ 20,736

Question 6

Kate and Chad are planning their wedding dinner and must select 3 of 12 entrees and 2 of 3 desserts for their guests to be able to choose from. How many different combinations of offerings are possible?

[   ]

Question 7

For her Halloween display, Margaret plans to arrange a row of alternating witch and ghost figurines. The row must begin on the left with a witch figurine and end on the right with a ghost figurine. Margaret plans to purchase either three of each type of figurine or four of each type of figurine, and each figurine will look unique. Depending on how many figurines she purchases, which of the following could be the number of ways that she could arrange her display?

Indicate all such values.

☐   6
☐   24
☐   36
☐   72
☐   576
☐   720
☐ 40,320

Question 8

There are six cars in a motorcade. How many different arrangements of cars in the motorcade are possible?

○   6
○   21
○   72
○   120
○   720

Question 9

Mark can take three friends with him on a vacation and is listing the possible combinations of friends. If he has five friends to choose from and is numbering each possible combination sequentially beginning with 1, which of the following numbers will appear on his list of combinations?

Indicate all such values.

☐   2
☐   10
☐   15
☐   24
☐   60
☐ 120

Question 10

Twelve runners enter a race to compete for first, second, and third place. How many different combinations of winners are possible?

[   ]

Question 11

Sherry supervises a crew of maintenance engineers for an office building. If there are 5 experienced maintenance engineers and 3 apprentice engineers and the engineers are sent out on jobs in teams, which of the following must be true?

Indicate all such statements.

☐ There are 10 different 3-person teams of experienced engineers she could send.

☐ There are 3 different 2-person teams of apprentice engineers she could send.

☐ There are 2 different 2-person teams of apprentice engineers she could send.

☐ There are 10 different 2-person teams of experienced engineers she could send.

☐ There are 10 different 4-person teams of experienced engineers she could send.

Question 12

All employees at Company *W* are assigned unique employee ID codes that consist of numerals and letters from the alphabet. If letters can be repeated within the same code but numerals cannot, which of the following must be true?

Indicate all such statements.

☐ There are 2,600 possible different 3-character codes consisting of 1 letter followed by 2 numerals.

☐ There are 60,840 possible different 4-character codes consisting of 2 letters followed by 2 numerals.

☐ There are 650 possible 2-character codes consisting of 1 letter followed by 1 numeral.

Question 13

For his birthday, Brian will receive either three or four differently colored ties, either two or three differently colored shirts, and either one or two differently colored jackets. Depending on how many ties, shirts, and jackets he receives, which of the following values could be the number of ways he could make an outfit with one tie, one shirt, and one jacket?

Indicate all such statements.

☐ 6
☐ 8
☐ 9
☐ 10
☐ 12
☐ 16
☐ 18

Question 14

Paul and Allen are choosing ties out of a selection of three distinct red ties, five distinct green ties, and six distinct blue ties. If Paul and Allen each wear one tie, how many different ways could they wear ties of the same color?

[   ]

Question 15

How many different committees of 5 members can be chosen from a group of 8 people?

○ 28
○ 56
○ 118
○ 336
○ 6,720

ANSWERS
Drill 1

1. A
2. D
3. C
4. C
5. 468,000
6. D
7. D
8. D
9. C
10. 60
11. B
12. B
13. A, C, D
14. C, D

Drill 2

1. D
2. A, E, F
3. 504
4. 840
5. C
6. 660
7. C, E
8. E
9. A, B
10. 1,320
11. A, B, D
12. B
13. A, B, C, E, F, G
14. 56
15. B

EXPLANATIONS
Drill 1

1. **A** For Quantity A, there are 8 options for president and 8 options for vice president, giving you 8 × 8 = 64 total assignments. For Quantity B, once you pick a woman to be president, there are only 7 women left to be vice president, giving you 8 × 7 = 56 assignments. The answer is (A).

2. **D** This is a case of simply multiplying the three numbers given: 26 × 21 × 5. The total is 2,730, so select (D).

3. **C** Start by expanding out Quantity A. The expression $(5^2)(2^3)(3^2)$ is the same as 25 × 8 × 9, which equals 1,800. Next, solve for the number of possible outfits Sydney can wear by drawing four slots, one for each article of clothing. Place the number of options on each slot (5 × 12 × 10 × 3). Multiplying the options together yields 1,800.

   Alternatively, it is possible to factor out the items in the wardrobe to see that the two values are equal. Instead of writing 5 × 12 × 10 × 3, write out the factors as 5 × (2 × 2 × 3) × (2 × 5) × 3. Notice that there are three 2s, two 5s, and two 3s, which can also be expressed as $(5^2)(2^3)(3^2)$. Either way, the values are equal, making (C) correct.

4. **C** This question is asking for the total of menu options out of 6 dishes with 4 entrees or 2 entrees and order does not matter. Chicken and fish is the same as fish and chicken. The comparison is between 6Choose4 and 6Choose2. These quantities are equal (both 15), so (C) is the correct answer.

5. **468,000**

   List the number of possible options for each character in the password. There are 10 possibilities for the first digit, 9 left for the second, and 8 left for the third. There are 26 possibilities for the first letter and 25 for the second. There are 10 × 9 × 8 × 26 × 25 = 468,000 possible passwords.

6. **D** The problem starts with the phrase "at least three," which means that three, four, or all five students may attend. To solve this problem, work out the total number of arrangements for 3 students, 4 students, and 5 students, and then add them together. Since this is an arrangement question, order matters. Multiply the possibilities for each slot and do not divide by the factorial of the number of slots. If three students attend the meeting, the number of arrangements is 5 × 4 × 3 = 60. If four students attend, the number of arrangements is 5 × 4 × 3 × 2 = 120. If all five students attend, the number of arrangements is 5 × 4 × 3 × 2 × 1 = 120. To get the total number of possible arrangements, add together the three totals, which is 60 + 120 + 120 = 300. Choice (D) is correct.

7. **D** First find the number of groups of fish he can select. This is your number of slots: _ _ _ _. There are six fish he can choose for the first slot, 5 for the second and so on: $\underline{6}\,\underline{5}\,\underline{4}\,\underline{3}$. Since order doesn't matter, you need to divide by the factorial of the number of slots: $\dfrac{6 \times 5 \times 4 \times 3}{4 \times 3 \times 2 \times 1}$. Reduce your number to get 3 × 5 = 15 . For plants you have two slots so $\dfrac{3}{2} \times \dfrac{2}{1} = 3$. 3 × 15 = 45. The answer is (D).

8.   **D**   The problem asks only for possible combinations of five. Therefore, the order of the players does not matter, which makes this a combination problem. First, draw slots for the five starters and place the number of options available for each slot. The first slot has ten options. Since one player has already been chosen, there are only nine options for the second slot. Continue this process for all five slots (10 × 9 × 8 × 7 × 6). On combination problems, the product of those five numbers must be divided by the factorial of the number of slots. There are five slots, so the product must be divided by 5!.

$$\frac{10 \times 9 \times 8 \times 7 \times 6}{5 \times 4 \times 3 \times 2 \times 1}$$

Factor out equivalent values from the numerator and the denominator. For instance, the 3 and 2 in the denominator cancel out the 6 in the numerator. Divide the 10 by 5 to equal 2, and divide the 8 by 4 to equal another 2. After factoring, the equation should be simplified as 2 × 9 × 2 × 7, which equals 252. Choice (D) is correct.

9.   **C**   It does not matter in what order the members of these committees are selected, so remember to divide. Do this problem one step at a time. The number of two-person committees that can be formed from a group of nine people is $\frac{9 \times 8}{2 \times 1} = 36$. The number of six-person committees that can be formed from a group of nine people is $\frac{9 \times 8 \times 7 \times 6 \times 5 \times 4}{6 \times 5 \times 4 \times 3 \times 2 \times 1} = 84$. So the ratio of two-person committees to six-person committees is $\frac{36}{84}$. Reduce this fraction: $\frac{36}{84} = \frac{12}{28} = \frac{6}{14} = \frac{3}{7}$. Be careful of (D), which gives the ratio of six-person committees to two-person committees. Choice (C) gives the correct ratio.

10.   **60**   Because order does not matter, divide by the factorial of the number of things. The number of two-student combinations that can be created is $\frac{6 \times 5}{2 \times 1} = 15$.

11.   **B**   Start by finding out how many groups of three seniors can be chosen from the five seniors: $\frac{5\ 4\ 3}{3\ 2\ 1} = 10$. Next, multiply that total by the number of individual juniors with which those groups can be paired (7) to form the full committee: 10 × 7 = 70. Quantity B is greater.

12.   **B**   Note the word *arrangements* in Quantity B. Arrangement means that order matters. In this case, male and female actors are assigned different parts in the play that are not interchangeable. First figure out the number of arrangements for the male parts. The play has two parts for actors, so draw two slots. The first slot has five possible casting outcomes and the second has four (5 × 4). This yields

20 possible casting outcomes for the male roles in the play. Next look at the female roles. There are four roles and six potential women. Draw four slots, one for each role. Label those slots with the number of possible outcomes for each ($\underline{6} \times \underline{5} \times \underline{4} \times \underline{3}$). Therefore, there are 360 possible outcomes for the female roles. Multiply those 360 outcomes with the 20 possible outcomes for male roles to equal 7,200 different casting arrangements. Quantity B is greater, so (B) is correct.

13. **A, C, D**

   This problem is about combinations, because order doesn't matter. On a night when the pizza place offers only seven toppings, Sam has $(7 \times 6 \times 5) \div (3 \times 2 \times 1) = 35$ options, (A). When the pizza place has eight toppings, Sam has $(8 \times 7 \times 6) \div (3 \times 2 \times 1) = 56$ options, (C). And when the pizza place has nine toppings, Sam has $(9 \times 8 \times 7) \div (3 \times 2 \times 1) = 84$ options, (D).

14. **C, D**   Simplify this problem by dealing with the two combinations separately. To select 2 out of 7, 8, or 9 ice creams, calculate $\frac{7}{2} \times \frac{6}{1}, \frac{8}{2} \times \frac{7}{1}$, and $\frac{9}{2} \times \frac{8}{1}$ to yield 21, 28, or 36 possible combinations of ice creams, respectively. Now, so the same thing for sauces: $\frac{3}{2} \times \frac{2}{1} = 3$, and $\frac{4}{2} \times \frac{3}{1} = 6$, so you have 3 or 6 possible combinations of sauces. The possible numbers of different Deluxe Sundaes, then, are $21 \times 3 = 63$; $21 \times 6 = 126$; $28 \times 3 = 84$; $28 \times 6 = 168$; $36 \times 3 = 108$; and $36 \times 6 = 216$. Only (C) and (D) work.

Drill 2

1. **D**   This is a permutation because order matters. First, think about the positions for the 2 governors from Alaska and Hawaii. There are 5 pairs of spots they can occupy: first and second, second and third, third and fourth, fourth and fifth, or fifth and sixth. That gives you 5 possibilities; since either governor could come first, you have a total of $5 \times 2 = 10$ possible ways to arrange those 2 governors. Meanwhile, for each of those options, the other governors can assume any of the remaining spots, which equals $4 \times 3 \times 2 \times 1$, or 24 possibilities. The answer is thus $10 \times 24 = 240$, (D).

2. **A, E, F**

   If Jeff watches one movie, he has four different choices for that one movie, so (A) is a correct answer. To find the total number of arrangements of two movies, first write out two slots. For the first movie, he has 4 choices and a 4 goes in the first slot. For the second movie, he now has three choices and a 3 goes in the second slot. $4 \times 3 = 12$, so (E) is correct. There are 24 arrangements if he watches three movies: $4 \times 3 \times 2 = 24$. Choice (F) is also correct.

3. **504**   This problem deals with permutations because the order of the statues matters. Draw three slots for the three positions. You can choose from nine statues for the first spot, eight for the second, and seven for the third. Multiplying these values together gives you 504.

4. **840** There are 10 possible presidents. After the president is selected, there are 9 members left to fill the remaining 3 spots. Order does not matter, so the number of possibilities for the other three spots is $\dfrac{9 \times 8 \times 7}{3 \times 2 \times 1}$. Simplifying the fraction yields $3 \times 4 \times 7 = 84$. So, there are 10 possible presidents and 84 possible committees for each president. Multiplying them yields the total number of possible committees, 840.

5. **C** This problem is about combinations, because the order of the dishes does not matter. Since you're choosing 4 dishes, start by drawing 4 blanks. On top, write the number of choices: 12 choices for the first dish, then 11, 10, and 9. On the bottom, start with the size of the smaller group and count down: 4, 3, 2, and 1. Cancel the numbers on the bottom, and the numbers on top will multiply to 495.

6. **660** The order of entrees the guests choose from does not matter. Therefore, the number of different possibilities of entrees is $\dfrac{12 \times 11 \times 10}{3 \times 2 \times 1} = 220$. The order of desserts does not matter either, so there are $\dfrac{3 \times 2}{2} = 3$ possible different combinations of desserts. Multiplying the two together gives a total of 660 possible different combinations of offerings.

7. **C, E** This problem is about permutations, because the order of the figurines matters since they each look unique. You have two cases to consider here. Start with the option that Margaret buys three witches and three ghosts. In that case, she has 3 choices of witch for the first spot, 3 choices of ghost for the second spot, 2 choices of witch for the third spot, 2 choices of ghost for the fourth spot, 1 choice of witch for the fifth spot, and 1 choice of ghost for the sixth spot: hence, her total number of arrangements is $3 \times 3 \times 2 \times 2 \times 1 \times 1 = 36$, which is (C). If she buys four of each figurine, her number of arrangements is $4 \times 4 \times 3 \times 3 \times 2 \times 2 \times 1 \times 1 = 576$, (E).

8. **E** The order of cars matters, so you simply need to multiply the number of possible cars for each spot. For the first car, there are six possible, for the second, five, and so on. So your scratch paper should look like this: 6 5 4 3 2 1, which is equivalent to 6!, or 720.

9. **A, B** The order of friends doesn't matter. There are five friends to choose from for three spots, so the top of your fraction should read 5 4 3, and to correct for the order of friends not mattering, the bottom of your fraction should be 3 2 1. $\dfrac{5 \times 4 \times 3}{3 \times 2 \times 1} = 10$. Since he is numbering possibilities sequentially, the numbers 1 through 10 will be on the list, making (A) and (B) correct.

10. **1,320** In this case, order matters, so you simply need to multiply the number of possible runners for each spot. That should look like this: 12 11 10 = 1,320.

11. **A, B, D**

Starting with (A), there are 3 slots on the team, with 5 experienced engineers available for the first slot, 4 for the second slot, and 3 for the third slot. Order doesn't matter, so divide by 3! to get $\frac{5 \times 4 \times 3}{3 \times 2 \times 1} = 10$. Choice (A) is correct. For (B), you have 3 apprentice engineers available for 2 slots and once again, order doesn't matter. $\frac{3 \times 2}{2 \times 1} = 3$. Choice (B) is correct and you can eliminate (C), which contradicts (B). For (D) you have $\frac{5 \times 4}{2 \times 1} = 10$, so (D) is correct. Choice (E) is incorrect because $\frac{5 \times 4 \times 3 \times 2}{4 \times 3 \times 2 \times 1} = 5$. The correct answers are (A), (B), and (D).

12. **B** This is a permutation problem, so lay out your slots to fill and then multiply. For (A), you have 1 slot for a letter and two slots for numerals. There are 26 choices for your letter and 10 choices for your first numeral. Because you can't repeat numerals, there are 9 choices for your second numeral. Thus, the number of different codes that can be made is 26 × 10 × 9 = 2,340. Eliminate (A). For correct choice (B), you have two spots for letters and two for numerals, so you have 26 × 26 (letters can repeat) × 10 × 9 = 60,840. Choice (C) is incorrect because the number of different codes consisting of one letter and one numeral is 26 × 10 = 260. The only correct answer is (B).

13. **A, B, C, E, F, G**

Rather than writing out every possible outcome, see if you can express the answer choices as the product of 3 factors that could be the number of ties, shirts, and jackets Brian receives. Choice (A) is possible: 3 ties × 2 shirts × 1 jacket = 6 outfits. Choice (B) is possible: 4 ties × 2 shirts × 1 jacket = 8 outfits. Choice (C) is possible: 3 ties × 3 shirts × 1 jacket = 9 outfits. Choice (D) is not possible: you'd need a 5 as a factor to get to 10, and Brian can't receive 5 of anything, so eliminate (D). Choice (E) is possible in 2 different ways: 3 ties × 2 shirts × 2 jackets = 12 outfits, as does 4 ties × 3 shirts × 1 jacket. Choice (F) is possible: 4 ties × 2 shirts × 2 jackets = 16 outfits. And, finally, (G) is possible: 3 ties × 3 shirts × 2 jackets = 18 outfits. All of the choices except (D) work.

14. **56** This problem involves permutations, because the order matters since the ties are all distinct. Start with Paul wearing a red tie. He has 3 red tie choices and Allen has 2 remaining red tie choices, giving them a product of 6 permutations. For green ties, they have 5 × 4 = 20 permutations. For blue ties, they have 6 × 5 = 30 permutations. The grand total is 56 permutations.

15. **B** This is the number of combinations of 8 items taken 5 at a time (because the order does not matter). This number is equal to $\frac{8 \times 7 \times 6 \times 5 \times 4}{5 \times 4 \times 3 \times 2 \times 1} = 8 \times 7 = 56$.

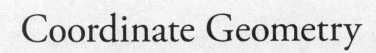

Coordinate Geometry

POINTS AND AREAS

A coordinate plane is simply any flat surface (a piece of paper, a chalkboard) that has been divided up into coordinates. The quadrants are as shown below.

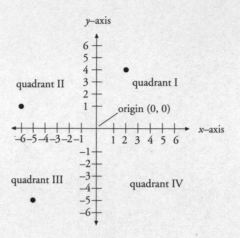

Some coordinate geometry problems will ask you to find the distance between points or the area of the shapes you make when you connect points. When plotting points on a graph, it is helpful to write the coordinates along the axis. This will turn the axis into number lines and make it easier to find the distances between points.

Here is an example.

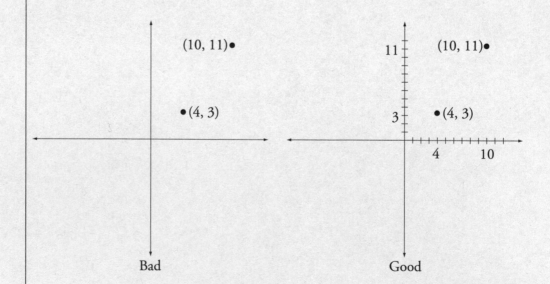

When you are asked to find the distance between these two points, you can use the distance formula or you can simply draw in a right triangle and use the Pythagorean Theorem.

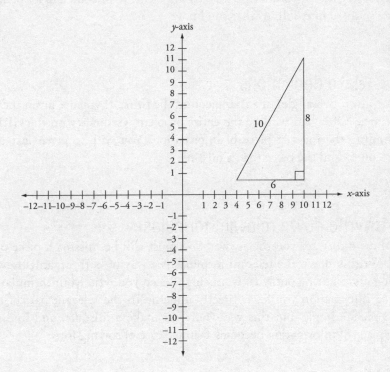

What would normally involve a long formula, and some calculations with the distance formula, becomes a simple process with a triangle, especially if it is a special right triangle. If you are finding the areas of shapes, they are the same old triangles, circles, and rectangles you find elsewhere on the test. The same rules apply. No matter what you are asked to find, it is still a geometry question, and you should still use your five steps.

Step 1: Draw your shape

In some cases the test will give you a shape, which you may or may not be able to trust, or it will give you a word problem and leave it up to you to envision the shape. As with every other part of the test, getting your hand moving is an important first step to beginning the problem. Get your shape down on your scratch paper so that you can begin working with it there. On Quant Comp questions involving geometry, instead of Plugging In more than once, you may have to draw your shape more than once.

Step 2: Fill in what you know

Whether you are given the shape or not, you will be given a certain amount of information regarding your shape such as the measure of some angles, lengths of some sides, or volume. Fill in what you know.

Step 3: Make deductions

If you are given two angles of a triangle, find the third. If you are given the radius, find the area. Often this will be the entire problem. Geometry on the GRE is all about finding the missing piece of information. You will be given just enough information to find the piece that is missing.

Step 4: Write down relevant formulas

If step three didn't get you the answer, you must still be missing a piece of information. Writing down the relevant formulas is a way of both organizing your information and figuring out what is missing. When you write your formulas down, fill in the information you have directly underneath the relevant part of the formula. It seems simple, but this way you can't make a mistake, and finding the missing piece of information becomes a simple case of solving for *x*.

Step 5: Drop heights/draw lines

If you're still stuck, you may need to manipulate or subdivide your shapes. If you have triangles, draw in the height. Have you created a 30-60-90? A 45-45-90? Or a Pythagorean triple? Try subdividing the shape or, if it's a three-dimensional figure, dashing in the hidden lines.

LINES AND SLOPES

You might see a question that asks about slope or gives the formula for a line. Questions about slope are terrific for Ballparking. Sometimes you can eliminate two or even three answer choices just by knowing the difference between a positive and negative slope.

Here's the difference.

positive slope

negative slope

slope = 0

The slope of a
vertical line is
undefined

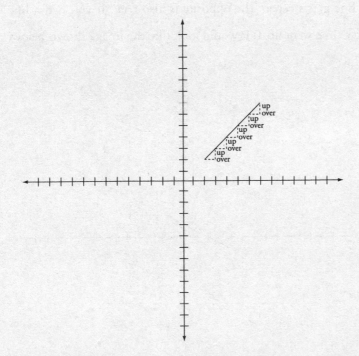

Rise: Positive
Run: Positive

Rise: 0
Run: Infinite

Rise: Negative
Run: Positive

Rise: Infinite
Run: 0
(can't have 0
on bottom of
a fraction)

Slope is defined as $\dfrac{\text{rise}}{\text{run}}$ or $\dfrac{y_2 - y_1}{x_2 - x_1}$. If you had a line that went up 1 every time it went over 1, it would look the image shown below.

The slope is equal to one $\left(\dfrac{1}{1}\right)$, and the line lies at a 45 degree angle to the x-axis.

If you had a line that went up 2 every time it went over 1, it would look like the image shown below.

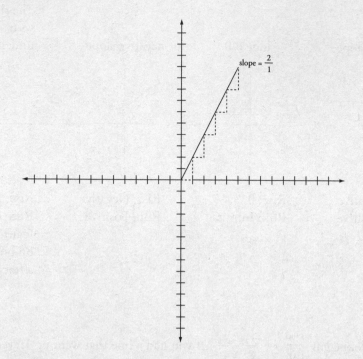

The slope of this line is $\frac{2}{1}$ or 2. Notice that the numerical value for the slope goes up as the line gets steeper. The opposite is also true. If you had a line that went over 2 every time went up 1, it would look like the image shown below.

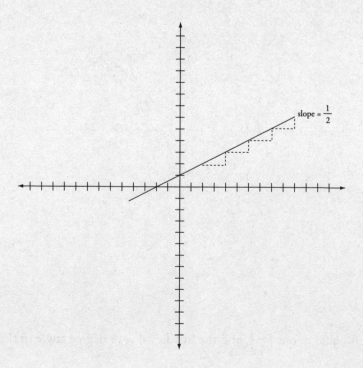

In this case, the slope is $\frac{1}{2}$ and you have a shallower angle.

A line at less than a 45 degree angle will have a slope with an absolute value of 0 and 1. A line that intersects the *x*-axis at greater than 45 degrees will have a slope with an absolute value greater than 1.

The formula for a line is $y = mx + b$. In this formula, *x* and *y* are the coordinates of a single point. *b* tells you where the line intersects the *y*-axis. *m* (or whatever value is being multiplied by *x*) tells you the slope of the line. With this information, you can accurately draw any line on a graph. ETS is likely to give you some of the information in this equation, sometimes as a picture, sometimes as a pair of points, or sometimes as an equation, and ask you to find the rest.

Remember three things.

1. With any two points, you can find the slope.
2. The coordinates of the origin are (0, 0). This is a point like any other and often the second point you need to find slope.
3. If you are given information as an equation, put it in the $y = mx + b$ format.

For example, you might be told that line l passes through the origin, and the coordinates of point *A* are (7, 4).

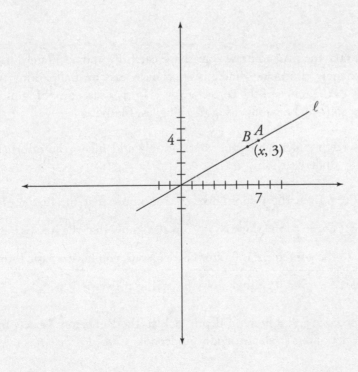

If you are asked to find the value of *x* at point *B*, draw it on your scratch paper like this.

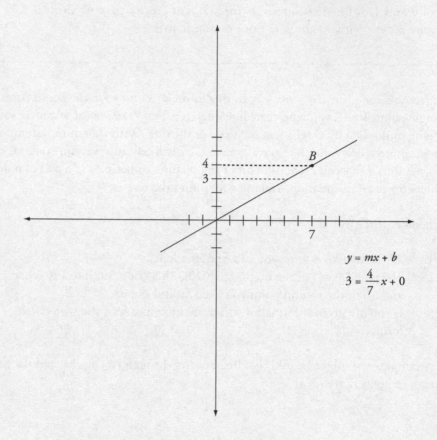

$$y = mx + b$$

$$3 = \frac{4}{7}x + 0$$

When you take the time to draw your shape carefully and accurately, usually you can immediately eliminate some answer choices just by Ballparking; you'll get some sense of the range of the correct answer. In this case, anything more than 7 is certainly going to be wrong, as is anything less than 4.

On your scratch paper, write out your formula and fill in the information you have directly underneath it.

You have been given the *y*-coordinate, 3. You know that the line goes up 4 for every 7 it goes over, so the slope is $\frac{4}{7}$. You also know that the line passes through the origin, so the *y*-intercept is 0. From here on out, you have a basic formula with one variable, $3 = \frac{4}{7}x + 0$. Simply solve for *x*. The answer is $5\frac{1}{7}$.

For more practice and a more in-depth look at The Princeton Review math techniques, check out our student-friendly guidebook, *Cracking the GRE*.

DRILL 1

Question 1

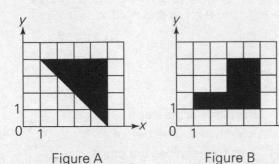

Figure A   Figure B

Quantity A	Quantity B
The area of the shaded region in Figure A	The area of the shaded region in Figure B

- ○ Quantity A is greater.
- ○ Quantity B is greater.
- ○ The two quantities are equal.
- ○ The relationship cannot be determined from the information given.

Question 2

Points P and Q are at $-\dfrac{4}{3}$ and 2, respectively, on a number line.

Quantity A	Quantity B
$\dfrac{1}{2}$	The midpoint of the segment PQ

- ○ Quantity A is greater.
- ○ Quantity B is greater.
- ○ The two quantities are equal.
- ○ The relationship cannot be determined from the information given.

Question 3

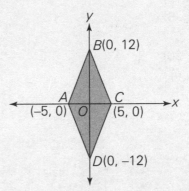

Quantity A	Quantity B
The perimeter of quadrilateral $ABCD$	The area of the shaded region

- ○ Quantity A is greater.
- ○ Quantity B is greater.
- ○ The two quantities are equal.
- ○ The relationship cannot be determined from the information given.

Question 4

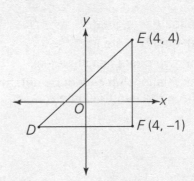

In the rectangular coordinate system above, if the area of right triangle DEF is 15, then which of the following are the coordinates of point D ?

- ○ $(-4, -1)$
- ○ $(-2, -1)$
- ○ $(-2, 4)$
- ○ $(1, -1)$
- ○ It cannot be determined from the information given.

Question 5

The line $y = 4x + 20$ intersects the x-axis at which of the following points?

○ (–5, 0)
○ (0, –5)
○ (0, 5)
○ (0, 20)
○ (5, 0)

Question 6

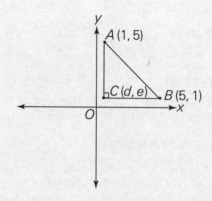

Line segment *BC* is parallel to the x-axis.

Line segment *AC* is parallel to the y-axis.

Quantity A	Quantity B
d	*e*

○ Quantity A is greater.
○ Quantity B is greater.
○ The two quantities are equal.
○ The relationship cannot be determined from the information given.

Question 7

To return to his home from City A, Cam drives 2 miles due east and then 3 miles due north. From his home to Town B, he drives 3 miles due east and 9 miles due north.

Quantity A	Quantity B
The shortest distance between City A and Town B	17 miles

○ Quantity A is greater.
○ Quantity B is greater.
○ The two quantities are equal.
○ The relationship cannot be determined from the information given.

Question 8

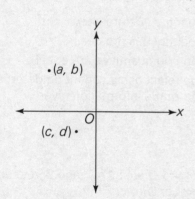

Quantity A	Quantity B
bd	*ac*

○ Quantity A is greater.
○ Quantity B is greater.
○ The two quantities are equal.
○ The relationship cannot be determined from the information given.

Question 9

Which of the following is the graph of the equation $y = -|-x|$?

○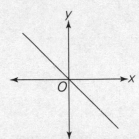

○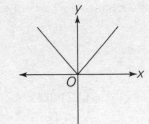

○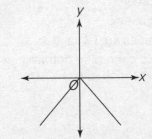

○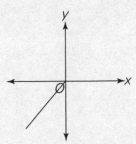

○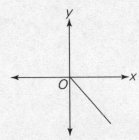

Question 10

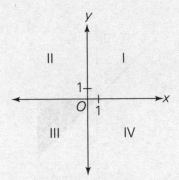

Points (a, b) and (c, d), not shown in the figure above, are in quadrants I and III, respectively. If $abcd \neq 0$, then the point $(-bd, bc)$ must be in which quadrant?

○   I

○   II

○   III

○   IV

○   It cannot be determined from the information given.

Question 11

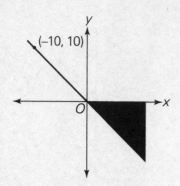

Which of the following pairs of coordinates corresponds to a point in the shaded region of the graph shown above?

- ○ $(9, -7)$
- ○ $(-9, -7)$
- ○ $(9, 7)$
- ○ $(7, -9)$
- ○ $(-7, -9)$

Question 12

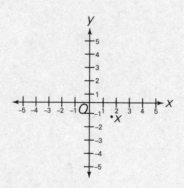

The coordinates of point X are (a, b).

Quantity A	Quantity B
$-a$	b

- ○ Quantity A is greater.
- ○ Quantity B is greater.
- ○ The two quantities are equal.
- ○ The relationship cannot be determined from the information given.

Question 13

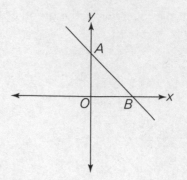

The equation of the line graphed on the rectangular coordinate system above is given by

$$y = -\frac{13}{12}x + 8$$

Quantity A	Quantity B
AO	BO

- ○ Quantity A is greater.
- ○ Quantity B is greater.
- ○ The two quantities are equal.
- ○ The relationship cannot be determined from the information given.

Question 14

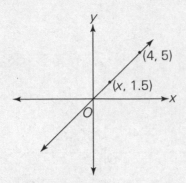

What is the value of x in the rectangular coordinate system above?

- ○ 1.0
- ○ 1.2
- ○ 1.4
- ○ 1.6
- ○ 1.8

Question 15

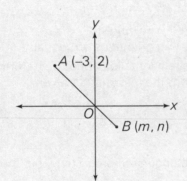

Quantity A	Quantity B
$-m$	n

- ○ Quantity A is greater.
- ○ Quantity B is greater.
- ○ The two quantities are equal.
- ○ The relationship cannot be determined from the information given.

Question 16

If the x-coordinates of the two x-intercepts of a parabola are $3 - \sqrt{2}$ and $5 + \sqrt{2}$, then what is the distance between them?

- ○ $2 - 2\sqrt{2}$
- ○ $2 + 2\sqrt{2}$
- ○ $8 + 2\sqrt{2}$
- ○ 2
- ○ 8

DRILL 2

Question 1

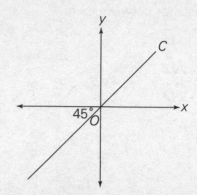

Point *D* (not shown) lies below line *C* in the rectangular coordinate system above.

Quantity A	Quantity B
The *x*-coordinate of point *D*	The *y*-coordinate of point *D*

- ◯ Quantity A is greater.
- ◯ Quantity B is greater.
- ◯ The two quantities are equal.
- ◯ The relationship cannot be determined from the information given.

Question 2

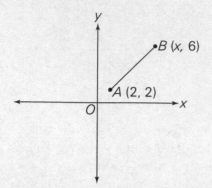

In the coordinate system above, the slope of line segment *AB* is $\frac{4}{3}$.

Quantity A	Quantity B
The length of line segment *AB*	*x*

- ◯ Quantity A is greater.
- ◯ Quantity B is greater.
- ◯ The two quantities are equal.
- ◯ The relationship cannot be determined from the information given.

Question 3

In the rectangular coordinate plane, the coordinates of points *A*, *B*, and *C* are (1, 4), $\left(7, 4 + 6\sqrt{3}\right)$, and (7, 4), respectively. What is the absolute value of the difference between *AB* and *BC* ?

- ◯ 6
- ◯ $4 + \sqrt{3}$
- ◯ $6 - 6\sqrt{3}$
- ◯ $6\sqrt{3} - 12$
- ◯ $12 - 6\sqrt{3}$

Question 4

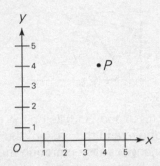

Point *Z* (not shown) lies inside the circle with center *P* and radius 2 (also not shown).

Quantity A	Quantity B
The *x*-coordinate of point *Z*	The *y*-coordinate of point *Z*

○ Quantity A is greater.
○ Quantity B is greater.
○ The two quantities are equal.
○ The relationship cannot be determined from the information given.

Question 5

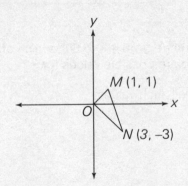

Note: Figure not drawn to scale

What is the area of triangle *MNO* in the figure above?

○ 3

○ 6

○ $4\sqrt{2} + 2\sqrt{5}$

○ $2\sqrt{10}$

○ $6\sqrt{10}$

Question 6

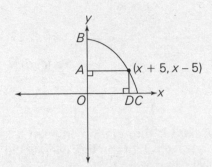

In the figure above, if *BC* is an arc in the circle with center *O*, then $AB - DC =$

○ -10

○ 10

○ $2x$

○ $x^2 - 25$

○ $\sqrt{2x^2 + 50}$

Question 7

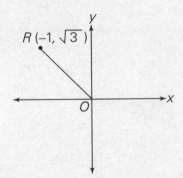

In the coordinate system above, line segment *OR* is rotated clockwise through an angle of 120° to position *OS* (not shown).

Quantity A	Quantity B
The *x*-coordinate of point *S*	$\sqrt{3}$

○ Quantity A is greater.
○ Quantity B is greater.
○ The two quantities are equal.
○ The relationship cannot be determined from the information given.

Question 8

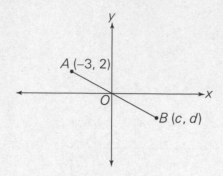

Line *AB* passes through the origin. If
$2 < c < 10$, which of the following could be
possible values for *d* ?

Indicate all such values.

☐ 2.0
☐ −1.3
☐ −1.8
☐ −3.1
☐ −5.5
☐ −6.8
☐ −10.0

Question 9

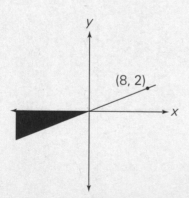

Which of the following points are located in
the shaded region of the graph above?

Indicate all such points.

☐ (6, 1)
☐ (−4, 0.5)
☐ (−4, −0.5)
☐ (−4, −4)
☐ (−6, 1)
☐ (−6, −1)
☐ (−6, −2)

Question 10

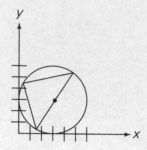

The points (0, 3) and (3, 0) lie on the circle in
the figure above and the base of the inscribed
isosceles triangle passes through the center
of the circle. What is the area of the triangle?

Question 11

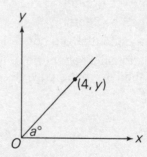

If *a* can range from 45° to 60°, which of the
following are possible values for *y* ?

Indicate all such values.

☐ 2
☐ 3
☐ 4
☐ 5
☐ 6
☐ 7
☐ 8

Question 12

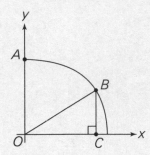

If point A is at (0, 8), point C is at (6, 0), and the distance from point B to point C is x, what is $\dfrac{x}{\sqrt{7}}$?

Question 13

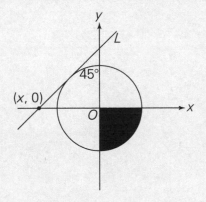

In the figure above, line L is tangent to the circle, which is centered at the origin. The area of the shaded region is equal to the circumference of a circle with a radius between 1 and $2\dfrac{1}{4}$. Which of the following could be values of x?

Indicate all such values.

☐   2

☐   −3

☐   4

☐   −5

☐   −8.5

☐   −12

Question 14

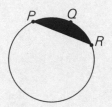

In the figure above, the circumference of the circle is equal to 8π, and the arc PQR is equal to $\dfrac{1}{4}$ of the total circumference. What is the area of the shaded region?

○ $16\pi - 16$

○ $2\pi - 8$

○ $8\pi - 8$

○ $4\pi - 8$

○ 4π

Question 15

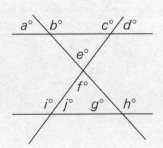

In the figure above, if $a = g$, which of the following must be true?

Indicate all such statements.

☐ $e = f$

☐ $i = d$

☐ $e = 90$

☐ $c + d = 180$

☐ $i + h = 180$

☐ $a + d + f = 180$

☐ $180 - i - h + e = 0$

ANSWERS

Drill 1

1. C
2. A
3. B
4. B
5. A
6. C
7. B
8. B
9. C
10. D
11. A
12. B
13. A
14. B
15. B
16. B

Drill 2

1. A
2. C
3. E
4. D
5. A
6. B
7. A
8. C, D, E
9. C, F
10. 9
11. C, D, E
12. 2
13. D
14. D
15. A, D, F, G

EXPLANATIONS
Drill 1

1. **C** Figure A contains 6 whole boxes plus 4 half-boxes, for a total of 8. Figure B contains 8 whole boxes. The answer is (C). Alternatively, the area of the right triangle in Figure A is $\frac{1}{2}bh = \frac{1}{2}(4)(4) = 8$ and Figure B contains a rectangle plus two units whose total area is $bh = (3)(2) = 6$; $6 + 2 = 8$.

2. **A** To find the midpoint, simply average the endpoints: $\dfrac{-\frac{4}{3}+2}{2} = \dfrac{-\frac{4}{3}+\frac{6}{3}}{2} = \dfrac{\frac{2}{3}}{2} = \frac{1}{3}$. Since $\frac{1}{2}$ is greater than $\frac{1}{3}$, Quantity A is greater.

3. **B** The axes split the quadrilateral into four equal 5-12-13 right triangles. So the perimeter is 4(13) = 52, and the area of each of the 4 triangles is 30 for a total area of 120. Quantity B is therefore greater.

4. **B** Subtracting the y-coordinates of the given points gives you the length of leg EF: 4 – (–1) = 5. The area formula for a triangle will give you the length of the other leg, DF: $\frac{1}{2}bh = \frac{1}{2}(b)(5)$; $b = 6$, to give an area of 15. Subtracting 6 from the x-coordinate of F gives you the x-coordinate of D, and D has the same y-coordinate as F. So the coordinates of D are (–2, –1); the answer is (B).

5. **A** On the x-axis, y = 0; eliminate (B), (C), and (D). Then Plug In 0 for y in the given equation. Solve for x: 0 = 4x + 20, so x = –5, and the answer is (A).

6. **C** Point C has the same x-coordinate as point A and the same y-coordinate as point B. The coordinates of C are therefore (1, 1), so the quantities are equal.

7. **B** Draw a rectangular coordinate system with City A as the origin, i.e., the point (0, 0). So Cam's home is at (2, 3). Going 3 miles east and then 9 miles north from his home puts Town B at (5, 12). Quantity A is the straight line distance from (0, 0) to (5, 12). Connecting these two points creates the hypotenuse of a 5-12-13 right triangle, so Quantity A is 13, and the answer is (B).

8. **B** Point (a, b) is in the second quadrant where points have signs of (–, +); thus, a is negative and b is positive. Point (c, d) is in the third quadrant where points have signs of (–, –); thus, c is negative and d is negative. So, Quantity A is a positive times a negative, which is negative. Quantity B is a negative times a negative, which is positive. Quantity B must be greater.

9. **C** Plug values into the equation and eliminate graphs that do not include those values. If x = 1, then y = –1; eliminate choices (B) and (D). If x = –1, then y = –1, eliminate (A) and (E). Only (C) remains.

10. **D** Plug In points in the appropriate quadrants. If $(a, b) = (1, 2)$ and $(c, d) = (-3, -4)$, then the point in question is $(-bd, bc) = [-(2)(-4), (2)(-3)] = (8, -6)$, which is in quadrant IV. Since "it cannot be determined from the information given" is an answer choice, Plug In again to confirm that the result will be in quadrant IV. The correct answer is (D).

11. **A** Use Process of Elimination to solve this one. First, only coordinate pairs with a positive x-value and a negative y-value will fall in the proper quadrant, so eliminate (B), (C), and (E). The line that divides the correct quadrant into shaded and unshaded regions has a slope of -1 because it goes through the origin and the point $(-10, 10)$. On this line, the absolute value of the x-coordinate equals the absolute value of the y-coordinate. In the shaded region, then, $|x| > |y|$, so (D) can be eliminated. Only (A) remains. Alternatively, realize that this figure is drawn accurately, because of the placement of $(10, -10)$, and plot all 5 points, eliminating all of those that fall outside the shaded region.

12. **B** Point X is at approximately $(2, -1.5)$. So Quantity A is about -2 and Quantity B is about -1.5; thus, Quantity B is greater.

13. **A** Although you have enough information to find the exact values of AO and BO, it's not necessary to do so to compare the quantities. The slope of the line is $-\frac{13}{12}$, which means that the vertical distance, or rise, is greater than the horizontal distance, or run, by a ratio of 13 to 12 (you're dealing with distances on a coordinate plane, so disregard the negative sign). Because AO and BO are equal to, respectively, the rise and the run of the same segment of the line, Quantity A is greater.

14. **B** Note that the line contains three points: $(0, 0)$, $(4, 5)$, and $(x, 1.5)$. The slope between any two of these points is the same. Remember that slope is change in y over change in x. Thus, $\frac{5-0}{4-0} = \frac{1.5-0}{x-0}$, or $\frac{5}{4} = \frac{1.5}{x}$. Cross multiply to find $5x = 6.0$. Divide by 5 to find $x = 1.2$. The answer is (B).

15. **B** Just because you don't know the values of $-m$ and n doesn't mean you can't determine which is greater. Using point A and the origin, you can find the slope of segment AB: $\frac{\text{rise}}{\text{run}} = \frac{-2}{3} = -\frac{2}{3}$. Now plug in coordinates for point B that will give you the same slope; the easiest way to pick them would be to simply rise -2 and run 3, bringing you to the point $(m, n) = (3, -2)$. So $-m = -3$, and $n = -2$, and Quantity B is greater.

16. **B** You don't need to use the distance formula, because the distance between the points $\left(3-\sqrt{2},0\right)$ and $\left(5+\sqrt{2},0\right)$ can be measured horizontally. Distance is positive, so subtract the smaller x-coordinate from the larger: $\left(5+\sqrt{2}\right)-\left(3-\sqrt{2}\right)=2+2\sqrt{2}$; the answer is (B).

Drill 2

1. **A** Plug In a few points that lie below line C, such as (0, –1), (–3, –4), (1, 0). In each case, the x-coordinate is greater than the y-coordinate, so Quantity A is greater. Alternatively, realize that the 45 degree angle and the fact that the line passes through the origin tells us that the equation of line C is $y = x$. So the region below the line is the graph of $y < x$. The coordinates of all points in that region must satisfy the inequality.

2. **C** Break this one into bite-sized pieces. You need x in order to find the length of AB, so find x first. If you insert the given values into the slope formula, $\dfrac{y_2 - y_1}{x_2 - x_1}$, you get $\dfrac{6-2}{x-2} = \dfrac{4}{3}$, so $x = 5$. Now you need to find the length of AB. Rather than using the distance formula, turn AB into the hypotenuse of a right triangle and find the lengths of the other sides. To make the triangle, add a new vertex at coordinate (5, 2). The length of the horizontal leg is $5 - 2 = 3$, and that of the vertical leg is $6 - 2 = 4$, yielding the familiar 3-4-5 triangle. The length of segment $AB = 5$, so the two quantities are equal.

3. **E** Draw the points and connect the points to form a right triangle. Subtract the x-coordinate of A from that of C to find the length of AC: $7 - 1 = 6$. Subtract the y-coordinate of C from that of B to find the length of BC: $4+6\sqrt{3}-4=6\sqrt{3}$. Notice that the ratio of AC to BC is 1 to $\sqrt{3}$. Therefore, ABC is a 30-60-90 triangle, and the length of AB, the hypotenuse, will be double the length of the shorter side (6), so $AB = 12$. The absolute value of the difference will be the positive value, obtained by subtracting the smaller value (BC) from the larger value (the length of the hypotenuse, AB): $AB - BC = 12 - 6\sqrt{3}$, which is (E).

4. **D** Plug In points. Since the circle has a radius of 2 and a center at approximately (4, 4), use points near the center of the circle. Points (3, 4) and (5, 4) both lie inside the circle. For point (3, 4), the y-coordinate is greater and for point (4, 5), the x-coordinate is greater. Choice (D) is the correct answer.

5. **A**   The slope of *MO* is 1, so it makes a 45 degree angle with the positive *x*-axis. Similarly, the slope of *NO* is −1, so it makes another 45 degree angle with the positive *x*-axis. The sum of the degree measures of these angles is 90, so *MNO* is a right triangle. Therefore, *MO* and *NO* are the base and height of triangle *MNO*. To find the area of the triangle, you need to find the length of *MO* and *NO*. Drop a perpendicular from point *M* to the *y*-axis, to form an isosceles right triangle whose hypotenuse is *MO*. Each leg of this triangle has length 1 so, $MO = \sqrt{2}$. Similarly, dropping a perpendicular line from the *y*-axis to point *N* creates another isosceles right triangle, whose legs have length 3, and whose hypotenuse is *NO*. Therefore, $NO = 3\sqrt{2}$. So the area of triangle *MNO* is $\frac{1}{2}bh = \frac{1}{2}\left(\sqrt{2}\right)\left(3\sqrt{2}\right) = 3$, and the answer is (A).

6. **B**   To find *AB*, find the radius of the circle and then subtract *OA*. If the radius is *r*, then $AB = r - (x - 5) = r - x + 5$. Similarly, $DC = r - (x + 5) = r - x - 5$. So $AB - DC = [r - x + 5] - [r - x - 5] = 10$, so the answer is (B). If you use POE, you can eliminate choice (A) because you know the answer has to be positive. If you selected (E), you selected the radius.

7. **A**   Drawing a horizontal line from point *R* to the positive *y*-axis forms a right triangle. The length of the leg that sits on the *y*-axis is $\sqrt{3}$, and the horizontal leg you just drew has length 1. The ratio of the legs is 1 to $\sqrt{3}$, so you have a 30-60-90 right triangle. Therefore, the hypotenuse (*OR*) has length 2, and the angle between *OR* and the positive *y*-axis is 30 degrees. The first quadrant includes 90 degrees total, so rotating *OR* 120 degrees clockwise puts *OS* on the positive *x*-axis, with a length of 2. Therefore, the *x*-coordinate of *OS* is 2, which is slightly larger than $\sqrt{3}$, which is approximately 1.7. The answer is (A).

8. **C, D, E**

    First, find the slope of the line, which runs through (−3, 2) and (0, 0). The slope is the change in *y* over the change in *x*, or $-\frac{2}{3}$. Therefore, the equation of line *AB* is $y = -\frac{2}{3}x$. To find the range of possible values for *d*, plug in the given range of possible values for *c* to the equation. If *c* = 2, $d = -\frac{4}{3}$, and if *c* = 10, $d = -\frac{20}{3}$. Any value between $-\frac{4}{3}$ and $-\frac{20}{3}$, or −1.33 and −6.67, will work for *d*. Therefore, the only right answers are (C), (D), and (E).

9. **C, F** First, find the equation of the line that defines the shaded region, expressed as $y = mx + b$. Using the origin and the one given point in the diagram, the slope m equals $\frac{1}{4}$, and the y-intercept b is 0. So $y = \frac{1}{4}x$ is the boundary line. Looking at the figure, if either x or y are positive, then the point isn't in the shaded region; you can eliminate (A), (B), and (E). For the other choices, Plug In the x-values. If the resulting y-value is less than the y-value in the choice, that point lies below the line and outside the shaded region. So you're looking for points for which $y \geq \frac{1}{4}x$. when $y \leq 0$ and $x \leq 0$. This is true for (C) and (F).

10. **9** The circle touches (0, 3) and (3, 0), so its center must be at (3, 3) and its radius must be 3. Since the base of the triangle passes through the center of the circle, the base of the triangle must be the diameter of length 6. Given the triangle is isosceles and inscribed within the circle, a line from the circle's center to the triangle's corner equals the triangle's height. This height must be the radius of the circle. The area of a triangle is 0.5 × base × height: 0.5 × 6 × 3 = 9.

11. **C, D, E**

Given that the angle ranges from 45° to 60°, you need to Plug In values for angle a and find a special triangle to solve for y. If a is 45°, the triangle's sides are $x, x, x\sqrt{2}$. It doesn't matter what the hypotenuse is; $x = 4$, which means y also is 4. If a is 60°, the triangle's sides are $x, x\sqrt{3}, 2x$. The shortest side of the triangle would be the one on the x-axis. Since $x = 4$, then $y = 4\sqrt{3}$ or approximately 6.93. So the correct answers range from 4 to 6.93. Choices (C), (D), and (E) are all correct.

12. **2** You need to find the length of a leg of a triangle. By finding the lengths of the two other sides, you can use the Pythagorean Theorem to find the third side. The hypotenuse of the triangle is the radius of the (quarter-) circle, which, since point A is at (0, 8), is 8. Since point C is (6, 0), the other leg is 6. From the Pythagorean Theorem, $6^2 + x^2 = 8^2$, so $x^2 = 28$, $x = \sqrt{28} = \sqrt{4 \times 7} = \sqrt{4} \times \sqrt{7} = 2 \times \sqrt{7}$, so $\frac{x}{\sqrt{7}} = 2$.

13. **D** Use line L to make a triangle, with points at $(x, 0)$, the 45° angle, and the origin. The angle at $(x, 0)$ must be 45° since the sum of the angles of a triangle is 180°. Since line L is tangential to the circle and forms 45° angles with each axis, a line from the point where line L and the circle intersect to the origin will form a right angle with line L. The smaller triangle formed—from $(x, 0)$, to where line L and the circle meet, to the origin—will be a 45-45-90 triangle, with two sides equal to the radius of the circle. Find the radius of the circle, and you can find x. The area of the shaded region is equal to the circumference of a circle with radius between 1 and $2\frac{1}{4}$. Circumference = $2\pi r$, so the area of the shaded region is between 2π and 4.5π, which means the area of the circle in the figure is between 8π and 18π. Area = πr^2, so the radius of the circle is between $\sqrt{8}$ and $\sqrt{18}$, which is to say between $2\sqrt{2}$ and $3\sqrt{2}$. 45-45-90 triangles have sides of a-a-$a\sqrt{2}$, where, in this case, a

is between $2\sqrt{2}$ and $3\sqrt{2}$. So the hypotenuse of the triangle, from the origin to $(x, 0)$, is between $2\sqrt{2}$ and $3\sqrt{2}$, and therefore between 4 and 6, so x can range from -4 to -6.

14. **D** For most shaded area problems, use the formula *shaded area = total area − unshaded area*. Since the figure for the problem does not include a center for the circle, give the circle a center O. Draw one radius from the center O to point P, and another radius from O to point R to create central angle POR. Since arc PQR equals $\frac{1}{4}$ of the total circumference, the central angle formed will be $\frac{1}{4}$ of $360°$; angle PQR is $90°$. From the information in the problem you know that circumference = 8π, so $r = 4$. The triangle POR is an isosceles right triangle with legs of 4 and an area of 8. The area of the circle is equal to πr^2, so the area of the circle is 16π. The total area taken up by the triangle and the shaded area together will be equal to $\frac{1}{4}$ of the area of the circle, or 4π. The total area is 4π and the unshaded area is 8, so the shaded area is $4\pi - 8$, which is (D).

15. **A, D, F, G**

Plug In for a. If $a = 40$, then $b = 140$, $g = 40$, and $h = 140$. Now Plug In for c. If $c = 100$, then $d = 80$, $i = 100$, and $j = 80$. You know that g, j, and f must add up to 180, so $40 + 80 + f = 180$, which means that $f = 60$, which in turn means that $e = 60$. Now check your answer choices to see which ones are true. In this case $e = f$, so keep (A). However, $i \uparrow d$, so you can eliminate (B), and (C) is also not true and should be eliminated. $100 + 80 = 180$, so you cannot eliminate (D). $100 + 140 \neq 180$, so (E) is incorrect. $40 + 80 + 60 = 180$, so keep (F) for now. You have three answers and since this is a must be true question, you should try another set of numbers and test the three choices with the new values to see if the choices are still correct. Choices (A), (D), (F), and (G) are the correct answers.

Essays

There are two essays on the GRE. They come first. Both are unavoidable. Unfortunately, very few programs care about your essay score. Before you spend time preparing for the essays, call the programs to which you plan to apply and ask them if they plan to use or look at your essay score. If they don't, skip this chapter. If your program is highly competitive, then all numbers count and you should keep reading.

The first of the GRE's two essays is the Issue essay. On this essay, you will be given two topics, called prompts, from which to choose, and 30 minutes to craft and write your essay. You will be given a specific task to perform, but essentially your job is to formulate an opinion on one of those prompts and to support it with well-chosen examples. It's really more like a debate team exercise than a writing exercise. You need to craft the strongest argument you can, and you have 30 minutes in which to do it.

On the second essay, you are the judge. You will be presented with someone else's argument, and it is your job to evaluate its strengths as an argument. Again, you will be given an argument and a specific assignment, but no matter what, you will have to be familiar with and evaluate the basic parts of an argument. It doesn't matter if you agree or disagree, only whether or not the argument is logically sound, and the issue is thoroughly considered and effectively presented.

Both of your essays will be scored on a six-point scale in half-point increments, and then the two scores will be averaged and rounded to the nearest half-point. If you score a 5 on one essay and a 6 on another, you will end up with a 5.5. A 5.5, by the way, puts you in the 87th percentile. You must score a 4.5 to put yourself above the 50th percentile or higher. Here is the breakdown of percentiles by score:

Score	Analytical Writing Percentile	Score	Analytical Writing Percentile
6	96	3	7
5.5	87	2.5	2
5	71	2	1
4.5	52	1.5	0
4	32	1	0
3.5	17	0.5	0

For both essays, it is critically important to consider the reader. ETS says that each reader will spend two minutes on your essay, but really, it's more like one. They call it "holistic grading" and claim that they consider the overall impact of the whole essay. You have a very short time to grab their attention, make a few strong points, and then wrap up. Your job is not to write the best essay ever. Not only do you not have enough time, but a beautifully written, crafted essay that takes a long time to develop and is full of deliciously subtle points may very well miss the mark. Your job is to give them what they're looking for, quickly and accessibly, so that they can give you the score you want.

Because this is a standardized test, it is not about opinion. It is not the reader's job to respond personally to your arguments or your opinions. In fact, they have a very specifically defined scoring rubric. They are looking at three things: the quality of your thinking, the quality of your organization, and the quality of your writing. Each one counts equally. All three must be present to some degree to score in the top half. An essay in the bottom half, scoring a 1, 2, or 3, will be missing one or more of these three components. It may be well structured but too narrow or obvious in its thinking. The thinking might be great, the writing pretty good, but organizationally it might be a disaster.

Since each of these three factors is so important, we want an approach that gives all three their due. No matter which essay you are working on, you must devote time to thinking, organizing, and writing.

THE ISSUE ESSAY

You will be given two prompts to consider. Each prompt will give a strongly worded point of view on some subject accessible to all. This means that they won't ask about *Hamlet*, but they might talk about education, society, or personal growth. Other topics could include anything from law, society, or trust to art, change, or technology. In fact ETS lists all of their topics on their website, www.ets.org. Go to GRE → General Test → Prepare for the Test → Analytical Writing → Analyze an Issue → Pool of Issue Topics.

Here are some examples of the type of prompts you will see for your Issue essay:

Topic: *Most people would agree that buildings represent a valuable record of any society's past, but controversy arises when old buildings stand on ground that modern planners feel could be better used for modern purposes. In such situations, modern development should be given precedence over the preservation of historic buildings so that contemporary needs can be served.*

Instructions: Write a response in which you discuss the extent to which you agree or disagree with the statement. In developing your point of view, consider ways in which the statement might or might not hold true and explain how these considerations affect your point of view.

Topic: *No one can possibly achieve success in the world by conforming to conventional practices and conventional ways of thinking.*

Instructions: Write a response in which you discuss the extent to which you agree or disagree with the statement. In developing your point of view, be sure to consider and address opposing views to your position.

Topic: *Students should memorize facts only after they have studied the ideas, trends, and concepts that help explain those facts. Students who have learned only facts have learned very little.*

Instructions: Write a response in which you discuss the extent to which you agree or disagree with the statement. In developing your point of view, consider the effects of implementing a policy based upon the statement and how the effects impact your position.

Step 1: Thinking

The essay topics are fairly general in nature. Education, for example, means lots of different things to different people and you could take your essay in a number of different directions. One of the most common mistakes test takers make is to write the essay on the first three examples that come to mind (while sitting in a cubicle at the test center). These examples are not necessarily the best, the most interesting, or even within the writer's area of expertise. They also tend to be simplistic, similar, and often really obvious.

To avoid this trap, force yourself to spend time thinking. Specifically, use your scratch paper to make a chart. On one side write "I agree" and summarize the prompt. On the other side, write "I disagree" and summarize the opposing argument. Now force yourself to brainstorm four examples for each column. It's likely that you will have no trouble filling up one column, but you may struggle on the other. Push yourself to complete it. It is when you really push your thinking that your essay gets interesting.

If you run out of ideas during your brainstorm, use this simple checklist. Ask yourself, "How is this true for me, my family, children, the elderly, my school, my community, my employer, my state, my country, my species, nature, science, or history?" By using this checklist to generate examples, you will automatically begin to see the issue from multiple perspectives. This will add richness and depth to your thinking.

Of course, the examples you choose need to be good ones. The best place to start is with things you know. Think about your job, your life, or your major in school. Work from your areas of strength or expertise and the ideas will come more easily and be far more powerful. You might think that the Holocaust and Gandhi's march to the sea are perfect examples, but if you don't know much more than the basics about either topic, you run the risk of sounding trite and simplistic. No one wants to sound trite when talking about the Holocaust.

When you come up with a general example, make sure you always attach it to a specific. If the topic is education and your point is that it is necessary so that history does not repeat itself, get specific. Which history, whose education. A general essay is short and average. An essay that rests upon clearly defined examples is longer and far more convincing.

Yes, you can write the essay in the first person. It is your job to have an opinion on the subject and to express it.

Step 2: Organizing

Now that you have this great list of ideas and examples, it's time to craft an essay. At this point, do NOT pick a point of view. *Pick your best three examples.* The point of view is irrelevant; it is your examples that make your essay powerful. It doesn't matter if you pick examples from both sides of the agree/disagree divide. If you have examples from both sides, it simply means that you will disagree with the prompt and that your thesis statement will be some variation of "this is often true but not always."

Rarely will you see a topic with which you agree wholeheartedly and for which you can't come up with a few powerful exceptions. In fact, an essay that acknowledges that there are two sides to an issue, and that takes time to address some of the opposing points of view, will be far more powerful. Instead of saying, "You are wrong and I disagree," you are saying, "I understand your point of view; here's why I think my point of view is better." Which one gives your argument more authority?

Pick your best three examples. These will be the ones about which you know the most, about which you are the most excited, and which can be linked together in a common thread. You might choose three examples that could sit on either side of the agree/disagree divide depending upon the point of view. You might pick three different scales and show how the topic affects a child, a family, or a country. You might want examples from wildly different fields such as software development, literature, and psychology. If you have brainstormed well, you will have plenty of interesting things from which to choose.

Once you have three good examples, you can craft your thesis statement to accommodate your examples. This way your examples will appear to be perfectly selected to support your thesis. Isn't it nice to have the perfect examples ready just when you need them? Now, write your thesis statement out on your scratch paper. Another common mistake is for essay writers to lose the thread of their argument halfway through the essay, or to stray from their thesis statements. This happens when you fail to make a plan and stick to it. Most people are actively thinking about what they're going to write next while they're already writing! This causes all kinds of errors, oversights, and meandering essays. Don't do it.

> Do not think about what you're going to write, while you're already writing. Make a plan before you start, and stick to it.

When you write out your thesis statement, you don't have to go into detail. You've got four more paragraphs with which to do that. Just tell the reader what you intend to prove and give him or her some sense of how you're going to do it. Your first paragraph will be short, to the point, and no more than three sentences. If your topic is censorship and your examples are spam parental controls on

Internet portals, the dominance of a few major corporations in news production, and access to a free press in China, then that is all you need to say in your intro. You have plenty of time to get to specifics in your body paragraphs.

On your scratch paper, write out your thesis statement, your three examples, one or two words here will do, and then a few words to remind yourself why each example is proof of your thesis statement. You don't need a whole sentence, just a few words such as "children, Internet, some censorship—good" or "children, Internet—children too sheltered, don't learn to censor selves."

When you begin to write your essay, these little guidelines will become the topic sentences of each of your supporting paragraphs. They will ensure that your essay stays on track and that the job of each example is clear to the reader.

Step 3: Writing

Now that you have three beautifully chosen examples, a point of view perfectly supported by the examples, an outline, and even your topic sentences, you are ready to write. In fact your essay, at this point, is 80 percent written. All you need to do is flesh out your paragraphs, come up with a conclusion, and you're done. The great thing about this is that it leaves you free to really focus on your writing.

ANALYSIS OF AN ARGUMENT

On the Issue essay, it was your job to craft your own Argument. On the Argument essay, your job is the opposite. You will be given someone else's argument and it is your job to break it down and assess it. In some ways, this is not difficult. The argument you will be given will be filled with some pretty obvious flaws. Here are some examples:

The following appeared in a memorandum from the new president of the Patriot car manufacturing company.

In the past, the body styles of Patriot cars have been old-fashioned, and our cars have not sold as well as have our competitors' cars. But now, since many regions in this country report rapid increases in the numbers of newly licensed drivers, we should be able to increase our share of the market by selling cars to this growing population. Thus, we should discontinue our oldest models and concentrate instead on manufacturing sporty cars. We can also improve the success of our marketing campaigns by switching our advertising to the Youth Advertising agency, which has successfully promoted the country's leading soft drink.

Write a response in which you discuss the specific evidence needed to evaluate the strength of the argument and how the evidence would affect the argument.

The following appeared in a memorandum from the owner of Armchair Video, a chain of video rental stores.

Because of declining profits, we must reduce operating expenses at Armchair Video's ten video rental stores. Raising prices is not a good option, since we are famous for our special bargains. Instead, we should reduce our operating hours. Last month our store in downtown Marston reduced its hours by closing at 6:00 P.M. rather than 9:00 P.M. and reduced its overall inventory by no longer stocking any film released more than two years ago. Since we have received very few customer complaints about these new policies, we should now adopt them at all other Armchair Video stores as our best strategies for improving profits.

Write a response in which you consider possible alternative explanations for facts cited in the argument, and explain how your explanations effect the argument.

The following is an editorial that appeared in the *County Register* of the cities mentioned in this piece.

In each city in the region of Treehaven, the majority of the money spent on government-run public school education comes from taxes that each city government collects. The region's cities differ, however, in the value they place on public education. For example, Parson City typically budgets twice as much money per year as Blue City does for its public schools—even though both cities have about the same number of residents. It seems clear, therefore, that Parson City residents care more about public school education than do Blue City residents.

Write an essay in which you propose a series of questions to ask to further evaluate the argument that has been presented. Explain how the answers to these questions might affect the conclusion of the argument.

Breaking Down the Argument

There are three basic parts to any argument. They are as follows:

> The Conclusion: The conclusion is the main point of the argument. It is the thing the author is trying to prove. It is the author's recommendation or action point.

> The Premises: If you identify the conclusion and ask, "Why?" the answer you get will be the premises. They are the facts or reasons the author uses to back up his or her conclusion.

> Assumptions: You can't point to the assumptions because they're not there. The assumptions are the unstated conditions that attach the premise to the conclusion. There are hundreds of these.

When you begin to break down an argument, you should use the formal language of arguments. First identify the conclusion of the argument you've been given, and then identify the premises and then some of the missing or weaker assumptions.

There are a number of types of arguments that you will see often. Once you identify the type of argument being made, spotting the flaws is easy.

Causal

A causal argument assumes a cause-and-effect relationship between two events. Sales are down, for example, because of a change in demographics. To weaken a causal argument, you need only point out some other potential causes for a particular event. Perhaps sales are down because the overall economy is down, or because the product suddenly has competition. To strength a causal argument, you need to show that other potential causes are unlikely.

Sampling or Statistical

In these arguments, one group is assumed to be representative of a whole population. Members of the group that was surveyed all said that they prefer lite beer because it is less filling. To weaken this argument, you need to show that the group surveyed does not represent the whole population. Perhaps they surveyed beer drinkers at a restaurant, where they were also eating diner, rather than beer drinkers at a bar. Perhaps they surveyed at a liquor store right after lunch. To strengthen this argument, you need to show that the sample population is, in fact, representative of the whole.

Analogy

Arguments by analogy claim that what is true for one group is also true for the other. Voters in Cleveland prefer one candidate; therefore, voters in Detroit will too. To weaken these arguments, you need to show that these two groups are not at all analogous. Perhaps Detroit is the hometown of the rival candidate; perhaps one candidate favors the auto industry and one does not. To strengthen these arguments, you must show that the two groups are quite similar indeed.

The overall process for crafting your essay will be the same as it is for the Issue essay. Almost invariably you will end up criticizing the argument you have been given, although it is often a good strategy to use your conclusion to point out ways in which the argument could have been improved. Throughout your essay you want to use the language of arguments. This means naming conclusions as conclusions, sampling arguments as sampling arguments, premises as premises, and assumptions as assumptions.

Thinking

Begin by identifying your conclusion or conclusions and then the major premises upon which it/they rest. For each premise, note the type of reasoning used (sampling, causal, or some other type), and the like flaws associated with that type of reasoning. This is as much brainstorming as you will need.

Organizing

Rank these premises by the size of their flaws. Start with the most egregious and work your way down. The outline of your essay will look something like this:

The author's conclusion is Z. It is faulty and more research/information is needed before the suggested action is taken.

The first and biggest flaw is premise Y. It's possible that it is true, but it rests upon the following assumptions. Can we really make these assumptions? What about these alternative assumptions?

Even if we assume Y to be the case, there is premise X. Premise X draws an analogy between these two groups and assumes that they are interchangeable. Can we really make this assumption; what about these alternative assumptions…?

Even if we assume X to be true, there is also W. W is a sampling argument, but the author not only has not proved the sample to be representative, but he/she points out that this might not be the case! Perhaps, as noted, blah, blah, blah.

In conclusion, this argument is incomplete and rests upon too many questionable assumptions. To improve this argument, the author needs to show A, B, and C: before the building is to be torn down, the company is to change tactics, the community is to devote resources, or the school is to reorganize its curriculum.

Writing

Feel free to have fun with this essay. Reading essays can get pretty boring, and a smart, funny critique of a faulty argument can be a welcome break. You might say, "If I were the president of company X, I would fire my marketing director for wasting my time with such a poorly researched plan," or "What the marketing director of company X should have done is…." It is okay to have personality as long as you get the Analysis-of-an-Argument job done at the same time.

For a more in-depth look at the techniques for the Argument essay and some sample essays, see *Cracking the GRE*.

ISSUE ESSAY DRILL

Here are some examples of the types of prompts you will see for your issue essay.

"One should not expect respect for disregarding the opinions of others. Only when every point of view is taken into consideration should people take action in the world."

"An increased number of laws or rules, ironically leads to a diminished sense of morality and impoverished relations among people."

"An idea alone, no matter how great, is meaningless unless it is put into practice."

"The value of ancient works, no matter how great, cannot be accurately judged because modern standards are not relevant and ancient standards cannot be known."

"When something is judged as ugly or lacking in style, it is only because it is being perceived by someone other than its target audience."

"Truly innovative ideas tend to come from individuals, because groups tend to work toward consensus and the status quo."

"It is far more important to define what you are for than what you are against."

"Education consists of making errors."

"The unknown is necessary."

"Skill alone, no matter how great, does not guarantee a masterpiece."

"To respect a symbol is to contribute power to a cultural institution; to worship a symbol is to bring about its eventual end."

"Success means a greater ability to communicate one's essence."

"A student who wishes to succeed in business school should study anything but business while in school. The additional perspectives gained by studying other fields of knowledge are too valuable to pass up."

"Unexamined conservatism is far more dangerous than reckless change."

"If a student can return home comfortably, a school has not done its job."

ARGUMENT ESSAY DRILL

Here are some examples of the types of prompts you will see for your argument essay.

The following appeared in a memorandum from the regional manager of the Taste of Italy restaurant chain:

> *"After the first month of service, the new restaurant in the Flatplains Mall, which uses the Chipless brand of wine glasses, has reported a far lower rate of breakage than our other restaurants that use the Elegance brand. Since servers and bartenders at all of our restaurants frequently report that breakage is a result of the type of wineglass, and the customers at the Flatplains Mall restaurant seem to like the Chipless style of glasses, we should switch all of our restaurants to the Chipless brand."*

The following appeared in an internal memo circulated among the partners of a small graphic design firm:

> *"When the economy was growing, there were more graphics jobs than there were designers and many designers could make more money working as independent contractors, than they could as salaried employees. As we too were growing and needed more designers, we were forced to pay higher salaries to recent design graduates than we had paid in the past. Now that the market is shrinking, we can save lots of money by cutting back the salaries of all designers on staff to match current market rates. Service sector companies and manufacturing companies have both been able to successfully cut wages in a down economy without harming production. We should too."*

The following appeared in a report to the board of a company that produces men's sporting apparel:

> "While national television advertising is increasingly expensive, it would cost roughly the same amount to reach the same number of people by buying print advertising space in various magazines. Since launching our newest TV ad campaign, sales have gone up significantly, but not in those markets which are served only by print ads. We should, therefore, increase our investment in TV ads and should not renew our magazine contracts once they are up."

The following appeared in an internal memo circulated among the partners of a small design firm:

> "We, the four partners of Max Design, have made the company what it is. When we are hired by a client, it is our taste and style that the client is paying for. In the last two years we have grown significantly and now have project managers handling many of our recent contracts. In my opinion, the work put forth by the teams led by the product managers is not as good as the work put forth when it was just the four of us. At other design firms of a similar size, the principals remain personally involved in all projects. Therefore, from now on, all decisions for all projects, no matter how minute, should be signed off by one of us."

The following appeared in an email written by the head of the market research division to the president of a major candy company:

> "In the last four years the gross sales in the candy market have remained static, but ice cream, another confectionary product, has experienced huge increases in gross sales. Specifically, the growth of boutique ice cream brands specializing in unusual savory ice cream flavors such as pink peppercorn, basil, and ginger, has exploded. In response, we have tested some savory flavored candy chews at a number of national gourmet food fairs. The response to our free samples has been extremely enthusiastic. Therefore we should jump to the forefront of this trend and launch our savory candy chews nationally at all retail outlets."

The following was a memorandum by the campaign manger for a state senate candidate:

> "Contributers to nearly every major blog in the state, both democratic and republican, agree that a proposal to increase tolls on the major highways going through our state is a good thing. They don't all agree that the increased revenue should go toward the same thing. Some say we need more technology in the schools, others favor subsidizing insurance

for the unemployed and independent contractors, and some say it should just be used to cut income tax. However, they all agree that the tolls should go up. Certainly this will cause more commuters to take public transportation, encourage businesses to ship by rail rather than truck, and save on road maintenance fees. Our chief competitor, who accepts major contributions from the trucking companies, opposes the toll increase. We should, therefore, come out strongly in favor of it."

The following appeared on the op-ed page of a local newspaper:

"As violent crime rates have slowly inched up in our city, it is time for city officials to take a stand to protect citizens from harm. The first step is to gate and lock downtown parks after dark. Keys can be passed out to apartment owners and other local residents to ensure that they have continued access to these public spaces while protecting against people who are using the park for things other than the recreational activities for which these public spaces were designed. This approach has been taken in three of the five suburbs that surround this city and polls of both homeowners and police departments in all three report higher property values and lower crime rates. The city needs to act now before we reach a tipping point."

NOTES